People, Communication and Organisations

People, Communication and Organisations

Desmond W Evans

PITMAN PUBLISHING
128 Long Acre, London WC2E 9AN

© Desmond W Evans 1986

First published in Great Britain 1986

British Library Cataloguing in Publication Data
Evans, Desmond W.
  People, communication & organisations.—
  (Pitman Polytech)
  1. Communication in management
  I. Title
  658.4'5   HF5718

ISBN 0–273–02588–0

Printed in Great Britain at The Bath Press, Avon

Contents

Acknowledgements

The author and publishers have made every effort to trace ownership of all copyright material and to obtain permission from the owners of copyright.

In particular, the author wishes to acknowledge his indebtedness to Macdonald & Evans and their authors, for permission to access the following texts as references and for permission to use charts and diagrams taken from them:

Administration in Business 2nd edition, Josephine Shaw, 1984
Data Processing 5th edition, R. G. Anderson, 1984
Office Management 5th edition, J. C. Denyer, revised by Josephine Shaw, 1980
Organisation and Methods R. G. Anderson, 2nd edition, 1980
Pocket Guide to Programming John Shelley, 1982

The author also wishes to thank the following for permission to reprint material:

Chichester College of Technology
Oxford University Press
Penguin Books Limited
West Sussex County Council
J Sydney Webb and T J Lowi
The IEEE (USA)
Scientific American
McGraw-Hill Inc
G Langley
EMI Records Limited
Hoover Limited
The Plessey Company plc
The Coca-Cola Company

Atlanta Georgia
West Sussex County Council
BBC Radio Light Entertainment
Michael Joseph Limited
John Offord (Publications) Limited
Fretwell-Downing Data Systems Limited
Select Offices Chichester
C H Longley (Rinnai UK)
British Telecom International
The Institute of Bankers
Professor Alec Rodger
NFER Publishing Company
Chichester & District Angling Society
US Bureau of Labor Statistics
Dr Peter Zorkoczy
Invalid Children's Aid Association
Ron Grant Advisory Teacher Reading
Charmian Goodson
Eileen Spooner } for their advice during the production
Kathie Cotton } of the text
Allun Clark

Finally, the author would like to thank Pitman Publishing for facilitating the inclusion of extracts taken from the author's previous publications:

People & Communication
All In a Day's Work *
Communication at Work

* Produced in collaboration with Ron Dauber, and to whom thanks are also due.

Introduction

You are coming to the study of people and the ways in which they operate in organisations at a most exciting time in the history of business administration!

Whether you are studying as a prelude to a career in commerce, industry or the public service, or whether you already have a career and are studying part-time, it will not have escaped your notice that the societies of the developed world are in the midst of a revolution as far-reaching in its implications as the first industrial revolution which began in Britain in the 19th century. Only this time, the industrial revolution is not based on steam engineering and the faster production methods it created but on electronic technology and an 'explosion of information' which information technology – based on the microprocessor or 'silicon chip' – has made possible. Nothing has burst upon societies and cultures with the same radical impact since the mid-15th century when the art of printing with movable type was first introduced into Europe.

It took nearly 400 years for half the population of Great Britain to become literate after the introduction of the printed book in the middle of the 15th century. The first microprocessor to be sold commercially was marketed by the Intel Corporation in 1971. In only 15 years, many millions of microcomputers have been sold around the world and are in daily use today from primary school levels upwards. This contrasting experience provides some idea of the speed with which modern societies move to embrace new technologies today!

The aim of this book is to help to prepare you for the exciting challenges you will undoubtedly face in your working life during the last quarter of the 20th century, and to acquire the practical skills you will need. It deals with acquiring effective communication skills, understanding the range and scope of information technology systems and equipment and the processing of information and data. It also looks at the organisation of work and ways of improving its effectiveness, the means of motivating people at work, the techniques and tools of business administration and the development of human relations skills.

This book is dedicated to you, and to your making a really strong contribution to improving the effectiveness of the business or public service enterprise you join. Provided you keep up a steady work effort and, above all, maintain an enquiring mind and inquisitive approach to your studies, you will undoubtedly enjoy them and build a sound foundation for your future career.

Good luck and good studying!

Desmond Evans
September 1986

1 How to study effectively

Introduction

By the time you set about pursuing this topic, you will have almost certainly 'studied' for a number of assessments or examinations, since by the term 'study' we may simply mean 'follow a course at school or college'. At the end of such a course may have loomed public examinations – sat in examination halls and preceded perhaps by classwork or homework, which will have contributed to the overall result.

For the teachers and examiners involved in such examinations there occurs an annual bout of depression which is the result of seeing bright and able students fail in the examinations and assessments they take, as a result of an inability to study effectively. Some students regrettably never master the vital skills of effective studying, whether full-time students doing nothing else, or part-time, mature students returning to college after a period at work.

Why should this be so, given that almost all students want to learn and to absorb the skills and expertise being imparted? There is no single, simple answer, but almost certainly the root cause lies in their inability to organise:

1 their time
2 their environment or location for study
3 their learning resources
4 a systematic and coherent approach
5 the records and notes they keep for future reference.

In order that you in particular, and as an individual in your class group, make a good start in this important area, this Topic has been included early in the text so that it may influence all that follows. Even if you fancy yourself as a 'pretty useful studier' it will do you no harm to read through this section – you may pick up some further useful tips!

Organising your time

There is a well-known proverb which goes:

If you want something done in a hurry – ask a busy person!

Behind this seeming contradiction lies the fact that busy people – managers, teachers, government officials – have to make prompt decisions and are used to regulating their working day very closely. Thus, for example, they will buy in one minute the picture postcard which takes the holiday-maker half an hour to choose!

One of the best ways of organising your time is to make out a timetable of your waking hours for the whole week and then to fill in those times taken up with: eating, travelling, lectures, socialising or relaxing.

The time which is left is then clearly seen as available for study and will include such times as:

- private study periods between lectures
- 'twilight' times between 4.00 pm and 6.00 pm
- time while travelling on bus or train (not ideal)
- time after tea or supper
- time during week-ends

and if you are a skylark who can rise cheerfully at 6.00 pm in the mornings, time before breakfast!

Clearly, the more time you have entered in your timetable for socialising and relaxing, the less there will be for study and so from the outset you must decide where your priorities lie. Similarly, if you have to pursue a part-time job in order to help finance your studies, then you must be particularly disciplined in maintaining your study times. An example indicating the sort of timetable which may be devised is shown on page 2.

Having produced your own timetable, it is not just a matter of putting in some study time where the blanks occur, but of analysing critically the pattern of your living week and of assessing where and how you can best accommodate your study time.

A perfectly fair question in this context is: How much study time is enough? There are unfortunately no simple or easy answers since much depends on your own ability, skills, experience and time availability. However, as a rule of thumb guide, a full-time student should be prepared to commit some 12–15 hours per week to studying and assignment production, while a part-time student ought to devote some 6–8 hours to study outside of, and in addition to, classroom lectures.

In organising your own weekly study times on your timetable, you should adopt the following guidelines:

Study timetable of Frances Jones

	Monday	Tuesday	Wednesday	Thursday	Friday	Saturday	Sunday
7.00 am 8.00 am		GETTING UP, BREAKFAST				PART-TIME JOB	GETTING UP + BREAKFAST
8.00 am 9.00 am		AND TRAVEL					
9.00 am 10.00 am	LECTURE	LECTURE	LECTURE	LECTURE	LECTURE		STUDY TIME:
10.00 am 11.00 am	LECTURE	PRIVATE STUDY: WRITE UP NOTES	LECTURE	PRIVATE STUDY: ASSIGNMENTS	PRIVATE STUDY: LIBRARY		ASSIGNMENT PRODUCTION
11.00 am 12.00 am	PRIVATE STUDY LIBRARY	LECTURE	PRIVATE STUDY LIBRARY	PRIVATE STUDY: ASSIGNMENTS	LECTURE		
12.00 am 1.00 pm	LECTURE	LUNCH	LECTURE	LECTURE	LECTURE		
1.00 pm 2.00 pm	LUNCH	PRIVATE STUDY: ASSIGNMENTS	LUNCH	LUNCH	LUNCH		LUNCH
2.00 pm 3.00 pm	LECTURE	PRIVATE STUDY ASSIGNMENTS	LECTURE	LECTURE	PRIVATE STUDY: WRITE UP NOTES		
3.00 pm 4.00 pm	LECTURE	LECTURE	LECTURE	LECTURE	LECTURE		STUDY TIME
4.00 pm 5.00 pm	TRAVEL +	BADMINTON IN GYM	PRIVATE STUDY LIBRARY	LECTURE	TRAVEL +		FLEXIBLE USE
5.00 pm 6.00 pm	TEA			TRAVEL +	TEA	FREE	
6.00 pm 7.00 pm	STUDY TIME	TRAVEL +	FREE	TEA	FREE		
7.00 pm 8.00 pm	READING	TEA		STUDY TIME WRITE UP NOTES			
8.00 pm 9.00 pm	FREE	FREE	FREE	FREE	FREE	FREE	

Make sure you have *three* main types of time:

(*a*) for writing up your notes at the end of each day – Mondays to Fridays

(*b*) for accessing reference books in your school, college or public library

(*c*) for extended periods to produce assignments.

Clearly, the different study tasks involved in these three types of time needed will involve you in ensuring that different locations are available. Obviously, you will need to tailor your reference checking times to those times and days in the week when your library is open. On the other hand you can write up your notes at home in the early evenings while lectures are still fresh in your mind. Lastly, you will need to ensure that your location for assignment production is one which is attractive to work in but free from interruptions.

The illustrated timetable above provides a specimen which takes all these factors into account.

While on the subject of time in relation to study, it is well worth keeping the following advice firmly in mind:

Individuals have different biological clocks and while some people are 'skylarks' others are 'owls'. Having made this observation, however, it should be remembered that most people work in a higher mental gear in the mornings than in the afternoons, and that mental work in the evenings, quite naturally, after the efforts of the day, takes place at the lowest level of mental energy. This being broadly the case, it is a mistake to think that brilliant work is going to be begun at ten or eleven pm and continue into the early hours of the morning! Always remember that these special hours are reserved for those who either cannot or do not wish to study at much more effective times.

Shorter periods of study are generally more effective than longer ones. In other words, it is usually better to work hard and without interruption for one or two hours than to stick doggedly at studying for periods of two to four hours without a break. It pays to organise study times so that they are not all bunched up, say, from 9.00 am to 3.00 pm on Sundays with the rest of the week free. When we come to consider how our memories work, we shall see how the brain needs time to digest information and how 'overstudying' in periods which are too long causes 'mental indigestion'!

In our consideration of time as the most precious study resource, it is important to plan in an organised way how to ration it out evenly between the various study subjects or units which go to make up a complete course of study. In the study timetable of Frances Jones, there are four possible slots for assignment production, totalling nine available hours, and eight slots totalling nine-and-a-half hours for other kinds of study such as reading, notes, revision etc.

In evolving an effective pattern of study which can be maintained conscientiously over one or two academic years, it is important,

1   to have available more study slots than are needed. This allows for flexibility within the week, so that the unexpected invitation to a disco or party may be allowed for, and
2   to have available a variety of study slots within any given week in which to put current study activities, like the assignment due for the coming Monday or the need to re-read a chapter on consumer law which proved thorny. In this way weeks which include a great deal of writing may be just as readily coped with as well as those with a lighter load.

Thus in any given week, Frances Jones knows where she can devote three or, if needed, four study slots to produce written assignments, two of which – since they take place in school/college time – also provide access to the library and course teaching staff.

By the same token, Frances has at her disposal eight slots to divide between, say, the six units of study she is pursuing, for:

- follow-up further reading
- reference-checking in the library
- re-reading and writing up of notes
- gathering information for assignments
- discussing a group assignment with fellow students.

Further, by keeping the Sunday afternoon period flexible, Frances can spend some time thinking about what needs to be reinforced or followed up from the past week, and what particular unit or topic studies should be planned for what study slots in the coming week.

Important

The presence of some $18\frac{1}{2}$ available hours of personal study time in Frances' timetable does not mean that she will be studying for all those hours, but that they are available to use in a flexible weekly study plan which may extend to some 12–15 hours of study in all.

Also, by making out such a weekly timetable structured around meal-times, lecture-times, travelling times and socialising times, Frances will ensure that she keeps to a regular pattern of study which is also flexible. The development of regular study times within the week is essential if work is to be handed in on time and if she is to avoid the trap of falling behind with handing in work, since this can rapidly lead to her demotivation with the course altogether.

Finally, in your use of time and overall study planning, it is essential that you have from each of your subject lecturers two central schedules of information:

1   the course syllabus or outline of aims and objectives to be met, and
2   the broad diary sequence of when what sort of assignments are going to be set throughout the academic year. This diary may be modified as the course progresses, to take into account unforeseen situations such as, for example, the teaching of report writing taking longer than anticipated.

Nevertheless, with these two study aids, you will be able to plan your general study strategy both in termly and monthly time-spans.

Though much of these observations about the effective use of time may seem – and indeed are – simple and straightforward, it is always a source of dismay for teachers that some otherwise able students find it so difficult to design and then stick to such a weekly plan. So take the above advice to heart and do not let yourself become the sort of student who always seems disorganised and short of time!

Organising your study environment

Having taken practical steps to make study time properly available outside the classroom, the next important step towards effective study methods is to consider carefully the location *where* the 'pearls of wisdom' are to be cultured!

Broadly speaking, these are the following places where it is likely that you will study:

- in your own study/bedroom or 'den'
- on the dining-table in the dining room or through-lounge
- on the bus or train travelling to and from school or college
- in your school/college/public library
- at your friend's house
- at work during the lunch period.

Certainly there are other locations where studying is possible but probably difficult and one of the first cardinal rules for finding and then using regularly productive study areas is to be honest with yourself about the effectiveness of some of the places you have used to study with little to show for it. For example, the above checklist includes some ideal study situations and others which may be far from suitable.

Certainly the best of study environments outside school or college is your own personal bedroom/study to which you can retire knowing that you will be left alone to get on with it. Not all students are so fortunate, however, and may well have to share a room with a brother or sister. In this case, an alternative location may be needed.

One student in this situation found an ideal solution in doing most of his studying in the college library each day, after lectures and before going home. In this way squabbles and upsets at home were avoided.

While the expanse of the dining-room table may be

ideal across which to spread books and files, this site is no good at all if your studying has to compete with the family's TV entertainment. Even a budding Sir Isaac Newton would have found it difficult to resist the temptations of the latest pop or rock show or first TV showing of a searing and passionate Hollywood film. So unless you can commandeer the dining-room or lounge for yourself alone, avoid it – family leisure time and your studying will not mix.

While we have all seen young school pupils feverishly copying maths homework from a friend's exercise book while travelling on the bus into school, this is to be viewed rather as the study location of the desperate rather than the organised student. Firstly, reading and writing on a bus journey may well make you feel sick and secondly, the bustle of the journey in peak commuting times is likely to distract you constantly. However, some students who have long train journeys daily in rural shires may well be able to do some useful light reading in this time.

The use of the library as a study centre is going to be essential during your course but you must make sure you learn to get the best out of it by becoming fully confident in using the filing systems under which titles and authors are recorded, and the Dewey Decimal System by which knowledge is classified – see page 11. Similarly, it will pay handsome dividends if you take the trouble to win the confidence and goodwill of the librarian and staff, as opposed to their wrath for being a constant loud chatterer!

This point leads on to a central one in terms of library study:

Do avoid becoming one of a small clique of three or four students who use the library (if they are allowed to get away with it) as a gossip-shop. Hours can drift by during the week's private study periods in sotto voce discussions of boyfriends, girlfriends, favourite groups, summer holidays and the like without a book being opened or an assignment begun!

Try to find a place away from any such nuisances and determine to make the best use of the library's facilities and your private study time.

Going to a friend's house for the evening to do some joint studying can certainly help to make a difficult patch more bearable in a demanding unit or topic, but only if some worthwhile work gets done. It's no good at all kidding yourself that you are busily engaged in earnest study if all you are really doing is idly leafing through notes or textbooks to the blasting decibels of your friend's favourite tapes. What is worthwhile, though, in this particular context is to test each other's recall of factual data which has to be remembered or to try out your approach to an 'open-ended' problem on a sympathetic ear. At all events, you must be the honest evaluator of such a study routine.

If you are studying and working full-time then you may find it possible to make legitimate use of your plan of work, but keep in mind that studying in the firm's time (other than via day-release) is cheating and could land you in trouble, and that your break times are needed for just that – a break. However, you may well be able to manage a little reading over lunch-times or, by arrangement, stay on after normal finishing time to make good use of a quiet environment.

Designing your study location

While you will be unable to make drastic structural alterations to your study locations, there is much you can do to your home study location to make it a place where you like to be rather than grudgingly have to be. Moreover, it is well worth taking the trouble to review your study room or area at the outset of a one or two year course of study since you have committed yourself to spending a lot of time there!

The following checklist provides you with the basic factors to consider in planning your study location:

Light

Natural and artificial. Is there enough of it? Does it fall where needed on to your books and files or does the location of your desk or table cause you to block much of it out with your head and back? Remember that a good reading lamp (100 watts) is essential for working in artificial light.

Heat

Not usually a problem in summer except in the occasional glorious summers about which we ought not to complain! But winter is a very different matter. If your study is cold you will not want to enter it, or if you do, stay in it for any length of time. If you cannot afford to use up expensive heating for yourself alone, then do not feel awkward about dressing up with extra sweaters, or even long-johns under trousers. Firstly, who's to know, and secondly making best use of your own body-heat by conserving it makes good sense. At the other extreme, don't allow your study to become an upstairs hothouse in winter. Nothing will send you to sleep quicker than an airless 28 degree Centigrade fug!

Noise

It is dangerous to give advice to students about noise when some of it turns out in fact to be highly prized and sensitively performed music – even if it can be heard three blocks away!

You must therefore make your own mind up about what are noises that irritate and distract you and what are truly helpful aids to study – whether hi-fi music or the Walkman variety. Serious advice is, however: give silence a fair try as the background to your home studying. The chances are that you will come to cherish its support of clear-thinking and prolonged concentration.

Even so, if you find that having some companionable music to accompany your studying makes you less lonely, and the alternative of rejoining the family downstairs less of a temptation, then play on!

Interruptions

These are to be avoided at all costs. You must educate your nearest and dearest to accept that during your study periods you really are 'out of bounds' or incommunicado. A notice over your door-handle barring all-comers may help. Also, if friends telephone, ask your family to get into the habit of taking numbers so you can ring back later. Without being rude, callers to your house should be discouraged during study periods, so make sure your friends know when you are 'not at home' during the week.

Desk, chair and bookshelves

The next area to review is your immediate study area. Naturally, you will need to make the best use of your existing furniture and the geography of your study room. The following guidelines will help you to set up an effective study location you will enjoy using:

1 Your working-surface – desk or table top – should be sufficiently large to cope with several open books and ring binders as well as your exercise paper pad or keyboard. Nothing interrupts the study process quicker than constantly having to hunt around for references under piled up books and files.

Your working area must also be well lit and free from glare, whether from natural or artificial light.

2 The relationship between your chair and desk top is also important. You should seek to obtain a chair which provides firm support and which gives you a comfortable writing or typewriting position. If your chair is too low, you will soon find your arms and shoulder-blades aching. Too high, and your back will soon object to your hunching over your work!

You may be able to purchase cheaply a good second-hand adjustable typist's chair to solve these problems.

3 It is important that you install a sufficiently large range of bookshelves on which to store your resources of texts, photocopies and notes etc. At the outset ensure that you allow for sufficient space for your future acquisitions throughout your period of study.

A helpful tip when storing books and files is to decide upon a logical sequence for them – perhaps by subject area – and then to make sure that you always return a book after use to the same place on its shelf. This will save you valuable time and avoid irritation when you next need the book.

In the same spirit, you should label the spines of your ring-binders and box-files or lever-arch files so that you can locate material quickly and easily.

4 While on the subject of books and files, do take the following advice to heart at the beginning of your studies:

Adopt at once the practice of transferring notes, handouts, photocopies and any other material you have collected at school or college into a file system in your home study on a daily basis, once you have finished with it for the time being.

It is most dangerous to keep all your notes and study material in a single subject file all year and to carry it daily backwards and forwards. You would not be the first student to be devastated by the loss of such precious information shortly before examinations and revision time!

Organising your notes and handouts

Some ill-advised students are so neglectful when it comes to taking, revising and storing notes that what they end up with is so scanty that it scarcely needs any organising! The conscientious student soon realises, however, the value of such memory-joggers and guidance aids during a long and demanding course of study.

It pays, therefore, to give careful thought to the most effective way of organising these important study resources.

There are several ways in which your study materials – notes, handouts, photocopies, newspaper cuttings, etc, can be systematically filed and indexed, so you know where to put your hand on even a single piece of A4 paper promptly and reliably.

One simple method to adopt is to store your index in a card index filing system under subject or unit headings. An individual card may look like this:

Unit: People in organisations	
Major topic:	Meetings
Sub topic:	Format and content of Chairman's agenda.
Resources:	1. Notes 25. 1. 19XX 2. Specimen of Agenda 3. Handout on Content Approach
Location:	PIO Boxfile
Other sources of information:	'People, communication and organisations' D. W. Evans, Pitman (1986) 'Meetings' L. Hall, M & E Handbooks, Macdonald & Evans (1985)

At the outset of your studies you may think setting up such a filing system or database a chore and scarcely worth the trouble, but as your study material builds up, and as you begin to produce assignments in which the content of various units is integrated, you will soon reap the benefit of your own means of quickly accessing useful information.

Indeed, nothing is more infuriating in the later stages of your studies than to have only a vague recollection of a super chapter or article you could use but cannot locate, or to have taken the trouble to produce equally super notes that you put away somewhere and cannot lay hands on just when you could use them to good effect!

As an alternative to the card-index system you may wish to consider putting your materials index on to a computerised database using one of the commercially available packages. This is an ideal way of organising your sources of information if you have access to a computer at home.

Golden Rule

Not even an Einstein can carry in his or her head all the information collected during a period of one or two years' study!

So you *must* determine, right from the start, to acquire, store and review from time to time your notes and other study aids – conscientiously!

Using study materials effectively

As the diagram illustrates, there are nowadays many sources of information about people working in organisations and how they communicate, which may be used as helpful sources of study information in addition to and complementing textbooks like this one.

As part of your regular study routine, you should make sure that you include the following good practices in your daily and weekly studies.

- Read and 'skim-read' the business sections of a good daily and Sunday newspaper. Cut out relevant articles for future reference. Remember that newspaper articles are up-to-the-minute, brief, and mostly straightforwardly written.
- Make a habit of checking in advance in television and radio programme magazines such as Radio Times and TV Times to see what helpful programmes are shortly to be broadcast. Make arrangements to view or listen, and to record by audio or video means, any programme which looks likely to be particularly helpful. But in doing so always ensure you conform to copyright laws!
- Photocopy any useful diagrams, articles, charts etc from books or magazines in your library. (It is useful to keep a supply of coins by you for this purpose for your library's photocopier.) By and large copyright is not infringed by the taking of a single photocopy of material for study/research purposes. If in doubt, check with your librarian first.
- Always be on the look-out for good specimens of actual documents in use – circular letters, agendas, invoices, balance sheets published by public companies etc. You can check out by this means how successful organisations view their printed communications and compare them with others to obtain an informed view of current practices. Also,

---

Range of possible study aids

1   Pen and file paper produced notes

2   Handwritten or typed assignments

3   Duplicated handouts

4   Tape-recorded audio observations

5   Cuttings from newspapers, periodicals, magazines

6   Library books, newspapers, journals and audio-visual aids

7   Single photocopies of pages of books, magazines, journals
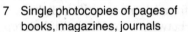

8   Video tapes of TV documentaries or features

9   Copies of photographs, drawings, graphs, charts, etc.

10   Educational computer software packages

11   Free handouts at exhibitions, displays, and public sector information offices

---

IF YOU CAST A WIDE AND IMAGINATIVE NET, THERE IS A WIDE RANGE OF STUDY AIDS AND MATERIAL AVAILABLE TO YOU, MUCH OF IT INEXPENSIVE OR FREE!

such a collection will provide you with practical help on the design of forms and documents and how to present information with visual effect.

- There are now a number of software packages available in schools and colleges which will provide invaluable assistance in helping the student to acquire both useful study skills and marketable career skills. These are packages such as the spreadsheet, database and file assistant.

In this context, it will pay handsome dividends – whether or not you pursue them as part of your course – to acquire keyboarding skills and the ability to operate a micro-computer. The chances are that you are already some way along this path, but if not, now is the time to get started!

How to take effective notes

As we have seen, a wide range of potentially useful audio-visual study material is available. Nevertheless, the textbook and specialist book still remain a central source of study data and information. Similarly, though modern courses of study involve the student in active learning situations – role-play, project, business-game and so on, nevertheless, there are times when it is necessary to take notes in class of an oral presentation of information.

The advantages of securing coherent notes for future revision have already been aired and this section aims to provide practical help in both the oral and written situation.

Taking notes of an oral presentation

Taking notes of what someone is saying as he or she says it is a demanding task. Practice is required and, as the proverb goes, makes perfect. The following pointers will help you to develop such skills promptly, provided you make a determined effort.

1 Make sure you arrive for your class on time. Miss the beginning of an oral presentation and you may never catch up and grasp the gist!

2 Arrive for the lecture organised. This means having a reserve pen or ball-point, sufficient note-paper and any other helpful 'tools' such as a ruler and eraser. This advice may seem extremely basic but teachers and students are always being asked to loan just such items.

3 Make sure you sit where you can obtain a good view of the black/white board or OHP screen.

4 Listen to what is being said *actively* and with concentration. Try to avoid 'switching off' or allowing your attention to wander.

5 Seek to establish the structure which the teacher is using to present the information in.

It may be that the lecture follows what is called an expositional pattern (that is, it sets about imparting information in a logical sequence) from the delivery of generalisations and principles or theories to the citing of examples or illustrations to support an initial,

general view. Such a structure usually centres upon factual information. In your notes, therefore, you will need to ensure that you set down in sufficient detail the general principles or major points and the main examples.

Remember that teachers tend to repeat their points and that their presentations often follow this structure:

Tell 'em what you're going to tell 'em.
Tell 'em.
Tell 'em what you've told 'em!

This being the case, the good teacher will give you plenty of opportunities to secure the most important points.

Another kind of structure used in oral presentations is the one called 'argumentative'. In this sense the label means the presenting of both sides of an argument, case, or discussion. This being so, the sort of structure likely to be followed is:

(*a*) Introduction of major issue or issues.
(*b*) The arguments for – the pros.
(*c*) The arguments against – the cons.
(*d*) A brief summary of the pros and cons – major points.
(*e*) A decision on which case is stronger or more logical or more justified – the outcome or conclusion.

6 Never remain a passive listener! If you fail to grasp a point during the oral delivery in an informal classroom situation ask your teacher to go over it again – there is absolutely no point in making copious notes about something you don't understand!

Also, if the teacher is going too fast (or too slow) tell him or her in polite terms that this is so. All teachers have a vested interest in your success, so they will not mind your helping them to help you.

7 Inevitably in an oral presentation the speaker will sometimes repeat points, digress into an anecdote or provide information that is 'padding' or trivial. Seek to 'edit' such information out of your notes as you take them so that you only record the most important points a single time.

8 Remember to make a note of any important questions and explanatory answers which may add further information to your notes at the end of the presentation.

9 *Always* go through your notes of an oral presentation within twenty-four hours so that, once you have digested the lecture, you can correct, revise, add to or delete information in your notes and make them a fully coherent set of notes which are going to be of some value to you in one or two year's time. Otherwise you may find that your initial note-taking work has been a waste of time!

How to find out

Your library and your study texts

Having spent some time on examining how to study effectively, it is now necessary to consider in some detail the ways of getting the best out of your library and the textbooks you will wish to use, or borrow, for study use.

Using your library to best effect

Obviously, if the library in question is your school library which you have inhabited since transferring to secondary school, then you will already know a great deal about it. However, you may be new to a college library and, in any case, a 'refresher' examination of library organisation will do no harm!

At the outset, it is important to realise that there are various kinds of knowledge available to the serious student and that a library is a centre or treasure-house for all sorts of knowledge – factual, philosophical, religious, imaginative and so on. This being so, it is necessary to understand that you do not need, nor do you have the time to learn by heart, everything you will encounter during your studies. You must therefore acquire the skill of finding quickly the precise location in your library of the sort of information you need, and learn to make value judgements along these lines:

What information
1   is important enough to make careful notes of for future use?
2   do you need to be aware of via browsing and skim-reading?
3   do you need to be aware of and know the location of in case of future detailed need?

If you regularly employ these three yardsticks, you will soon become proficient in using your library's reference section during the production of an assignment, in searching its non-fiction shelves expertly with an informed understanding of the Dewey Decimal System, and in checking out regularly in its newspaper and journals section for useful articles or extracts. Most libraries, however they are organised geographically, incorporate the following sections or divisions:

Fiction   An area set aside for fictional novels and stories.

Non-fiction   An area in which the universal body of knowledge is set out according to a carefully devised classification system. In most UK libraries the Dewey Decimal System is employed. (See below.)

Reference section   An area which contains the year-books, dictionaries, directories and books of specialised reference of interest to public service officials, engineers, linguists, musicians and so on. These books are not usually allowed to leave the library.

Newspapers and journals   Many libraries take out subscriptions for daily and Sunday newspapers, magazines, journals and newsletters etc. spanning a wide range of specialist interest. For example – *The Economist* for those interested in business, politics and the economy, *Computer News* for those involved in computer use and so on. A brief list is set out below.

New additions   Librarians are always keen to advise their clientèle of new additions to the library stock and it is well worth keeping an eye on this area for an up-to-the-minute book on a topic central to your studies.

Catalogue and index section   This is the place where the library keeps its index of all the books, reference texts and other study materials it holds. Some libraries still employ card-index systems in wooden cabinets for this purpose and others use more extensively a computerised system for recording: the works an author has produced, the extent of the library's stock on a particular subject, helpful information such as date of publication, Dewey Decimal and ISBN references and so on. Make sure with your teacher's and librarian's help that you learn to use the cataloguing system in your library as quickly as possible if you are not entirely expert as yet.

Information technology   Many libraries today also provide rooms or booths having micro-computers and viewdata facilities to scan the databases of Prestel, Oracle and so on. Make sure you know how to take advantage of such equipment.

The Dewey Decimal System

The father of the modern library indexing system was Melvil Dewey (1851–1931). He was an American and invented the 'Dewey Decimal System' while working at a training library in Albany in 1876.

Dewey's system is based on dividing all human knowledge into ten broad categories. Each category is identified by a three-digit code number coming before a decimal point:

000. general books	600. technology
100. philosophy	700. the arts
200. religion	800. literature
300. social sciences	900. geography, history
400. language	B biography,
500. science	autobiography

Within each section of one hundred points, the broad area of, say, languages is sub-divided into a series of specialist areas. Thus books on the English language are to be found in the 420s. Alternatively, in the applied science section, books on business English applications are in the 651 section. Further degrees of specialisation are indicated by the use of numbers *behind* the decimal point:

651.74 English for business students
651.77 committees
651.78 report writing

while a further area of specialisation is introduced at a slightly later point: 653.424 Pitman 2000 Shorthand Dictation Practice.

In this way, the Dewey Decimal System is able to expand to include modern technologies like micro-electronics or newly-devised shorthand systems.

Model: how to take effective notes

To illustrate the suggested approach to taking notes and to itemise important factors, the preceding section has been set out below in note form

HOW TO TAKE EFFECTIVE NOTES 12.9.19XX

Source: People, Communication and Organisations   D.W. Evans, Pitman
ISBN. 0273 02588 0

Checklist of Points of Note

Always title notes in capital letters.

Always date your notes and record their source fully — you may wish to find original in the future.

Effective notes to be taken in two contexts:
  Orally delivered lectures/presentations
Summaries of written word: texts
magazines etc.

Notice statement on the two major contexts.

1.0 Taking Notes In An Oral Situation

Note the use of initial capitals and underlining for section headings.

  1.1 Make sure arrive on time - or fail to grasp opening points.

It helps to number sections and points for easy absorption of information.

  1.2 Arrive organised - with reserve pens and all needed 'equipment.'

  1.3 Ensure seat gives good view of board or OHP.

The points made are abbreviated from full, grammatical English, but not so much that their meaning is lost.

  1.4 Always listen actively - avoid 'switching off.'

  1.5 Seek to spot early likely structure of lectures:

    1.5.1 Expositional
    logical structure, from general to particular, often factual main points with illustrations.

Note the way that the notes are indented across the page to aid visual impact and show the relationship of major points to sub-points.

    1.5.2 Argumentative
    presents two-sided case - pros and cons thus:

      - intro main issues
      - pros points
      - cons points
      - summary both sides.
      - come down on one side.

Notice underlining of important sub-point headings.

  1.6 Teachers usually repeat information to aid students to absorb points via:
    tell 'em : intro
    tell 'em : main delivery
    tell 'em : repeat summary

Don't be afraid to put notes into your own words. Include an example if it makes a good point or aids understanding.

Libraries using the Dewey system display their books in consecutive order, starting with the 000s and ending with the 900s. In most libraries, books which are not lent out, but retained for reference are kept in a separate area, but indexed in the same way.

It should be noted that the Dewey system is not international. The Americans have now replaced it with their Library of Congress system which uses a series of numbers and letters to break down knowledge in a similar way. In Great Britain, however, the Dewey Decimal System is widely used, save in some universities.

Once you have mastered the logic behind Dewey's system, it will now take you only a minute or two to locate the section you need. The table on page 11 will show you how the ten categories are further broken down.

The catalogue system

It is difficult to generalise about library cataloguing systems, since many libraries employ different variations on the Dewey or Library of Congress theme.

Most libraries now employ a form of computer-based cataloguing, and organise the records of the books they stock under the main headings of:

author or **subject**

Under the author section, the authors are listed alphabetically and each book is listed below its author. Under the subject section, books are indexed according to where they come in the Dewey or Library of Congress coding.

Some libraries record this information on cards filed in labelled boxes, others hold the information in large ring-binders of modified computer print-out.

Golden Rule

If, at any time, you are unable to find what you want quickly – ask the librarian! No one knows his or her library better, and he or she will prove a helpful information source.

It is important, when one's work relies upon sources of information, to build up a checklist of useful reference books. Of course the nature and scope of such a checklist will depend on the type of job – the solicitor will need to know where to find information relating to law in all its aspects, the production manager will need to know where to check on established rules for manufacturing different types of machine. The office worker will need to know about postal charges, directories of organisations and companies, specialist dictionaries and business reference books.

The following list is intended for such an office worker. It is by no means exhaustive, but will provide a basis from which to build:

Dictionaries
Oxford Shorter English Dictionary
English Pronouncing Dictionary
The Pergamon Dictionary of Perfect Spelling
Cassell's New Spelling Dictionary
Dictionary of Acronyms and Abbreviations
A Dictionary of Modern English Usage
Fontana Dictionary of Modern Thought
Oxford Dictionary of Quotations
Pitman Dictionary of Shorthand

Use of English
The Complete Plain Words
Roget's Thesaurus
ABC of English Usage
Usage and Abusage
The King's English

Directories
Kelly's Directories of Streets
Kelly's Directory of Manufacturers and Merchants
Current British Directories Yearbook
Guide to Current British Periodicals

Yearbooks
British Standards Yearbook
The Post Office Guide
Whitaker's Almanac
The Municipal Yearbook
Social Sciences Yearbook
BBC, ITV Handbooks
Various Trades' Handbooks e.g. Engineering

Business reference books
ABC Railway Guide
Who's Who
Who Owns Whom
Kompass
Titles and Forms of Address
How to Find Out About Secretarial Practice
Basic Medical Vocabulary
Businessman's Guide
The Secretary's Yearbook
Business Terms, Phrases and Abbreviations

Encyclopaedias
Encyclopaedia Britannica
Larousse Illustrated International Encyclopaedia

Hotels and restaurants
Egon Ronay's Lucas Guide Yearbook
AA Guide to Hotels and Restaurants in Great Britain and Ireland
The Good Food Guide

Newspapers
The Times
The Financial Times
The Guardian
The Daily Telegraph
The International Herald Tribune

Periodicals
Business Education Today
Office Equipment News
Commerce International
New Society
Economist
New Statesman
Journal of the Institute of Bankers
Caterer and Hotelkeeper
Computer News

Using study texts effectively and economically

Having made it your early business to explore the geography of your library and its various stocks of study resources – including any IT resources – it is now necessary to become proficient in the skills of extracting the information you need from a variety of books quickly and economically. For example, you certainly will not have the time to read each and every useful

Dewey book classification outline

000 General Works
030 Encyclopaedias
070 Journalism

100 Philosophy
150 Psychology

200 Religion
220–280 Christianity
290 Non-Christian Religions

300 Social Sciences
310 Statistics
320 Political Science
330 Economics
340 Law
350 Public Administration
355–359 Armed Forces
360 Social Services
370 Education
380 Commerce
385 Railways
390 Customs, Folklore
391 Costume

400 Language
420 English Language
430 Germanic Languages
440 French
450 Italian
460 Spanish
470 Latin
480 Greek
490 Other Languages

500 Science
510 Mathematics
520 Astronomy
530 Physics
540 Chemistry
550 Earth Sciences
551.5 Meteorology
560 Palaeontology
570 Life Sciences
580 Botanical Sciences
590 Zoological Sciences

600 Technology
610 Medicine
620 Engineering

630 Agriculture
635 Gardening
640 Household Management
641.5 Cookery
650 Business Practices
658 Management
660 Chemical Technology
670–680 Manufacturing
690 Building

700 The Arts
710 The Landscape, Town Planning
720 Architecture
730 Sculpture, Metalwork
740 Drawing
745 Decorative Arts
745.5 Handicrafts
746.44 Embroidery
750 Painting
760 Graphic Arts
770 Photography
780 Music
790 Recreations
792 The Theatre
793–799 Sports and Games

800 Literature
810 American Literature
820 English Literature
830–890 Other Literatures
See 400–490 Languages

900 Geography, History
910 Geography, Travel
913 Ancient World, Archaeology
914 European Geography and Travel
915–919 Other Continents
See 930–990 History
929 Genealogy
930 Ancient History
940 History, Europe
950 Asia
960 Africa
970 North America
980 South America
990 Australasia
998 The Polar Regions

B Biography and Autobiography

book you encounter from cover to cover, and it would indeed be senseless even to try! This being so, it is helpful to know what information you can glean from the format of a text to help in saving precious time and effort.

In developing a useful approach to this aspect, always consider, before settling down to read a text, the following questions:

- What do I need this book's information for?
  – detailed study, background reading, awareness, skim-reading etc.
- Do I need to absorb all the information it provides, or only some of it?
  – a particular chapter or section, a helpful appendix, a useful diagram, chart or graph.
- At what level is the text pitched and is it suitable for my purposes?
  – 13-year-olds, BTEC National level students, university students or PhD postgraduates.
- How up-to-date is the information in the text?
  – only months old, one year, two years or ten years.
- How much does it matter that the information is not right up-to-date?
  – totally, fairly, not much, not at all.
- How long will it take to extract the information in the text and is it worth the effort?
  – well worth it, worth it, not worth it (find a shorter and more readily assimilated text).

Posing such questions while leafing through a text and sampling extracts of it will help you to get best value for your time and effort, always allowing for the range and age of books available to you.

To find the answers to the sort of questions posed above, it helps to be familiar with the customary layout or sequence of non-fiction texts:

Title page
Publication details
Table of contents
List of illustrations
Sequence of chapters or sections
Preface
Acknowledgements
Chapter summaries
Footnotes
Appendices
Bibliography
Questions/assignments and answers
Index

As you can see from the above checklist, there is more to the structure of a textbook than meets the eye! Below you will find some illustrations of these components to help you to become familiar with them; most readers – as opposed to students – tend to make straight for the chapters.

Parts of the textbook explained

The title page

As a conscientious student you are soon likely to develop a permanent crick in your neck from trying to read the titles of library books from their upright spines as they range along library shelves! But it pays to make a thorough search via titles and authors' names. If you got on well with a particular author check to see what else he or she may have written in your library's cataloguing system.

Publication details

Make sure you have checked the date of the book's publication and make a note of the book's Dewey Decimal Number and ISBN number so that you can locate it again quickly.

Look for reprint and subsequent editions details. A book which is frequently reprinted and revised indicates that it has proved very popular and this may well mean that it is well written and worthwhile.

Preface

Take the trouble to read the book's preface or prefaces – these will very often give you a quick insight into the author's or editor's attitude to the subject or his basic approach to it and this will help you to decide whether to invest some of your time in reading it or looking elsewhere. The preface also provides an outline in many books of the structure of the text.

Acknowledgements

Here the author publicly thanks the owners of the copyright of books, magazines, newspapers etc from which extracts have been printed in the book.

Consequently, the information provided in an acknowledgement section may help you to identify other books and sources of information helpful to your studies.

Table of contents

Always take the trouble to scan the book's table of contents carefully. It forms in effect the bare skeleton of the book's 'body', and you should think carefully about whether you need to read and make notes on all the book, or only on one or two of its chapters. In this way it is often possible to save time by going straight to what is directly and immediately relevant to your needs, and then perhaps doing the same in other books so as to obtain, say, two or three experts' views on interview techniques or staff appraisal before you make your own mind up. Such a technique of study will ensure that you acquire balanced views and arguments or approaches reinforced by the unanimity of several specialists.

List of illustrations

In some books a list of illustrations or diagrams is provided. It is well worth checking through it and turning to likely sources of relevant information with a view to making a photocopy. The Chinese have a proverb:

A picture is worth ten thousand words!

Thus the retention of a chart, map, diagram or illustration in your study notes may well prove invaluable later in your course.

Sequence of chapters or sections

Some books are constructed in a careful sequence and this makes it difficult to read a middle chapter without having any knowledge of preceding ones. In this situation you should 'skim-read' what comes before and after the chapter you wish to read and make notes so as to get the feel of the author's overall approach. (See below for skim-reading guidelines.)

Some authors go to the trouble of including chapter summaries at the start of each chapter, and these are a boon for the student who can thus obtain a quick outline of the content so as to judge whether it is relevant or useful.

If there are no such chapter summaries in evidence, adopt the technique of reading the first and last paragraphs of a chapter before committing yourself to reading all of it. In this way you will often obtain a shrewd notion of its content by means of the main points made in an introduction to the chapter and the major aspects chosen as part of its closing and summarising chapter.

Footnotes

Authors include footnotes as a means of providing additional information or explanation of a particular point or as a means of indicating further sources of information. It is worth reading them – even if they are sometimes set in fine print!

Appendices

The appendix – usually placed near the end of the book – is often a very helpful source of information. The function of the appendix is to act as a location or storage point in the book of particular data which has a relevance to all or part of the book's subject-matter. For example, a book on retailing may include as an appendix salient extracts of various consumer and trades description laws. Alternatively, an appendix might comprise a list of useful addresses. Often the appendix lends itself to photocopying as a means of follow-up reference or source of detailed information on a matter of background relevance.

Bibliography

The word bibliography stems from Latin and Greek and means 'a list of books'. Authors who have made reference to books in their own text very often list them in alphabetical order of author's surname or clustered under topic headings. A bibliography is of great help to the student as a shortcut to other useful texts which has been compiled in a list by the author as part of his service to his reader and thus is always worth consulting!

Questions/assignments and answers

Some texts include (at the back) a section of questions or assignments to undertake, and may also provide answers. It may be that as a formal part of your course you are requested to undertake some of these to gain practice and to try out new-found skills. If you should come across such a section in a book you locate in your library, it is well worth browsing through them, and sometimes making notes of the major assignment topics, since, when you think about it, the book's author has identified these topics as sufficiently important to include in the assessment section – so they must be worth noting!

Another value of such a section is that it provides you – if answers are also included – with an opportunity to undertake some self-testing during your course.

Index

The inclusion of an index in a text is particularly helpful to the discerning student. It provides an opportunity to glean relevant information quickly and without having to read or scan a series of chapters.

As the example below illustrates, an index is compiled alphabetically in subject order with page numbers supplied after the entry.

```
limited partnerships   24
liquidity   17, 178, 181, 210
    world   224
liquidation   31
Liverpool   5, 54
livestock   2
living standards see standard of living
Lloyd's   186
loan stock   30
loans see bank loans
local government   20, 114, 120
localised unemployment   55, 77–8, 135, 137–8
location of industry   52–6
```

The supply of an individual page number usually means that the topic is referred to on that page but perhaps only in passing, by name. The reference which implies a number of pages:

217–229

means that the topic is handled and discussed throughout the pages cited: in the above example, in 13 pages.

Example of publication data

PITMAN PUBLISHING LIMITED
128 Long Acre, London WC2E 9AN

A Longman Group Company

© Desmond W Evans 1978, 1984

First published in Great Britain 1978
Reprinted 1979, 1980, 1982 (twice), 1983
Second edition 1984
Reprinted 1986

British Library Cataloguing in Publication Data
Evans, Desmond W.
  People and communication. – 2nd ed.
  1. Communications in organisations
  I. Title
  658.4'5   HM131

ISBN 0 273 01972 4

Text set in 10/12 pt Sabon Roman
Printed and bound in Great Britain
at The Bath Press, Avon

1. Before you do anything:

   Check carefully when it was first written and whether you are looking at a recent edition.

If you think you will want to use it again make a note of its ISBN number and its Dewey decimal classification.

It may be that the text is not sufficiently up-to-date — if so, proceed no further!

Publication details from
'People and Communication' Second Edition by
D. W. Evans published by
Pitman Publishing Ltd

Contents

2. Go next to the book's Table of Contents. Study now the structure of the book in this helpful 'skeletal' outline to see if you need to refer to all of it or only one or two sections. In this way you can save yourself much time!

3. While you are studying the contents section, skim through it to see what other chapters or parts could be worth noting (in your notebook!) for a future topic, of your course.

Table of Contents extract from
'Office Management' by J. C. Denyer
revised by Josephine Shaw,
Macdonald & Evans
Fifth Edition

Example of an index

4. Before delving into chapters check (usually at the back of the book) if there is an index. If so, this can take you directly to the particular area you wish to research.

Notice that single page references usually are quite restricted while those hyphenated deal with a topic at length.

Also, a good index provides helpful cross-references, or explanations.

Thus there will clearly be some extended data in this part of the book worth checking.

Indexes also provide cross-references:

bits, *see* Computer binary digits

here the reference to 'bits' of information in computer form are shown as being dealt with under the index heading 'Computer binary digits'. The entry for this subject in the index supplies the page references.

As you can see, the index provides a direct shortcut to detailed information which would otherwise be 'buried' in thousands of words of text. A good practice, therefore, when researching information for an assignment, is to make sure you consult the indexes of the books you locate. This regular study habit will save you hours of time during your course and almost certainly result in your finding a wide range of useful data.

Summary

The above checklist of book components has, all being well, shown that there is more than meets the eye to extracting information from library texts. If you use the guidelines suggested regularly and conscientiously, you will soon become accomplished in locating and extracting helpful information quickly and simply.

Developing reading skills

It must seem rather strange to come upon the above title of a topic on reading when you have almost certainly read thousands upon thousands of words in your life so far! Nevertheless, it is important at the outset of an extended course of study to reconsider the ways – rather than way – that reading may be undertaken.

It is therefore helpful to consider the ways in which we all read, depending upon the circumstances in which the reading takes place, and to incorporate such approaches *consciously* in study reading routines.

Examples

1 Very quick reading of an important letter to get to the essential message as quickly as possible – as in a letter about a recent interview for a job or place at college or university.

In this circumstance, the non-essential, 'leading-up' and congratulating or 'letting down lightly' parts of the letter are initially glossed over in a first reading and only taken in more carefully at a second reading, because only the essential message is initially important.

2 Scanning paragraphs quickly with the eye being used almost like a satellite camera which only stops when a key word or phrase is spotted.

This sort of reading is done when, for example, a student is leafing through a magazine or journal of articles to check whether there is one worth stopping to consider in a slower more detailed way.

Such a 'skim-reading' technique is very helpful to 'pre-digest' possibly useful information, but it must be made clear that it is not a substitute for careful, painstaking reading.

3 Reading for clear understanding and remembering is a much slower business. People like accountants,

lawyers, doctors and professors, whose daily lives require the reading of long, specialist and often complex documents will read the same piece perhaps three times:

First: fairly quickly to get the gist of it.

Second: slowly to absorb the meaning fully.

Third: fairly quickly to get the feel of the structure and logical sequence and to summarise mentally the main points.

4   Reading for note-taking combines the approaches suggested in 2 and 3 above. In addition, it requires pauses at paragraph intervals to allow information to be digested and then noted. Thus the technique of reading a passage or chapter may be summarised as follows:

- first skim-read the whole piece to get the feel of its approach and in so doing let key words and phrases 'hit' your eye and consciousness
- then read the first and last paragraphs to check introductory issues and summarising closing points
- it may be necessary to read the whole chapter first at a steady pace before attempting to make notes of it
- next read the passage a paragraph or 12–15 lines at a time
- make your notes of this paragraph or section in your own words, seizing upon major points, names, dates and other essential factual data
- continue this practice until you complete the chapter
- lastly, re-read your notes to make sure you have omitted nothing of importance, while the chapter is fresh in your mind. Also check that your notes make sense and will also make sense in six months' time!

Summary

'Topic 1: How to study effectively' has outlined a number of tips, guidelines and useful practices to assist you in swiftly settling into a happy and productive routine. Of course, every student is different and will naturally develop habits and routines in step with his or her life-style and general approach to learning. The advice set out in this Topic results from much teaching and studying experience and should provide you with a helpful start to your studies in general. To summarise, 12 golden study rules are set out below which you should always keep in mind:

12 Golden Rules for effective studying

1   Organise your time each day and each week with care and forethought to make best use of it. It pays to work to a regular study timetable.

2   Avoid starting to study late in the evening or when you are tired. You must have an alert and sharp mind to study effectively.

3   It is better to study in a series of 3–4 1 hour periods with 15–30 minute breaks in between than to attempt to 'slog' without a pause or break through study stints of 3–4 unbroken hours.

4   Take the trouble to organise your study area or room so that it is comfortable and conducive to regular periods of work, free of interruptions and distractions. Keep it tidy at all times!

5   Always ensure your main body of notes are kept safe at home, secure from loss.

6   Take the trouble to devise a database or index system so as to be able to find quickly what you filed months previously and so as to provide a memory-jogging index of what study data you have amassed.

7   Always be on the look-out for useful study material from the wide range of audio-visual sources around you.

8   Take proper care with developing note-taking skills and make a regular routine of writing up your notes clearly while they are still fresh in your mind, so as to provide you with useful data you will be able to understand months later.

9   Take the trouble to learn how to use your library's available resources to the utmost, particularly its indexing and cataloguing system. Make friends with the librarians – they are a precious source of help and also have feelings and sensitivities!

10   Learn how to get information from texts quickly and economically.

11   Practise consciously the various reading skills discussed.

12   Remember that like life, the process of studying has its ups and downs and the greatest aid to your success is 'stickability' and determination!

Build-up tasks

1   Re-read the section of Topic 1 which deals with the production of a personal weekly study timetable and then design your own.

Go over it with your teacher and when you both consider it neither too easy-going nor over-demanding, copy it for display in your study area and for insertion in your travelling ring-binder so as to help you to establish a regular pattern of weekly study.

2   Browse through your school or college library's reference section and select ten reference books you think likely to be of use during your course of study.

Back in your classroom discuss your choice with your fellow students and make up a checklist of those which seem to be of most help, with brief notes on what information you and your fellow students have discovered they contain.

In this way you will quickly build up a useful outline knowledge of your library's reference resources.

3   Design either as the format of an index card or as an entry format on a micro database package a cataloguing system for storing the information about the study materials you collect during your studies.

Establish your own study materials database in your study area and maintain it as you acquire handouts, photocopies, tape programmes, etc.

4   As a group activity at school or college, design and implement a study materials database for the core Units of your course of study which all your class can have access to.

You should consider carefully the sort of documentation you will need to produce as paper forms on which to collect the information prior to processing it, and then how the database may best be classified and its information organised for eventual distribution.

5   Check through the current copies of the *Radio Times* and *TV Times* to see what radio and television programmes due to be broadcast may be worth recording. Make arrangements to record them by audio-visual means, either at home or at school or college.

Set up a rota of three to four students in your group whose job it will be to act as a tv and radio monitoring panel for four weeks at a time and to publish in your classroom details and dates/times of relevant programmes as a class informational service.

6   Make a careful study of the Units which go to make up your course syllabus, and with your teacher's help, draw up a checklist of the major study topics for each Unit.

This checklist will prove a useful reference when you come across a book or article in your searches which relates to a topic to be dealt with at a later date. You will then be able to make a note of its precise location to come back to, or you may decide to make a study copy of the material there and then.

7   Find out the precise location in your library and the exact Dewey Decimal number for books in stock under the following headings:

Business Law
Business Practices
Public Administration
Business Finance
Manufacturing
Commerce
Design of Manufactured Goods

8   Survey the periodicals, journals and newspapers which your library takes on regular subscription and list those which you think likely to be of particular help in the future after you have made a brief examination of their contents.

Compare your list with those drawn up by your fellow students.

Case study

'You can't afford to be wrong'

The following interview recently took place between Tina Barker, a top secretary, and David Jackson, an educational researcher:

DAVID JACKSON   Let's turn to sources of information. When you were following your business education course did you make much use of your college library?

TINA BARKER   Well, not enough – initially! When I first started at the college, I used to walk past the library and feel somehow 'put off' by the rows and rows of books. I suppose it looked a bit intimidating. We were all given an induction and the library staff were very helpful, but even so, I just didn't make the effort to get to grips with the way it was organised and then, of course, I felt I didn't want to have to ask basic questions about where to find books.

DAVID JACKSON   Did your failure to use the library have any adverse effects?

TINA BARKER   Oh, yes! It wasn't long before my work suffered. Both the teaching staff and I knew that I wasn't doing any proper research for essays or checking up on half-remembered facts and so on.

DAVID JACKSON   Well, Tina, what caused you to change your attitude towards using the library?

TINA BARKER   Oh, I almost blush to tell you even now! I was brought up with a jolt when I was asked to produce a programme introducing a distinguished speaker invited to the college to give a talk to students in my department. Well, I thought I knew how he spelled his name and also, I'd somehow missed the fact that he'd been knighted in a New Year's Honours List. He really was an eminent person in the business field, with a string of letters after his name – all of which I could have checked and included in the programme, which in the event was duplicated in something of a rush. Well, you can imagine my embarrassment! People were definitely not amused, and I just wanted to hide! From that day on I vowed I would become expertly acquainted with the library and its information and reference services. It was a salutary lesson, and one which has stood me in good stead in my own secretarial career.

DAVID JACKSON   Did you find that being familiar with library services helped you in your job?

TINA BARKER   Absolutely! You see, in my view there are basically two types of knowledge – firstly, simply knowing a thing for sure, and secondly, knowing how and where to look up and find out about something when you're not sure or simply don't know. In my present job, I work for a senior manager with contacts and associations in all sorts of fields – local government, the civil service, manufacturing companies and overseas organisations. I never know what he'll want to find out about next – it could be exporting regulations to Brazil or the name and address of the Chief Executive of the Berkshire County Council. And in such matters – I found out early – you can't afford to be wrong!

Also, my principal's interested in what is absolutely new on the market and in what our competitors are doing, so I often have to refer to the specialist trade journals and magazines – which incidentally are taken by my local public library!

DAVID JACKSON   What about the librarians themselves, do you use their expertise?

TINA BARKER   Very much so. In fact, I'm frequently on the telephone asking for some rather obscure piece of information and they're most helpful, and their expertise saves me an awful lot of time. And even when they don't have the book or journal I need, they'll obtain it for me. In fact I don't think I could do my particular job without the help they provide.

DAVID JACKSON   Thank you, Tina, that's been a most interesting account. It's funny, isn't it, how sometimes an isolated incident can cause people to change an attitude completely. And in your case, I'm sure it was all to the good.

Assignments and discussion topics

1 Read the above case study concerning the experiences of a former student and in a group discussion, consider the following questions:

1.1 What is it about libraries which some students find so off-putting and daunting?

Is it that some students fail to take the trouble to find out what a help a library can be sufficiently early in their courses and then don't like to 'lose face' by showing they feel intimidated and embarrassed by not knowing how to locate a book or use the cataloguing system?

1.2 Do some students use their sense of discomfort at being in a library as an excuse for underlying laziness?

1.3 What do you think could be done in your school or college to encourage students to make more effective use of the library?

2 In pairs or groups of 3–4 students, carry out a careful survey of the range of services and resources which your library offers and produce a leaflet or brochure including suitable diagrams and illustrations which would appeal to other student groups within your centre. Your aim in producing this leaflet should be to encourage doubtful library users to overcome any hesitations in using the library's facilities to the full.

Your leaflet should not include more than 250–300 words in total.

2 How to use a dictionary and thesaurus

How to use your dictionary effectively

One of the main reasons why many people continue to suffer from the limitations and frustrations of having a restricted vocabulary at their disposal is, quite simply, that they cannot be bothered to look up and digest the meaning and information about a new and unfamiliar word in a good dictionary! If you really *do* wish to improve and extend the range of your active vocabulary, then you must take the trouble to carry out this essential work each time you meet an unknown word and then to make the effort to introduce it into your talking or writing as soon as possible. Your constant companions from now on should be your pocket notebook and your pocket dictionary – supported by your larger dictionary on your study or work desk.

There are a number of helpful and informative dictionaries on the market and, as with most purchases, you will tend to get what you pay for. It is a false economy where a dictionary is concerned to consider price as the only factor – your studies are likely to be amply rewarded by purchasing the best you can afford.

The following checklist includes some of the principal features you should take into account before buying your dictionary.

1   *Current edition*   Check when the dictionary was last revised or a new edition published. There have been so many new words added to English recently that a dictionary which has not been revised for ten or so years will be very much out of date when it comes to current usage and popular meaning of words.

2   *Pronunciation*   Most dictionaries include an introduction which explains the signs and symbols used to indicate how words are pronounced. Make sure you read through this carefully. For example, the sign′ immediately after a syllable means that it is the stressed one:

con′trast   exhil′arate   psychol′ogy

The sign ĭ is used to signify a short, unstressed syllable:

arĭthmetĭc   cŏntĭněn′tal   ĭllŭ′strĭous

The sign – is used to convey a long vowel sound of a syllable:

lī′lac   refri′gerāte   contribū′tion

A dot over an ė indicates that it is pronounced 'igh':

nak′ėd   mag′nėtize

Such an introduction will also provide help on general pronunciation and the way in which a phonetic (how the word sounds) system is employed in the dictionary entries.

3   *Plurals*   The plural form of words is also an essential part of an entry in a good dictionary and is often shown as:

goose n. (pl. geese pr. gēs)

Here the plural spelling of the word is shown and its pronunciation indicated by the symbol for a long 'e'.

4   *Abbreviations*   A checklist of the various abbreviations used in the dictionary will also be found as a rule in the introduction of a good dictionary. Such a list will include a range of letters to signify the part of speech of the entry – **n** for noun, **v** for verb and so on. Also, the word's origins (etymological roots) will be shown in the section *Where English came from* – MHG would mean Middle High German, for instance.

Your efforts in learning what the abbreviation symbols mean will be amply repaid in strengthening your word power and confidence in using words.

Many dictionaries also provide an appendix or other form of checklist of commonly used abbreviations or acronyms (words formed from the first letters of a title, e.g. BBC for British Broadcasting Corporation). Often to be found in such checklists are entries like:

GP – General Practitioner   RSVP – Répondez S'il Vous Plaît   TUC – Trades Union Congress   etc – et cetera

5   *Tables of weight, volume, distance, conversion*   The good dictionary will often include various tables which set out the principal points of, say, imperial or metric

measurement, the metric system of measuring areas and volume or the conversion of inches into centimetres and so on.

6   *Words of foreign origin*   In addition, it is usual to find foreign words listed with a detail of their pronunciation in English, and what anglicised pronunciation is commonly accepted:

Marseilles   'Marsales'

Otherwise the pronunciation in the foreign language is mirrored:

coiffeur: kwahfer′   pièce-de-résistance   pērs de rāze′st

7   *The addenda*   As you can imagine, the compilation of a dictionary takes a long time, and during its course, a number of words may have extended their meaning or new ones may have been coined. Others may have been omitted in error. Thus an addenda or 'additions' section is often to be found at the back of dictionaries, and is well worth browsing through – 'bug', for example, is likely to be shown as a concealed microphone as well as the general word for a type of insect, or 'pad' as the launching platform for a rocket and not merely as a compress on layered cloth!

Extracting the meaning of a typical entry

The following entry is taken from the seventh edition of *The Concise Oxford Dictionary* and it has been selected to show you how a typical entry is made up, and what may be learned from it.

---

swine *n.* (*pl.* same). **1.** (US, formal, or Zool.) = PIG 1, whence **swī′**nERY[3] *n.; *PEARL[1]*s before swine*. **2.** person of greedy or bestial habits; (colloq.) unpleasant thing. **3.** ~-**fever,** infectious intestinal virus disease of pigs; ~-**herd,** one who tends pigs; ~-**plague,** infectious bacterial lung-disease of pigs. **4.** Hence **swī′**nISH[1] *a.* (esp. of persons or their habits). [OE *swīn,* = OS, OHG *swīn,* ON *svín,* Goth. *swein* f. Gmc **swīnam,* neut. (as n.) of a. f. IE **suw-* pig]

From an initial survey of this entry, the reader might be forgiven for thinking that he or she needs a dictionary to decipher the dictionary entry! Phrases like:

'infectious intestinal virus disease of pigs'

takes some sorting out and words like 'bacterial' and 'bestial' do indeed tend to 'hit us between the eyes'! Never mind, the same dictionary can deal with these too.

In looking at the entry, 'swine', it is worth noting that the alphabetical arrangement of the words in the dictionary follows a strict system. Clearly all the words starting with *a* come before all those starting with *b*

and so on. Moreover, within each letter section – a, b or c etc – the system also is enforced:

aback comes before *acacia*

simply because the second letter of *aback* is b and that of *acacia* is c. In the same way, the entry '*abbreviate*' comes before *ABC*, because the third letter of *abbreviate* is a b (the other two being identical) and that of *ABC* is a c.

The next entry against 'swine' is: n. This abbreviation, as we know, means that the word swine is a noun or the naming word of something.

We also learn from (*pl. same*) that the word swine does not change in its plural form – for example 'Many swine browsed in the meadow'.

The entries which follow after the numbers 1.2.3.4. illustrate different meanings or uses of the word and show how it may be used in conjunction with another (*swine-fever*) to form a further word of different meaning.

The entry takes the trouble to inform us that the word swine is used formally in the United States and in Zoology to mean pig and that in the USA (as opposed to elsewhere) the word *swinery* is used for a place where pigs are housed.

A further part of the entry refers to the proverbial expression taken from the Bible of casting pearls before swine.

The smaller numbers 1,2,3,4, invite us to check the entry in the dictionary, for example, for ISH.

Lastly, the entry concludes by showing us the origin of the word *swin* from the Old English, or the Old Saxon and Old High German *swin*, the Old Norse *svin* and the Gothic *swein*.

It is remarkable how much information surrounds a simple five-letter word, but then it has been around in English for a long time! Of course, you will not always wish to study a dictionary entry in such detail – you may simply wish to check on the spelling of a word or a particular meaning or use of it. Nevertheless, it is worth knowing precisely what sort of information you may expect to obtain from the entry of a word in a reputable dictionary:

1   its correct spelling (or spellings)
2   its accepted pronunciation (or alternative pronunciations)
3   how it is spelled in the plural, including accepted alternative spellings
4   what part of speech it is, and what parts of speech its derivative words are (e.g. swine, n. swine-fever, n.)
5   in what ways it is used and what meaning (or meanings) it has
6   how it is linked to other words or expressions to form words (especially hyphenated ones of an extended meaning)
7   the origins of the word from old (or current) languages.

Bear in mind that the word *swine*, though it has served to show some of the major factors of a dictionary entry by no means includes all the signs and symbols which may be employed, so do spend some time browsing through those in your dictionary's introduction.

Here are some you may expect to find:

app. apparently   Bibl. Biblical   c. circa (about the time of)   colloq. used colloquially or as slang   sl. slang   sp. spelling   P proprietary name (e.g. hoover)   D disputed usage

Provided that you are prepared to devote some time to familiarising yourself with your dictionary's system of codes and symbols, you will find it a lifelong friend as well as a most helpful and informative tool. Correspondingly, your word-power will increase, and with it your self-confidence and ability to capture and hold other people's attention.

Build-up tasks

1   Find out how the following words are pronounced in English:

raison d'être   charabanc   lingerie   vol-au-vent

2   Find out what the following abbreviations stand for:

AAA   cl. do.   exc.   HRH   Mme NALGO
prop.   WHO   UNESCO   E&OE   prov.   pp

3   How many meanings can you find out for:

peer   rig   grave   fair   catch   bind

4   Find out what the following prefixes and suffixes mean: (note: prefix is that part of a word which comes first, and suffix that part which comes last.)

Prefixes	Suffixes
pre-	-ist
bi-	-ism
hyper-	-ious
contra-	-graph

While you are investigating, check out the origins of these prefixes and suffixes.

5   Use your dictionary to find out and list the proverbial expressions associated with the following words:

pride   blue   die   fine   fool

6   By using your dictionary, find out whether the following words are:

(a) all one word   (b) joined by a hyphen   (c) two separate words

race/track   race/horse   post/card   sea/breeze
ladies'/tailor   stomach/ache   under/ground
all/right

How to use an English language thesaurus profitably

An English language thesaurus of words and phrases may best be described as a giant key which can unlock a vast treasure-house of English vocabulary and expressions. Learn how to use this straightforward key and you will gain access to a fascinating way of extending your vocabulary quickly and painlessly!

Peter Mark Roget, the most famous of the thesaurus compilers, was born in 1778, and was a doctor by profession. He developed a life-long passion for words and for classifying them into helpful categories as an aid for writers, public speakers and – in fact – anyone with an interest in developing a wider vocabulary.

Roget's *Thesaurus* has become a faithful friend and companion for all whose stock-in-trade is words. Even the most fluent journalist or politician sometimes becomes stuck for an alternative to a particular word or expression he would like to use again but does not wish to repeat exactly for fear of becoming repetitive or boring. Similarly, inexperienced writers suddenly notice that they have used the same tired old phrase three times within eight lines of text – in either case, the thesaurus can resolve the problem by offering a series of lists of words and phrases collected in groups, sharing a similar or identical root meaning and branching out in a logical progression to words more distant from the root word. Consider the following example taken from Roget's Thesaurus, updated to meet current language needs:

> **556. Artist – N.** *artist*, craftsman *or* -woman 686 *artisan*; architect 164 *producer*; art master *or* mistress, designer, draughtsman *or* woman; fashion artist, dress-designer, couturier, couturière; drawer, sketcher, delineator, limner; copyist; caricaturist, cartoonist; illustrator, commercial artist; painter, colourist, luminist; dauber, amateur; pavement artist; scene-painter, sign-p.; oil-painter, watercolourist, pastellist; illuminator, miniaturist; Academician, RA; old master; art historian, iconographer; aesthetician.
>   *sculptor*, sculptress, carver, statuary, monumental mason, modeller, moulder.
>   *engraver*, etcher, acquatinter; lapidary, chaser, gem-engraver; typographer 587 *printer*.

Here we find set out in an organised form some 60 alternative words or phrases which derive from the root idea of *artist*, and almost certainly we should find an alternative word here for *artist*, whether in the field of painting, sculpture or printing.

Similar groups of words set down as nouns, verbs, adjectives or other parts of speech (these are dealt with in detail in the grammar and syntax sections which follow) are displayed throughout the thesaurus according to the following classification:

PLAN OF CLASSIFICATION

Class	Section	Heads
1 Abstract Relations	1 Existence	1–8
	2 Relation	9–25
	3 Quantity	26–59
	4 Order	60–84
	5 Number	85–107
	6 Time	108–142
	7 Change	143–155
	8 Causation	156–182

PLAN OF CLASSIFICATION continued

As you can see from the above table, Roget broke down his thesaurus into these parts:

1   A class given over to such abstract ideas as, relationships, time, change etc.

2   A class for the words associated with space, form and motion.

3   A class for words to do with all forms of matter.

4   A class about the intellect of the mind, about thought processes and the communication of ideas.

5   A class for the exercise of the will or freedom of choice.

6   And lastly, a class on emotion, religion and morality.

As you will have noticed, some classes are divided into divisions. Also, each class has a further sub-division entitled 'Section' and each section is made up of a series of numbered heads. Thus, Class Four has two divisions, the second called: *Communication of ideas*. This division is further sub-divided into three sections, the second of which is termed *Modes of communication*, and contains 24 different heads. The first, numbered

522 starts with a list on *manifestation* – as of spirits appearing, and goes on to include words to do with exhibits, displays and so on. The third heading, 524, deals with the idea of *information*, and provides words and ideas such as: viewdata, computer, hearsay, broadcasting and so on.

However, the user of the thesaurus is most unlikely to approach the use of the thesaurus in this way. He or she is much more likely to turn straight to the back of the thesaurus, to the Index. Here, the root words of the 990 heads which make up the thesaurus are listed alphabetically. Suppose, for example, we wanted to find an alternative to the word 'information' we would look it up in the alphabetical list, and, lo and behold, find against it the reference 524 n. This means that we should turn to Head number 524 in the book and find that alternative nouns or naming words for information are set down there. The further use of this Index is that it supplies, under the root word, different meanings or versions of the idea:

inform
  inform 524 vb
  educate 534 vb
– against
  inform 524 vb
  accuse 928 vb

Thus in the area of the idea *inform* we are given two places to look; either under 524 vb, where the idea is basically 'to tell', or under 534 vb, where the idea is 'inform meaning to educate'. Alternatively we might be seeking the list of words where the idea is to 'inform against someone'. In this instance, we are referred to Head 928.

Should we turn to Head 928, we would find it starts with: *Accusation* and goes on with *complaint*, *charge*, *home truth* and so on. Having exhausted the nouns or naming words for 'to inform against', it proceeds to list adjectives like: *accusing*, *incriminating*, *suspicious* etc, and then provides verbs like: *to accuse*, *challenge*, or *defy*.

In this way, the thesaurus can supply help, whether you are looking for another word for 'accusation' as a noun, or for the verb, 'to accuse'.

And, as if this were not enough, the Head 928 provides for certain words a cross reference to another Head in the thesaurus. For example, if the sense of the word we seek in Head 928 for 'accusation' is to reproach someone, or cause them to think again about an action, then we are referred to Head 924. A section under 924 begins with the word 'reproach' which includes *hard words* and *reprimand*.

In this way, the reader is able to travel backwards and forwards through the thousands of words of the thesaurus until just the right alternative word or phrase is found – and this can be a godsend to a tired brain!

Summary

To summarise, then, all you need to be able to use an English language thesaurus successfully are:

1 The price of an average paperback or a library ticket.

2 The ability to spell reasonably, so as to use the alphabetically set out Index.

3 The ability to leaf through a numerical sequence between 1 and 990.

4 The ability – gained from this book – to identify a word as a noun, verb, adjective etc.

5 And, most important, a sufficiently open mind actually to go out and find one and 'get the hang of it'!

> If you do master the way to 'read' all the parts of the entries in your dictionary, and do learn the simple rules of using a thesaurus, and do refer to both regularly, your mastery of English words and vocabulary range must improve!

So, having gained access to a thesaurus, move on now to the thesaurus assignments.

Build-up tasks

1 Consider the following sentences:

(a) One sure way out of the recession lies in a definite growth in the economy. This . . . could be achieved in a number of ways.

(b) Acquiring the business to produce this growth, however, is by no means easy. In order to . . . increased business, it is necessary to be competitive across a range of world-wide markets.

Assume that you do not wish to repeat the word 'growth' in the dotted space in (a) nor the word 'acquire' in the dotted space in (b). Consult your thesaurus to find two suitable alternative words which would fit in (a) and (b).

2 Follow the same approach to find appropriate alternative words for each of the dotted spaces in the following passage. The numbers beginning the dotted spaces refer to words shown after the passage, to provide you with the sense of what is wanted:

It is always a pleasure to be introduced by you, Mr Chairman, and indeed, it is with great 1 . . . that I stand before you all this

evening to talk about improving one's English. Many experts have put forward their methods for 2 . . . either written or spoken English skills but there is no quick or simple route to this worthy destination. Indeed, the 3 . . . is sometimes full of pitfalls and often goes uphill! The person who wishes to 4 . . . in correct and acceptable English must possess the qualities of patience and determination.

He or she must 5 . . . work through a progressive programme of study which will provide plenty of opportunities for practising accuracy and style. It is certainly in the 6 . . . of writing that progress and development are to be won.

With the help of your thesaurus, find an alternative to the word given below which will fit in each of the numbered spaces:

1 pleasure 2 improving 3 route 4 communicate
5 patiently 6 practice

3 Using your thesaurus, find suitable alternatives for the words or phrases underlined in the following sentences:

(a) The young girl looked extremely <u>agitated</u> as she waited for her driving-test.

(b) The ballroom formation dancing team appeared extremely <u>lively</u> as they went through their routine in front of the judges.

(c) As he felt rather depressed, he was not <u>in a sociable frame of mind.</u>

(d) The chairman ran the meeting in a most <u>dictatorial</u> way.

(e) The bomb-blast left a scene of <u>havoc</u> never before witnessed in such a quiet village.

(f) From the look on her face, it was clear that she <u>had resented</u> the remark made by the angry customer.

4 Again, with the help of your thesaurus, find a suitable alternative for the following definitions (either as a single word or as a phrase – a small group of words.):

youngster:	when taken to mean someone young, poorly dressed and presumably fending for himself.
mistake:	meaning when something has gone wrong as a result of carelessness on someone's part.
evil:	as if in league with the devil.
to be cheeky:	as, for example, a child being disrespectful to adults.
to voice:	when, for example, speaking carefully so that each syllable is clearly understood.

3 The communication process

Introduction

'I've always believed in calling a spade a spade . . .'

'I don't believe in beating about the bush . . .'

'Always speak my mind . . .'

'I fancy I'm pretty clear-minded . . .'

'Communication? No problem – it's the other people round here . . .'

It's a fact of life that we all consider ourselves to be good communicators. After all, by the time we start work we've been at it for at least sixteen years, and we manage to get what we want. Or do we? Part of our self-esteem, that image of ourselves which acts as a kind of defence-mechanism in the face of the bruisings of this world, requires that we see ourselves as straight-talking, level-headed, able, honest, and above all, effective communicators.

Yet how often do we fail to see ourselves as others see us?

'Trouble with Harry, he always calls a spade a shovel . . .'

'Like a bull in a china shop at the last meeting . . .'

'Every time she opens her mouth, she puts her foot in it . . .'

'Janet's all right, she just has a talent for rubbing people up the wrong way . . .'

'He's all right as long as it's only the computer he's talking to!'

All too often there is a difference between what we say and what we think we have said, and between how we feel we have handled people and how they think they have been treated. When such 'gaps' occur between the intent and the action often it is stated that there has been 'a break-down in communication'. Sometimes the breakdown is allowed to become so serious that the gap becomes a chasm – relatives in families ceasing to speak to one another, managements and trade unions refusing to meet and governments recalling ambassadors when relations between states reach a low ebb.

In fact, whenever people communicate, either as individuals or within groups, problems inevitably occur – instructions may be impossible to carry out, offence is taken at a particular remark, a directive is ambiguously phrased, or people's attitudes are coloured by jealousy, resentment or frustration.

During the past fifty years, industrial, commercial and public service organisations have grown prodigiously to meet the needs of advanced technological societies. Sometimes as many as 10 000 people work on one site, or one company employs more than 50 000 people. Multinational companies send electronic messages on facsimile transmitters around the world at the press of a button. Clearly, good communications are essential to the efficient operation of any organisation, and vital to the fulfilment of all those who commit their working lives to it.

For this reason, management specialists and behavioural scientists have devoted much thought and energy over recent years to analysing the problems caused by bad communication practices, and to creating good communication climates, and systems.

As a result of the current structure of societies and economies, most of us will spend our working lives in an organisation – for many of us it will be a large one. If we are to understand our working environment it is essential that we become good communicators with effective social skills.

Theory and process

When communication specialists began to study the theory and process of communication methodically, they developed an approach to the mechanics of communicating which is, perhaps, best expressed as a cycle. Essentially, 'messages' are 'sent' and 'received' and confirmation of their receipt and interpretation is returned by a 'receiver' to a 'sender'; effective communication is always a two-way process.

As a result of carefully performed experiments and the patient compilation of case-histories of various communication practices, management specialists and behavioural scientists came to appreciate that what appeared on the surface to be a simple and straightforward process was, in fact, both involved and subtle. After all, if the workings of one human mind are complex, how much more so must be the various interactions and relationships of two, or even many minds, in the process of communication!

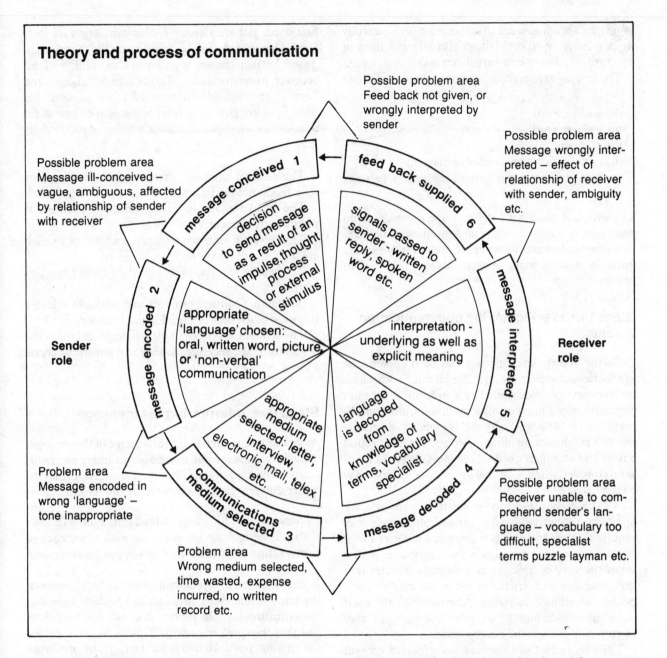

Theory and process of communication

Possible problem area
Feed back not given, or
wrongly interpreted by
sender

Possible problem area
Message wrongly inter-
preted – effect of
relationship of receiver
with sender, ambiguity
etc.

Possible problem area
Message ill-conceived –
vague, ambiguous, affected
by relationship of sender
with receiver

message conceived 1

feed back supplied 6

decision
to send message
as a result of an
impulse, thought
process
or external
stimulus

signals passed to
sender – written
reply, spoken
word etc.

message encoded 2

message interpreted 5

appropriate
'language' chosen:
oral, written word, picture,
or 'non-verbal'
communication

interpretation –
underlying as well as
explicit meaning

**Sender
role**

**Receiver
role**

appropriate
medium
selected: letter,
interview,
electronic mail, telex
etc.

language
is decoded
from
knowledge of
terms, vocabulary
specialist

**communications
medium selected 3**

message decoded 4

Problem area
Message encoded in
wrong 'language' –
tone inappropriate

Possible problem area
Receiver unable to com-
prehend sender's lan-
guage – vocabulary too
difficult, specialist
terms puzzle layman etc.

Problem area
Wrong medium selected,
time wasted, expense
incurred, no written
record etc.

Simply expressed, the cycle of communicating proceeds through a number of stages during which a message is conceived by a sender, encoded and relayed via a particular route to a receiver who then decodes and interprets it and finally confirms to the sender that it has been understood. This process is set out in more detail in the diagram.

Stage one: conceiving the message

The first stage in the communication process is the decision made by a sender to communicate a message. Some messages are sent involuntarily – such as a scream of fright or gasp of pain. Others are the result of an impulse which occurs so quickly that the sender is barely conscious of having decided to say or do anything. Yet others may be the result of a careful process of reasoning. Some messages are the product of an internal reasoning or emotional process and some of an external stimulus.

The very act of articulating an idea in words, expressions or gestures is in itself a development of originating the idea itself. Even so, it is not uncommon for people to conceive ideas which when uttered are regarded as 'half-baked', or for someone to regret at the moment of speaking a conceived message:

'I really put my foot in it!'

Moreover, in the electronic office, where messages are very rapidly 'switched' to remote locations or copied by high-speed printers, it is vital that messages are carefully conceived. In the words of the proverb – 'Think before putting mouth (or one might add, keyboard) in gear!'

Stage two: encoding the message

Before a message may be sent to its recipient, the sender needs to encode it in an appropriate language. The language may take the form of a sympathetic grunt, an abrupt gesture of impatience or a carefully written letter or report. It may also take the form of a picture, symbol or non-verbal expression or gesture.

The languages of communication include the following:

the spoken word

the written word

the number

the picture, drawing, symbol or diagram

the non-verbal communication: expression, gesture, posture

The eventual success of the message depends in no small part upon the choice of an appropriate language. At a sales conference, for example, a chart may express instantly what a long, spoken address may fail to impart.

Stage three: selecting the communication medium

Once the appropriate language has been chosen, the sender needs to select the right medium through which to transmit the message. The choice of a medium depends upon a number of, sometimes, quite complicated factors. The proximity and availability of a colleague in a neighbouring office may suggest a head round a door and a spoken word. If the message is disciplinary, however, then a formal, private interview may be required.

Some messages need to be written – contracts are an obvious example – and geographical distance may require that the message is transmitted in letter-form, or via an electronic message-switching system. Sometimes the very complexity of a message dictates that it is produced as a written report which may be composed and studied in stages. Alternatively, the need for a quick exchange of attitudes and opinions may suggest a meeting as the best medium.

The likely effect of a message upon its receiver will also influence the choice of medium. Bad news, for example, is much better broken in a private interview than more impersonally in a letter.

Some major factors influencing the choice of the communications medium are:

potential effectiveness

need for tact

simultaneous reception of information by recipients

need for a written record

confidentiality

need for instant feedback

complexity of message

time

cost

need for speed

Stage four: decoding the message

Before a message can be absorbed or acted upon it first needs to be understood. Many messages are ineffective because the sender failed to realise that the language he had chosen was beyond the ability of his receiver to comprehend. Terms like 'officialese' and 'jargon' are frequently employed when someone has used inappropriate language. Some of the reasons for a failure by a receiver to decode a message successfully are:

The receiver does not share the sender's language (e.g. he cannot read a graph).

The sender's vocabulary (words or phrases) is unknown to the receiver.

The sender's sentence structure and use of English are too difficult for the receiver to grasp.

The sender is a specialist and the receiver is a layman.

Education, cultural pursuits and outlooks create a language block between sender and receiver.

The sender uses over-simple language and thus condescends to the receiver causing resentment to create a block.

Stage five: interpreting the message

As well as comprehending the language of the message, the receiver also needs to be able to interpret it correctly. The underlying import of a message may be rather different from the words actually spoken:

'Sorry about old Jonesy. Liked him a lot. I daresay they'll be looking for someone with experience of marketing to head up the division pretty soon now.'

It doesn't need a crystal-ball gazer to 'read between the lines' of the above message and to determine that the sympathy for 'old Jonesy' does not run very deep and that the speaker perhaps 'fancies his chances' for the arising post! In point of fact, many messages are capable of more than one interpretation – the apparent meaning and the underlying one. Often we speak sarcastically, with innuendo or *double-entendre*. Sometimes we reveal innermost thoughts unconsciously. Also, the context in which a message is sent affects the way in which it may be interpreted. 'Have a bit of a clean up' may mean one thing on a routine Friday afternoon, but quite another on the day before the managing director's visit! Problems of interpretation also arise when there is 'bad blood' between the sender and receiver:

'Get on with it right away, would you!'

may be interpreted by a receiver who dislikes the sender as a deliberate attempt to 'needle', and may result in a task being deliberately left as a means of passive retaliation. In this situation, however, it must not be forgotten that the sender may also be at fault for having 'encoded' the message in a provocative way.

Impact of information technology on the communication cycle

The rapid growth of electronic office equipment and telecommunication systems in commerce and public administration has had a marked effect upon the communication process.

For example, more information is now exchanged by communicators in remote locations using computerised telephone networks to channel either voice-based or computer-based messages. Mastery of telephone techniques in particular has become an even more important communication skill to acquire as a result.

Similarly, the increasing use of word processors in offices to produce multiple copies of circulars, reports or sales letters has placed great emphasis upon the need for first-class English language skills on the part of word processing operator. Undetected mistakes in spelling, punctuation or grammar may nowadays very rapidly be duplicated and perhaps sent out to hundreds of customers or associates nationally!

Again, with the growing use of organisational computers to provide a single 'library' of office information for general use, it becomes essential to avoid the insertion of faulty data into the system which will degrade the value of such a database.

Thus the main thrust of information technology in an office context is to make the acquisition of good communication skills essential for all who work or intend to work in offices or who interact in the course of business with office staff.

Stage six: providing feedback

All the stages so far outlined are important, yet the need for feedback is perhaps the most essential. Feedback provides a means of reassuring a sender that:

A message has been received
It has been comprehended
It has been correctly interpreted
The receiver is ready for the next part.

Such feedback, when positive, may be signalled by a nod, smile, a written acceptance of an invitation or a series of agreeing murmurs at the other end of a telephone line. Alternatively, it may be negative – a stifled yawn, a restless fidgeting, an angry silence or vociferous clamour.

Either way, such a feedback is essential for a successful communication process, since it serves to confirm to a sender that he is on the one hand 'pitching' the message successfully, or on the other that an alternative language, medium or totally different approach is called for. Whether positive or negative, if correctly interpreted, feedback is always productive to the alert and sensitive sender.

It is therefore important to be able to recognise the signals and read them correctly.

Routes of communication

In developed organisations, communications flow down, up and across, from board-room to shop-floor and back, between departmental managers or between sales assistants. They also move diagonally between different levels of different departments:

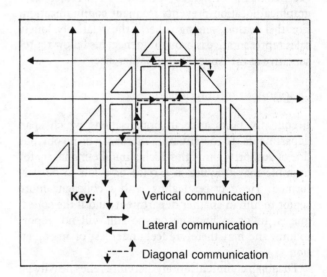

Key: ↓ ↑ Vertical communication

→ ← Lateral communication

- - -↑ Diagonal communication

Vertical communication

This term is used to describe the principal channel for routing directives, instructions and policies from top decision makers down through the organisation to the people who, at various levels, will implement them.

Correspondingly, the term describes those upward channels through which flow ideas, suggestions, criticisms and queries from the retail branch, factory floor or middle management.

To an organisation, an upward communication flow is just as important as a downward one. When downward communication becomes an avalanche and upward communication a tremble, then, sooner or later, an organisation will suffer from poor morale, low productivity and potentially explosive frustration in its employees.

The downward flow of communication is most frequently channelled through an organisation's 'line of authority', from manager to subordinate in a 'reports to' relationship.

Lateral communication

The most frequent and routine communication occurs between people who operate at the same or similar levels. For example, sales assistants behind a counter may share an on-going dialogue as part of the daily serving of customers. Similarly, clerical staff in a large county council office need to interact constantly in the course of their business. Lateral communication occurs at all levels of an organisation and is generally marked by the increased frankness and ease with which groups at similar levels – peer groups – communicate. The reason is that they are less affected or inhibited by the 'chain-of-command' situation which employees tend to experience when communicating with superiors.

Sometimes, however, lateral communication between peer groups may be adversely affected by attitudes of rivalry or jealousy. At other times remote geographical location prevents frequent communication. For this reason, among others, the relatively lonely sales representative is brought to meet his fellow representative at the Annual Sales Conference.

Diagonal communication

Frequently tasks arise in organisations which span departments. In this situation there may be no obvious line of authority through which a middle-manager, for example may 'require' a service or a job to be performed. He may be dealing with a colleague more senior to him in another department, and if the colleague is junior to him, he or she still will not report to him, and may therefore feel under less of an obligation.

Diagonal communication, therefore relies heavily on reservoirs of cooperation and good-will which the proficient communicator will have been careful to nurture by way of the friendly greeting or brief chat to this and that colleague on his journeys through the company's offices.

Summary

One of the most demanding tasks in any organisation lies in keeping all communication routes as open as possible. They are the veins and arteries carrying the organisation's life-blood.

The routes or channels along which communication flows may be classified in another way:

formal
informal
grapevine
bypassing

Formal

This description is applied to those communications which are routed through what have been called 'official channels'. For instance, a written memorandum from a managing director to his departmental heads to call a meeting, or a written report from a regional manager to his sales manager are termed 'formal communications'.

This route, understandably, is used to disseminate an organisation's directives and instructions for execution, since it is reinforced by the authority of those executives who act as 'staging-posts' in relaying such requirements.

Informal

A surprising amount of communicating is done in organisations informally even when it is official. That is to say that much information is passed on by word of mouth among interested colleagues who have received it from various sources – briefings, memoranda, visits, reports and so on. Spontaneous gatherings around a desk may spark off the exchange of such informal information. Informal meetings act in the same way. Usually, however, even when staff communicate informally there is an underlying presence of line authority in that they may share a restricted access to certain types of information, and unwritten rules exist to ensure that it does not leave a particular set of people.

Grapevine

'Hello, Grapevine? I'd like to scotch a rumour. . . .'

Every organisation has its grapevine. The term describes the interleaving branches of a totally unofficial communication system which has been constructed informally and which is constantly changing.

Users and distributors of grapevine sources of information find their material in the form of confidential letters left unattended on desks, accidental, careless remarks, loud voices coming from behind closed doors or sudden changes in established routines and practices. The basis of the grapevine is gossip and rumour. It is often the cause of misplaced resentments or unfounded fears. It flourishes more particularly in organisations in which communication channels are more closed than open. Like the real grapevine, it is extremely hardy, and flourishes on many different types of soil. Unlike the real grape, however, its fruit is seldom sweet!

Bypassing

Sometimes the urgency or importance of a communication requires that its sender, perhaps a managing director or sales manager, chooses a route which bypasses any intermediate management or supervisory stages. For example, the managing director may wish to send an individual letter to all company employees regarding rumours of a proposed merger, or a sales manager may wish to relay direct to all sales staff details of a new bonus scheme.

Most middle managers are mindful of their authority, which is sometimes uneasy in between top management and junior staff. Too frequent bypassing of them in the communication process tends to lead to resentment. This route, therefore, is used judiciously.

Using the process effectively

Research has proved that, with effort and application, communication techniques may be improved out of all recognition! The first step in becoming a more efficient communicator is to be more aware – of what you are trying to achieve and of the abilities, outlooks and interests of other people with whom you communicate. Next it is important to remember the circumstances in which the receiver is likely to receive your message – the telephone line may be bad, the receiver may be busy, he may have 'got out of the wrong side of the bed', he may be preoccupied or he may be prejudiced.

The following guide-lines and approaches are intended to help you to think more consciously about developing good techniques and avoiding pitfalls during the communication process:

As a sender

1   When composing the message decide carefully what sort of action or response you desire from the receiver.
2   Choose a language or combination of languages – spoken or written word, picture or symbol, non-verbal expression – most suitable for your needs and the situation.
3   When encoding the message take time to structure your ideas logically. Give thought not only to the choice of language but also to the way you use it.
4   Select the most appropriate medium – letter, telephone-call, meeting, electronic mail, telex message or interview etc. Think carefully about which medium (or combination of media) is most likely to help you to achieve your aim.
5   Ensure that your chosen language is fully comprehensible to the receiver. Put yourself in his or her position. Try to ascertain your receiver's abilities and limitations.
6   Take care that your message is not capable of being misinterpreted. Avoid vagueness, ambiguity, sarcasm, pettiness or innuendo.
7   Check that you are receiving the desired feedback – answers, confirmations, indications of attitudes.

As a receiver

1   Give an in-coming message all your attention. Avoid being side-tracked or distracted. Read, look or listen positively and with concentration.
2   Check that the sender's chosen communication medium is meeting your needs. Don't settle for a bad line, an interminable wait for a letter or incoherence in a speaker. Help the sender to put his message across effectively by letting him know tactfully if the medium is inappropriate.
3   Ensure that you comprehend the message fully. Take the trouble if part of the message's language is unfamiliar to check a reference, word or concept. Seek confirming feedback from the sender if the message is unintelligible by asking for explanations or repeats.
4   Take care to interpret the message correctly. Check whether there is any underlying or implied meaning in the message. Think carefully about what its implications might be before you act upon or divulge its contents. Learn to attend to *how* something is said as well as what is said.

Mastery of the media

As office communication systems become more sophisticated, it is important for sender and receiver alike to master the range of available communication systems or media within the organisation.

Whether a computerised Private Automatic Branch Exchange is to be used in order to set up a head office telephone conference, or a desk-top computer terminal to switch data from one location to another, it is impossible for the office communicator to make effective judgments about the suitability of one channel of communication as against another – in terms of time, cost, rapport etc – unless he or she has confident mastery of *all* the available media.

5 Avoid the temptation deliberately to misinterpret a message as a means of retaliating against its sender. If you are not on good terms, endeavour to thrash the matter out with goodwill. Try to realise when you are being hostile to a message and why.

6 Provide the sender with sufficient feedback, so as to reassure him that you have received the message, understood and interpreted it in the way the sender intends.

The media of communication

The electronic revolution, following its mechanical predecessor has brought profound changes to the way that organisations communicate. The 'communications explosion' is still resounding through the second half of the twentieth century. The developments in telecommunications, computers and information technology have revolutionised the business world. Executives speak of 'drowning in a sea of bumf', the shrill of telephone bells punctuates some offices incessantly and computer print-out has the capacity to paper the walls of many an office tower block! The world of Victorian copper-plate, hand-written invoicing already seems centuries old.

The sheer range of communications media, their sophistication and the technology which makes instant communicating possible, place heavy demands upon those who communicate within organisations. The manager must control and direct the flow of communication which he generates and receives; the secretary must become proficient in the use of a wide range of business systems and pieces of business equipment; he or she needs to have mastered often very complex record storage and retrieval systems. The following diagram illustrates the broad extent of the manager's and secretary's business activities and the range of communications media available, together with some of the communicating 'tools'. Every employee within an organisation is making constant value-judgments about what to communicate, how to do it, what medium to choose, and what 'tool' or equipment to employ. Moreover, being successful in one's job means mastering the media and equipment rather than allowing them to master you!

Communication: the functions, the media, the tools

The manager

reads
speaks
listens
drafts

informs
explains
persuades

decides
delegates
consults
proposes
suggests
organises

classifies
analyses
evaluates

selects
summarises

appraises
assesses

plans
thinks

Written communication
letters, memoranda,
reports, minutes,
press-releases etc.

telegrams, telex
messages, abstracts,
wp text, etc.

Oral communication
conversations, interviews,
meetings, conferences,
public addresses

telephone-calls, intercomm
video link-ups

Non-verbal communication
reinforcing expressions,
gestures, postures

Communication tools: voice, face, body, dictaphone, audio tape-recorder, video tape-recorder, typewriter, telephone, intercomm, film, public-address system, pocket calculator, word processor, facsimile transmitter, electronic photocopier, computer, business accounting and duplicating machines, overhead projectors, poster, noticeboard, house journal, micro-film, micro-fiche equipment etc.

The secretary

reads
speaks
listens

takes shorthand
transcribes
types
word processes

proof-reads
edits

disseminates
filters

informs
explains
consults

processes data
files data
extracts and
disseminates data
classifies
evaluates

confirms
arranges
assists

Talking point: Behind every good communicator stands a competent and versatile technician

Advantages and disadvantages of principal media

	Advantages	Disadvantages
Written communication Letter Memorandum Report Abstract Minutes Article Press release etc.	Provides written record and evidence of despatch and receipt; capable of relaying complex ideas; provides analysis, evaluation and summary; disseminates information to dispersed receivers; can confirm, interpret and clarify oral communications; forms basis of contract or agreement.	Can take time to produce, can be expensive; communication tends to be more formal and distant; can cause problems of interpretation; instant feedback is not possible; once despatched, difficult to modify message; does not allow for exchange of opinion, views or attitudes except over period of time.
Oral communication Face-to-face conversation Interview Meeting Oral briefing Public address Oral presentation Telephone call Conference Training session etc.	Direct medium of communication; advantages of physical proximity and, usually, both sight and sound of sender and receiver; allows for instant interchange of opinion, views, attitudes – instantaneous feedback; easier to convince or persuade; allows for contribution and participation from all present.	More difficult to hold ground in face of opposition; more difficult to control when a number of people take part; lack of time to think things out – quality of decision-making may be inferior; often no written record of what has been said; sometimes disputes result over what was agreed.
Visual communication Non-verbal communication – expression, gesture, posture Diagram Chart Table Graph Photograph Film slide Film Video tape Model Mock-up etc.	Reinforces oral communication; provides additional visual stimulus; simplifies written or spoken word; quantifies – provides ideas in number form; provides simulations of situations; illustrates techniques and procedures; provides visual record.	May be difficult to interpret without reinforcing written or spoken word; requires additional skills of comprehension and interpretation; can be costly and expensive in time to produce; may be costly to disseminate or distribute; storage may be more expensive; does not always allow time for evaluation.

Talking point: Effective communication is usually the result of a careful selection of the appropriate medium, or combination of media available

The communication process and information technology

Though it is important to remember that only people can communicate and not machines – however sophisticated – the advent of information technology (IT) in the world of business and public administration has had a profound effect upon the *media* of communication, that is to say the channels through which messages are transmitted and received.

Today it is impossible for the effective communicator to ignore the wonders of electronics in the realms of telecommunication and information processing. The introduction of the microprocessor or silicon chip by the American corporation Intel in 1971 as a commercial proposition had many unforeseen consequences in the design and production of office and telecommunication equipment, as indeed did the development some years earlier of the laser beam, which was initially called 'the invention looking for an application'! Today its applications include acting as a channel for telephone messages and as a means of printing letters on paper.

Consider, as an example of the pace of change during the past 15–20 years, the following passage.

In the 1960's and early 1970's secretaries worked hard to acquire shorthand and typewriting skills and were rightly proud of their hard-won expertise which enabled them to take dictation at 100 plus words per minute and to type out the transcription as a letter, say, at some 40 to 50 words per minute. In terms of the available technology in those days, however, the skills of the secretary were badly let down by the slow pace of the distribution service. The completed letter would probably have lain in an out-tray for several hours awaiting collection by a clerk from the mailroom. Once franked and posted, the letter might take up to two or three days to arrive at its intended destination. Thus the pace and productive efficiency of the secretary was largely nullified by the time taken to route messages along the channels of distribution.

Of course, in the 1960s and 1970s there were telex machines and the Post Office's telegram service available for the transmission of urgent messages, but these were not cheap, nor were they available for the commu-nication of messages on the scale of the millions of business letters posted daily in the UK and abroad.

Now 'we have the technology!' British companies like Telecom Gold market a service which enables clients to keyboard written messages into office – or even portable computers – and, at the press of a button, to relay them via a central computer to their intended destination, such as the desk-top computer of a manager several hundred miles away. The problems of the delay in the distribution of the message have been overcome as a result of IT.

In a similar way, photographs, plans, diagrams and text can be sent across the world at the speed of light by the facsimile transmitter as radio waves or electrical pulses to be reconstituted at their destination as a precise copy of the transmitted original. In this way, a chemical engineer in London could send modifications to a plan of a refinery being constructed in the Middle East, so that, for example, the benefit of a last-minute improvement in design may be incorporated into the building within hours!

Nearer home, developments in local area networks (LAN), have enabled staff in multi-storey office blocks to intercommunicate via desk-top computers without moving from their desks and to 'switch' text and data around for each other's use and attention. By the same token, the micro-computer on the manager's or secretary's desk may be connected to a mainframe computer with huge resources of memory so as to gain access to vast amounts of information maintained at the organisation's headquarters which may be hundreds of miles distant. Indeed, this mode of communication is now being used by multinational companies on a global scale. This sort of interaction between computer and

IT creates 'The global village'

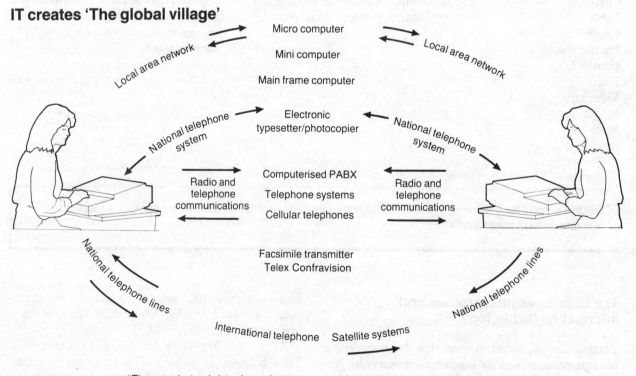

"The new electronic interdependence recreates the world in the image of the global village".
The Gutenberg Galaxy, Marshall McLuhan

users is made possible by the establishment and maintenance of a database – a comprehensive storehouse of data and information constantly being updated and modified which in informational terms *is* the organisation!

These illustrations of the impact of Information Technology upon the ways in which messages may nowadays be created, transmitted, received and stored indicate the radical nature of the changes taking place in communication techniques. The effective manager, secretary, word processing operator or clerical assistant cannot afford to ignore the implications of IT in the office environment. Rather, he or she should be grasping every opportunity to acquire the technical know-how needed to feel comfortable and secure in this electronic world, since its impact, already extensive in business and public administration, is fast becoming all-embracing!

Discussion assignments

Discuss the following extracts from conversations:

'I've never been so insulted in my life! All I wanted was to try the set on approval and I was informed over the phone that this was entirely possible. When I arrived your assistant asked me for a deposit against possible damage – anyone would think I was a hi-fi vandal!'

'Listen here, Smith, just because you won the Alfordale contract you think you're the bees-knees round here! Let me tell you, some of us in this office were winning contracts when you were still in nappies! So don't come so condescending with us – we won't wear it!'

'Well, you see, I'm new here . . .'

'I don't know, it's all very frustrating. Sales are up in the air because of the extra paperwork. Accounts are complaining about the costs. Marketing are determined to push it through at all costs. And Personnel maintain we can't staff it. Still, I daresay it will sort itself out . . .'

'Don't ask me, I only work here!'

'The trouble with Jonesy is, he ain't got the nerve to sort out the late-comers – too many of his golden boys among 'em. But I'm telling you, this place don't get started properly until half-past nine in the morning – and he calls 'isself a manager!'

'No, sorry. You're the sixth person to ask for the blue one this week. Trouble is, we don't get much call for the blue ones . . .'

'I've had just about enough! This is the fifth week running that they've messed up my pay-slip. They ought to bury that wretched computer down the deepest coal-mine. They must know when the thing's gone wrong! Look, answer my phone for me will you? I'm going over to wages to sort this out right now!'

'Nothing to do with me, chum. Try Servicing . . .'

'It's no good, Harry, you've just got to take the bull by the horns, or there'll be no factory. If you'd grasped the nettle six months ago it might have been easier. As it is, you'll have to handle it the best way you can. But it's got to be done!'

'You're wasting your time. Take it from me. Just keep your head down, wait for pay-day and keep your nose clean. I mean, if your idea was any good, they'd have thought it up years ago, now wouldn't they?'

'I don't care who you are! There's nothing in my contract says I have to put up with your carry on!'

'Can't you read the notice? It says "No refunds on sales goods". I mean, if they didn't mean it, they wouldn't have put it there, now would they?'

'Look, Jenkins, when I want advice from you I'll ask for it. OK?'

Talking points

1   How is the communication process likely to be affected by the growing presence of IT electronic equipment in offices and the increased use of IT based telecommunications systems in the next few years?

Can you foresee any problems stemming from a growing dependence upon a highly sophisticated technology?

Will this technology change the ways in which organisations are staffed and structured? If so, in what ways?

2   In the 1960s a communication specialist, Marshall McLuhan, commenting on the rapid rise of the channels of mass communication, like television, radio and film, observed shrewdly:

The medium is the message.

What he was driving at was that people's personal, social and working lives were being deeply influenced by the advent of mass communication techniques irrespective of *what* these media communicated.

Is this situation even truer today with the development of desk-top micro-computers, 'intelligent photocopiers' and televised meetings of remotely located executives and the like?

Is it more important than ever to think carefully about what is to be communicated and with what intended outcomes before reaching out for the 'instantaneous communications button'?

3   Are the developments in communications technology likely to lead to people turning away from 'in the flesh', face-to-face modes of communication, in favour of communication by VDU computer terminal, facsimile transmitter or computerised telephones and intercoms?

If this were to be so what would be lost in your opinion?

4   'In the end, people will reject the computer age in favour of a return to old-fashioned, honest-to-God talking to each other and letter-writing with pen and paper – thank goodness!'

Can the clock now be put back, and should it, even if it could be?

'No, I didn't get it sorted out. He just waffled on about spirals and escalations or something. They always tie you up with words. Anyway, I'm going to be looking for something else now ...'

'Yes Mr Theobald. Of course Mr Theobald. No, no, ... it was nothing really. It was just that ... No, I know. I realise you're busy ... Yes, I know I can see you any time ... No. Sorry to have troubled you.' (Puts down 'phone.)

Discussion topics

1 'If people concerned themselves less with communicating and more with doing some actual work, we might get something done round here!'

2 'You're either a born communicator – "gift of the gab" and all that – or you're not!'

3 'The trouble is, once you get everybody chipping in their two-penn'orth, you get further away from a decision, not nearer.'

4 'You either believe in all that communication mumbo-jumbo or you don't. Either way, I don't think it makes any difference.'

5 'As far as I can see, a lot of the communication thing goes on without people being aware of it. If that's the case, it doesn't seem to matter whether you develop these techniques or not.'

6 'I can't see how communication techniques affect me. You see, in my job I'm asked to do something and I do it. Simple as that.'

7 'It's all right, I suppose, if you're a manager, but if you're at people's beck and call like me, you don't get much chance to be a whatdoyoucallit, "communicator chappie".'

8 'All this new technology just gets in the way of good, old-fashioned plain speaking!'

Build-up tasks

Theory and process: check your progress

1 Why do people generally imagine themselves to be good communicators?

2 What are the six main stages in the communication cycle?

3 Describe the main features of each stage in your own words. Draw any illustrative diagram which will help to explain the process.

4 How many communication 'languages' can you identify?

5 Draw up a list of the principal media for communicating. Outline the main advantages and disadvantages for each.

6 What is the importance of feedback in the communication cycle?

7 Outline the nature of the problems which may occur at each stage of the communication cycle.

8 List the main communicating activities of:
(a) the manager
(b) the secretary

9 What has been the effect upon communication processes of the 'information technology revolution'?

Routes

10 Explain what you understand by vertical, lateral and diagonal communication routes.
11 What do you understand by formal, informal, bypassing and grapevine routes of communication?

Activities

1 Compose a written case-history (the description of a problem which actually occurred) stemming from your own experience of a communication break-down. Take care to keep places, people and events anonymous. Read your case-history to the group and explain why you think things went wrong.

For example, you could choose a shopping experience, a telephone-call or a conversation in which you were involved.

2 Devise a dialogue including a number of inappropriate communication practices or attitudes.

Your dialogue may either be in written form and duplicated or tape-recorded. Present your dialogue to your group for analysis and evaluation.

3 Draft a manual of helpful hints and tips on effective communication for the new junior staff joining your organisation (which may be of whatever type you choose).

4 Devise a scene built around one of the following situations:
(a) a customer complains about a shoddy article recently purchased
(b) a sales representative neglects to send in his sales report two weeks running
(c) a member of staff is causing resentment because of arrogant behaviour and disciplining is called for.
After consultation and rehearsal, members of the group should simulate the scene for the group to analyse and evaluate.

5 Write an essay entitled:
The causes of communication break-downs in organisations and ways of preventing them.

6 Draw up a checklist of points giving advice to newly-appointed sales assistants in your company's departmental stores on how to serve customers successfully.

7 Devise a case study (an open-ended presentation of a problem) based on your knowledge of communication problems and experience.

You may like to perform this task either as an individual or in a small group.
Suggestions for themes:
(a) a personality clash
(b) a blockage in a communication route

(*c*) a misunderstanding
(*d*) a wrong approach
Your case study may then be duplicated or tape-recorded for your group to analyse and discuss.

8 Interview a number of contacts – parents, relatives, friends or neighbours – privately and ask them what they consider to be the most important aspect of communication. Present your findings (anonymously compiled) to your group and compare notes. Draw up a comparative check-list. See if there is any connection between occupation and choice of important aspect.

9 You have been asked to write an article for your firm's house magazine entitled:
'How information technology is changing the communication process.'

First carry out your research in your library and/or at work and write a suitable article of about 750 words.

10 As a means of sharing information and promptly extending your group's awareness of developments in office equipment, as individuals (or in pairs) research one of the following and then deliver a 3–5 minute talk to your group on how it works and its principal uses:
(*a*) a cellular telephone
(*b*) a telex machine
(*c*) a plain paper copier
(*d*) an electronic memory typewriter
(*e*) a micro computer
(*f*) a facsimile transmitter
(*g*) a computerised telephone switchboard
(*h*) a database software package
(*i*) a word processing software package.

Assignment case studies

A high price to pay!

Dick had worked in the Office Administration Department of the head office of Buy-rite Supermarkets Ltd for the past ten years. He'd started off as a junior clerk and was now responsible to the Senior Administrative Officer, who herself reported to the Assistant Officer Manager.

Dick was fairly conscientious and tended to keep himself to himself. He prided himself on a faultless record in producing the weekly schedules of selling prices which were distributed to each branch manager, and displayed a certain touchiness if anyone strayed into what he considered his 'patch' or questioned his performance.

He liked to recall to his fellow-clerks in the pub the occasion when he'd 'put one over' Miss Jameson, the Senior Administrative Officer, when she had queried the price of butter on the schedules:

'Forgot clean about the government subsidy she had,' Dick would say, 'came over all highty-toighty. When I told her she should do her homework first. Still, what d'you expect from a woman? Think they know it all. Still, I soon put her right!'

The other clerks would smile politely but kept their own counsel.

About six months ago, as the company's business had grown, it was decided that Dick should be given a junior assistant to help generally and to learn the job.

'I don't need any help Mr Richards,' Dick had said to the Office Administration Manager. 'That'll be the day when I'm not on top of my job!'

Nevertheless, John was appointed as Dick's assistant, and Dick was asked to bring the youngster along and show him the ropes. John was rather quiet and rather self-conscious about a stammer he would develop when nervous.

'Here you are,' Dick had said to John on his first day, giving him a bulky folder, 'when you've memorised

these prices you can come and find me. Carry 'em all in my head I do. Never been caught out yet!'

Some weeks later, Dick was overheard shouting at John:

'Come on! Spit it out, you daft beggar! Why didn't you remember that two-pence off? I told you about that yesterday. – It's too late now, all the schedules have been duplicated. You m-m-m-might well be sorry! Here, give 'em me!'

Later that morning, Dick was called into Mr Richards' office and confronted with the fact that a complaint had been made about his treatment of John.

... 'That's a lie!' said Dick. 'In any case, people have got to learn from their mistakes. Anyway, who's complained? Come on, you tell me! I don't see why I should have to justify myself for some anonymous Johnny. Was it the lad?'

The Office Administration Manager indicated that John had said nothing and that he wasn't prepared to divulge his sources:

'But I will say this; this is the second complaint I've received and called you in over in the last two months. If there is another instance I shall further implement the provisions of the current employment legislation.'

To which Dick replied:

'Well, you know what you can do with your Act! Keep your job! I don't have to work in some kind of police-state outfit!'

And with that he stormed out.

Assignment

What was the nature of Dick's shortcomings? Were they entirely his fault? Did Mr Richards handle the interview correctly? Could the outcome have been avoided? Make a written analysis of the case study outlining problems and causes. Alternatively, analyse the case study in syndicate groups and discuss your findings in your full group.

Case study

Clean sweep at Visco

Jim Peters joined the head office of Visco Computers Ltd as Office Manager on 27th July 19—. His appointment was in no small way due to his record of achievement in a smaller company which had been in need of office reorganisation. At 28 Jim was ambitious and an extremely hard worker. He was given to making a total commitment to any work in hand and expected a similar commitment from those who worked for him. In his previous appointment he had a reputation for being hard but fair. His staff had been young and keen to benefit from the rapid progress the firm had been making. The Visco company, a much larger organisation, was one of the first in the computer industry after the war and after early successes had lost its lead in the market. Staff relationships were generally good and staff turnover low. The managing director had a favourite saying: 'What we lack in "whizz-kids" we make up for in continuity!'

Some six weeks after his appointment, Jim Peters sent the following memorandum to all office staff:

Subject: Office Reorganisation

You will doubtless recall my first staff meeting on 4th August 19— when I informed the department of the poor performance I had noted on arrival and that changes would need to be made.

Despite the introduction of an open-plan office to accommodate a centralised secretarial service, efficiency and productivity still leave much to be desired.

Staff are still wasting time in idle gossip and showing little consideration for others in the open-plan working area. Moreover, it is apparent that little effort is being made to promote the effectiveness of the reorganisation.

You are therefore reminded of the obligations implicit in your contract of employment in supplying a degree of commitment related to your remuneration. I shall expect to see an immediate improvement generally in the productivity of the work of the department.

Within three hours of the distribution of the above memorandum, Jim was called into the managing director's office. A stormy interview ensued. Jim was informed that Visco was not another HMS Bounty and that there was no room for any Captain Blighs. Jim's answer was that he expected support in remedying what he saw as an acute problem, 'a cosy and cushy complacency'. If his resignation was required, it was immediately available.

Assignment

Discuss or answer in written form the following questions:
1   Did Jim go wrong in his approach?
2   If so, where?
3   What would you, as Jim, have done to resolve the situation?
4   Consider Jim's memorandum. Re-write it if you consider it less than appropriate.

4 Organisations: their structures and functions

Introduction

The term 'organisation' covers a multitude of industrial, commercial, service industry and public service activities. Indeed, the word is an abstract label for any group of people who come together and interact with one another in order to achieve a set of predetermined ends or aims.

In our very complex society there are organisations, for example, which recover the natural minerals we need and turn them over to other organisations to serve as fuels or raw materials for manufacture into something else. Then there are the distributive and retailing organisations which take over the finished manufactured goods and take them to where they can be sold and then sell them to many different kinds of customer. In addition, organisations like insurance companies, banks and solicitors provide valuable services to the productive and retailing industries by supplying sources of finance, financial security, the underwriting or financial cover of risk-taking, and legal advice and representation.

Such organisations, which act in the sector of the economy which aims to buy and sell so as to make a profit are called **private sector organisations**.

There are, of course, millions of people employed in the United Kingdom who work for the **public sector organisations**, those which are financed out of central or local government taxes and which provide a very extensive range of services such as:

Government Departments like Defence, Employment, Health and Social Services, etc
The Inland Revenue Service
Customs and Excise
Immigration
Public utilities such as British Rail and the National Coal Board.
Her Majesty's Prisons and Detention Centres
Job centres, libraries, schools, colleges, etc.

In fact there are many national networks in the public sector which coordinate the activities of tending the sick, coping with unemployment, providing a transport service and so on. Such national organisations are responsible for carrying out the bills or laws enacted by successive British governments and may be considered as a kind of infrastructure of government – a series of interlocking meshes or cogs which carry out much of the work of central government.

At a more regional and local level of public service there are the county, district, borough, city and parish councils, which with varying degrees of authority and power implement the authorised instructions of both central government and local elected councils. Such organisations have traditionally been concerned with the management of various functions and activities:

● running schools, FE colleges and polytechnics within county boundaries
● maintaining roads and thoroughfares
● running county police forces
● providing a fire service
● providing a housing service

and many other kinds of provision.

There are clearly, then, very many different types of organisation, or groups of people at work today in the UK, which have been structured to serve a host of different purposes, from the greengrocer shop in the precinct shopping centre employing two or three people, to the national utility like British Rail, employing tens of thousands of people from Holyhead to Dover and from Penzance to Aberdeen!

As a result of such contrasting factors such as size, geographic location and nature of activity, profit-making or public service-giving, organisations take on very different shapes and structures. Moreover, they are not designed with particular people put into certain places at various ranks or levels within the organisation where they remain for ever, but are constantly changing and evolving as they anticipate events in the economy and society, and react to them.

Organisational structures

Thus the structure of any organisation is very much the product of 'what it was, what it is and what it would like to be'. That is to say that structures are not static but constantly evolving.

In industry and commerce, organisations are continually alert to the 'needs of the market-place'. The development of a new technology or manufacturing process may have far-reaching consequences for a manufacturing company. Changes in the purchasing behaviour of consumers may radically alter the pattern of trading of a retailing organisation – for example supermarkets, hypermarkets and fast-food cafés have mushroomed over recent years. In the public sector changes in society are mirrored in, say, the restructuring of local government, the integration of some central government departments, and the privatisation of public corporations.

The forms which commercial organisations take depend very much upon the scope of their activities. For example, some companies carry out the entire process of manufacturing goods, marketing them, and distributing them to their own retail outlets:

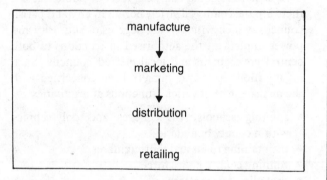

When the whole operation is undertaken within one company, it is said to be 'vertically integrated'.

Other companies specialise in one activity only – manufacturing or distribution or retailing. In such instances a company either makes for others to distribute and retail, acts as a distributing 'middle-man', or buys in for retailing goods which a distributor or wholesaler has purchased from a manufacturer. The advantages of vertical integration stem from extensive control and the potential for greater profits, whereas the specialist is able to concentrate expertise and experience within a specific part of the trading area.

Such differences of approach affect the shape of a company's organisational structure. A manufacturing company may look like this:

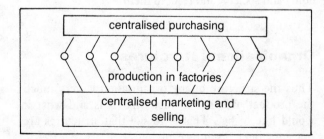

A retailing company may be structured differently:

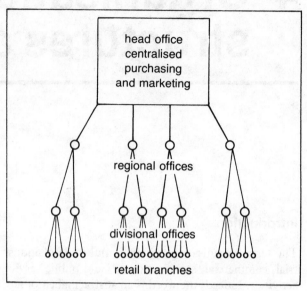

And a distributing company may take this form:

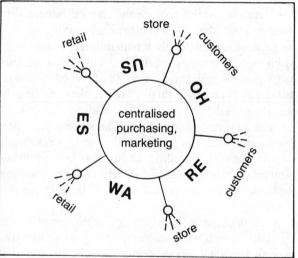

Thus the manufacturer may not need a dispersed sales force, the distributor avoids the complexities of the manufacturing process, and the retailer concentrates on direct selling to the consumer. In this way, different communication needs are established, ranging from maintaining good shop-floor industrial relations to keeping retail customers satisfied.

Organisations tend, therefore, to become 'product intensive' or 'people intensive'; that is to say that the constraints imposed upon them come from making things, where assembly-line flow, quality-control and the meeting of deadlines and output targets are crucial, or from dealing with people, servicing their needs, where selling techniques, customer satisfaction and consumer behaviour are central to the activity.

Of course, whether the organisation concentrates on manufacturing or sells to consumers in the High Street, it will need to care about people's needs, about its own employees and its customers.

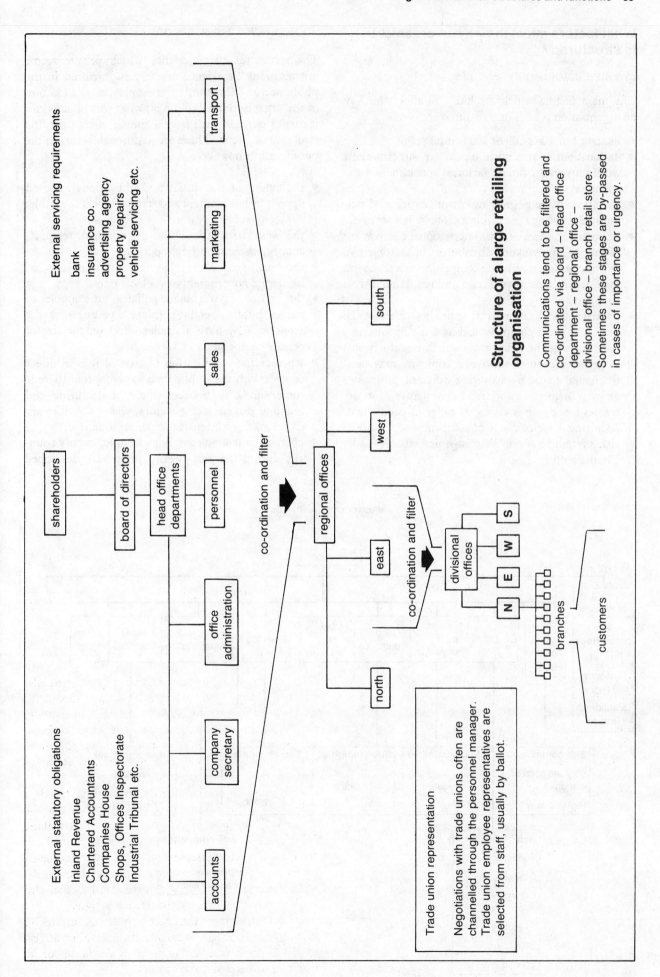

Structure of a large retailing organisation

External servicing requirements
bank
insurance co.
advertising agency
property repairs
vehicle servicing etc.

External statutory obligations
Inland Revenue
Chartered Accountants
Companies House
Shops, Offices Inspectorate
Industrial Tribunal etc.

shareholders
board of directors
head office departments

accounts
company secretary
office administration
personnel
sales
marketing
transport

co-ordination and filter

regional offices

north
east
west
south

co-ordination and filter

divisional offices

N   E   W   S

branches

customers

Trade union representation

Negotiations with trade unions often are
channelled through the personnel manager.
Trade union employee representatives are
selected from staff, usually by ballot.

Communications tend to be filtered and
co-ordinated via board – head office
department – regional office –
divisional office – branch retail store.
Sometimes these stages are by-passed
in cases of importance or urgency.

What factors affect the way an organisation is structured?

Private sector organisations

The main factors which are likely to affect the way an organisation is built or structured are:

- its size: 1 or 10 or 100 or 1000 employees?
- its location: in one office block? ten supermarkets within a region? fifteen factories spread across the country?
- its nature: mining? growing? manufacturing? distributing? retailing? providing a professional service?
- its clientèle: three or four international companies? twenty to thirty major distributors or factors? two to three hundred retailing companies? ten thousand mail-order housewives? two million High Street shoppers?
- its past shape, its current structure, its future needs: the structure a company had as a family business may not suit the chain store which bought it out; to grow or even to survive, a company may need to change shape by acquiring different businesses or by transforming the traditional nature of its activities i.e. by diversifying its range of products or acquiring a varied range of companies to spread its risk of failure – not all companies will do badly simultaneously.

Public sector organisations

The structural characteristics which private sector organisations experience are largely mirrored in the public sector – the number of employees, the location of the organisation's buildings, what sort of activities it carries out, etc, will have a similar effect upon the structure or shape. These are additional factors in the public sector, however:

- the extent of the duties and obligations imposed upon it by government and statute, which the public authority *must* carry out;
- the boundaries of its authority: national, regional, county, district, borough, parish;
- the amount of income it has to spend either supplied by central government or via local rates;
- the impact of government policies, for example, to reduce public spending. (Note a recession in the economy may have a similar effect on the size of private companies.)
- whether the organisation or part of it is in direct contact with the public or not. (Note that there is some similarity between the manufacturing and retailing private sector factors, where activities are either machine intensive or people intensive.)
- changes in technology. For example, county councils during the past twenty years have developed

Structure of a County Council

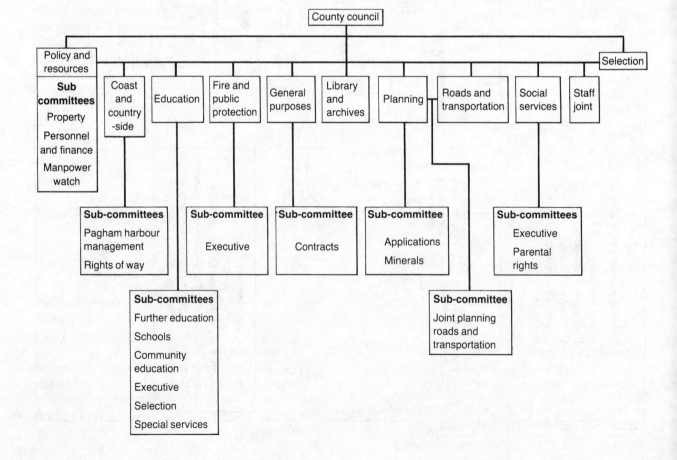

Computer Services Departments. (As indeed have private organisations.)

- changes in society's expectations. Citizens expect to be told more about local and central government activities so more meetings are open to the public and more councils now have public relations units and officers.
- increasing complexity of the work to be carried out. Many County Councils now have senior Planning and Resources Committees to help Chief Executives in making policy decisions.

Hierarchies

Apart from the structures which are determined by an organisation's general activities – whether in the private or public sector, whether selling goods or services – most organisations are internally structured.

Perhaps the most significant aspect of organising people into groups which have specific aims and functions is that either intentionally or unconsciously a 'pecking-order' is established. Few groups operate successfully without leaders and followers. Organisations are no exception. When organisations are composed of 'layers' or gradings of personnel they are termed hierarchies. A popular way of expressing this concept is the organisational pyramid.

The structuring of organisations into hierarchies is in many ways inevitable – although some organisations are evolving other structures, such as the franchise system. The need for important decisions to be made by people with expertise and experience, in consultation very often with those affected, together with the need to provide a person with sufficient authority to execute a decision, results in the 'pyramid effect'; by this means a small number of senior managers or officials are given the responsibility of directing an organisation's activities. It should be pointed out, however, that they are also, by dint of office, made accountable for its success or failure!

Specialist divisions

As the example above illustrates, the other source of the pyramid effect in organisations is the division of the total operation into specialist departments, all of which are answerable to a more senior co-ordinator.

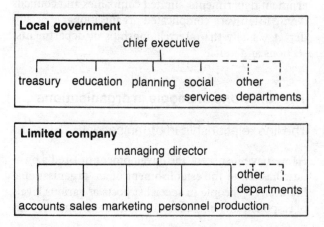

Each department will have its own pyramid structure of head, senior, middle and junior staff, and career hopes and expectations will cause employees to seek to climb the pyramid.

There are problems – in communication, administration and effectiveness – which are attributable to the size and the complicated grading of authority in some hierarchic structures. To avoid such complications many organisations deliberately limit size and grant extensive independence to departments.

A structure evolves

First, it is necessary to examine how communication paths and systems are established in organisations. For a model, let us consider the story of Fred Parkins, greengrocer. Fred started out by selling fruit and vegetables in a small shop he rented. Though he had other worries, his communication paths were straightforward, in that he dealt directly with everybody:

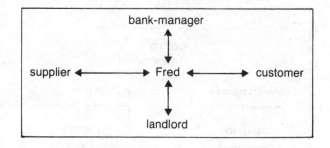

As a result of his hard work and enthusiasm, Fred's business prospered – he took on Harry, a sales assistant. This one act transformed Fred's communication system. He had become an employer, and soon found that he was no longer able to see to the needs of each customer personally – frequently he had to delegate, and communicate his requirements to Harry.

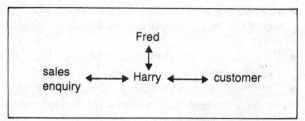

And Harry now first handled some of the sales enquiries. Clearly, Fred's business success now very much depended upon Harry as well, and it became important for both to communicate effectively.

Fred's business prospered further, and he decided to open another shop. Harry was put in to manage it, and Fred, meanwhile, had trained another assistant, Jack, to manage the founding shop. His organisational structure looked like this:

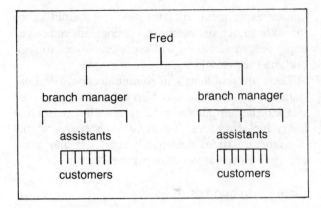

Part of the price of Fred's success was that he could no longer manage all the administration himself. He found it necessary in the end to appoint a number of administrative personnel. His organisation had become more complex.

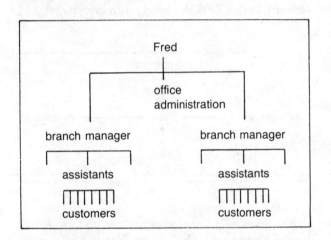

Fred found that he had generated a number of new problems with his extra business:

- In some ways he felt he had 'lost control' and missed serving his customers.
- He did not always get to know about customers' complaints until events had taken a serious turn.
- His two branch managers did not always like it if any of the assistants approached him directly about problems.
- Relations were not always good between the shop and office staffs.
- There was a certain amount of unproductive rivalry between the branch managers – for example when one branch was re-fitted.
- His instructions had a way of becoming distorted and misinterpreted by the time they reached the assistants.

In other words, Fred, in building up his organisation, encountered many of the communication problems common to most organisations. His problems stemmed from his having to learn to achieve his aims and objectives *through* his employees and overcoming many of the problems which occur when people work in groups which are structured as hierarchies.

Organisational functions

So far we have seen how the structure of an organisation varies according to its size, dispersal of its parts, and the scope and nature of its activities and that external constraints or economic conditions will have distinct effects upon the way the organisation is built up. Also, the term 'hierarchy' has been used to describe the pyramidic steps or levels of an organisation – rather like the steps up an Aztec pyramid. The reasons for such a stepped hierarchy have been suggested as stemming from the need for the control and authority of certain functions to be placed within the hands of fewer people as the staffing within the hierarchy becomes more senior: via section heads, heads of departments and directors. Bear in mind, however, that other forms of organisational structure do exist; i.e. the workers' co-operative, run on more democratic lines; the franchising arrangement where a central organisation sells its product or name to individual and almost totally independent operators, who enjoy much more freedom than does the traditional departmental head; or the subsidiary company within a group of companies, controlled by a 'holding company'.

We have also seen how communication and organisational problems may grow as the small sole trader or small partnership type of organisation evolves into a larger limited or public company, where the top decision-makers are five or six steps removed from their customers or members of the public.

What has not yet been fully made clear is that the single most important factor in the structuring and allocation of functions within organisations arises from the inevitable need to delegate authority and responsibility from the most senior member of the organisation downwards, as the organisation expands in terms of personnel and the establishment of multiple sites, branches or offices. Hence the creation of specialist divisions and departments in organisations as a means of making possible the undertaking of a myriad of tasks large and small, and of ensuring that the clearly allocated responsibility for success and achievement is not lost beneath a tangle of job responsibilities and overlapping involvements.

In order to clarify to all concerned in an organisation how it is structured, and who has what functions, government departments, limited companies and councils devise often very complicated organisational charts to depict visually the interrelationships of departments, sections and units.

The functions of people in organisations

The line relationship in organisations

As we have just seen, the development of Fred's business has led to the establishment of an 'organisational hierarchy' – people in specialist posts at various levels of responsibility and authority within the organisation,

Examples of organisational structures

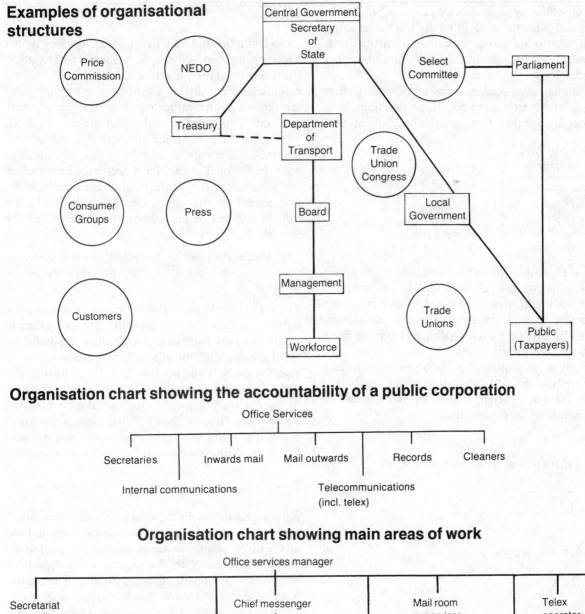

Organisation chart showing the accountability of a public corporation

Organisation chart showing main areas of work

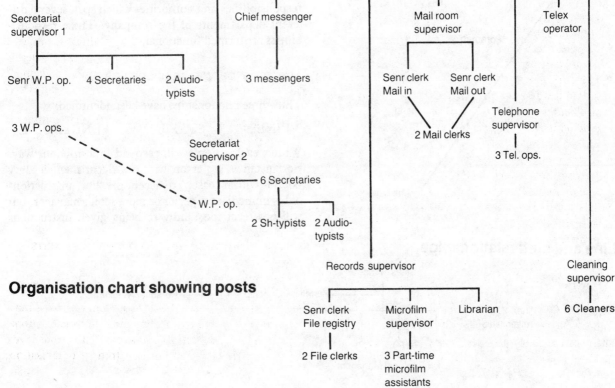

Organisation chart showing posts

many of whom as supervisors and managers have a responsibility for the work of others and for ensuring that through other people as well as from their own hard work, the organisation's policies and objectives are met.

In the retail organisation whose organisational chart on page 39 we are examining, these functions have been identified at the following levels or grades of staff:

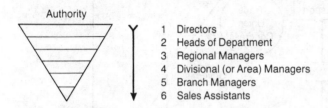

Authority

1 Directors
2 Heads of Department
3 Regional Managers
4 Divisional (or Area) Managers
5 Branch Managers
6 Sales Assistants

There is evident in this list of job designations a clear line of authority, from director to sales assistant, and as this is a selling organisation, the 'line of authority' is traceable through the six grades or levels of staff. People who have such a relationship through the direct giving and acceptance of instructions to do with the job of selling, as illustrated in the organisational chart under discussion, or with manufacturing goods in a factory are said to belong to the '*line management*' or '*line function*' of the organisation:

Line management function

Works Director

Works Manager

Direct 'line' authority

Foreman

Charge hand

Machine operator

Line and staff relationships

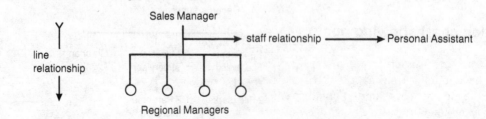

Sales Manager

line relationship

staff relationship ⟶ Personal Assistant

Regional Managers

The staff relationship in organisations

As well as a line function in organisations there is also a relationship between people, termed a 'staff relationship'. For example, a senior manager in a retail or manufacturing company will often have a senior assistant known as an administrative secretary or personal assistant. This assistant will report to, say, the Sales Director and carry out his instructions and requests, but the assistant does not have a 'line relationship' with the regional or divisional personnel reporting to the sales manager. The assistant, when relaying an instruction on the telephone, will therefore often explain that his or her authority is directly derived from the boss:

'*Mr. Jenkins has asked me* to remind you that your sales report must reach him by Tuesday morning's first post at the latest.'

Thus a staff relationship within an organisation lies outside of the line relationship. Another example would be of the management consultant appointed by the managing director of a company as a specialist to examine current efficiency within the company. His authority stems from the MD and he reports solely to the MD. Consequently, the consultant would not be able to instruct a departmental head, although in practice it would be customary in such circumstances for the departmental head to offer his full co-operation.

Functional responsibilities

In larger organisations there are activities which spread across the entire operation. A nationwide organisation may employ people to act as company inspectors or to work in a personnel department which reports to the managing director directly. Such staff are given responsibilities and authorities which span several different departments of the company. These responsibilities are termed functional.

The three 'people' relationships

Thus three relationships have been identified:

LINE   STAFF   FUNCTIONAL

Within each, people will respond in a different way. For instance, a person within a department is duty bound (within reason) to accept the 'line' instructions of his immediate superior or more senior manager, but will not react too kindly to being given instructions from the head of another department. A person in a staff position will normally advise people rather than instruct them and the person in the functional role will take pains to keep line heads fully informed and avoid 'ruffling feathers' by acting with too heavy a hand. The member of staff, for instance, with a company-wide role on office safety (Health and Safety At Work) will report any defects to a departmental head for putting right, or report back to the MD directly for a general instruction to be sent from the MD's office in the case of an important matter.

Furthermore, the establishment of an organisational hierarchy embracing line, functional and staff relationships will inevitably cause more complexity and protocols in the ways in which people communicate with each other. As we have already discovered in the process of expansion in Fred's business, his 'line' deputies – the branch managers – soon came to resent it if he went over their heads or bypassed them in order to instruct more junior staff directly. Similarly, it would be a rash head of department who tried to give orders to the staff of a different department. So you can see that in order to fit into the people network of a large organisation, a new employee needs to know about these relationships and to respect the patterns of behaviour they expect and require.

People's roles and jobs in large organisations

1 The shareholders

The customer is decidedly the most important factor on the organisation chart but we shall consider first the shareholders. Since in limited companies the shareholders in effect own the company, they will naturally monitor the weekly, monthly and annual performance of the organisation in which their money is invested. Each company will have registered its articles and memoranda of association with the Registrar of Companies and these will determine the rights of the shareholders (together with various Companies Acts) to appoint and vote out of office the directors of the company and to make certain other decisions such as whether to accept an offer to buy the company from a rival competitor and so on. Thus the shareholders exercise much power and the company directors of public companies take pains to ensure that organisational information is properly and meticulously provided for them, especially in the form of the annual presentation of accounts and the chairman's report on the year's business prior to the annual general meeting of the shareholders.

2 The board of directors

Each limited company – whether public or privately owned – will have its board of directors. This board may comprise the members of a family – grandparents, parents, sons, daughters, brothers or sisters whose con-

certed efforts over several generations have enabled a family business to grow. Very often, however, family businesses are absorbed by being purchased by large chainstores or national companies looking for additional outlets for their products with established customers or 'goodwill'. In this way, boards of directors may eventually become peopled by professional business men or women with no personal ties or family bonds.

However the board of directors is made up, its primary function is to act as the top decision-makers for the company and to oversee its entire operations as well as to take on the legal liabilities which a limited company must accept. Indeed, 'the buck stops with the board of directors'!

Customarily, members of the board of directors assume particular responsibilities – for finance, for marketing and selling, for personnel, for office administration and so on. At the head of the board will be the managing director whose job it is to act as the overall co-ordinator at the very tip of the organisational pyramid. In some limited companies there is also the role of company chairman above the managing director, but often this role is non-executive, that is, lacking the authority to carry out actions, and sometimes the roles of chairman and managing director are combined in one person.

The number of times the board meets is governed by its articles of association, but usually it meets monthly so as to review progress and to plan the next phases of policy. Instructions are then issued via the managing director's office or the offices of the designated directors to the heads of department for execution. For example, it may be that a piece of research carried out in the testing unit of a large retail toy-selling company discovers that soft toys being imported from a certain foreign country are potentially dangerous. The board may well then agree, having discussed the matter, to stop buying toys from this particular country until the safety standards become acceptable. Such a decision will affect all sorts of people both outside and within the organisation and will need to be communicated to the purchasing staff, to the accounts staff, to the sales staff at regional, divisional and branch level, so that orders are stopped, explanations given, the offending toys withdrawn from sale and so on. It might even be necessary to publish warnings in the press for such toys to be returned for a refund in order to keep goodwill and meet legal requirements. As well, it may be necessary to ensure the maintenance of goodwill with the offending toys' foreign suppliers, since its other products may be being sold quite happily by the company.

The board of directors will also spend time carefully monitoring the current performance of the company, using indicators such as the ratios which accountants have devised for checking on how well sales are going in relation to the extent of the company's working capital, and so on. They will be carefully monitoring the activities of rival firms so as to be able to respond promptly to price-cuts, new products or intensive sales promotions etc. They will also be conscientiously planning the future direction of the company for the years ahead, projecting, with the help of marketing experts within the company, what products will be in vogue and demanded by what type of customer in two, three or five years' time and deciding on how to meet the demand most effectively and profitably. Such activities are acknowledged in the term 'devising corporate strategy'.

Naturally, the board can only see the activities of a large company in overview terms, but its appetite for brief, accurate and up-to-the-minute information is insatiable, for without it the board is powerless when it comes to the making of good decisions!

3 The heads of department

Immediately beneath the board of directors come the heads of department.

How a company organises its departmental structures – how many departments, and the scope and range of their functions – depends entirely upon the sort of business the company is in. In the example under consideration, the activity is retailing and the number and activities of its departments reflects this retailing role.

Clearly, organisations need to regulate and monitor the ways in which money flows in and out of the company (accounts department) the whole operation of selling (sales department), the means of bringing products from factories or wholesale markets to the company's outlets or branches (transport), and so on. Usually the administration of these functions in a large regional or nationwide organisation are grouped together for ease of inter-communication in a head office.

Each head of department will have a detailed brief or job description which will list the nature and extent of the activities for which he is responsible within his department. For example, the sales manager will certainly have a responsibility to draw up in consultation with the board a sales budget for the financial year which will forecast how much money the company will turnover in sales. Such a forecast would then be divided into the various regions of the national company and the regional managers be given targets to achieve broken down by quarter, month and week. A large preoccupation of the sales manager will be to ensure that realistic sales targets are met. This will involve him in devising and maintaining a careful system of monitoring the performance of the regional, divisional (or area) sales managers and through them the work of branch managers and sales assistants. In order to do this sort of work effectively, there must be a good and fast system of reporting back to the sales manager in operation so that corrective action, if needed, can be taken in time should sales be slumping.

Thus a head of department is responsible to the board of directors for the performance of his depart-

ment and for the part it plays in attaining the company's aims and objectives. In very many ways this function is crucial to the organisation's success, for the departmental head has the daily, weekly and annual job of transforming broad-bush policy set by the board of directors into activities and undertakings which are much more specific. For example, a decision to introduce a new set of products to the company's existing range will involve customers being informed of the new products, sales representatives being trained to sell them, price structures being devised to ensure that sufficient quantities are sold at the right profit and sales information about the new products being in the right place at the right time. Much of the preparatory work in this context will have been carried out by the marketing department, but it will be for the sales personnel to make a success of actually converting the new products into profit and fresh stocks!

4 Departmental personnel

As the functions people undertake in organisations proceed further down the stepped hierarchy, so the extent of their authority becomes more restricted and the scope of their work more limited and specialised. For instance, the departmental accounts manager will have the responsibility to keep the accounts for the entire organisation – all sales, all purchases, all operational costs, all payroll, all credit control and so on. Within this span of control, however, will be sections which are run by section heads and which concentrate upon just one of these activities – only looking after company purchases, or only being concerned with ensuring that staff receive the right pay on time.

By the same token, part of a personnel department may only be concerned with personnel records maintenance or with the job of recruiting people as others leave or retire.

In this case, as you might expect, there comes to exist organisational hierarchies *within* departments as well as across the whole company:

The example below taken from *Office Management* by J C Denyer and Josephine Shaw, Macdonald and Evans, illustrates in organisational pyramid form the structure of the accounts department of a large organisation, which totals 46 staff. At the topmost tip of the pyramid is the Department's head, the Chief Accountant. In this organisation he has five immediate lieutenants or section heads, each one responsible for a particular area of work. To each of them work three senior accounts clerks and beneath them a further five accounts clerks.

The inverted pyramid to its side shows how the scope and responsibility of the department's tasks grow the higher up the organisational pyramid staff work.

This particular pyramid of staff is said to indicate a 'line management' function (see below) since each member of staff is connected to the one above in a line or sequence which stems from the most senior

Pyramid structure of an accounts department

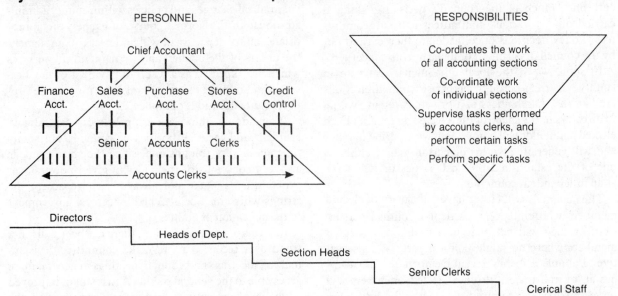

directors and where each member of staff in the stepped line has a responsibility for helping to ensure that company policy is carried out.

If the roles of the sales department staff are considered in a similar way, then the division of responsibility can be seen to be arranged not merely in the scope of job responsibilities, but also in a geographical structure, where responsibilities are given first for national activities (the sales manager), then for regions (regional managers), then for districts or areas (area managers) and finally for individual stores or branches (store managers).

In this way, the span of control which a manager has over his immediate subordinates is restricted to some six or seven people:

work of more than six or seven other people. Thus it becomes essential for functions to be divided into specialist groupings and for work to be delegated down through the organisational hierarchy in a logical and clear manner.

Finally it is well worth considering the communications problems which may develop when the head of a sales department of a national company is some five or six organisational hierarchy steps away from the firm's customers – in other words, messages and communications have to flow up and down the organisation through five or six layers or levels of management for sales manager and customer to communicate or to understand each other's needs or preoccupations!

Organisational structure of a sales department

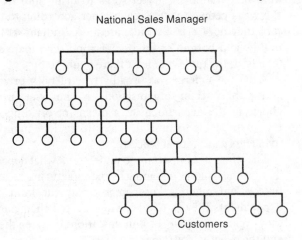

National Sales Manager:	7 Regional Managers
Regional Manager:	6 Area Managers
Area Manager:	6/7 Stores
Store Manager:	7 Departments
Store Department Head:	6 Floor Supervisors
Floor Supervisor:	6/7 Sales Assistants

In reality, the line management structure of a national retailing chainstore group does not always work out as neatly as the above illustration, but it is a firm belief of management studies experts that a single manager cannot effectively communicate with or manage the

A county council

Though the workings of a county council are in some ways very similar to those of a private sector retailing organisation (both have departmental specialisms and stepped hierarchies) in other ways they are very different, since much of the council's decision-making is carried out by various committees and sub-committees. Policy decisions once made are then carried out by the council department or departments concerned.

In some ways, the local inhabitants who vote in county, district, borough or parish council elections are like the shareholders of a private company voting in directors in the shape of the 'elected members'. Each elected councillor will enjoy a four-year period in office and will generally give his or her allegiance either to one of the established political parties or will serve as an independent councillor.

Thus councils will either have a majority of elected members who embrace a particular political persuasion, or they will be made of a coalition of elected members where no single political party – Conservative, Labour, Liberal–Social/Democratic Alliance – has an overall majority. Once elected, members will serve on particular committees, such as the Education Committee or Joint Planning and Transportation Sub-Committee.

In essence, each council committee oversees the work of a particular department or departmental section. For instance, there will be a committee to co-ordinate the work of the education provision overall within a county, and there will be sub-committees to oversee in detail the work of the primary schools, secondary schools and further education colleges, who report to the co-ordinating education committee.

In order to carry out the instructions of the elected members decided in committees and agreed at council meetings there is the body of employees known as county council officers or staff. As you would expect in an organisation with wide-ranging responsibilities, police, fire-protection, education, roads, social services and so on, the staff are organised within specialist departments (*see* chart on page 40):

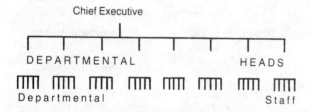

In some authorities, senior consultative teams have been set up to advise the chief executive which operate above the departmental head level, but by and large, there is a clear line management relationship between departmental staff, departmental heads and the chief executive.

Clearly, as part-time officials, the elected members are not always in a position to have absorbed all the detailed knowledge of the day-to-day running of, for example, a large planning department and so they inevitably take and accept a great deal of advice from, say, the county surveyor or director of social services. Nevertheless, councils are very conscious of their

power as elected representatives and often do introduce very radical changes and policies within county administrations. In the normal course of events, the appropriate county department will undertake to implement the orders of the council and to maintain the services which are expected as a result of payment of the local rates, and in response to central government rate support grant allocations of money.

Interestingly, the relationship between central government and local authorities or councils can sometimes be a very fraught one, since the shire councils are very conscious of their locally given powers over expenditure and are not always eager to accept the strings which may be attached by central government to the allocation of grants.

In terms of communication, there has been a distinct trend over recent years to make committee decision-making meetings and council meetings in general more accessible to the general public. As a result of improved educational opportunity during the past fifty years, the public is much more articulate and vocal in its interest and occasional criticism of councils' decisions and councillors are having to pay much more attention nowadays to public relations and effective communication practices to ensure that local inhabitants and ratepayers understand the need for particular policies.

Like the articles of association of a private sector company, the standing orders of a county council act as a rule book by which council meetings are run. These rules on whether the meeting is legally entitled to take place, and what may be acceptable as relevant debating matter or otherwise are involved, and need to be mastered by councillors if they are to take an effective part in the meetings which are regularly held.

What departments do

So far we have tended to view the organisation as a kind of pyramid in shape, so as to bring into focus the ways people relate to each other according to the jobs they do. Certainly there are more 'indians' at the middle and bottom of the organisation than there are 'chiefs' at the top. Or at least there ought to be!

What has emerged as broadly true of both private and public sector organisations is the widespread choice of the department as a means of dividing up into manageable sections the work to be done in order to meet organisational objectives.

Therefore it is important to understand what departments tend to carry out and why manufacturing, distributing and retailing companies create the kinds of departments they do, and having created them, how they organise and effect communications between them and the eventual customer.

The needs of any private sector company, in departmental structuring terms, may be listed as follows:

The accounting function
Recording, interpreting and presenting financial information concerning the company's activities. This

involves the day-to-day maintenance of records concerning all the company's selling activities in both cash and credit, or customer account terms, the details of all purchases made, including goods returned as defective etc, the transactions of moneys banked or drawn from the bank, the records of outstanding debts and amounts owed by the company to its creditors; the weekly and monthly compilation and distribution of pay to staff; the keeping of records required by the Inland Revenue, the provision of reports and advice to senior management about company performance and forecasts of future financial situations.

The sales function

Organising the sales of company products or services; administering and monitoring the performance of the sales force; setting sales budgets and targets and organising staff so as to meet them at a profit; taking care of after sales service and customer complaints.

(Note: in some firms this last operation is handled by a Service Department.)

The company secretary function

Administering the company's directors' meetings, keeping company records required by law, ensuring that company activities comply with the Companies Acts and general business legislation.

The office administration function

Ensuring that all departments and personnel are supplied with the equipment, stationery and materials needed to carry on the company's business; monitoring the cost-effective use of office equipment and resources; anticipating future requirements; ensuring that the various Offices Acts and Health and Safety At Work Acts are enforced.

The personnel function

Administering the selection, induction, training, relocation and termination of company staff; maintaining personnel records, maintaining staff welfare and counselling services; advising on salary structures and policies; acting as an industrial relations service to management; administering staff assessment and appraisal schemes, co-ordinating the company's pension fund and payments.

The marketing function

Devising company strategies and policies in terms of ensuring that the company's range of products or services continues to find a ready market at a profit:

> The right goods or services at the right place at the right time for the right customer creating the right profit.

Overseeing product research and design; carrying out ongoing market research and collecting market intelligence about customers' wants and needs and rival firms' activities; co-ordinating advertising and publicity for the company; maintaining the best channels of distribution of the product or service; advising on product specification and the structure of prices for products.

(Note: in some companies there is a separate public relations function, and in some companies the marketing and sales functions are combined in a single department.)

The transport or distribution function

Ensuring that the company's transport/haulage/distribution needs are effected as efficiently as possible. Usually this involves maintaining the company's fleets of heavy goods vehicles and staff cars economically and reliably. Part of this demanding function is to co-ordinate the buying, servicing and re-selling of vehicles, or of leasing them; the planning and execution of cost-effective distribution; the inspection of vehicles in the context of legal requirements and so on.

The management services function

Maintaining an efficient and reliable computer services unit for all arms of the company; providing an organisation and methods (OM) service which is constantly monitoring performance and supplying advice for improving efficiency. Acting in an advisory capacity for job evaluation and work study.

(Note: there is no easily defined range of functions undertaken by this type of department since some or all of them may be undertaken by other departments. However, a management services department, reporting to the managing director, is able to provide objective advice across a wide range of company activities.)

The production function

Ensuring that products are manufactured as cost-effectively as possible within the limits set down by the required specification; planning the production process so as to ensure that plant and personnel are used as efficiently as possible by avoiding peaks and troughs in production; designing and making equipment which will carry out production processes; maintaining plant so as to minimise hold-ups in production; making sure that staff are versatile and able to perform a variety of tasks in case of need – for example sickness cover; liaising with marketing in the areas of research and development and producing prototypes and test products; keeping pace with changes in technology – robotics, computer aided design and manufacture etc so as to maintain a profitable manufacturing function and to provide goods customers want with up-to-date features and specifications.

This checklist is by no means exhaustive, nor does it set down the departmental functions in 'tablets of stone', since private sector organisations are notably individualised and some departments display a structure which, 'like Topsy, just growed' from small, historical beginnings!

Integrating the departmental activities

Though it is helpful for organisations to divide their activities into separate departments in order to encourage specialist skills to develop, it is essential that senior management and heads of department work as a team and ensure that they actively promote a system of communication within the organisation and outside it which works to pull the enterprise together as a single unit of activity.

And indeed, in larger organisations, this is easier said than done. There are a number of communication problems which arise when organisations grow and have to divide the range of their activities into manageable sections, as we have already come to realise. The following checklist reviews some problems already identified and also includes further problem areas which departmental structures tend to create:

1   *The basic problem of size*   It is so much easier to get a message across to 10 people rather than 10 000 without it becoming distorted in the process.

2   *The problem of geographic dispersal of staff and buildings*   It is difficult to relate to other people as part of one big team if you never meet them or get to know them in any way.

3   *The problem of relating to people who are engaged in some other set of activities*   For example, it may be difficult for sales staff to understand the accounts staff's preoccupation with regular and detailed returns of a financial nature such as expenses or petrol receipts. Again, if a member of staff's only contact with another department's personnel arises from mistakes occurring in his monthly pay, it may be difficult for him to sympathise with the difficulty they may be experiencing with a new payroll software package.

4   *The problem of inter-departmental rivalry*   Because of the separated nature of departments there arises a tendency for staff to identify strongly with their own department and its head (with whom they communicate closely) and to see only their own activities as supremely important and those of other departments either as inefficient, poor by comparison or even a drag upon their own efforts:

> If only Personnel had the wit to select the right staff, we wouldn't be in this sales target mess!
> or: You've got to be an accountant to get on here!
> or: The trouble with the sales reps is they think the whole company revolves around satisfying their whims and fancies – never did an honest day's work in their lives!

While such comments are made and resentments or jealousies allowed to flourish, the corporate or total company effort is being constantly undermined.

5   *The problem of specialisation and concentration upon a part of the whole organisational operation*   If organisations are to flourish, it is inevitable that the vast range of activities within them – across seven or eight different departments – will be broken down into small sets of tasks such as managing the despatch of mail, ordering company stationery, filing customer records,

updating price lists etc, etc. Yet this very approach of dividing tasks into smaller areas with restricted levels of responsibility can result in the staff concerned becoming very 'blinkered' and limited in their understanding of what the firm is doing as a whole, with little interest in anything happening outside their own particular corner:

> Sorry, can't help you. I just look after the transport records.
>
> Who ? Never heard of him! Can't work in this office!
>
> Look, if you've found a mistake in the adding up, that's Accounts' problem! They don't come round here helping us out!
>
> Charlie! There's a bloke on the phone says he's enquiring about some order that's adrift...
>
> Oh, tell 'im we're Packing, and he's got the wrong extension – and come and give me a hand instead of skiving on that blinkin' phone all day!

6   *The problem of the hierarchic structure of organisations*   By their very nature, organisations shaped like pyramids will have fewer people being promoted as the grades of job become more senior – ten company directors may oversee the work of a company of twenty thousand personnel. There may arise therefore, among some staff, a sense of having been unjustly passed over in the promotion stakes or a feeling that, given the chance, the machine operator could do a better job than the foreman, or the section head than the departmental manager. Thus there needs to be a constant effort upon the part of managers and supervisors in organisations to minimise as far as possible these counterproductive feelings and attitudes by means of good communication practices, fair opportunities for advancement and what is known as leadership from the front, where the boss earns the respect of his staff by his or her example and extra effort and know-how.

7   *The problem of complexity of the communications process*   As organisations grow, they tend to become more bureaucratic and unwieldy in the processes they design to acquire, store and distribute information. Like parliament, sometimes new rules and regulations are invented without older ones being cancelled, so that employees become so bogged down in, for instance, filling in endless returns for the higher tiers of management that sales suffer and customers are put off.

8   *The problem of rapid changes in technology*   While Information Technology (IT) has brought many blessings, including the eradication of some monotonous and repetitive clerical tasks, it has meant that people right up the organisational ladder have had to acquire new skills and specialisms at a time in their working lives when grasping new concepts and techniques can cause unease and worry about loss of face in front of younger staff educated in the new technology at school, college, polytechnic or university.

Communication practices and integration

The above checklist of problem areas serves to illustrate some of the daily communication and human relations difficulties which organisations may have to overcome in order to achieve success. For example, the customer on the telephone who has been routed to the wrong extension is not going to make allowances for the fact that he is talking to a junior packer and not a skilled sales receptionist. He regards the company as a single entity and himself as a customer of all of it!

The following discussion topics will help you to concentrate upon identifying the kind of activities which would help to prevent communication problems like those illustrated above from arising, or to find a solution to such problems once they have become apparent.

Discussion topics

In a group of about five or six students, choose one or more of the following topics and spend about 10 to 15 minutes discussing each and noting the main conclusions reached. Then, in turn, compare your conclusions with those of the other groups by electing a spokesman to summarise your discussion:

1 In what ways could communications among employees in a large organisation be supported and strengthened?
2 Supposing that you had to improve communications between distant factories and offices, all belonging to one firm, what suggestions could you make to aid the communications process?
3 How could communications between separate departments be improved in order to create better morale and a total sense of putting the customer first?
4 What causes rivalry among people? Can it be minimised by changing communications processes? If so, how would you seek to achieve co-operative working relationships among people?
5 What is meant in the sense used in the above checklist by the term bureaucracy? How does the increase in rules and regulations affect communication practices in your view? What would happen in a large company without any rules and regulations governing work routines?
6 Why is it that older and senior staff sometimes feel uneasy about new practices and technologies? Where would you start, for example, in introducing a new system of information handling – like a linked set of desk-top computers in a traditionally-minded organisation – at the top, in the middle or at the bottom and why?

You may wish to consult parents, relatives or working friends before starting these discussions, and you should bring to bear as appropriate any personal experiences arising from a full or part-time job you may have.

Summary

In this Topic, the relationship between the structure of an organisation and the range of activities it pursues has been examined. The differences between the getting of raw materials, manufacturing, distributing, retailing and providing services have been highlighted, and the similarities and differences between the private and public sectors considered. In either case, the central and crucial role of the customer or local citizen has been seen to be of paramount importance. Profit depends upon a steady stream of satisfied customers and efficient public service is measured by continuous esteem and regard for its community work by the people affected. Moreover, in times of recession on a country-wide level, the very survival of private small businesses, national limited companies or public corporations depends upon what marketing experts term 'customer orientated' corporate policies or in other words: *always* putting the customer first. In this context, the development of good communication principles and practices is essential.

In the latter part of this Topic, emphasis has been placed upon describing the characteristics of organisations, such as hierarchies, types of functions of personnel at differing levels, and the kind of activities which various private sector departments are likely to pursue. In addition, some of the main problems associated with communication in organisations have been identified and attention has been given to investigating the solutions to such problems.

This necessary introductory spadework will have raised a number of issues and controversial points which will need following up and examining in greater detail. Moreover, if it is to be of value, this follow-up work must be practical and not just theoretical, and it must include the current situations and practices of real firms and government agencies in your own locality.

Thus the Build-Up Tasks and Assignments which follow have been designed with this approach in mind. Having gained some insights into the functions and structures of organisations and the roles of people within them, it is for you to build on this in the light of what you can discover about *real* organisations and the *real* people working in them.

Build-up tasks

1 Design an up-to-date organisational chart of either:
your firm
your college
your school
On your chart illustrate clearly any line, staff or functional relationships you discover. When completed, share your chart with other members of your group and explain its major features to them. In this context, you may wish to produce your chart in the form of an overhead projection, coloured foil or transparency and give an oral presentation about it to your group.
2 Using the local information facilities in your area, first research the necessary information and then draw up an organisational chart of one of the following:

your county or borough council

a large local manufacturing company

a large local retailing or distribution company

Provide brief explanatory notes to accompany your chart and circulate your findings among your group.

3　By arrangement with your teacher, arrange to interview a local private or public sector manager about the nature of his job, the communications activities he has with others inside and outside his organisation, and the sort of problems in this context he encounters and how he tackles them. Deliver your findings as a 5–10 minute talk to your group.

4　Find out the different ways in which communications are channelled and distributed in your firm, school or college and devise a diagram which best illustrates your findings.

5　First undertake your research, then write an article of about 750 words to explain clearly one of the following:

(a)　What information resources and facilities are available to the inhabitants of your locality and what types of information are on offer?

(b)　The work of your county's planning department.

(c)　The services offered by your local Citizens' Advice Bureau.

(d)　The work of your local Job Centre and how it relates to area, regional and national Department of Employment organisational networks.

(e)　How your local hospital is administered.

6　Either write brief notes for your file, or give your group a brief oral explanation of one of the following specialist terms:

organisational hierarchy

vertical integration

the line relationship in organisations

the span of control in management

7　In small discussion groups, make a checklist of the sort of communication problems you are currently experiencing in your own firm, school or college and how you think they might best be overcome. Discuss your conclusions as a general group.

8　As a general group, consider the following and discuss your own views on the matter:

'On the one hand, organisations tend to be divided into specialist units, divisions or departments as a means of organising the work to be done, yet on the other hand, it is said that integrating the whole range of an organisation's activities is essential for success. How can these two statements be reconciled and through what kind of policies and activities?'

Case study

Hopgood Sports Limited

Jack Hopgood's problems can be summed up in one word – success!

Four years ago, following a modest pools win, he started up on his own, as a retailer of sports and camping equipment. He rented a shop in Westleigh High Street, which, to begin with, he ran on his own. Within a year, Hopgood Sports Limited was in full swing. Jack had taken on two full-time assistants – Les Green, aged 36, and Beryl White, aged 48. Les soon proved an enthusiastic salesman, becoming Jack's 'right-hand man', while Beryl,

a placid but conscientious employee, took on much of the book-keeping and office work.

Two years ago, Jack felt the time was right to open a second shop and he chose premises in the Rosegreen Shopping Precinct, a busy shopping centre in an affluent Westleigh suburb. For some time, Jack travelled between his two branches, since he felt that Harry Pritchard, aged 22, was insufficiently experienced to manage at Rosegreen on his own. Besides, Jack just loved to sell and talk to his customers! About eighteen months ago, the turnover at Rosegreen justified the appointment of a junior sales assistant. Jack appointed Carol Brooks, aged 17. Also, Saturday was always busy and so two part-time staff helped out – Linda Warren at the High Street branch, and Bernard Lincoln at Rosegreen.

With an eye to the changing patterns of consumer purchasing, Jack saw his chance to open a camping shop on the site of a busy self-service petrol station on the London Road, just north of Westleigh. He arranged with the owners to pay rent and a percentage of the profit in return for the floor-space on which the camping shop was situated. The current arrangement is that the petrol station staff take the money for the camping goods, which Jack keeps stocked up in self-service merchandisers opposite the petrol sales till. Jack is not very happy with the level of sales, however, and is convinced that they would increase dramatically if someone in his own employ were put in to sell the camping products full-time, particularly as the more expensive items are not selling and the petrol station personnel lack the required sales expertise.

'Behind every successful man stands a woman!' In Jack's case, it is definitely Mrs Elsa Hopgood, who handles all the account customer sales, processes the ordering of stock and attends to much of the increasing business administration of Hopgood Sports Limited. Recently, however, her enthusiasm seemed distinctly wilted:

'I don't know, Jack, I can't see the point of our having such a successful business if it means we both have to work a twenty-five hour day! You seem to spend your time tearing about all over the place and our "Book At Bedtime" is usually this month's accounts! Take it from me, you're heading for a breakdown or something if you don't sort out the business! You can't tell me we can't afford some extra help. Anyway, look at the business opportunities we miss because no one can ever get hold of you – you're always on the way to somewhere else! You've just got to learn that you can't go on for ever doing it all on your own – you want to do more thinking and proper administrating instead of just buzzing around in circles. Besides, I want a holiday next month on the Costa Brava! The one you promised me two years ago!'

Never a woman to waste her breath, Elsa Hopgood's pointed comments caused Jack to do his first real thinking about Hopgood Sports since he had established the three outlets.

'She's right – as usual,' mused Jack. 'Now how could I organise things properly? Not only for the present, but also to allow for future expansion over the next five to ten years...'

Assignments

1　In the light of Jack's current business situation, what should he do to follow up Elsa's advice?

In small discussion groups, make out a checklist of actions needed and put them into an order of priority. Then compare your checklist with those drawn up by other groups.

2 What do you consider to be the advantages and disadvantages of a small trader owning a cluster of some 3–4 retail shops in separate locations in a large town, as against him owning a single, larger store centrally located. What current shopping trends and environmental factors would have to be taken into account in making a decision as to maintaining several small shops or changing to a single larger store?

Follow-up assignments

3 Find out what facilities exist within your district to aid small businessmen and women in setting up a business and ensuring its survival.

4 Having given some thought to the problems encountered by a small, growing business, interview a local retailer and try to find out what makes up his or her current preoccupations. Find out what factors enable a small business to keep going in the light of fierce competition from national chainstores.

Case study

'As I see it . . .'

Bettadecor is a large national company in the home decorating and furnishing retail and distribution markets. The company has over 150 branches throughout the country linked by divisional and regional offices. Its head office is in London and its national marketing headquarters are based in Bristol. The company has recently computerised its sales and accounts systems from a newly-established computer centre in St Albans. The growth of Bettadecor has been swift and is the talk of city financiers.

(Scene inside the Hightown retail store)
'Been waiting long?'
'About ten or fifteen minutes – everyone seems to be dashing about . . . but . . . three of 'em in there, engrossed in something or other . . . Well, I dunno. I think I'll call back . . .'

(The Divisional Office of the western district of the Southern Region)
'Could you put me through to the Regional Manager's Office, please. Hullo? Miss Davidson? Ah. Jack Griffin here . . . I was wondering whether you got my order for the new Peterson wallpaper range . . . Yes I know you sent out a questionnaire . . . Well I sent in an order about two weeks ago, asking for 300 extra rolls in about 30 patterns under the special arrangement . . . only I'm being badgered for them. Oh, there's a new special order form. How many copies? You're kidding! . . .'

(Bettadecor's Head Office. The Transport Manager meets the Assistant Accounts Manager in the corridor)
'How's tricks, Harry?'
'Don't ask! I've just done an exercise on town and country mileage. Could help to cut servicing costs. But you'd never believe the trouble I've been having getting the returns in from the branches. They must need cushions or something – sit on things so long!'
'Yeah, you don't need to tell me. Between ourselves, this computer's giving me grey hairs – we sent a processing manual to every branch, but the mistakes! It's not as if the new invoices are very different from the old ones. Dave Pritchard's tearing his hair out at St Albans. . . .'

(Sales Manager's Office at the Quarterly Regional Managers' Sales Meeting. The Sales Manager is speaking.)
'Frankly, it's extremely disturbing. The company seems to have lost all impetus. The figures for the second quarter are simply not good enough. But before anyone starts blaming the computer, there are some questions I'd like answers to about the new order processing scheme to speed special orders. . . .'

(The Manager's Office of the Newtown retail branch)
'Fred, flip the closed sign on the door, will you. And come in here and give me a dig out with these sales analysis sheets. They've been on the phone from Divisional Office. Jack Griffin's been on the warpath. Wants 'em yesterday, or, preferably, the day before!'

Assignment

What do you see as Bettadecor's fundamental problem? How is it manifested? What could be done to improve matters? Can you draw any conclusions about problems which beset large companies as opposed to small ones?

Write an analysis of the kind of problems which Bettadecor are experiencing and what could be done to improve matters. Alternatively, discuss the case-study in syndicate groups and discuss your findings in a full group analysis session.

5 People in groups

'Man is a social animal.' This self-evident truth has provided a basis of enquiry and analysis among anthropologists, sociologists and behavioural scientists alike. Wherever we look, from kindergarten to old people's nursing homes, we see individuals coalescing into groups and groups inter-acting with one another.

What makes a group? Certainly it is quite different from a random collection of individuals waiting for a bus or train. Firstly, a group has an identity which its members recognise. This identity may be formally acknowledged, as in a committee or working-party, or it may be totally informal, as in a children's gang or a set of commuters using the same train compartment daily. The establishment of a group identity leads anyone to being an 'insider' or an 'outsider' as far as the group is concerned.

The next aspect affecting the creation and composition of groups is that all human beings share the need to belong to one group or another. Very few people survive long periods of isolation. Indeed, long periods of solitary confinement have been proved to be positively injurious. Similarly, few actively seek the life of the hermit or recluse.

Belonging to a group involves an individual in accepting and being accepted. The whole purpose of some groups seems to lie in maintaining a jealously guarded exclusivity and in setting often very extensive formal or informal entry 'exams'. What the individual has to demonstrate is that he or she accepts and is willing to comply with the 'norms' of the group – that is to say the established outlooks, attitudes and behaviour patterns which the group displays. For example, it would be a reckless probationary golfer who never replaced divots, frequently picked up other golfers' balls, cheated on his scorecard and always wore his spiked shoes in the teak-floored club lounge! It is only by clearly demonstrating similar ideas and behaviour that an individual becomes accepted by a group.

In society groups exist in many forms. The basic, indeed fundamental group is, of course, the family. Extensions to this group are formed through relatives and close family friends.

Yet further, separate groups are readily identified in the local sports or social club, residents' association or parent-teacher association.

'Any chance of joining your group?'

As well as possessing a discernible identity and norms of behaviour, groups also exist to achieve aims and objectives, whether commercial, cultural, sporting or community centred. Such groups will evolve, either formally or informally, procedures for choosing leaders and will also establish 'pecking-orders' which derive not only from official status, but also from length of membership, degree of assertiveness or demonstrated expertise. Most cricketers, for example, defer to the club's fast bowler or move aside to allow the 'Father of the House' to reach the bar.

It is interesting to note that within any group of reasonable size sub-groups will also exist or come together temporarily. Within a music society, for example, there may lurk a secret, hard-core nucleus wishing to oust Gilbert and Sullivan and to put Mozart on the throne! Such a group may only be identified when the future programme comes up for discussion and they form a solid caucus at a meeting. Once the

The attributes of a group

Identity	It is identifiable by its members and (usually) by those outside it
Norms of behaviour	It requires its members to conform to established norms or patterns of outlook, attitude and behaviour
Purpose	It has aims and objectives either clearly defined or intuitively understood which direct its activities
Hierarchy	It evolves either formally or informally a leadership and 'pecking-order' or hierarchy which its members accept
Exclusivity	It has the power to grant or deny admission and also to expel anyone from membership
Solidarity	It demands loyalty of its members and is capable of experiencing internal conflict while displaying an external front
Capacity for change	Its life may be either long or short. It may form, disintegrate and re-form depending upon external circumstances and stimuli.

purpose has been achieved, however, such a group may disperse as quickly as it was formed.

Groups at work

The characteristics of groups outlined so far are also to be found in company or public service organisations. Companies strive to establish a corporate identity among their employees and to build a corporate image through advertising and publicity to make themselves readily and pleasingly identifiable to the general public. Both private and public service organisations encourage staff to feel more involved and committed by circulating house journals, newspapers and magazines and by staging social and sports events. Also, in many organisations there is tremendous loyalty and a will to survive in members facing external competition and adverse circumstances.

If it is true that work-centred organisations embody characteristics shared by most groups, how are they to be identified? Firstly, it should be pointed out that, although an organisation as a whole may have a recognisable identity and character, the whole is, in fact, made up of many smaller groups, and, within them, sub-groups. As we have discovered, organisations are divided into specialist divisions, which themselves may take on the characteristics of a distinctly identifiable group – 'the marketing wallahs', 'those whizz-kids from R & D', 'the Scrooge brigade in accounts'. Indeed, groups are often formed as a kind of self-defence and means of survival in the face of other groups. In addition, within any specialist or departmental group there will form sub-groups of people who associate together for a variety of reasons – shared activities, outlooks, physical proximity, common goals and so on. The following represent some of the reasons why groups are formed within work organisations:

1 It is difficult as an individual to feel a part of a large organisation.
2 People need to have a sense of belonging and to feel that they make a meaningful and accepted contribution somewhere.
3 People are drawn together by striving to achieve common goals and objectives.
4 People often form groups by reason of daily proximity and shared work-places.
5 Common expertise may be the basis of a group as may also be common outlooks and interests.
6 Positions in similar grades may also form a group characteristic.
7 People may wish to join a group because its activities make it look desirable.

Some groups within organisations are created and then develop extremely tight-knit relationships as the result of a formal activity. For example, a committee may be set up to make an investigation or develop a product. Though its members may not, initially, know one another very well, being drawn from different departments and levels, nevertheless, if the work is protracted, and if the members become thoroughly committed to the group's defined goals – especially if the committee faces external criticism – then very often it will become distinctly recognisable as a group. Other groups, however, are formed quite informally, springing from likings which A and B and C may have for one another. Such groups are often found within departments, but may also span them.

Relationships at work

The employee, whether as part of a group or as an individual, will create, maintain and develop a number of different relationships at work with those people with whom he has contact. The nature and extent of such relationships obviously depend a great deal upon the employee's job and position in the organisation's hierarchy. The diagram indicates the wide range of relationships which, in this case, a manager may have with people both inside and outside his company. (See page 56.)

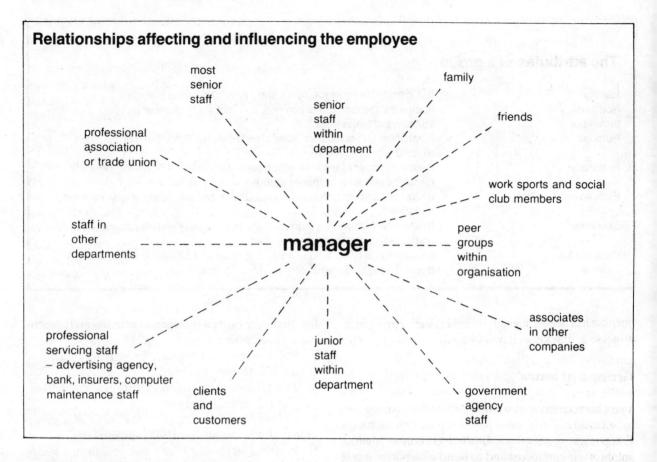

Relationships affecting and influencing the employee

- most senior staff
- senior staff within department
- family
- friends
- professional association or trade union
- work sports and social club members
- staff in other departments
- **manager**
- peer groups within organisation
- professional servicing staff – advertising agency, bank, insurers, computer maintenance staff
- clients and customers
- junior staff within department
- associates in other companies
- government agency staff

What the employee communicates and how he communicates is very much influenced by the nature of the relationship between sender and receiver. Indeed, the success or failure of communication depends upon both sender and receiver perceiving that a relationship exists and that it places constraints upon the communication process. We regard the polite handling of a difficult customer by a sales assistant as 'professional'; we admire the way a resourceful secretary handles her boss, who may be under pressure; we applaud the manager who executes an unpopular directive without alienating his subordinates. Each in his or her way has seen a relationship and has used communicating skills to overcome a problem without transgressing the protocols, etiquettes or conventions which undoubtedly characterise the relationship.

Conflicts

When communication goes wrong the fault may lie in any one of a number of different areas:

1   The communication process may break down in any one of the six main stages.
2   The wrong communications medium may have been chosen.
3   The route for communication may have been disrupted by 'interference' of one kind or another.
4   The context or background of a situation may have been misread.
5   Arising more particularly from 1 above, the relationship between sender and receiver may create a conflict in one or other or both.

This last area may cause deep-seated problems. One main reason for such conflict is that all members of an organisation embody within themselves a number of different obligations and responsibilities which come to the fore at different times, depending upon which particular duty they are discharging and with whom they are relating, whether to a group or an individual.

Jim Harper's problems

Take Jim Harper, for example. Jim works as senior clerk in the production department of a large manufacturing company. He is also the representative of an office staff trade union. For some years he has been actively involved in the works sports and social club and has recently been elected its chairman. He is also a husband and father. As the diagram above illustrates, all these duties or 'roles' overlap and together go to 'make up' Jim both at work and at home.

The various roles of Jim Harper

In some parts of each of his roles there is no problem – Jim is able to carry out his duties without feeling tension or conflict. But there are also areas which overlap, where aspects of one role and the relationships it creates with other people impinge upon another role with accompanying difficulties. Imagine, then, how Jim would feel in the following situations:

1   He has been asked to work late on the night he promised to take his family to the cinema – a treat they had all been looking forward to.

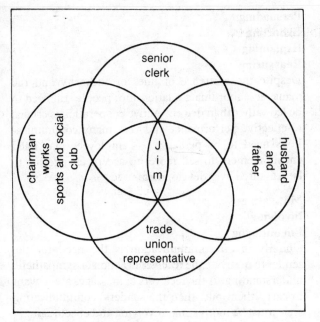

2 His trade union is in general dispute with employers over a pay settlement.

3 His departmental manager is appointed to the works sports and social committee saying, 'Don't worry about me, Jim, just treat me as another committee member'.

4 As trade union representative he is given confidential information to the effect that the company is likely to require the sports field for the expansion of the works.

The conflicts which are bound up in such situations are not easily resolved and membership of any organisation, in whatever capacity, is likely to involve the employee in similar, difficult circumstances. Resolving such problems requires much communication expertise and reserves of goodwill and mutual sympathy on both sides of a relationship.

Effective communication, then, is totally bound up with an understanding of how people behave in groups or as individuals and also with an appreciation of the ways in which relationships – managing director/senior clerk, foreman/operative, secretary/principal – affect the process of communication. For example, the managing director, because of his power and status may only get to hear what his staff think he wants to hear; the departmental group which represents the older, long-service staff may express resentment at the changes being energetically introduced by a newly-appointed young manager; the machine operator may have a disagreement with the foreman in fuller and franker terms than he would with the production manager.

Thus communication tends to be coloured by a number of factors based on group attitudes and person-to-person relationships:

1 Communication with a superior tends to be more formal or guarded than with an equal: 'I'd better be careful what I say here.'

2 Communication with a subordinate tends also to be formal and restrained: 'I don't wish to lose my authority by becoming too familiar.'

3 Communication with an equal tends to be fuller, franker and less restrained: 'What I tell Charlie will not affect my position.'

4 Informal groups may not always communicate directly, but 'let their feelings be known' in various ways.

5 People expect other people to communicate in ways associated with their position and mutual relationship:

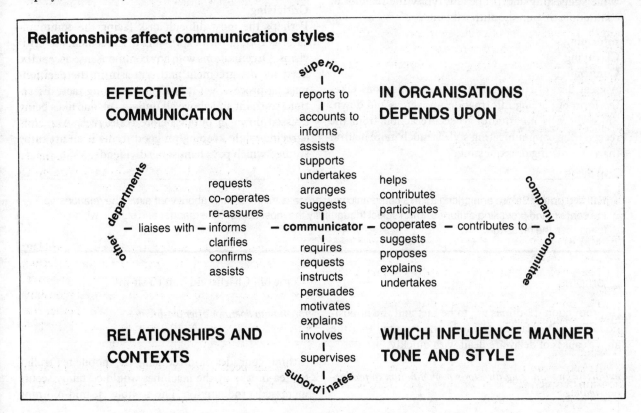

'The boss don't stand for no nonsense,' or, 'Janet? Oh, yes, always polite. I'd be sorry to lose her.'

Styles of communication

Directing
Instructing
Requiring
If the objectives of an organisation are to be achieved then orders and directives need to be sent down the authority line which are clearly expressed. The authority of the sender backs up the 'requiring' message which the subordinate is expected to accept.

Accepting
Undertaking
Executing
Effecting
Accepting and undertaking – doing – are central to the subordinate's role. In fact the directing/accepting relationship is the lynch-pin of organisational communication since it lies at the heart of the contract between the employee and the employer. Acceptance of employee status requires self-discipline and if the receiver cannot accept and undertake courteously phrased instructions he or she is probably in the wrong job!

Requesting
Suggesting
Proposing
Nevertheless, some directives are more tentatively phrased – especially when the receiver's active goodwill is central to the task. Requesting also characterises those liaising relationships between departments, while suggesting and proposing typify the manner of communicating up the authority line.

Informing
Clarifying
Confirming
A great deal of communication in organisations takes the form of passing information up, across and down. Since there is no attempt to secure action from the receiver the communicating style is much more neutral than in directing or requesting.

Persuading
Exhorting
Explaining
Reassuring
Despite the existence of lines of authority and the manager/subordinate relationship, people still need to be led rather than driven. Active cooperation is crucial to effective performance and very many communications need to be persuasive – employees may need encouragement to sell more, to accept changes or to be reassured over developments.

Motivating
Involving
Encouraging
Underlying *all* communication is the need for the sender to motivate the receiver to action or sympathetic understanding. If the receivers of messages are to want to carry them out, then the senders' communicating style must be motivating, involving and encouraging.

Helping
Assisting
Cooperating
Contributing
In many relationships where the communicator makes a contribution to a group activity – meeting, task-force or working party – then the communicating style needs to display a willingness to help, contribute and cooperate. In this way a team-spirit will be built up without which little will happen. Also, the communicator must be willing to accept criticisms and modifications to his or her contributions.

Questioning
Disagreeing
Criticising
Perhaps the most difficult task facing the communicator is coping with expressing disagreements or criticisms. Organisations with any commonsense accept the need for disagreement and criticism in the decision-making process, yet it is an area needing tact, discretion, restraint and above all timing – no one likes being dressed down in public before colleagues. Also, disagreeing while keeping on good terms is an art to be studied which pays handsome dividends!

Talking point: Before embarking upon a communicating process think carefully about your aims, the relationship, the context and prevailing attitudes. Then select thoughtfully the most appropriate manner and style in which to express the message.

Examples

'If production deadlines are to be met and the imposition of penalty-clauses avoided, it is essential that the above causes of delay are dealt with quickly.'

extract from managing director's memorandum to production manager

'Come on, Charlie, this ain't a sit-in!'

foreman to operator after tea-break

'I think your idea of introducing the mobile tea-trolley for tea-breaks by the machines would certainly secure increased productivity. The trouble is, mid-morning and afternoon tea-breaks have become traditional in the eyes of the men. . . .'

production manager to organisation and methods officer at a meeting

'It is therefore recommended that a working party be set up to investigate the feasibility of introducing a local area network to link our range of electronic office equipment.'

extract from an investigatory report from data processing manager to board of directors

'So I was wondering, Jack, if we could possibly borrow your slide-projector for the Bristol presentation.'

assistant sales manager to training officer over the 'phone

'This one's a tricky one, John, so I decided to ask you to handle it.'

extract from briefing of a personal assistant by the marketing manager

'I very much regret the trouble you have been caused and assure you that the defect is being given urgent attention at the company's Birmingham works. The machine will be delivered to you no later than . . .'

extract from regional sales manager's letter to a customer

'I appreciate that Mr Jenkins – it's just that no one appears to be controlling the flow of work and the girls are being pressured late in the afternoon and left with little to do in the mornings . . .'

extract from a secretarial supervisor's conversation with office manager about the recent introduction of a typing pool

'I know – and you know – that the company, and indeed the country, have been going through a difficult trading period. Equally, I know that the strength of Allied Products lies in its ability to meet a challenge. It hasn't been easy, and I can give you no guarantee that it will get better at all quickly. What I do know is that if anyone is going to lead the company into a better tomorrow, it is you, its sales representatives. And so my closing message to you all is: the company is proud of what you have done during a difficult year and will back you all to the hilt in the coming months; but it will only be your determination and continued enthusiasm which will turn the corner during the next year. I know I can rely on you!'

conclusion of managing director's address to the Annual Sales Conference of Allied Products

'If it will help, I don't mind staying on to type the letter – Monday's my stay-at-home night anyway.'

secretary to manager late Monday afternoon

Talking point: A major cause of communication failure occurs when the receiver considers the manner, tone or style of the sender's message inappropriate– . . . He can't talk to me like that!' . . . 'Cheeky young puppy' . . . 'I can never take him seriously' . . . 'if only he'd come out and tell you what he really wants'. . . .

The communicating manager

The role of the manager in any organisation involves the acceptance of many responsibilities. It also places a number of constraints upon the person who manages, whatever his or her title or designation. Certainly the manager needs to be a good communicator, since communicating lies at the heart of what the manager is doing, achieving given objectives through other people. The following table indicates some of the principal managerial qualities; they all direct or influence what the manager says, writes or does and the manner in which it is done and add up to what is an asset in any organisation – the communicating manager:

As an executor of tasks

decision-making
problem-solving
accountability
authority
initiative
anticipation
effectiveness

That the manager often acts under pressure to achieve objectives imposed from above is not always fully appreciated by his subordinates. Such accountability imposes strains, tensions and conflicts reflected in daily inter-personal communication. Helping the manager – who usually is only too aware of his problems – is a duty of the subordinate. In such ways teams are built and climates established essential to enjoying life at work.

As a leader

delegating
motivating
developing
involving
counselling
reconciling
healing

It is, however, the manager's responsibility to provide the lead and impetus in building a team based on cooperation and goodwill. This involves trust on both sides. The communicating manager needs to make constant efforts to be aware of the expectations, needs and anxieties of his team. Indeed, as much time may be needed to develop and hold the team together as in achieving tasks, since the latter is wholly dependent upon the former.

As a subordinate

integrity
loyalty
discretion
tact
diplomacy
self-discipline

The manager is also, usually, a subordinate. Much of his effectiveness relies on the development of personal qualities, reflected in communication practices, which result in his being trusted. Access to confidential or privileged information assumes qualities of tact, discretion and integrity – and the total subordinate role requires a high degree of self-discipline.

As an information source

informing
disseminating
listening
relaying
interpreting

If his team is to perform effectively, then the manager needs to keep sources and routes of information as open as possible, allowing for obvious needs such as security and confidentiality. He will need to develop skills in ascertaining what his team needs to know in order to perform and then to supply that need.

As a contributor to the organisation's development

thinking
planning
proposing
suggesting
querying
disagreeing

The manager is also a contributor to his organisation's development. If he is to be of benefit, then he needs to put his experience and expertise to use by thinking about what he is doing, putting forward suggestions and proposals, criticising constructively and using instances of disagreement to re-appraise what he is doing as well as to cause others to think about what they are doing.

The communicating secretary

The secretary's role has been significantly enlarged in recent years, partly as a development of information technology, and partly as the result of the changing economic and social climates regarding women at work. Nowadays, the secretarial post is much more frequently a route to executive responsibility. In any case, secretaries have always been lynch-pins or sheet-anchors in many an organisation. Many discharge responsibilities out of all proportion to their designations as assistants to senior managers, and are, in effect, executives in their own right. Moreover, the scope of the secretary's role is enormous, embracing not only the routine duties of dictation, typewriting or filing, but also coping with unexpected potential disasters, using initiative and resourcefulness and often, extreme delicacy and discretion. Good secretaries are treasured by managers in all organisations, since their price is truly 'above rubies'! Perhaps the best definition of the secretary's role is as the hub of a communications wheel around which a manager, staff – in fact a whole department – may revolve.

As a subordinate

loyalty
integrity
discretion
tact
cooperation

The secretary is often, literally, 'at the right hand' of her principal, acting in co-ordination with and as an extension of the manager. In addition to qualities like those already outlined in the manager as subordinate, the secretary needs to be particularly aware of the need for personal loyalty.

As a supervisor

delegating
checking
maintaining standards
helping
developing

Very often the secretary acts as a supervisor to junior staff, and is, consequently, in a similar position in many ways to the manager. She will need to set high standards by personal example, yet be accessible to staff, many of whom may be young, diffident and inexperienced, and so also has a responsibility to enrich and develop the staff in her charge.

As an executor of tasks

accuracy
precision
editing
efficiency

Much of the secretary's work lies in written and oral communication, in producing as finished products the manager's messages. Such work entails painstaking care, and may include the discreet editing of rough drafts.

As an assistant

ability to cope
initiative
resourcefulness
perceptiveness
helpfulness

In addition to the routine range of secretarial duties, the secretary is very often given, or assumes the role of assistant or confidante to her principal. In fact very many management functions are, in reality, carried out by a team of two. Thus taking an interest and being committed may soon lead to a creative and fulfilling assistant's role.

As receptionist and 'filter'

charm
intelligence
poise
grooming
perception
alertness

Most secretaries have an involvement in reception work. In this role they may be understudies for an absent principal and may form a lasting first impression on a visitor or client. Also, alertness and perceptiveness may prove invaluable in relaying information or attitudes regarding customers or competitors who visit or telephone. Also, the secretary needs to be resourceful in deciding what she can deal with and what needs her principal's attention.

Conclusion

Nowadays people acknowledge much more readily the central part which good communication techniques can play in overcoming the problems which occur when objectives are to be achieved by people working in tiered structures or hierarchies.

This is not to say that all problems related to work are easily overcome – newspapers provide evidence to the contrary every day. Nevertheless, systems and processes are being improved. In many organisations employees are consulted and involved far more extensively than in the past. In the area of industrial relations, managements and unions have developed sophisticated 'negotiating machinery' and government agencies have been created to arbitrate where necessary.

The improvements in education during the last 100 years have resulted in individuals being more aware and articulate, with the result that, both as managers and as subordinates, they have more insight and perception of 'the other fellow's point of view'. More recently, the study of human behaviour and human relations has revealed much more of the psychology involved in human communication processes – of 'what makes people tick'.

In addition, organisations in recent years have been casting a much more critical eye over their systems and structures. Management specialists and consulting industrial psychologists are able to demonstrate the problems deriving from a line of authority which is too long or the problems arising from groups which are too big or from doing work which is unsatisfying. There is now a greater appreciation of the fact that people like, on the whole, to work in small, closely-knit groups; there is also more understanding of the need for people to be given the initiative to solve problems or to effect manufacturing processes in their own way.

For this reason many organisations are now more loosely controlled from the centre and more independence is given to subordinate parts. The trends of the future, resulting from the findings of the communication and behavioural sciences, may well be away from the giant corporations and back to smaller, locally based manufacturing or servicing units.

One thing is certain, however. Whenever people, even in comparatively small numbers, are put together in a working environment, human nature will ensure that problems ensue! Overcoming the problems of human interaction in the world of work is, in effect, what business communication is all about.

This module aimed to set out some of the main theories and principles which underpin good communication techniques and to indicate some of the problems which only developed social skills and positive human relations attitudes will overcome.

All really worthwhile skills not only take time to learn, but also need daily practice to maintain. Communication is no exception.

The chances are that you already are, or shortly will be working in an organisation. Whether you love it or hate it, whether you become fulfilled or frustrated in your working life, will depend very much on how well you manage to put good communication skills into daily practice. Doing so requires self-discipline and dedication and the benefit of experience – plus the counsel of those who 'have been around' if you are wise enough to seek it.

But the effort is worth it – especially if you consider that you will probably spend some 80 000 hours of your life at work!

Build-up tasks

1   Draw up a definition of a group (in not more than 50 words) which in your opinion satisfactorily describes your present class. Compare your definition with those compiled by fellow students.
2   Write a paragraph to explain in your own words why people tend to form groups at work.
3   First do your research, then explain to your group in a five minute lecturette *one* of the following topics:

   (*a*) The characteristics of a group.
   (*b*) What is meant by 'role-conflict' in the work-place.
   (*c*) What is meant by the term 'peer group pressure'.

(*d*) How the hierarchic structure of posts in organisations influences the styles in which people communicate.

4   In pairs, draw up a list of 8 personal qualities which an employee should possess in his or her relationships with others at work e.g. respecting confidences. Put your list in what you see as an appropriate order of priority, then compare your list with those drawn up by others in your group. Ascertain which qualities are most frequently identified. Can you draw any conclusions from this exercise?

Discussion topics

1   Do you see the formation of informal groups at work – that is, those which arise spontaneously as opposed to being formed by management – as helpful or unhelpful in 'getting the job done'?
2   *Should* the tone or style of a person's communication be influenced by the status or seniority of its recipient?
3   What potential conflicts may arise when a manager is also a member of a professional trade union? In such an instance, is the manager in a different position from the machine operative who is a trade union member? If so, why? If not, why not?
4   Why does the concept of 'us and them' arise in some organisations? What sort of strategies could be introduced in communication practices to avoid this sort of polarisation into two sometimes hostile groups?

Group activity

In small groups of 3–4, devise a set of 5–6 questions which will provide answers to what sort of outcomes people seek to obtain from their work. Then interview about ten people in different types of employment and note down (preserving anonymity) what sort of outcomes are identified. In a general discussion, consider how being a member of a group at work is relevant to the outcomes which have been identified.

Case study

He only arrived yesterday!

Harry, Jim, Sue and Nicky all work as junior clerks in the office administration department in the head office of Electrix Motors Ltd. The company manufactures a wide range of electrically powered motors for use in industry. At present, all four are sitting round a table in the staff restaurant having their mid-morning coffee break.

HARRY: What do you make of the new feller then?

SUE: What new fellow do you mean?

HARRY: You know, the stuck-up blond-haired feller who's just joined us in the office!

NICKY: Oh, him! *I* think he's rather dishy, actually! Wears his hair short, well-dressed, blue eyes . . .

HARRY: Yeah, that's the one! Right stuck up, if you ask me!

JIM: Well, what's he done to you, Harry? He only arrived yesterday!

HARRY: Fancies himself, that one! There I was, doing some collating for Mr Jenkins – a batch of sales instructions for the reps – I had all the sets of pages set out in numerical order. Anyway, he just walked by me and said he knew of an easier way to do it! I mean, I don't suppose he knows where the main entrance is yet! Telling me how to do my job!

SUE: I'm sure he wasn't, Harry. Perhaps he *did* know a better way, though. And even if he did, perhaps he was, you know, just trying to be friendly, to get to know you . . .

HARRY: Well, he's going a funny way about it.

NICKY: Who has he been assigned to?

HARRY: Miss Fox, I think. She'll soon sort him out, mark my words!

JIM: Well, I had a brief word with him yesterday afternoon – just after he had come out of Miss Fox's office. Didn't seem a bad sort to me. Bit sure of himself, perhaps. Still, it's bound to take him a while to fit in – find his way about.

NICKY: Does he play badminton by any chance? Perhaps I should see if he wants to join the Sports Club?

SUE: Well, I know someone he's made a hit with. And I reckon that someone will soon be having a spot of trouble with some collating, if I know that someone!

NICKY: Oh, be quiet, Sue. I'm only, well, just thinking he might be glad to join the badminton group, just to make a few friends here.

HARRY: Well, if that doesn't beat all! She'll probably be offering him my place in the team by next week.

JIM: Well, Nicky, here's your chance to ask him. He's just coming this way with a cup of coffee in his hand.

SUE: Go on, Jim, ask him to join us. I'm sure Harry's *dying* to get better acquainted.

JIM: No sooner asked than done . . . Hello, Peter, isn't it? Come and join us. This is Sue French, Nicky Wilson, Harry Jackson, and I'm Jim Thomas – we met briefly yesterday afternoon . . .

Assignments

Discussion topics

1   Do you think Harry's initial response to Peter is justified?

2   How would you describe Nicky's attitude to Peter? Is she likely to make a sound judgment about Peter?

3   What would you say to Peter if you were Miss Fox, telling him about starting to work in the office administration department?

Written assignments

1   Carry on writing the dialogue of the meeting of Peter with his new colleagues, until they go back to the office. Assume that Peter is anxious to start off on the right foot with the junior clerks.

2   Write an essay outlining the sort of problems someone is likely to encounter when joining a new group of fellow-students or work-mates. Suggest how such problems might best be overcome.

Case study

'I shouldn't really tell you this but . . .'

Charlie Watson had worked for many years in the Office Administration Department of Britaware Cutlery Limited as a senior clerk. Hazel Perkins had been there almost as long and had worked her way up to typing pool supervisor. Not long after Mr Simon Walker, a young but able administrator, had been appointed Office Administration Manager at Britaware. Charlie and Hazel met in the staff restaurant:

'Afternoon, Hazel.'

'Oh, hello, Charlie. Come and sit down. How's the world treating you these days?'

'Not very often! Too busy trying to keep up with the new ordering system His Nibs has devised. He must think I've got overdrive or something!'

'I'm not surprised. A real new broom by all accounts. A little bird just told me he wants to bring in some new sort of filing system. Though I daresay there's nothing wrong with the old one. Still, I expect you'll have something to say about that, Charlie.'

'Too right I will! Anyway, where d'you get that from? First I've heard!'

'Never you mind! Still, I thought you'd like to know. And, another thing. (Hazel leans across the dining-table to whisper into Charlie's ear.) Don't breathe a word of this, but Mabel – you know, works in the M.D.'s outer office – told me she'd heard that our Mr Walker left Dixon's under a bit of a cloud! Some talk of him and a dolly bird secretary who left just before he did. Not many weeks after their Christmas party! . . .'

'No! Well, well, well. The girls upstairs had better watch out then! Mind you, I'm not surprised. I've seen him and that Carole Waters looking – well you know – funny at each other come to think of it. Flighty piece if ever I saw one. You'll be keeping your eye on her, I'll be bound!'

'I've got her number, don't you fret! Listen, I shouldn't really tell you this but Mr Walker told me in confidence – now I know I can rely on you – that as soon as he's got time, he's going to introduce a new Saturday working rota system for the typing staff. Something to do with the Works order book being full. I told him the girls wouldn't stand for it but he said it was all a matter of how it was put to them. Still, if the girls get wind of it, there'll be a right dust up, you mark my words! So don't breathe a word!'

'Course not! What d'you take me for? Well, I'd better be getting back upstairs – see what else is new!'

Later that afternoon, Charlie wandered over to the typing pool with a sheaf of papers in his hand and gave Susan Greenford the following instructions:

'Do this little lot soon as you can Sue.'

'I shouldn't really, Mr Watson. Miss Perkins doesn't really like us to. . . .'

'Don't you fret! She's got other things on her mind at present. By the way, how's your boyfriend, Gary? Still mooning over each other every Saturday morning in Carlo's Coffee Bar? You tell 'im from me, he wants to make the most of his Saturday mornings!'

'How d'you mean Mr Watson?'

'Never you mind! You know what they say, "Absence makes the heart grow fonder!"'

'Oh, I haven't got the time to listen to your riddles Mr Watson, I've got work to do!' With that, Susan attacked her typewriter determinedly.

But Charlie's innuendo *did* form the last piece of the jig-saw that perceptive Susan Greenford had been assembling for some little time. And the picture she had pieced together did not please her at all. . . .

Assignments

1   In groups, consider the above case study and then discuss the following questions:

(a) What has the Britaware 'grapevine' to do with Charlie and Hazel's conversation?

(b) To what ends are Charlie and Hazel using the 'grapevine'?

(c) How do Charlie and Hazel match up to your idea of senior departmental staff? Make a checklist of the shortcomings you think they display.

(d) What do you see as the dangers of talking about departmental colleagues and business in the way that Charlie and Hazel do?

(e) Can you envisage any ways in which the conversation could rebound on Charlie and Hazel?

(f) What do you think might have prompted Charlie and Hazel to talk in the way they did?

(g) What consequences do you see in indulging in 'grapevine gossip' and acting as a staging-post for grapevine rumours?

Compare your group's views with those of other groups in a general group session.

2   Make a checklist of the qualities which all organisational employees ought to possess, which you think Charlie and Hazel clearly lack.

Follow-up assignment

In a general group discussion, explore the nature of the relationship between employer and employee, manager and subordinate. Try to establish a generally acceptable code of behaviour and standards which you think someone preparing for a career in business or the public service ought to stick to – through thick and thin, in good times and bad.

6 Introduction to information technology

Introduction

> **Definition of information technology**
>
> 'The acquisition, processing, storage and dissemination of vocal, pictorial, textual and numerical information by a microelectronics-based combination of computing and telecommunications.'
>
> Department of Employment
> Information Technology Leaflet

Information technology means simply the application of technology to information. But this is not a new idea – we have been applying technology to information for a very long time (look at the chart on pages 70 and 71!) However, it has created a lot of excitement lately because of the rapid advances in the technology that is associated with microprocessors.

The term 'information technology' now covers the whole range of office/factory communication including telecommunications which is carried out by means of equipment based on the electronic microprocessor or silicon chip. In manufacturing, the terms 'CADCAM' (Computer Aided Design, Computer Aided Manufacture) and 'Robotics' are also now widely used to describe IT activities.

The microprocessor

The microprocessor is a very complex collection of microcircuits which are capable of moving around electrical impulses or signals, and these impulses themselves represent bits (items) of information. In this way, the microprocessor is able to add, subtract, multiply and divide and to perform a host of calculations at very high speeds. Indeed, calculations which would literally take a human mathematician years to solve are completed by microprocessors in seconds! No bigger than a thumbnail and no thicker than an ice-cream wafer, the microprocessor now easily out-performs the massive computers of the 1950s, which weighed tonnes and occupied entire rooms.

Manufacturers in both the industrial and commercial fields were quick to see the amazing business potential of the microprocessor – it was tiny, and so fitted into small products such as pocket calculators or digital wristwatches; it was made in large mass-production batches and was therefore extremely cheap; it was robust and particularly free from faults, since it possessed no moving parts. Moreover, it was powerful and could handle the computer needs of small businesses readily. Such revolutionary design features were made possible by advances in electronic technology.

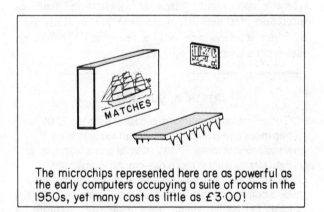

The microchips represented here are as powerful as the early computers occupying a suite of rooms in the 1950s, yet many cost as little as £3·00!

The mass media – newspapers, TV, magazines – were also quick to appreciate the immense technological and social impact of this new technology. The 1970s were referred to as 'The Age of the Chip'. Articles were entitled, 'Chips with Everything!' Even the valley in California where the technology was pioneered become known across the world as 'Silicon Valley'. Within a few years, products abounded with microprocessors as control- or information-giving mechanisms – pocket calculators, watches, cookers, radios, musical instruments, factory presses and drills. The microprocessor quickly found its way into almost every facet of industrial or commercial work.

So fast was this process in the mid-1970s, that historians and industrialists already referred as early as 1976–77 to the 'microelectronics revolution' which was transforming commercial and everyday life.

'This is the second industrial revolution. It multiplies man's brainpower with the same force that the first industrial revolution multiplied man's muscle-power.'

J Sydney Webb
Executive Vice-President TRW Inc

'There can no longer be any question that the industrial nations of the world are producing another technological revolution of historic importance. It may well emerge as the single most important influence in the development of a post industrial society.'

T J Lowi, IEEE, 'Transactions on Communications', October 1975

This 'technological revolution' has had a profound impact on business communications during the past decade. Nowadays, desk-top terminals which can act as word processors, data processors, 'windows' into large computers, or as powerful computers in themselves are thought commonplace. Terms such as 'electronic mail' and 'message switching' in an interconnected network of machines are regularly used by office workers who only a few years ago had no idea what a word processor was!

'IT' IN A NUTSHELL!

'Today's microcomputer at a cost of perhaps $300 has more computing capacity than the first large electronic computer ENIAC. It is 20 times faster, is thousands of times more reliable, consumes the power of a light bulb rather than that of a locomotive, occupies 1/30 000 the volume and costs 1/10 000 as much. It is available by mail order or at your local hobby shop.'

'Microelectronics', Robert E Noyce
Scientific American, 1977

What *is* a silicon chip?

The popular term 'silicon chip' used to describe a microprocessor conveys the idea of its smallness, but the term 'layer sandwich' might better describe the complexity of its construction!

A silicon chip is made up of layers of silicon and other added materials which have embedded upon them complex electrical circuits. These circuits interconnect in three dimensions, like tracks running up, down and across a 'layer sandwich' as it were.

The essential concept to grasp is that tracks and 'gateways' of metal are interconnected without any

moving parts, but in such a way as to allow pulses of electricity to be moved around extremely rapidly so that the information represented by them may be stored or moved to various locations as the program or calculation of which they are part demands.

In order to achieve such microscopic complexity, original drawings some 100 times larger than the microchip are first produced. The circuits they represent may be interconnected in up to 20 layers or wafers of silicon.

Once the plans have been produced, they are reduced by a process known as photolithography and etched upon the wafers of silicon – a material capable of conducting electricity only in its pure form. The process of etching ensures that only the tiny tracks representing the desired circuit are left adhering to the silicon and allied material bases. At intervals, other impurities are added to the silicon in order to control its conductivity and create transistors which are used to regulate the flow of electricity and to act as switches.

Silicon chips are now mass-produced in dust-free factories. The economies of this mass-production technique of manufacture have enabled the silicon chip or microprocessor to be sold extremely cheaply – for a matter of a few pounds each. This factor, in combination with the general reliability of microprocessors, has provided the main impetus for the electronics revolution of the past decade, where a single tiny microprocessor may embody more computing power than the bulky computers of the 1950s which occupied whole rooms!

How did information technology (IT) come about?

Though it took only a few years in the 1970s to develop and market the microprocessor, its origins may be traced back some 150 years to the beginnings of telecommunications in the 1830s (see time chart on pages 70 and 71). The strands which make up the new information technology include the widespread use of electricity as a means of powering equipment and transmitting signals, the development of telegraphy and telephony, the evolution of the typewriter from mechanical upright to electronic word processor, the invention of the Cathode Ray Tube (CRT) TV and – most importantly – the invention of the electronic digital computer. Further strands include the development of telex and facsimile transmission as well as xerography or photocopying.

It is important to appreciate the origins of the new information technology, and to realise that it has taken a century and a half for the developed countries of the world to adjust – both in business and in social terms – to the incredible innovations and changes which information technology is bringing about. It is also important to accept that people and businesses do not change at the same rate – while a go-ahead multi-national organisation may already have introduced a fully integrated electronic office, the proprietor of the firm next door may only just be contemplating buying an electronic typewriter!

The following paragraphs trace the pathway of technological invention which has led to the development of information technology.

The telegraph

The first commercial use of electricity in Britain occurred in 1839 when the Cooke and Wheatstone telegraph was opened in London. This remarkable development paved the way for national and international telegraphic networks which opened up a host of business links and opportunities.

The telephone

On 10 March 1876, Alexander Graham Bell, 'father of the telephone', relayed the first words by telephone. Some five years later, the British Post Office was offering a public service for both telegraph and telephone users. Indeed, the widespread development in the 19th century and in the first half of the 20th century of sophisticated telephone networks has proved to be of crucial importance in the establishment of a modern means of conveying electronic messages, since today many computers 'talk to each other' by courtesy of telephone lines! Such interactive links are better known nowadays as 'area networks'.

Radio communication

In 1901, many of the secrets of radio waves yielded to Guglielmo Marconi, when he successfully transmitted radio signals from Cornwall to Newfoundland. Within 25 years, newspaper pictures were being radioed across the Atlantic!

The typewriter and Qwerty keyboard

Undoubtedly, the most used item of office equipment in the past 100 years has been the 'Qwerty' typewriter. Developed from a design by Scholes, the first commercially marketed typewriter was produced in the USA by the Remington Corporation in 1874. Two years later, the shift key was introduced to enable the typing of both upper and lower case letters. The early typewriters were, of course, manuals and the first electric typewriter was developed in the 1920s. In the 1960s, electric typewriters with memories were introduced. Soon such models were given TV screens and word processing was introduced. From the 1960s onwards, the pace of invention and innovation quickened dramatically.

Telex and facsimile transmission

The teleprinter and telex were developed in the 1920s in response to a growing thirst for international news,

and as a result of international business connections requiring instantaneous communication. From telex grew the ability to scan drawings, photographs, plans, etc electronically and to send the information as electrical signals across the world. In this way, modern facsimile transmission evolved.

Computers

Today, computer scientists talk about 'fifth generation' computers and are not so far away from the introduction of 'voice input', where the spoken word may be used to program the computer instead of a high-level programming language allied to a machine code converting information into a series of 0s or 1s!

Today's computer roots lie in the 18th and 19th centuries, when a number of attempts were made to construct mechanical adding machines – notably by Charles Babbage, the father of computing, who laid the foundations for automatic counting. Another 19th century development was 'symbolic logic', which George Boole evolved to help problem-solving, and a renewed interest in the binary system of counting.

The need to be able to reduce problems to a logical sequence of steps and the ability to perform calculations in binary arithmetic are both central to current computing techniques. However, it is not only numbers which are capable of being represented by binary numbering codes; letters of the alphabet may also be so represented. By these means of binary mathematics, a number of computer languages have been developed such as BASIC (Beginner's All-purpose Symbolic Instruction Code) and COBOL (Common Business Oriented Language). Other languages with more mathematical, science or business orientations have also been devised to enable the computer user to interact with the computer by written programs.

The difference between the decimal and binary numbering codes			
Decimal code	Binary code	Alphabetic code	Binary code
1	1	A	1000001
2	10	B	1000010
3	11	C	1000011
4	100	D	1000100
5	101	E	1000101
6	110	F	1000110
7	111	G	1000111
8	1000	H	1001000
9	1001	I	1001001
10	1010	J	1001010

It was not until the 1940s and 1950s that the modern electronic computer evolved. The first computers – ENIAC and EDSAC – (see the time chart on pages 70 and 71) were very bulky and heavy. They occupied whole suites of rooms and weighed many tonnes. They were often out of order because they relied on thousands of valves. But work they did, and complex calculations at great speed became a reality.

Since the 1960s, there has been a process of miniaturisation in computer design made possible by the development of the transistor – a solid state type of valve – and subsequently by the microprocessor. Thus today's desk-top microcomputer is many times smaller yet more powerful than its early predecessors! Speed of information is another factor which has developed with incredible leaps and bounds. Today's 'hard disc' which stores some parts of a computer's memory may embrace several hundred million bits of information, each one locateable in less than a few hundredths of a second!

Developments in information technology

In order to understand the new technology, it is important to be aware of what may be termed the three phases of the introduction of electronics into the office.

Phase one

In the 1970s, the first business machines using the new technology tended to be 'stand-alone' word processors or microcomputers. In other words, they were not connected to any other electronic machine and tended to be 'dedicated' to one function only – say word processing or data processing.

Phase two

The second phase of development was to group word processors together in a 'shared logic' system. This meant providing a number of word processor operators with a visual display unit (VDU) and keyboard, each of which was connected to a central processing unit (CPU), and one or more printers – the word processor workstations 'shared the logic' of the CPU and printer.

Such an evolution enabled secretarial servicing units to be set up which were able to provide secretarial support for up to, say, 30 principals – managers or executives – through a team of administrative secretaries and correspondence secretaries, the former generally performing administrative secretarial functions, while the latter worked the word processors. Such a unit would be managed by a supervisor.

As will be seen later, this development has within it a number of consequences for business communication, not least of which is the need for the word processor operator to possess an extensive active vocabulary adequate to meet the text generated by a wide range of executives.

Same main strands of the new information technology

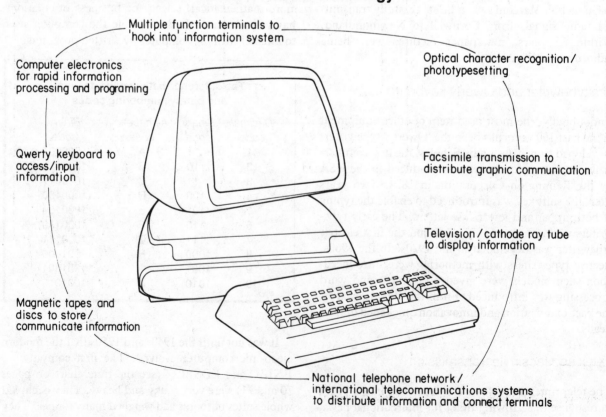

Multiple function terminals to 'hook into' information system

Computer electronics for rapid information processing and programing

Optical character recognition / phototypesetting

Qwerty keyboard to access/input information

Facsimile transmission to distribute graphic communication

Television / cathode ray tube to display information

Magnetic tapes and discs to store/ communicate information

National telephone network / international telecommunications systems to distribute information and connect terminals

Phase three

A third phase is now developing in which all the items of electronic equipment – word processor, microcomputer, telephone system, mainframe computer and intelligent photocopier – are all 'convergent' or interconnected in a total electronic communication system. The illustration shows how the office and remotely located factory may be linked via a common electronic communication system.

Integrated IT office system

Text production retrieval and storage : word processing		Electronic facsimile transmission
Information/data production, storage, retrieval : microcomputing	Office manager secretarial and clerical support staff	Audio / visual 'teleconference' mock-ups
Electronic photocopying and phototypesetting		Oracle, Ceefax, Prestel information services
Local, national, international telephone communication		'Electronic mail' inter-office communication

'I warned you this might happen, Hopcroft, if we left them switched on overnight!'

Development of Information Technology timechart

pre-3500 BC	Signs and speech
c 3500 BC	Earliest known writing (cuneiform), Mesopotamia
63 BC	Tiro, Rome invents a shorthand which is taught and used to record speeches
100 AD	Paper invented in China
c 300	First parchment book
c 1450	Paper mills in England. Invention of moveable type in Europe
1476	W Caxton, book printed in English
c 1590	Invention of lead pencil
1714	Henry Mill, patent for a typewriter
1837	Samuel Morse (USA) produces his first telegraph
1839	First British commercial use of electricity: Cooke and Wheatstone's telegraph lines open in London
1843	Principles of facsimile transmission patented by A Bain
1852	B Dancer, invention of microfilm
1867	James Maxwell proves the existence of radio waves
1868	Scholes develops his typewriter, forerunner of modern typewriter
1874	Remington Corporation (USA) markets the developed Scholes typewriter
1876	First words transmitted on a telephone by Alexander Bell
1878	Bell predicts the current telephone network
1882	Vertical filing systems introduced
1897	First Cathode Ray Tube (CRT) invented by K F Braun
1901	Guglielmo Marconi sends radio signals from Cornwall to Newfoundland
1913	Vacuum tube amplifier (the valve) produced by H D Arnold. First long-distance telephone cable laid
1920	First electric typewriter in commercial use
1925	John Logie Baird produces first real television
1928	Baird demonstrates first colour television pictures
1931	Page-printing teleprinter introduced by Creed
1936	British Broadcasting Corporation (BBC) starts the first public television service in the world
1946	ENIAC – Electronic Numerical Indicator And Calculator – the first modern electrically powered computer demonstrated, Pennsylvania, USA

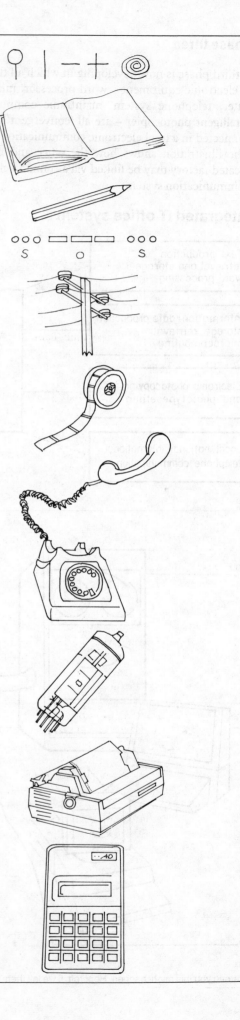

1947	The transistor is invented by Brattain and Barden
1949	First computer (EDSAC) with stored memory is demonstrated in Cambridge, England
1950s	Start of long-distance direct dialling of telephone calls Photocopying devices on general sale
1956	IBM Corporation develops computer disc drive
1958	First satellite radio message
1960	Laser light beam developed by T H Maiman (initials standing for: Light Amplification by Stimulated Emission of Radiation)
1964	IBM Corporation markets its Selectric Typewriter with memory function – forerunner of word processing equipment
1966	ITT Corporation (USA) develops fibre-optics technology
1967	British Post Office introduces its Data Processing Service
1971	Intel Corporation (USA) produces first commercially applicable microprocessor Floppy disc drive introduced for computer programming
1970s	Rapid development of microcomputer-based equipment and systems – microcomputer, stand-alone word processor, optical scanner, etc
1974	Xerox Corporation introduces the 'daisy' print wheel
1979	British Post Office transmits its Prestel viewdata service
1980	British Post Office begins to introduce its 'System X' computerised telephone network
1981	British Telecommunications Act: establishes British Telecom as public corporation separated from the Post Office. Also permits the introduction of private enterprise into telecommunications
1980s	Developments in information technology proceed apace – more powerful microprocessors, area networking for electronic mail, etc, experimental work on voice input into computers, 'wristwatch TV', improved 'bubble' memory for microcomputers, fibreoptic transmission of messages, work with electronics at 'faster than light speeds', widening of information technology education in Great Britain from primary schools upwards

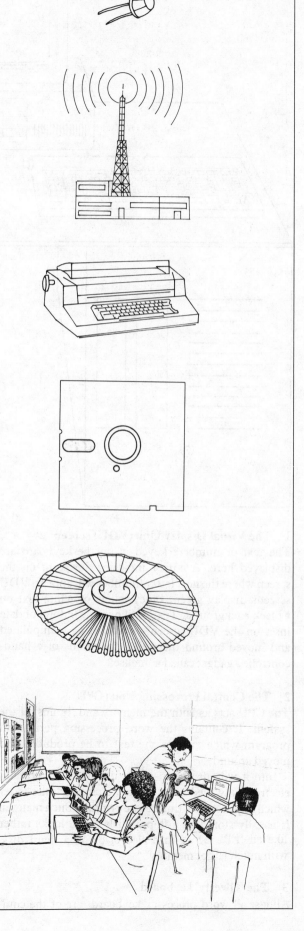

How a word processor works

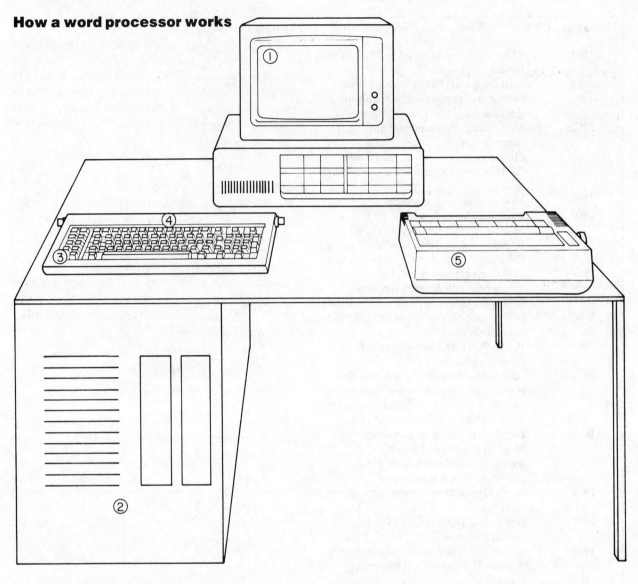

1   The Visual Display Unit (VDU) screen

The text or numbers keyed in on the keyboard are displayed here. A cursor indicates the point on the screen where the next letter/number will appear. VDU screens display green, blue, yellow or white text on a black background. Text or 'ikons' – windows of data inset on the VDU screen – can also be manipulated and moved around the screen by means of a hand-controlled gadget called a 'mouse'.

2   The Central Processing Unit (CPU)

The CPU acts as both the memory and 'brains' of the system. It contains the word processing permanent program which enables the text to be produced and moved around.

Into it will also be inserted, during the operation, electronically filed copy of, say, a circular sales letter which requires updating before printing. Such material is usually stored on a floppy disk which looks rather like an 'EP' record in a sleeve, or on a 'hard disk' with much larger memory.

3   The 'Qwerty' keyboard

Almost all word processor keyboards are of the com-

mon 'Qwerty' type and are used in much the same way as those of a manual or electric typewriter. In addition to the Qwerty and functional keys, the keyboard will also include a numeric pad which deals with the numerical facilities of word processing.

4   The functional keys

These keys are used to give the commands to the CPU which then performs the functions of text editing such as 'Erase', 'Move Text', 'Edit', etc.

5   The printer

The printer is activated whenever 'hard', i.e. paper copy of the electronically displayed text is needed. Such printers incorporate 'dot-matrix' or 'daisy-wheel' mechanisms capable of printing the text at hundreds of characters per minute. Current technology is also employing laser beams to perform this function as well as a system of ink-jet printing to speed the process.

Such a printer is capable of printing 'correspondence quality' text as 'one-off' copy or as multiple copies of, for example, reports, minutes or form/circular letters.

Nowadays, when such word processing systems form part of an integrated computer network, such documents may be relayed to remote locations many miles away in what is known as an 'electronic mail' system.

How a computer works

Computers work under the control of a program of instruction which is a step-by-step solution to a problem. Programs are used to process items of data which are put into the computer and later converted into outputs or files.

Putting information into the computer

Programs or data may be put into the computer by means of the terminal's keyboard. The program is displayed step by step on the VDU screen and then proceeds into the store of the CPU for processing.

Inputting a pre-written program

A program previously devised may be recorded on a floppy disc and loaded into the CPU whenever it is required, using the terminal.

The functions of the CPU

The CPU is the 'brain' of the system. It controls the operation of all the programs ('software') and of the computer 'hardware' or allied equipment. It has the facility both to store information and to move it around in order to complete the computing function – such as putting a random list of names into alphabetical order.

The CPU is the main part of the microprocessor.

Additional storage capacity

Information such as personnel records, stock items, sales orders, etc may be kept in additional files and updated or modified as required.

Getting information out of the computer

While processing the information, the computer will, in order to make it intelligible at the 'output' stage, convert it into English text, mathematical formulae, etc or graphical display.

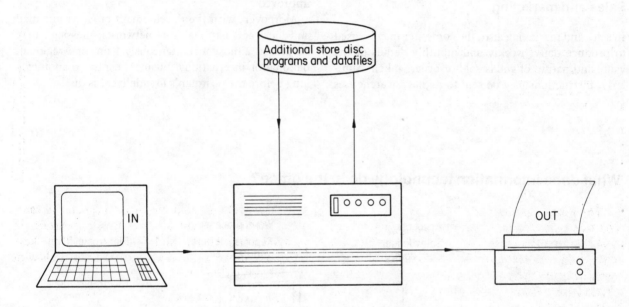

Programs may be written in high-level languages (BASIC, COBOL, FORTRAN, etc) and translated into special programs – machine language – represented by binary digits: 0 and 1 which form 'bits' or 'bytes' (items) of data. The CPU performs the desired arithmetic calculations or logical decision steps at lightning speed – the particular quality of the computer which makes it such an invaluable tool.

Data and programs held in store by the computer

Some programs (such as word processing packages) may be held permanently in store by the computer. Such a use of the computer's memory, however, may limit the range of tasks it can undertake.

Ins and outs

Note: There are various ways of getting information into and out of a computer.

IN
- Punched tape or cards
- Using the keyboard
- Floppy disc or cassette
- Optical Character Recognition (OCR)
- Voice input (in the research stage)

OUT
- Paper printout
- VDU screen display
- Intelligent copier
- Facsimile transmission
- 'Switched' electronic mail

IT office applications

In the past decade, the rapid introduction of electronic office equipment has made possible a host of labour- and time-saving operations. In fact, there are few office and management functions today which have not been affected by information processing.

Accounting

In accounting, for example, the entire company's pay-roll operation for weekly or monthly paid staff may be readily processed on computer, which adds in at regular intervals the various factors which go to make up the payslip – gross pay, income tax due, super-annuation, overtime worked and so on until a net sum is computed. Such records are then printed on a pay-slip, the correct amount of banknotes and coinage worked out and the whole process kept on record dur-ing the 52 weeks of the year. Such an operation has cut down extensively the laborious task of manual pay-roll computing.

Sales and marketing

In sales and marketing also, the computer may be used to produce daily, weekly and monthly details of the value and nature of goods sold or orders taken. Simi-larly, instructions may be sent to regional warehouses for orders to be packed and despatched to a range of locations within a district or sales region.

The marketing manager is also now able to use one of a number of modelling programs which will quickly answer a series of 'what if' questions – What if the sales price is raised? What if the products are sold only to certain credit-worthy dealers? and so on.

Office administration

In office administration terms, the flow of documents into and out of internal offices and to and from external contacts is made much more rapid and efficient by the sensible use of word processing. Numerous revised drafts of reports are handled by the editing function, where only those parts of the report which need modi-fying are changed. Computer terminals nowadays can handle not only word processing needs but can also call up information from a computer's main memory. The same terminals can be used to add new data to the computer's store of data. Thus access to company records is made much swifter and security is greatly improved.

Moreover, with the development of electronic mail and local and national area networks, messages may be passed almost instantaneously from one regional, national or international business centre to another – long before the postman's first delivery is due!

What does information technology do in the office?

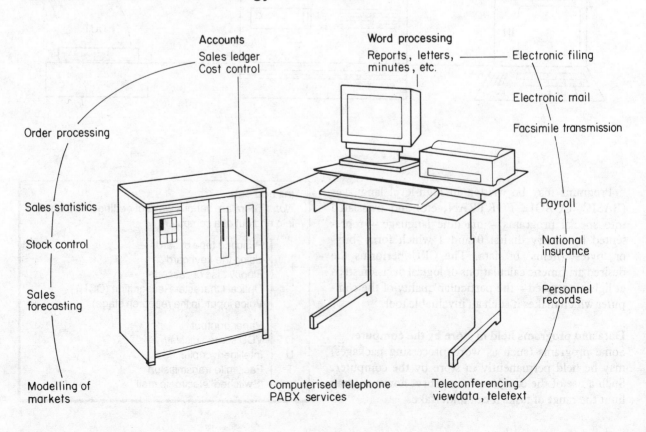

Accounts
Sales ledger
Cost control

Order processing

Sales statistics

Stock control

Sales forecasting

Modelling of markets

Word processing
Reports, letters, minutes, etc. ——— Electronic filing

Electronic mail

Facsimile transmission

Payroll

National insurance

Personnel records

Computerised telephone ——— Teleconferencing
PABX services ~~~ viewdata, teletext

The electronic office of tomorrow

The illustration shows the latest developing trends in information technology, which are discussed in further detail below.

1 Mainframe computer linked to Local Area Network (LAN)

The trend in electronic office technology over the next few years will be towards increasingly integrated systems or networks of office information processing machines. Such a system has been called a Local Area Network (LAN). At the hub of such a network is the organisation's mainframe computer with a wide range of programs and information readily accessible. Other terms used to describe this integration of all IT office equipment are 'convergence' and connectivity!

By means of telephone lines, new telecommunication channels such as fibre-optic systems or by commu-nication satellite, the new office will communicate swiftly either within the multi-storey office block, or across miles of countryside, or right across the globe! Thus messages can be 'switched' from one form of electronic machine to another whether they stand side-by-side or are located far apart.

2 The visual display unit (VDU)/text and data processing (DP) terminal

The crucial item of office equipment in a network infor-mation system will be the intelligent terminal. Such a terminal will sit on top of the office member's desk or 'workstation' and will embody both a VDU and a keyboard. Upon the VDU will be displayed either words or numbers, diagrams or graphs, pictures or cartoons in black/white or colour.

As well as forming the access point into the network system, the terminal will also be able to display view-data or teletext material such as the BBC's Ceefax,

The electronic office of tomorrow

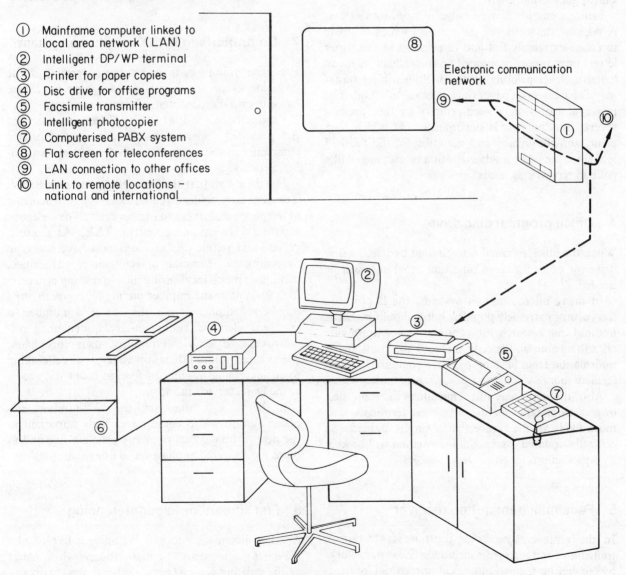

① Mainframe computer linked to local area network (LAN)
② Intelligent DP/WP terminal
③ Printer for paper copies
④ Disc drive for office programs
⑤ Facsimile transmitter
⑥ Intelligent photocopier
⑦ Computerised PABX system
⑧ Flat screen for teleconferences
⑨ LAN connection to other offices
⑩ Link to remote locations – national and international

Electronic communication network

Administrative / secretarial workstation

IBA's Oracle or the Prestel information service. Such services provide 'pages' of information on the TV screen, selected from continuously updated banks of information. The Prestel viewdata system provides for two-way communication.

In addition, the terminal will act as a computer in its own right, without the need to use the mainframe; it is this computing ability which gave rise to the term 'intelligent terminal'.

3   The electronic printer

An important adjunct of the terminal is the electronic printer which is used to obtain 'hard' or paper copies of any information displayed upon the terminal's VDU. Thus the printer may record outgoing information. It should be pointed out, however, that in the future it is much more likely that information will be electronically stored in computers' memories rather than upon pieces of paper. And though the truly 'paperless office' is still some years away, it is technically quite feasible today!

Printers employ a wide range of printing devices. A popular device is the daisy wheel which is made to rotate extremely fast and to print on to the paper letters or numbers positioned on the ends of its many 'petals'. Other printing devices include ink-jet spraying of characters on paper or laser beam 'etching'. The principal attraction of such printers are the speeds – several hundred words per minute – at which they print, and the quality and versatility of the finished job, since the print-heads may often be exchanged like golfball typewriting heads.

4   Office program disc drive

When the office terminal is to be used by itself, a disc drive (or other means of inputting programs) will be needed.

In many microcomputer systems, the floppy disc has become extremely popular, but it should be borne in mind that research still continues apace to provide cheap, reliable and speedy methods for transferring information from file storage into a computer's short-term memory.

Also, though it may suit some offices to retain their own discs or tapes for use with their terminals, it is more likely in the future that a single, unified and centrally updated database of information will be kept by organisations for employees to access.

5   Facsimile transmitter/receiver

In the representative office illustrated, a facsimile transmitter and receiver is included. The system works by converting textual, numerical or pictorial information recorded on paper into electrical signals which are sent over telephone lines or via satellite telecommunication 'beacons' to remote locations where they are 'decoded' back into their original form and printed.

Such a facility is of enormous help to architects, engineers, construction staff, designers and draughtmen who are able to receive in a matter of minutes amended diagrams or updated plans despatched from the other side of the country or the world.

6   The intelligent photocopier/high-speed printer

In tomorrow's office, the intelligent photocopier/high-speed printer will also be a boon. It will be able not only to copy documents in the conventional way, but also to receive directly from a computer data which it is able to convert into a printed form and then to duplicate as required.

Such a machine will be able to produce some 1000 characters per second by means of a laser and to provide copy of an extremely high quality.

7   Computerised PABX telephone system

For some time now, there has been a growth in the provision of private telephone exchanges which are based upon a digital system of message routing.

Furthermore, the 1981 British Telecommunications Act provided opportunities for consortia of private companies to construct networks for message switching/networking use.

For their own part the Post Office, and now British Telecom, have undertaken an extensive restructuring of telephone exchanges to incorporate the new electronic reed relay switching system (TXE). As a result, private and public organisations now have access to a rapidly growing number of telephone-based facilities, including: much less waiting time in making or receiving calls; automatic number finding for regularly used numbers; automatic call dialling if a number is engaged; telephone audio-conferencing enabling executives to take part in meetings from their office chairs; access to centralised dictation systems; direct dialling to an increasing number of foreign countries; access to the Datel service and so on.

In the office of tomorrow, the computerised telephone system will become increasingly important as the new technology allows more calls per line and as more sophisticated applications are devised.

8   Flat screen for teleconferencing

Another information tool in the office is likely to be the flat TV screen, about a metre square, which hangs on the wall and is used (among other things) to display office personnel in various locations who are taking part simultaneously in a 'teleconference'. A teleconference is a televised meeting where TV cameras transmit pictures and sound to various locations so that managers may communicate with each other without leaving their offices. Such a system would prove costly in transmission terms but is, again, technically quite feasible.

9 & 10   Network link to other offices and remote locations

Whatever type of communication network evolves, office staff will need to continue to communicate with each other, as well as with the central mainframe computer. Equally, there will continue to be clients and customers in other organisations with whom communication will take place either via terminal, facsimile transmitter, telex, telephone or the like. It is therefore of central importance for such networks to communicate without delay or complexity both with other offices within a single building or site and with other more distant locations, both nationally and internationally.

It's getting me really down, Doctor, my user doesn't even say 'Good morning' any more, and he keeps looking across at the 5th Generation Mark II Model and thinks I don't notice! ...

At the heart of information technology – people!
When seeking to understand the marvels of the new electronic technology – microcomputers, word processors, facsimile transmitters, network systems – it is all too easy to become preoccupied with the equipment and machine aspects of information technology and to forget that, at the heart of all communication processes, whether face-to-face conversation or computer printout, are people!

An old but still true axiom states that organisations are not the fabric of office blocks or office suites, but are made up of the complex interrelationships of people – of customers, sales representatives, typists, managers, suppliers, and so on. Moreover, the most sophisticated computer system, no matter how colossal its memory, remains an inert, lifeless tool until people provide it with data to process and until people interpret its outputs and responses.

Certainly the wonder of computer electronics lies in the incredible speed and accuracy with which information may be handled and used to resolve problems or to classify data. What would take many thousands of man-hours to compute is nowadays printed at high speed only seconds after a large computer has been given a problem to consider and to answer. Yet it is the staff of offices, factories and public departments who have to absorb and to utilise this increasing high-speed delivery of information – to make sense of it in terms of the range of activities of their organisation.

At best, electronic office equipment provides a series of tools which help people to do their jobs more efficiently. The good communicator should regard the new technology only as a means to this end and not as an end in itself!

Assessment questions

1   In what industrial and commercial fields does the microprocessor now play an important part?
2   Why was the new information technology taken up so quickly by industrial and commercial organisations?
3   In what ways has the invention of the microprocessor proved so important?
4   Draw up a checklist of the kind of office activities in which text/data processing equipment is now used?
5   Explain briefly what a silicon chip or microprocessor is.
6   By what means is it possible to make microprocessors so small?
7   List the principal technological developments which led to the construction of the first microprocessor.
8   Why was the development of the telephone so important for current information technology?
9   Explain briefly how facsimile transmission works.
10   What do you understand to be the difference between mainframe, mini and microcomputers?
11   List some of the ways of inputting information into a computer.
12   Explain what you understand by the term 'Local Area Network'.
13   What is meant by the term 'electronic mail'?
14   Describe the difference between ink-jet and daisy-wheel printing methods.
15   Outline briefly what a word processor is and how it works.
16   List as many services as you can recall offered by a computerised telephone network.
17   What is meant by the term 'teleconference'?
18   Explain the difference between viewdata and teletext.

19   What do the following stand for:

    a BASIC

    b COBOL

    c CADCAM

20   Explain briefly what is meant by the following terms:

    a hardware

    b software

    c hard copy

    d peripheral

    e floppy disc

    f daisy wheel

21   Give a brief outline of the services offered by:

    a Ceefax

    b Oracle

    c Prestel

22   What does the term 'intelligent' mean in connection with a computer terminal?

23   Write a paragraph to explain in simple, layman's terms how a computer works.

24   Write a short essay entitled 'What I think the office of the future will look like'. Give your reasons for the forecasts you make.

25   Draw up a schedule which identifies the main applications of information technology in the modern office. Write brief explanatory notes for each application on your checklist.

Assignments and discussion topics

1   You have been asked by your firm's training officer to draft an entry for the organisation's *Junior Staff Handbook* on *one* of the following topics:

    a How a computer works

    b What is meant by 'word processing'

    c Major uses of information technology in offices today.

2   First carry out your research then compose an article entitled: 'A brief history of information technology'.

    As a group, decide upon the best article and suggest that it be used in your school or college as a learning resource. Keep in mind the value of illustrating your article.

3   First undertake your research then give a 10-minute talk to your group on one of the following:

    a The development of the microprocessor

    b The service offered by Ceefax and Oracle

    c Developments in communication networks

    d The services of Euronet, Ethernet and Micronet

    e The latest developments in information technology.

4   First update your knowledge, then draft an entry for your company's staff handbook on the facilities provided by your recently installed computerised telephone service.

5   First find out about the range and nature of services offered by a computer bureau, then design a leaflet aimed at conveying the information you think important to potential users of the bureau.

6   Assume that a 'shared logic' word processing system is soon to be introduced in your head office. Compose a memorandum to all managers explaining the nature and scope of the services which will be available to them.

7   Having undertaken your fact-finding, design a pamphlet to be sent to businessmen outlining the main services offered to them by British Telecom.

8   Find out what IBM (UK) Ltd's 'PROFS' system is and how it may be used in an office context

9   Assume that you are the assistant of the office administration manager of a manufacturing company making a range of cooking utensils. Your firm, Cookware Limited is considering installing a minicomputer with up to 24 terminals in order to process all company information in a progressive manner.

    Your head office employs some 70 staff in the following departments: sales, personnel, marketing, accounts, office administration, production, transport.

    Also, there is the company's factory on the same site, which employs some 200 production staff.

    The firm's customers are spread across the country and many of them have access to computers and possess telex equipment and facsimile transmission facilities.

    Choose *one* of the company's departments and, in the role of assistant, write a report for senior management on how the move to full computerisation is likely to aid that department. Your report should also indicate some of the problems which might occur in such a move.

    Before attempting this assignment, you should seek to interview friends, relatives or contacts working in computerised firms.

Discussion topics

1   Organisations which do not computerise as soon as possible will lose out to their competitors who do.

2   Trade unions representing office workers are wrong to view information technology developments with suspicion.

3   Information technology by the year 2000 will have totally changed the office as we now know it.

4   'The impact of information technology is being overrated. Essentially people don't like these electronic gadgets. The whole thing will die out like a nine-day wonder!'

5   'If information technology is to help business and public service organisations to operate more efficiently, it is necessary to start the educational process of potential employees in their primary schools.' What steps would you take to educate people for the information technology age?

6   'Developed societies are in danger of pinning too many hopes for new jobs on the IT revolution.'

Case studies

Teletext, Viewdata, Prestel

Teletext is the name given to the system which permits a limited number of pages of text to be transmitted by TV broadcasting stations together with their program emissions; these special signals are transmitted using lines which are not being used for the ordinary video signal. A special decoding unit in domestic TV receivers permits selection and display on the screen. All the information is transmitted on a cyclic repetition basis by the broadcasting station without any need for communication back to the TV transmitter from the domestic receiver. There is bound to be some delay between choosing a particular information frame and the display of that frame on the screen; to minimise this delay a restricted number of frames are transmitted, only a few hundred.

Teletext services are provided in Britain by both the BBC and ITA: Ceefax and Oracle. In addition to the separate information frames, some broadcast TV programmes are accompanied by a teletext display of spoken dialogue so that these TV programmes may be enjoyed by the hard-of-hearing.

Viewdata, sometimes called 'videotext', is similar in appearance on the screen but is an interactive service. Viewdata has been operational in Britain since 1979. The UK service is now called Prestel; it uses a slightly modified domestic TV receiver in conjunction with an ordinary public telephone line in order to provide an interactive computerised data retrieval service (see diagram). Generally similar systems have been designed in France and in Canada.

Prestel service is provided in Britain by a computer network organised to store frames of information which are transmitted (over the telephone line) at 1200 bit/sec when requested by the customer. A reverse channel at 75 bit/sec is provided to allow the customer to select the frame required or to provide answers to questions set in the information frame itself. This bit rate is sufficient for manual keyboard operation.

The database information is provided by many specialist companies. Some pages of information have to be paid for, some are free. Some companies put information on the database on a restricted access basis, e.g. only Prestel customers from their own organisation are permitted to call up these particular frames.

One present major difficulty is that the viewdata systems used in different countries use different procedures, codes and signals and cannot interwork with each other: e.g. customers using British Prestel cannot access the Canadian Telidon system. The Prestel system was the first of its type to be developed and uses an 'alpha-mosaic' method of constructing letters from small squares of colour; that is why they seem odd to those who are used to normal TV definition pictures. Telidon, much later in the field, uses an alpha-geometric method of constructing letters, with lines and curves as well as squares of colour, so it is able to give an easier-to-read page of text and better diagrams than Prestel. Some countries are experimenting with hybrid viewdata/teletext systems by which the interactive or 'command' signals from the customer to the computer are sent via a telephone line but the called-for page of information, text or picture, is transmitted by a radio signal, coded, stored and displayed only by the customer asking for this particular page.

Considerable activity is taking place in some international bodies to define standards which would permit interworking between generally similar services around the world. Among the bodies involved in discussions are CCITT (International Telegraph and Telephone Consultative Committee), CCIR (International Radio Consultative Committee), ISO (International Standards Organisation), CEPT (Conference of European Posts and Telecommunications Administrations) and EBU (European Broadcasting Union).

Improvements are continually being made to Prestel services; one which will have a significant effect is Picture Prestel which allows the insertion of a still picture of colour television quality into an information page. The only restrictions which affect this are the cost of the extra memory required in each terminal, and the time taken to transmit the required amount of data on a low-bandwidth telephone circuit. When digital transmission systems and digital exchanges such as System X have been brought into wide-scale use it will be possible for high-definition Picture Prestel to be transmitted very much more rapidly than is now possible.

Prestel Gateway is an extension of ordinary viewdata services which provides for greater interaction with users and enables Prestel customers to obtain access to computer networks managed by other organisations. For example, among the banking services available to Prestel Gateway users are:

Accessing statements and ordering chequebooks
Handling loan enquiries and showing repayment
  options
Stopping payment on cheques
Amending standing orders
Effecting transfers of funds

Airline and tour operators are among those who find Prestel interactive services most useful; it is possible now to display on the screen all possible alternative flights and for tickets on a particular flight and for accommodation to be booked, all by a single call.

Prestel users are able to do their shopping via supermarket computers, examine the choice of available items, check prices, make a note of special offers and then order the goods, all without leaving the comfort of their own homes.

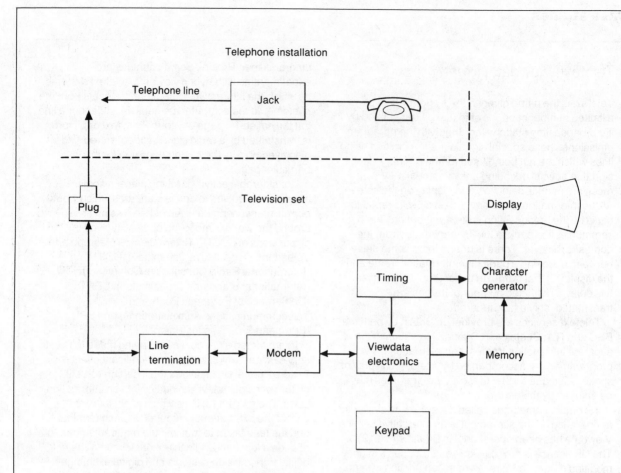

Telephone installation

Telephone line

Jack

Television set

Display

Plug

Timing

Character generator

Line termination

Modem

Viewdata electronics

Memory

Keypad

A typical Prestel terminal

Assignment

The extract on page 79 from *Telecommunications Primer* by Graham Langley contains some 900 words.

Your principal, Mr Arthur Donaldson of Telemax Office Systems Limited – a company which sells its expertise on office communication systems to a wide range of organisations – has asked you to provide him with a note summary of about 300 words, with headings, numbered points etc of the extract. He intends to incorporate it in a presentation he is giving to a large public company, on the likely impact of teletext and viewdata communication systems on the business world.

Produce a suitable note summary after you have researched the extract, to ensure you understand its technical points.

Travel or communicate?

Many office workers now spend their working days sitting before computerised workstations, typing on keyboards which print characters on to the screen of a visual display unit. Even when the task is to prepare an ordinary letter for mailing, the actual printing process now often takes place in a separate print room; when the letter as shown on the screen is exactly what is needed, the typist keys a 'print' key and the computer does the rest.

If typists had a similar workstation at home and took a batch of rough drafts back with them, they could no doubt do their work just as well in the comfort of their own home. The workstation could be linked with the office computer when necessary through the ordinary telephone system, on a dial-up basis.

Many people might perhaps be very unhappy if they had to spend most of their working days at home, alone: they would miss the social side of office life, the gossip sessions and cups of coffee, and all the interactions which can lead to increased job satisfaction and greater efficiency. But for those people who could do a good job of work in their own time, at their own pace, a home-based workstation might be an ideal arrangement.

People all over the world now talk about the paperless office as if it were bound to come soon, and indeed many electronic business devices are already widely used. In Britain it is still rare, however, to see VDUs on the desks of senior executives; in the USA this is not at all uncommon, at least in companies dealing with technologically advanced matters. Possibly today's commitment to paperwork here in Britain is associated with 'the briefcase complex'; some executives appear to feel that, if they do not take a case full of papers home with them for study, they are in some mysterious way not really part of the team, not pulling their weight – and perhaps about to be declared redundant.

Increased use of recorded speech in office communication is, however, likely to become common. As the cost of electronic memories falls and the cost of human secretarial services rises, it would seem logical to be able to store messages digitally in the form of speech. These messages could go straight to the addressee as soon as he or she becomes available and thus avoid processing by secretaries. They would of course still remain in store for reference as long as necessary. The humble telephone answering machine is a small step in this direction. Some executives still dry up and promise to call later rather than leave a message on an answering machine, but familiarity with such devices rapidly results in user confidence.

It is, however, in reducing travelling time and costs that electronics really comes into its own. Many companies now use telephone conference calls involving several executives, at different locations. A third party can be brought into a conversation merely to clear up a point under discussion. Most modern telephone switching systems provide features of this type.

If meetings are held regularly involving staff from two different locations, it is often economic to equip rooms specially as conference studios using a form of closed-circuit television called Confravision or 'teleconferencing' to link the two locations. Cameras can if necessary be directed to focus on the person doing the talking or can be used to give close-ups of plans or drawings which are the subject of discussion. It takes very few such conferences to save the money otherwise spent in travelling and hotel accommodation.

Radio-paging is already common in many countries. Some of these will merely 'bleep' to indicate that the user should phone the office; others can give simple coded messages on a strip of liquid crystal diodes (like a digital wrist watch) or can even pass on a voice message as soon as the user indicates that this can safely and securely be done.

The use of viewdata services such as Prestel is another efficient way of eliminating the need for physical travel. Prestel can be used on a completely interactive basis to enable questions to be put to people at a distance and their answers obtained immediately. It is highly likely that, within a few years, enterprising merchants will establish Prestel calls to major customers every morning so that their orders for goods may be placed for rapid delivery, with no paper copies of orders at all, no travelling to warehouses, and direct charging to the purchaser's account with no bills and no cheques.

Assignment

1   Do you think that workstations at home are likely to replace or extend the work habits currently existing in business offices? In your opinion would such a development be an advance or a setback for office employees?

2   What useful functions do you think working in groups fulfils for people, apart from 'getting the job done'?

3   Do you discern any disadvantages which might accompany electronic, rather than 'in-the-flesh' communication between people?

4   Draw up a checklist indicating the advantages and disadvantages of the trends in electronic communication referred to in the article 'Travel or Communicate?'

5   Assume your organisation is considering setting up its own teleconferencing network nationally from locations in Glasgow, Bristol, Birmingham and London. Role-play a meeting in which the advantages and disadvantages of such a development are aired and produce minutes for the meeting. You should assume that the organisation is a large national advertising agency with offices in the cities mentioned.

7 The letter

Introduction

'Ah, Mrs Parker, could you make a few notes – there are a number of things I'd like you to tie up. . . Firstly, we've had an enquiry through Miss Jones down in Plymouth – Atkins Ltd are interested in the new range of fabrics. Better ring them up and describe the patterns and outline the price-structures. Now, these overdue accounts. Send Mr Jenkins round to see the firms concerned to ask for the money. Forty-four of them. Well, tell Mr Jenkins not to hang about! Oh, and Bentley's. What were the revised buying terms we agreed last month? Was it an extra 5% and $3\frac{3}{4}$% settlement, or an extra $3\frac{3}{4}$ and 5? Well, it was something like that. Anyway, Miss Johnson wants to know. Tell her to make an intelligent guess and say they'll let us know if we're wrong. Now, about the Motor Show. Ring round all our customers. What do you mean you won't have time? We always ask them! Ring round all our customers and say we'll be exhibiting on Stand 146. Invite them for the usual hospitality. It's on the 13th . . . or is it the 31st? Well, ask Mr Jenkins to check on his way through Birmingham.'

Imagine the crazy chaos which could overwhelm today's hard-pressed executives if they suddenly had to do without that most essential of written documents – the business letter!

Telephone networks would soon be jammed as hundreds of thousands of organisations tried to pass messages to customers and creditors, accountants and suppliers. Communications would have to be passed by word of mouth without the written record to act as a subsequent memory-jogger. Costs would soar and efficiency would go by the board as organisations in the private and public sectors endeavoured to find alternative means of routing the thousands of millions of business and official letters which the Post Office handles in Great Britain each year.

Developments in paper-making technology, supported by electronic printing and copying processes have resulted in the letter becoming one of the major means of written communication between companies and public sector departments and their host of daily contacts.

The modern business letter is used as a means of making enquiries, confirming information, collecting outstanding debts, selling, advertising, tendering, giving quotations, complaining and answering complaints. It is also used as a means of relaying the thousand and one 'one-off' messages which arise from the specialisations and situations which make up the day-to-day business of the commercial and public service worlds.

In many instances, the letter forms the only contact between organisations and acts as ambassador or salesman or both. Managers set great store by the appearance of the letters they send, since they know that the reputation of their organisation may depend entirely upon the appearance of such letters – whether upon the image evoked by the printed letterhead or upon the typescript. They also realise how important is the composition of the message in eliciting a positive response from the letter's recipient.

As more and more organisations join together their computer, word processing and data processing activities to form a single communication network, the trend towards paperless 'electronic message switching' – relaying messages electronically between remote locations – is certain to grow. However, such a comprehensive national network is still some way off, and for a number of reasons, letters conveyed on paper will continue for some time to form the basis for much written communication between organisations and their associates and customers.

A mastery of the skills of letter writing, and an appreciation of the displayed letterhead and letter layout are therefore essential to the efficient communicator.

Format

The letterhead

The letterhead is basically the printed part of the letter sheet. Its design is extremely important, and skilled graphics designers take great pains to produce a format of letters and colours displaying the trading-name, logo, address and other legally required components of a company or institution, which will create an appropriate image of that concern for the letter's recipient.

In recent years the development of a 'corporate image', by which the company's activities are publicised in designs for uniforms, stationery, company vehicles, shop-fronts, packaging and so on has played an important part in transforming companies' services or products into household words. The total effect of the design of the letterhead (as a result of the type, coloured inks, paper colour and quality of paper employed) is to create a sense of, say, reliability, modernity, efficiency or flair.

The letterhead indicates the nature of an organisation's activities, where it is located and how it may be reached by letter, telephone, telegram or telex. In addition to this, the letterhead also includes certain other information required in law as a result of the Companies Act 1948, Sec 201, and the European Communities Act 1972, Chap 68 Sec 9, para 7:

> The company's trading name
> Its status as a limited company, if appropriate
> A list of company directors, if founded after 23 November 1916
> The address of its registered office
> The company's registered number
> The location of registration e.g. England, Scotland.

All this information must be displayed legibly and there are also stipulations covering any changes in directors' names and the indication of nationality in certain instances. The legal requirements are to protect the letter's recipient from difficulties of identification or communication resulting from unscrupulous dealings.

The logo

One particularly fascinating element of letterhead graphics design is the logo. Simply explained, the logo is a visual symbol or device which communicates memorably what a company or institution does, or with what it would like to be associated.

Local authorities, for example, often use the heraldic coat of arms of the county or city with which they are associated.

Many companies utilise the same symbol both as a letterhead logo and as a registered trade-mark on their range of products. The electrical giant EMI, for example, still uses on some of its products the old 'His Master's Voice' symbol of a dog listening to an early gramophone. HMV is now part of the EMI group. And the 'Hoover' symbol, which has perched on millions of vacuum cleaners, has been a household word for many years.

Letterhead example

In arriving at an effective design, a university bookshop might well wish to associate its wares with the consumers on whom it relies for much of its business, bringing both together in a visual statement of its activities (*see* page 84).

Letter layout

Just as much care is devoted to the letterhead design, so also is particular attention given to the overall appearance of the typescript when it is set out beneath the letterhead. One business communication researcher ascribed as much as 25% of the business letter's total impact to its visual appearance. Thus the graphics designer, secretary, word processor operator and typist have an extremely important combined role to play in the production of an elegant, crisp letter.

Many organisations have developed personalised ways of displaying their letters, and display conventions vary from one company to another – especially since, ultimately, there are no absolute rules governing letter layout, but rather sets of generally accepted conventions which are consistently applied, and which most letter-writers agree to accept. Thus the elements

Student Bookshops Ltd

21-25 High Street
Oxford OK19 4QZ

Telephone: Oxford 46912 Telex: 8694173
Telegrams: Stubooks Oxford

Directors: K. Harris (Managing) H. Klein (U.S.A.) J. Jermyn P. Weston
Registered Office: 12-20 Richmond Street London WC2B 4TZ
Registered No: 694892 Registered in England

Letterhead components

Trading name	must be registered and displayed
Logo	see page 83
Postal address	see annual Post Office Guide
Post code	now incorporated in postal address
Telephone number	either preceded by name of town or city or STD code if universally used e.g. 01-632-1000
Telegraphic, cablegram address	usually an abbreviation of trading name with city location
Telex number	see British Telecom's Directory of Telex Numbers
Reference entries	some companies include in letterhead 'Your ref: Our ref:"
Names of directors	
Address of registered office	see reference previous page for details of legal display requirements
Registered number	
Registered location	

of letter layout are constantly subject to change, as one practice is superseded by another in order to achieve greater simplicity, speed of production or pleasing appearance.

The following models indicate in outline the principal shapes of currently popular typescript letter-layouts, which are used in conjunction with whatever letterhead design a company or institution has chosen to adopt.

Fully-blocked

All the typed entries commence from the left-hand margin, forming a 'vertical line' down the page.

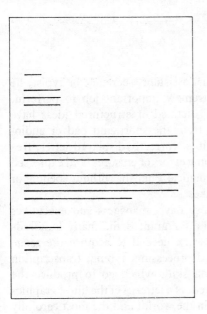

Blocked

The date is displayed near the right-hand margin and the complimentary close to the right of a central position. Otherwise as for 'fully-blocked'.

Semi-blocked

The date and complimentary close are situated to the right of centre and each paragraph is indented.

Open and closed punctuation

An integral part of the appearance of the typescript section of the letter is the use of either an 'open' or 'closed' punctuation system at the end of the lines of type outside the main body of the letter – the letter references, date, recipient's name and address, complimentary close, writer's name and official designation etc. (See The Typescript Component – The Recipient's Address.)

When the open punctuation system is employed, particularly in the Fully Blocked layout, *all* punctuation outside the body of the letter is omitted. The absence of commas and full stops enables the letter to be typed more quickly, thereby increasing the typist's productivity. 'Closed punctuation' is the name given to the practice by which the type outside the body of the letter is normally punctuated.

Paper and envelope sizes

The most frequently used sizes of letter stationery are A4 (approximately the size of this page), and A5, half the size of A4:

A4 = 11.7″ × 8.3″ or 297 mm × 210 mm
A5 = 8.3″ × 5.8″ or 210 mm × 148 mm

Paper sizes used for stationery and some printed matter range from A0 (841 mm × 1189 mm) to A10 (26 mm × 37 mm).

In the Post Office Guide, the range of envelope sizes which the Post Office prefers (POP) is listed. The maximum envelope size allowable is 2′ × 1′6″, and the minimum is 4″ × 2¾″ (610 mm × 460 mm and 100 mm × 70 mm respectively).

Envelope size reproduced below: quarter DL size,
normally 110 mm × 220 mm.

```
Mr. R. J. Thompson,
Better Business Equipment Ltd.,
14 Broad Street,
MAIDENHEAD, Berks,
SL6 1FH
```

The envelopes most frequently in use are coded:

DL = 110 mm × 220 mm and
C6 = 114 mm × 162 mm

The envelope address

In the 'Method of Address' section of the Post Office Guide, full details are given of the preferred method of addressing envelopes. A frequently used example is shown below.

The typescript component

The typist's role

The importance of the word processor operator's or typist's role in the production of a letter cannot be over-emphasised. As the last link in the letter-producing chain, after the graphics designer and dictator, whether as personal assistant, secretary or typist, he or she has an extremely important job to perform. Sometimes poorly dictated or structured ideas have to be transcribed from the shorthand pad or audio-cassette into a legible, correctly displayed letter, free from unsightly typing errors or erasures, and expressed in accepted, grammatical English, without spelling or punctuation mistakes.

During their busy days, managers and executives are inclined to take for granted the many hundreds of hours of hard work needed to acquire the range of shorthand, word processing, typing, transcription and communication skills which go to produce the typescript component of a letter. Yet the finest graphics letterhead design in the world, and the most carefully constructed letter message will all count for nothing in the face of a sloppily typed and error-ridden typescript. And so the typist's contribution, though sometimes under-valued, must never be under-estimated.

Typescript components check-list

Letter references	commonly author, typist, filing ref.
Date	day, month, year
Recipient of letter	company, institution or individual
Recipient's address	name, street, town, county, post-code
Attention reference	identifying specified recipient
Salutation	greeting prefacing letter message
Subject-heading	brief summary of letter's theme
Letter message (main body)	letter message, or content
Complimentary close (or subscription)	closing assurance e.g. Yours faithfully
Signature space	location of author's signature
Author's identity	typescript of author's name
Author's official designation	author's title or job designation
Enclosure reference	indication of accompanying material
Letter copy(ies) reference	indication of recipients of copy(ies)
Continuation sheet details	page number, date and recipient's name

The letter reference

The need to file correspondence, whether originals or copies, for future reference requires that each letter carries two reference entries:

Our ref

Your ref

'Our ref' prefaces the reference given to the letter being dictated, the outgoing letter, while 'Your ref' indicates the reference given to an incoming letter which is being acknowledged. Commonly both references have the following components:

1   the letter-writer's initials
2   the letter-typist's initials
3   a coded file reference

The first and second parts of the reference are separated by a solidus:

Our ref   HT/JN

Sometimes the typist's initials are typed in lower-case:

Your ref   LMK/pb

and the following filing reference perhaps indicates an account file:

Our ref   HT/JN   WA 151

Sometimes the reference entry is simply indicated by, 'Ref'. Often, the typist types the letter reference prefixes, although some companies include them in the letterhead.

The model letters on pages 89, 101 and 103 show where the letter references may be located.

The date

The date on business or public service letters is displayed in the order:

day   month   year

For example,

16th July, 19—

Sometimes a comma separates the month from the year, but increasingly, the date is being displayed without the 'th', 'st', or 'nd' and 'rd' after the day, and also without the comma:

16 July 19—

Neither the month nor the year should be abbreviated as 'Jan' or '84' and the abbreviation 16/7/84 should be reserved for sales slips, or invoices etc.

In the United States the date is usually set out as:

July 16th 19—

but the European practice as set out above should be adhered to.

The locations of the date on the letter-sheet are shown in the model letters on pages 89, 101 and 103.

The letter's recipient

Letters may be addressed to entire organisations or departments, as well as to an official function within a department or lastly to a personally named individual:

Gourmet Restaurants Ltd

The Department of Employment

Wessex County Council

The Accounts Department,
Gourmet Restaurants Ltd.

The Education Department,
Wessex County Council.

The Sales Manager,
Gourmet Restaurants Ltd.

The County Architect,
Architect's Department,
Wessex County Council.

Mr P J Harrison,
Managing Director,
Gourmet Restaurants Ltd.

J P Knight, Esq, MA, Dip Ed,
Assistant Director of Education,
Education Department,
Wessex County Council.

The recipient's postal address follows on directly beneath the various forms of identifying the letter's recipient, whether, as shown above, it is a company, local authority, department or individual, either addressed by his or her name, or by official designation only.

Styles of address

The following are the principal styles of address currently in use:

male recipient   Mr, Esq, Dr, Sir, Lord
female recipient   Miss, Mrs, Ms, Lady, Dame
male partnership   Messrs

Note that 'Messrs' is sometimes used as a courtesy style to address companies where a personal name forms the basis of the trading name:

Messrs H G Cartwright & Co

In the case of Messrs prefixing a partnership, it is followed by the names of the partners:

Messrs Trueman and Wellstead

Note also the following styles of address:

Sir *Richard* Hargreaves
Lord Chilgrove

Some women in business prefer to use 'Ms' as their style, since it indicates neither single nor married status, thus preserving a personal matter for a private life.

Frequently the recipient of a letter has letters or qualifications after his or her name. Some people spend years of hard study to acquire the degrees, diplomas or awards which appear after their names, and it is important to take care in setting them out correctly, even if this means making a preliminary call to an executive's secretary to check.

In broad terms, orders and decorations precede degrees and diplomas, which are themselves followed by memberships of professional bodies:

James Gray Esq, OM, DFC, MSc, MBIM

Note that men with letters after their name are usually addressed as 'Esq' (as above). Mr is rarely used in this case. Ladies with letters to their names are styled thus:

Miss P Singleton, MA,
Mrs H Grantham, BMus, DipEd,
Or the style 'Ms' may be used in either case.

The recipient's address

The recipient's postal address follows immediately beneath the name of the recipient or his department. It is set out in the sequence: street or road, town or city, county and, lastly, post-code. In the case of larger conurbations (listed in the Post Office Guide) the county may be omitted.

In order to avoid commencing the letter's message too far down the page, it is a common convention to restrict the postal address to no more than five lines whenever possible.

The combination of personally identified recipient, designation, organisation and postal address will look like this:

Open punctuation version:

```
Mr R O Jefferson
Marketing Director
Fleetway Transport Ltd
14 Queen's Road
MANCHESTER    M60  2DA
```

Closed punctuation version:

```
Mr. R. O. Jefferson,
Marketing Director,
Fleetway Tansport Ltd.,
14 Queen's Road,
MANCHESTER.    M60  2DA
```

For further examples of layouts of the recipient's address consult the model letters on pages 89, 101 and 103.

Note that when a letter is written to an organisation

Location check-list

1 Letterhead

Trading name ●

Postal address ●

Telephone number ●

Telegraphic address ●

Logo ●

2 Typescript component

References ●

Date ●

Recipient ●

Recipient's address ●

Salutation ●

Subject-heading ●

Body of letter with
indented paragraphs for ●
semi-blocked layout

Complimentary close ●

Signature ●

Writer's identity ●

Job designation ●

Enclosure reference ●

Copy reference ●

3 Letterhead – legal requirements

List of directors,
includes a United States citizen ●

Address of registered office ●

Registered number of company ●

Location of registration ●

Student Bookshops Ltd

21-25 High Street
Oxford OK19 4QZ

Telephone: Oxford 46912 Telex: 8694173
Telegrams: Stubooks Oxford

Your ref: ND/TM
Our ref: KH/SV WC 1

7th June, 19--

N. Dawson, Esq., M.Sc., D.M.S., M.B.I.M.,
Management Studies Department,
Cherwell College of Further Education,
West Grove,
OXFORD   OK12 3BG

Dear Sir,

MANAGEMENT STUDIES BOOK EXHIBITION

Thank you for your letter of 28th May 19--, in which you invite
our Oxford branch to mount an exhibition of management studies books
early in the coming autumn term at your college.

Mr. Peterson, branch manager at Oxford, has passed your letter
to me, and I am delighted to accept your kind offer and appreciate the
extension of the facilities of your main lecture hall to my company.

I should be grateful if you would notify me in due course of the
proposed date for the exhibition, the number of students for whom we
should plan and the nature and levels of their courses.

I look forward to hearing from you, and enclose a copy of our
current management studies catalogue to give you an indication of the
scope of our stocks.

Yours faithfully,

K. Harris.

K. Harris
Managing Director

enc.

copy to: Mr. J. Peterson

Directors: K. Harris (Managing) H. Klein (U.S.A.) J. Jermyn P. Weston
Registered Office: 12-20 Richmond Street London WC2B 4TZ
Registered No: 694892 Registered in England

or department, the official nominated to deal with it may be indicated by typing the following 'leader' above the salutation:

For the attention of:

with the specified person's style and name following on the same line.

Components of the letter

Salutations and complimentary closes

Bracketing the letter's message, which comprises the body of the letter, are the Salutation and Complimentary Close.

Conventions exist to follow certain salutations with particular complimentary closes (see table). Some pairings are regarded as more formal and some less so. In addition, there exists a protocol or etiquette which determines their use. 'Dear Sir,... Yours faithfully,' is reserved, broadly, for situations in which the letter is formal, where dictator and recipient have not met, and where their respective positions in their hierarchies differ in vertical terms. 'Dear Mr,... Yours sincerely,' is considered more friendly (hence its use in sales or advertising letters) and can show a closer, established relationship. While pairings such as, 'Dear Jim,...

Table of linked salutations and complimentary closes in use

Salutation	Complimentary close
Dear Sir, Dear Madam, Dear Sirs, Dear Mesdames,	Yours faithfully,
Dear Mr Green, Dear Miss Sharp, Dear Mrs Howes, Dear Dr Ivors, Dear Lord Chilgrove, Dear Sir Richard, Dear Lady Hatton,	Yours sincerely,
Dear Jim, Dear Jenny,	Sincerely, Kind regards,
My Dear Susan, My Dear Harry,	Affectionately, Best wishes,

Note that: 'Yours truly' as an alternative to 'Yours faithfully' is no longer used.

The salutations and complimentary closes other than, 'Dear Sir,... Yours faithfully,' or 'Dear Mr Green,... Yours sincerely,' are becoming less bound by conventions as contemporary letter-writers give their letters a more personal stamp.

Kind regards, Jack' or 'My Dear Susan,... Sincerely, Janet' display a close relationship within the working environment.

The subject-heading

Dear Sir,

SEMPERFLO DISPENSERS

The subject-heading summarises the theme of the letter and not only focuses the reader's interest, but also aids mail sorting and filing. Examples are shown in model letters on pages 89, 101, 102 and 103.

Signature, identity and designation

The complimentary close is followed by a space for the letter-writer's signature, which in turn is followed by a typescript entry of his or her identity and job title or designation to assist the letter's recipient in replying:

Yours faithfully

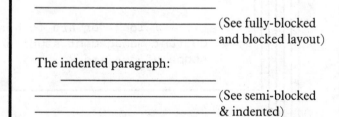

R J Enwright
Production Manager

Note that when letters are signed by, say, a secretary for his or her principal, 'for' is commonly inserted before the typescript name. Although derived from a legal context, p.p. is also used in this case.

The letter's paragraphs

The fully-blocked paragraph:

———————————————————————
——————————————————————— (See fully-blocked
——————————————————————— and blocked layout)

The indented paragraph:

    ———————————————————
——————————————————————— (See semi-blocked
——————————————————————— & indented)

The letter's message is divided in the body of the letter by one of the paragraph layout conventions. Each paragraph is commonly separated by 2 spaces.

Enclosure(s) and copy(ies)

It is essential that material accompanying the letter is 'signalled' to the reader:

enc. encs. Enc. Encs.
enclosure enclosures

The above methods are currently in use. See model letters on pages 89 and 103 for location points.

When letters are copied in order to inform a third

party, usually within the writer's organisation an acknowledgement prefaced by:

    copy to
    copies to
    cc

is given at a suitable place on the page.

The continuation sheet

At the head of page 2 and subsequent pages of a letter the following information is typed:

    recipient's name, page number, date

Status of the letter

When the letter's contents are confidential the following 'warning headings' may be prominently displayed on both the letter-sheet and envelope:

CONFIDENTIAL or
PRIVATE AND CONFIDENTIAL

Note: if the heading PERSONAL is used the letter will only be opened by the person to whom it is addressed.

Common categories of letter

Although it would be impossible to categorise the myriad of different uses to which business and public service letters are put, nevertheless, it is helpful to be acquainted with the more common categories which recur frequently.

As the brackets indicate, some letters are 'paired' in a sequence of broaching a matter and of responding to its implications – the enquiry is answered, the sales letter wins an order, the complaint is adjusted or the order is confirmed. Sometimes letters are produced in a related series, like the three-part collection letter series making a request for payment in progressively more stringent terms.

In some circumstances the frequency with which certain categories of letter are despatched makes it worthwhile having them produced on a word processor. Standard paragraphs may thus be used in all letters, and variables such as names, addresses and amounts of money typed on individual letters by the word processor operator or by means of 'mailmerge' software. Such letters are called 'form letters'. Their advantage lies in the time that may be saved in producing virtually identical letters individually. Letter writers must, however, decide in which situations a form letter may be appropriate, since in some situations a 'one-off' personal letter may be more suitable.

Common categories of letter

Area	Letter classification	Explanation of use
General	Enquiry	to seek information, confirmation
	Acknowledgement, Information	to provide information, confirmation
	Complaint	to seek redress of a deficiency
	Adjustment	to rectify a complaint
Financial	Collection 1, 2, 3	to obtain settlement of a debt
	Letter of credit	to authorise an advance of credit
	Financial standing	to check credit-worthiness
	Solicitor's letter	to procure debt settlement etc.
Sales, Advertising	Sales letter	to sell goods or services
	Follow-up sales letter	to remind of sales offers
	Unsolicited sales letter	to advertise goods or services
Orders, Estimates	Order	to place an order for goods etc.
	Confirmation of order	to confirm a submitted order
	Estimate	to submit a projected price
	Tender	to submit a contractual price
Appointments	Application	to apply for a post
	Resignation	to confirm resignation from a post
	Reference enquiry	to seek confidential particulars
	Reference reply	to provide confidential particulars
Circulars	Circular to personnel	to reach a group, organisation
	Circular to customers	or company customer in one despatch
Special category	Letter requiring especial tact	to convey delicate information etc. tactfully

Content

Structuring the message

1   The opening paragraph – puts the message into a context

The function of the opening paragraph is to put the detailed message into a clearly defined context, either by initiating an action, by responding to a received stimulus or by introducing the next stage in a sequence or exchange.

This may be achieved by:

1   Acknowledging the date, receipt and subject of any received correspondence

2   Supplying the reason for the letter being written

3   Providing essential names, dates, locations or other data to put the message into context.

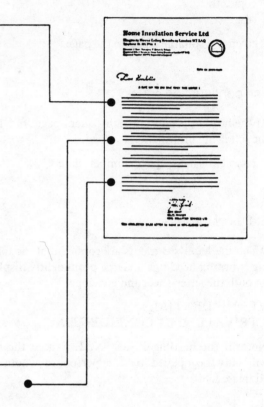

2   The middle paragraph(s) – develops detailed message

In the middle paragraph(s) the detailed data which comprises the letter's message is logically, briefly and clearly set down. For example, the precise nature of a complaint may be described, the benefits of goods for sale enumerated, the chronology of payment requests reiterated or the essence of bad news gently imparted.

In complex letters, several middle paragraphs may in turn, deal with one principal aspect of an involved message. This will make it easier for the reader to assimilate.

To aid impact, some data may be displayed in tabular form, perhaps as a table of discounts, schedule of supplementary benefits, list of selling points or specification of building materials.

3   The closing paragraph – states action needed

In addition to providing a résumé of the main points of a complex letter's message, the essential function of the closing paragraph is to state simply and unequivocally what action the writer needs from the recipient.

The time and effort needed to send a letter require that it promotes an active desire in its recipient to act upon its message, whether by paying a bill, ordering some perfume or meeting a rates demand.

Since the action statement is the entire reason for writing letters other than informational ones, the requirement or request for action appears virtually at the letter's end, thus remaining uppermost in the recipient's mind, followed only by a courteous closing statement.

Analyses of structures

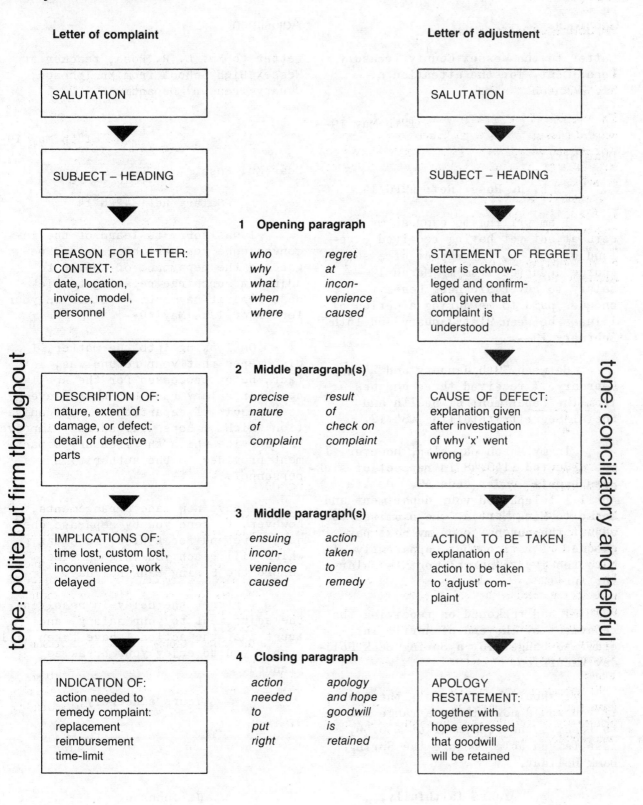

Letter of complaint

Letter of adjustment

tone: polite but firm throughout

tone: conciliatory and helpful

SALUTATION

SALUTATION

SUBJECT – HEADING

SUBJECT – HEADING

1 Opening paragraph

REASON FOR LETTER:
CONTEXT:
date, location,
invoice, model,
personnel

who   regret
why   at
what   incon-
when   venience
where   caused

STATEMENT OF REGRET
letter is acknow-
leged and confirm-
ation given that
complaint is
understood

2 Middle paragraph(s)

DESCRIPTION OF:
nature, extent of
damage, or defect:
detail of defective
parts

precise   result
nature   of
of   check on
complaint   complaint

CAUSE OF DEFECT:
explanation given
after investigation
of why 'x' went
wrong

3 Middle paragraph(s)

IMPLICATIONS OF:
time lost, custom lost,
inconvenience, work
delayed

ensuing   action
incon-   taken
venience   to
caused   remedy

ACTION TO BE TAKEN
explanation of
action to be taken
to 'adjust' com-
plaint

4 Closing paragraph

INDICATION OF:
action needed to
remedy complaint:
replacement
reimbursement
time-limit

action   apology
needed   and hope
to   goodwill
put   is
right   retained

APOLOGY
RESTATEMENT:
together with
hope expressed
that goodwill
will be retained

Remember!

When writing a letter of complaint, remember that the recipient must receive clear details of the transaction and a careful explanation of the faults complained of. He must also be informed of what action is expected to put the matter right and any deadline required.

Correspondingly, the adjustment letter must, while expressing regret at the inconvenience caused, take pains to explain *why* things went wrong and what is *speedily* being done to put them right, especially since the customer's goodwill is the lynch-pin of commerce.

Model letters

Complaint

Letter to the Wessex County Treasury Department, for the attention of Mr. Johnson.

12th May 19--

Dear Sir,

L. R. Ross. Ref: 42PG 14

I am writing to express my concern at not yet having received a refund of £56.36, in respect of a surcharge deducted from my March 19-- salary to cover sickness benefit cheques paid to me during a period of illness between 21st January and 15th February 19--.

Between 30th January and 24th February, I received three cheques from the Department of Health and Social Security totalling £84.12.

In my March pay-slip, however, I was deducted £140.48 in respect of sickness benefit under code AG. On 4th April I telephoned your department and spoke to Miss Martin, who promised to adjust the surcharge on my next paycheque. I notice that, apparently, I have received a normal month's salary for April.

I had reckoned on receiving the repayment by the end of April, in order to budget for a Spring Bank Holiday excursion.

I should be grateful, therefore, if you would now kindly arrange for me to receive the repayment of £56.36, less tax payable, before the Spring Bank Holiday.

Yours faithfully,

L. R. Ross
Wessex High School

Adjustment

Letter to Mr. L. R. Ross, teacher at Wessex High School from Mr. Johnson, County Treasury Department.

18th May 19--

Dear Mr. Ross,

Salary Ref: 42PG 14

I was sorry to learn of the inconvenience you have been caused regarding the repayment of £56.36 to adjust a surcharge relating to sickness benefit payments outlined in your letter of 12th May 19--.

On looking into the matter, I discovered that your refund was, in fact, being processed for the April computer salary run, but was delayed as a result of departmental reorganisation which, I hope, will shortly improve the service which the Treasury Department provides to the authority's personnel.

I have now made arrangements, however, to send you by separate cheque, a refund for £56.36, less tax, which will reach you in good time before the Spring Bank Holiday.

I regret the delay in resolving the adjustment to your salary, and trust that the action I have taken will enable you to enjoy your break as planned.

Yours sincerely,

J. Johnson
Treasury Department
Wessex County Council

Tactful letters

Perhaps the most difficult of all letters to write are those whose messages must either affect the reader adversely, or which require great tact or delicacy, so as not to offend the recipient – particularly when the writer hopes to elicit action in spite of difficult or unwelcome circumstances. Many managers or officials find themselves all too frequently having to impart bad news, having to say 'no' gracefully, or to communicate an unpopular directive.

The diagram illustrates how a four-paragraph structure could be employed to break bad news to a recipient – perhaps of failure in a promotion application, or a transfer to a different position with less authority, or the closing-down of a branch-manager's store because of falling turnover. The permutations are numerous.

Although the letter-writer's aim is basically to convey the bad news clearly and unambiguously, he or she has an equal obligation not to wound the recipient's feelings by insensitivity, indifference or terseness. As the diagram illustrates, the letter must be carefully structured to cushion the impact of the bad news, which can neither be baldly stated in the first paragraph, nor 'tacked on' to the closing paragraph almost as an after-thought.

The context and circumstances surrounding the bad news are used carefully to prepare the reader for what is to come. Similarly, once the bad news has been imparted (towards the end of the second paragraph in the diagram), the writer must take pains to ensure that some positive factors are found, with which the reader may identify and so not be left feeling entirely overlooked, discarded, incompetent or passed over.

The most difficult task is to avoid any sentiments which may be interpreted as being insincere. And, as may be readily imagined such letters require careful drafting and scrutiny before despatch.

Now turn to page 101 and study the model letter which aims to convey disappointing news tactfully.

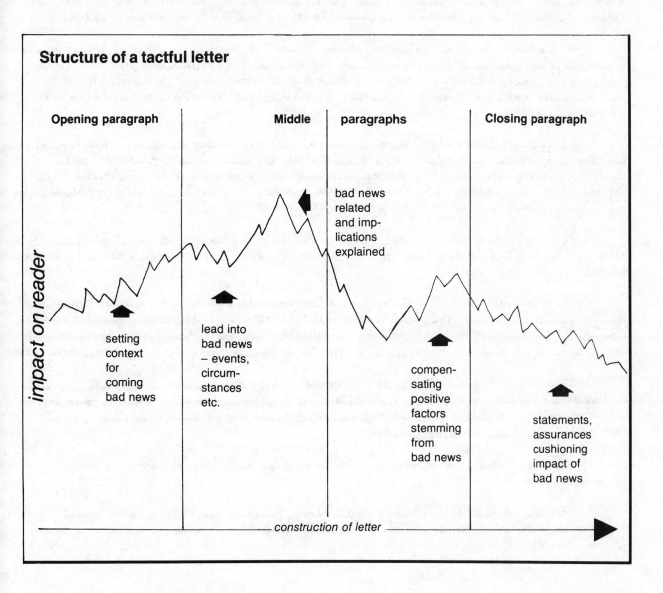

Structure of a tactful letter

Opening paragraph   **Middle**   **paragraphs**   **Closing paragraph**

impact on reader

bad news related and implications explained

setting context for coming bad news

lead into bad news – events, circumstances etc.

compensating positive factors stemming from bad news

statements, assurances cushioning impact of bad news

construction of letter

FINOSA FABRICS LTD require a PRIVATE SECRETARY to the EXPORT SALES MANAGER (EUROPE)

A knowledge of two EEC foreign languages is required and experience of export sales procedures is an advantage. The successful candidate will work on her own initiative and be able to handle incoming telephone calls and documentation from French or German agents. He or she must also be prepared to travel abroad.

The company provides excellent conditions of service, including four weeks' paid holiday per annum subsidised insurance and restaurant facilities. Salary negotiable according to age and experience.
Apply in writing to: The Personnel Manager, Finosa Fabrics Ltd, 4 York Way, London WC2B 6AK

Applications to be received by 30 May 19—

Model letter of application

Dear Sir,

I should like to apply for the post of private secretary to your Export Sales Manager recently advertised in 'The Daily Sentinel', and have pleasure in enclosing my completed application form and a copy of my curriculum vitae.

The advertised post particularly appeals to me, since my own career aspirations and education have been specifically directed for the last two years towards a secretarial appointment in the field of export sales.

In the sixth form at Redbrook High School I specialised in Advanced-level German, French and English and proceeded in September 19   to Redbrook College of Technology, where I embarked upon a bilingual secretarial course leading to the Commercial Secretary's Diploma in Export Studies.

The course includes intensive commercial language studies (I am specialising in German), communication, office administration and export studies with particular emphasis on E.E.C. procedures and documentation. In addition, the Diploma course provides shorthand, word processing and typewriting components, including work in the special foreign language.

I anticipate achieving a good pass in the June Diploma examination and attaining shorthand and typewriting speeds of 100/50 w.p.m., having already secured passes at 80/40 w.p.m.

During my full-time education, I have travelled extensively in the Federal Republic of Germany and in France, and have become familiar with the customs and outlooks of both countries. In August 19   I gained a valuable insight into German business methods during a month's exchange visit to a Handelsschule in Frankfurt-am-Main.

Assisting my father for the past two years in his own company has afforded me an opportunity to use my own initiative and to obtain helpful work experience in areas such as sales documentation, customer relations and the use of data processing in a sales context.

If called, I should be pleased to attend for an interview at any time convenient to you.

My course at Redbrook College of Technology finishes on 30th June 19   and I should be available to commence a full-time appointment from the beginning of July onwards.

Yours faithfully,

Jane Simmonds. (Miss)

(Note: It is usual for letters of application such as the one above to be handwritten.)

Commentary

Jane Simmond's letter of application begins by acknowledging the source of the advertisement, makes a formal application statement and refers to relevant enclosures.

In her second paragraph, Jane endeavours to establish a close link between her own career aspirations and vocational education and the essential nature of the advertised post.

Jane goes on to draw particular attention to those aspects of her more recent education which she considers have equipped her with a sound preparation for the post.

In case her prospective employers may be unfamiliar with them, Jane outlines the relevant course components of the Diploma, emphasising those parts which would be most likely to interest her potential principal.

Jane endeavours to display self-confidence without immodesty, and evidence of existing achievement.

Since she lacks full-time work-experience, Jane makes the best of her travels and knowledge of the countries relating to the advertisement. She also includes mention of a course of study which has provided relevant insights.

Realising that her lack of work-experience could prove a stumbling-block, Jane emphasises the practical work-experience she has had, and highlights aspects of it which she hopes will be relevant to her application.

Availability for interview is made as easy as possible.

Since she needs the job, Jane displays a willingness to start just as soon as possible after the end of her course, thus demonstrating her 'earnestness of intent'.

Assignments

1 In syndicate groups, study Jane Simmonds' letter from the point of view of Finosa's Personnel Manager and consider the following questions:

Has Jane's letter succeeded in arousing your interest? If so, why? If not, why not? Does Jane's letter succeed in meeting the aims suggested in the commentary? Do you have any criticisms to make of Jane's letter in terms of the information supplied, its structure, its tone and style? Could it be improved upon? Does it adequately match the requirements implied in the advertisement?

2 Draft letters from Finosa to:
  a call Jane Simmonds to attend an interview
  b inform Jane Simmonds of her failure to obtain the post after interview
  c offer Jane Simmonds the post after interview

3 As Jane Simmonds, assume that, while awaiting news from Finosa after interview, you have been offered, and accepted a post with another company as a result of an earlier application. Write a letter to Finosa appropriate to the situation. Invent a suitable home address.

Style

Language

Essential to conveying the letter's message effectively is the form of language used – the style in which the letter is written.

Immediately any written form of communication is employed problems occur which are much more easily

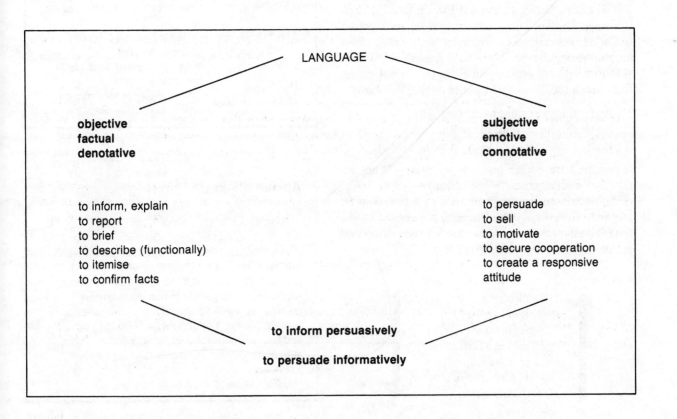

LANGUAGE

objective
factual
denotative

to inform, explain
to report
to brief
to describe (functionally)
to itemise
to confirm facts

subjective
emotive
connotative

to persuade
to sell
to motivate
to secure cooperation
to create a responsive attitude

to inform persuasively

to persuade informatively

overcome in, say, face-to-face oral communication. The transmission, assimilation and feedback cycle of the oral conversation are supported and reinforced by a range of non-verbal communication signals such as the smile, nod, gesture or posture. In oral communication offence caused by misunderstandings over inappropriate tone or ambiguity is much less likely to occur and much easier to put right. Correspondingly the permanence of the letter as a written record and the absence of the supportive effect of non-verbal communication mean that special care must be given to the way in which the letter's message is expressed. The construction of the message, the 'what', should be carefully organised in the letter's structure, and in the same way, the 'how', the choice of words expressing the message, should be just as carefully chosen so that the letter's basic aim is reinforced and the desired action from the recipient thereby generated.

Some letters are written principally to convey information, while others are active selling 'weapons' in the armoury of the advertising manager, and seek to persuade. Yet others may seek to inform and persuade simultaneously.

Simply put, style may be defined as 'the most effective words in the most appropriate order', and the letter-writer must be continually checking to ensure that the words he or she is using are creating the right effect, whether it be to inform objectively, or to sell subjectively:

The emulsion paint embodies a vinyl additive which improves both its covering capacity and durability.

Wondacover! Its warm and satiny vinyl finish makes it go on great! And then go on and on and on!

The Latin, Saxon, Norse and French roots of English have rendered it extremely rich when it comes to finding alternatives or synonyms to express an idea or sentiment, and, in *The King's English*, H W and F G Fowler have synthesised three proverbial guidelines which the letter-writer would do well to follow:

1 Prefer the short word to the long
2 Prefer the Saxon word to the Romance
3 Prefer the single word to the circumlocution.

When the letter-writer poses the question, 'What action do I wish to generate?' he is thinking of the effect of his words on his recipient. His style will also be affected, however, by the 'strength dimension' of the letter's context and the relationship between writer and recipient, where the writer may be:

directing
requiring
requesting
asking a favour
seeking help
in dire need of
'baling out'.

The recipient

As well as developing a style in a letter appropriate to its aim, the letter-writer must also keep firmly in mind the kind of person for whom the letter is intended:

how old is the recipient?

what sort of education?

what kind of business background?

what professional interests?

what tastes, preferences, leisure interests?

what prejudices, *bête-noires*?

The response of the recipient is bound to be affected by a wide range of factors which have moulded his or her life and experiences – either a wealth of practical experience, or a lengthy higher education, a specialism in a narrow field, or a succession of varied appointments, either a metropolitan, sophisticated life-style or a traditional, rural background.

Use this plan and your letters will always 'IMPRESS'!

I DEA	– Decide upon the principal aim(s) of the letter
M ETHOD	– Structure the letter's main points in a plan
P ARAGRAPHS	– Follow the opening, middle and closing scheme
R ECIPIENT	– Remember who will receive the letter
E MPHASIS	– Guide the letter's progress to its action statement
S TYLE	– Employ a style appropriate to the letter's aim(s)
S AFETY	– Check the letter for errors or omissions before despatch

---

Above all, keep thinking!

... 'Ah, take a letter, please, Miss Smith ... Bombay Animal Supplies Ltd, etc ... Dear Mr Singh comma subject-heading Order No. 8692 ... Letter begins ... Further to my order of 21st August 19— comma please supply comma in addition comma three elephants open bracket Indian close bracket comma two tigers open bracket striped close bracket comma three cobras with hoods if possible and two mongooses ... er no, mongeese ... No, start again ... and one mongoose. Letter ends Yours etc ...
P.S. Please send another mongoose.' ...

To remain indifferent to the recipient's personality is to run the risk of communication breakdown, perhaps by using terminology and syntax which the reader does not understand, or to cause unpremeditated offence by tactlessness or by an insensitive reference. Whatever the cause, failure to write specifically for the letter's recipient may cause him or her to ignore the letter's message and to refuse to act upon it.

Examples

Don't

In view of the recent increase in postal rates and because of rising labour costs, a surcharge of 10% will be levied to cover the cost of postage and packing.

Although the holiday which you request is now fully booked, the latter holiday to which you refer is still on offer, together with Holidays 164 and 169 in our Sunny Days brochure, although the former is more expensive than the latter.
   I trust this information will help you to make your choice. .

The aerial to which you refer is no longer available from stock, since the radio was withdrawn six years ago. I suggest you try local stockists.

We are unable to deliver the goods you ordered before mid-July.

Our new range of wall-coverings are advantageously priced. We also supply on request our merchandiser free-of-charge.

The extent of rate-relief for which rate-payers are eligible is dependent upon the level of earnings in gainful employment.

I regret that I shall be unable to keep our appointment on 21 March 19—, as I have to see one of our larger account customers.

Dear Sir,
   Your application for a reduced-fare omnibus pass is awaiting process pending receipt of a photostat birth-certificate in compliance with public transport departmental regulation 46, our letter 16 June 19— ref. AT/TG refers.

... but do

Keep it brief but polite
A 10% surcharge is, regrettably, payable on orders under £2.50 to cover postage and packing.

Keep it clear and simple
I regret to inform you that Holiday 161 is fully booked. You referred, however, to Holiday 179, which is still on offer, and I also strongly recommend Holidays 164 and 169 in our Sunny Days brochure. Of the three holidays, number 164 is more expensive, but features additional attractions. . .

Be helpful
The radio, model XL49, was withdrawn from our product range six years ago. I have located a spare aerial at our Oxford service depot, however, and have made arrangements for it to be posted to you c.o.d.

Be positive
The goods you ordered will be delivered by 16 July 19— at the latest.

Be persuasive
Not only will our new range of wall-coverings give you a much better deal, the free-of-charge merchandiser ensures they sell themselves!

Avoid officialese
The amount of rate-relief to which you are entitled depends on how much you earn.

Be tactful
I am sorry to have to ask you if we may postpone our appointment for 21 March 19—, as a matter has arisen requiring my personal attention.

Remember the recipient
Dear Sir,
   I should be grateful if you would kindly send a photocopy of your birth certificate as soon as possible to enable us to send your reduced-fare pass by return of post.

Don't

We acknowledge receipt of yours of 15 January 19— re our new upholstery fabrics catalogue.

I am obliged to inform you that your claim against warranty in respect of your hair-dryer cannot be met, since accidental damage lies outside the terms of the conditions laid down.

On receipt of £6.50 the company is prepared, without prejudice, to undertake the repair of your hair-dryer, although it accepts no responsibility to ensure that such repairs are efficacious.

Dear Sir,

Sorry we haven't been round yet to fix your TV. The van has been on the blink since Monday, and the service engineer is off with 'flu.

As you can imagine, things have been a bit tricky lately, but we hope to send someone round before Saturday.

Sorry about the waiting.

Yours truly,

Dear Sir,

I am writing to complain about the way I was treated by your counter-clerk last Thursday, when I came in to enquire about a tax rebate, to which I feel I am entitled, since I have been off work for the past three weeks, as a result of an industrial accident, which was occasioned by the negligence of a colleague, although I do not hold him personally responsible. . .

Dear Mr Green,

I am sorry to have to advise you of the delay in delivery of your personal Ariel 64 home computer by next Wednesday as promised.

Unfortunately the Sales Department have lost your original order and efforts to find it at the company's Computer Centre have so far failed. . .

. . . but do

Avoid clichés

Thank you for your letter of 15 January 19—, in which you request our new upholstery fabrics catalogue.

Be courteous

I am sorry to inform you that your claim against warranty for a replacement hair-dryer cannot be met, since upon inspection, it was discovered that the appliance had, apparently, suffered from accidental damage.

The company would, however, be most happy to undertake the repair of your hair-dryer at a nominal charge of £6.50. As I feel sure you will appreciate, however, such repairs do not carry our guarantee.

Avoid over-familiarity

Dear Sir,

Please accept my apologies for the delay in repairing your television set.

Our service engineer is ill with influenza, and the service van has suffered repeated breakdowns, now traced to an electrical fault.

Nevertheless I am very hopeful that a service engineer will be able to call before Saturday.

I hope the delay will not prove too inconvenient.

Yours faithfully,

Avoid irrelevance

Dear Sir,

I wish to complain about the way I was treated by your counter-clerk when I came in on Thursday 14 April 19— to enquire about a tax rebate.

After a long, but admittedly unavoidable wait, I was curtly informed that . . .

Don't blame other people

Dear Mr Green,

I am sorry to have to advise you of the delay in delivery of your personal Ariel 64 home computer by next Wednesday as promised.

Unfortunately there is a temporary delay in supply, but I am following up your order personally and will contact you as soon as possible . . .

Wessex County Council

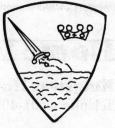

County Hall High Street
Avalon Wessex DO14 6QZ

Telephone: Avalon 86000

Education Department Ext: 247

Your ref:

Our ref: HPK/AT HCS 41

12 February 19--

P K Harrison Esq BSc Cert Ed
Headmaster
Highgrove Comprehensive School
AVALON
Wessex   AV12 4KA

Dear Sir

PROPOSED EXTENSION TO THE SCHOOL LIBRARY

As a result of recent discussions between the Wessex Education Committee
and the Education Department arising from the reduction made in the
rate-support grant for the coming financial year, I am now able to tell
you the decision on the proposed extension to the Highgrove Comprehensive
School Library.

After having given careful thought to what money will be available to
the secondary education sector, and bearing in mind other essential
renovation and maintenance obligations, it is with regret that I inform
you of the Committee's decision to postpone the building of the proposed
library extension.

I realise that this decision must come as a disappointment to you,
especially after the work which both you and your library staff have
put into the design of the proposed provision.

Nevertheless, I feel sure that you will appreciate the difficulties facing
the Education Department at this time, and I should welcome an opportunity
of discussing with you ways and means by which additional library facilities might be provided within the existing accommodation.

I shall look forward to hearing from you when you have had an opportunity
of re-appraising the distribution of your accommodation resources.

Yours faithfully

H P Knight MA Dip Ed
Assistant Director of Education
Wessex County Council

copy to: Director of Education

This letter is typed in
FULLY-BLOCKED LAYOUT

with

OPEN PUNCTUATION

Home Insulation Service Ltd

Kingsway House Ealing Broadway London W7 5AQ
Telephone: 01-401 3986/9

Directors: J. Kent (Managing) P. Brown A. Wilson
Registered Office: Kingsway House Ealing Broadway London W7 5AQ
Registered Number: 846971 Registered in England

Date as post-mark

Dear Householder

A SURE WAY YOU CAN SAVE MONEY THIS WINTER!

Will your bank-balance get blown away by an
'over-draught' of cold air again this winter?

Our research has proved that up to 30% of all money
spent on home heating virtually goes up in smoke!

The guilty culprits are ill-fitting, single-glazed
windows and doors, poor insulation in the lofts and attics
and exposed cavity walls.

Can you afford to let yet another year go by with your
heating bills far larger than they need be?

Or will you be sitting pretty when winter winds rage,
secure in the knowledge that your family, home and income
are being protected by Home Insulation Service's unrivalled
products?

Our FREE expert advice and NO-OBLIGATION quotations
are tailor-made to suit the insulation needs of YOUR home.

Our policy specifically excludes high-pressure
salesmanship and gives you a 7-day 'make-your-mind-up'
period.

Special low-interest credit facilities are also
available to suit your pocket.

ACT NOW! Ring 01 100 9000 <u>free of charge</u> and our
specialist insulation consultant will arrange to visit your
home <u>when it suits you</u> to give you an on the spot FREE
QUOTATION!

REMEMBER: a FREE phone-call <u>now</u> to 01 100 9000 could
prove the wisest investment you ever made - and your family
will love you for it all winter long!

Sincerely
John Grant

JOHN GRANT
SALES MANAGER
HOME INSULATION SERVICES LTD

This UNSOLICITED SALES LETTER is typed in SEMI-BLOCKED LAYOUT
on a word processor.

Registered Office:
42 Warrington Road
Liverpool LW4 9RT
Registered No. 468973
Registered in England

Telex: 349764
Telegrams: Lancstyre L'pool

Directors
A. Rowe (Managing)
F. Piercey
T. Rowlands
S. Wainwright

LANCASHIRE TYRE DISTRIBUTORS LTD

42 Warrington Road, Liverpool LW4 9RT
Telephone: 051-423 6934/5/6

Ref: SGS/JB/ATC 16   14 May 19--

H. R. Baxter,
Proprietor,
Ajax Tyre Centre,
Stretford,
MANCHESTER.   MS14 3RF

Dear Sir,

OVERDUE ACCOUNT: £1492.43

     In spite of the copy statement and reminders sent to
you on 3 April, 21 April and 7 May 19--, your account for
February 19-- totalling £1492.43 remains outstanding;
enclosed please find a final statement.

     As previously stated, the period of credit extended to
your company was agreed as one calendar month from receipt
of statement.

     Unless the above overdue account is settled in full
within seven days, I shall be compelled to instruct my
company's solicitors to undertake the necessary legal action
to recover the debt.

                         Yours faithfully,

                         S. G. Simmonds
enc.   Accounts Manager

This COLLECTION LETTER, the last of a series of three, was
typed in SEMI-BLOCKED LAYOUT with CLOSED PUNCTUATION, on a
word processor.

☐ Items which are inserted via word processing into a standard form letter of
   collection according to the state of the individual customer's overdue account

Assessment questions

Letter format

1   What contribution do the letterhead and logo make to the impact of the business or public service letter?
2   What parts of the business letter are required by law for some companies? Can you remember the names of the Acts concerned?
3   Describe two principal methods of setting out the typescript component of the business or public service letter.
4   What are the two acceptable methods for setting out the letter's date?
5   How are letters usually referenced under 'Your ref.', 'Our ref.'? How does the letter referencing system contribute to the filing and retrieval of letters?
6   Describe the difference between the 'open' and 'closed' methods of letter punctuation. What advantages does open punctuation provide in letter production?
7   List the various ways in which the letter's recipient may be styled in the recipient's address.
8   Specify the technical terms for the letter's 'greeting' and 'signing-off'.
9   Complete the following: a Dear Sir, ... b Dear Mr Smith, ... Describe the circumstances in which you would use the former and the latter.
10   List the appropriate methods for styling a man, a married woman, and a single woman with letters after their names.
11   What is the order by which letters after a person's name are set out?
12   What is the function of the subject-heading?
13   Why are the letter's paragraphs separated, most frequently, by double-spacing?
14   Why are the letter-writer's name and job-designation typed beneath his or her signature?
15   How should a secretary sign a letter on behalf of an absent principal?
16   How does the typist indicate that a letter is accompanied by additional material?
17   How does the typist indicate that a copy of a letter has been sent to a third person?
18   What are the components of the recipient's address on the envelope?
19   How should an envelope indicate that its contents are only to be read by the recipient specified?
20   Make a check-list of as many of the letter's components as you can remember.

Letter classification

21   What is a letter of adjustment?
22   Why are collection letters produced in a series?
23   What is an unsolicited sales letter?
24   Under what circumstances might a circular letter be used?
25   What is a form letter? What are the advantages and disadvantages of its use?
26   List and describe the use of as many different classifications of the letter as you can remember.

Structure

27   What is the usual function of the opening paragraph of the letter?
28   Outline the type of information most generally provided in an opening paragraph.
29   What is the function of the middle paragraph(s)?
30   What considerations should be borne in mind when planning the content of the middle paragraph(s)?
31   What is the function of the closing paragraph?
32   What do you understand by the term 'action statement/request'?
33   Outline the typical paragraph structure of:
     a a letter of complaint
     b a letter of adjustment
34   Describe the way in which a tactful letter might be structured which conveys bad news to its recipient.
35   Describe the considerations to be borne in mind when planning the structure of the letter's message.
36   What effects upon the structuring of letters have resulted from the widespread use of word processors?

Style

37   What sort of difficulties in communication face the letter-writer which are more easily resolved in oral communication?
38   What do you understand by 'objective, denotative language'?
39   What do you understand by 'subjective, connotative language'?
40   Outline the sort of message which might be expressed in the language referred to in:
     a Question 38
     b Question 39
41   Why is the English language so rich in alternatives and synonyms by which an idea might be expressed?
42   Can you remember the three style guide-lines advocated by H W and F G Fowler? Set them down.
43   What factors of the letter's context might affect the tone which the letter-writer adopts in influencing the recipient?
44   Why is it important to keep the recipient's personality and background firmly in mind when choosing the language in which a letter is expressed?
45   Specify the aspects of the recipient's make-up which should be borne in mind.
46   In planning and composing a letter, why is it of paramount importance to have arrived at a clear idea of the letter's overriding aim(s) before commencing to write or dictate?
47   Can you remember the key words in the planning and expression of a letter signified by the mnemonic, 'IMPRESS'? Set them down.

Case Study

Excelsior – for people on the move!

Mr Harold Langstone, Office Administration Manager of Tuffa Tools Limited, 14–16 Fordingley Road, Westport, Midshire WP12 5AG, is due to retire in four weeks' time.

As his assistant, you organised a 'whip-round' in the company's head office to purchase a suitable retirement gift for him. He has dropped broad hints that an overnight bag would be especially welcome, as he intends to spend the early months of his retirement visiting friends and relatives.

Accordingly, you bought an Excelsior Model XD overnight bag from Bags Galore, 32 High Street, Westport, Midshire WP3 2FD on March 2nd 19—. It cost £28.34 and was fully guaranteed for two years. When showing it to your office colleagues, the zip fastener jammed shut, and defied all efforts to ease it. On returning with the bag to Bags Galore, you were told by the shop assistant who had served you that they were unable to replace it, as it was the last one they had in stock and was referred to for the first time in your hearing as 'an obsolete model'.

The assistant suggested that you write to Excelsior Limited, Longmoor Road, Stoke-on-Trent, Staffordshire. Though sympathetic, the assistant informed you that she could not refund your money, but that you could expect Excelsior to supply an alternative bag through Bags Galore.

Preliminary assignment

Find out the legal position regarding your purchase of the overnight bag and what your legal rights are.

Main assignment

As a result of your investigations in the Preliminary Assignment, compose a letter using a simulated Tuffa Tools letterhead to the manager of the Bags Galore Westport branch outlining your experience and indicating how you would like the matter to be resolved.

Follow-up assignments

1   As the manager of Bags Galore, write a letter answering the one received in the Main Assignment, indicating the action you are taking to adjust the complaint.
2   Compose the Bags Galore manager's memorandum to all sales staff informing them how they should handle customer complaints.

Build-up tasks and discussion topics

1   Imagine that your principal has recently heard about a new electronic typewriter marketed by 'Electronic Business Equipment Ltd', Queensway House, Great Russell Street, London WC1 3AQ, which embodies a memory and self-correcting facility together with an interchangeable daisy wheel print facility.

Write a letter to enquire about the availability, performance and cost of this machine. Provide a suitable letter-heading. Note that your company prefers to use the semi-blocked letter format.

2   Assume that you are Mr Peter Jones, Sales Manager of 'Electronic Business Equipment Ltd'. Write a letter which embodies an appropriate letterhead replying to the letter outlined in Question 1 above, providing a suitable recipient's address. Bear in mind that you have published a brochure advertising the 'EBE Moderna' typewriter referred to above. Also, demand has greatly exceeded supply, and at present, there is a six weeks' waiting period for delivery. Your company has a nationwide sales force, and demonstration machines are available. Use the fully blocked open punctuation format.

3   Your company recently purchased a beverage dispensing machine from Semperflo Beverages Ltd of Highdown Industrial Estate, Birmingham BS3 4RA. Since its installation it has repeatedly broken down, and your company has no alternative means of providing for coffee-breaks etc.

Write a letter of complaint with a suitable letterhead employing the closed punctuation semi-blocked format.

4   As Sales Manager of Semperflo, you learned upon investigating the complaint outlined in Question 3 that the defect was caused by faulty installation by subcontractors whose services you no longer employ.

Write an appropriate letter of adjustment, with letter-heading, to redress the complaint, providing recipient details as necessary, using the blocked format.

5   Write a final letter of collection to R J Hill Esq, BSc, Econ, ACMA, Accounts Manager of Maxi-Markets Ltd, whose head-office is at 14–18 Richmond Way, Edinburgh E14 6ST.

Maxi-Markets are a chain of retail supermarkets. Your company has been supplying their Newcastle branch with a range of delicatessen sausages. Your company is owed £436.13 in respect of purchases invoiced for the month of September 19—. Your letters are neither being acknowledged nor replied to.

Provide your letter with a suitable letterheading and adopt an appropriate format.

6   Your company sells a range of household cleaning products which are sold on a cash basis by door-to-door salesmen and women.

Recently your company decided to adopt a change in policy by offering householders an opportunity to inspect your products by appointment at times suitable to them.

Draft an unsolicited sales letter, embodying an appropriate letterhead, which actively promotes these points:

Your company manufactures and retails a wide range of brushes, polishes, detergents and shampoos.

Your policy is to keep prices down by 'cutting out the middle man'.

Sales representatives are well-trained and able to demonstrate your products.

By returning in the envelope provided a detachable slip, customers can specify a date and time for representatives to call.

You are making a special offer of a free tin of furniture polish to all customers who reply with an appointed time.

You may add any additional supportive material. It may be helpful to collect and discuss a range of unsolicited sales letters before attempting this question.

7 Your company has employed Mr Fred Jenkins for the past 17 years. During that period, Mr Jenkins, who is well-liked in the company, has had a variety of jobs mostly of a handyman, storeman nature. Currently he is in charge of your mail-room, but recently his disability occasioned by injuries sustained during military service has worsened. His doctors have advised him that he should give up his job or run the risk of a severe deterioration in his health. He has a small disability pension, but is 58 years old, and male personnel in your company are not entitled to a pension until aged 65.

Mr Jenkins could be kept on in a part-time capacity if his health improved. Ex-gratia payments are at the managing director's discretion.

As personal assistant to the managing director, you have been asked by him to draft a suitable letter to Mr Jenkins, who is at home following a set-back. You have been told to use your discretion and submit the draft when the managing director returns from a visit.

8 Assume you are personal assistant to Mr Richard Brown, Sales Manager of Sceptre Garages Ltd, a company with a chain of garages specialising in car sales and servicing, motor-accessory retailing, petrol trade and retail sales, and general parts and body-repair sales to the trade.

In six weeks' time your branch at Midchester is to be relocated at 8–16 Bedford Road, Midchester, Bucks ME12 2BG. Telephone: Midchester 4631/2.

The new premises afford the following advantages:

Showrooms for 15 new cars
Sales area for 50 used cars
Ample customer parking
A diagnostic centre
Large body repair shop
10 self-service petrol pumps
8 while-you-wait tyre, battery and exhaust fitting bays
A motor-accessory supermarket.

Write a circular letter:
a to trade customers

b to account customers
to advise them of the forthcoming relocation. You may add any additional material you consider justifiable.

Choose a format you think appropriate, supplying a letterhead and logo.

9 Write a letter in support of your application for the post which you hope to obtain either at the end of your studies, or as your next appointment. Assume that your letter is accompanied by a completed form of application and a copy of your *curriculum vitae*.

Such letters are customarily hand-written

10 Design a letter of collection to be sent to any library user who has books long overdue indicating the fines already accumulated and the action to be taken if the books are not returned in 7 days. Underline those parts of the letter which the word processing operator would need to insert individually in each letter.

Discussion topics

1 Are the days of the paper letter despatched to clients, associates and customers numbered as a result of developments in electronic message-switching?
2 Are the pains taken in letterhead and logo design worthwhile?
3 Are the conventions governing letter format unnecessarily complex, or do they contribute positively to the letter's impact?
4 In what ways does Mr Harris in his letter on page 89 try to initiate a good relationship with Mr Dawson?
5 How does Mr Ross in his letter of complaint on page 94 manage to maintain a polite but firm tone in his letter?
6 In what ways are the extracts in the left-hand columns on pages 99 and 100 inferior to those preferred in the right-hand columns? Do you agree in every case?
7 How does Mr Knight endeavour to break his bad news tactfully in his letter on page 101?
8 What advertising techniques do you detect in the unsolicited sales letter on page 102?
9 What aspects of the collection letter on page 103 reveal a formal, reserved tone?
10 What advice would you give to someone about to begin a job involving much letter-writing?
11 Why is it so important that the letter is pitched at a level appropriate to its recipient?
12 In what situations would you consider the letter to be the only suitable medium in which to transmit a message?

Gayglo burns fingers

In order to promote a new range of eye make-up, Gayglo Cosmetics Ltd recently placed a series of advertisements in women's magazines to offer a free mascara kit (brush, mascara disc and mirror in a plastic wallet) to all women ordering the new pack of Gayglo eye-liners, cost £4.50. The total cost value of the mascara kit was 56p on the basis of an order for 12 000 kits. Gayglo had anticipated a demand for some 12 000 kits and had budgeted some £9000 for the whole promotional venture. To Gayglo's consternation, however, more than 30 000 replies were projected on the basis of the initial level of demand. As the advertisements had already been published, there was no way of reducing the demand. To meet the demand for an additional 18 000 kits would mean that a loss would be incurred on the first production run of the eye-liners, since in making the original offer, Gayglo had banked on establishing repeat-purchases of the eye-liners. The company's directors reached a conclusion that their only solution was to refund the postage to the disappointed customers for their mascara kit orders, and to send out a form letter explaining the situation as tactfully as possible as orders came in.

In such circumstances should Gayglo have absorbed the cost of the additional kits to maintain its favourable public image?

Given the directors' decision, what should the form letter aim to do?

Could any mitigating factors be introduced? Draft an appropriate letter, either singly or in syndicate groups, which you think most suitable. Then discuss and justify your draft.

Goodfellow says 'No'

In order to help out a friend, Robin Goodfellow recently stood in as a stage-manager for a local amateur production of *Cats*. Although he had no previous experience, Robin was an undoubted success with both the back-stage crew and cast. So much so, that shortly afterwards he received a letter from the honorary secretary of the Newtown Players offering him the permanent position of stage-manager. Robin was flattered, but had too many business and social commitments, and did not wish to commit himself to the many nights of rehearsal and production involved. Neither did he have any wish to offend the Newtown Players' committee, partly because his friend was a member, and also because some of his business associates were patrons of the Players.

What sort of letter-plan should Robin devise before drafting a letter replying to the invitation?

How could he best excuse himself tactfully? What tone should he adopt?

As Robin Goodfellow, draft a suitable letter to Miss Penny Haslemere, Honorary Secretary, Newtown Players, 'Cawley House', Cawley, Near Newtown, Herts CW12 8MG.

Trouble bubbles at the Cauldron

Recently production at the Cauldron Engineering Ltd's factory has been declining dramatically. The root of the trouble is a long history of industrial disputes. Both management and factory-workers have been to blame for the deteriorating relations which have left both sectors mutually antipathetic. Yesterday the board of directors held a meeting after productive consultations with the unions involved to try to find a peace formula. It was decided to send out a circular letter to all company personnel outlining the gravity of the situation. Unless a solution is made to work, large-scale redundancies seem inevitable, as the factory is losing money. The basis of the management offer is that, provided production is increased by 15% within four weeks and at least maintained at that level, the company would re-introduce overtime working, re-negotiate productivity bonus payments and make substantial investments in re-tooling, which is much needed.

What would be the letter's main aims? What tone should it adopt?

Draft an appropriate letter, either singly or in syndicate groups and then evaluate each version.

Approach check-list

Don't

Allow a letter to become formless

Lapse into long-windedness

Allow the letter to become obscure or ambiguous

Let the message become irrelevant or trivial

Opt for jargon, officialese or deliberate complexity

Ramble or 'butterfly' around the message

Adopt a tone which is aloof, hostile, over-familiar, condescending or mixed with slang expressions

Talk down to the letter's recipient or baffle him or her with inappropriate language

Be vague or ineffectual, or overlook the action to be generated by the letter

Ever allow a letter to degenerate into rudeness, sarcasm, offensiveness or tactlessness

Allow the language to become stale, cliché-ridden or hypocritical

Settle for a half-hearted or indifferent approach

Allow a letter to be despatched which contains careless errors either in its composition or in the typescript

Forget that a letter provides a written record – don't commit to paper what you may later regret having written

Do

Keep the basic aims firmly in mind

Plan the letter's points before starting to write or dictate

Aim for brevity

Ensure that ideas are clearly expressed

Keep to the relevant points

Prefer the simple to the complex

Check that the message is logically structured

Adopt a tone appropriate to the letter's aim

Remember who will be receiving the letter and adopt the appropriate vocabulary, syntax etc.

Be positive

Write a clear action statement or request

Take care at all times to ensure that the letter is courteous and tactful

Take trouble to keep the language fresh and sincere

Use your powers of persuasion when it matters

Check carefully for careless mechanical errors –
spelling
punctuation
usage

Remember that every letter is an ambassador

Multi letter-writing assignment

Leisure Press Limited

Situation

The sales of *Home Hobbies*, a monthly magazine aimed at 'do-it-yourself' home improvers have slumped badly in recent months.

The magazine is written, printed and marketed by Leisure Press Ltd, 42 Regency Crescent, London SW1 4TD.

Home Hobbies is produced monthly and marketed by direct subscription to householders responding to unsolicited sales letters followed up by calls from the company's representatives.

At present the 64-page magazine costs £10.50 per year and is supported by a wide range of advertising. The peak circulation nine months ago was 84 000 copies per issue.

The managing director is of the opinion that what is needed is some 'young blood and fresh ideas'.

Assignments

1   For the past two years Leisure Press Limited has used the services of the Grafix Advertising Agency. The Home Hobbies account is being managed by Mr Peter Cos, senior accounts manager. His address is:

Grafix Advertising Ltd
Grafix House
22 Hampstead Park Road
London
SW1 4TD

As assistant sales manager, you have been requested to draft a letter for the sales manager, Mr John Lloyd's signature, expressing your dissatisfaction with the current unsolicited sales letter used to promote the sales of *Home Hobbies* to householders.

You would like Grafix to submit for your approval two specimen unsolicited sales letters, one for young, married house-owners, and another for established householders. You will need to outline your ideas clearly.

2   The management of Grafix takes the letter from Leisure Press (Home Hobbies Dept) very seriously, and the managing director calls a meeting to see if a 'brain-storming' session will come up with some new ideas for the unsolicited sales letters. Your group should simulate the meeting (syndicate groups may be used), produce two suitable drafts, and set them out with a suitable covering letter to Mr Lloyd.

3   For the past two years, you have been a regular subscriber to *Home Hobbies*. Unfortunately, for the past six months delivery of your copies has been late and two copies never arrived. On another occasion, an 'enclosed' free gift of a tape-measure was not included.

Write a letter of complaint to the sales manager of the Home Hobbies Department at the London address, outlining your complaint and what you would like done to remedy it.

4   As sales manager of Home Hobbies Department of the Leisure Press Ltd compose an answer to a letter you have received from the customer making the above complaint. The problem has arisen because of staff turnover in your despatch section. Conditions of service have now been improved.

5   Compose an appropriate letter of application in response to the following:

ASSISTANT SALES MANAGER required by LEISURE PRESS LIMITED for *Home Hobbies* Magazine Dept.

Energetic, well-educated young person with business administration ability needed to assist sales manager of successful magazine. Top conditions and excellent salary for right applicant. Drive and ideas more important than experience.

Apply in writing to:
The Personnel Manager
Leisure Press Limited
42 Regency Crescent
LONDON
SW1 4TD

The above letters should include letterheads and may be composed either by individuals or by syndicate groups. The assignment should conclude with a group evaluation and analysis session.

8 Internal communication: memoranda, notices, reports and summaries

Introduction

This section will examine those types of written communication which are most frequently used by companies and institutions as *internal* channels of communication: memoranda, notices, reports, abstracts and summaries.

Some of the means of communication listed above are used externally as well as internally in the same way as the letter, while one, the memorandum, is *only* used within an organisation.

Fig. 1 illustrates how internal communications within a commercial company are organised.

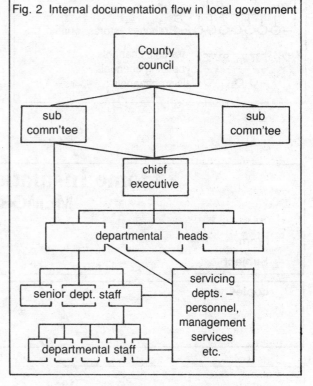

Fig. 2 Internal documentation flow in local government

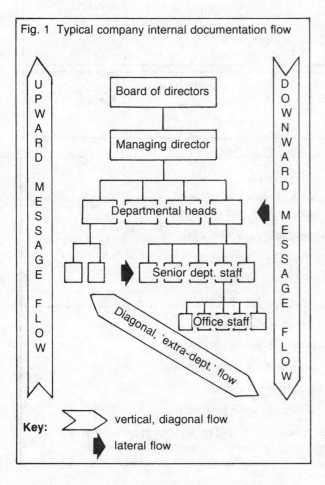

Fig. 1 Typical company internal documentation flow

UPWARD MESSAGE FLOW

DOWNWARD MESSAGE FLOW

Board of directors

Managing director

Departmental heads

Senior dept. staff

Office staff

Diagonal, 'extra-dept.' flow

Key: ▷ vertical, diagonal flow

▶ lateral flow

The structure of institutions such as a county council is similar to that of industry or commerce – policy decisions initiated by county councillors (board of directors) are implemented by the various departments which report to a chief executive (managing director). See Fig. 2.

The recording and storage of the details of a host of policies, decisions and routine daily business is essential to the efficient running of hierarchic organisations – though it is equally essential that the flow does not become a torrent! The internal flow of documents, vertical, lateral and diagonal can keep widely dispersed offices, branches or outlets constantly in touch with one another, as Fig. 3 indicates.

Fig. 3 Internal documentation flow in an inter-office context

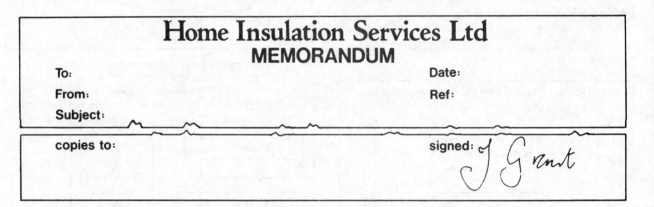

```
Head
office

Regional        Regional        Regional
office          office          office

Divisional
offices

Branches, stores, outlets
```

Key: ——————— hierarchic channels
- - - - - - bypassing channels
–O–O–O–O liaising channels

The memorandum

Format

The format of many memoranda begins with the name of the company or institution, although this is probably unnecessary since the document is intended for internal use only. The title 'Memorandum' is usually centred at the head of the page. The names, and sometimes job designations, of author and recipient are displayed after 'To' and 'From', omitting courtesy titles. The date is set out as for the letter – day, month, year, and often a space is allocated for entering a reference for administrative purposes. The essence of the message of the memorandum is briefly stated after 'Subject', and space must be given for the inclusion of 'cop(y)-ies to', 'enclosure' and, if company practice, for a signature.

Although typists learn a helpful format for setting out a memorandum on blank paper, there is no single, universally accepted memorandum format. Many organisations adapt the basic format indicated below, or add to it location points for the inclusion of information which they require as part of their individual administration. The inclusion, for example, of a space for the writer's signature or initials is optional,

---

Home Insulation Services Ltd
MEMORANDUM

To: **Date:**

From: **Ref:**

Subject:

copies to: **signed:** J Grant

Memorandum component check-list

Organisation's name	Some organisations' names appear above 'Memorandum'.
'Memorandum' heading	'Memorandum' is usually employed as a central heading.
'To'	'To' precedes the space for the recipient's name.
'From'	'From' identifies the writer of the memorandum.
'Date'	The date is entered as for the letter: day, month, year.
'Reference'	Some memoranda carry a reference for filing purposes.
'Subject'	The memorandum's theme is briefly stated after 'Subject'.
'Signed'	Some memoranda include a space for the writer's signature.
'Cop(y)-ies to'	Memoranda should indicate the recipient(s) of copies.
'Enclosure'	Memoranda should also indicate accompanying material.
Memorandum's message	The memorandum's message is set out in spaced paragraphs in the same way as the letter's, but salutations and complimentary closes are dispensed with.

although there are sound reasons for ensuring that no memorandum is despatched before its author has seen it in print and authorised its despatch by the initialling or signing of the memorandum. Also, the format of a memorandum will in some companies depend upon the degree of intended formality. For example, computer-relayed messages printed on a desk-top printer may well have the effect of a memorandum but may not adhere so strictly to traditional conventions of layout. It is important therefore for the effective office communicator to learn the conventions of communication and format followed by his or her employer.

Page size

Memoranda are usually produced in two standard sizes: A5 – 8.3″ by 5.8″ or 210 mm by 148 mm (about the same width as this page, but half its depth) and A4 – 8.3″ by 11.7″ or 210 mm by 297 mm (approximately the same size as this page). A5 memoranda are used when the message is brief, conveying a single major point, and A4 memoranda are employed, sometimes with continuation sheets, when messages are involved and complex, perhaps including schematically set out components.

Colour-coded filing systems

Instead of using a number of white sheets for the carbon-copies of a given memorandum, some organisations have adopted a colour-code for memoranda copies similar to that illustrated. The advantages of this system include prompt identification for filing, and speedy interpretation for possible action on the part of a recipient. For example, the recipient of a blue-coded copy

would know immediately that it was for him to read, but not act upon, whereas the recipient of the top copy of the same memorandum might need to act instantly upon its contents.

Application check-list

The memorandum provides an extremely useful channel of communication for transmitting unsolicited ideas or suggestions upwards in an organisation, as well as enabling policy decisions and routine instructions to flow down the hierarchic structure of a company or institution. Additionally, the memorandum is employed laterally or 'diagonally' between departments to seek advice, assistance or cooperation. By means of the copies despatched, memoranda also help to keep interested personnel 'in the picture' regarding a situation or development in which they are not required to act directly.

Some of the principal uses of the memorandum are to:

send unsolicited suggestions or ideas upwards
instruct, require, advise downwards
request, seek help or cooperation
confirm, especially following a telephone
    conversation or discussion
seek information, confirmation or advice
clarify, explain, introduce
amend or modify existing policies or practices
brief, or inform via copies

Production process

Note: Increasingly, internal messages are being displayed and stored electronically by means of desk-top

Colour-coded filing systems

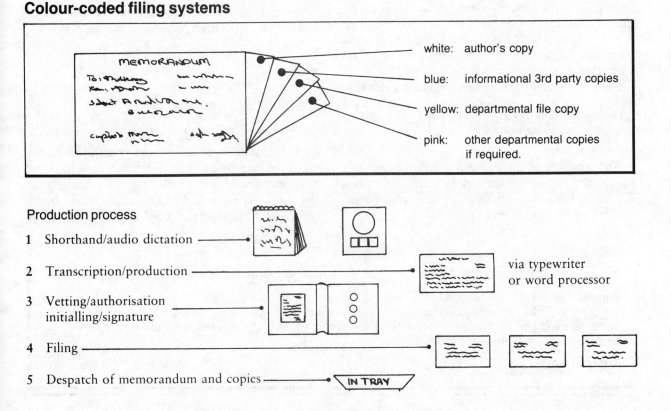

white: author's copy

blue: informational 3rd party copies

yellow: departmental file copy

pink: other departmental copies
         if required.

Production process

1   Shorthand/audio dictation

2   Transcription/production — via typewriter or word processor

3   Vetting/authorisation initialling/signature

4   Filing

5   Despatch of memorandum and copies — IN TRAY

visual display units (VDUs) and the memory of the company computer. Thus the flow of paper around the organisation is being modified by electronic 'message switching' and filing systems or the extended use of microfilm storage methods.

Content

The *Concise Oxford Dictionary*'s definition of the memorandum is, a 'note to help the memory'. Such a definition emphasises the brevity of many memoranda messages and focuses attention on their *supportive* function in helping personnel to recall, plan or act upon the flow of business activity.

In view of the space-restrictions deliberately imposed on authors by the A5 paper size, it is essential that the content of any message is condensed, so that only its essentials and any arising action requirement are transmitted to the recipient. Some memoranda, however, are produced on A4 paper and may run to a number of continuation sheets. Therefore, it is wrong to think of the memorandum solely as a means of transmitting short, 'one-point' messages.

The heading of the message after the entry, 'Subject' serves to pin-point the reason for the memorandum's production:

Regional Sales Meeting: 3rd June 19—
Reduction Of Days Of Credit
Revised Personnel Induction Procedure
Reorganisation Of Reprographic Service

and such headings, as well as summarising the subsequent message, also assist in allocation, ranking for action and filing.

Memoranda convey many different types of message: procedures to be followed, policies to be implemented, changes in established practices, clarifications or confirmations, motivation or exhortation of staff, disciplinary action, requests for assistance or liaison with other staff or departments.

Some memoranda are written by one individual to another, others by one department to another, yet others by an individual (perhaps a senior executive) to a large body of staff at different levels in the organisational hierarchy.

The structure of the memorandum's message will vary according to its context but the following diagram illustrates the three principal content components which form the basis of many memoranda.

Memorandum	
Subject:	SYNTHESIS OF THEME
Para 1: or (sentence)	**1** Puts message in context past – present – future
	2 Identifies the related components – people, places, events, time: who, why, what, when, where?
Para 2: or (sentence)	Details the essence of the memorandum's message.
Para 3: or (sentence)	**1** Identifies clearly the action either required or requested of the recipient.
	2 Puts a time-scale or deadline on the completion of the action – '... *by* ...'.

Written confirmation

Perhaps the most important single aspect of the memorandum's application lies in its provision of a *written* record (for retention, future reference, circulation etc.) of previously conducted oral communications – conversation, telephone calls, meetings, informal corridor encounters and so on.

It is therefore essential that the content of the memorandum in such circumstances is factually accurate, unambiguous, devoid of inference or 'side-swipes' and fair to quoted third parties.

Style

The dictates of context

The style of memoranda varies enormously. Directives, for example, from a managing director or chief executive may be couched in formal, depersonalised terms and delivered with all the crisp authority of an electronic typewriter. On the other hand, hasty, handwritten messages produced on a 'memo-pad' and

---

Copy to: The Reader – for future action.
'Memos and all other documents should always bear dates and initials. One of my colleagues once spent a twelve-hour night working on an undated document which turned out not to be the current draft. Why he was not convicted of mayhem remains a mystery.'

Robert Townsend, *Up the Organisation*

passed to a colleague's desk may be written in a much more personalised and familiar language.

Factors affecting style

The style of the language in which the memorandum is couched depends very much upon the following:

1 **The context of the message** – a crisis, congratulation, reprimand, routine order etc.
2 **The status, personality or background of the recipient** – high/low position in organisation, higher education, practical background etc.
3 **The nature of the message** – factual, informational, congratulatory, persuasive, soliciting, requiring etc.
4 **The urgency or priority of any action needed** – crisis, routine re-stocking order, need for liaison or cooperation, instructions for all staff etc.

Appropriateness

In such varying situations the mechanics of the style will be different:

1 **Syntax** – sentence length may be longer or shorter, may include or exclude subordinate clauses or phrases.
2 **Vocabulary** – the choice of words will vary enormously: some may be complex technical or specialist words or phrases, others may be deliberately factual, devoid of emotive overtones (in an explosive situation), still others may be engaging and familiar in a persuasive role.
3 **Tone and nuance** – the shades of meaning, or connotations given to the message's component parts will differ, depending on whether the message is factual or persuasive, the situation is 'fraught' or routine, the recipient responsive or obstructive.

Reaching the recipient

The style of the memorandum is also very much dependent upon the kind of recipient:

1 **Fellow specialist** 'in the know' – understands specialist, 'jargon' terminology.

2 **Peer group** – colleague(s) among whom is an unconstrained familiarity and directness.
3 **Junior personnel** – where the difference in authority, experience and 'reports-to' situation affects the way in which a communication is made.
4 **Range of staff within hierarchy** extending from senior to junior levels, where age, experience, background require a 'consensus' style approach avoiding obscurity, condescension or a patronising tone.

Message situations

The choice of either subjective or objective language or a mixture of both will also be decided by the nature of the memorandum:

1 **Informing** – where the message may confirm a revised discount, call a meeting or raise an order.
2 **Directing** – where action requirements are 'passed down the line' (persuasion may also be needed here to secure active cooperation).
3 **Requesting** – where there is no 'line-control' and colleagues may need 'wooing' for their help.
4 **Motivating** – where senior management needs, perhaps, to boost morale, exhort or persuade in engaging, motivating terms.
5 **Suggesting** – where junior executives attempt to 'sell' an idea to busy, sceptical seniors.
6 **Confiding** – where closely-working executives exchange highly personalised information informally and directly.

One last word!

No reference to style would be complete without mention of a simple, short word which matters so much when the cooperation of colleagues is sought: 'Please'. It pays ample dividends to remember that courtesy – even to long standing colleagues – is *always* important:

'Would you please ensure that I receive your report by the 21 March 19––.'

Models for analysis

Jim Grainger is a good salesman – he could sell ice to eskimos – but when it comes to routine paperwork, Jim is a laggard! Despite exhortations at a recent Area Sales meeting, he still isn't submitting his weekly reports on time.

Which of the following alternatives do you think his Area Sales Manager should send to Jim to motivate him to meet his Monday deadline? What criticisms can you make of the memoranda you reject? Or are they all inappropriate?

A Further to the Area Sales Meeting of 13th May 19--, you are reminded of my
reference to punctuality in despatching weekly sales reports. This reference was occasioned by the need for the efficient compilation of Area Sales
figures, Head Office statistics and Company Bonus Scheme returns.

I note, however, that I am still not receiving your returns by first post
on Mondays. Unless your performance improves, I shall be compelled to take
the matter further.

B At our last Area Sales Meeting on 13th May 19--, I stressed the need for
all sales representatives' weekly sales reports to reach me by the first
post Monday mornings.

You will recall that I emphasised the importance of sending in weekly reports
on time, not only to allow me to appraise the area sales situation, but also
for our Head Office to produce national sales turnover statistics and monthly
bonuses.

I should, therefore, be grateful if you would ensure that your weekly sales
report reaches my office in time for me to deal with the Area Sales Report
without delay.

C At our last Area Sales Meeting on 13th May 19--, I mentioned how important
it was for your weekly sales report to reach me early on Mondays. My own
sales picture, company sales figures and the monthly bonuses all rely on
my receiving sales representatives' reports in good time.

Your own territory is playing an important part at the moment in our area
sales recovery programme, and for this reason I am relying on you to send me
those figures for Mondays' first post, so that I can finalise my own report
to Head Office.

I know you won't want to hold up my report unnecessarily, and I set too much
store by your ability and enthusiasm to feel that I need to remind you
again.

D I'm concerned about not receiving your weekly sales report on time. You
remember I raised the problem at our last Area Sales Meeting on 13th May 19--,
and told everyone how important it was to send in their reports to me by
first post Mondays.

Well, I don't seem to be receiving yours until Tuesday or Wednesday, and so
I'm held up in sending my own report to Head Office, giving our own situation and supplying information for our overall sales and bonus scheme.

It would certainly help me on a Monday, if I had your figures along with
everyone else's. I know I can rely on you to rally round.

Keep up the good work!

Examples A-5 memoranda

NEWSHIRE COUNTY COUNCIL
Memorandum

Ref: HT/JR CS 46

To: B. Martin, County Surveyor.

Date: 24 February 19--

From: H. Taylor, County Information Officer

Subject: ACCEPTANCE OF PRESS RELEASE: RE-ROUTING TRAFFIC

I write to confirm our telephone conversation of 22 February 19-- regarding the submission of a press-release to the 'Newtown Evening Post' concerning the re-routing of traffic in the centre of Newtown.

I received confirmation today from the editor that the press-release and map would be given space on the front page of the edition for Friday 4 March 19--. As I assured you during our telephone conversation, the explanatory statement accompanying the map will be published in full.

As you requested, I have now arranged for copies of the press-release and map to be available for distribution in Newtown public libraries and the information kiosk in the pedestrian precinct.

I enclose a final draft of the press-release for your files.

H.T.

enc.
copy to: K. Mills, Chief Executive.
         P. Allsop, Printing Dept.

---

memorandum

to All Sales Representatives.   **from** M. Franks, Sales Manager.

ref MF/kg SGC 116   **date** 8 August 19--

subject Achievement of Sales Targets: July 19--

I want to thank you all for the superb sales performance you achieved in surpassing the company's national sales turnover target for July 19-- by £205.00.

The difficult trading situation experienced throughout the building trades sector during the past three months has made your successful efforts especially praiseworthy and particularly satisfying for me.

I am confident that, with our continuing determination and enthusiasm, not only shall we achieve our national sales target for 19--, but also that I shall need to review the sales bonus targets next year!

Well done, one and all!   *M.F.*

A-4 memorandum

MEMORANDUM

TO   All Company Personnel   **REF** SK/RD

FROM S. Kilbride, Managing Director   **DATE** 7 September 19--

SUBJECT A PROPOSAL TO INTRODUCE A FLEXIBLE WORKING HOURS SYSTEM

For some time past, the board of directors, in consultation with senior members of staff, has been considering the introduction of a system of working known as 'Flexible Working Hours', or, 'Flexitime'.

Under this system, personnel work an agreed total of hours each week or month (in the case of Kaybond Ltd. $37\frac{1}{2}$ hours each week), within a frame-work of agreed starting and finishing times which allow for commencing work before the current 9.00a.m., and continuing after the present finishing time of 5.30p.m. to a maximum of $7\frac{1}{2}$ hours each day.

In addition, <u>all</u> personnel are required to work during a 'core-time', say, between 10.00a.m. and 3.50p.m. excluding a lunch-break.

At the request of the board of directors, I have been asked to furnish you with a schedule of possible flexible working hours (enclosed), together with a detailed explanation of the scheme which the board would like you to digest, with a view to its implementation after a period of discussion and trial if the consensus views received prove favourable.

Broadly, staff would be required to work $7\frac{1}{2}$ hours each day, between 8.00a.m. and 6.15p.m., with a core-time from 10.00a.m. to 3.50p.m., and a minimum lunch-break of 45 minutes to be taken between 12.00p.m. and 2.15p.m. Thus the time available within which personnel may choose to work a period of $7\frac{1}{2}$ hours totals $9\frac{1}{4}$ hours each day, after a 45 minute lunch-break has been subtracted.

In this way, a 'late-starter' may elect to commence work at 10.00a.m. and to finish at 6.15 p.m. Alternatively, an 'early-bird' may begin work at 8.00p.m. and end at 4.15p.m., both having worked the required $7\frac{1}{2}$ hour period, both having taken a 45 minute lunch-break during the period 12.00p.m. to 2.15p.m.

There are distinct advantages, it is felt, to be gained from embarking upon a flexible working hours scheme; from the company's point of view, both punctuality and productivity would improve since peak rush-hour times could be avoided and staff could elect to work at times best suited to their 'internal clocks': similarly, the office would be manned for longer periods to take in-coming sales enquiries, and the pressure on the staff restaruant would be relieved. From the viewpoint of company personnel, greater opportunities would be afforded to <u>plan</u> work and leisure times; shopping journeys and the collection of children from school would be made easier and there would be quieter periods during the working day for uninterrupted, concentrated work.

A detachable form has been included with the schedule referred to; you are requested to give serious consideration to the proposed introduction of the 'Flexitime' scheme and then to deliver your conclusions on the form provided to your departmental head no later than Friday 20th September 19--. Additional information may be obtained from your head of department or the Personnel Manager. I anticipate that I shall be in a position to provide you with a decision by 8th October 19--.

encs.

Designing an effective notice

While the letter and memorandum tend to receive more attention in examining internal communications within organisations, the importance of the notice is not to be undervalued. As part of a staff noticeboard, it has an important part to play in interpersonal communication. All too often, however, it happens that no one is delegated to keep the noticeboard tidy and up-to-date, with the result that notices in some firms are seen to be frayed, yellowing, pinned haphazardly on top of others so that their entire credibility suffers and staff ignore them. Given an efficient treatment, however, the internal notice can provide an inexpensive and prompt means of disseminating certain types of information, usually that which affects significant proportions of staff, which is not confidential and which does not need to guarantee notice and assimilation by everyone.

Notices may take on a range of formats, from the extra copy of an A5 memorandum affixed to the noticeboard to an especially printed version on coloured paper including an element of graphics design.

Essential features

Whatever the intention of the notice, its designer should keep the following production guidelines firmly in mind:

- Make sure the paper size is large enough for the message but not so large as to swamp the noticeboard. People will have to read the text from a distance of 2–3 feet and will not bother with tiny, cramped wording.
- Give it a sufficiently bold and clear set of headings to arrest the attention of its intended recipients:
  ATTENTION ALL SQUASH LOVERS!
  and to convey its title:
  JOIN OUR NEW AEROBICS CLUB NOW!
- Keep the text of the notice short, sharp and to the point, avoiding long-winded constructions and lengthy words – the art is to impart the message as quickly, clearly and simply as possible.
- Make sure the notice indicates clearly what the recipients should do if any action is needed and who – name, job title and telephone extension – the contact person is to obtain forms or further details from.
- The notice should be 'topped and tailed' with the date of its composition, the name and designation of its author and, as appropriate, the signature of the person authorising its display.

Note that in some organisations each notice is given a display life period entered on it: 'Display from 1 June 19–– to 14 June 19––.' Then the person maintaining the board knows when to get rid of outdated notices.

The following example illustrates these main points:

```
                ATTENTION ALL OPERA BUFFS



        EVENING PERFORMANCE OF DON GIOVANNI BY W A MOZART
                 FESTIVAL THEATRE KENT OPERA
                 7.30 P.M. THURSDAY 14 JUNE 19—


        An amazing group discount deal has been struck with the Festival Theatre management
for the single performance of Mozart's Don Giovanni being performed by the excellent
touring company of Kent Opera. This is a traditional production in beautiful costumes with
classic sets.

        The performance starts at 7.30 p.m. prompt and is scheduled to finish at about
10.45 p.m. Afficionados will recall the splendid review this production received in last
Sunday's 'Despatch'.

        Tickets cost £5.50 each and are available from:

                Maureen Connolly
                Accounts Department
                Ext:  234

        SUPPLIES ARE LIMITED SO DON'T MISS YOUR CHANCE TO ENJOY THIS
                 MARVELLOUS PRODUCTION


Sue Jones, Social Club Secretary                              28 May 19—

Authorised:  K. Jones,
             Communications Officer

Display from:  28 May to 14 June
```

The report

The commission and production of reports plays a crucial part in achieving the goals which organisations set themselves. The more important decisions become, whether about people, finance or production, the more it is likely that specialist reports will be required by decision-makers to ensure that the process of decision-making is informed, impartial and considered.

The popular conception of a report is of a long, schematically set-down document, full of 'paras' and 'subparas', punctuated by references such as 'B 4 (iii) d', and it is true that some complex reports do require a logical referencing system. The format and methods of reporting are, however, many and varied, both spoken and written, and produced in a number of different contexts.

Classification and context

1 Regular and routine reports
   equipment maintenance report
   sales report
   progress report
   safety inspection report
   production report etc.

2 Occasional reports
   accident report
   disciplinary report
   status report etc.

3 Especially commissioned reports
   investigatory report
   market-research report
   staff report (personnel)
   market forecasting report
   product diversification report
   policy-changing report etc.

The range of reporting may be illustrated by the following two examples:

Situation one

Susan Spicer, personal assistant to the Sales Manager, Mr Jones, has just emerged from a meeting on administering a new bonus scheme. By chance, she encounters her principal, the Sales Manager.

'How did the meeting go, Susan?' she is asked. What follows will be an orally communicated report which synthesises the main features of the meeting as Susan saw them.

As the example on page 119 illustrates, Susan displays the care and attention which she devoted to her role of substitute at the meeting.

She follows the order of the items discussed at the meeting and dispenses with those parts which she does not think sufficiently important – so she is having to use her judgment as she goes along, selecting only the main and relevant points as she sees them in the context of Mr Jones' and the sales department's needs and interests. Susan also structures her oral report to proceed from the most important to the least important – she realises that Mr Jones is a busy man and has no time for trivia. In addition, she is particularly careful to ensure that Mr Jones is made aware of action which is shortly expected of him, particularly since the instructions come from a representative of top management, Mr Jackson. Lastly, Susan checks that no further action is expected from her, so that she may dispose of the meeting, as it were, in her mental checklist of 'matters outstanding', and move on to the next job.

Logic not magic!

There is nothing magical about the ability to deliver effective oral reports. The secret is to listen alertly as a participator in all office business, to make careful notes, to develop a clear memory, and to practise delivering information in a fluent, organised and logical sequence.

Example of an oral report

Susan Spicer, giving an oral report of a departmental managers' meeting she attended in place of her boss, Mr Jones, Sales Manager.

'As you requested, Mr Jones, I sat in on yesterday's meeting for you, which Mr Jackson (Deputy Managing Director) chaired. Only the production manager couldn't attend.

'Matters were very much routine until Item 5 on the Agenda – "Proposal to form a Training Department." Mr Jackson set out the background which you know about. One important development has taken place, though, that affects us directly. It seems that the budget won't stretch to building a new training centre, so we're likely to be asked to give up our storage rooms on the ground floor. However, the main point was that all the departmental heads are in favour – Mrs West submitted a summary of production's views. Mr Jackson asked the Personnel Manager to submit a detailed scheme for discussion at the next meeting. Heads were asked to submit suggestions to Mr Jackson by next Wednesday.

'There wasn't anything else particularly important, except that the introduction of the staff holiday rota arrangements were given the go-ahead.

'Under Any Other Business, Mrs Davidson complained about the poor response to the forthcoming Social Club Dance, so I've asked Julie to do her best to sell some more tickets.

'I think that was about it. Is there anything you'd like me to follow up?'

Clear beginning At the outset, Susan confirms those present and who chaired the meeting.

Development of essential and relevant points in the middle Aware of the scope of Mr Jones' interest, Susan skips over some early items of no relevance to the sales department – her report selects the particularly relevant points.

Confirmation of action Mr Jones must take himself She anticipates those areas in which her boss must make a response and provides the key details, and deadlines.

Descent to more minor points Susan also confirms that action may now be taken on the rota system.

Confirmation of conclusion and request for further instructions arising from the meeting Nearing the end of her report, which has gone through the same sequence as the meeting's business items, Susan relays details of action she has taken on her own initiative. She closes by asking if there is anything further she should do arising from the meeting.

Situation two

Later the same day, Susan is called into the Sales Manager's office:

'I'm worried about the steady fall in sales turnover at our Bournemouth branch, Susan. You'd better have a thorough look at the situation, get down there and let me have a report on what's gone wrong and how we put it right. Oh, and I'll need it by next Wednesday. I'll write to put the Regional Sales Manager in the picture.'

Such orally communicated instructions, or 'terms of reference' define the limits within which Susan may act, and are usually confirmed in a memorandum. Having collected and classified the information, Susan will present it to the Sales Manager as a written report to assist her principal in making a decision – whether to close the branch, redeploy staff or institute a hard-hitting advertising campaign.

In addition to the orally-delivered or detailed, investigatory reports, there are numerous routine reports the formats of which are designed to allow information to be inserted into boxes following questions or to permit a tick or cross to show a 'satisfactory/unsatisfactory' message. Such 'check-list' reporting systems save time and simplify routine reporting procedures.

Format

The format of written reports varies considerably. Some may run to hundreds of pages, such as those produced by Royal Commissions, others may be quite short and set-out on an A4 memorandum sheet. Some may be produced as a succession of paragraphs of continuous prose, while others may be displayed under a series of headings and sub-headings with lists, tables and diagrams.

The following table indicates some of the principal contexts and forms in which reporting takes place.

The choice of format for a report is most important. Therefore, before producing his report the report-writer should decide carefully which layout will best relay his message.

In some circumstances the powers of persuasion and emphasis of a direct oral report may outweigh the advantages of producing a written document – particularly when a time-factor is an over-riding consideration. Similarly, when more than one recipient is concerned, a report may best be delivered orally at

Reporting applications

Messages in letters or memoranda

Oral briefings or reporting back

Minutes of meetings

Routine 'check-list' reports

Progress reports – architects' site meetings

Annual reports to shareholders

Profiles of candidates for interview

Sales reports

Newspaper reports/news releases

Technical reports

Balance sheets for annual audit

Statistics in various visual formats

a meeting, where the information may easily be verified, confirmed, questioned and examined.

In many situations, however, the sheer wealth and complexity of report data require that it be transmitted in a written form, so that recipients keep a record for reference, and have repeated access to it and so assimilate it more easily. Moreover, in the context of the meeting, it is common practice to circulate reports in advance to allow participants to arrive at the meeting prepared to discuss a report's contents on an informal basis.

The following check-list provides a guide to the components which, in various combinations, form the parts which go to make up the whole of a range of different report formats:

Component check-list

1 Title
2 Author
3 Identity of report's commissioner
4 Date
5 Reference
6 Contents, pagination
7 Status e.g. Confidential
8 Background/history/introduction/terms of reference
9 Method/procedure/*modus operandi*
10 Information/findings/data input
11 Conclusions/synopsis/synthesis
12 Recommendations/suggestions for action
13 Footnotes
14 Appendices
15 Index
16 Circulation list

The extended formal report

This format is used for high-level, extensive reports by central or local government and large companies.

Layout

Sectionalised with schematic organisation and referencing.

Format key: extended report (see Component check-list)

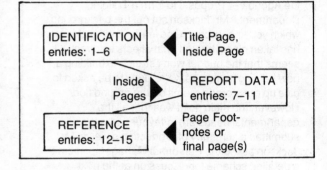

Principal components

1 Title page
2 Contents, pagination
3 Synopsis of findings
4 Terms of reference
5 Procedure
6 Sectionalised findings
7 Conclusions
8 Recommendations
9 Appendices
10 Bibliography

Note: Where a reporting committee cannot agree, some members may submit a 'Minority Report'.

The short formal report

This format is used in formal reporting situations (mostly internally directed) where middle or senior management reports to senior or top management.

Layout

Sectionalised with schematic organisation and referencing.

Principal components

1 Title page or heading
2 Terms of reference
3 Procedure or identification of task
4 Findings
5 Conclusions
6 Recommendations (where required)
7 Appendices (if appropriate)

Note: This format should be reserved for situations where the context, nature and complexity of the data warrant a formalised report.

The short informal report

The short, informal format is used when the information is of a lower status and less complex than that of the 'short formal report'. It is frequently used in 'subordinate reporting to departmental head' situations. (See model on page 125).

Layout

Usually three-part and less elaborately schematic in its organisation.

Principal components

1 (variously styled) background
                       introduction
                       situation etc.
2 (variously styled) information
                       findings etc.
3 (variously styled) conclusions
                       action required etc.

Note: Any recommendations required are usually included in the final, 'conclusions' section.

The memorandum report

The memorandum format is used for internal reporting, especially within and between departments. Its format is extremely flexible, since the 'title' information is contained in the memorandum heading and the space of the sheet below 'Subject' may be employed in a variety of ways to display the content of the report.

Layout

Heading as for memorandum. May be sectionalised with headings and include tabulated information.

Principal components

No pre-determined components – the format of the memorandum report may be structured to suit the nature of the data.

Display techniques

```
D O U B L E   S P A C I N G   O F   C A P I T A L S      used for titles, title
                                                         pages etc.
USE  OF  CAPITALS                                        used without underscoring
                                                         for main section headings.
Initial Capitals Underscored                             used to introduce sub-
                                                         headings within a main
                                                         section.
Initial Capitals Without Underscore                      with use of space around
                                                         it, this form of heading
                                                         may be used for minor
                                                         headings.

Use of numbers and letters for referencing
schematically:

Roman Numerals: I,II,III,IV,V, etc.)                     best employed to intro-
Capital Letters: A,B,C,D,E, etc.   )                     duce main section head-
                                                         ings.
Arabic Numerals: 1,2,3,4,5, etc.                         used to introduce sub-
                                                         sections after Roman
                                                         numerals or capital
                                                         letters are used for main
                                                         sections.
Lower Case Letters: a,b,c,d,e, etc.              )       used to introduce minor
Lower Case Roman Numerals: i,ii,iii,iv,v, etc.)          points; used in conjunc-
                                                         tion with indentation.

(Note that such letters or numbers are sometimes
 displayed within brackets thus; (i), (a).)
```

Alternative referencing system

In the Civil Service and Local Government an alternative system is frequently employed, which utilises a system of numbered sections: 1. 2. 3. 4. etc. to introduce major sections of the report. Successive sub-sections within a major section are referenced: 1.1, 1.2, 1.3, etc. and subordinate points or paragraphs within such sub-sections are referenced by the addition of a further full stop and number: 1.2.1, 1.2.2, 1.2.3, 1.2.4, etc.

In the references illustrated immediately above, the points being referred to would be the first, second, third and fourth points of the second sub-section of the first major section. This system has the advantages of using only one 'code', the Arabic numeral system and full-stops, and is economic to display.

Use of space and indentation

Apart from considerations of logically discriminating between major and minor sections or points, the use of space – either by centring titles, or leaving lines blank above and below a section heading – is extremely important in enabling the reader's eye to travel more easily down the page and to take in the impact of the report more readily. Long paragraphs of continuous prose are extremely difficult to digest, particularly when the information they contain is specialised or technical. The use of progressive indentation, similarly helps to convey the report's information quickly.

The impact of word processing on report formats

The word processor is ideally suited to the production of reports because of its formatting and editing facilities. It not only incorporates all those features available on more conventional typewriters, but also makes available many additional ones. For example, individual words, phrases or sentences may be emboldened for extra impact; right-hand margins of text may be justified to make the displayed item more visually appealing; and the time-consuming problems of tabulation and centring of text may also be overcome in a trice through the formatting wizardry of the word processor.

Similarly, the push-button editing facilities permit words to be erased, inserted, moved or brought into the text as standard sentences or paragraphs.

The general appearance of a report in terms of its format, structure and visual appeal has thus been much improved as a result of recent developments in word processing technology.

Content

Title page headings

All reports are prefaced with certain information which is displayed either on a title page (in the extended, formal report) or as a series of headings (in the memorandum or short, informal reports):

1 The subject of the report, displayed as its title
2 The identity of the report's recipients
3 The identity of the report's author
4 The date at completion
5 A reference (optional)
6 A circulation list
7 An indication of priority or confidentiality as required.

Structure of the short formal report

The structure of this report is divided into four or five sections (depending on whether recommendations have been asked for in the 'Terms of Reference'). The report is set down schematically as the following diagram broadly illustrates:

```
I     TERMS OF REFERENCE

II    PROCEDURE

III   FINDINGS
      1 Main Section Heading
      2 Main Section Heading
      3 Main Section Heading
          a Section 3 Sub-Heading
            i  Sub-point of a
            ii Sub-point of a

IV    CONCLUSIONS

V     RECOMMENDATIONS
      1 First main recommendation
      2 Second main recommendation etc.
```

The principal features of the schematically organised report to remember are that each section or point has a code for reference:

I or II or V or, III 3 a ii.

Also, headings are either in upper case, initial capitals underscored or initial capitals only, depending on whether they introduce a major section or a subheading. Lastly, as points become more detailed, they are progressively indented.

I   TERMS OF REFERENCE
In this first section of the report, the author details the scope of the report, or its 'parameters', within which he may investigate. Sometimes the report's commissioner asks for recommendations; at other times they are made by the recipient(s) of the report.

II   PROCEDURE
Having outlined the report's scope, the writer identifies the means he or she adopted to collect its data:
　　by scrutinising documents
　　by interviewing personnel
　　by visiting branches

by observation
by examination, analysis etc.

III FINDINGS
Here the detailed information which has been collected is sifted for relative importance and relevance and classified under appropriate headings, usually in descending order of importance, where the most important comes first.

IV CONCLUSIONS
In this section a résumé or synopsis of the principal findings is written, and is particularly helpful to those who may not wish to read the entire report.

V RECOMMENDATIONS
Having classified the detailed information of the report and summarised its main conclusions, the writer's last duty, if required, is to identify the means by which a problem may be solved or a deficiency remedied, so that decisions may be made or advice acted upon.

Structure of the short informal report

The content of this report falls into three principal sections, equating to a 'beginning, middle and end', and may be used in a variety of situations where the subject of the report is neither too long nor complex. Its sections may be variously titled but the three sections may be considered as follows:

> 1 Background outlined
> 2 Problem/situation analysed
> 3 Problem/situation resolved

The content of each section is detailed in the three boxes below.

> **1 First Section – headed:**
>
> Background or
> Introduction or
> Situation etc.
>   This opening section puts the report into a context and briefly outlines the essential background information needed to make the detailed information which follows in the middle section intelligible to the reader.

For example, if the report were entitled, 'Report on the Prevention of Wasteful Use of Stationery', the first section might well indicate a situation in which waste of stationery had been detected and a dramatic increase in stationery costs discovered. This section would also indicate who had commissioned the report, its author and any further details corresponding to the 'Terms Of Reference' section of the Short Formal Report.

> **2 Middle Section – headed**
>
> Information or
> Findings or
> Analysis of problem etc.
>   This section displays systematically the detailed information which has been collected by similar methods to those identified in the 'Procedure' section of the Short Formal Report.

The detailed information of this middle section may be organised as a series of continuous prose paragraphs beneath sub-headings, which may also contain numbered lists or tabulated information. Generally the input of this section is not sufficiently complex to justify a highly schematised, indented layout.

> **3 Final Section – headed**
>
> Conclusions or
> Action required or
> Resolution etc.
>   In this last section the main points of the report are summarised as conclusions and any actions required, recommendations or means of resolving a problem outlined. Thus the 'Conclusions' and 'Recommendations' sections of the Short Formal Report are combined.

The final section may be set out as a single continuous prose paragraph (or as a series of paragraphs), or may itemise its main points in a numbered list of sentences or phrases.

Structure of the memorandum report

If the subject may be treated analytically, the structure of the Memorandum Report will correspond to that of the Short Informal Report. Indeed, the A4 memorandum sheet, and continuation sheet(s) if needed, may be used for the Short Informal Report.

Additionally, the structure of the Memorandum Report is extremely flexible, and by employing the various display techniques available in typescript, it may be used for a range of internal reporting situations.

Detailed information in the form of charts, graphs and tables is often placed at the end of a report as an appendix.

> Illustrated below are the section headings for a candidate profile in a job application situation:
>
> 1 Personal details
> 2 Education
> 3 Qualifications
> 4 Experience
> 5 Personality/disposition
> 6 Interests
> 7 Circumstances

Each section will be displayed in whatever manner is easiest for the reader to absorb.

Style

The style of report-writing should be factual and objective. In the case of investigatory and analytical reports, the decisions to be made and actions to be taken should be based on information and recommendations devoid of self-interest or bias.

The author of the report should not allow prejudices or emotional responses to intrude into the presentation of the Findings, Information or Recommendations sections of the report. Even when opinions are presented, these should be supplied in an *informed* and balanced way.

In practice, however, it is difficult for the report-writer to avoid influencing his or her report by subjective value-judgments, whether made consciously or subconsciously. Indeed, it is often the case that the member of personnel assigned to investigate and to report upon a situation is chosen on the basis of possessing a sound reputation in matters which require judgment. Subjectivity or bias may be exercised, not only in the style in which the report is written, but also in the *selection* of points or topics to be included and in the omission of other material which may be deemed irrelevant or too trivial to warrant attention.

Some reports may be couched in entirely denotative language, devoid of rhetoric or persuasion. Frequently, however, the report writer is seeking not only to inform but also to persuade. Therefore, the report writer must always be on his guard to avoid subjectivity creeping in.

Most experienced senior executives, usually the recipients of reports, have a developed sense for detecting unfairness, biased selection or partiality in a report, the effect of which is usually to detract from the reputation of the writer. It is therefore extremely important when choosing the style of writing for a report to check continually, both in the organisation of the data and the use of language, for signs of inappropriate subjectivity or partiality.

Impersonal constructions

One important convention employed particularly in the writing of formal reports is the use of impersonal constructions to convey information. The use of 'I' or 'we' and their respective cases is avoided. Instead, ideas are expressed, not with a first, but with a *third* person subject. Instead of writing:

I found that . . .

constructions are preferred such as:

It was evident that . . .

or,

The statistics revealed that . . .

The underlying reason for preferring such impersonal constructions lies in the exclusion of any subjectivity associated with 'I', 'me', 'my', 'mine' and 'we', 'us', 'our', 'ours'.

Both before drafting a report and during composition, it is helpful to keep in mind a check-list of guidelines or yard-sticks to ensure that the end product accords with the intentions or aims which are to be met:

Style check-list

1   What is the principal aim of the report – to inform by presenting a body of facts, to persuade by supplying a distillation of opinions, or both?

2   What sort of people are the report's recipients? Are they specialists who will understand specialised or technical language, or laymen for whom facts must be presented simply?

3   What is the context of the report? Does it require the use of formal language, or may points be made informally and familiarly?

4   What sort of language will be appropriate? Should the report be couched in objective terms, using impersonal constructions and the passive voice? Should its vocabulary deliberately seek to avoid connotative, emotive meanings? Should technical and jargon words be avoided, or may they be employed? Should sentences be kept short and simple, or may they contain provisos and modifying ideas?

5   How should the data be organised? Are the themes of the major sections all relevant and important? Is the material of each section connected and related to its heading? Does the complexity of the report's data require the use of a detailed schematic format?

6   Do the recommendations or suggestions given derive from the Findings rather than from personal bias?

7   Have formatting techniques been used to display information clearly and in a logical sequence so as to help the reader to digest the data easily and grasp the connection between various sections and points?

Model of a short informal report

```
CONFIDENTIAL

FOR:   Mrs K Pearson, office manager

FROM:  Christine Fellows, personal assistant

Ref:   CF/AB

12 August 19--
```

REPORT ON THE PREVENTION OF WASTEFUL USE OF STATIONERY ①

1.0   INTRODUCTION ②

On Tuesday 28 July, you asked me to investigate the current wasteful use of stationery in the department and to suggest ways in which it might be ③ used more economically in future. My report was to be submitted to you by Friday 14 August 19--.

2.0   INFORMATION ④

2.1   Stationery Use Investigated ⑤

The range of departmental stationery investigated comprised: headed letterpaper and memoranda, associated copy paper and carbon paper, envelopes, duplicating masters and copy paper, and photo-copying stationery.

2.2   Stationery Associated with Correspondence/Internal Mail

The suspected increase in wasteful practices was confirmed upon investigation. I spoke to executive staff who confirmed that a   ⑥ significant proportion of typescript was being returned for retyping because of careless errors and poor standards of correction and erasure.

Observation and discussion with secretarial staff confirmed that   ⑥ clerical and executive staff in particular are using printed stationery and unused envelopes on occasion as message pads.

Regarding envelopes, white ones are being used where manilla would serve, and much non-confidential internal mail is being sent in sealed envelopes. No member of staff appears to be re-using envelopes.

Carbon paper is not generally wasted but staff complain of its limitations in reproducing multiple copies.

2.3   Duplicating and Photocopying Stationery

The spirit duplicator is in need of servicing and staff are wasting extensive amounts of duplicating paper as a result of a fault which creases the paper.

Though the increase in photocopying is in line with departmental work ⑦ (an increase of 11% in the last quarter) staff are tending to photo-copy when duplication would be more economical and to despatch individual copies for information purposes when a single circulated, initialled copy might suffice.

2.4   Increase in Stationery Costs

I analysed the cost of departmental stationery, comparing this year's second quarter with the first, and this year's consumption to date against last year's.

The stationery bill for the second quarter of this year is 29% higher ⑧ than for the first quarter (Jan-March: £321.15 April-June: £414.28).

Allowing for increases in price, the department's stationery bill for this year to date against an equivalent period last year is some 18% higher - £736.44 compared with £623.26 last year. This increase does not appear to be justified by an equivalent increase in the output of the department. Moreover, the rate of increase is rising. ⑨

```
    3.0   CONCLUSIONS (10)

          The investigations I have made do justify the concern expressed about
          excessive waste of office stationery and its impact on departmental
          running costs.

          The increase in careless use of stationery is not confined to one section (11)
          but is to be found, in different forms throughout the department.  If
          action is not taken immediately the department is unlikely to keep within (11)
          its administration budget.

          I should therefore like to recommend the following measures for your
          consideration:

          3.1 A meeting with senior secretarial staff should be called to discuss the (12)
              gravity of the problem and to obtain their cooperation in improving
              secretarial performance.  A refresher course could be mounted by the
              training department.

          3.2 Control of stationery issue should be tightened; sections should be (12)
              required to account quarterly for stationery if this proves practicable
              in principle.

          3.3 Departmental policy on internal mail procedures and message recording (12)
              should be revised and all staff notified.

          3.4 An appraisal should be made on the possible savings to be made resulting (12)
              from the introduction of NCR pre-printed forms (memoranda etc) and from
              restricting access to and use of photocopying facilities.
```

Reference heads section

The report is clearly headed with the appropriate information for despatch and filing.

Note the use of the CONFIDENTIAL classification resulting from the nature of the report's information, since some staff are clearly open to criticism.

A report's title(1) should always indicate briefly yet clearly what it is about.

Introduction section

This section(2) establishes concisely: What? Who? When? Why?

Note that from the outset it is clear that the report will include recommendations for action(3).

Information section

The INFORMATION section(4) could be made up simply of continuous prose paragraphs, but the inclusion of sub-headings(5) helps to break down the information into more easily digested sections, which emphasise the particular areas of investigation Christine Fellows thought important.

Note that the first sub-section identifies and defines the range of stationery to be investigated. In so doing, an effort has been made to break down the range into logical groupings.

Much of the report's information relies on Christine's observations and discussions with staff(6) and, in the report, takes the form of assertions. Mrs Pearson would need to rely on Christine's judgment – it is important, therefore, that in reports(7), investigators are just and fair, and as far as possible, support their assertions(8) by quoting facts, figures or clearly evident practices. This reassures the report's reader that the report is based on fact, rather than opinion or purely personal views.

To this end, Christine has taken the trouble to examine the department's spending on stationery over the past 18 months. Her factual financial evidence is hard to ignore, and has the effect of emphasising the need for urgent action.(9)

Conclusions section

In the short informal report, the CONCLUSIONS section(10) provides a summary of the main factors(11) which arise from the INFORMATION section, and also relays to the reader any suggestions or recommendations(12) which may have been asked for.

Note: In more complex reports, these two aspects, of summarising the findings of a report and then of specifying recommendations are in two separate sections.

In terms of the report's visual impact on the reader, it might have been helpful for Christine to have headed each recommendation with a suitable 'label':

Secretarial staff

A meeting with senior ...

Such display techniques are a matter of personal judgment, since there are, in fact, no hard and fast rules governing report format; it is a matter of using most effectively the display facilities of the typewriter and setting out information in a logical and clear manner.

Model of memorandum report

MIDSHIRE COUNCIL
Memorandum

<u>CONFIDENTIAL</u>

To: Director of Education

Ref: HJK/RT   DE 156

From: Personnel Services Manager

Date: 12th August 19--

Subject: Appointment of Personal Assistant to Director of Education
Candidate Profile: Miss Jean Harris

PERSONAL DETAILS

> Full Name: Jean Olivia Harris   Date of Birth: 22nd April 19--
> Age: 24   Status: Single   Nationality: British
> Address: 14 Highmoor Drive, Midtown, Midshire. ME12 4TG

ATTAINMENTS

> Secondary School: September 19-- to July 19-- Waverely College.
>   'A'-levels: English Lit A, History B, Sociology B.
> University: October 19-- to June 19-- Cumbria University.
>   Graduated B.A. Hons in English Literature,
>   Second Class.
> Post-graduate: September 19-- to June 19-- Midtown College of F.E.
>   R.S.A. Diploma for Personal Assistants: Distinction

GENERAL INTELLIGENCE

> Miss Harris's academic record evidences a lively intelligence and her
> success in higher education courses suggests an ability to deal with
> problems conceptually and analytically. Reports from Cumbria University
> and Midtown College of F.E. confirm initiative and resourcefulness in
> problem-solving situations.

SPECIAL APTITUDES

> During her post-graduate course, Miss Harris did particularly well in
> shorthand and typewriting, achieving 110w.p.m. and 50w.p.m. respectively,
> and gained distinctions in Communications and Administration.

> While studying at Cumbria University, Miss Harris served on the Students'
> Union Education Committee and published a paper entitled, 'The Future
> of Higher Education - Freedom Now!'

INTERESTS

> An accomplished violinist, Miss Harris is Honorary Secretary of the
> Midtown Orchestral Society. She also enjoys sailing and is interested
> in industrial archeology.

DISPOSITION

> Reports indicate a tendency towards impatience with viewpoints commonly
> identified with the 'establishment' but also reveal a willingness to
> modify a point of view when faced with a superior argument. Miss
> Harris's personality has been variously described as 'forceful' and
> 'dynamic' and she is generally held to possess a cheerful, outgoing
> personality and a good sense of humour. She has been universally
> described as a young woman of integrity and loyalty.

CIRCUMSTANCES

> Since completing her course at Midtown College of F.E., Miss Harris
> has been staying with her parents and would be immediately available
> for employment if successful in her application.

signed........................

Specimen short formal report

CONFIDENTIAL

FOR: P J Kirkbride, Managing Director   REF: HTD/SC/FWH 4

FROM: H T Dickens, Chairman, Flexible   DATE: 14 February 19—
       Working Hours Working Party

REPORT ON THE PROPOSAL TO INTRODUCE A FLEXIBLE WORKING HOURS SYSTEM IN HEAD OFFICE

1.0 TERMS OF REFERENCE

   On 7 January 19— the managing director instructed a specially set up working party to
   investigate the practicality of introducing a system of flexible working hours in all
   head office departments, and to make appropriate recommendations. The report was to be
   submitted to him by 21 February 19— for the consideration of the Board of Directors.

2.0 PROCEDURE

   In order to obtain relevant information and opinion, the following procedures were
   adopted by the working party to acquire the information in the report:

   2.1 Current office administration literature was reviewed. (Appendix 1 Bibliography
        refers.)
   2.2 A number of companies were visited which have adopted flexible working hours
        systems and the views of a wide range of staff were canvassed.
   2.3 Current departmental working loads and practices were observed and evaluated.
   2.4 Soundings of likely staff responses were obtained from departmental managers and
        senior staff.
   2.5 The cost of introducing a flexible working hours system was considered.

3.0 FINDINGS

   3.1 Principles of the Flexible Working Hours System

        The essence of a flexible working hours system consists of establishing two
        distinct bands of working hours within a weekly or monthly cycle and of ensuring
        that staff work an agreed total of hours in the cycle.

        3.1.1 Core Time Band

               During this period (say 10 15 am to 3 45 pm) all staff are present at work,
               allowing for lunch-time arrangements.

        3.1.2 Flexi-time Band

               Periods at the beginning and end of the day (say 7 45 am to 10 15 am and
               3 45 pm to 6 15 pm) are worked at the discretion of individual staff
               members in whole or part, allowing for essential departmental staff
               manning requirements.

3.1.3 Credit/Debit Hour Banking

According to previously agreed limits and procedures, staff may take time off if a credit of hours has built up, or make time up, having created a debit to be made good. Most companies require that the agreed weekly hours total (in the case of head office staff $37\frac{1}{2}$ hours per week) is reached but not exceeded, though some firms adopt a more flexible approach, which permits some time to be credited/debited in a longer cycle.

3.1.4 Recording Hours Worked

In all systems, it is essential that logs or time-sheet records are kept and agreed by employee and supervisor for pay and staff administration reasons.

3.2 Discussions with Departmental Managers

Most departmental managers were in favour of introducing a flexible working hours system, anticipating an improvement in both productivity and staff morale. The sales manager saw advantages in his office being open longer during the day to deal with customer calls and visits. Reservations were expressed by both the office administration and accounts managers arising from the likelihood of increased workloads to administer the system.

3.3 Sounding of Staff Opinion

Discreet enquiries were made via senior staff regarding the likely response of staff at more junior levels.

3.3.1 Summary of Favourable Responses

Secretarial staff in particular would welcome the means of tailoring their work and attendance to fit in with their principals' presences and absences. Many staff would enjoy working when they felt at their personal 'peaks'. Over 35% of female staff are mothers with children of school age, and would probably welcome the opportunity to fit their work around family responsibilities and according to seasonal daylight hours. Weekday shopping opportunities would be improved and travelling in peak rush-hour times avoided.

3.3.2 Summary of Unfavourable Responses

Few staff at junior levels intimated an unfavourable response but more senior staff were concerned about key personnel not being available when needed for consultation etc. Older staff seemed less enthusiastic and any introduction of flexible working hours would need to be carefully planned and full consultation carried out.

3.4   <u>Cost of Introducing a Flexible Working Hours System</u>

The increase in costs of heating, lighting and administration of the system would be offset to some degree by a decline in overtime worked and the cost of employing temporary staff to cover for staff absences, which may be expected to reduce. (Appendix 3 provides a detailed estimate of the cost of introducing and running a flexible working hours system.)

4.0   CONCLUSIONS

In the working party's view, the advantages of introducing a flexible working hours system outweigh the disadvantages. Head office service to both customers and field sales staff would improve; staff morale and productivity are also likely to rise. Administrative costs do not appear unacceptable and senior staff have the necessary expertise to make the system work. Of necessity, the working party's view was broad rather than detailed and the introduction of any flexible working hours systems should allow for the particular needs and problems of individual head office departments to be taken into account as far as possible.

5.0   RECOMMENDATIONS

As a result of its investigations, the working party recommends that the Board of Directors gives active consideration to the following:

5.1   That the introduction of a flexible working hours system be accepted in principle by the Board and staff consultations begin as soon as possible with a view to establishing a time-table for implementing the change.

5.2   That all departmental managers be requested to provide a detailed appraisal of their needs in moving over to a flexible working hours system and of any problems they anticipate.

5.3   That a training programme be devised by personnel and training departments to familiarise staff with new working procedures and practices.

5.4   That a code of practice be compiled for inclusion in the company handbook.

5.5   That arrangements be made to inform both field sales staff and customers at the appropriate time of the advantages to them of the introduction in head office of flexible working hours.

Assignment

Compare the visual impact of the layout of this report with that of the A4 memorandum layout shown on page 116

Summaries

One of the most essential needs of business is for the succinct presentation of ideas, information or opinion. The communications revolution of the past one hundred years has resulted in incredible mechanical and electronic advances. The wide-spread use of telephones, telex, typewriters, word processors, computers, and so on speaks for itself.

Such universal adoption of communications equipment has meant that managers and secretaries are deluged by a flood of documentation and oral communication. The pressure on people's time and the increase in data production and relay costs have impelled organisations to develop sophisticated summarising techniques which, by reducing communication to bare essentials, achieve an essential saving in reading, processing and assimilation time as well as a reduction in expenditure.

The plight of the senior executive amply illustrates the need for good summarising practices. If an organisation is to benefit from the years of experience and developed expertise present in such people, it must appreciate that their time is a precious asset. Such executives need not only to keep abreast of activities and developments, but must also regulate their contact with the large numbers of colleagues, associates or subordinates who make pressing demands upon their time.

In order to cope, senior managers need to avoid time-wasting minutiae and to encourage those in contact with them to discipline themselves, both orally and in writing. Ideas, factual reporting, feed-back or suggestions should all be condensed to a main core which represents the main points of a complex problem, a synthesis of a discussion or meeting, or a brief analysis of an involved situation.

All those who produce information in such circumstances need to acquire summarising skills broadly identified as:

comprehension
classification
analysis
evaluation
selection

Essentially, they will exercise their powers of discrimination in deciding which parts of a given piece of material need to be extracted and relayed in a particular format to meet the needs of a third party.

Indeed, one of the most valuable assets of the executive, personal assistant or secretary is the ability to relay the essence of a 'message' which will involve meeting the following objectives in whole or part:

1 Ability to comprehend a range of information, data or opinion
2 Ability to identify salient points for a particular purpose
3 Skill in analysing and evaluating material to distinguish the essential from the trivial
4 Practice in working objectively so that personal attitudes do not influence selection processes
5 Skill in using language to convey the tone or attitudes of the original
6 Familiarity with business practice to ensure that appropriate formats are used when reproducing data

Whether we realise it or not, the techniques of summarising pervade the whole range of communication activities. For many of us that schoolday scourge, the précis, was the first 'baptism of fire' in acquiring the skills of summarising, yet it is not used to any extent in business, though the skills it develops are valuable in a host of situations. The following table indicates just some of the communication contexts which involve the application of summarising techniques:

Applications of summarising techniques

Relaying to a principal the outcome of a meeting
As chairman, summing up a discussion at a meeting
Passing a message, either orally or on a message pad
Designing an advertisement for a job
Delivering the chairman's report at a company's annual general meeting
Producing a sales report
Writing a letter or memorandum conveying information or a point of view
Relaying instructions from above to subordinates
Editing a press-release for inclusion in a newspaper
Writing an article for inclusion in a house magazine
Drafting a notice or circular
Using the telephone – particularly over a long distance!
Interviewing a candidate for an appointment
Giving a briefing to a group, working party or task-force
Getting across a point of view or suggestion
Despatching a telegram or telex message

Many oral and writing situations arise daily requiring summarising techniques

Though the summarising process is present in so many communications channels, nevertheless there are a number of documents produced frequently in an organisation which require a specific summarising technique:

Documents needing specific summarising techniques

Précis	a faithful, selective miniature reproduction
Summary	selective reproduction of *required* data
Abstract	selective data from long article, paper
Abridgement	shortened version of a book, thesis etc.
Précis of documents, correspondence	summary of a series of related documents
Minutes	summary of decisions (background) of a meeting
Conclusions, synopsis sections of the formal, extended reports	summary of main points of 'Findings' section (or Synopsis), introductory essence of report
Telemessage, Telex message	abbreviated message reduced to essentials
Press release	submission to newspaper of newsworthy item

(For a more detailed examination of minutes see the 'Meetings' module.)

Note the difference: The précis seeks to reduce a passage to about a third, and aims to retain both its major features and attitudes in a faithful, miniature reproduction. The **summary** selects points to meet a specific brief or requirement and is therefore selective of the passage's material, extracting only those points relevant to a desired purpose. The **abstract** is also selective, reducing a much longer article or passage far more extensively, but again, its length is determined by the *specifically directed* requirements of its recipient.

Principles of summarising

Stage one

Check that you understand clearly the requirement or brief – which may only involve *part* of the item for summarising.

Stage two

Read the item *thoroughly*, since you cannot summarise what you do not fully grasp. Read for:

a The general drift or meaning
b For the meaning of individual words or phrases
c For the structure of the item and the development of its ideas or arguments.

Stage three

Give the item a title conveying the essence of the summary. This will act as a yard-stick against which to measure points for importance and relevance.

Stage four

Select the principal points, keeping the 'terms of reference' of Stage One in mind. A useful technique is to identify the 'key topics' of paragraphs as a starting point.

Stage five

Check your list of points against the original in case something has been overlooked. Check your points against your title for relevance.

Stage six

Establish which format is appropriate for the summarising version – schematic layout or paragraphed continuous prose.

Stage seven

Compose a rough draft leaving room for subsequent refinements and using your own words to convey the sense rather than copying phrases or sentences; remember that you need not find alternatives for specialist terms like 'inflation' or 'wage-freeze' etc.

Stage eight

If you are limited to a specific number of words, it is wise to aim to exceed this limit in a rough draft by some 10–15 words in the context of a passage of 300 words to be reduced to some 110, since it is easier to prune further than to insert extra points into a rough draft.

Stage nine

Check the rough draft to ensure that the points are linked in connected sentences that read smoothly and where the progression is logical and intelligible. Then polish into a final version by improving vocabulary, syntax, tone etc. Ensure that the final version has been checked for transcription errors of spelling, punctuation etc.

Stage ten

Add the details of the item's sources, the author's name and status, as well as your own. The summary may be passed to its recipient by means of a covering memorandum. All such work should bear a completion date, to indicate that it is current work.

The acid test

The acid test of all summarising work is that its recipient can clearly understand it without ever having seen the original!

Example

Let us assume that the material of page 131 is required to be summarised to form a guide for would-be summarisers. It comprises some 470 words, which we shall try to reduce to 160.

The requirements of our brief require that we keep our summary simple and present only the main points in a way which will help the reader to follow them easily.

A first reading indicates that the passage deals with the need for executives and their assistants to develop expertise in summarising in order to cope with the flood of communications and to make best use of the time available.

The second reading will, perhaps, produce a number of words and phrases which require careful scrutiny:

succinct	time-wasting minutiae
deluge	synthesis
data production	exercising their powers
saving in reading,	of discrimination etc.
processing and	
assimilation time	

Some dictionary work may be needed, or in an examination situation intelligent guesses may be required by looking at the *context* of difficult words or phrases.

Structurally, the passage embodies five stages:

1 Introduction – communications revolution
2 The communication flood
3 The plight of senior executives and how assistants may help
4 An identification of the main areas of summarising techniques
5 A check-list of the basic skills needed by the summariser.

The title required in Step Three might be:

'Summarising Techniques: Why They Are Needed And How They Are Applied In Organisations.'

Following the structural plan, the main points are then listed, using the title as a yard-stick of relevance.

Main points list

The main points check-list will appear, broadly as follows:

First para
1 Summarising – essential need in organisation – need for *brief* statement of info, ideas
2 Communications revolution – reliance on wide range of business equipment

Second para
3 Communications revolution – flood of documentation, inc. oral comms.
4 Consequence – pressure on person's time and increase in production and distribution costs
5 Essential reduce flow to be able to cope

Third para
6 Senior executives – their time and expertise wasted if spent on trivialities
7 Calls on their time must be rationed to 'core material' and brief analyses

Fourth para
8 Those who summarise – need to acquire skills in: comprehension, evaluation, selection
9 Must have ability to discriminate to meet a *specific* requirement

Fifth para
10 The summariser needs to develop these specific skills:

(*a*) Comprehension
(*b*) Recognition of main points
(*c*) Analytical skill
(*d*) Objective working
(*e*) Facility with language
(*f*) Sound knowledge of business practices
(*g*) Familiarity with document formats

Note: In terms of the target 160 words, the notes are rather generously written, but since they are not for personal use, they need to be intelligible to the reader.

The rough draft

The next stage, having established a format, would be to compose a rough draft:

The ability to summarise effectively is essential in organisations ~~if personnel are to cope~~ *to enable personnel to cope* with the flood *of information* ~~brought about~~ *caused* by the communications revolution and the *consequent* wide-spread use of business equipment.

Organisational personnel are being 'flooded' by oral and written communications, causing staff to waste time and ~~resulting in~~ increasing *the* costs *of* ~~in the~~ produc~~tion~~ *ing* and distribut~~ion of~~ *ing* information.

Senior executives cannot use their time and expertise *effectively* if forced to waste time on trivialities. Calls on their time must be rationed and communications reduced *by those servicing them* to 'core material' or brief analyses.

To help senior ~~executives~~ *staff*, those who summarise need to acquire skills in comprehending, evaluating and selectively reproducing data~~/~~ *. T* they must learn to discriminate.

Specifically, ~~they should develop their expertise in the following areas:~~ *expertise is needed in:*

comprehension

~~recognition of main points~~ *selection*

~~analytical skills~~ *analysis*

objective ~~working~~ *writing*

~~facility with language~~ *fluent expression*

sound knowledge of:business practice

~~familiarity with~~ document formats   (143 words)

The next step is to include the title and any other helpful headings and to polish the rough draft, taking care not to exceed any prescribed word limit.

The final version

The final version will then appear like this:

SUMMARISING TECHNIQUES: WHY THEY ARE NEEDED AND HOW TO APPLY THEM IN ORGANISATIONS

Background
The ability to summarise effectively is essential in organisations to enable personnel to cope with the flood of information caused by the communications revolution and the consequent wide-spread use of business equipment.

The current situation
Organisation personnel are being 'flooded' by oral and written communications causing staff to waste time and increasing the costs of producing and distributing information.

The senior executive's problem
Senior executives cannot use their time and expertise effectively if forced to waste it on trivialities. Calls on their time must be rationed and communication reduced by those servicing them to 'core material' or brief analyses.

Skills needed by the summariser
To help senior staff, those who summarise need to acquire skills in comprehending, evaluating and selecting data. They must learn to discriminate.

Specifically, expertise is needed in:

comprehension
selection
analysis
objective writing
fluent expression
sound knowledge of:
   business practice
   document formats
(160 words)

Last word

More communication fails from being too long, than from being too short!

When summarising . . .	. . . but do
Don't	Check your brief carefully before starting
Skimp the reading stages – the original *must* be clearly understood	Check unfamiliar words
Include items in your points list which are trivial, repetitious, and, broadly, illustrations or examples	Convey fairly the author's own attitudes and outlooks
Abbreviate your points list too dramatically or allow yourself to be verbose	Measure your points list against relevance and importance to theme
Allow your own personal views to obtrude into the summary	Cross-check against passage and chosen title
Forget that it takes at least twice as many words on average to expand a points list into continuous prose	Convey the sense rather than the wording of the original
Try to 'borrow' phrases or sentences from the original – they won't fit into your smaller version comfortably – and you may use them wrongly	Think of reducing the original to its basic 'skeletal' form
Allow your rough or final version to suffer from 'over-compression', where the meaning is lost in a kind of shorthand language	Keep essential illustrations short – use collective nouns when possible
Allow your summary to look like a list of unconnected and hence meaningless statements	Bear in mind that authors tend to repeat main points several times and 'say it only once'
Overlook the fact that the recipient may never see the original. Your version must stand on its own two feet and not rely on a reading of the original to render it intelligible	Make a draft before attempting a final version
	Ensure that your tone and style are appropriate either to the author's approach or the recipient's needs – e.g. factual or persuasive
Forget that the context dictates the format of the final version – a schematic layout may be essential for quick reference in a meeting	Ensure that the rough draft to final version stage is free from mechanical errors – spelling, punctuation, syntax
	Choose an appropriate format ·

Précis of documentation or correspondence

Sometimes it is necessary to produce a summary of an exchange of letters or of a number of related documents. Such techniques involve selecting only the most essential points and connecting them as follows:

1 Specifying the context, authors' names and designations and organisations in a title section.
2 Proceeding chronologically showing dates and authors and the essential point of each document or letter.

The abstract

In compiling an abstract, it is extremely important to act only upon the requirement of your briefing – do not produce a précis when the recipient has asked for a particular aspect to be synthesised from points dispersed in the original. Follow the method shown on page 132. Remember that you will need to be far more stringent in excluding non-essential material, and that a schematic presentation may be needed for the abstract to be used in a discussion or meeting. Lastly, always cite the source, authorship and date of the original, together with your name, status and the completion date.

Assessment questions

The memorandum

1   How does the use of the memorandum differ from that of the letter?

2   What are the main components of the memorandum format?

3   What are the limitations of a memorandum set out on A5 paper?

4   What sort of message does the memorandum tend to convey?

5   List the various stages of producing an interdepartmental memorandum.

6   What considerations govern the construction of a memorandum subject-heading?

7   Outline the composition of each of the three parts of the suggested structure of a memorandum.

8   What aspects of the recipient's make-up should the memorandum-writer keep in mind?

9   What communication factors would affect the style in which a memorandum is written?

10   What dangers do you think might stem from an executive sending too many memoranda throughout his organisation?

11   In what circumstances might it be necessary to send a memorandum?

The report

12   What principal functions does the report perform in organisational communication?

13   What are the differences in use and format between a routine report and an especially commissioned, investigatory report?

14   In what situations might it be appropriate to deliver an oral as opposed to a written report?

15   What are the main components common to the majority of reports?

16   What are the principal differences of format of:
(*a*)   The short informal report?
(*b*)   The short formal report?
(*c*)   The memorandum report?

17   What are the advantages of using a schematic layout in report-writing? Identify two methods for schematic referencing.

18   When would you opt for the short formal report format?

19   What do you understand by the headings:
(*a*)   'Terms of reference'?
(*b*)   'Procedure'?

20   What considerations would you bear in mind when classifying the data collected for the Information or Findings section of a report?

21   What principal features of style should the report-writer adopt when writing a report?

22   How has the introduction of the word processor in offices affected the production of reports?

Summarising communication

23   In what ways are summarising communications employed in organisations?

24   How can summaries help senior executives?

25   List some of the communication activities which require summarising techniques.

26   Identify some communication documents which specifically require summarising techniques.

27   List the ten stages of summarising.

28   What advice would you give to someone about to commence a summary?

29   What do you understand by:
'Précis of Documentation or Correspondence'?

30   When is a précis of correspondence likely to be required?

31   What is an abstract?

32   What is the 'acid test' by which the success of a summary may be gauged?

Build-up tasks and discussion topics topics

The memorandum

1 Recently there have been several instances in your company when confidential information about your products and activities has been secured by rival firms. As a result, your office administration manager has asked you to draft a memorandum to all office staff reminding them of the need for maintaining security and confidentiality at all times, and outlining the procedures they should follow.

2 A fire-drill in your offices last week revealed a number of alarming inadequacies. Many members of staff behaved quite indifferently; others seemed to have no idea of what they should do, while one or two simply did nothing at all, saying that they were 'far too busy'. As a consequence, you have been detailed to draft a memorandum to all staff aimed at emphasising the possible dangers in remaining indifferent to company regulations in case of fire and at securing an improved response.

3 As assistant sales manager you recently clashed with the deputy works manager at a marketing meeting over the need to have a batch of refrigerator motors produced by what he thought was an impossible deadline. Now you need to secure his cooperation, following complaints feedback from your sales representatives, to reduce the time taken by the Works to repair defective refrigerators sent back under warranty.

Draft a memorandum which you think will result in the repair time being reduced.

4 After deliberating on ways to overcome persistent late-coming on the part of the factory and office staff, your managing director decided three weeks ago, in the spirit of industrial democracy, to introduce clocking-in and off for *all* company staff, himself included! Your departmental office staff did not particularly welcome such an innovation, and feelings since have been running high. You have therefore been requested to draft a memorandum to departmental staff aimed at improving the situation and securing cooperation while reiterating the need for punctuality in all staff.

5 Write a critical evaluation of the four alternative memoranda on page 114 and justify which version you consider as being likely to secure the punctual submission of Jim Grainger's sales reports.

6 Analyse the three memoranda on pages 115 and 116 from the point of view of the style in which they have been composed and comment on the ways in which the choice of words and syntax is likely to contribute to the effectiveness of the memoranda.

7 Assume that you are a departmental head at Kaybond Ltd, and that your staff have indicated that they are not keen to work under the proposed flexible working hours system. (See model memorandum, page 116.)

Write a memorandum to S Kilbride, managing director, outlining the staff's response to and misgivings about the proposal and stating clearly what you consider to be the best next step.

The report

8 You work as a trainee manager in the Gifts Department of a large departmental store. Three days ago, one of the sales assistants was involved in a difficult situation with a customer who wished to make an account purchase but who did not have her account credit card with her. Following company regulations, the assistant declined to give credit, whereupon the customer became abusive. You witnessed the scene and have been called in by the departmental manager to report on what you saw.

Deliver your oral report. (Note this assignment may be carried out in a role-playing situation.)

9 Gourmet Enterprises Ltd is a company manufacturing a wide range of kitchen utensils. After initial rapid expansion, the company did badly last year. Profits slumped and its share of the market fell by a third. The company's factory is in need of investment and there has been some industrial unrest. Fortunately, the company's small but resourceful research unit has just developed and patented a revolutionary new inner coating for saucepans, fryingpans etc. which enables them to be cleaned by a wipe with a cloth – thus doing away entirely with the need to wash them up. As chairman of the Board, draft that part of your annual report releasing news of this development, bearing in mind that you and your co-directors are anxious to keep your seats on the board and need to win back the confidence of the shareholders.

Before attempting this assignment collect a number of company annual reports, extracts of which often appear in newspapers. Discuss their style and tone.

10 Recently your superior, the office administration manager, expressed his dissatisfaction with the number of different ways in which your department's secretaries and typists are unilaterally producing letters and memoranda in widely differing formats.

He thinks it should be possible to standardise such formats in a way which would make a more economic use of time and human resources. At the same time he thinks that guide-lines could be established to assist new staff on an induction and familiarisation programme. The active cooperation of departmental executives would, however, be needed.

As his personal assistant, he has asked you to look into the matter and to submit a written report to him indicating the nature and extent of the problem he has perceived, together with your recommendations for implementing an acceptable and workable system for producing letters and memoranda.

Research current commercial practices and then compose an appropriate report.

11 Last week a row broke out among the office personnel in your department over the drawing up of the annual summer holiday staff rota.

In past years it has been the practice to approach senior and long-service staff first and to follow an informal and delicate 'pecking order'.

Two weeks ago, however, the senior clerical officer,

over-worked and under pressure at the time, delegated the job to a relatively new and inexperienced subordinate. Unaware of the customary procedure, he compiled a list on a 'first come, first served' basis, and then circulated the list without any consultation.

Several members of staff took exception to the way in which the rota had been drawn up and a row occurred which had the effect of polarising attitudes between senior and junior, older and younger departmental personnel.

In order to retrieve the situation and to improve departmental staff relations, your office manager has informed staff that he is currently 'looking into the matter', and has asked you, his deputy, to investigate the situation and to produce a written report for him, establishing what went wrong and why, and suggesting how the current problem may best be resolved and how an equitable procedure may best be established for the future.

Write a suitable report, adding any additional authenticating material you consider appropriate.

12 Your company, Powa Tools plc, manufactures a wide range of electric tools for the home DIY enthusiast, and is currently considering the introduction throughout its head office of a fully integrated system of desk-top micro 'intelligent' terminals linked to a mainframe computer. Such a move is intended to make the company's communications more effective, since operators of the terminals will be able to consult the computer for up-to-date information, use its word processing program and enter data into the computer's memory. Certainly this is the intention of the managing director, Mr Geoffrey Adams.

Located in the head office complex are the following departments: Research and Development, Sales, Marketing, Personnel, Accounts and Office Administration.

Currently, the head office is using a range of electronic typewriters, one stand-alone word processor in Office Administration, and three terminals connected to a mini-computer in Accounts.

As Personal Assistant to Mr Adams, you have been asked to investigate the implications of installing a fully integrated system of computer-based communications and to submit a report which Mr Adams intends to use as a basis for discussion at a forthcoming heads of department meeting. Mr Adams has posed the following questions to aid the production of the report:

(a) What is such a system likely to be good for?
(b) What couldn't it do?
(c) What would be the likely cost?
(d) Would there need to be a special unit set up to run it?
(e) What about staff training?
(f) What about security and control of information?
(g) What are likely staff reactions to such a proposal?

(h) How is the present system likely to improve on what there is at present?

Before attempting this assignment, you should interview your teaching staff for their views and suggested sources of information and, by arrangement, the staff of any local organisation which has introduced a similar computerised communication system.

Having produced your report, you may wish as a student group to role-play the heads of department meeting which Mr Adams calls.

Discussion topics

1 What do you think some executives mean when they refer to 'memo warfare'?

2 How can the proper use of the memorandum improve internal communication in organisations?

3 What advice would you give to someone new to a job involving the regular writing of memoranda?

4 What problems do you think could result from sending 'blind copies' of memoranda to an organisation's personnel?

5 Some organisations distribute memoranda which are neither signed nor initialled by their authors. Can you see any dangers arising from this practice?

6 Some senior executives consider the production of a detailed investigatory report to be one of the most demanding tasks which an executive can be given. Why do you think this might be?

7 What contributions do a precise referencing system and an indented schematic layout make to the communication of report data?

8 Why is so much store set by 'objectivity' in report-writing? Can a report ever be truly objective? Does it matter?

9 What problems do you envisage in the collection of data for an investigatory report of a controversial or delicate nature? What could the report-writer do to avoid embarrassments, confrontations or indelicacies?

10 Assignments involving summarising techniques are sometimes viewed with distaste by those deputed to undertake them. Why should this be so?

11 What do you think is the best way to acquire summarising skills?

Case study

The Bournemouth problem

'I'm getting seriously concerned about the slide in sales at Bournemouth, and from what I hear, there's also a staff problem there. I think the time has come to get to the heart of the matter. I want you to have a good look at the picture as we have it here at Head Office, and then get down there and find out what's gone wrong. Let me have a report by Wednesday week, in time for my meeting with Mr Green (the regional manager for the Southern Region). Oh, and you'd better let me have your own views on how the matter can best be put right. Now, about this draft advertisement . . .'

It was with these words that Harold Grafton, managing director of Countrywide Food Stores Ltd, briefed his personal assistant on the need for an investigatory report into the slump in sales at the Bournemouth branch.

After having carefully researched the relevant documentation at head office – sales statistics, personnel files, marketing reports and the like, and having visited the Bournemouth branch, Harold Grafton's P.A. uncovered the following information:

After a steady increase during the last five years, sales have dropped by 31% during the past nine months.

Company advertising and sales promotion has recently been criticised by a number of branch managers and divisional managers.

Customer relations at Bournemouth suffered for two months as a result of a faulty cash-register which has now been repaired.

Branch stocks are replaced by a system of drawing from a regional warehouse to ensure fresh stocks, quick turnover and avoidance of shortages.

A rival company opened six months ago a branch some three-quarters of a mile away, which has been engaging in price-cutting and extensive sales-promotion.

Mrs Harris, the branch manager, was appointed 12 months ago. Her background was sales assistant, assistant branch manager and temporary branch manager at three of your company's branches in Lincoln, Harrogate and Warrington.

A memorandum from the Central Southern Divisional Manager drew attention four months ago to the increasing demands of head office regarding the completion of a host of returns issued by various head office departments to all branches.

Telephone and customer serving techniques leave much to be desired at the Bournemouth branch.

The fixtures and fittings of the branch are old and were put in as a 'temporary' measure some three years ago.

Basically, office administration, merchandising and branch appearance are satisfactory if unremarkable.

An urban redevelopment plan is at present responsible for the demolition of 500 houses about half a mile from the branch as part of an urban renewal and rehousing scheme.

Marketing Department wrote a eulogistic report about the business potential of the area when a decision to purchase was being made three years ago.

Company branches at Poole and Christchurch are eclipsing the Bournemouth branch's turnover.

Assignment

As Harold Grafton's personal assistant, draft a suitable report according to his brief above, incorporating whatever aspects of the above information you consider relevant, and adding any appropriate, additional material you wish.

Case study

The Sherbury Leisure Centre

For several months public unrest has been growing in the town of Sherbury, county town of Wealdshire, about the lack of leisure amenities and facilities in the town, particularly for young people. A recent police report revealed that cases of vandalism had risen by 32% in the last 12 months, and teenage arrests for drunk and disorderly behaviour by 24%. Social workers have also expressed their concern about the mounting incidence of teenage alcoholism, and teenage gangs roaming the town centre and housing estates, bred as they see it, from boredom deriving from little or nothing to do in the evenings. The town's two youth clubs are oversubscribed, and there have been incidents when older teenagers have attempted to disrupt youth club activities when denied entrance.

During the past six weeks the local weekly newspaper, *The Sherbury Chronicle* has been campaigning for improvements in leisure facilities, with hardhitting editorials under headlines such as, 'Council Fuddy-duddies Forget Their Youth'. The paper has also carried a lively correspondence on the subject. Readers' views have ranged from the sympathetic to the condemnatory – 'Sherbury's years of indifference towards the needs of the young are now bearing a bitter fruit,' and, 'In my youth people were too tired from a hard day's work to worry about whether they could play ping-pong or not. As a ratepayer I fail to see why I should subsidise the indolent by forking out for some white elephant Leisure Palace!'

Some town councillors have been actively canvassing for a Leisure Centre to be built to provide what they consider as sorely lacking amenities. At a recent council meeting, Councillor James Hillingdon referred to 'the shocking state of affairs that exists when a town of this size should have nothing to offer its young people in the evening but violent films from its one cinema and the alcoholic beverages from its ten central public houses.'

Local sports clubs and associations have been making representations to councillors and to County Hall officials. Some sports enthusiasts are travelling thirty miles or more to find the amenities they seek. The existing facilities are predominantly those for outdoor sports on recreation park pitches or for a few indoor sports such as judo in the small and over-crowded Community Hall at the western end of the town. The activities which have been suggested for inclusion in any future Leisure Centre include table-tennis, badminton, basketball, tennis, swimming, judo, karate, volleyball, ten-pin bowling, snooker and billiards, gymnastics and for older members, yoga, relaxation classes and keep-fit courses, together with a club-room for darts, dominoes and other 'less strenuous pursuits'.

A rough projection has put the cost of building a Leisure Centre at £1.8m, for a centre suitable for existing needs. Two sites have been identified as suitable. The first is at the end of the Charles Bowley Memorial Recreation Park, in the town's southern suburb, and the second is a central site which would require the centre to be built as a multi-storey building. Obviously, to meet the costs the rates would have to be increased, although it might be possible to secure a grant from central government, and local sports clubs have intimated that they would group together in a cash-raising drive.

As a result of the mounting pressure to provide a Leisure Centre, Sherbury's Chief Executive has decided to form a working-party made up of representatives of the Planning, Architect's and Education departments, including the Youth and Community Officer, the Sports Advisory Office and co-opted representatives from local sports clubs and associations. He has asked this working-party to investigate the need for a Leisure Centre, to make projections as to its likely building and maintenance costs, suggestions as to its location having regard to parking and transport considerations, proposals as to the kind of activities it should house and the kind of rooms or halls it should contain. Lastly he wishes the working party to make recommendations which could be submitted to the Council. As secretary to the working party you have been asked to draft the report.

Case study

Civic catering news

Employ a vending machine . . .

Ralph Braybrook talks to Douglas Lee

We started something when we told you, in the May issue, how Lyons Maid's Russell Boorer felt about wasted potential catering sites. Douglas Lee, catering advisor to the big GKN Sankey vending machine concern, shares his views to a great extent and has entered the arena.

'What,' he asks, 'about those coach parks where 8000 or so people disgorge in a day and head straight for the toilets. Just the place for some impulse buying by people who have sat long hours in a coach.

'Look at it this way,' he says to civic caterers. 'We can help you compete on more equal terms with your commercial competitors. After all, you can employ a machine on a coach park or some similar site at no extra cost throughout the 24 hours. There is no argument with a machine about unsocial hours.

But, he hastens to say, it is no good putting in vending and leaving it at that. 'People must be more sensitive to service through a machine than through a service counter. The machine is dead, thus presentation must, if anything, attain a higher standard than normal kitchen standards.

Particularly where there is a captive audience, and where people will be using the machines day after day, a good image has to be established, he says. 'Yet people do not pay sufficient attention to customer requirements. They feel that a machine comes in and takes over and their responsibilities are at an end.'

Constant attention to the needs of the people you are feeding is essential,' he says. 'Too long vending of food has been looked upon as a second-class catering operation.'

This view was confirmed by his predecessor, Ron Lawrence, who though now in retirement, is still associated with the company. He said, 'If you give a second-class service of food through vending equipment you might just as well not bother to put the food in at all. It does not take any longer to do the job properly; in fact, it takes less because no time is wasted in catching up on mistakes. Yet it is terribly difficult to get this over to some wooden-headed caterers.'

At one time, he said, it was possible for a company like theirs to insist on certain standards.

Another essential, said Douglas Lee, is for caterers to get away from the habit of merely banging machines against a wall. A great deal depended upon environment. For example, in a sports centre, vending units should be close to the area of activity, furnishings should be good – a few well-placed seats made a lot of difference – and decor was all-important. 'If you are going to give people decent food in vending machines, you must let them eat it under decent conditions.'

There was a tendency, when aiming to save labour, to try and save everything else as well; to take automated selling to its ultimate. Saving labour did not necessarily mean becoming spartan. 'One must not become too grasping, and interchange of menu is all important.'

Given that, there was very little feeding that could not be carried out through vending machines, and much of his company's success in the past had been in basing food vending on the 'home' kitchen. On the caterer preparing the food in-house, that is. This, he said, vested direct control in the catering manager, from the point of view of portioning, price structure and quality. Though, of course, in smaller establishments, vending was based entirely on hand-snacks and beverages.

He could see a trend away from the main meal to the snack type of item, but, whether one was selling meals or hand-snacks and wrapped confectionery, it was vital to go through the same merchandising techniques.

He pointed out that, in most staff canteens, most items were provided at an overall loss. But beverages and snack items were profit makers and could ease their subsidy. 'In addition,' he asked, 'does everyone feel hungry and thirsty at the same time? That is why we like the system of open vending, where people can feel like a snack and go and get it at will.'

He foresees a great increase in leisure activity and, through vending, it was possible to feed people round the clock. Moreover, it was essential to encourage impulse buying by having, say, a snack machine next to a beverages machine. 'If they go to one it is likely they will also use the other.'

He could see instances where, at a seaside resort, for example, it would be viable to install vending for weekend trade only. After all, the machine would last longer and was costing no more. However, he added that it was of paramount importance that sites should come under frequent inspection.

He foresaw vending moving into such establishments as schools, where costs were such a problem, especially where they were multi-purpose buildings that were in use in the evenings, or in instances where senior pupils studied on their own and did not keep normal school hours.

'Give vending the first-class image it should have and there is no feeding requirement it cannot meet,' he says. And he is not averse to talking to people like yourselves about the possibilities.

Assignment

Your company, Leisure Catering Co Ltd, supplies a wide range of catering equipment to both private companies and council authorities.

Your principal, Mrs K Peterson, sales manager, has asked you to read the above article and to draft for her a summary of the business potential of vending machines in council-run leisure complexes and the educational institutions market.

Mrs Peterson is shortly to attend a meeting of representatives of the Association of County Councils. Having recently negotiated an exclusive agency with a major manufacturer of vending machines she is keen to promote their use.

Your summary should be appropriately set out and should not exceed 300 words. (N.B. Some of the reported speech in the article will need modifying.)

9 Introduction to information and data processing

Introduction

One of the major effects of Information Technology upon the world of business has been to bring into sharp focus the concept of the organisation – whether in the private or public sector – as a *system* either for manufacturing, distributing or retailing goods (or doing all three in one large operation) or for providing a service.

The concept of the organisation as a system is not new. In fact teachers of management studies have been using this notion of the organisation for many years, and before the advent of IT in business. It is convenient when handling ideas about how organisations work, and how they might work more effectively, to use the systems concept and to understand what the systems approach means and how it has been influenced and developed by the widespread introduction of the computer to process data or information.

What is meant by a system?

Firstly, it is important to keep in mind that the concept of a system when applied to organisations is primarily an abstract idea or a form of model in the human mind drawn up to explain and account for what happens in organisations. Real life is never as tidy nor as symmetrical as a systems model, with neat boxes and arrows all leading around in flawless circles or squares!

However, by looking at an organisation as a system either for manufacturing or for providing a service, a degree of clarity may be given to what are often complex processes or interactions of human beings. Let us then consider a simple model of a system, shown below.

In the model information is taken into the system where it is then absorbed and where it has an impact or effect upon either people or existing information, modifying people's understanding, attitudes or outlooks, or simply adding to the fund of available information. The processing of the input may lead to an output – a letter of complaint to an organisation will cause an investigation, perhaps spark a change in procedures, and be followed up by a letter of adjustment to rectify the complaint.

In many systems the inclusion of a feedback function is considered to be important in order for the effect of the whole process to be monitored. Consider the example on page 143 of feedback in a systems approach in the context of production.

The diagram illustrates simply a systems approach within a manufacturing environment. In addition to the input, process output and feedback phases, there may need to be a modification phase in the light of the information received from the feedback obtained. If productivity were no better despite the introduction of the new equipment and the training of operators, then an investigation of the whole process would be needed to find out what had gone wrong – whether the equipment was faulty, the staff in need of more training, or whether there was underlying resentment of the new production rates and so on. The result would be a modification at the input or process phases, to change the machine or alter the manufacturing process.

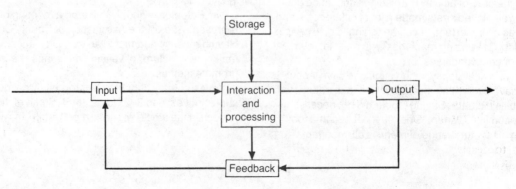

A production systems model

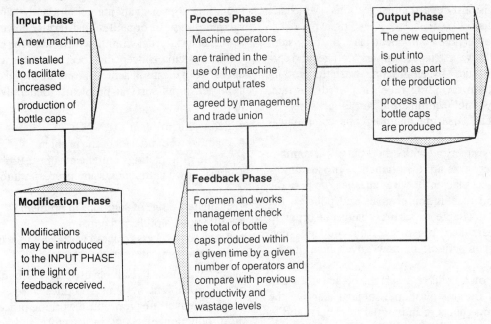

Input Phase

A new machine is installed to facilitate increased production of bottle caps

Process Phase

Machine operators are trained in the use of the machine and output rates agreed by management and trade union

Output Phase

The new equipment is put into action as part of the production process and bottle caps are produced

Modification Phase

Modifications may be introduced to the INPUT PHASE in the light of feedback received.

Feedback Phase

Foremen and works management check the total of bottle caps produced within a given time by a given number of operators and compare with previous productivity and wastage levels

"You'll soon fit in, Blenkinsop. As you can see, DP is pretty straightforward here ... "

The systems concept in organisations

The above examples illustrate how the systems approach works in relation to two commonly occurring situations – the processing of information in organisations and the introduction of a new manufacturing process in a factory. In fact, the systems approach may be used to describe the entire range of activities of an organisation and the following guidelines will help to illustrate the components of a systems view of an organisation. Viewed as a system, the organisation will:

- possess defined goals which it aims to achieve through the attainment of specific objectives.
- exist within a particular environment which has perceptible boundaries.
- interact with other systems across respective boundaries – in the jargon of systems management, the system will be 'open', meaning it is subject to outside influences.
- within the system a mechanism of controls will exist with the purpose of ensuring that the pre-set goals are attained and counter-productive activity eliminated.
- the function of the control mechanism is to maintain a stable equilibrium which promotes the attainment of the goals.
- within the system, sub-systems will exist which interact in the setting and achieving of the organisation's aims and objectives.
- also within the system will be essential variables which are needed to sustain the survival of the organisation: for example, the influx of money from goods sold, the obtaining of raw materials, plant and equipment with which to manufacture.
- once in being, the system acts to protect itself from external (or internal) activities which would prevent it from reaching its goals – for instance, the introduction of a new product by a competitor might lead to the organisation setting up a massive special sales offer on its own similar product to stifle the infant competitor at birth!

Such are the principal characteristics of the systems view of an organisation when described in the abstract. This set of characteristics may be amplified by adding to them some further features which are more easily recognisable from our previous studies:

- the organisation is logically structured in component parts – divisions, departments, sections – which act as sub-systems.
- acting together, the component parts of the system work to achieve set goals (company policies and corporate strategies) by eliminating wasteful production or action, avoiding repetition or duplication wherever possible, eliminating bottle-necks, resolving conflicts, ensuring unambiguous communication, etc.
- within the system and with others outside it communication networks are maintained to process information/data efficiently. By means of periodic reviews and redefinition of goals and policies, the organisation is able to secure change in order to meet threats and pressures from outside, e.g. increased competition or new government taxes, etc.
- by means of a collective system of activities and responses, the organisation is able to survive the comings and goings of individual members, and to adapt to social and cultural changes and developments in technology and market trends whether of a local, national or international significance.

In such terms, the systems view becomes more familiar and intelligible as a way of interpreting the activities of organisations. In the systems view, organisations are dynamic and not static. That is to say, they are always in the process of change, like a chameleon responding to ever-changing colours and shapes in its surroundings. In organisational terms, however, it is 'external or internal stimuli' which cause the changes.

The systems concept has been used for a number of years as a means of achieving a rational and objective approach to all sorts of problems. Generally it seeks to:

- define the problem
- define the boundaries of the problem
- identify interacting components of the problem
- break down components and processes into sequential parts
- evaluate a range of solutions to problem
- settle upon a preferred outcome
- refine the process to avoid waste and to achieve the most economical solution.

Such an approach can be used to reach decisions, design document systems, produce a research and development strategy, produce working procedures in the production of goods in a factory and so on. As you have almost certainly already decided, such an approach would be ideal for use in conjunction with computers – and you would be right!

The method used in data processing is to utilise a system of logic to define a problem and then to resolve it. The symbols on page 145 are used to construct an algorithm or flow-chart – terms used to describe the

The organisation's systems boundaries

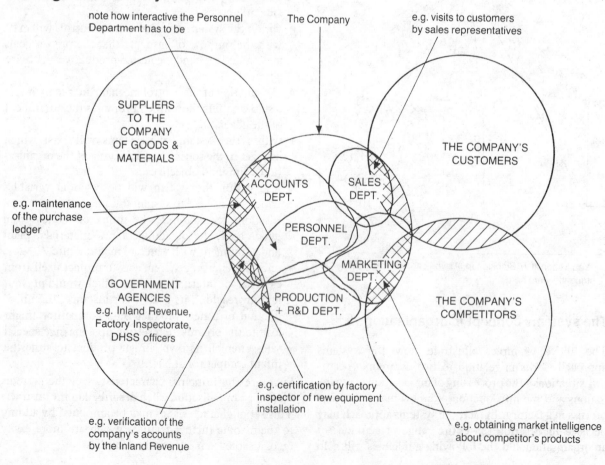

way in which 'decision paths' are put into a pattern or sequence which may be transformed into a computer program.

In effect, the flow-chart is designed in such a way that the computer may only be faced with a yes/no decision, represented by the on/off switch of electrical current. Thus computers are at bottom very simple machines – it's just that they can make an incredible number of such yes/no decisions each second!

The following are the conventional symbols used to construct a flow-chart:

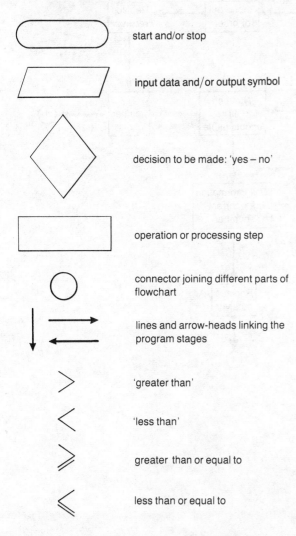

start and/or stop

input data and/or output symbol

decision to be made: 'yes – no'

operation or processing step

connector joining different parts of flowchart

lines and arrow-heads linking the program stages

'greater than'

'less than'

greater than or equal to

less than or equal to

The following are the customary processes adopted in devising a program for operation with a computer:

1 the task is discussed and the desired outcome(s) identified.

2 the task is broken down into stages in narrative English, care being taken to identify when options or choices of action occur:

    example: mixing cement
    is mixture too wet? yes/no
    if yes – add more sand/cement mix
    if no – carry on to next step

3 then the task is converted into a flow-chart using the symbols illustrated above

4 the flow-chart is converted into a computer lan-

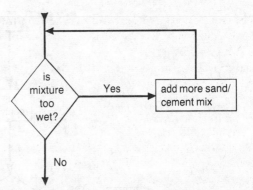

guage which can be 'fed' into the computer as a program. Some popular computer languages are BASIC, COBOL, PASCAL, FORTRAN (see page 147)

5 the program is tried out on a computer to see that it works effectively and that its logic functions correctly

6 'debugging' checks are made to identify any errors and the program is refined and 'polished' before being ready to use.

The solution to a simple problem – using a public telephone – is set out on page 146 as a flowchart or algorithm, which illustrates a number of the symbols used for the different stages.

(Source: *Pocket Guide to Programming*)

Computers and their languages

As we have already discovered, the whole basis upon which computers operate consists of their ability to interpret the high-speed switching on and off of sets or series of electronic impulses which are circulated around the computer via 'gates' which open and close. Because of this inherent characteristic, the binary code is an ideal medium in which to develop instructions which the computer could understand since it consists solely of the numbers 0 or 1 set down in a series which, in the table below, are seen to correspond to our more customary decimal number system or A–Z alphabet system:

Decimal Code	Binary Code	Alphabetic Code	Binary Code
1	1	A	1000001
2	10	B	1000010
3	11	C	1000011
4	100	D	1000100
and so on.			

Thus the letters of the English alphabet are themselves converted into the binary language which the computer can understand. The binary code is referred to as 'machine code' when used in this way. The term 'bit' in computer parlance is a contraction of the label 'binary digit' which refers to a single 0 or 1, and the term 'byte' or 'bite' refers to a kind of sense group of binary digits which form letters or sub-divisions of words or symbols.

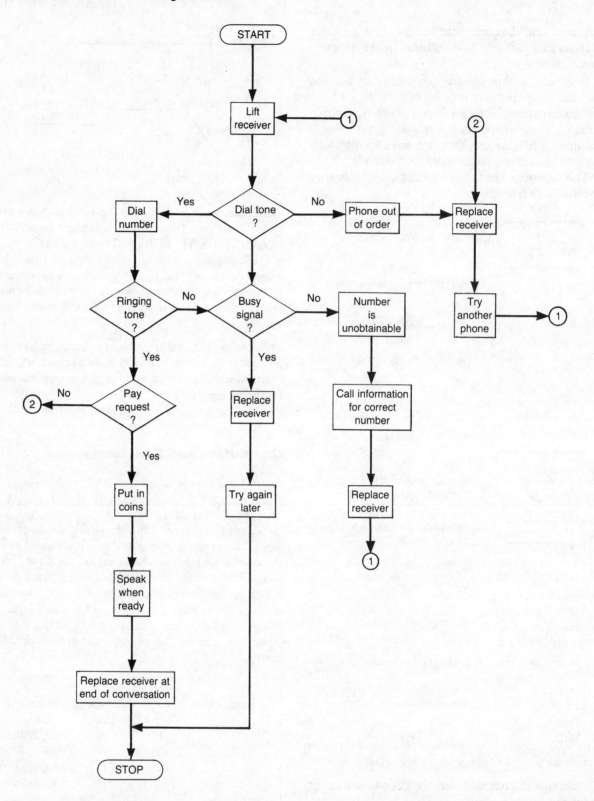

As you can imagine, it is very laborious for computer programmers to have to convert, say English, into the machine code language the computer can understand and so intermediate 'low-level' languages have been devised to process more easily and swiftly the messages and instructions that programmers write in 'high-level' computer languages which are much nearer to the English used in everyday life.

Today there are a wide range of high-level computer languages in use, together with what are called 'authoring languages' which programmers use to construct lessons or learning programs which allow the user to follow complex routes from the start to the end of the lesson on the computer's monitor, depending on whether he supplies a correct or incorrect answer. The following table provides a list of some of the more frequently encountered high-level languages.

The advantages of designing a high-level language which entirely resembles English as it is spoken or written are obvious and will provide its originator with the proverbial 'crock-of-gold' by making programming a much more readily accessible skill to millions of

Abbreviation	Meaning	Application
BASIC	BEGINNERS ALL-PURPOSE SYMBOLIC INSTRUCTION CODE	Used for general-purpose program writing, especially by computer hobbyists.
COBOL	COMMON BUSINESS ORIENTED LANGUAGE	Devised for use in commercial applications.
FORTRAN	FORMULA TRANSLATION	Developed for scientists, this language is suited to handling mathematical symbols and formulae.
PASCAL		An advanced language for general programming.
ALGOL	ALGORITHMIC LANGUAGE	For mathematical and scientific use.
LISP	LIST PROCESSING	Used particularly for applications involving text processing.

people. However, there are very extensive problems to be overcome in converting the highly complex shades and nuances of the meaning of English words and the grammar and syntax in which they are structured into a form of language which the computer can interpret and respond to. Needless to say, this is an area of research, along with voice-recognition by computers and hence operation and control by oral means, which is very much pre-occupying computer engineers and scientists today.

Summary

This section on data and information processing has sought to explain the links which exist between a systems view of organisations and the development of computerised data processing systems. Both the abstract approach to explaining how organisations work and the rational and objective logic of computer programs share a common view of work processes and operations – that inputs or incoming information can be classified and sifted in such a way that logical conclusions may be reached and actions set into motion (outputs) through the means of objective reasoning and decision-making.

Appeals to the emotion, persuasive or impassioned argument have no place in the systems view or data processing. It is therefore important in this first part of Data/Information Processing to appreciate that, while the advent of data processing and the construction of ways of processing information electronically have been instrumental in making businesses more efficient, neither computers nor their software can provide *all* the skills needed to manage organisations successfully – the 'people skills' of human relations management and the evaluative and analytical capacities of the human brain still far outreach any computer. After all, who interprets and uses the computers' conclusions – people in their working roles!

Consider instead, the many advantages which fast and virtually error-free data and information processing can bring to an organisation as a 'tool-box' for accountants, personnel managers, works managers, sales representatives and secretaries alike, which they can use to construct all sorts of information devices to aid the attainment of the organisation's goals.

Manual data processing systems

Though the use of computers – from the massive mainframe computers used in multinational companies to the relatively humble micros employed by the small traders – is daily becoming more widespread, there are still plenty of firms in business today which employ manual systems of data processing allied to a form of machine accounting. Similarly, there are still large numbers of organisations which employ the punched card technology of early computerised data processing. For such reasons, and to develop an understanding of the evolution of data processing, this section will examine the principal developments in data processing from manual systems to current integrated computer software packages for processing data.

Firstly, let us return to the concept of an office as an information processing unit. The office staff, in conjunction with office equipment, have to carry out the following operations in order to effect information processing efficiently:

1 Incoming information has to be scanned and classified – for example as having top priority or only a marginal and non-essential value.

2 It has to be allocated to the appropriate organisational section or unit for action. Here the message must be absorbed and interpreted and its impact upon any other existing information noted and suitable responses made.

3 The message must be stored or filed for future reference and in case of any future liability kept along with any subsequent and internally produced message it has prompted in case of need.

4 The effect of this incoming message in terms of modifying existing data must be understood and the existing body of organisational information modified accordingly. (In modern data processing terms this information is termed the organisation's database of information.)

5 The actions and effects caused by the incoming

Sales documentation: manual system – monthly cycle

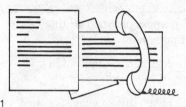

1
SALES ORDER RECEIVED
by letter, telex, telephone sales rep's order book etc.

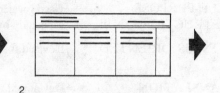

2
REQUISITION NOTE RAISED IN STORES
to authorise the movement of the goods to the Despatch Dept.

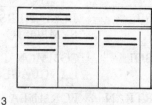

3
STOCK CARD AMENDED
the card relating to the bin or shelves where the goods are kept is amended and a reduce balance shown.

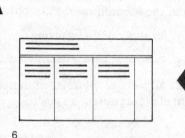

6
TRANSACTION ENTERED ON CUSTOMER'S SALES LEDGER CARD
the total of the invoice will be added to the current month's sales to the customers and a cumulative total brought forward.

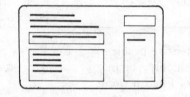

5
DELIVERY/ADVICE NOTE
this note (often an unpriced NCR copy of the invoice) is taken by the goods deliveryman to the purchaser as proof of delivery and a signature obtained.

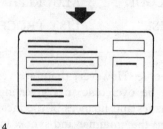

4
SALES INVOICE IS RAISED
this will include quantity, description, price and customer's account number and VAT due on the sale.

6A
CREDIT NOTE RAISED
if the goods prove faulty or damaged on arrival, then a Credit Note may be raised to refund the amount charged.

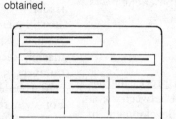

7
STATEMENT OF ACCOUNT DESPATCHED AT END OF TRADING PERIOD (e.g. MONTHLY)
this will itemise the invoices raised during the month and present a total amount due, together with any settlement discount terms which may apply. VAT will also be included with cash invoice transaction.

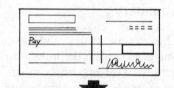

8
THE CUSTOMER WILL DESPATCH A CHEQUE IN PAYMENT WITH A REMITTANCE ADVICE NOTE
this payment is recorded within the sales ledger and the amount taken from customer's account ledger card, thus reducing the balance owing — remember that subsequent invoices will have been raised before the statement in 7 is due for payment.

PROCESS STARTS AGAIN

message must be monitored and controlled to ensure that they are effective – some feedback must be built into the information processing system.

Clearly, given such a general scenario for processing information, one of the most significant classifications to introduce is to divide messages into two sorts: those which are routine and those which are 'one-off'. For the routine kinds of message, documentary systems may be readily devised – forms may be designed which will act as media upon which to communicate and store the information, as the above diagram illustrates.

Sales order documentation the manual way

The above diagram illustrates the principal documents which are produced in a sequence or cycle to record a sales transaction with an account customer. The production of such documents is geared to whatever period of credit the account customer is given – often this is a calendar month, so that purchases made on account in one month are payable by the end of the subsequent month. In periods of high inflation, however, this period may be shortened and increased settlement discounts given to induce quick payment.

The point of sale

Often an account order is taken by sales representatives in the course of following their daily rounds to account customers, and they will have an order book in which to record the order which will be designed to relay the information needed in the stores and accounts departments. It may be that special details are needed if the order is to be tailored (in a manufacturing process) to a customer's individual requirements.

Requisitioning the goods

In larger companies (as opposed to family-run small businesses) the stores area may, in fact, be a large warehouse holding thousands or even millions of pounds worth of goods such as a Littlewoods or Grattan's mail-order warehouse. Consequently, security is very important and authorisations such as the sales requisition note are needed to permit the removal of the goods from the warehouse.

Despatching the goods

Again, in a larger firm, the sales order may be just one of a whole lorry-load of orders which are to be delivered over a region of the company and will thus form part of the despatch manager's data and be entered on to schedules for loading on to a particular vehicle and to be signed for by its driver, who in so doing signifies his personal responsibility for the goods while in transit. Such procedures also provide checks against theft and pilferage of goods within the organisation's premises.

Raising the sales invoice

This is a centrally important sales document, since it provides the details of the sale in terms of the quantity of the goods, any model or parts code number they may possess, their list-price cost, details of any discount given as part of the arrangements made between seller and customer and a confirmation of any settlement discount which the customer may rightfully deduct from the subsequent statement if it is paid within the agreed credit period.

The sales invoice will also show the correct name, address and account number of the account customer and will be given a unique number of its own in order to identify it among what may be, in the course of a year, many thousands of its fellows.

In some companies it is the practice to ensure that priced invoices are sent to an authorised member of the customer's staff – either a branch manager or an accounts member of staff to ensure that confidential selling and buying arrangements remain secret and kept from unauthorised eyes.

The delivery/advice note

For this reason, the delivery note which the delivery-man leaves with the customer while showing the quantity and description of the goods will have the priced part of the note left blank. This is possible by the use of 'no carbon required' paper forming the basis of both the invoice and the delivery note (usually printed in contrasting colours). The sales order clerk

will write or type the sales order once only on to both copies via the NCR process and the part of the delivery note which would pick up the pricing information is effectively blanked out.

Recording the transaction in the sales ledger

In the manual system, each account customer will be given a ledger card on which the essential information of the invoice will be recorded – the date of the issue of the invoice, the code of the goods and the price of the goods. The total of the invoices thus recorded in each month is shown as a cumulative total. As additional invoices are issued, so the total grows. At the end of the trading period – say each calendar month – the ledger for that month is closed off and the invoice entry totals are checked and converted into a statement of account. Note that during the month some goods may have been returned as defective or delivered in error. These credit note details are also entered on the customer's ledger and the running balance of money owing reduced accordingly.

The monthly statement

Each month, then, the customer receives what is, in effect, a summary of the previous month's trade between them and the supplier. An appropriate member of the customer's staff will scrutinise the statement to make sure that it agrees with the retained delivery and invoice notes which will have been recorded in a similar way in the customer's purchase ledger. All being well, the statement will prove an accurate representation of what is owed for the current accounting period, and having deducted any settlement discount due, the clerk will authorise the production of the cheque to be remitted in payment.

As you can imagine, in companies with many account customers, there could be a mad scramble towards the end of each month in order to prepare and despatch statements punctually. This being so, some companies spread out their accounting due dates across a month so that various customer statements are sent out during the whole month so as to avoid a regular month-end bottle-neck.

The routine cycle revolves

Of course, while the accounts department is recording the daily and weekly account sale transactions in order to send out correctly drawn up month-end statements, the sales representative is out in the field, busily acquiring fresh orders. Thus the cycle of the monthly account sales process revolves in a kind of circular motion from the despatch of one statement to the next.

However, not all account customers are regular and steady 'good payers'. Their businesses may fall upon hard times, a cash-flow problem may occur when the proprietor has insufficient cash to pay his monthly

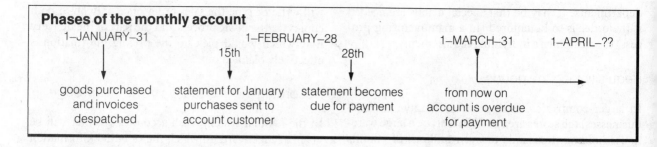

Phases of the monthly account

1–JANUARY–31	1–FEBRUARY–28		1–MARCH–31	1–APRIL–??
	15th	28th		
goods purchased and invoices despatched	statement for January purchases sent to account customer	statement becomes due for payment	from now on account is overdue for payment	

debts – he may have allowed too much credit to too many people who in turn are not paying him. The reasons for account customers not paying their debts are legion, but the data processing system must be able to act if a good account customer appears to be becoming a bad one!

Such evidence is likely to be spotted in the non-payment of the amount shown on the statement by the due date (*see* above table).

When the account rendered in the middle of February for January's purchases remains unpaid by the beginning of March, then a response will need to be made by the supplier. Clearly courteous follow-up enquiries initially are the order of the day, since a good customer may be in temporary difficulties or some good reason for the delay may be the case. If not, then no extension of credit will be justified and the first action to be taken will be for a stop to be put on the giving of any further credit – sales representative, stores manager and accounts staff will be advised to prevent any further goods being supplied on account until the money owing is paid. Further the credit status on the customer may be reviewed or terminated. Increasingly formal collection letters (*see* page 103) will be despatched to the customer, allied to visits by the sales representative to obtain payment. Ultimately the debt may require legal action to be taken either in the County Small Claims Court or through the issue of a bankruptcy writ to recover all or part of the debt.

The area of credit control in a data processing system concerned with account sales is very important – failure to act promptly and to have an established procedure to deal with bad debts may cause the suppliers themselves to go out of business.

Computerised data processing

The advent in the 1950s of the commercial computer revolutionised the ways in which data – especially routine data – could be processed in both public and private sector companies. For example, the transfer by hand of individual transactions from one accounts ledger to another could be effected in a trice and thus a great deal of time-consuming and error-prone drudgery could be taken over by an uncomplaining computer which would work round the clock!

And company accountants were not slow to see the advantages in using a computer to process much of their financial data which in the case of large organisations, amounts to millions of individual transactions annually. The uses to which computers have been put since the 1950s to process data include:

Applications of computers

Private sector organisations	Public sector organisations
maintaining company payroll	issue of rate demands and maintenance of records
controlling stock movements	maintenance of driving licence records
maintaining the accounts ledgers: sales, purchase, nominal, etc	keeping the electoral register up-to-date
processing sales orders	running the public library loans records
add-listing purchases in supermarkets and re-ordering stock automatically	maintaining Inland Revenue tax files and records
booking foreign holidays and airline flights	keeping Department of Health & Social Security records
running the national clearing banks cheque clearance systems	sending out gas, electricity and water bills and recording payments made.
and so on in a very extensive list!	

Since the early computers were introduced into commercial and public sector use, there have been a number of radical developments and improvements in the ways in which the computers employed are able to accept, store and disseminate the data involved.

The following chart illustrates some of the ways in which data was rendered into an appropriate form which computers were able to accept and read since the early days of computerised data processing:

Media for inputting and storing data

The punched tape

Here the data – i.e. details of sales invoices – was transferred into a series of punched holes placed in meaningful permutatiions and locations on the tape which the computer read and then acted upon. Special machines were designed to punch the holes on the tape and used by DP operators much like a typewriter.

The punched card

Here the concept was similar, but the cards were stronger and easier to handle. Data was punched on to the cards as a series of rectangular holes which the computer could read as letters or numbers (see opposite).

Magnetic tape

Much stronger than the paper tapes, and capable of holding very much more data, magnetic tapes became a popular input medium in the 1960s and 1970s on mainframe computers.

Data is held on the tape as dots and read by the computer very much like a hi-fi tape recorder 'reads' an audio-cassette. The major shortcoming with this method of inputting data was that it took the computer a comparatively long time to access data at either end of the tape, which has to be spun backwards and forwards at high speeds until the computer finds the right point on some 2400 feet of tape!

The floppy disc

Very familiar to the micro or personal (PC) computer user is the floppy disc which is usually $5\frac{1}{4}$ inches square and is made of a material similar to that used in magnetic tape. It is capable of retaining up to 500k bytes of data in a 'dual density, double-sided' format. Indeed some such floppy discs may hold much more information and are used by specialists.

Some computer manufacturers have designed machines to use more compact 3 to $3\frac{1}{2}$ inch 'microfloppy' discs.

The discs rotate at high speeds within the computer's disc-drive and data is read by a reading head as the disc crosses the oblong aperture in its casing.

(Some earlier versions of personal computers employed cassette tapes and tape drives to input data but this method is now largely obsolete in view of the time taken to input the data.)

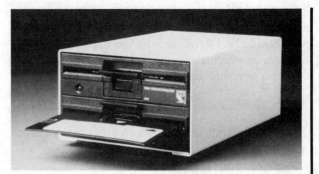

Hard discs

Mini and mainframe computers have for some time stored data on exchangeable 'hard discs' which come in a set or pack and which are capable of holding up to 300 megabytes of data. Additional megabytes of capacity are available if disc drives are linked 'on-line' in a series. They are extremely fast in retrieving data or accepting new data on to an appropriate file since the computer's read/write head can move across the spinning disc without having to read intervening information already on the computer.

Micro-computers are now capable of storing data on a form of hard disc called a Winchester disc. As the data is stored within a sealed case, the data is less likely to become contaminated or destroyed accidentally by careless use or by dust, moisture etc. Further, the Winchester disc holds much more data and works much faster than the floppy disc.

Storing and processing data via computers

Once the data has been converted into a binary code which the computer can process in as little as a nano second (one thousand millionth of a second!) it is either stored in the computer's central processing unit (CPU) or moved around the computer's microcircuitry as a means of adding, subtracting, multiplying, dividing, reconstituting, amending, extending or otherwise modifying existing data which is then stored on the computer's storage medium – floppy, hard or Winchester disc.

For example, the computer will hold on to data in its short-term storage banks until a process has been carried out, when the data will be transferred to its long-term storage medium.

In current computer configurations, data can be accessed, modified and returned to storage in extensive and far-flung networks, where a microcomputer may act either on its own as an intelligent terminal with its own CPU and inputting media, or as a terminal directly linked to a mainframe computer, capable of obtaining (subject to security clearance) any information on the mainframe and modifying it (again, subject to security and access checks). In this way, an enormous database of information may be made readily available to, say, a regional or district manager in a remote part of the country.

Processing data

There are a number of ways in which data may currently be processed. Essentially, the data is either a set of new information – new sales to an account customer, or new purchases of stock made by the company – which has to be fed into the computer's storage system to keep records up-to-date, or it is data of this type which has already been collected and held but which is to be extracted and delivered in a meaningful way so as to effect a particular company activity. For instance, the hours worked by hourly paid staff, including any overtime and bonus payments need to be computed and then any deductions for income tax and national insurance etc made, so that a pay-slip may be printed correctly indicating the gross and net pay due. On the other hand, the data to be processed may need to be fed into the computer on the spot and an immediate answer given. For example, the would-be holiday-maker in the travel agency will want to know immediately whether his or her holiday in Costa Del Mar is available from July 14 to July 28 and whether there are four seats available on outward and returning flights on those days.

Batch and real time data processing

In the case of the payroll data processing, this can be done at a suitable point in the week or month and a 'batch' of data may be processed all at once – perhaps overnight when computer use is at its lowest. The holiday-maker won't wait that long! He or she wants to know straightaway, and so airline companies and holiday tour operators have to maintain on computer a database of information about hotel accommodation, airline seats, coach seats etc, which is in a constant process of change as hotel rooms and suites are booked and seats on aeroplanes reserved. And all this has to meet customer expectations of a 'while-you-wait' service at the computer terminal in the travel agency. Such a computer operation is termed 'real-time' data processing. Once the rooms and seats have been booked, and the deposit paid, they are not available for the next travel agency clerk who interrogates the holiday tariff of, say, Sungold Holidays using Mediterranean Airlines. Similarly, once stock has been identified as having been sold and due for removal from a distributor's warehouse it is taken off the listing of available stock items and a re-order request simultaneously recorded. In this way, holiday-makers should not be disappointed in finding their airline seats occupied on arrival months later at the airport, nor should sales staff inadvertently sell the same goods twice over!

On-line data processing

This form of processing enables computer terminals to access data often held on remotely located central computers. Not only may information be acquired to read on a terminal's VDU so as to check the availability of a good or the current state of a customer's bank account or credit status, the centrally held information may also be updated in the light of a local transaction. For example, the purchase of goods on account in a departmental store may result in the details being posted directly on to the customer's computerised account file on the company's remotely located central computer. Thus on-line processing enables data to be inputted as transactions occur, rather than in a series of batch runs.

Time sharing

When on-line access is made available in large organisations, it is important that the computer's CPU is large enough to cope with dozens of terminals all operating simultaneously. This method of processing or calling up data is referred to as a 'time-sharing' system. It is only made possible by the installation of a powerful computer memory or storage unit and the computer's almost magical ability to switch at high speeds from one user to another while still maintaining overall control of total usage.

Fully integrated accounts packages

One of the far-reaching results in the design and development of computer software has been the introduction of 'turnkey' computer programs which are capable of masterminding virtually the entire accounting function within a company.

Not only will such programs process the data relating to the various accounts ledgers – sales, purchase, nominal etc, and produce trial balances and profit and loss accounts, they will also make available various financial reports to meet management accounting demands such as: what is the current average credit period in days, or what is the current cash flow situation?

The diagram of Fretwell-Downing Data Systems Limited's integrated Business Management System on page 154–5 illustrates in helpful detail how a software program can be designed to integrate certain financial operations – here the maintenance of a sales order processing, stock control and accounts system.

Notice that the program is able to provide a number of different ways of accessing the stored information:

1 via on-line review
2 via printed report
3 via outputs specifically stipulated by the user

In order to satisfy chartered accountants and the Inland Revenue, such sophisticated electronic accounting systems need to be able to demonstrate what is termed an audit trail. This is a system which can prove the integrity of the accounting effected electronically by tracing a process step-by-step from the original document (say a customer's printed order), to the payment of the arising invoice forming part of a given printed statement.

Other checking processes are maintained by the users of such programs including a system called 'check digit' verification, which is the addition of a specially calculated number on the end of, say, an account number or payroll number as a means of ensuring regularly that the system is functioning correctly.

Fretwell-Downing Data Systems Ltd

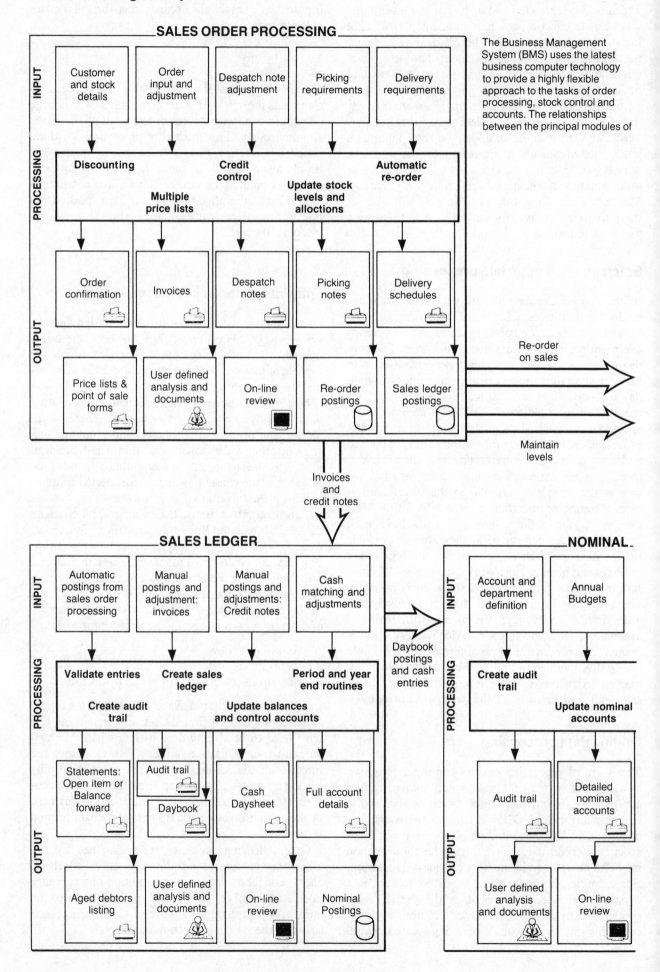

The Business Management System (BMS) uses the latest business computer technology to provide a highly flexible approach to the tasks of order processing, stock control and accounts. The relationships between the principal modules of

Sales Order Processing with Invoicing, Purchase Order Processing, Stock Control, Sales Ledger, Purchase Ledger and Nominal Ledger are illustrated here. The choice of modules and their specific components within the BMS framework can be geared to precise user requirements.

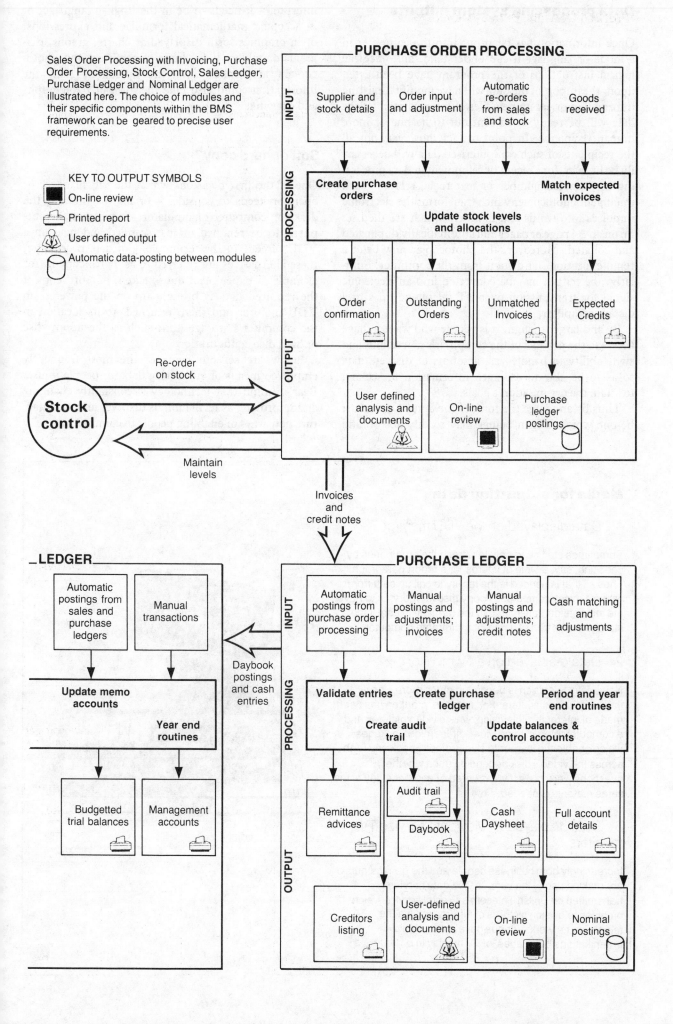

Data processing system outputs

Once information has been put into the computer in a mode or language it can understand, and once the logical instructions of the program have been acted upon, the import of the data will have modified existing information or set up new files of information and the data will be ready to be sent out to its one or more human recipients. In point of fact, however, not all the recipients of such computerised data will necessarily be human, for a recent development in data processing has enabled number or text to be relayed to an intelligent photocopier which transforms the electronic impulses into words and numbers which are then set up on an A4 page or pages and automatically duplicated and collated. Moreover, the photocopier may be at a remote location, far distant from the computer! Similarly, the output may be converted into an electronic signal for transmission over BT telephone lines to a distant computer.

By and large, though, it is people who want to have access to the product of the computer's marvellous and swift ability to handle vast amounts of discrete data so as to be able to use such information in seeking to attain the organisation's goals.

Thus by and large the form of the output data must be one which human beings may readily absorb and interpret – it needs to be in the English language, or in accepted mathematical formulae and expressions, or in graphics form displayed as charts, graphs, diagrams or tables. If facsimile transmitters and photocopiers are linked into the operation, then the information could also take the form of photographs and drawings.

Soft or hard copy?

One of the first decisions which the DP manager or operator needs to consider – or for that matter, the desk-top computer manipulator – is whether the output is to be retained or just scanned and read on a VDU screen. In the terminology of data processing, these alternatives are referred to as 'hard' copy if, for example, a paper print-out is taken, or 'soft' copy if the required data is brought up on the powered-up VDU monitor and then 'returned' to its location in the computer's storage unit, such as the floppy disc or hard disc configuration.

Below are set out some of the most frequently employed means of outputting data for people to use. Bear in mind that technology is constantly changing and improving as fertile minds discover and manufacture new ways of enabling people to communicate.

Media for outputting data

1   Data displayed on the VDU monitor

Sometimes staff need only to refresh their memories by checking, say, a table of figures, or a report paragraph. Thus all that is needed is the facility to call up data from within a micro-computer's floppy disc memory, or to have the information transmitted to the terminal in use, if the storage unit is part of a mini or mainframe computer.

2   Data displayed on a TV monitor

Nowadays television is becoming much more closely involved with computers. For instance, mention has been made of interactive television, where video pictures and a computer interact to provide self-learning packages which enable the learner to skip promptly back and forth across the video's disk depending upon whether questions were correctly answered or another study of the same material is needed.

3   Data displayed on viewdata service TV monitors

Increasingly both business people and the general public are making use of the various viewdata services transmitted by British Telecom's Prestel service which provides television pictures of information via the telephone network. Various private and public organisations buy 'pages' of TV display in order to

transmit information which people are prepared to pay for. The London Stock Exchange is a good example of a vigorous market for information – prices of stocks and shares – which changes by the second.

A growing number of private companies and associations – travel agents, airlines, solicitors – are buying user facilities of private viewdata systems which make up-to-the-minute information, or swift access to large databases of information in the case of the legal profession, available on demand.

4 Television text transmission

Not to be confused with viewdata services, the BBC and IBA provide television text services respectively called Ceefax and Oracle which are available to viewers who buy television sets with the facility to receive pages of information on, say, current West End theatre productions, the latest Test Match cricket score, the latest weather forecast and so on. These systems are not interactive with the viewer.

5 Data in printed form

Many computer users require a copy of a particular set of data which can be read or referred to away from the computer's VDU. Commonly such data is transformed from electronic display into hard copy by means of a printer.

Today there are a number of different types of printer, starting with the humble dot-matrix printer, which performs on continuous stationery by producing the letters or numbers to be read as a series of dots produced on paper by a print head pressing on a continuous ribbon, much like a typewriter functions. Such printers are very hardworking and produce copy for internal organisational use.

```
THIS IS AN EXAMPLE OF DOT MATRIX PRINTING


   The dot matrix printer provides an inexpensive means of
   printing text for internal and house use.
```

When letter-quality printing is needed, say to produce a letter for despatch to a customer, a more sophisticated form of printer is used which employs a daisy-wheel to imprint the text upon the paper. Feeder mechanisms form part of such printers to enable sheets of A4 headed stationery to be processed continuously if a circular is being produced.

```
      THIS IS AN EXAMPLE OF DAISY WHEEL PRINTING

   The daisy wheel printer provides a quality printout,
   suitable for letters and documents.
```

When extensive runs of print-out are required, then the printer is likely to be a laser printer. Such printers are capable of printing at very high speeds and of automatically bursting and collating continuous stationery into multiple copies of reports etc.

6 Data photocopied

There is a wide range of photocopiers on the market today which employ the 'plain paper copying' process, also known as xerographic copying. Such photocopiers range from compact desk-top machines which require the paper to be hand-fed as single sheets, to sophisticated suites of equipment often linked to a computer or incorporating a computer in its own configuration. The facilities available across this spectrum include enlarging and reducing of copy, printing in colour, setting text by OCR (Optical Character Recognition), automatic page setting and formatting, selection of desired typeface, simultaneous copying on both sides of paper, copying in sizes varying from A5 to B4, accepting copy in electronic form direct from a computer for transforming into text etc.

Indeed, national newspapers are now produced in a continuous electronic process from the writing of the news item or copy on a VDU screen, which can display simultaneously on a split screen the relevant Reuters news service story being edited, to electronically transmitted ready copy for printing on computerised presses!

Microfiche reader

7 Data displayed on computer output on microfilm

For some time the use of microfilm and microfiche to store information on was relatively eclipsed by the focus of attention on computerised DP. However, the advent of the 'paper flood' as opposed to the promised 'paperless office' in many large electronic data processing organisations has led to heightened interest in the storage of, in particular, archival data on microfilm which is managed and made available by means of a computer controlled process by which the computer's electronic output is directly filmed as text etc on the microfilm sheets and stored until needed.

Should a further paper print copy of an individual microfilm page be required, the equipment is able to produce one.

8 Data transmitted from computer to computer/electronic device

Bear in mind that sometimes a computer's output may not take the form of text, number or graphics which people can read.

In order to effect electronic mail processes and message switching or 'packet switching' (a means of sending large chunks of message very quickly along telephone lines) so that far-distant computer terminals can pick up transmitted messages, then the output mode will often take the form of electronic impulses or signals routed along British Telecom or Mercury wires of fibre-optic lines. The British Telecom Gold system is explained opposite.

Example: BT Gold at work!

1   A sales representative after her day's work in the field, sits in her hotel's lounge before dinner and keyboards into her pocket-size computer a series of messages for various head office sales staff situated some 200 miles away.

2   She then tears off the small roll of paper which has provided her with a hard copy of the messages for filing or records.

3   Next she goes to the hotel's telephone booth and connects the normal public telephone to a modem device which will convert the computer's electronic data into signals which can be transmitted along BT lines. All set, she dials the telephone number of the BT Gold computer and in a trice her messages are transmitted to the central computer's memory.

4   Each message has an electronic address and can be routed to the recipient's desk-top computer terminal. In this example it could be the Sales Manager, to seek the immediate despatch of an urgently needed large order as soon as possible the next morning.

5   Once the messages have been accepted for re-routing, the charges are recorded and the sales representative can go into dinner relaxed, knowing that her messages will be picked up and dealt with as soon as the office opens next morning – while she is off to the next customer!

The use of the modem allied to the national and international network of telecommunication services is revolutionising flexible communication, any time, anywhere.

Organising the process

Understandably, the very sophisticated software programs which often take thousands of hours to develop require a painstaking system of procedures and 'protocols' or rules of operation if they are to be maintained around the clock and from the 1st January to 31st December throughout the year. Indeed, the modern Data Processing Department will customarily be staffed night and day and senior managers are used to occasional callouts at night if, say, a local thunderstorm brings the entire DP system to a halt! Indeed, in many DP departments proud notices are displayed heralding the fact that the entire DP provision has only been (usually partially) out of action for two hours in three months! The chart below illustrates a typical computer department's organisation which is based on project development.

As you can see, the organisation requires the development of computer projects as the department's prime function. The structure of the organisational tree shows a split between project development and general maintenance operations led by two managers. On the operations side, most of the work lies in preparing the data for entry into the computer in various shifts of work. The project side, with its two team leaders and Organisation and Methods specialist, reflects the creative and analytical nature of the tasks involved in creating computer systems which will make available the kind of information which line managers in other parts of the organisation may need.

Creating a computerised DP system

As we have already discovered at the beginning of this Topic, the establishment of any system in the systems management approach requires logical and objective

Computer Department organisation based on project development

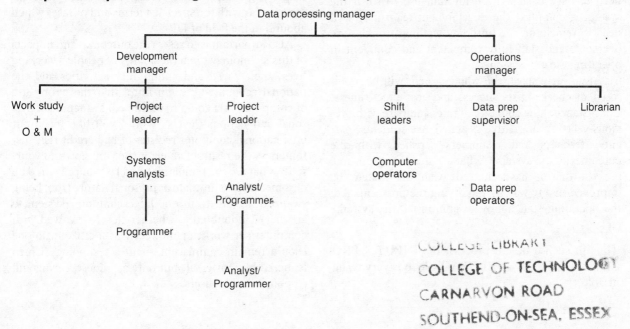

thinking so that irrational elements, waste and duplication may be avoided. This is also true in setting up a system which will use computer-processed data to perform a particular task.

We can identify six main stages in this process:

1   Performing a feasibility study
2   Detailed system analysis and design
3   System definition
4   Program specification
5   Implementation
6   Review

1   Essentially, the feasibility study establishes whether the proposed new system – say a system for marking a certain examination paper via computer – is technically possible, is administratively possible, and is educationally acceptable, and then whether the proposal is financially and administratively worthwhile in terms of its cost and the time and effort taken to put it into operation.

2   If so, a specialist at converting what managers want into a delivery system via computer, namely a systems analyst, will enter into detailed discussions with the personnel involved to design a system which will do what is needed. Such an analysis will cover who inputs what, where and how; who needs what output information and in what form, what security measures are required and what the overall time-scale is and so on.

3   Next a detailed manual – in effect the masterplan for producing the system will be designed – and the sequence of steps and processes defined carefully.

4   Having been given this 'blueprint' to work from, the programmers then proceed to write out the program in order to make the computer perform as required and to process the data as expected. In its developmental stage, various parts of the program will be tested, 'debugged' and checked against the system definition's specifications.

5   The subsequent implementation stage may require staff training prior to the installation of the system. Explanatory operations schedules and manuals will need to have been written for staff use. Also, if the system is complex, the development team may well need to remain on site until any teething troubles are overcome and staff fully competent and confident in operating the new system.

6   At an early stage, the whole system will be monitored to check on its success and cost-effectiveness. For instance, how do pass-fail rates compare with previous years or alternative systems? Are students, parents, teachers and examiners satisfied with the outcomes of the system? What are the savings in time or cost that it has achieved? Can the system be improved in any way by modifying the program? Are the operating staff happy to administer the system? etc.

Thus in such a design process, the INPUT – PROCESS – OUTPUT – FEEDBACK loop is very recognisable.

Summary

This Topic has supplied a general overview of a very important area of business and public sector activity. Most large organisations – banks, multinationals, national chainstores, county councils, central government agencies like the DHSS and DoE are totally reliant upon the reliable and prompt processing of data. Indeed, recently in the USA, a survey established that if the various national networks of computers were to break down as a result of widespread sabotage or the like, then the entire social system would be gravely affected in a matter of hours as airline and railway schedules collapsed, banks closed, supermarkets ceased trading, power-stations switched to emergency systems and so on. The central importance, then, of efficient computerised data processing upon our daily lives is not to be under-rated, nor the skills of the systems designers undervalued, simply because we grow accustomed to error-free electronic DP transactions every day.

The scope of this Topic has only been able to provide an overview of a wide range of specialisms. All being well, it has enabled you to concentrate upon the contribution which computers and allied data and information processing systems are making in the world of business and public service. Also, it has pointed to the necessary limitations of the data processing service when human relations and personal interactions are concerned. Thus it is important to keep the marvels of IT technology in perspective – without the presence of human beings to interpret and make use of the computers' work, it is entirely without value or meaning. Correspondingly, to ignore the impact of electronic data processing upon the working and daily lives of whole populations would simply be the act of a King Canute, and equally foolish and futile!

The next, important step is to build upon this introductory Topic by perhaps your pursuit of a specialist study unit on data and information processing, by pursuing the area of study through visits to organisations employing computers to process data, and by becoming familiar with the specialist terms and phrases which abound in the field of DP.

Also important is to assess the outcomes and impacts of this technology upon the quality of people's working lives, their social and community activities and the national economy. Bear in mind that the wrong use of computer data could have dire consequences at personal and national levels. Would you like to be put on a national computer register of bad credit risk customers as the result of an error, but unknown to yourself? What are the regulations and laws to prevent data of sometimes an intimate or personal nature from being swapped around from one large computer system to another? Undoubtedly, whether closely involved with computers at work, or indirectly as a citizen, no one should remain complacent about a technology which is incredibly powerful, but only as honest, caring and responsible as its users.

Mastering the jargon!

As part of your efforts to absorb the specialist terminology of IT and DP, look up the following terms and make a note of their meaning for your files:

cybernetics
a backing-file
source document
master file
control report
Electronic Fund Transfer (EFT)
grandfather tape or disc
a Kimball tag
MIS (Management Information System)
multi-font
a modem
peripheral
teletex (NOT teletext)
TEL-time data collection terminal
a closed-loop system
ASCII
audit trail
check digit
DATEL
EAN bar code
intelligent terminal
LAN (Local Area Network)
a menu-driven package
a mouse
OCR (Optical Character Recognition)
relational database
windows
electronic work study

As a means of sharing the researching load, each student in your group could take one of the above terms, research it, and then write a brief definition of about 200 words. The group as a whole could compile a card-index of such definitions for general access, or alternatively, produce a database of such terms on a word processing or database software package. In this way, a helpful source of reference during your course of study could be developed and expanded.

Build-up tasks

1   Write a paragraph of about 250 words, including any diagrams you think helpful, to explain the systems approach to problem solving.
2   Make up a check-list of the main characteristics which define an organisation in systems terms.
3   Design a flow-chart which would enable a programmer to write a program to:

either: Run a bath using a hot and cold tap to a depth of 12 inches and having a temperature of 28 degrees C.
(Assume the bath has a built-in thermometer.)
or: In front of you is a pile of bank-notes amounting to exactly £300. Randomly mixed are:

8 × £20.00 notes
10 × £10.00 notes
4 × £ 5.00 notes
and   20 × £ 1.00 notes

Design a flow-chart to separate the notes into four separate piles, one for each denomination of note.

4   First carry out your research into one of the following computer languages and then deliver a five minute talk to your group on what you have discovered about its main features and applications:

BASIC   FORTRAN   PASCAL   COBOL   LISP   PROLOG

5   As part of a concerted effort to improve its records and understanding of employment trends locally, your school/college has decided to place on computer details of the first full-time jobs which leaving students obtain. Also, to keep in touch with those who do not immediately find employment, the system needs to be able to keep track of those students looking for employment.

Design a form, together with any follow-up documentation, which you think would record the relevant information. Consider the implications of using the form as a basis for inputting the information into a computer.
6   When you have completed the task in 5 above, carry out some research into the structure and applications of database software packages used with microcomputers. Consider how such a package might be used to store and access the information obtained about the job placements of full-time students.

Compose an appropriate report, with recommendations for your head-teacher or principal.
7   Choose one of the data processing activities in the table on page 150. Through your teacher, make arrangements to interview a local manager involved in the activity – for example, the manager of a local travel agency using a real-time holiday booking service – and find out about the principles of the system, and what advantages it offers.

Then produce an illustrated article based on your findings for circulation among your group, and perhaps for publication in your school/college magazine. Remember that your readers will not be DP experts. If an alternative DP system is easier for you to access locally, then write about that one, having agreed it with your teacher. As an alternative to writing an article, you may wish to give an audio-visual aided presentation to your group of between 5 and 10 minutes.
8   Carry out your research, and then write an illustrated article for your company's house magazine (with a general readership) entitled, 'A short history of data processing: from paper tape to voice input!' Your article should begin with the developments in data processing in the late 1950s.
9   Write a paragraph on each to explain in your own words the difference between:

Batch Processing   Real Time Processing
On Line Processing   and Time Sharing

10   Assume you work in the advertising department of British Telecom and form part of a group which promotes the Prestel service. Having assembled your material, compose a circular sales letter to be sent out to senior managers of large organisations to explain the advantages of becoming a Prestel user. When you have completed a draft of your letter, find out how the merging process works which combines the body of a letter with

various filed names and addresses on a word processor and in small groups, set up one of the circular letters to be merged with ten names and addresses you have put on the mailing file of the WP mailshot package.

11   Assume that you work in the Records Department of a national building society. You have been asked to find out how 'Computer Output On Microfilm' works as a means of setting up an archive system for large numbers of documents, some of which may need to be accessed fairly regularly and, on occasion, copied on to paper for management reference.

Having undertaken your research, you have been requested to submit a report outlining the salient features of the system and its possible suitability for the Records Department. Compile a suitable report.

12   You are the personal assistant of the very busy National Sales Manager of Nordic Office Equipment Limited. The company employs some 50 sales representatives throughout the UK calling on companies of all sizes and in widespread locations. The Sales Manager has just heard of the British Telecom Gold message switching system via computer. He has given you a brief to do two things:

(a) to compose a factsheet outlining the service's main features on not more than two sides of A4 in typescript, set out for easy reading

(b) to produce a 10 minute audio cassette describing the BT Gold's major features and advantages that he can listen to in his car on the way to the annual Sales Conference of the sales force. This year's theme is:

Achieving Greater Efficiency!

13   Your company, Supaswift Computer Services Limited, is a computer services bureau which undertakes a varied range of work for small business, such as preparing weekly payroll and associated documentation for auditing records, processing market research statistics, analysing sales by product etc.

In order to meet 'one-off' requests for programs which will 'drive' individualised data processing requests, your firm employs a number of computer programmers under the supervision of a systems analyst. Also, there are a number of junior staff whose function it is to input data into the computer in various forms, according to the needs of particular jobs.

Firstly, carry out your research into the major responsibilities of:

a systems analyst
a computer programmer
a data preparation operator

Then, compose a suitable advertisement for insertion in the local press to attract suitable applicants for *one* of these posts.

In consultation with your tutor, you may, having been supplied with further information, wish to produce the job specification associated with the advertisement you choose to devise, as well as a simulated job description. Before doing so, however, find out what sort of firms in your locality provide the kind of service outlined in this task and try to base your documents on an actual, existing job.

Discussion topics

1   Has the advent of widespread use of data processing systems in manufacturing, retailing and service industries like banking brought only benefits to the consumer? In your view, are there still any shortcomings to be set right or improvements to be made?

2   Is there any real point in using the systems approach to describe the functions of organisations, or does it lead to over-simplification on a massive scale?

3   Is there a danger of the extensive application of DP techniques leading to the deskilling of jobs and the demotivation of employees on a large scale? What might be done to avoid this tendency – if indeed you agree that it exists?

4   What changes are likely to occur in larger organisations as a result of the comprehensive introduction of DP processes, when the managing director and departmental heads can obtain all the information they need at the press of a button?

5   What new and – as yet – untried applications of DP can you anticipate as being 'just around the corner'?

6   'Nowadays people have to put up with computers and DP because they're supposed to cut costs! But off the record everyone'll tell you they'd much rather get back to dealing with people face-to-face. Come back the good old days – all is forgiven!'

Is this just a soured view of modern IT effects on interpersonal communication practices, or is there a grain of truth in the cynicism expressed?

Case study

What are you reading these days?

In your school/college, thanks to the generosity of the Parents and Teachers Association (PTA) and Board of Governors, an annual allocation of some £5000 has been promised for the next five years in order to improve the range and currency of the books in the library.

This financial support has been particularly welcomed by the head/principal because the nature of the curricula of the courses being studied is currently undergoing radical change – due in no small part to the impact of Information Technology in fields such as business studies, engineering, food technology, science and technical design.

A proposal has been put forward to introduce a computerised system for recording the loans of books from the library. It is felt that if substantial amounts of money are to be invested in the purchase of new stocks, then some improved information ought to be made available on the lines of:

- building up a profile: what sort of student borrows what sort of book?
- what sort of books are most frequently borrowed?
- what is the frequency of borrowing of books in general? What case is there for buying multiple copies of books?

Before considering the installation of a computer and software package which might undertake this work, it is sensibly considered that a feasibility study should be undertaken to see whether the introduction of a computer system to monitor and analyse book loans is viable.

You form one of a group of 4–5 students who have been invited to carry out this feasibility study and the questions which are particularly needing answers are:

Is the installation technically feasible?

What additional time and effort would it require? Or could it make the recording of loans simpler and easier?

What are the likely costs of introducing such a provision?

What are the implications for staff training and development? Could existing library staff manage the system?

What would be the kind of information which could be obtained from the system? Would its acquisition be worth the effort and cost?

What are the estimated maintenance costs annually?

Are there any implications regarding the Data Protection Act?

In order for you to undertake this feasibility study, you will need to:

(a) through your teacher secure the goodwill and support of your librarian and head teacher/principal;
(b) elect a group leader to co-ordinate the project's work;
(c) allocate specific tasks to individual group members;
(d) agree a diary of deadlines to achieve.

The composition of the findings and recommendations of your feasibility study should be submitted to your head teacher/principal.

Case study

You'd better take a photograph . . .

Your group of 4–5 students forms a purchase analysis section reporting to the Office Administration Manager of Mercury Records Limited, a national company manufacturing long-playing records and compact discs for the pop record market. You are based in the company's head office, which comprises the following departments:

Sales   Production   Marketing   Accounts
Personnel   Distribution   Office Administration

The Office Administration Manager is currently preparing a report for the board of directors about replacing the company's ageing and obsolescent photocopiers, since the business has outgrown their capacities.

So far he has established that Sales, Accounts and Office Administration are each making approximately 500 A4 plain paper copies each day in the course of their normal activities, while Personnel and Distribution are each making some 50–100 copies each day. Marketing are in a different situation. Though their throughput is lower than that of the large user departments, they need to have such facilities as enlarging and reducing, colour printing and excellent reproduction of photographs and drawings to assist the work of the advertising staff, etc.

In the suite of the Managing Director, some highly confidential letters and documents need copying on a small scale each day for circulation to directors and departmental heads etc.

Your purchase analysis section has been given the following brief by the Office Administration Manager, Mr Bill Dawson:

I want you to find out what sort of photocopier would best meet the needs of each of the four user groups so far identified and to obtain the sales literature and current prices for two models in each category which you think would do the job. With each set of brochures I want you to produce a single sided A4 factsheet which summarises the main benefits of each of the two models you have selected, including prices, and whether these are for outright purchase or monthly rental.

I will then submit these, with my report, at the next board meeting – and remember, the directors are busy people, they'll want clear and simple information set out so that a sensible decision can be readily arrived at!

With these terms of reference in mind, in syndicate groups of 4–5 students, carry out the survey of photocopying equipment needed and produce the required factsheets and supportive brochures.

10 Oral, visual and non-verbal communication

Introduction

Our lives are moulded by the way we communicate in speech with others and man's highest artistic and technological achievements derive from his ability to communicate orally with his fellow man.

In the modern business world, the spoken word is used far more frequently in shops, offices and factories as a communication channel than are the written, numerical or visual media. In many organisations oral communication may take up 60–70% of the manager's or secretary's working day in a host of different situations:

face-to-face conversations
interviews, meetings
telephone-calls, briefings
customer reception
public address

But, in spite of the varied and extensive use of the spoken word at work, the techniques which enable people to speak and listen effectively are often taken for granted – until something goes wrong:

'I could have bitten my tongue off!'

'Better let Linda handle the negotiations – David's likely to speak first and think afterwards.'

Such comments are heard all too frequently in organisations, where the inability to use the spoken word with precision, tact or persuasion may cause unintended slights. Of course, being human, everyone is bound to make occasional mistakes – what *is* important is to learn from them by studying how to use the spoken word tactfully and effectively.

What, then, are the principal skills of effective speaking and listening?

Any message passes through six stages, from sender to receiver, from being conceived, encoded and relayed, to being decoded, comprehended and acknowledged. What characterises oral communication particularly is the rapid interchange between being a speaker and a listener when two or more people talk together. In addition, the whole process is amazingly subtle. The way in which the spoken word is transmit-ted and understood may be affected by a wide range of factors – expression, gesture, intonation, choice of words, the background to the situation, the relationship of sender to receiver and so on.

Also, the extremely rapid exchange of ideas in dialogue or conversation means that people need to 'think on their feet'. They have to consider the likely effect of what they are saying, or about to say, upon the recipient of the message and to listen actively to what is being said. In other words, oral communication requires a conscious effort, both in judging in advance the impact of what is about to be said, and in monitoring the receiver's feedback to assess how the message is being received.

The following table illustrates the skills of oral communication which the speaker and listener need to acquire:

Speaking skills
Mastery of the mechanics of speech
Logical structuring of the message
Choice of an appropriate style
Effective delivery
Awareness of the message's context
Understanding of the recipient(s)

Listening skills
Active concentration when listening
Correct interpretation of visual
   signals – expression, gesture
Sending of feedback signals

An ancient Chinese proverb runs:
'Open your mouth, that I may know you.'

Are you revealing the best parts of yourself every time you speak?

The voice in action

The process of speaking

The physical process of human speech is the result of millions of years of evolution. It requires coordination of the muscles and nerves controlling diaphragm and lungs, tongue, palate, lips, teeth, nose and 'mouth box'. Air is forced out of the lungs, past vibrating vocal chords and expelled through the nose and mouth. The sounds produced by the vibrating vocal chords are then 'moulded' into the components of human speech by a complex series of positions of lips, tongue, palate, teeth and cheeks, working together to produce vowel sounds like 'eh', 'uh', 'ooh', or consonants like 'tuh', 'buh', 'guh' or 'kuh', and so on. The process relies upon air being expelled from the lungs during speech.

Articulation and pronunciation

The process of learning to speak is imitative – babies absorb and mimic the sounds they hear around them, first from their mothers and then from their families. Later, as children, people tend to imitate the speech they hear in the streets or playgrounds they play in.

It is only in later life that we become aware of different modes of articulating or pronouncing words or expressions. Indeed, the whole topic of spoken English is a controversial one, since we naturally defend and hold to the speech patterns most deeply embedded in our consciousness. It is always the other person who has 'a plummy voice', 'speaks all lahdidah' or suffers from 'lazy speech'.

What matters more than the variations in pronunciation, however, is that people's speech should be understood – not just by a close, local circle of family and friends – but by people from geographically distant national regions, and, where the language is common, from other countries.

Thus clearly articulated expression *does* matter – not from any misapplied sense of snobbery which one social group may have for another, but simply, and essentially so that, for example, two participants in a long-distance telephone-call may understand each other and carry out actions, instructions or requests unambiguously!

The language of childhood:

S'mine! 'T'ain't!
Gotny swee's?

or its adult extensions:

Skay spoz
Thernks orfly

will, inevitably, contribute to oral communication breakdowns if personal speech habits allow words to become badly slurred, syllables clipped or omitted or vowel sounds completely modified.

Accent

One of the glories of English is the range of accents with which it is spoken internationally. Few can resist the lilt of the Scot, the soft brogue of an Irishman or the musical rhythms of the English-speaking African or West Indian. The English language would be infinitely poorer without the modifying influences of place and time which maintain English as a living language.

It is important, however, for the effective oral communicator to realise that a strong local accent which is perfectly intelligible in his or her own community may be extremely difficult for a colleague to understand who lives and works five hundred miles away. By the same token, it is a perceptive and sensitive communicator who restricts the use of his or her accent's dialect words to those who share and know them.

The area of articulation, pronunciation and accent is indeed a sensitive one. Adults tend to assume that anyone who does not share their mode of expression will not share their views and there are historical and sociological reasons why groups with different speech patterns may view each other, if not with hostility, then with caution.

Perhaps the best advice to oral communicators is to speak with their natural accent and internalised patterns of pronunciation, as long as they are sure that they are being understood and satisfied that their attachment to their way of speaking is not a cover for maintaining bad habits of speech which ignore the needs of their listeners.

Consider, for example, two versions of a receptionist paging an employee on the company's public address system:

'Will -ah Mistyeah Seempsone plee- yerse com-ah teyew re-ah-cerption-ah. Mistyeah Herndcock would-ah laik a word-ah wiyath heem.'

or,

'Wu' Mister Sums'n plees cum ah reception. Smister-ancock'd lika wordivim.'

On the one hand there is the artificial, imagined accent of 'posh speech' and on the other an ugly and slurred habit of speaking. Neither is pleasant to the ear, and both would be lucky if Mr Simpson ever arrived at reception!

Intonation and speech rhythms

Effective speaking relies, not only upon the clear articulation with which words may be pronounced, but also upon the way in which we raise or lower our voices as we speak and upon the pace of our words – whether we say them slowly and deliberately or quickly and cheerily.

Whether a spoken message is understood at all, and the way in which it is interpreted depend a great deal upon the emphasis and intonation given to its component syllables.

Consider, for example, the simple sentence:

I don't know him.

Its meaning is apparently clear and simple, yet by emphasising any one (or two) of the four words, the sentence takes on quite different shades of meaning:

(a) *I* don't know him.
(b) I don't *know* him.
(c) I don't know *him*.
(d) I *don't know* him.

In (a) the implication may be that, 'whoever does, I certainly don't' (and have no wish to). While (b) may imply that, 'while I have met him, I do not accept that I know him and do not wish to be involved in any commitment.' The emphasis in (c) may be that 'I do not consider him worth getting to know'. And (d) strongly refutes, after being pressed on the matter, any suggestion of the speaker knowing 'him'.

Moreover, by stressing the word '*know*' and raising the voice on the word 'him', the statement has not only been turned into a question:

(e) I don't *know* him?

but also carries the sense that the speaker not only knows 'him' well, but that notion of his not knowing 'him' is incredible.

The subtleties which intonation, and emphasis may bring to conveying the meaning of the spoken word are clearly evident in this one example. And, as we shall see later, such subtleties may be further enlarged by the addition of non-verbal signals such as facial expression or gesture.

One of the fascinating aspects of the spoken word is the way a speaker builds up his phrases or expressions into units of speech. Users of direct speech build up a bank, not of single words, but rather of expressions or phrases which occur frequently and which may precede or follow other such units:

. . . not at all. . . .
. . . wonder if you would mind . . .
Excuse me, please. . . .
. . . it's a matter of. . . .
. . . come straight to the point . . .

Such units of speech help to link ideas and also, because of their very familiarity act as 'pauses' while the speaker frames his next idea. Sometimes stock expressions are used by a speaker as a substitute for a sincere conversation contribution:

. . . so long as you've got your health and strength . . .
. . . none of us getting any younger. . . .
. . . takes all sorts . . .

In such circumstances these stock expressions are called clichés and are usually irritating to the listener.

In order to test the effect of intonation, emphasis, voice level and pauses upon the spoken word, consider this example:

I was térribly sórry | to hear the

news | of yóung Jím's | cár áccident. ||

How ís he? || I dó hópe | it isn't

ánything ┊ sérious.

Key: ╱ ╲ rise and fall of voice

┊ | ‖ length of pause

—— emphasised words

╱ highly stressed syllables

Much depends upon how we express ourselves in direct speech. As the above example indicates, key words and phrases are intensified by the use of emphasis, stress and a rising voice level, while the endings of speech units and sentences are indicated by the voice falling. Questions are signalled by a rise in the ending of the sentence and pauses are used partly to identify speech units, partly for breathing spaces and partly to signify the end of one sentence and the start of another. Failure in any of these areas may be interpreted as a lack of concern, or even hypocrisy in the example of Jim's accident. The human ear is extremely finely attuned to pick up inappropriate voice levels or emphases, especially when these are accompanied by facial expressions which do not match the situation.

It is not an over-statement to say that intonation, emphasis and phrasing are crucial to effective oral communication. One speaker may be described as, 'dynamic', 'a real enthusiast', 'extremely persuasive', 'very authoritative'; while another is regarded as 'dull as ditch-water', 'lacking in conviction' with the ability to 'bore the pants off' people.

Such judgments are accorded, not only about what someone has to say for themself, but how they say it. And indeed, unless the speaker wins their listener's attention with the 'how' from the outset, they may never create the climate in which to convey the 'what'!

Projection

Those people, like actors, lecturers or public speakers, who regularly communicate to large groups in theatres or auditoriums, soon feel the need to project their voices. Ensuring that one's voice carries over a wide area requires a correct posture to enable the diaphragm to function properly, an 'open' position of the head and throat to allow the voice to carry readily, and a voice pitch which helps the voice to travel. Successful voice-projection also involves taking the accoustics of hall or room into account, and in some cases will require accentuated articulation. The shy speaker must avoid speaking too softly into his chest, while the extrovert must learn to speak more slowly and take care not to batter the listeners' ears with harsh, grating tones.

Effective voice projection is particularly important in business – it is often the speaker whose voice commands attention at, say, a meeting, who frequently wins the day. Having something worth saying is one thing. Reaching one's listeners compellingly is quite another!

Practice pieces

1 Check the clarity of your vowels, diphthongs and consonants by tape-recording the following sentences by yourself:

Blue Skies Tours mean fine, warm days!

Mining underground often requires working in confined spaces.

Tempered steel displays both strength and elasticity.

Strict adherence to company regulations is essential.

Advertising is quickly becoming an integral part of people's lives.

Picking grapes is a popular choice for a working holiday.

Baking bricks is a back-breaking business!

Play back your recording and check that:
the open vowels are really open
-ed, -ing endings are not clipped
'h's' have not been omitted
's' and 'z' sounds are clear
syllables have not been slurred
consonants are clearly sounded

2 Study the following extracts from three different work situations. Consider how you would use intonation, emphasis, pauses and voice-levels to make them as effective as possible when spoken. Re-write them using the key signs employed in the 'Jim's car accident' example. Then record them on to tape and submit your version for evaluation by your group:

'I wanted to speak to you about a personal matter as you know I have been with the company now for eighteen months as far as I know my work has always been satisfactory and I feel that I have been a conscientious employee I should therefore like to ask you for an increase in my salary.

'I have called you in to discuss a most serious matter with you during the past three weeks I have received a number of complaints from customers upset by your apparent rudeness while serving them I propose to outline the circumstances of each complaint from the customer's point of view and then to ask you for your own account of what allegedly took place.'

'Charlie we're in trouble Johnson's have just phoned a large order in but they must have it by tomorrow morning I told them I couldn't promise anything until I'd spoken to you is there any chance of your fitting in another production run I'd certainly appreciate it if you could use your influence.'

3 The following passage is the closing section of a managing director's address to his Annual Sales Conference. Study it carefully and then record it on to tape for play-back analysis. Your aim should be to fire the sales representatives with enthusiasm during a difficult period:

'I know – and you know – that the company, and indeed the country, have been going through a difficult trading period. Equally, I know that the strength of Allied Products lies in its ability to meet a challenge. It hasn't been easy, and I can give you no guarantee that it will get better at all quickly. What I do know is that if anyone is going to lead the company into a better tomorrow, it is you, its sales representatives. And so my closing message to you all is: the company is proud of what you have done during a difficult year and will back you all to the hilt in the coming months; but it will only be your determination and enthusiasm which will turn the corner during the next year. I know I can rely on you!'

Check the recorded versions for the following:
audibility – clarity
delivery – pace, emphasis
commitment – sincerity
ability to enthuse
Where any version may be considered to have fallen short, try to decide the reasons for its lack of success.

4 As a means of gaining practice in using the spoken word effectively, form pairs in your student group and make a recording on audio or video equipment of one of the following situations. When the recordings have been made, play them back to the group for comment and discussion of such factors as: clarity, fluency, persuasiveness, rapport, effectiveness, etc.

Before attempting the recording, the pairs of students should make notes of their aims and objectives and of their roles or attitudes in the situation. Also, a few 'trial goes' may be needed.

(a) Choose a piece of office or school equipment which you know well and, as a salesperson, seek to sell it to a prospective customer who has to think carefully before spending money on office equipment.

(b) Sally Jones, audio-typist, is normally conscientious. Recently, however, her work has become untidy and marred by messy erasures. Her supervisor decides the time has come to tackle her on the subject!

(c) Recently, the wholesaling chain of Office Supplies Limited went over to a computerised system for rendering accounts to its credit consumers. Jim/Jane Harris, a customer of long standing, keeps getting demands to pay an account of £243.22 which he/she paid several months ago. Peter/Petra Ford is the sales representative of Office Supplies who has to take the brunt of the complaint when making a call on Jim/Jane's store.

Non-verbal communication

'So what went wrong? . . .'

'Good morning, may I help you?'

'Here's the crucial point.'

'Search me.'

'Hi, Joe, what'll it be?'

Non-verbal communication either reinforces the spoken word or acts in place of it

Non-verbal communication (NVC) is a fascinating area of study It concerns the many ways in which people communicate in face-to-face situations, either as a means of reinforcing or of replacing the spoken word. Sometimes people employ non-verbal communication

techniques consciously, at other times the process is carried out unconsciously. In many instances, the response is involuntary. A sudden shock, for instance, may result in someone draining in facial colour, opening his or her eyes wide and becoming slack-jawed.

Non-verbal communication may be divided into three main areas, with rather technical labels for readily observable activities or responses:

Kinesics

Facial expressions

smiles, frowns, narrowed eyes transmitting friendliness, anger or disbelief etc.

Gestures

pointing fingers, 'thumbs up' sign, shakes of the head, transmitting an emphasising focus, congratulations or disagreement etc.

Movements

quick pacing up and down, finger-drumming, leisurely strolling, transmitting impatience, boredom or relaxation.

Proxemics

Physical contact

shaking hands, prodding with the forefinger, clapping on the back, transmitting greetings, insistence or friendship.

Positioning

keeping a respectful distance, looking over someone's shoulder, sitting close to someone, transmitting awareness of differing status, a close working relationship or relaxed mutual trust.

Posture

standing straight and erect, lounging, sitting hunched up, leaning forward, spreading oneself in a chair, transmitting alertness and care, self-confidence (or even over-confidence), nervousness or ease.

Para-linguistics

feedback sounds of surprise or agreement of annoyance or impatience –
'uh-uh', 'whew!', 'oops!', 'tsk', 'tut-tut' etc.

A heightened awareness of what people are 'saying' non-verbally greatly assists the manager or secretary to read a situation and to act – perhaps to head off a personality clash or to calm an irate customer.

NVC and effective communication

Working successfully in an organisation requires that staff develop human relations skills by becoming more aware of how other people are reacting or feeling. Specifically, it requires the ability to 'read' a situation quickly and correctly. Though information and attitudes may be readily conveyed by means of the spoken word, the constraints of courtesy and staff relationships may result in the spoken message masking how someone is really feeling or relating. At other times, a correct interpretation of NVC signals may allow the interpreter to act positively.

For example, the sales representative who recognises that the nods, smiles and approaching movements of the prospective customer mean that he or she is won over, is able to proceed confidently to close the sale. Equally, the secretary who correctly interprets her principal's frowns and toe-tapping as he or she reads a report, may rightly decide to postpone until a more favourable moment her request for a salary increase! Moreover, the receptionist who recognises annoyance in the hurried approaching steps of a member of staff who bursts into the office, eyes narrowed, chin jutting forward and mouth down-drawn, will have the commonsense to ensure that her opening words are calming:

'I'm very sorry, Ms Jones is out at the moment. Is there anything I may do to help meantime?'

rather than exacerbating:

'Ms Jones is out. I'm afraid you'll have to call back.'

Thus the ability to recognise NVC signals and to modify responses in their light is essential to the maintenance and promotion of good human relations within an organisation as well as being a valuable tool in helping the manager, secretary or clerk to achieve objectives involving direct personal contact with others.

Expression, gesture and movements

Facial expression

The human face is capable of conveying a wide range of expression and emotion. Various parts of the face are used to convey signals:

Facial components	A range of responses
Forehead – upward and downward frowns	ACCEPTANCE
	REJECTION
Eyebrows – raising or knitting, furrowing	ENJOYMENT
	DISLIKE
Eyelids – opening, closing, narrowing	FRIENDSHIP
	HOSTILITY
Eye pupils – dilating	INTEREST
Eyes – upwards, downwards gazing, holding or avoiding eye contact	DISINTEREST
	ANGER
	LOVE
	SYMPATHY
Nose – wrinkling, flaring nostrils	JEALOUSY
	ASSURANCE
Facial muscles – drawn up or down, for grinning, teeth clenching	NERVOUSNESS
	AGREEMENT
	DISAGREEMENT
Lips – smiling, pursing, drawn in	ATTENTION
	BOREDOM
Mouth – wide open, drawn in, half-open	ACCEPTANCE
	DISBELIEF
Tongue – licking lips, moving around inside cheeks, sucking teeth	SURPRISE
	FEAR
	IMPATIENCE
Jaw/Chin – thrust forward, hanging down	FRUSTRATION
	ENVY
Head – thrown back, inclined to one side, hanging down, chin drawn in, inclined upwards	EMPATHY
	EASE
	DISCOMFORT
	ALERTNESS
	STUPOR
	PAIN
	PLEASURE
	ECSTASY
	TORMENT
	SATISFACTION
	DISPLEASURE

Though the above check-list of responses may not, perhaps, be manifested in every office or factory, it does indicate the incredible range of emotions and feelings visible in the human facial expression!

Assignment

Choose a number of varying responses from the above check-list and, from the list of facial components, make out a description of how the individual parts of the face would act together to form the particular expression for each response.

Gesture

Apart from actors, politicians and public speakers who may rehearse a telling gesture to emphasise a point, many of the gestures which people employ as they speak or listen are used unselfconsciously. When the speaker becomes excited, for example, sweeping movements of the arms or the banging of a fist into an open palm may act to reinforce what is being said. Alternatively, the propping of the head upon a cupped hand may signal that what is being said is boring and failing to interest.

Of course, some gestures are consciously and deliberately made. The car driver who points a finger to their head with a screwing motion is demonstrating what they think about the quality of someone's driving!

The range of gestures which utilise head, shoulders, arms, hands, fingers, legs and feet is indeed wide. Though frequently supporting the spoken word, gestures may either be used, consciously, to replace speech, as, for example, with the finger placed in front of the lips urging silence. Unconscious signals from the listener – the brushing of the hand across mouth and chin may be 'saying', 'I'm not sure that I go along with what is being said'. On the other hand, someone may seek to calm a meeting which is becoming heated by consciously patting down the air with both open palms which transmit the sense of, 'Steady on, let's not lose our tempers over this!'

Commonly used gestures

The following gestures are seen regularly in daily life, either reinforcing or substituting for the spoken word:

Head

nodding sideways to urge someone along
nodding up and down
shaking sideways
inclined briefly
cradled in one or both hands

Arms and hands

widely outstretched
jammed into trouser pockets
firmly folded across the chest
holding the back of the head with fingers laced
making chopping movements with the side of the hand
hands pressed together in 'praying' position
one or both hands held over mouth
flat of hand patting desk-top
hand brushing something away in the air
both hands placed open upon the chest

Fingers

running through the hair
drumming on table-top
stroking mouth and chin
stabbing the air with forefinger
clenched into a fist
manipulated in an arm-wave
patting the fingertips together with the fingers of both
    hands out-stretched
rubbing the thumb and fingers together

Legs and feet

leg and foot making kicking motion
foot or toes tapping the ground
moving legs up and down while seated

Posture

The way people 'arrange their bodies' as they stand or sit may also be extremely communicative. The candidate at interview, for example, who sits hunched into a chair with arms tight, hands clenched, and legs and feet pressed and folded together is probably 'saying' very 'loudly' to the interviewers, 'I am feeling extremely nervous.' By the same token, the interviewee who lolls and sprawls in the chair may be revealing an unpleasant over-confidence and familiarity. As a general rule, the body frame is more widely spread in a relaxed position, whether seated or standing, when someone feels at ease, and is more tightly held, with arms and legs together when discomfort, nervousness or tension is being experienced.

The ability to interpret such signals and to act as necessary to disarm or reassure is invaluable in promoting good human relations.

> ### Assignment
>
> Add to the above examples of gesture and posture and then describe the sort of messages sent through each example and identify the contexts in which they may be seen.

Communicating face-to-face

Face-to-face communication is the oxygen in the life-blood of business and public service organisations. Despite the efficiency and speed of modern telecommunications – essential in their way – there is no totally acceptable substitute for people talking and reacting in close, direct contact. How often at work are sentiments expressed such as:

'Pop into my office and we'll talk it over.'

'I'm sure we can thrash this out round a table.'

'I'm glad I've bumped into you, Jane, I'd like your opinion on . . .'

Communicating face-to-face embraces a wide variety of situations:

private discussions in offices
encounters in corridors
conversation over lunch in staff restaurants
taking part in meetings
selling across the sales counter
explaining on the factory floor
discussing in the large open office
speaking at conferences
questioning at interviews

Courtesy

The effective communicator is always courteous. Avoid:
interrupting,
contradicting,
'showing off' to impress others,
making someone 'look small',
losing your temper,
being condescending,
showing boredom or impatience.

Listening

Failing to listen to someone is not only a grave discourtesy, but also may result in your looking silly or making a *faux-pas*.

Pay attention, consider the implications of what is being said. Look at the speaker, provide him with feedback to show you are following.

Styling

Strive to ensure that the manner in which you speak is appropriate to the circumstances.

Choose your words and expressions carefully, mindful of the personalities and backgrounds of others present.

It is easy to give offence but difficult to overcome its effects.

Thinking

It is vital to think before you speak – once a statement is uttered it may be difficult to retract.

If you agree with a point, try to develop it constructively; if you disagree do not become over-assertive. Show that you can see more than one point of view.

Remember, it is better to say a little which is considered, than a lot which is superficial.

Mannerism

Avoid irritating, unpleasant or discourteous mannerisms of speech, gesture or posture.

Do not distract by 'fiddling' with a pencil, doodling or indulging in other distractions.

Timing

Choose the right moment to speak; sometimes it is better to let others have their say first.

Listen for the drop in a person's voice, look for a smile or nod which may indicate that someone has finished making a point.

Be alert for the signs a person makes when he wishes to end a conversation or interview.

Know when you have won and leave promptly!

Structuring

If others are to follow your argument and value what you say, it is important that you structure your points logically, and express them in connected phrases and sentences.

It is also essential that you do not speak for too long at a time; people will quickly reject what you have to say if you deprive them of the opportunity to have their say too!

Reacting and contributing

One of the quickest ways of alienating others is to show no reaction to what they have said. Enthusiastic agreement or determined disagreement both indicate that there is an interest and commitment present.

Ensure you make some positive contribution to the dialogue – if you have nothing to say, people will assume that you have nothing of value to contribute and may assess you accordingly.

Also, the context of the dialogue may render it formal or informal. A 'natter' over lunch will be expressed in words very different from those used at a formal appointment interview. Also, the way in which a dialogue develops will depend entirely upon its context and the relationship of its participants, who may be conversing with the aim of directing or requesting, informing or persuading, congratulating or disciplining.

Whatever the circumstances, the reason why most people prefer most of the time to communicate face-to-face is that such a medium best provides them with 'a total impression' in a way that written communication or telephone calls do not. This impression derives not only from what is being said, but from the whole manner of a person's delivery, including non-verbal communication factors. Moreover, the medium permits instant feedback, the means of asking snap questions and of, sometimes, obtaining prompt answers!

In face-to-face contact many 'tools' of communication are working in concert: intonation of the voice, facial expression, gesture, posture and movement, all of which provide a much fuller and often more accurate indication of the import of any given message.

Factors affecting face-to-face communication

What, then, are the most important factors which affect and influence direct personal contact? Whether the context is formal or informal and whether there has been an opportunity to plan beforehand will clearly make a difference. The following check-list includes some of the main ingredients necessary for effective face-to-face communication:

Check before you speak!

1 *Plan beforehand* – have supporting notes and documents to hand.

2 *Explore opposing points of view* – look at the situation from the other point of view and have counter-arguments ready if needed.

3 *Check out the location* of the contact – it helps to be familiar with surroundings, whether for a meeting or interview.

4 *Exclude interruptions and distractions* – frequent telephone-calls or staff interruptions prevent concentration.

5 *Consider the person or people you will be seeing* – it pays to be as well informed as possible about colleagues, associates or customers, and to know 'what makes them tick'.

6 *Select a mode of speaking appropriate to the situation* – being over-familiar and 'chatty' or reserved and formal may prove blocks to effective communication, depending upon the context of the dialogue.

7 *Check your appearance* – dress is another way of signalling what we represent, or how we wish to be accepted.

The telephone

Telecommunications systems in general, and the telephone in particular have become indispensable tools for communicating the spoken word in business today.

Indeed, the range of telecommunications services now offered to the businessman is amazingly wide and still growing fast!

People and organisations are now linked nationally and globally by networks of satellite, radio, undersea cable and land-line which provide telephone, telex, computer and video conference links. Moreover, the extensive development of computerised telephone networks both nationally and internationally, because of fibre optics technology and computerised telephone exchanges, is resulting in the provision of a much more sophisticated telephone service, and many organisations now operate their own private network system over remote locations. The introduction of microprocessor facilities into telephone services has made possible, for example, the automatic calling of engaged numbers until a line is free, the abbreviated dialling of frequently sought telephone numbers, as well as a wide range of automatic message recording features. The near future will almost certainly bring a video-telephone service to business and domestic users.

For some time to come, however, the oral-aural telephone network will continue to be the most widely used of the telecommunications systems, and a mastery of telephone techniques is essential for those planning a career or already working in industry, commerce or government.

The first, and indeed principal factor to be borne in mind by the telephone user is that the medium is oral and aural but *not* visual! As has been already discussed in the section on non-verbal communication, one of the main benefits of face-to-face communication is being able to see facial expression, gesture and posture which help enormously to convey the significance or implications of what is being said.

Telephone users, however, often refer to the 'disembodied voice' which is much more difficult to understand and which may be prone to communication breakdowns for a number of reasons including:

the spoken message is inaudible
the spoken word is misheard
the spoken message is misinterpreted because required
    feedback is not forthcoming

To become an effective user of the telephone, therefore, requires the acquisition of specialist skills ranging from distinct articulation of the spoken word to expertise in handling sophisticated telephone equipment. Such skills are particularly important in view of the dehumanising effect which using the telephone may have on people who cannot see the person they are talking to!

The following check-list indicates the principal skills which using the telephone successfully involves:

Plan carefully what you aim to achieve from your call and what you wish to say, whether you are seeking or providing information, requesting assistance or confirmation or endeavouring to convince or persuade.

Identify what action you seek from the recipient of your call and ensure you have worked out in advance any relevant deadlines.

Organise your material. Make a checklist of what points you wish to make for instant reference and to guard against any omission – especially important when telephoning long-distance. Locate and have to hand any files or documents to which you may wish to refer. Nothing is more irritating or calculated to lose the thread of a conversation than having to break off to rummage for a letter or report.

Check the sequence of your points. Does your explanation follow a logical order? Is your approach tactful? Does your effort to persuade culminate with the most telling arguments?

Know who you need to speak to. Valuable time may be lost and frustration experienced if you are 'shunted' around a large organisation because you do not know who deals with your specific enquiry. Although this process is inevitable at times, keeping your personal telephone directory and noting both names and extension numbers will prove invaluable and save time at the switchboard.

Make sure that your call will not be affected by interruption or distracting noise which will interfere with the flow and audibility of your call.

Dial the required number carefully, or relay it to your operator clearly. Expense is often incurred by obtaining a wrong number through mis-dialling or misreading directories.

Knowing how to make and to receive telephone calls: greetings, identifications, message-taking, obtaining confirmation, providing feedback, closing the call, passing messages on.

Using the spoken voice effectively: articulation, clarity, warmth, friendliness, courtesy, charm, persuasiveness.

Employing telephone reception techniques: routing, filtering, message-taking, appointment-making, relaying information.

Planning telephone calls: organising the message, having supportive documents to hand, being aware of time and costs, synthesising essential information, ensuring the transmission and receipt of all required information.

Being fully conversant with the equipment and systems in use within the organisation: use of internal and external telephone directories, switchboard facilities etc.

Using the telephone sometimes has a dehumanising effect on people. . . .

Techniques of using the telephone

Making a telephone call costs time and money. It can also be an extremely frustrating experience if undertaken without forethought and preparation. The following guide-lines will help you to make effective use of the telephone in your working life and to use its advantages to their fullest extent:

Before telephoning

Familiarise yourself with the main telephone systems in use. It helps to know how, say, PMBX or PABX systems are used in organisations, and will save you from starting your message several times before reaching the appropriate recipient of your call.

When contact is made

Bear in mind whether you are likely to be connected to a telephone directly or via a switchboard.

Wait for an identifying greeting from the answering recipient. Return an offered greeting and identify yourself and, if appropriate, your organisation:

'Good morning, Mrs Ford of Britco Ltd speaking, I'd like to speak to Mr Jones, please.'

If you are being connected via a switchboard, the operator will ask you to hold:

'Just one moment, please, Mrs Ford,'

and will then contact the relevant extension. If Mr Jones is available to speak to you, the operator will say:

'Putting you through now,'

and you will be in contact either with Mr Jones, or his secretary. If Mr Jones has a secretary, one of her duties will almost certainly be to filter his calls, and so you should not be put off by a polite request from the secretary asking you to state the nature of your call. If it should be confidential, you may reply to such a request with a courteous:

'I should like to speak to Mr Jones personally upon a confidential matter.'

Sometimes the person you would like to speak to may be engaged or out. A decision must then be made whether to ask an assistant or secretary to pass a message on, or whether to call back later.

Once connected to your desired contact, keep the following in mind:

Do not rush your message. The recipient may be taking notes of your points.

Remember the nature of the medium. Ensure that you speak clearly and make good use of intonation and emphasis to impart friendliness, warmth, co-operation or goodwill.

Spell out any proper names or trade names. Repeat any number series or codes.

Pause fairly frequently for responses confirming that your message is being understood. Seek such feedback if it is not forthcoming:

'Have I made that clear?'

Check your notes as you speak to avoid errors or omissions.

Make notes of any arising information you receive.

Emphasise the action you desire, any urgency or deadlines to be met, at the end of your call, but remain courteous. Using the telephone effectively means retaining the goodwill of the recipient.

Seek confirmation at the end of your call that its main points have been understood.

Be brief. Using the telephone is expensive, so do not allow your call to become protracted. (Remember the times when telephoning is cheaper and make your calls during that period whenever possible.)

Always check before ringing off that you have made a note of the identity and telephone number of the person to whom you spoke. This information is invaluable if your requested action is not progressed and you have to make a follow-up call.

Be polite. Remember to thank the recipient of your call for his time, help or interest. In this way the future calls and requests you will make are much more likely to be met with cooperation.

After the call has been made

Check your notes and expand them if necessary before becoming involved in anything else. Inform any interested colleagues of any developments or results of your call. Make a note in your diary to check on any progress relevant to your call.

The ability to take an incoming telephone call efficiently is one of the most important aspects of oral communication.

The nature of the medium makes demands upon the call-taker which do not arise in face-to-face contact. Your voice and manner, for example, may provide a

'Trying to connect you.' . . . Eeny, meeny, miny . . . mo! . . .

prospective customer with his first – and perhaps only – impression of your organisation. It is therefore of the utmost importance that you develop a professional approach to answering the telephone, so that, whatever the circumstance, you are unfailingly courteous, helpful and efficient. After all, you never know who may be making the call!

Before taking a call

The roles of the switchboard operator, secretary and manager differ widely in terms of call-taking. Broadly, the operator provides a routing service, the secretary a filtering and assisting role and the manager a decision-making role, though there is, of course, a wide area of overlap in the secretarial and management functions.

Nevertheless, the following guide-lines will help you to develop a good telephone-answering technique – essential to effective communication in organisations:

Organise your working area so as to enable yourself to handle telephone calls quickly and efficiently. This means having to hand:

telephone message pad
writing implement
internal telephone directory
appointments diary

Having to hunt for a pencil and writing messages on scraps of paper is not only time-wasting, but can be potentially disastrous if important messages go astray.

Ensure you are thoroughly familiar with the telephone equipment in use within your organisation. Cutting someone off because you do no know how to transfer a call creates a bad impression and is avoidable:

As far as possible, try to ensure that when your telephone rings there is no distracting level of noise around you. In addition, you should always ensure that confidential conversations take place in confidential surroundings – even if it means calling someone back.

During the call

Anyone taking calls direct from outside lines should have a courteous identifying greeting for the caller:

'Good morning, Gourmet Restaurants, may I help you?'

It is good practice – and many firms insist upon it – that the greeting is standardised and is neither too curt nor too involved.

Staff within an organisation employing a PMBX system will know that an initial greeting has been given from the switchboard, and should offer name, designation and department in whatever combination is most appropriate:

'Mr Brown's personal assistant speaking.'

'Miss White, sales manager's secretary.'

'Johnson, County Surveyor, speaking.'

Sometimes only departments are identified:

'Accounts Department'

but it is an elementary courtesy to let a caller know to whom he is talking. Some call-takers deliberately avoid providing their identity on the assumption that if anything goes wrong they are shielded by anonymity. Such tactics are, however, quite indefensible and demean their user.

It is important to identify the caller, and in many instances his organisation. Secretaries performing filtering duties may also need to ascertain diplomatically the nature of the caller's business. Such information may then be relayed to a principal who may, or may not decide to be 'available'. Additionally, if the call is routine, it may be dealt with by the secretary, thus saving the principal's time. Over-zealousness should, however, be avoided in this regard, since it may become a prime cause of a communication block that both principal and caller may justifiably resent.

When taking the details of the call, it is vital to listen attentively. Some telephone messages are extremely important and may require instant action – after all, speed is one of the main advantages of the telephone system.

Do not hesitate to slow the caller down, to ask for spellings or to request that a point be repeated:

'Could you spell that name, please.'

'I didn't catch your last point, would you mind repeating it – it sounded important.'

Ensure that you have a telephone message pad handy and that you make it an unbroken rule to use it consis-

tently. Organisations design their own pads or obtain them from stationery suppliers. The illustration on this page shows the information generally included in such message pads.

```
┌──────────────────────────────────────────┐
│           TELEPHONE MESSAGE              │
│                                          │
│  Time: 10.30      Date: 14.6.8-          │
│  Message For: Mr. Dixon                  │
│  Caller: Mrs Jean Mills                  │
│  Address: Bella Boutiques Ltd.           │
│           14 King Street,                │
│           LONDON WC2A 4ND                │
│  Tel No.: 01-642-9461    Ext: 242        │
│  Message: Unable to make 11.00           │
│  appointment tomorrow. Will              │
│  ring back at 2.30 p.m. to               │
│  arrange another day.                    │
│                                          │
│  Message Taken By: John White            │
└──────────────────────────────────────────┘
```

Some message pads also contain boxes to be ticked to save time for routine message-taking situations.

TELEPHONED		WILL CALL BACK	
CALLED TO SEE YOU		PLEASE CALL HIM	
WANTS TO SEE YOU		URGENT	

Noting names and addresses as well as telephone numbers is important since the recipient of the message may wish to write to the caller rather than telephone back.

As the caller relates the message, make sure that you provide them with reassuring feedback:

'Yes. Quite.' . . . 'I see.' 'Oh no, it won't be any trouble' . . . 'I'm not sure I agree entirely' . . .

Remember that the caller cannot see you and needs, therefore, spoken signals to enable them to continue the message in the knowledge that it is being understood.

When you are speaking, always remember to talk clearly and distinctly. Telephone lines are sometimes bad and it is easy for words to be confused. Adopt a helpful and alert approach and use your voice to impart warmth or charm. Avoid using words or expressions which are over-familiar or slang:

'Yeah. Okay.'

'Geddaway! You're kidding!'

Keep in mind, too, that it is very easy on the telephone to become more aggressive, brusque and rude than in face-to-face situations; similarly, there is a greater tendency for the person at the other end of the line to take what you say amiss, since he or she is only *hearing* what you say.

Never allow someone near you to distract you with a gesticulation, whispered instruction or by putting some papers in front of you. Not only are such actions discourteous to you, but may result in your missing a vital point.

Do not keep the caller waiting on the line unnecessarily. Such behaviour creates a bad impression, the more so because your organisation is not paying for the call.

At the end of the call, check that your telephone message is correct by briefly repeating the main points to the caller. Bear in mind that what seems elementary in telephone technique theory is easily overlooked in practice. Moreover, once the call has been concluded, it is embarrassing to have to telephone the caller back to ask for a piece of information they have already given but which you overlooked or could not decipher from your notes. Similarly you will appear rather ineffectual to your principal if you noted a name but not an address or telephone number or time:

'There's a Mr Smith coming to see you tomorrow from a firm in Birmingham. I forgot to ask the name. . . . anyway, it's definitely tomorrow. . . .'

After the call has been made

Check that the message is clearly taken down without omissions. Pass it *directly* to its recipient or ensure its delivery by placing it prominently on their desk if they are out and remind them on their return.

Carry out any additional duties connected with the call by entering, for example, an appointment in a diary or fetching out files or documents needed for your principal to make a call on their return to the office.

Dictate or draft any memorandum or letter arising from the call, if time and priorities permit, as soon after the call as possible, while matters are still fresh in your mind.

Make a note, if applicable, in any forward planning system to ensure that progress is checked or initiated actions carried out. In this context it is important to keep in mind that most telephone calls are made to instigate action on the part of the receiver. Your own personal reputation and the image of your organisation will suffer if any expected follow-up is slow in coming or not forthcoming at all.

Reception skills

Although some people make the important duties of receptionist their full-time occupation, almost every office worker at some time or another acts as an unofficial receptionist.

'Just a minute . . .'

A customer once telephoned the book department of a large store to enquire whether a particular text had arrived which had been on order for some weeks. A young voice answers,

'I'm afraid Miss Stanshawe's at lunch.'

The caller then asked if there was any means of checking – from a goods in or order processing ledger – whether the book in question had arrived, but was met with the same response,

'Well, you see, Miss Stanshawe's at lunch.'

Whereupon the caller asked if the sales assistant would mind having a look to see if there was any sign of the book. The assistant said,

'Just a minute . . .'

After about ten minutes of waiting, the caller heard a second, young voice whisper,

'Go on. You can put the 'phone down now. He's bound to have rung off!'

What does the above situation reveal about the inadequacies of the book department's and store's management?

The skills of reception are important. You never know when you will be left to 'hold the fort' or deal with an unexpected visitor or telephone-call.

The following sections summarise the main responsibilities of reception work so that clients, customers or colleagues are left with an abiding impression of courtesy and efficiency!

The reception area

It goes almost without saying that the reception area or foyer should appear smart and well-cared for at all times. The reception area and the receptionist provide an all-important first impression of the organisation for the visitor who will inevitably make value-judgments about a firm's efficiency, reliability and modernity by what they see and hear around them upon arrival.

Consequently, foyer furniture, fixtures and fittings should always be kept well polished and dusted. Ashtrays should be frequently emptied and cleaned, and newspapers and magazines kept tidy and up-to-date – a firm which hoards old magazines may also do the same with outmoded ideas! Also, utensils for refreshments should be kept clean and readily available. Some companies provide instant hot-drink dispensers for this purpose.

Telephone situations

The following telephone situations may be used as the basis for role-playing simulation exercises or developed for group discussion and analysis purposes.

It is helpful to tape-record simulations for subsequent evaluation, or to duplicate dialogue transcriptions, for members of the group.

1 Mr Jones, an impatient, but important client, calls to speak to Mrs French, Sales Manager, who is out. Her secretary takes the call.

2 An irate customer succeeds in being connected to the General Manager of Home and Leisure Departmental Stores Ltd. He proceeds to complain vehemently about a defective television set he purchased from his local branch and the company's failure to rectify matters.

3 A prospective applicant rings in response to the current advertisement for a shorthand typist in the Office Administration Department. The Personnel Manager's secretary takes the call. Her principal is at a meeting.

4 You receive an urgent 'phone-call, as Personal Assistant to the Managing Director, from the Personnel Manager wishing to inform your principal that important negotiations with trade union negotiators have just broken down. The officers of the union are about to recommend an immediate strike with official backing if their demands for a new bonus incentive scheme are not met. The Managing Director is with a client company discussing a new product.

5 The Personal Assistant of the County Treasurer receives a telephone call from one of the Treasurer's personal friends who insists on speaking to him. He is at an important meeting and has left instructions that he does not wish to be disturbed. The friend maintains that he wishes to speak to him upon a personal and confidential matter and will not, apparently, be put off.

6 The secretary of the Chief Buyer of Smartahomes Building Contractors Ltd, receives a call from a Sales Representative wishing to speak to the Chief Buyer about a new line. The Buyer tells you, the assistant, to handle the call.

7 As the manager of a selling organisation, you are engaged upon the telephone with an important but extremely long-winded customer. What techniques could you adopt to end the call without seeming discourteous?

8 You are trying to obtain a number to make an urgent call but you keep getting a wrong number. What do you do?

Desk tops and working surfaces, including workbooks and documents should always be kept clean and tidy and clear of clutter or personal belongings. In addition, the whole of the foyer area should be tastefully decorated and well-lit; and the caring receptionist will take pains to ensure that seasonal flower arrangements provide a pleasant, eye-catching feature.

In short, the reception area should always seem as though it had just been prepared for the next visitor – who is *always* a VIP!

The receptionist

Smartness, alertness, courtesy and initiative are the watchwords of the good receptionist. Top-flight organisations hand-pick their reception staff because they realise how important their functions are, whether in public/customer relations, message-relaying or security.

The receptionist should take a pride in his or her appearance: well-pressed clothes, well-groomed hands, attractive make-up or clean-cut features as well as carefully dressed hair will certainly not go unnoticed and communicate a great deal by themselves! Even more important is a ready smile and friendly turn of phrase – even in the middle of a crisis or at the end of a long day. In fact, the whole manner and bearing of the receptionist should clearly communicate at all times the kind of corporate (or company) image which the organisation wishes visitors to receive and hold in their minds.

The receptionist's job skills

In terms of job skills, the receptionist needs to be an expert in a variety of areas. Firstly, the telephone switchboard system must be thoroughly learned, so that in-coming and out-going calls are quickly and flawlessly dealt with. The receptionist must also be able to 'keep cool' when lights are flashing and three visitors arrive simultaneously!

The receptionist must also take pains to get to know as many members of staff as possible, so that a personal touch may be added to routine communications:

'Good morning Mr Charlesworth, I have Miss Watkins on the line for you.'
'. . . Just one moment, I'll see if Mr Foster is available. He deals with our stationery.'
'Would you mind taking a seat? Miss Jones, the Managing Director's personal assistant will be down in a moment to take you to his office.'

or to deal with an emergency:

'Could you get Mr Weston, security superintendent, to reception at once please. I'm having difficulty with a caller who appears to be drunk!'

In the course of the job, the receptionist must know how to use a wide range of reference books and directories – the firm's internal telephone index, British Telecom telephone directories, Kelly's Directories, rail and airline timetables will certainly be among them. Receptionists may also have to transfer appointments made by staff into their own diary for future reference. This means they will be aware of all expected visitors and for reasons of security they may be required to record the arrival and departure times of all callers. No potential industrial spy or unwelcome visitor should be allowed to roam around design offices, laboratories or workshops unaccompanied.

Some firms expect the receptionist to maintain records of all outgoing telephone calls, so that they may be charged to the appropriate department. Moreover, telephone calls or callers may result in the receptionist having to take messages to be passed to relevant members of staff. And in case the receptionist should ever feel bored or lonely, many firms provide a telex or secretary needs to obtain answers to a number of pertinent questions:

The PA and secretary as receptionist

In many companies personal assistants and secretaries also carry out the duties of receptionist. From their outer offices, they can act as 'interceptors' of both visitors and telephone calls for the boss. In such instances, it is important for staff to remain courteous and polite – even when denying access to the principal because a visitor has called without an appointment, or because the boss just does not wish to see him!

In order to carry out such reception duties, the PA or secretary needs to obtain answers to a number of pertinent questions:

Who is the caller? Which organisation does he represent? What is the nature of his business? Is it urgent? Can I handle it or should I refer to the boss? Should I note down any particulars? Should I inform the boss of the caller's presence?

Answers to these and other similar questions need to be found before the caller may be ushered into the principal's presence or put through to their telephone extension. Throughout the process, constant tact and discretion are needed, rather than the rude bluntness of:

'What's yer name? Who d'yuh work for? And waddja want?'

Coping with the waiting visitor

Sometimes it is necessary for a visitor to be asked to wait in a reception area or outer office until the person they wish to see is free. At such times, it is the duty of the receptionist to make the visitor comfortable and to ease the waiting time with remarks such as:

'I'm sure Mr Goodson won't keep you waiting long.'

'I'll just see if Mr Goodson has been delayed . . .'

'May I offer you a cup of coffee while you're waiting?'

'Have you read this week's *Time* magazine? It's in the rack beside you. I believe there's an interesting feature on . . .'

Oral aspects of meetings

The way in which organisations have developed over recent years has resulted in the meeting being used much more frequently for decision-making and problem-solving. This has come about largely because of the pressures imposed upon business and government to adopt more participative and open styles of management and employee involvement.

Some managers feel that meetings are a poor way of arriving at decisions, preferring the process of consulting individuals and then making up their own minds. The opponents of 'management by meetings' would point to the extensive use of people's time – often with little to show for it, the cost in terms of the combined salary total per hour of those present, and the poor quality of decisions made, based on consensus and compromise. They would also refer to the tendencies of some meetings to deepen rifts between people and departments rather than to heal them. There is more than a little truth in such points of view.

Nevertheless, most organisations consider that the advantages outweigh the disadvantages. Meetings *do* tend to improve communication between people and departments by 'keeping people in the picture'. They also help people to feel involved, and to consider that their contributions matter. Moreover, when it comes to implementing decisions, those who have shared in the decision-making process are much more likely to use their influence and authority to help put into practice what has been decided in principle.

Meetings, then, both formal and informal, are used as a communications medium to:

plan	future policy, strategies
design	systems, regulations, processes
analyse	past performance, activities and problem situations
develop	new products, promotions, structures
negotiate	salaries, conditions of service, work methods
persuade	motivate personnel, explain changes

Progressive organisations also use the meeting to bring together different departments and staff to solve problems in a way which serves to integrate companies or departments and to break down traditional, sectional interests. Thus meetings may take place under the group title of:

working party
task force
study group
management committee
negotiating panel

Whether the meeting is formal and interdepartmental or informal and within a departmental section, it is likely to have aims to meet and to require the active participation of all present. In addition, although the process may not be specifically referred to, the meeting will, if it is to be successful, result in the modifying of the opinions and attitudes of at least some of those present.

Thus there is present in all types of meeting an element of persuasion or 'winning over'. This means that the participant must develop a number of skills and professional practices if he is to make a positive and effective contribution.

Being informed

It is essential that all relevant 'homework' is done before the meeting – reading minutes and reports, obtaining briefings, researching files and documents, appraising situations. Appearing misinformed or 'behind the times' invalidates the force of any contribution.

Being aware of other participants

Very few people attend meetings with entirely open minds; people may have hobby-horses, pet projects, confirmed attitudes or 'axes to grind'. They may also have 'soft spots', susceptibilities. If they are to be won over, or their support gained, then consideration will need to be given to 'where they stand' and 'what they stand for'.

Being ready for opposition

For any contribution to be accepted it must be able to withstand challenge and opposition from those with conflicting points of view. Views, standpoints and positions must therefore be critically examined and the ground prepared for answering criticisms.

Being an effective speaker

The ability to speak effectively is nowhere put to a more rigorous test than in a meeting. The following rules-of-thumb illustrate areas involving such skills:

Listen first Each meeting develops its own climate. Its temperature may become boiling or frosty. By listening and waiting, you will be able to assess not only the general climate, but also the moods and attitudes of individuals. Test the temperature first, before diving in!

See where the land lies Most meetings tend to comprise sub-groups or caucuses allied to achieve common objectives. While speaking or providing feedback, others may reveal where sympathies or antipathies lie.

Timing If your contribution is to be effective, then timing the moment to speak is all-important. Personal judgment is important here to perceive when a developed argument proposed by another is failing, or when the ground has been prepared and participants are sympathetic or amenable.

Succinctness More good ideas fall by the wayside by being 'oversold' in protracted explanations than are dismissed by reason of their brevity. Keep your points short and simple. Use any previous arguments to support your opening statement, justify your points with generally appreciated examples and stress your main contention when closing.

Involving others If other participants have shown a like-minded point of view, ensure you make reference to their contributions. In this way you will broaden the base of your approach and may win helpful allies.

Overcoming counter-arguments When people are behaving reasonably and rationally, the most convincing means of persuasion is the use of a superior argument. If, therefore, your approach seems more logical, rational and justifiable, then the opposing arguments must be analysed and shown to be inferior.

It is in this situation that human relations skills are at a premium. No one likes to see his own argument demolished or derided. Moreover, such an argument may well be the 'sheet anchor' of four people out of a committee of ten. The whole process requires, therefore, the capacity for 'gentle persuasion' rather than the brutality of the battering ram!

Loss of face One of the hurts which goes deepest and which people least forgive is when someone causes them to 'lose face' in the company of associates or colleagues.

It is deceptively easy to make someone 'look small' by treating what they have said with scorn, contempt or heavy sarcasm. Additionally, the hierarchical structure of an organisation may make it difficult for them to reply in the same vein. Some actions may make an enemy, or at least an opponent, for long after the meeting – even though nothing further may be said! Consideration for others and the ability to construct 'face-saving' formulae, approaches and remarks is one of the most important skills which those who take part in meetings need to acquire.

Integrity not obduracy Holding to a point of view generally challenged by others may require a great deal of courage and integrity, and, in general, commands respect. It is important, however, that you look objectively at your attitudes in such circumstances. Stubborn resistance to persuasion may indicate a closed mind, pettiness or even spite. The mark of the mature person is that he has the strength of personality to defer to a superior argument – graciously!

Courtesy Each participant at a meeting is inevitably being assessed by his peers. People are quick to label behaviour as boorish, arrogant or rude. Bad habits in this regard are easy to acquire by:

Interrupting someone by 'talking over them'.
Exchanging leers, winks or grins with a neighbour as a means of criticising what is being said.
Showing annoyance by 'switching off' or sulking silently.
Showing boredom by lounging or doodling.

Engaging in a conversation while someone else is talking.

Losing your temper.

Belittling others when speaking yourself.

Failing to show the chairman due respect.

Monopolising the proceedings by being long-winded.

Failing to pay attention, and then showing it.

Looking constantly at a clock or watch.

Good manners displayed by attentiveness, politeness, consideration of other points of view and respect for the rule of procedure are the hall-marks of the effective participator.

Being an effective note-taker and relayer of information

The business of any meeting is only partially concluded when it closes. For decisions to be effective, participants may either be expected to implement actions themselves, or to relay information back to their own sections or departments. Thus it is essential that the main points of the meeting are noted clearly. From such notes you may be required either to deliver an oral report to your superior, or to disseminate information informally to colleagues.

One attitude to guard against: participation in meetings provides automatic membership to a small, perhaps even élite group within an organisation. Such membership may also result in your acquiring information not generally known. It is a natural tendency, therefore, to keep such information to yourself or to release it in small portions, while enjoying the status which goes with having knowledge not given to others. Of course, some meetings deal with confidential matters and expect that members respect the fact. However, your membership of a meeting group may be to act as an information disseminator. Hoarding information is a common cause of communication breakdown, is resented by those around you and reflects insecurity rather than efficiency.

Assessment questions

The spoken word

1   Make a list of situations in which oral communication commonly occurs in organisations.

2   Outline the principal skills involved in speaking and listening effectively.

3   Explain briefly the physical process involved in the act of speaking.

4   Explain the importance of the following in using the spoken word successfully:

(a) articulation, pronunciation
(b) accent
(c) intonation, emphasis
(d) voice levels

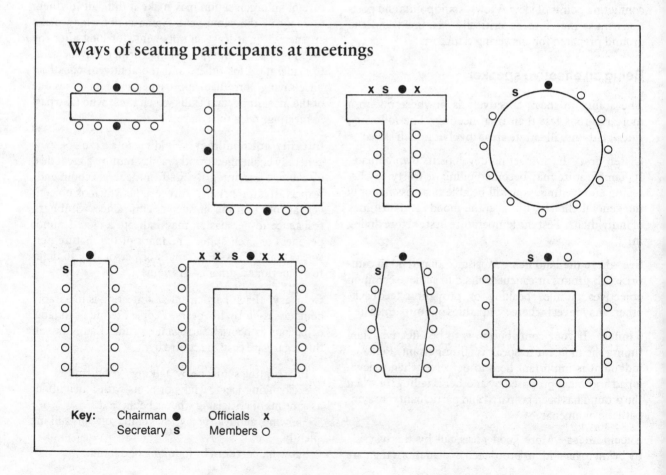

Ways of seating participants at meetings

Key: Chairman ●   Officials x
       Secretary s   Members ○

5 What is voice projection? How is it achieved? When is it necessary?

Non-verbal communication

6 What do you understand by the term 'non-verbal communication'?
7 What NVC activities are involved in:

(a) kinesics
(b) proxemics
(c) para-linguistics

8 What is the connection between non-verbal communication, speaking and listening?
9 Outline briefly the NVC signals you would associate with:

(a) nervousness
(b) anger
(c) impatience
(d) boredom

The interview

10 How would you define an interview?
11 List as many uses of the interview in organisations as you can recall.
12 Make a check-list of the preparations made before a job application interview by:

(a) the interviewee
(b) the interviewer

13 What advice could you give to an interviewee about being interviewed?

The telephone

14 What are the main differences in communicating by telephone as opposed to communicating face-to-face?
15 Find out the difference between PMBX and PABX.
16 What effects upon the telephone system have resulted from the development of public and private computerised telephone networks?
17 What advice would you give to someone new to an organisation:

(a) in taking calls
(b) in making calls?

18 Explain the difference in greeting a caller:

(a) by a switchboard operator
(b) by an internal extension user

19 Why is feedback especially important in telephone use?
20 What do you understand by the term 'filtering'?
21 List the component parts of the telephone message pad.

Oral aspects of meetings

22 What are the advantages to organisations of oral communication through meetings?
23 How does the process of communication differ between a group meeting and a one-to-one face-to-face interview?
24 What advice would you give to someone whose new job will involve him taking part in frequent meetings?
25 What constitutes discourteous behaviour at meetings?
26 What obligations does a participant of a meeting have after it is over?
27 Summarise a 'golden rule' which you think all oral communicators should follow.

Build-up tests and discussion topics

1 Make a tape-recording of members of the group discussing one of the Discussion Topics on page 182. Analyse the tape for evidence of irritating speech mannerisms. Consider how the manner of delivery of any points could be improved.
2 Enact the following situations in role-play simulation:

(a) a door-to-door salesman selling brushes or polishes
(b) a sales representative selling office stationery
(c) a sales assistant selling cosmetics

First, make notes on product details, selling benefits and prices, then sell the products to a sceptical consumer. Record the transaction on tape and then analyse the language used for persuasiveness and effectiveness.
3 Deliver a short talk to the group on one of the following:

(a) How to address a group
(b) Taking part in meetings
(c) Using the telephone effectively
(d) Coping at interviews
(e) The impact of information technology upon the work of the office

Two or more members of the group may deliver the same talk. Listening group members should assess each talk for subject-matter, organisation, delivery and effectiveness.
4 An employee in your company is persistently late in arriving for work. Several warnings have had little effect. Simulate the disciplinary interview between manager and employee called to resolve the matter. The employee is aware that others are also late in the mornings.
5 Morale in your organisation is low. Working conditions have deteriorated because of lack of investment. Managers are hard-pressed and irritable. Staff turnover is high. Productivity is low. A meeting of departmental heads has been called to suggest solutions. Simulate the meeting.
6 Two members of staff have been at loggerheads recently over what each considers as an intrusion of the other into his job. One orders office stationery, while the other supervises secretarial staff and ensures they are equipped to work efficiently. Each accuses the other of inefficiency. Matters come to a head and the manager decides to sort the matter out. Simulate any resulting interviews and analyse your solutions.
7 Make contact with a large local organisation. Find out what types of meeting it conducts, how frequently and in what areas of work. Summarise your findings in an oral report to your group.

8   Interview members of your organisation on their attitudes to taking part in meetings. (It will help to design a small questionnaire.) Collate your findings and report back orally to your group.

9   Select one of British Telecom's services. Research the service and then write an article for your organisation's house journal describing the range of the service and its current costs.

10   Find out about British Telecom's Confravision service. When you have gathered your material, draft a memorandum to be sent to senior staff outlining its advantages and how the service may be obtained.

11   Assume you work for an organisation using a PMBX system with 10 external lines and 40 extensions. Find out how the system operates and then compose a leaflet to be given to new junior staff explaining how they should use the system and practise good telephone techniques.

12   Recently you have received a number of letters from customers unhappy about the way they have been treated on the telephone when making a complaint about your firm's products. You have called a meeting of all staff to explain to them your company's new procedure for handling telephone complaints. Draft the procedure in notice form. Explain its principal points orally to assembled staff.

13   An irate customer telephones to complain about the non-delivery of goods promised faithfully two days ago. The delay has been caused by an unofficial 'go slow' in the factory. Simulate the telephone call.

14   Examine the diagrams of seating arrangements for meetings. Decide which plan would be most appropriate for which sort of meeting. Suggest any short-comings in any of the seating plans illustrated. (See p 180.)

15   Simulate a committee meeting of your student association. Discuss any of the following agenda items:

(a) Increasing student participation
(b) Extending the scope of activities
(c) Voluntary help in the community
(d) Organising a special event for charity

16   Tape-record one of the discussions from the Discussion topics list. Analyse the progress of the discussion and its conclusions. Establish how far arguments were rationally based and how far emotionally biased. Try to establish the quality of the conclusions reached. Make notes of the proceedings. Deliver an oral report to someone who was not present; ask him or her to validate it against the taped transcript.

17   Write an article for the *Receptionists' Quarterly Journal* about non-verbal communication and how the ability to recognise and interpret NVC signals can help receptionists in their work.

18   Hold a discussion with your whole group. Seek to establish what the group considers to be the most important factors influencing the ability to use the spoken word successfully. Produce a report of the discussion.

19   One of the effects of electronic information technology in the office is the more frequent 'spoken word' contact between people in remote locations – via centralised dictating systems, telephone conferences or private telephone networks. With this trend in mind, draw up a set of guidelines intended for junior office staff defining what you consider to be good oral communication practice in situations which are *not* face-to-face.

Discussion topics

1   Effective oral communication techniques tend to be overlooked because people are loath to admit – even to themselves – that they are less than expert in any aspect.
2   The way a person speaks is a highly personal matter. People are best left to 'sort things out' for themselves.
3   Studying the way people communicate non-verbally is rather like hitting them below the belt.
4   Too much consideration of oral communication techniques destroys natural, unselfconscious rapport between people.
5   The interviewing process, since it is quite artificial, rarely arrives at any meaningful conclusions.
6   In the interview situation, there is, inevitably, a conflict between truth and self-projection.
7   The interview process is loaded against the reserved, quiet and introverted. Yet more often than not they may be better in the job than the brash, assertive or plausible candidate.
8   The telephone is an interrupting inconvenience in organisations far more frequently than it is a time-saving helpmate.
9   There's far too much mystique preached about using the telephone – you just pick the thing up, make contact and talk!
10   The ability to use the telephone is generally taken for granted. Yet the national bill for its misuse and abuse must run into millions.
11   Meetings are usually little more than opportunities for people to confirm their innate prejudices to each other.
12   Nothing is achieved through meetings that couldn't be done more quickly, cheaply and with much less fuss by a series of individual conversations.
13   Contributing effectively at meetings has more to do with listening than with speaking.
14   Meetings are for bureaucrats. The doers are usually out of the office, busily doing!

Case studies

Temperature soars at Freshair!

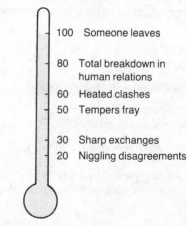

Friday 15th March had begun quietly for Jean French, personal assistant to Mr Trevor Jones, Managing Director of Freshair Conditioning Limited. This was just as well, since most of the senior managers were attending the one-day seminar on Value Added at Porchester House.

THE VALUE OF VALUE ADDED TO YOUR BUSINESS

A one-day Seminar at Porchester House, Cranbrook given by Management Consultancy Services Limited Friday 15th March 19——

PROGRAMME

0930—0945	Assembly and Coffee
0945—1000	Welcoming Address. Mr Paul Dixon, Managing Director, Management Consultancy Services Limited
1000—1100	What is Value Added? Professor Richard Mason, Faculty of Management Science, University of Wessex
1100—1115	Coffee
1115—1215	Introducing Value Added to Your Business, Gordon Hayward, MSc, ACMA, AMBIM, Management Consultancy Services Limited
1230—1330	Lunch
1345—1445	Seminar Study Groups
1500—1530	Open Forum
1530—1615	Plenary Session
1615	Closing Address Mr Paul Dixon

Freshair's progress in the field of air-conditioning and ventilation had been meteoric. The key to its success lay in the excellent design work of the research and development team and the aggressive marketing and selling of its products. The result was a growing demand for Freshair's systems – a demand which was daily increasing the already heavy workload of the small management team.

Temperature rises

Jean French was busy helping to prepare Freshair's Annual General Report when she was interrupted by the ringing of her telephone:

'Any chance of seeing Mr Jones, today, Jean?' The request came from Peter Simpson, a leading designer in the Research and Development Department.

'I'm afraid not. He's not due back from Porchester House until five this afternoon. Is there anything I can do to help?'

'Not really. Thanks all the same. It's just that Fred Bolton's coming the old acid again over the Metallia Engineering design. Thinks we can just wave a magic wand to suit his customers' slightest whims! I'll leave it for now – I'd forgotten the seminar.'

Jean frowned as she put down the telephone. It was common knowledge that Peter Simpson and Fred Bolton (Assistant Sales Manager) were like oil and water – their different personalities made it very difficult for them to blend or mix. Peter was conscientious and something of a perfectionist – Freshair's success owed a very great deal to his imaginative and effective design work. Fred Bolton, on the other hand, was an aggressive and

dedicated salesman, whose customers always came first. He and Peter Simpson had clashed frequently.

Jean felt that the problem had been made worse in recent months because Mr Rowe, who headed the Research and Development Department had tended to ignore the growing animosity between the two. 'As if we didn't have enough to do,' he'd said to her one day. 'Why can't people just get on with the job? I mean, if Peter just got on with designing and Fred with selling, things would be fine!' Jean had wondered whether she ought to discuss the situation with Mr Jones, or whether she ought to mind her own business. In the event, she had said nothing and there had seemed to be a lull. . . .

Heatwave

At 11 o'clock the phone rang again. It was Peter Simpson on the line:

'Jean? Peter. Look, Bolton has been in here again! And this time I've really had enough of his finger-stabbing and rudeness! I tell you, Jean, if somebody doesn't get him off my back – I quit! In fact, I quit anyway!'

Jean's heart sank. 'Peter, I'm sure things are not as bad as they seem to you just now. Have you spoken to Mr Rowe?'

'You're kidding! When Fred and I were having our barney just now, he bolted for his office like a frightened rabbit!'

With an effort at transmitting calmness and reassurance Jean said, 'Look, Peter, would you please just stay by your phone for a few minutes. I'm sure that matters can be resolved. I'll call you right back!' Peter reluctantly agreed.

On Jean's desk were a copy of the Value Added Seminar programme and a copy of a memorandum sent by Mr Jones the previous day to senior managers. (*See* page 184.)

'I've called you in because I'm not too happy about the way things have been going here lately. . . .'

```
                              MEMORANDUM


   To:    All Senior Managers              Ref:   TJ/JF

   From:  T Jones, Managing Director        Date:  14th March 19—


   Subject:  VALUE ADDED SEMINAR
             PORCHESTER HOUSE  15th MARCH 19—


   The following staff will be attending the one-day seminar on the subject of Value Added
   concepts in business organisations tomorrow:

        Mr T Jones     Managing Director
        Mr P Knight    Accounts Manager
        Mr D Banks     Sales Manager
        Mr S Kirby     Production Manager
        Mrs W Young    Personnel Manager

   Mr Rowe will deal with any urgent business during the day. You are requested to consult
   with your departmental head on any important matters today, so as to avoid problems
   arising during tomorrow's seminar.
```

Assignments

1 In a role-play sequence, resolve Jean French's dilemma.

2 In groups, consider the case study carefully and agree upon a plan of action which Jean French should initiate to try to save the situation. Make notes of your solution and compare it with those reached by other groups.

3 Write a detailed analysis of the problems facing Freshair. Give your own suggestions for resolving the immediate problem and your ideas on tackling the wider issues.

4 Should Jean have informed Mr Jones of the growing animosity between the two managers, or should she have considered it none of her business and kept quiet?

Follow-up assignments

1 Find out how a one-day seminar tends to be organised. Explore the idea of your group mounting one to involve other groups. Choose a topic related to communication studies. Invite visiting speakers, lecturing staff or students from your group to address the participants. Share the administrative arrangements among your group members.

2 Discuss the following topic in a general group session:

'One of a manager's most difficult tasks is to ensure that his staff work amicably together. If personality clashes are inevitable in organisations, it is his or her job to see that they are kept under control and not allowed to interfere with the organisation's objectives.'

Are personality clashes inevitable in organisations? What can managers do to prevent them from arising? Faced with one, what communication principles should a manager adopt in seeking to resolve it?

Professor Arnold's breakdown

Today is the day of Auto Components Ltd's Annual Sales Conference, which has been organised by Mr Charles Dutton, sales director. The conference is to follow this programme:

Auto Components Limited

Annual Sales Meeting

0930–1000 Assemble in coffee lounge
1000–1015 Opening Address by Mr G. Rose, managing director
1015–1100 'Profitable Retail Marketing' Professor James Arnold
1100–1145 'Better Selling Techniques' Mr Paul Hendrix
1145–1230 Open forum
1230–1400 Lunch
1400–1530 Study groups
1530–1545 Tea
1545–1630 Plenary session

The Annual Conference is taking place in the company's Conference Room at its Head Office. The time is 0935. Mr Dutton is already in the Conference Room making final arrangements with Mr Hendrix. Professor Arnold has not yet arrived.

At this moment the telephone rings in the office of Mr Dutton's personal assistant. It is Professor Arnold, ringing from a public telephone box opposite the Hare and Hounds, Barringford, a rural village some 23 miles from Head Office. When the personal assistant takes the call, Professor Arnold explains that his car has broken down; he sounds agitated and proposes to walk down into the village to see if he can find a garage or a bus.

Assignment

Either:
Discuss what action the personal assistant should take.
Or:
Simulate the telephone conversation and any ensuing telephone calls or actions.
Auto Components has a modern, extensively installed PMBX switchboard system.

'A little something I dreamed up!'

Hotex Furnishings Ltd is a company which manufactures and sells a range of furniture and fittings to hotels and restaurants. The firm was founded by Sir Alfred Gaskin, a forthright and determined person and a confirmed entrepreneur. Much of the company's success has been due to his efforts.

The personal secretary to Mr John Chesterton, managing director, has, among her responsibilities, the job of looking after bookings of the directors' dining suite, which seats 10 people, has its own drinks cabinet and is serviced by Mrs Rosina Carter, an extremely capable but rather temperamental staff restaurant manageress.

Today, Mr Chesterton has called a working lunch meeting in the dining suite for eight of the company's marketing executives at 12.45 p.m. At present he is holding an important meeting with accounts staff preparing for the annual audit.

The time is now 11.30 a.m. The telephone rings in the personal secretary's office of Mr Chesterton's suite. It is Sir Alfred on the line:

'Hello, Carol? Sir Alfred here. I'm at the Phoenix Hotel. I've been selling the directors here our new line in dining tables and chairs, and I'm pretty sure I've won them over. But it needs a few final touches. So I want you to contact Mrs Carter straight away and tell her I'm bringing six guests and myself over for drinks and lunch at about one. I shall need the dining suite, of course. You know the drill. I realise it's a bit short notice, but this could mean a really big order if they buy for their chain. See if you can get Mrs C. to pull something out of the bag. Must go now or I'll be missed!'

Assignment

Either discuss how the personal secretary should resolve the situation.
Or:
Simulate any subsequent arrangements made over the telephone.

Pulses race over communications at Pulsar!

A meeting has been called at Pulsar Electronics Ltd to discuss the proposed appointment of a Communication Officer, whose job would be to coordinate company communications. Present at the meeting are: John White, Managing Director and Chairman; Kay James, Personnel Manager; David Kean, Sales Manager; Lawrence Carr, Marketing Manager; Caroline Brooks, Office Manager; Harry Brent, Production Manager; Jean Bates, Company Secretary and Peter Short, Accounts Manager.

Chairman:
Right. Everyone's here. I think we should start. As you know, I have called this meeting to discuss the proposed appointment of a Communication Officer. The company's growth and dispersed buildings have made internal communication more difficult. It has therefore been suggested that someone working full-time to coordinate communication would improve the situation. Who would like to start the ball rolling?

Harry Brent:
I'm going to lay my cards on the table. I think the idea, though fine in principle, will never work in practice. I remember when we tried employing a trouble-shooter in the Works. The thing was a flop because the operatives still went through their union channels and management went up the traditional line.

Lawrence Carr:
Just a moment, Harry, I'm not sure a Works trouble-shooter and a Communication Officer are quite the same thing. As I see it, this new post will enable someone to coordinate areas like the house magazine, notices, internal publicity generally and to act as an advisor to senior staff – like yourself.

Peter Short:
That's all very well, Larry, but I think Harry's got a point. Without sufficient authority this new Officer will be a loose floater. Departmental heads will still keep control of any important communications.

Kay James:
Peter and Harry are both right – to a degree. As I see it, this new post is a natural for Personnel Department. After all, we already run the house magazine and are deeply committed to personnel communications.

Harry Brent:
Oho! Another lieutenant for Kay's Commandos in the pipe-line! Do I detect a take-over bid?

Chairman: (cutting in)
That was uncalled for, Harry. I wonder though whether attachment to any particular department would be appropriate in this case.

Kay James: (ruffled)
Well, so far all we've had from some quarters (looking hard at Harry) is a completely negative attitude. At least mine was a *constructive* proposal. . . .

David Kean:
In my view, I think we're all looking at this from too personal a position. Larry's right. There are a number of important functions going by the board because none of us has the time to devote to them. Obviously the job would call for tact and initiative, and clearly there would be overlap in, say, Personnel and Training. But surely the value of a new post would be to have an expert, independent and with no departmental axe to grind. I see no reason why he or she could not report to the M.D.

Caroline Brooks:
I've been sitting here listening, because I had no fixed views when I came in. If you don't mind my saying so, everything seems to be proceeding a little too fast. Surely the best approach would be to establish whether departmental heads are for or against in principle – since their cooperation would be essential – and then to draw up a job specification and description which 'a' would work and 'b' other heads would accept.

Harry Brent:
Never underestimate a woman! If *you* don't mind my saying so, Caroline, I think you're trying to push us into a quick decision before we've even had time to have a proper exploratory discussion. How can we decide in principle before we've had a chance to examine the situation fully. It's a big decision. I don't think we should rush into it. . . .

Assignment

Assess the contribution of each member.
Comment on the Chairman's role.
Suggest how you think the meeting *a:* would end and *b:* should end.
Carry on the meeting by role-play simulation.

Multi-media assignment

All out at Alumix?

Before attempting this assignment you will need to research the following: Dismissal and Grievance Procedures; Summary and Unfair Dismissal; Industrial Tribunal Procedures.

Situation

For the past three weeks, the wife of Mr Fred Jackson, a machine operator at Alumix Alloys, has been seriously ill. Fred has been very worried about her and is currently on a course of tranquillisers prescribed by his family doctor, but is still at work.

Fred operates a machine that needs constant attention, and Alumix's company regulations state that a relief operator must be summoned to take over temporarily if the machine is left for any reason. If left unminded, the machine could cause serious injury to other factory workers, and three weeks ago, Alumix had issued a works reminder about the dangers.

Feeling rather agitated, and in need of a smoke, Fred leaves his machine, thinking he'll only be away 'for a few minutes', and goes into the staff restroom. He has only been there a minute or two when he is startled by the appearance of Mr Alfred Parker, the foreman for his part of the factory. Fred becomes extremely upset and is unable to express himself very clearly. Mr Parker is known as a strict but fair man.

Mr Parker reports the absence of Fred from his machine to the assistant works manager. Both consider Fred to have been in breach of company regulations.

The management of Alumix take a serious view of the situation. Fred is summoned to the Works Manager's office, and following the company's procedures is summarily dismissed for negligence.

Fred returns to his locker in a very upset state, claiming to his friends that he was not given a chance to state his side of the case. At this stage the shop steward of Fred's trade union, the Allied Workers' Association, arrives and asks Fred to put him in the picture. The shop steward's view is that Fred has been 'unfairly dismissed', and he determines to take the matter to his branch.

Meanwhile, word of Fred's summary dismissal has spread round the factory like wildfire! The factory staff have decided to take matters into their own hands and are threatening an unofficial walk-out, claiming that Fred is being victimised. Extremely concerned, Mr Parker tries to telephone the Works Manager, but obtains no reply. He therefore, determines to ring Mr French, the company's Personnel Manager. He is out, but his Personal Assistant, Miss Sally Barnes takes the call.

The following day, the Works Committee, including trade union representatives, seeks and obtains a meeting with the management of Alumix to try to sort out the problem.

Assignments

1   Face-to-face encounter
Simulate the encounter between Fred and Mr Parker. Two of Fred's friends, taking a legitimate break enter the restroom and join in.

2   Dismissal interview
Simulate the interview between Fred and the works management personnel.

3   Briefing conversation
Simulate the conversation between Fred and the shop steward, Mr Tom Harris.

4   Telephone call
Simulate the call between Mr Parker and Sally Barnes and any subsequent action taken.

5   Meeting
Simulate the meeting between the Works Committee and management.

Several weeks pass (you may at this stage assume that the meeting between the Works Committee and management was unsuccessful). Both Alumix and the Allied Workers' Association think they have a strong case, and Fred's dismissal is taken to the local Industrial Tribunal for judgment.

6   Hearing

Having prepared a case, a management and union team simulate the hearing before the Industrial Tribunal panel.

11 Applications of Information Technology

Introduction

Over the past 150 years, the lead-time – the time it takes between making a scientific discovery and marketing its applications commercially – has been growing ever shorter. And the incredible speed with which microprocessors have been introduced into equipment in use in factories, offices, shops and warehouses, not to mention private homes is ample evidence of the eagerness with which new technologies are nowadays adopted.

In this context it is well worth recalling that the first microprocessor or 'silicon chip' was introduced commercially by an American corporation, Intel, in 1971. In just 15 years, the newly-emergent 'IT' technology has fundamentally changed production processes, office information systems, telecommunications, the workings of the mass media – newspapers, television, hi-fi etc, the way people shop, and even enabled the customers of one bank to organise their affairs from their own homes via their television screens and allied equipment!

Already the applications of Information Technology are abundant and this Topic will provide a broad overview of the current major applications in the areas of the commercial office, manufacturing company, retail distribution and service industries such as banks and solicitors' practices. It is important to keep two factors, however, firmly in mind. Firstly, with the technology developing so quickly, it is impossible to predict what amazing new products and techniques will hit tomorrow's headlines – already work is underway to introduce a 'flat-screen' electronic office desk-top which will enable managers to scan different types of information appearing before them electronically as opposed to various sheets of notepaper, photographs, or paper-based diagrams. Similarly, research into voice-activated computing proceeds apace with the proverbial rainbow's end crock of gold awaiting the first company to introduce a computer system which will respond fully to voice commands. More imminent is the introduction of optical computer operations, where the equivalent of the hard or floppy disc will be read optically. Here the advantage will be that information will be able to be stored far more abundantly in the same sort of space and accessed far more quickly.

In factories the introduction of robotics and computer aided design and manufacture (CADCAM) has been revolutionising manufacturing practices for the past 3–5 years – 'hand-made by robots' was a popular television advertising slogan of one motor-car manufacturer in the early 1980s – and now some high-tech companies are already introducing fully integrated computer-directed manufacturing operations combining the production process, the purchase and stock-control of parts, the costing and accounting functions and the despatch and distribution of the finished product!

In effect, the ordinary citizen may be forgiven for finding the extremely swift pace of technological change and innovation difficult to grasp and assimilate. Nevertheless, everyone contributing to the working life of his or her community must either meet this challenge head on and conquer it, or accept a seat on the sidelines to watch other developed countries reap the benefits which the 'post-industrial', IT led society can bring.

The second factor which must be kept firmly in mind is the need for everyone involved in IT to sustain a critical awareness of the limitations of the technology and the dangers which are implicit in it if due checks and controls are not properly maintained. Indeed, with the wonders of the technology still unfolding it almost seems presumptuous to refer to its limitations. Still, it is worth remembering that the most sophisticated computer in existence has a long way to go yet to replicate the capacities of the human brain in its reasoning, evaluating and interpretive powers. Furthermore, however capable the computer technology in operation, it remains a tool for human beings to make use of. IT is not an end in itself and we should all be careful about allowing it to reform our cultures and lifestyles in ways we may come to regret.

In sum, while becoming conversant with the major applications of IT in business and the public service, we should not allow ourselves to be over-awed by the technology nor remain passive in our attitudes to the changes it is spearheading in society in general.

A robot fits a front screen: cameras mounted on the robot head control positioning. Reproduced by kind permission of British Leyland (Austin Rover).

At the centre of IT – the computer

This section heading may appear so obvious as to scarcely be worth repeating, yet its function is to remind us of the fact that the computer, whatever its form:

Mainframe

Mini

Desk-top micro

is being used increasingly today, not as a stand-alone device, but as means of linking together all kinds of peripherals to form a networking system by which people may readily intercommunicate, whether on different floors of the same multistorey office block, or located on different sides of the globe. The diagram on page 191 illustrates this networking facility. As you can see, comparatively recent developments of computer-centred applications have linked micro-computer terminals to mainframe computers so that a company's database may be accessed through a manager's desk-top micro (subject to customary security clearance procedures). Additionally, the desk-top terminal can act with its own 'intelligence' – its own operations system and software packages – as a tool in its own right. Thus managers nowadays have the flexibility to switch in and out of the central network at will.

Additionally, the capacities of the facsimile transmitter for international communication of photograph, drawing etc and the textual communication abilities of the telex machine have now been linked to the computer network and the word processing function. Similarly, the plain-paper office copier has been connected to the computer network to produce duplicates of, say a report, from electronically inputted text direct from the computer. By the same token, a host of telecommunications services allied to computing – such as the high-speed transmission of digitised data – have also played an important part in the introduction of a highly sophisticated electronic data communications network on a local, national or international basis.

Putting the IT network to use

In order to survive, companies have to make a profit and thus the IT technology, however versatile and sophisticated, has to demonstrate its ability to contribute to the cutting of costs and the increasing of profits. It is therefore rightly judged on its outcomes and results.

Bearing this in mind, consider the kind of activities that a typical head office of a national UK company now using computers and allied IT equipment perform:

Sales Department:

Handling sales enquiries

Production of annual sales forecasts broken down into regions, districts and branches.

Sales analysis on a weekly/monthly basis identifying product breakdown, profit leaders, slow-moving items etc.

Results of sales promotions and special offers.

THE IT COMPANY NETWORK FOR LOCAL TO GLOBAL COMMUNICATION

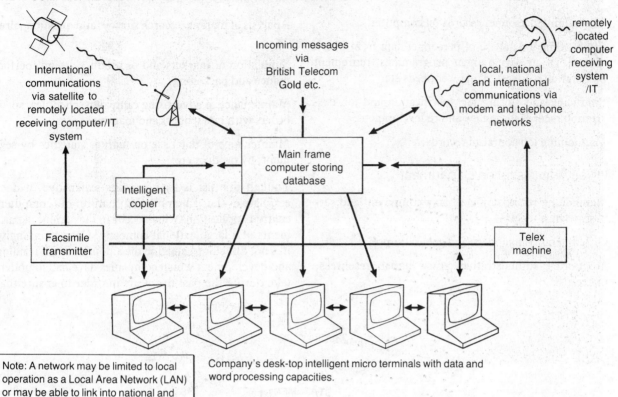

Note: A network may be limited to local operation as a Local Area Network (LAN) or may be able to link into national and international networks.

Company's desk-top intelligent micro terminals with data and word processing capacities.

Monitoring of sales representatives' calls, new business, expenses etc.

Monitoring of general sales performance daily, weekly, monthly and comparing actual performance to forecast performance – 'sales to budget'.

Accounts Department

Maintenance of an integrated accounts system: sales ledger, purchase ledger, nominal ledger, payroll, stock control etc.

Maintenance of credit control system and recovery of bad debts.

Supply to senior management of one-off or regular status reports on, for example, cash-flow, profits, expenses, days of credit of account customers etc.

Supply to company's chartered accountants of details of the company's books to facilitate the annual presentation and auditing of the accounts.

Production Department

Maintenance of purchasing records and status of stocks.

Monitoring of production outputs and wastage rates.

Quality control systems for minimising defective production.

Production planning – matching output capacity to forecast and actual demand.

Calculating operative' hours of work, bonuses etc – see links with Accounts Department and payroll.

Using computers in the manufacturing process to control machining, drilling, assembly, paint-spraying etc.

Control of goods moving out of the factory – see also links with Despatch Department.

Research and Development

Using computers to produce designs, computer models and three-dimensional projections of potential products.

Using computers to store informational databases and approved designs for future reference.

Using computers to access the databases (at a fee) of other research establishments – for example foreign universities and research institutes.

Testing product performance via computer simulation to check design and performance features.

Using the computer to record and evaluate product tests.

Providing tool-room specialists with product specifications from which to make the machines to manufacture the product or to reprogram existing robotic (CAM) plant.

Personnel Department

Maintaining personnel records on computer.

Establishing a database of personnel data from which to design staff development programmes, retirement preparation courses, manpower needs etc.

Producing and storing job specification and job description records for review and redevelopment.

Maintaining job appraisal records.

Office Administration Department

Maintaining records on company equipment and servicing dates.

Ordering office stationery and general supplies.

Monitoring administrative costs, human resources, materials.

Marketing Department

Analysis of market research surveys and questionnaires etc.

Simulation of markets and of product design, performance and packaging.

Maintenance of advertising campaign schedules, space orders with newspapers and magazines etc.

Maintenance of database on market statistics by segment, by product etc.

Though this list is by no means exhaustive, it does emphasise the all-embracing nature of computer-centred applications which occur in the various departments of a large national company. Correspondingly, it is not difficult to imagine the amount of staff training and development which companies have had to undertake during the past five years in order to ensure that

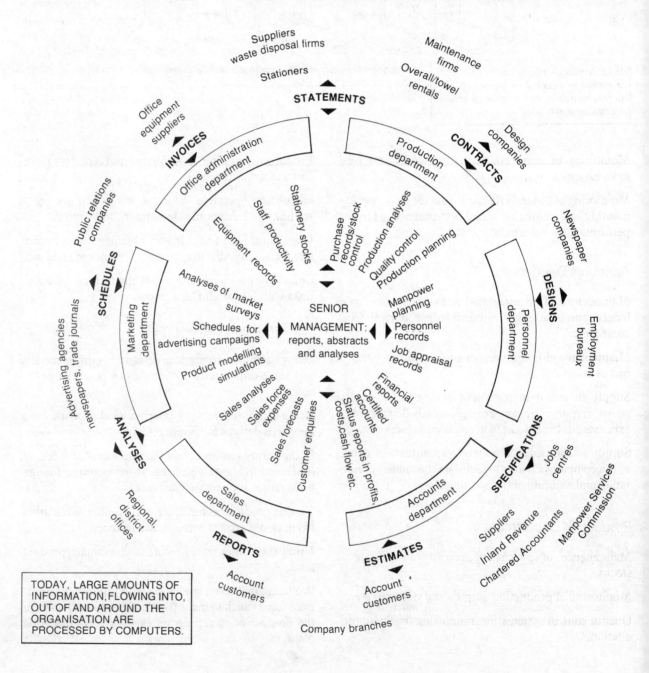

TODAY, LARGE AMOUNTS OF INFORMATION, FLOWING INTO, OUT OF AND AROUND THE ORGANISATION ARE PROCESSED BY COMPUTERS.

competitors did not overtake them by becoming more adept at using the new technology profitably, whether in the making, selling or distribution of products.

Also, the widespread application of IT in companies is having the effect of modifying their shapes and organisational structures – new posts are being devised, such as Company Information Manager, responsible for overall company communication systems and procedures, or Word Processing Supervisor, in charge of a unit of word processing operators working for as many as thirty managers or executives. Also, companies are having to employ staff as data preparation operatives to input all the data into the company computer, as well as a Database Systems Manager to ensure that an extensive and sophisticated company database is not corrupted and does *not* 'go down' or become unavailable because of machine failure. The increasing reliance upon advanced technology is also leading to the design of jobs such as Technical Support Officer/Assistant. Such staff are on hand to assist managers in getting the best from their IT equipment.

At the head of the company, directors are having to become far more 'computer-literate' in order to be able to make intelligent requests on what information is to be stored and in what form it is to be presented for evaluation. One company in the UK has recently installed a fully equipped IT boardroom with a series of computer VDU screens mounted around the walls between confravision and viewdata screens so that board meetings can access up-to-the-minute information presented in straightforward and visually interesting formats.

Talking Point 1

If senior managers can obtain the information they need from the programs designed by a few systems analysts and inputted by a team of junior data preparation operatives, is there a future for the middle manager or senior clerical officer in large organisations? Can you see the traditional organisational pyramid shape of companies in staffing terms changing in the light of current IT applications?

Talking Point 2

Having reviewed the above checklist of the various applications of IT in a national company, consider the following questions:

1   Can you identify areas in the checklist where IT applications are likely to lead to either cutting costs or increasing profits?
2   Is there a danger that the extensive introduction of IT systems may actually increase the amount of paper in the company's offices, need more staff to run them and lead to a more time-consuming administrative process?
3   If so, what checks could be introduced into a large firm to ensure that IT applications were proving cost-effective?

Electronic office equipment and IT applications

In the 1960s a communication specialist, Marshall McLuhan wrote that 'the medium is the message'. He was saying that the import of a message and how it is received and understood by its recipients was influenced by the medium in which it was transmitted. For example, the massive exposure on television of the United States moon-walker shots soon led to such wonders of space technology being taken for granted. In other words, over-exposure by television tended to downgrade the occasion's unique majesty.

Nowadays electronic wonders of a smaller scale occur daily in our offices and factories by courtesy of microprocessor technology and, human nature being what it is, they come to be regarded as commonplace and 'old-hat' just as quickly as the technology which put man on the moon! Nevertheless, it is important that we appreciate how IT systems and equipment are influencing and affecting the ways managers and company staff communicate and how new practices are changing the ways in which firms and public sector departments operate. The following sections highlight the major features of the electronic equipment which influence communications practices and promote effectiveness and profitability.

IT equipment and its applications

1   The mainframe computer

Rightly considered as the giant of the computer family, the mainframe computer is a powerhouse of computing functions allied to an enormous memory or data storage capacity running into hundreds of megabytes. Not only does the mainframe computer co-ordinate the work of dozens of terminals, grouped together or remotely located, it also holds archives and records equivalent to many millions of A4 typescript pages which it can readily access for review or production of hard copy.

Today, many national and multinational companies are employing mainframe computers to house an integrated database of virtually all the information in the company's ownership. Such a database approach to information processing means that items of information need only be entered into the computer once, and subject to security checks and procedures, may become instantly available to all the organisation's personnel, wherever they may be located. Such an approach, properly run and maintained means that information is constantly updated so as to be accurate and current. Ready access to it saves precious time and frustration and improves the quality of decision-making across the board of the company's activities. Also, the duplication of filing systems and the proliferation of paper-based documents is either avoided or kept in check. Indeed the mainframe computer used in this way does bring nearer the paperless office concept.

A further advantage of the mainframe lies in its capacity to meet the needs of dozens of workstations simultaneously by means of an ingenious system of 'switching' users in and out of its system only made possible by its incredibly swift operational ability.

2   The mini computer

As its name suggests, the mini computer system can supply most of the mainframe services but on a smaller scale – say to some 30 to 50 workstations within a multi-storey office block. Like the mainframe, the mini can also communicate with microcomputer terminals and support a network of mini and micro terminals. Its memory capacity is generally measured in five to fifty megabyte terms.

3   The intelligent microcomputer terminal

The term 'desk-top' has come to be used frequently to describe the microcomputer so as to provide an indication of its compact size and the environment in which it is used – as an office tool much like the typewriter. Yet not so very long ago a large room would have been needed to house the equivalent memory store!

The widespread introduction of the microcomputer has meant that managers and their assistants have won much more flexibility in accessing computer support than used to be the case when some firms' computers were managed by central computer departments, whose staff were looked up to as mystical gurus managing an exotic information system, and where extended access to the computer was frowned upon.

The practice today in which microcomputers may either perform as terminals forming an output of the mainframe computer, or independently as small computers in their own right provides the best of both worlds, since departments or sections within departments can access (if mainframe services are available) a vast database of information, or can work from micro software programs like word processing, spreadsheet or office administration packages, independently of the mainframe provision.

This relative independence from centralised control has resulted in junior and middle management being able to introduce innovatory ideas and practices which have then been absorbed into company policy. In this way, the micro has done much to make UK businesses both large and small more efficient and effective, while also improving the morale of such staff.

4   The electronic typewriter

The developments in typewriter technology over the past ten years have tended to be eclipsed by the advent of word processing via dedicated word processing machines and then via microcomputers. However, it is the electronic typewriter that has topped the sales of office equipment for the past two years in the UK, particularly where the electronic typewriter incorporates a memory.

The success of the electronic typewriter may be ascribed to its familiar and straight-forward operation and perhaps to the conservatism of some office administration managers and typists reluctant to jump into the IT 'deep end', preferring to edge down the steps of the 'shallow end' via the small memory capacity (8k is typical) of the memory typewriter.

Perhaps the real reason for the popularity of the electronic typewriter is its versatility, for it can be employed as a customary typewriter, as a simple word processor and in many cases even as the printer connected to a microcomputer. Further, in price terms the electronic typewriter is very competitive when all its features are taken into account.

Current technology favours the interchangeable daisy wheel allied to the correction ribbon, automatic paper feed and a range of helpful features such as the emboldening of key words, automatic underlining, centring and right-hand margin justification. Many memory typewriters will also tabulate automatically and construct boxes to contain tabulated and columnar textual or numeric information.

Most useful is the memory capacity of the electronic typewriter which enables text to be displayed on some machines on a liquid crystal display screen so that errors may be corrected before being committed to paper. Alternatively, the electronic typewriter's memory functions can facilitate the correction of text by 'lifting errors off the typed page' and substituting the correct text via the stored text duly corrected, and with the help of the correction ribbon. Typically, memories are some two lines long, though top end of the market machines incorporate much larger memories and can store form letters and particular document formats against future use.

Such machines are particularly useful if the text being produced largely comprises 'one-off' letters or memoranda etc and some users consider the electronic typewriter much easier to operate than a word processor. Clearly it is a case of 'horses for courses' when deciding whether to use an electronic typewriter or word processor. Such decisions will depend upon the nature of the task – a 30 page report requiring, say, three drafts is much more sensibly produced on a word processor. The busy office with a varied range of duties will almost certainly utilise both electronic typewriter and word processing equipment.

5   The facsimile copier

The technology which speeds copies of photographs, drawings, cartoons, typescript – in fact any kind of image produced on paper – around the world in seconds is not new. Nevertheless, developments in microtechnology have brought about improvements and reduced the time taken to effect the process.

In effect, the facsimile copier is a machine which can scan or read the imprints on, say, a sheet of A4 which is fed into it and convert the image – photograph, plans or letter etc – into a series of electronic signals which are then despatched to a receiving facsimile machine via telephone or satellite telecommunications. The incoming signals are then interpreted and reconverted into an identical copy of the original and printed on to paper already loaded into the copier. Modern facsimile transmitters are generally referred to as FAX machines and transmit their signals in digital form. At the present time facsimile copiers are graded into four series, I, II, III, and IV, where a series I machine takes some 5–6 minutes to scan and transmit a sheet of A4 and where a series IV machine can perform the same function in about 4–5 seconds.

The advantages of facsimile transmission for national and multinational firms and for international exporting companies are many. For example, a firm of industrial architects based in London may be constructing an oil refinery in Saudi Arabia. With the aid of facsimile transmission, last-minute amendments to blueprints may be sent direct to the site office near the Persian Gulf coastline and be received in seconds for inclusion in that day's construction programme. Similarly, copies of legal contracts, advertising designs, graphs and charts may be sent wherever suitable reception equipment is sited. The Chinese proverb, 'One picture is worth ten thousand words' provides all the rationale needed to ensure that facsimile transmission remains an important part of the future IT communications tool-kit!

6   Telex

Like facsimile transmission, telex communication systems have been around a long time – about 50 years. Telex messages are transmitted both nationally and internationally via telephone networks which in worldwide transmissions incorporate undersea telephone cable lines or the more recent technology of communications satellites. The telex sender first makes contact with the receiving machine by 'dialling it up' to ensure that the message about to be transmitted may be received. The telex message is then typed on a keyboard very similar to the querty keyboard and virtually simultaneously it is printed out by the receiving machine on to continuous stationery which may be cut to size.

As the illustration on page 196 shows, a telex message looks rather like a mixture of memorandum and telemessage. At the head of the message are the date and time of transmission 86–02–03 – the 3rd of February 1986. This is followed by the notation of the telex addresses. The sender's telex address being 86402 CHITYP G, and the recipient's 5417710+. The message itself is kept to a minimum while maintaining normal courtesy.

Large organisations tend to save up their telex messages by storing them for transmission overnight when telex transmission costs are much cheaper. Also, when converted into either punched-tape or digital signals, telex transmissions may be sent at high-speed so that costs are kept to a minimum. British Telecom provides the UK telex service on a rental basis, where access to the national and international telephone networks is rented out to users who are supplied with telex directories. For larger users British Telecom have introduced Telex Plus, a service which sends 'telex circulars' to multiple destinations on behalf of clients, thus avoiding the creation of bottle-necks on, say, the client's single machine.

An 'up-market' version of telex (although using different IT based equipment) is BT's Teletex service. This allows senders to transmit electronically top quality correspondence, reports etc over long distances which are reproduced via letter-quality word processing equipment at the receiving end. The Teletex service ensures that important documents intended for senior decision-makers are presented in an appropriately crisp and duly elegant manner. And here it is worth bearing in mind that 25% of a document's impact is ascribed to its visual appearance.

British Telecom also provide a telex onward transmission service for small users for whom the rental of the telex equipment would not be economic. This service is called TextDirect and may be accessed through a personal computer. For larger users, BT provides a Telex Manual Services support arm. TMS offers a range of services including a kind of international telex subscriber enquiry service and a sales promotion, direct mailing provision.

7   Viewdata systems

Viewdata provides a communication system through a television screen which acts like a kind of window, allowing the user to access through a series of menus – like computer software package menus – sets of 'pages' which are transmitted to the TV screen through

Specimen telex message

```
86-02-03 12:33  ←————————— date and time of despatch of telex
007  ←——————————————————— 'signature' of telex sender
CF179 12.34  ←—————————— British Telecom acknowledgement
86402 CHITYP G  ←————————— Telex address of sender (Secretarial Services Bureau)
KEY+5417710+  ←——————————— Telex address of recipient (54 = Sweden)
17710 PRIMUS S
17710 PRIMUS S

5399 86-02-03 12:33  ←————— Telex reference number

REF 86032  ←—————————————— Bureau client's reference

TO: H TOENER

FROM C.H. LONGLEY (RINNAI U.K.)

AM ARRIVING STOCKHOLM MON. 10 FEB. FLT SK526 AT 1505 HRS. AND AM
BOOKED STRAND HOTEL.  REQUEST APPOINTMENT TUES. MORNING 11 FEB. AM
CATCHING EVENING FERRY TO HELSINKI.

REGARDS
17710 PRIMUS S
86402 CHITYP G*
```

This message was despatched by a Secretarial Services Bureau on behalf of a client.

Reproduced by kind permission of Select Office Services, Chichester and Mr C H Longley (Rinnai UK).

the telephone network. British Telecom provides a viewdata service which is called Prestel. The system enables advertisers to promote their services on particular 'pages', and for government agencies likewise to employ the service to broadcast information to users. For example, a polytechnic may use Prestel to disseminate information about its degree courses, or the Scottish Tourist Board may take Prestel 'space' to advertise Scottish holidays. All kinds of information is made available on Prestel, such as weather forecasts, opera company programmes, Stock Exchange share prices and the like.

Prestel makes possible a *two-way* intercommunication, since with a computer keyboard linked to the system, users can interrogate the visually displayed databases for additional information, and may even send messages to the advertisers, for example, to request a particular holiday brochure to be sent to them in the post!

British Telecom are able to make a 'Prestel-type' service available to private users such as banks and stock-broking firms which wish to be provided with the latest, up-to-the-minute information relating to international finance and the money markets. Recently one national company of retail chainstores acquired such a system to give branch managers details of price changes, special offers and other similar information hourly and daily.

8 Photocopiers and printers

When the term 'photocopying' is used nowadays, the copying system being referred to is almost certainly that termed xerography, a process developed some 50 years ago in the United States. Also called 'plain paper copying' this process relies upon electrical charges which cause patterns (effectively printed words, diagrams, photographs etc) to be formed upon a light sensitive material. These images are then transferred on to a powder or toner which through a heat process is fixed on to each page copied from the original. In current xerographic copying processes, multi-coloured copies can be obtained by using different colour toners sequentially.

Plain paper copiers are manufactured in a wide range of sizes, from simple, desk-top models into which single sheets are hand-fed to large, sophisticated stand-alone versions which have high-speed duplication capacities allied to functions such as collating and binding, as well as page enlarging or reducing facilities.

The applications of photocopiers are many and varied. At one end of the spectrum, the desk-top model is invaluable for reproducing a single copy of an incoming letter to circulate for information to, say, section heads. For bound copies of reports destined for senior management and directors, then the larger machine with automatic collating and binding facilities is needed. Also, the high speed photocopier is ideal for duplicating circular sales letters or leaflets which have been produced using a word processor or lettering kits to obtain a master, since the process is relatively cheap and remains within the control of the organisation.

The prudent office administration manager, however, will take pains to establish a system for monitoring photocopying facilities and to ensure that the respective costs are borne by appropriate sections or departments, since open access to high-speed photocopiers often results in a frightening growth in a company's reprographic costs!

Printers

Information Technology has revolutionised the printing processes employed in modern offices and publishing companies alike. Historically, office printing work tended to be farmed out to local jobbing printers who used typesetting equipment to produce letterheads for notepaper, notices or leaflets. In the world of newspaper publication, linotype printing technology was formerly used to transform a typed line of text into individual letters or matrices which were then aligned to form a moulded line of text using hot metal. In this way pages were built up to be incorporated into the newspaper's presses. Such systems have now been superseded by the introduction of IT into the world of newspaper printing, where computers with word processing features are employed to create the text and to design the newspaper page simultaneously. This information is then passed electronically to the computer-controlled printers which can even print a colour picture taken directly under licence from a television news broadcast!

Just as IT is changing radically the production processes of newspapers, so it is transforming the ways in which text and graphics are printed in the office.

At present there are four principal printing techniques allied to computer-linked printers:

1 dot matrix print head
2 daisy wheel print head
3 ink jet
4 laser device

The humble work-horse of the quartet is the dot-matrix printer. This printer is inexpensive and ideal for in-house printing and internal drafts of text. It works by transforming the electronic signals despatched by the print commands in the computer into a series of instructions in the dot-matrix printer which cause a series of dots to be imprinted on the page of paper, line by line, which resemble alphabetical letters, numbers or symbols. This is achieved by a print head which 'hammers' the dots on to the paper through an impregnated continuous ribbon.

The daisy-wheel variant follows a similar approach, but employs a kind of spoked cart-wheel or daisy-wheel. At the end of each spoke sits a letter, number or symbol which is pressed through the ribbon (much like the traditional typewriter ribbon) to impress the image of the letter via the ink in the ribbon on to the paper page. The advantage of this type of printer is that sets of daisy wheels may be kept so as to make various typefaces available for use on a single document if need be. Both the dot-matrix and daisy-wheel printers have features in common such as emboldening of text and automatic underscoring, but it is the daisy-wheel printer that is generally used to produce letter-quality text.

The ink-jet printer is a relative newcomer to computer linked printing and works by 'spraying' the letters or numbers on to the page. Its major advantage lies in the speed at which it can perform. Likewise the laser printer is also employed for high-speed, large volume printing. Its technology relates to xerography in that the images picked up by a light-sensitive reader are then converted into electrical signals which affect a laser beam as it scans across a photosensitive drum to produce an electrostatic series of images which become the text or graphics printed on to the page in a manner similar to that used in xerographic printing.

What is exciting about the development of the laser printer is that it can be used in much the same way as a photocopier and may be linked to a computer/word-processing system and thus incorporate many of the word processor's editorial features as well as the capacity to receive data from remote locations for printing.

In large companies with extensive computerised data processing functions, large, stand-alone laser printers are employed to cope with the hundreds of meters of continuous computer paper which is used daily to produce computer print-out reports. Such equipment is also able to collate and bind such documents automatically.

9   Telecommunications

The advent of IT has radically transformed the telecommunications industry over the past ten years. Indeed, without the existing national and international telephone networks, most of today's electronic message switching and high-speed data transmission would not be possible, and the success of telephone research engineers in extending the traffic or number of calls received on existing systems while developing new transmission vehicles like fibre optic lines and System X exchanges is not to be undervalued.

The telephone has become such a familiar instrument that we tend to take for granted the massive investment in high technology that supports it. For example, how readily may a manager become impatient when the telephone service takes a few seconds longer than usual to effect a direct connection between him or her, one of three million people living in Greater

Features of electronic telephone systems

1	Abbreviated dialling	Frequently used numbers may be obtained by a 'shorthand' three digit version of a particular number.
2	Absent extension answering	Unanswered calls are routed to as many as five extensions until connection is effected.
3	Call waiting signal	The extension user on the phone can be advised that another caller is waiting to be connected.
4	Camp on busy/ring when free	A call is held over 'in suspense' until the recipient's line becomes free without the caller having to hold – he or she is called up automatically.
5	Direct dialling	Incoming calls can be routed to a known extension independently, without switchboard interception.
6	Transfer and enquiry	A call can be held while another is dialled if in the same area and the first call recontacted, or calls can be transferred by the subscriber.

A number of additional features are available as part of the computerised telephone switchboard service which now offers commercial users a highly sophisticated and flexible communications system.

Birmingham, with the desired contact, one of eleven million people living in Greater London!

The system that has underpinned such telephone connections for many years is called the Private Automatic Branch Exchange (PABX) system. Telephone calls made between offices are routed through the telephone exchanges of British Telecom to switchboards which in turn route the incoming call to one of as many as 600 internal extensions (*see* above).

The existing telephone network system is currently being upgraded by British Telecom so as to provide enhanced telephone and electronic message switching services. It is now possible, for example, to purchase computerised switchboard systems which incorporate a number of additional services for the user as a result of developments in IT.

The international telephone user

British Telecom's International Division supplies a wide range of services for the business user, including an International Direct Dialling service to some 160 countries. A further service is BTI's International 0800 direct dial freephone service which allows foreign customers or sales representatives to telephone companies in the UK without having to pay for the call, which is billed direct to the company in the same kind of way that Freepost operates.

Data communication

In addition to its telephone service for the transmission of human voice calls, British Telecom provides a range of services for the routing of data, whether in textual or digital computerised form.

The BTI International Packet Switching system allows personnel abroad to transmit data to the parent computer direct. The Datel Service is provided by BT to link remotely located computers and allied equip-

ment via UK national and international telephone networks and will transmit both text and computerised data. It is especially useful for the transmission of high-volume data.

Increasingly, large multinational organisations are finding it worthwhile to lease their own, private networks from companies like British Telecom or Mercury so as to ensure that data and messages are promptly and efficiently relayed between offices and countries. One such private network service offered by British Telecom is Primex, which can make connections with public telecommunication services while masterminding the routing of privately networked data. Another is called Satstream and offers a private international leaseline service via telecommunications satellites. Satstream not only copes with the transmission of speech, text, data and facsimile messages, but can also handle very high volume data transmission direct from sender to recipient internationally.

Teleconferencing

Teleconferencing or videoconferencing facilities have been provided by British Telecom for some years through studios maintained in larger UK towns and cities. Essentially, people are linked together visually and audially through interconnected television monitors and television cameras. In this way, a sales conference may be held of, for example, a dozen regional sales managers without them having to travel out of their respective 'patches' to a London head office. With the support of IT, such teleconferences may now be organised internationally and may be supported by simultaneous facsimile transmission of diagrammatic or photographic material. BT now offer this service from companies' own offices as an alternative to their own studios.

In a similar way, national and international audio

conferences can be set up via an operator to connect a team of businessmen via existing telephone lines and exchanges.

9   Cellular radio and radio paging

Grouped together within the title of 'mobile communication systems' are the two-way communication systems of cellular radio and the one-way radio paging service.

Radio-paging via 'bleepers' has been in use for some time in hospitals, universities and large private and public institutions to call up the attention of doctors, maintenance engineers or caretakers, whose jobs involve them moving around a large building or campus. Having been alerted by the bleeper, the person sought has to access an internal telephone extension and call up the switchboard operator to find out whom he should telephone or see. Recent developments of this system permit short messages to be displayed on an LCD screen built into the pocket radio pager receiver.

Cellular radio is a genuinely two-way radio-telephone communication system which operates on local frequencies. First introduced in 1985, the service will extend nation-wide by 1987 and is provided by Racal-Vodafone and Cellnet principally. Radio-telephone calls are routed through a system of interlocking 'cells' by computer. At present subscribers tend either to be people 'out in the field' like on-site architects or building contractors or high-level business executives using the radio-telephone while driving or being driven to an appointment or air terminal. The comparative current exclusivity of the cellular radio system is not unconnected with the cost of acquiring the equipment and the cost of using it. However, as costs fall and more frequencies are made available, then the market is bound to grow in those sectors where personnel do not spend their working lives seated comfortably next to an office telephone extension.

Retailing, distribution and IT

Just as the information processing systems in offices have undergone far-reaching changes in the past decade, so also has IT radically changed the practices of retailing and distribution companies. Where only a few years ago the emphasis was upon manual, labour-intensive administrative systems, nowadays in hypermarkets and supermarkets fully integrated IT systems are employed to control cashing-out, stock-control, sales and product analysis and stock re-ordering at remotely located depots!

Such integrated procedures depend extensively upon a highly disciplined system of pricing policies

Communications flow in the 'less paper' office environment

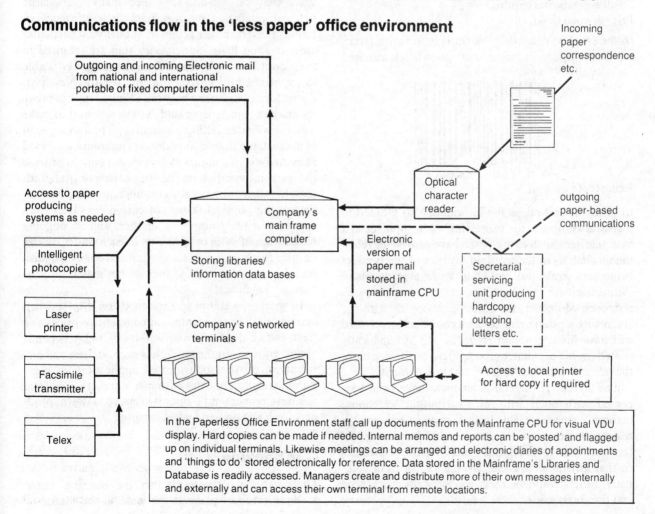

Example of a Kimball Tag

and structures, product codes, sophisticated delivery schedules from wholesalers or the company's distribution arm, and the installation of costly computerised tills and bar code scanning equipment.

Before the introduction of the optically read bar-code, retailers relied in larger organisations upon the Kimball tag to supply sales information and analysis. The tags are attached to garments, household goods etc and carry a series of codes in the form of punched holes and imprinted letters. Sales assistants collect the tags as each item is sold and they are subsequently processed by computer to yield their information upon:

Total sales
Sales by product
Stock adjustments required
Price of goods sold, etc

In the same way, another system is in use with larger retailers which reads magnetic strips on labels attached

![Example of a bar code showing 5 000201 461100]

Example of a bar code

to products and relays the information so gleaned to a central computer for processing via a sophisticated cash register. Such cash registers are capable of relaying an analysis of the required features of the product being sold while also providing aggregated details of sales during the day for stock re-ordering and despatch purposes. Moreover, the customer shopping with the chainstore's plastic registered account customer card will have his transaction recorded and automatically posted to his account by computer, to form part of the transactions listed in his monthly statement.

The advent of the computer must have been welcomed with open arms by distribution warehouse managers since it enabled much time to be saved in maintaining extensive stock control and ordering systems, as well as providing route-planning schedules so that itineraries to either customers' shops or company outlets could be most economically sequenced and the goods loaded accordingly.

Perhaps the most useful feature of the computer for the distributor lies in its ability to classify and reformat lists in a trice. For example, the various sales of tomato ketchup made by a supermarket chain's southern region branches can be fed into the computer by means of the systems outlined above. The computer is then able to aggregate the total sales by size and type so that a single order may be placed with the supplier. The same computer is able to store the day's or week's restocking order for tomato ketchup by individual branch and to issue it for loading and delivery along with a range of other items to be delivered at the same time. By the same token, the sales value of each product can be stored and a running total maintained so that at any time management staff are able to secure up-to-the-minute sales analysis figures on the basis of:

this week: last week
this month: last month
this year to date: last year equivalent period

As we may now readily appreciate from our study of data processing, all this information may derive from the single input of the bar code data at the point of sale.

Computers are also invaluable in retailing and distribution for highlighting both slow and fast-moving stock. In the high streets of the UK competition is fierce and the annual rent for a square foot of floor space may be considerable. For many years large national retailers have measured their efficiency in terms of the turnover achieved annually by particular areas of shop floor. Supervisory staff are required to keep careful records of sales and the computer is able to supply helpful analyses in this regard. New products, for example may be given a limited time to prove themselves before being sold out at a discount to make way for a better selling alternative. The buying staff of national retailing chains also rely on computer-based sales analysis in a number of ways, not only to provide the latest information on the sales of new or trial products but also to maintain customer profiles. For example, the physical stature of customers varies from one part of the country to another, and an ongoing monitoring of sales of garments in each outlet by size ensures that stocks are fast-moving and do not languish on sales gondolas because they do not match the customers' size needs.

In short, the ability to have goods on display when and where they are wanted, at competitive prices and fresh out of the factory or warehouse today depends almost entirely, in the nation's bigger retailers and distributors, on the sophisticated applications of computer services. And the customer stands to gain from this development of IT since it keeps costs down, products fresh and on hand when required.

IT in banking

There can be little doubt that the banking sector deserves pride of place at the head of the league of commercial, industrial and service sectors when it comes to applying IT to business activities.

During the past 20 years or so, banks all over the world have invested many millions of pounds, dollars, yen or Deutsch Marks into IT equipment and systems which have revolutionised the ways in which individuals and corporations use the banks' repertoire of services. Indeed, such commitment and enthusiasm for computer-based technology has helped to coin phrases like 'consumer banking' and 'plastic money'.

Perhaps the most pressing reason for such a widespread and committed investment in IT in the banking system was the sheer volume of transactions which have to be processed each day, each month and each year. For example, the UK major clearing banks handle well over two billion cheques each year and billions of pounds are spent annually in credit card transactions. In effect, the banks simply could not cope with today's volume of business without the support of sophisticated computer and data processing systems, parts of which now provide a 24 hour service 365 days a year.

The system employed to clear cheques between banks provides an excellent example of IT at work. Each cheque embodies a code in magnetic ink characters which may be read electronically to speed the data inputting phase. This code conveys each cheque's individual number, the number of the branch where the account is held and the customer's individual account number. When the operator processes the cheque he or she only needs to add the amount the cheque is made out for alongside the magnetic ink codes. The cheque then joins hundreds of others which are sorted into a series of slots, one for each clearing bank. Batches of cheques are despatched daily to central clearing offices where balances are maintained between the cheques a bank has to pay out on and the flow of money represented by cheques being paid into accounts belonging to its own customers. Each day a national clearing bank – thanks to IT – is able to pay or receive in a single transaction the difference between what it owes to another bank and what the other bank owes it. Such a sum, coming in or going out, may represent hundreds of millions of pounds for a single day's business!

While the clearing process occurs daily, the local bank paying out on a cheque and another branch crediting payment received, scrutinise cheques carefully as they return from the central clearing process and a three day waiting period is customary before a cheque is officially cleared.

Cash cards and automatic telling machines

Everyone possessing a bank account knows how irritating it is to have to wait in a queue for what seems like hours simply to cash a cheque because the person in front seems to be paying in what seems like ten years of takings from his family business!

The pressure on banks to provide prompt services for customers in a hurry – whether in their lunch hour or outside banking hours led to the introduction in the late 1970s to the installation by Barclays Bank in the UK of some 100 Automatic Telling Machines (ATM's). Such machines soon became a widespread and popular feature of all the High Street banks, as the familiar Saturday morning cashpoint queues of people waiting to access cash from their ATM set in the bank's front wall readily illustrates.

Such unstaffed facilities can only function because of an on-line, real-time computer system. The customer inserts a magnetic strip card into the cash dispenser which identifies them as a bona fide user. They then key into the dispenser's numeric key pad their personal identity number and the amount of cash required (there are restricted amounts specified, like £30.00 or £50.00). Before the notes issue forth, the customer's creditworthiness is checked by the dispenser interrogating the bank's mainframe computer to ensure that he or she has not exceeded the seven days' authorised withdrawal total.

Once satisfied, not only does the dispenser issue the cash to the customer, who hurries off presumably to spend it, but it instructs the central computer to make the necessary adjustments to the customer's bank statement. Further, the customer is issued with a hard copy paper receipt on the spot to check against his statement at the month's end. The effect of this IT has been to give the customer a better and more convenient service, while reducing staff costs and paperwork within the bank during opening hours. This unstaffed service has been more fully developed in West Germany, where the customer can interact with the bank's computer to obtain a visual display of his account or a hard copy of his current financial status as well as being able to amend standing order arrangements and the like. A similar service is currently being offered by the Bank of Scotland via customers' home television sets allied to a keyboard in viewdata fashion.

Credit cards

Just as the ATM cash dispenser has proved popular with the consumer, so also has the credit card industry. Indeed, worldwide, it is a billion pound industry, supported by intensive advertising campaigns such as the American Express series of TV commercials with the slogan 'That'll do nicely!' (as an expression of its universal acceptance as a means of payment) becoming a catchphrase.

The widespread use of the credit card, especially among travelling business executives, supported by an effective computerised billing system, has brought nearer the forecast cashless society, where all transactions will be facilitated by a plastic identity card which enables, say, a departmental store to transfer the cost of a three piece suite from the customer's bank account to its own. Indeed, such a trend would be welcomed by both retailer and banker alike since it should help to contain the costs of administering the sales transaction and make it more secure.

IT and international banking

Just as IT has transformed the world of the consumer in banking, so also has it provided the corporate banker with a wide range of facilities in an international context.

In 1973 the Society For Worldwide Interbank Financial Telecommunications (SWIFT) was formed by the American and European banking communities to make it easier and quicker to move money and financial data around the world. It is now used by over 50 countries worldwide. Indeed, some of its transactions are undertaken with such speed between one major international banking establishment and another that it is theoretically possible for a small country to 'go broke' and be rescued with a loan before anyone has appreciated the difference! In everyday terms, SWIFT supplies a wide range of facilities such as the transfer of funds for exporters and importers, the issue of letters of credit and the networking of messages, etc, all as a result of the international application of IT in the world of banking.

IT applications in business: what the future holds

It would be a brash clairvoyant who would care to predict just what the future holds for the continuing application of Information Technology in business as the 21st century approaches! Nevertheless, there are a number of trends and research programmes which may be identified in order to supply some clues and clear the IT crystal ball a little.

The Japanese have been working intensively for some time now on what they have termed the 'fifth generation' of computers. This development work is generally associated with the design of an artificial intelligence in computers to enable them to simulate the creative thinking ability of human beings and to evolve decision-making patterns arising from a rationale which they themselves have constructed. If such feats of computer engineering prove possible, then human society may well be somewhere near the point when it becomes possible to construct the android robotic butler beloved of science fiction writers.

Allied to the work on computer intelligence is the research into voice-operated computers. Already there are computers in the USA which can understand and act upon about 100 different voice-delivered commands, and speed emulation research is being conducted in the UK to aid those who suffer from being deaf and dumb. The problems associated with voice-operated computers are not to be underestimated, since it is proving difficult to design programs which will allow the computer to understand various regional ac-

cents and also the meaning associated with pitch and emphasis in the spoken word. Should this area of research prove fruitful, and should a programming language evolve which enables 'everyday English' to form the basis of computer programming and authoring languages, then IT as we know and understand it will seem like a Model T Ford set beside a Ferrari!

Much nearer at hand is the development of the home computing and data-interrogating console of equipment which links into a national message-switching network. This will make it possible for people to access the books and information of national libraries as pages of information presented in viewdata fashion. It can only be a short time before high-speed OCR readers are used to convert the printed word in books into the electronic word for VDU monitor display. Such developments are likely to transform the educational, cultural and recreational pursuits of the populace in unsuspected ways. The repetitive and boring 'munchman' computer game has already been replaced by far more stimulating interactive video/computer games which provide more sophisticated scenarios and game choices of action.

Also accessed from the home computer/information console will be information relayed from, say, the local supermarkets on fresh or new goods, current prices, special offers and the like. In a society in which both husband and wife work full-time, the ability to order goods and pay for them via a home computer and have them delivered within the hour may prove a tempting convenience.

Just as message switched electronic mail is becoming a familiar part of many business communications systems, so we can expect such a service to be available to every home in the near future, so that the familiar white paper envelopes with coloured stamps affixed to them which are delivered by hand may become objects for our grandchildren to peer at through a museum's glass case!

In other areas of IT, there may be a convergence which allies miniaturisation of existing microprocessors with the introduction of flat TV screen technology and cellular radio message routing. These three areas could bring about the wristwatch television and two-way intercommunicating device hitherto beloved of comic cartoonists.

In manufacturing industry we are likely to see dangerous mining operations being conducted with IT equipment operating drilling and hewing work by remote control. Factories are likely to become far more robotic in their production areas and manufactured goods better designed, safer and more efficient as the result of computer based design and testing developments.

The above paragraphs outline only a few of the possibilities which the wonders of IT can provide in the future. But in constructing rosy future scenarios for IT, it should be kept firmly in mind that at the centre of any society are its people. Thus the most demanding challenge facing western governments, multinational and national company directors, educationalists and trade union leaders alike is how to manage the further introduction of IT applications so that people as a whole are its beneficiaries and not, as in some cases, its casualties.

Assessment questions

1 What do these sets of initials stand for?

CADCAM LAN LCD OCR ATM SWIFT

2 In your own words, explain briefly how a network linking computers and other IT equipment works within a company context.

3 What is the difference between facsimile and telex transmissions? In what situations would a company use these facilities?

4 What do you understand by the terms 'digitised data' and 'packet switching'?

5 Make a checklist of the type of business activities likely to be handled by a computerised system in one of the following departments of a national manufacturing company:

Sales Accounts Production Research & Development

6 Make a checklist of the types of organisation and agency which are likely to communicate with a large company via computer or ancillary IT equipment and set against each the nature of the communication – for example, a supplier may send a priced catalogue updated by computer.

7 What new staff posts can you think of which have been created as a result of the introduction of IT into commercial, industrial and public service organisations? Describe each post's duties briefly.

8 What service does British Telecom's Confravision service provide?

9 Write a short explanation of the difference between viewdata and teletext.

10 What, in your view, did Marshal McLuhan mean when he wrote 'the medium is the message'?

11 What is meant by the term 'a fully integrated database' when used to describe a large organisation's information processing system?

12 Explain what an 'intelligent microcomputer terminal' is.

13 In your own words, outline briefly how the widespread introduction of microcomputers into companies has changed the nature of computer services provisions.

14 In what ways would you consider the electronic memory typewriter to be a versatile office communications tool?

15 If you were a business executive, how might British Telecom's Prestel service help you?

16 List four different services which a computerised telephone switchboard system can supply to someone using an internal extension.

17 What services are provided by Vodaphone and Cellnet?

18 Explain clearly the differences between cellular radio and radio-paging.

19 What is a Kimball tag? How is it used?

20 How does the bar code labelling system work in retailing?

21 How can a computerised system help to keep stock moving in a busy High Street retail chainstore?

22 What do you understand by the expressions 'plastic money' and 'the cashless society'?

23 Explain briefly how an automatic cash dispensing machine works.

24 What is a 'fifth generation' computer?

25 What is meant by the term 'artificial intelligence'?

Discussion topics

1 Currently, UK companies have been criticised for spending too little of their income on staff development and training. What dangers in the context of IT applications are likely to occur in UK trading if this trend is not reversed?

2 What do you see as the 'people problems' which would have to be identified and overcome when a firm decides to install a less paper office environment in a part of its organisation – say the accounts department?

3 'In a few years time, the IT available will enable everyone to work from home via a computer network.'

What advantages or disadvantages of this situation do you anticipate if such a forecast should come true?

4 What do you see as the major development which are likely to occur in the field of IT applications in business in the next ten years?

Build-up tasks

1 Make contact with the help of your teacher with a local firm using IT applications and find out what particular tasks the system is used for and what the staff see as the advantages which result. Write a short report for your group to read on what you discovered.

2 In syndicate groups of about 4–5, research into one of the following and then give a combined oral presentation of your findings to the group, using whatever audio-visual aids you consider appropriate:

2.1 How laser printers and laser photocopiers work and are used in business.

2.2 What a phototypesetting machine does.

2.3 The scope of the services provided by British Telecom's Prestel system.

2.4 The major IT applications used in a clearing bank's local branch.

2.5 How the field of retailing has been affected by the introduction of IT applications.

3 Write a short explanation, with diagrams, explaining the principles of xerographic photocopying.

4 Research one of the following British Telecom International Division's services and report back on it orally to your group.

Telex Plus   Primex
Satstream   TextDirect
Datel   City Direct
International Kilostream

Your presentation should not exceed ten minutes.

5   With the help of your teacher, make arrangements in pairs to go and interview county council, district council or borough council staff to find out how computers are used in local government.

You may wish to concentrate on the work of one major department. When you have assembled your facts, compose an article to explain your findings which would be appropriate for inclusion in your local weekly newspaper.

6   First do your research, and then write an article of about 750 words entitled: 'How Information Technology applications can help the small business'.

7   Find out how a 'mouse' and 'ikons' are used in connection with office computing software programs.

When you have done your research, assume that you have been asked as a Training Department assistant to produce three pages of A4 typescript and allied diagrams or illustrations to be inserted into the Office Administration Department's Training Manual to explain how this aspect of computer technology works and how it may be of value to administrative staff.

8   Each day, each month and each academic year, the department in which you are studying is spending money – either on consumable materials such as stationery or on equipment and repairs.

In pairs, explore what services a spreadsheet can provide, and having learned how to operate a spreadsheet with a microcomputer, design a system using the spreadsheet to show how a budget of money can be monitored as it is expended – for example for your department's outgoings – so as to provide an up-to-date record at any time of outstanding balances and in what areas the income was spent.

9   Assume that you work as assistant to the Sales Manager of a national company selling a range of office equipment to high street stores and in some cases direct to firms and educational institutions.

Today your boss greets you with these words:

You know, I'm just not satisfied that we are managing to communicate our sales statistics and analyses to our sales representatives in the field. I've just looked again at my monthly report to the sales reps, and it just looks too wordy and dull. What we could do with is one of those graphics software packages I've just been reading about in this month's 'Business Computer News'! Apparently they can transfer numbers and columns of figures into coloured pie-charts, graphs and what have you – now that's just the thing I need to give my reports some visual impact and appeal!

Needless to say, you are delegated to find out about the kind of services a graphics software package can provide. Your Sales Manager has asked you to devise a factsheet and to obtain any relevant catalogues or brochures which he can digest prior to raising the prospect of acquiring such a package at the next meeting with his regional managers.

Produce the appropriate factsheet in not more than 300 words and submit it with any suitable leaflets or brochures you are able to locate.

Case study

Powa Drills Company Limited

The Powa Drill Company Limited was originally founded in 1955 as a partnership between Charles Boxgrove, an ex-World War II army officer in the Royal Engineers, and Keith Mitchelson, a distributor of government surplus electrical equipment.

The partnership was started on a 'shoe-string' in a pair of prefabricated buildings adjoining Keith Mitchelson's Army Surplus Store in Uxbridge Road, Slough. In a post-war period of rapid expansion, the partnership prospered and was formed into a limited company in 1961. By 1968, the company had an annual turnover of £860,000, mainly in the commercial drill market of the construction industry. Powa Drill's hand-held drills were sold through a network of retail ironmongers over their trade sales counters.

In 1975 Keith Mitchelson died suddenly and, with the help of a bank loan, Charles Boxgrove was able to secure a majority shareholding in the company, and with it, the post of chairman of the board and managing director. At about this time, a local industrialist, Sir Harold Wentworth, bought shares in the firm and secured for Powa Drills the lease on a factory on the Slough Industrial Estate, since the company was in urgent need of additional space.

With Sir Harold's support, the company developed a plan in the late 1970s to penetrate the expanding market for DIY home-users of electric drills. Thus a design team was established, and a successful new product launched on 1 May 1980 called the 'Home-Maka Powadrill'. As a result of the innovative design of its gearing mechanism, the drill proved extremely versatile and sales quickly climbed.

To meet demand, a second factory was leased in 1981 on the Ritchfield Industrial Estate, Reading, and production was rationalised, with the commercial market range of drills being manufactured in Slough, and the DIY range in Reading. At this time, the company moved into a new head office building in Maidenhead, Berkshire, about equidistant from both factories.

In 1984, the 'knock-on' effects of the recession in the construction industry were felt, and Powa Drills found itself short of finance with which to redevelop and redirect its product range. Fortunately, a wealthy widow stepped into the breach. In her sixties, Mrs Harriett Finch-Barton was the widow of a retired merchant banker who had left her with a considerable amount of disposable assets. Partly due to Charles Boxgrove's powers of persuasion, Mrs Finch-Barton invested a considerable sum in Powa Drills and was appointed to its board of directors. She also proved a most valuable human asset, since it was she who persuaded the board to diversify into labour-saving, electrically powered garden tools – such as grass-cutters, strimmers, hedge-trimmers and rotavators.

At the end of 1985 a project was started at the Reading factory to develop a range of accessories built around the heavy-duty Home-Maka drill which would enable a wider range of functions to be performed, including cutting timber, sanding, effecting mitre joints and the like. By June 1986, the research and development staff were on the brink of bringing to a successful conclusion the prototype testing of a comprehensive kit, including metal bench, which would handle almost any job around the house in carpentry and general maintenance terms. The kit was scheduled to retail at around £150.

Currently, the company's structure is as follows:

Locations: Head Office: Powa Drill House, Cookham Road, Maidenhead.
Commercial and Garden Tool Factory: London Road Industrial Estate, Slough.
Home and DIY Factory: Ritchfield Industrial Estate, Reading.

Since the mid 1970s, the company's efforts have been concentrated upon production, marketing and selling. Thus the acquisition of office equipment and information processing systems had evolved somewhat haphazardly, as each department perceived a particular need. Moreover, the Office Administration Department was only reorganised in an effectively functioning form two years ago, and there was still a great deal to be achieved in formulating a coherent information processing policy.

Currently the company's office equipment comprises principally:

Reading Factory: 1 Olivetti Manual Typewriter (10 years old)
1 IBM Electric Typewriter (approx 8 years old)
Internal Public Address System
PABX Telephone Switchboard with 12 internal extensions and 3 outside lines.
Paging System for Managers and Foremen
Telex Teleprinter connected to Head Office

Slough Factory: 3 Imperial Manual Typewriters
PABX Telephone Switchboard System with 14 internal extensions
Internal Public Address System
Paging System for Managers and Foremen

Accounts Dept: 1 Olympia Manual Typewriter (8 years old)
2 IBM Electronic Typewriters (3 and 4 years old)
1 Burroughs Card Based Computer (purchased in 1972)
5 Olivetti Electronic Calculators (about 6 years old)
Various Add List and Mechanical Calculators
3 Philips Audio Dictation Systems (6 years old)

Sales Office: 2 Olympia Manual Typewriters (8 years old)
1 Imperial 5005 Dual Pitch Electronic Typewriter (3 years old)
2 IBM Golfball Electric Typewriters (4 years old)
1 North Star Horizon Micro Computer and Printer (7 years old)
4 Grundig Audio Dictation Systems (3 years old)
Assorted Pocket calculators

Office Administration: 3 Imperial Manual Typewriters (7–9 years old)
1 Imperial 5005 Dual Pitch Electronic Typewriter (4 years old)
1 IBM Electronic Typewriter
3 IBM Electric Golfball Typewriters (7–9 years old)
6 Philips Audio Dictation Systems (5 years old)
3 Olivetti Electronic Calculators
Rank Xerox Photocopier (Desk-top) (4 years old)

Personnel: 1 Triumph Manual Typewriter (9 years old)
1 Brother Electronic Memory Typewriter (2 years old)
1 Olivetti Audio Dictation System (5 years old)

The Head Office functions on a PABX telephone switchboard system and the receptionist operates the telex machine. In addition, there is a Rank Xerox photocopier for interdepartmental use, together with a conventional mailroom. There are some 24 internal telephone extensions with a total of 10 outside lines.

Recent Board of Directors Meeting

Item 6 on the Agenda is: Updating of communications system and future policy
Mrs Harriett Finch-Barton addresses the Board:

'I must tell you about my recent visit to the Information Technology Exhibition at the Barbican! It was a revelation, I don't mind telling you! We've got to accept the fact that, in information processing terms, we're still operating in the Dark Ages – what we need is a long hard look at the nature and scope of our current equipment and to move into a comprehensive and networked word and data processing system. I was talking to one of the exhibitors who reckons that it's quite possible to process five times the information with about half the staff! And the information is readily accessible to help the Board in making effective decisions. . . .'

Sir Harold Wentworth:

'I'm not so sure about the position with regard to trimming back on admin staff, but I think Harriett is right in principle. According to the last set of management accounts figures, we should have a not inconsiderable sum to invest in this sort of rationalising project.'

Stanley Jones, Accounts Director

'Well, I don't need to remind you about the age of our computing equipment – its replacement has been long overdue, and these current integrated software packages in accounting terms could save a lot of time, as well as providing more up-to-date information. I think it's high time we moved on this one.'

With little more discussion, other than general supportive remarks about the need to get abreast of IT developments promptly, the Board voted to install a suitable system as soon as possible.

Overheard in the Head Office ladies cloakroom:

'Well, I suppose we might as well start looking for another position. By all accounts, half of us in Office Admin will be made redundant when this new All Singing, All Dancing Network watchamicallit is set up!'
'I heard the screens are ever so bad for your eyes – imagine looking at a flickering green screen all day long!'
'And they reckon they can keep a check on how much you've typed in an hour!'
'No!'
'Yes! Take it from me, the best days are already over here!'

Peter Richards to Sue French:

'You going to this demo of the proposed computer system tomorrow?'
'What new system?'
'The one Stanley Jones has arranged in Accounts.'

'Be nice to know it was happening. What time is it?'
'I'm not sure – anyway, it's probably only good for number crunching if I know Stan!'

Senior Shop Steward at Reading factory, addressing monthly union meeting:

Machine Operator: What about this computer set up they're all talking about. I reckon it'll be used to jack up our piece work rates if we're not careful. I've heard tell Management's gonna use it to analyse productivity from top to bottom!

Senior Shop Steward (embarrassed): Don't you worry Sam, we'll not let 'em steal a march on this one – in fact, I've got it on the agenda for the next Works Committee Meeting.'

Voice from back: 'About time too!'

Jean Harrison to John Knight

'Confidentially, John, I think this whole computerisation thing is going to rebound on us if we're not careful – the whole place is rife with rumour and counter rumour. Surely there's a better way of going over to a more fully computerised set up than putting on a series of demonstrations without much prior notice or explanatory follow-up!'

Assessment Questions

1   How should the Board of Directors, in your opinion, set about the acquisition and installation of a suitable computerised information system?
2   What do you see as the major needs of Powa Drill in information processing terms?
3   What are the needs in interpersonal terms and for internal public relations which are highlighted by the case study when such an acquisition is being considered?
4   Can you suggest any restructuring of the company which might be undertaken as part of the installation/implementation of introducing an extensive computerised information processing system?

Assignments

1   Draft the minute of the Board Meeting which gives the 'green light' to acquiring the proposed system.
2   In syndicate groups, draw up a plan of the way the introduction of the new system should be undertaken.
3   Outline as a report to the Board the kind of system and implementation approach which you, as a hired consultant, would advocate to up-date the company's computer and information processing provision.
4   Write an essay which discusses the following:

'What interpersonal communication approaches are necessary at all levels of an organisation which contemplates a major move towards the installation of a "turnkey" information processing system?'

[This case study has been adapted from an original devised by the author subsequently made available to the London Chamber of Commerce.]

12 The job application process

In many ways, the time devoted to general and vocational education and training, which young people over some eleven to thirteen years in, may be regarded as a preparation for a worthwhile career. Of course, an education does more than prepare someone for the world of work but it is timely, in these days of ongoing high unemployment, to put the right degree of emphasis and importance upon the job application process, the success of which can crown many years of application, striving and personal effort.

Moreover, the ability to find a worthwhile post with good prospects is not built into people along with the fact that their genes may endow them with red hair or blue eyes! No, like many skills worth attaining, the process of applying for – and obtaining – a first job has to be carefully studied, practised and perfected!

Indeed, the trouble taken to acquire and maintain these skills will certainly not be wasted, for in some 40 years of working life, the average person will change jobs several times and many employees will be required to undergo promotion interviews as they progress up the organisation hierarchy.

The best way to prepare for a period in which jobs will be intensively applied for is to break down the process into its component sections and to examine each carefully before putting them back together and practising the entire sequence.

The job application process may be regarded as having two sides to it – the side seen by the applicant, and that seen by the employer. In both cases, it is important for each to know 'how the other half ticks' – for the employer's staff to have some feeling and understanding of the stress which job applicants undergo, and for the applicant to realise the time, money and effort which employers expend to endeavour to recruit the right person for the right job.

Firstly let us examine the process from the applicant's viewpoint. The phases of job application may be broken down into the following.

The applicant's viewpoint

1 The career exploration and counselling phase

A period of careful consideration given to the sort of sector or field in which the applicant has a genuine interest and to which he or she could dedicate most of his or her waking hours.

This process may take some time to unfold and it is sensible for young adults to obtain expert careers advice and to take the trouble to research various sectors personally. It can be equally fatal either to drift into a particular area of commerce, industry or public service or to 'follow in father's footsteps' just because that's what is expected.

2 The finding out where jobs are phase

Once the particular sector in which to find a good job has been identified – say publishing, personnel management, accounting, selling, manufacturing or the like – the next step is to discover how available jobs in a particular sector are advertised or publicised.

The following checklist provides an overview of likely sources of information about available posts.

In a national context

Some jobs are advertised nationally, especially if a large organisation is looking to recruit a number of trainees at one time. Therefore jobs are likely to be found advertised in:

National daily press *The Times, Guardian, The Daily Telegraph*, etc. (Some national dailies advertise certain sectors on particular days – *The Times:* secretarial posts on Wednesdays; *Guardian:* teaching posts on Tuesdays. So it pays to check out when likely advertisements appear.)

Sunday newspapers *The Sunday Times, The Observer, The Sunday Telegraph*, etc. Currently some of the Sunday newspapers produce as many as 10–15 pages of job advertisements. Many are for senior positions, but some do ask for trainees or advertise junior posts.

Professional and trade journals and newspapers In the UK there are literally hundreds of specialist journals and magazines published weekly or monthly for various specialist workforces, from doctors to plumbers, nurses to chemical engineers, lawyers to public health officers. Almost certainly there will be one for the area in which you are interested. It therefore pays either to become a regular subscriber of such a journal or to see whether it is taken by your local municipal, college or school library.

Television and radio   Occasionally organisations will take out commercials for jobs to be broadcast on the national broadcasting media; these are not very extensively used for advertising jobs but sometimes a worthwhile opening – especially in the public sector – may be spotted. Local radio stations sometimes adopt regular job advertising spots, however.

In a local context

The local daily and weekly press   The local equivalent of the national daily newspaper is often the weekly paper serving a district and concentrating on local news. Some larger towns do support evening dailies and occasionally a morning local paper. These newspapers provide a fruitful source of local job opportunities, although, each opening must be evaluated on its merits in terms of opportunities to progress and conditions of service, when smaller, local firms are set against larger, national ones.

Free newspaper   Increasingly weekly newspapers are springing up which depend upon their advertising revenue for their income and are thus delivered free to householders. Again local jobs are advertised in free newspapers, whose display advertising rates are often cheaper than those of the established local press.

Careers Centre   For young people up to the age of 18, the local Careers Centre provides not only expert advice, but also a job finding service, since local employers often send to the Centres copies of job advertisements, job specifications and details, or just simply telephone to provide information about a current opening.

Job Centres   Local Job Centres operate in a similar way, and advertise available jobs on window and reception display boards. Job Centre staff become very knowledgeable about local conditions and openings and their advice is worth obtaining.

In addition, Job Centres act as information agencies for details about Youth Training Schemes, Job Training Schemes for mature students and local Community Projects, which are offered by the Manpower Services Commission.

Private Employment Bureaux   Increasingly, privately owned employment bureaux are opening not only in London but in larger provincial towns and cities. They act as a kind of broker between the employer and the applicant, and often work closely with local personnel officers. Theirs is a highly competitive world and they have to maintain high standards in order to survive. Usually they earn a fee from the employer if someone registered with them is appointed by a firm. But it always pays to be absolutely clear about any financial commitments being accepted whenever a job applicant registers with a private employment bureau, and to scrutinise fully any document requiring a signature.

Word of mouth   In many organisations the fastest route that confidential communication takes is the company grapevine!

It may well be worthwhile in this respect for the job hunter to alert suitable friends and relatives and ask them to keep eyes and ears open for an opportunity to be quickly followed up even before it appears in the national or local press.

Self advertisement   An additional and very productive strategy for the job applicant to adopt while examining the national and local media for job advertisements is to devise a suitable personal letter of 'unsolicited application' and to send it with a current curriculum vitae to a whole range of national and local employers. It turns out sometimes that the arrival of such a letter coincides with the decision to create a new post or look for a replacement for a member of staff who has been promoted or who has retired or resigned. Such actions also demonstrate the applicant's initiative to a potential employer.

3   Responding to an advertisement phase

Sooner or later, an advertisement is spotted which excites the individual who decides to apply for the advertised post.

Even at this early stage, some essential questions need to be posed and answered by the applicant:

- Am I ready to apply?
  Nowadays employers can afford to set high demands for their job applicants to meet and many will expect a curriculum vitae – a schematic checklist of education, examination successes, experience etc (*see* page 219) – to accompany the written application. So ideally, the CV should have been designed, vetted and flawlessly duplicated before the first advertisement is responded to.
- What do I know about this employing organisation? Does it enjoy a good reputation for the way it treats its staff?
- Does the job appear to give scope for personal development and prospects for advancement? Or does it seem a dead-end post?
- What clues does the advertisement provide about conditions of service – pension scheme, holidays, pay, hours of work etc?
- Do I know to whom I shall be applying or am I expected to reply to a box number? It is generally preferable to know who you are dealing with when offering your services.
- Am I expected in the first instance merely to send off for an application form and further details of the post? If so, only a short, polite letter asking for them is needed initially. An official letter of

application is expected to accompany the completed application form.

- Do I really want this job? Or shall I be wasting everybody's time by turning it down if it is offered to me?

4 The detailed application phase

This phase will involve three major tasks:

- completing the application form effectively
- composing a letter of application
- doing further fact-finding research about the firm and the advertised job.

Here, the following tips may prove useful:

Look up the company in *Who Owns Whom* and its directors or main board directors in *Who's Who*. This can forestall any faux pas about certain countries or pastimes which are close to the corporate heart or form the interviewer's pet hobbies!

Look the firm up in *Kompass* to see what they make if they are in manufacturing. Check their position on the stock market if they are a public company – are their shares rising? Or falling?

Ask friends and relatives what they know or can find out about the company and its trading record. Will it still be about in two years' time or will you have been made redundant and have to start all over again?

5 The preparation for interview phase

All being well, you will have been shortlisted for an interview and advised so by letter specifying a given date and time.

A short and courteous letter of acceptance should be directly despatched and then preparations begin in earnest! Your application documents have worked and you are almost certainly one of the last five applicants selected for interview.

The conscientious candidate will have kept photocopies of all the application documents to refresh his or her mind and will be drafting the sort of questions expected to come up at interview and deciding upon the answers to be given.

Careful thought will be given to what constitutes the appropriate outfit or suit to wear to the interview and timetables will have been double checked to ensure arrival at the interview location in good time. In this regard, the crafty candidate arrives early and, if possible, tours the company areas which are accessible to 'get the feel' of the place. Noticeboards, foyer areas and offices visible through glass partitions may reveal a great deal about the quality and image an organisation projects and maintains. If everything looks sloppy and disorganised then the chances of acquiring useful career skills may be slim. However, the organised firm will almost certainly lay on a tour in any case, and in such a firm the applicant is unlikely to get past the reception area without an escort!

6 The interview phase

This is the crucial part of job application, since all is either won or lost at the interview. To perform well, the applicant must:

- master nerves and shyness
- listen carefully to the questions posed
- respond fluently but without gabbling endlessly nor by uttering monotones
- avoid irritating speech mannerisms and physical movements like playing with a ring or scratching an ear.

In fact, the interview phase requires careful preparation and practice and is dealt with in detail on pages 216–18.

7 The acceptance phase

If the interview has gone well, the applicant is offered the post – either immediately at the interview or within a day or so by letter. The offer will be confirmed by letter in any case and by law has to be followed up within three weeks of employment commencing with a detailed contract of employment. The prudent interviewee therefore does not wait until it is too late to check up on salary, terms of notice on either side etc, but clarifies such central matters at the interview phase. It then remains for the applicant to respond with a formal letter of acceptance and to provide his existing employer with the required written notice – again usually by letter. Subject to the recruiting company obtaining acceptable references from the applicant's employer, the process is complete.

Except that the shrewd applicant does not spend the time left working out his notice by running down his present employer or giving voice to thoughtless criticisms of the firm and the people who run it. No company or manager is perfect, and who knows, perhaps the wheel will one day turn full circle, and the applicant wish to apply for a more senior post at his old company! As is usually the case, 'a still tongue makes a wise head' in such matters.

The employer's viewpoint

Just as the job applicant has his own set of activities to mastermind during the job application process, so indeed has the employer. As the chart on page 216 illustrates, the employing organisation – if it is a thorough and conscientious one – has to carry out a good deal of preliminary work before the advertisement for a particular post can be published.

The following sections outline the work carried out by the recruiting organisation:

1 The job creation phase

Long before a post can be brought to the attention of would-be applicants a decision has to be taken on

The Job Selection Process

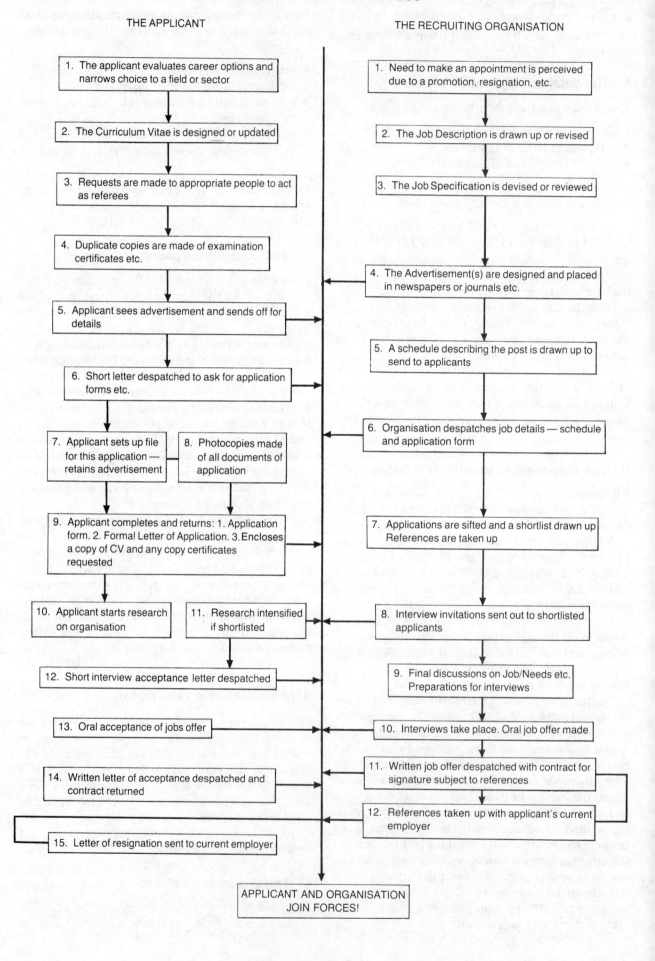

THE APPLICANT — THE RECRUITING ORGANISATION

1. The applicant evaluates career options and narrows choice to a field or sector

1. Need to make an appointment is perceived due to a promotion, resignation, etc.

2. The Curriculum Vitae is designed or updated

2. The Job Description is drawn up or revised

3. Requests are made to appropriate people to act as referees

3. The Job Specification is devised or reviewed

4. Duplicate copies are made of examination certificates etc.

4. The Advertisement(s) are designed and placed in newspapers or journals etc.

5. Applicant sees advertisement and sends off for details

5. A schedule describing the post is drawn up to send to applicants

6. Short letter despatched to ask for application forms etc.

6. Organisation despatches job details — schedule and application form

7. Applicant sets up file for this application — retains advertisement

8. Photocopies made of all documents of application

9. Applicant completes and returns: 1. Application form. 2. Formal Letter of Application. 3. Encloses a copy of CV and any copy certificates requested

7. Applications are sifted and a shortlist drawn up References are taken up

10. Applicant starts research on organisation

11. Research intensified if shortlisted

8. Interview invitations sent out to shortlisted applicants

12. Short interview acceptance letter despatched

9. Final discussions on Job/Needs etc. Preparations for interviews

13. Oral acceptance of jobs offer

10. Interviews take place. Oral job offer made

14. Written letter of acceptance despatched and contract returned

11. Written job offer despatched with contract for signature subject to references

12. References taken up with applicant's current employer

15. Letter of resignation sent to current employer

APPLICANT AND ORGANISATION JOIN FORCES!

whether and when to create it if it is an entirely new one, for example arising from the introduction of IT equipment, or on how it should be revised, modified and updated if it is an existing one just vacated. Interestingly, it is often at this stage that senior managers come to realise how much 'Old Jonesy' quietly got on with it, or how different his job has become from the one they thought he was doing! And this is one good reason among many for regular reviews of job specifications and job descriptions (see below). The reasons for jobs arising in a firm are many – a new store may be opened, someone retires, an employee's spouse is promoted to another part of the country and so on.

2 The job specification and job description

To avoid the chaos which ensues, not to mention the toes that get trodden on without their implementation, progressive organisations have for many years maintained careful records or statements about the jobs their staff do.

This process forms part of what is termed job analysis. This function is usually carried out either by an organisation and methods unit which forms part of a management services department, or is undertaken by the personnel department.

Briefly, each job is carefully monitored to establish in detail its component parts and also to determine the skills, qualifications and personal attributes which a person needs to enable them to do the job competently.

The job specification

It is the job specification which sets out as a schedule the skills, technical competencies, knowledge and experience which are needed to carry out the job. For example, a word processing operator would be 'profiled' in the specification as needing, among other attributes:

- twenty-twenty or corrected vision (the job entails a great deal of visual work);
- the ability to use a computer efficiently (indeed, the job centres upon manipulating text via a keyboard and VDU);
- a thorough knowledge of the word processing package being used in both theory and practice;
- a creative and imaginative flair (sometimes WP operators solve textual and display problems by manipulating the software in ways not mentioned in the manual);
- a methodical and conscientious approach to work (editing the MD's Annual Report is not a job for a 'slapdash artist'!);
- the ability to spell correctly and to proof-read well and so on.

There is no single, approved way in which to set out a job specification, but as you will have noticed from the examples given above, the specification identifies a number of factors needed which can be classified as follows:

1 Physical attributes or proficiencies
2 Manual skills
3 Knowledge skills
4 Personality and social skills.

Many job specifications are, appropriately, drawn up therefore according to the headings of the NIP Seven Point Plan (see page 219), specifying requirements in the areas of physical make-up, attainments, general intelligence, special aptitudes, disposition, etc.

The job description

The function of the job description is to set down clearly what a particular job consists of and to set it in a context. For example, a sales representative's job will customarily be set out according to sections such as:

1 The job's title.
2 If appropriate, its coded position on a league table ranging from the most junior to the most senior posts, so staff can place it promptly in the hierarchy.
3 A brief outline of its major role.
4 The identity of the person who supervises the work, i.e. the job holder's immediate superior in a 'reports to' function.
5 The identity of anyone reporting to the job holder, i.e. any subordinate staff.
6 The job description then proceeds to catalogue the major tasks involved.

For example the job description of the sales representative may include descriptions such as:

- follow a schedule of visits (to existing customers) on a monthly cycle to obtain sales orders;
- submit weekly (for receipt at District Office by Mondays) a sales report using the relevant report forms;
- keep proper records, supported by receipts of expenses arising solely and entirely from the requirements of the post. Submit such expenses records weekly;

and so on.

Of course, it is much easier to compile a job description for someone with an orderly and structured job than it is for an employee like an advertising copywriter who is expected to be creative every day and whose job is often self-directed.

3 Details for the applicants phase

Once the job specification and description have been designed or revised, the schedule detailing the main features of the organisation along with the principal benefits and requirements of the job may be drawn up and duplicated in anticipation of applications.

4 The advertising phase

How this is approached depends on a number of factors, including the seniority of the post, whether the organisation is large enough to support a personnel department to design advertisements and so on. For some managerial posts, large firms employ specialist consultancy firms which place the advertisement while not revealing the company's identity and which undertake the initial screening and interviewing to save the hiring company time.

However managed, someone has to assume responsibility for placing advertisements in what is potentially the most effective newspaper or journal (or mix of both).

The specimen advertisement below illustrates some of the major aspects of display advertising. But bear in mind that different posts require different approaches and different organisations have evolved preferred ways of advertising.

5 The shortlisting phase

The existence of a job specification does much to aid the sifting of applications, since it specifies what skills, attainments, knowledge, etc are deemed necessary. Some personnel staff draw up schedules to assist in the selection process by listing requirements under such headings as:

VITAL   IMPORTANT   USEFUL
NON-ESSENTIAL

They then measure applications against such a yardstick.

It is important for the applicant to bear in mind that he or she is often competing in this phase with

1 *Display advertisements need bold eye-catching headlines, allied to a visually interesting*

2 *logo or piece of artwork. Notice that this artwork sets a mood of upward success which is not daunting.*

The company knows that it is highly regarded so it displays its name prominently to attract high-calibre applicants.

4 *The advertisement's job title also needs to be displayed prominently.*

5 *This advertisement seizes upon four main 'carrots' to interest the applicant without becoming too detailed or involved. Notice that in this advertisement no 'hard' details are given about pay, hours of work etc.*

6 *Having conveyed what is on offer, the advertisement briefly sets out the salient features (which are looked for) in an applicant.*

7 *The name and address of the person to write to are clearly and fully displayed*

8 *Note that Sparks & Muncer PLC pride themselves on providing equal*

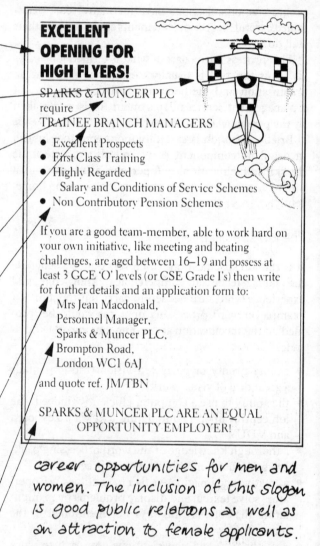

EXCELLENT OPENING FOR HIGH FLYERS!

SPARKS & MUNCER PLC
require
TRAINEE BRANCH MANAGERS

● Excellent Prospects
● First Class Training
● Highly Regarded
   Salary and Conditions of Service Schemes
● Non Contributory Pension Schemes

If you are a good team-member, able to work hard on your own initiative, like meeting and beating challenges, are aged between 16–19 and possess at least 3 GCE 'O' levels (or CSE Grade I's) then write for further details and an application form to:

Mrs Jean Macdonald,
Personnel Manager,
Sparks & Muncer PLC,
Brompton Road,
London WC1 6AJ

and quote ref. JM/TBN

SPARKS & MUNCER PLC ARE AN EQUAL
OPPORTUNITY EMPLOYER!

career opportunities for men and women. The inclusion of this slogan is good public relations as well as an attraction to female applicants.

DISPLAY ADVERTISEMENTS
should be
○ VISUALLY ARRESTING
○ SHORT ON TEXT
○ APPEALING IN TONE
○ EASY TO GRASP

as many as 100 fellow applicants and that sometimes pressure of work may cause the barely legible application or the long-winded one to be instantly discarded. In the same way, the 'tatty' or casual-looking application may be given short shrift!

Once a shortlist (or sometimes an initial 'long shortlist' if there are to be two sets of interviews) has been established, then the given referees will be contacted to provide a confidential reference about the applicant. As this takes time and effort, it is crucial for applicants to approach referees to ask for their support and willingness to act as referees *before* they receive reference requests out of the blue!

6   The interview phase

Prior to holding the interviews, the organisation will arrange final discussions to establish in fine detail exactly the kind of person they are seeking and to structure the interviewing process. Sometimes four or five managers may interview candidates in a sequence and compare notes. Sometimes they may act together as a panel. Nowadays employment law has resulted in (quite properly) a lengthy and sometimes costly procedure being needed before an employee may be dismissed. As a result, the applicant can be sure that the interviewing staff will have done their homework and be ready to ensure that the selection process provides a truly testing dialogue so that selection mistakes are minimised!

7   The job offer phase

Sometimes an interviewing panel will recall an applicant from a waiting room and make an orally delivered job offer at the close of the interview. Some firms, however, may prefer interviewing staff to 'sleep on it' and write to all candidates the next day offering the post to one of them. Yet others may wait to see if the first preference applicant accepts or rejects the post before contacting the second choice.

However tackled, the job offer will be made within a day or so of interview. It may be that the official contract for the job is enclosed with the letter offering the post. Applicants should always keep in mind that this is a binding document on both sides.

7   Approaching the applicant's current employer phase

It is a long established code of professional practice that recruiting companies will not approach an applicant's current employers without his or her permission. Nevertheless, oral or written job offers are often qualified by the phrases:

> . . . subject to the receipt of suitable references from your current employer.

This phase is almost always perfunctory in that candidates are rarely rejected after the job offer has been made, but it does illustrate the thoroughness of the job selection process from the employer's viewpoint.

Tips on writing a letter of application

We first saw Jane Simmond's letter of application for the post of Private Secretary to the Export Sales Manager of Finosa Fabrics Limited in the Topic on letter writing as an example of letter structuring. It is also a useful model to study in the context of applying for a job.

A letter which supports a completed application form and accompanies a curriculum vitae has a different job to do from the letter which is the only submitted application document. The latter is sometimes requested as the sole means of written application and has to do the job all by itself:

> 'Interested applicants are invited to apply by letter to . . .'

In the former case, the main functions of the letter of application are:

- To formalise the act of application. Jane Simmond's opening paragraph does that and gets it out of the way. Note the need always to refer to any enclosed documents – the application form and CV – to ensure they are not overlooked or misplaced.
- To act as a summary of what are considered the major strengths of the application. Bear in mind it does no harm to repeat them as a way of imprinting them on an employer's mind. He or she may be sifting through several dozen applications.

FINOSA FABRICS LTD require a PRIVATE SECRETARY to the EXPORT SALES MANAGER (EUROPE)

A knowledge of two EEC foreign languages is required and experience of export sales procedures is an advantage. The successful candidate will work on his or her own initiative and be able to handle incoming telephone calls and documentation from French or German agents. He or she must also be prepared to travel abroad.

The company provides excellent conditions of service, including four weeks' paid holiday per annum subsidised insurance and restaurant facilities. Salary negotiable according to age and experience.

Apply in writing to: The Personnel Manager, Finosa Fabrics Ltd, 4 York Way, London WC2B 6AK

Applications to be received by 30 May 19—

Model letter of application

Dear Sir,

I should like to apply for the post of private secretary to your Export Sales Manager recently advertised in 'The Daily Sentinel', and have pleasure in enclosing my completed application form and a copy of my curriculum vitae.

The advertised post particularly appeals to me, since my own career aspirations and education have been specifically directed for the last two years towards a secretarial appointment in the field of export sales.

In the sixth form at Redbrook High School I specialised in Advanced-level German, French and English and proceeded in September 19   to Redbrook College of Technology, where I embarked upon a bilingual secretarial course leading to the Commercial Secretary's Diploma in Export Studies.

The course includes intensive commercial language studies (I am specialising in German), communication, office administration and export studies with particular emphasis on E.E.C. procedures and documentation. In addition, the Diploma course provides shorthand, word processing and typewriting components including work in the special foreign language.

I anticipate achieving a good pass in the June Diploma examination and attaining shorthand and typewriting speeds of 100/50 w.p.m., having already secured passes at 80/40 w.p.m.

During my full-time education, I have travelled extensively in the Federal Republic of Germany and in France, and have become familiar with the customs and outlooks of both countries. In August 19   I gained a valuable insight into German business methods during a month's exchange visit to a Handelsschule in Frankfurt-am-Main.

Assisting my father for the past two years in his own company has afforded me an opportunity to use my own initiative and to obtain helpful work experience in areas such as sales documentation, customer relations and the use of data processing in a sales context.

If called, I should be pleased to attend for an interview at any time convenient to you.

My course at Redbrook College of Technology finishes on 30th June 19   and I should be available to commence a full-time appointment from the beginning of July onwards.

    Yours faithfully,

    Jane Simmonds. (Miss)

(Note: It is usual for letters of application such as the one above to be handwritten.)

- To emphasise the applicant's suitability to *this particular advertised post*. Consider that the application form will have gathered the information the *employer* seeks and that the CV must of necessity be an all-purpose document to support an application for different types of job. The specific advertisement will have asked for particular qualities or abilities and the written letter provides a chance to demonstrate their possession – as far as the applicant is genuinely able to do so.
- Good letters of application convey a sense of enthusiasm for gaining the advertised post without being either 'gushy' or 'swollen-headed' in reciting accomplishments. The tone of Jane's letter seeks to meet this requirement:

Specimen Job Description

Job reference:	PA/SD	Date: 21 January 19—

Job Title: Personal Assistant to Sales Director.

Responsible To: Sales Director.

Responsible For: The work of three clerical staff in Sales Director's Office.

Job Role: The post is primarily a staff appointment to provide administrative assistance to the Sales Director and to supervise the work of clerical staff within the Sales Director's Office.

Principal Duties: To maintain an efficient administrative service for the Sales Director having regard to the Sales Director's Office and the Director's ongoing programme of duties.

To prioritize each morning's mail; to ensure the confidentiality of incoming and outgoing correspondence as appropriate and to handle matters not requiring the Sales Director's immediate attention.

To process correspondence, internal mail and other material as required. To supervise the work of clerical staff in this regard.

To maintain an effective filing and records system both in traditional and electronic modes.

To ensure the smooth working of the Sales Director's diary and schedule of appointments.

To channel incoming telephone calls, using initiative to filter out those not requiring the Sales Director's personal attention.

To be in attendance for the purposes of minute taking at sales meetings.

To receive visitors hospitably.

To supervise the filing, reprographic work, records maintenance and general duties of the clerical office staff.

To undertake any further reasonable duties from time to time as may be deemed in keeping with the job designation.

Résumé of Conditions of Service: 37.5 hour week, Mondays to Fridays, 8.45 a.m. to 5.15 p.m. 1 hour lunch-break by arrangement.

Four weeks paid holiday annually plus bank holidays.

Notice of termination of employment: two weeks on either side.

Instituted: 1 September 19—   Revised 21 January 19—

Authorising Officer: J D Norton, Personnel Director.

'the advertised post particularly appeals to me since . . .'
'I gained a valuable insight into German business methods . . .'
'If called, I should be pleased to attend for an interview at any time . . .'

- The accompanying letter of application should be kept fairly short – the equivalent of one side of A4 is suggested – and should be written by hand. Firstly since this is still established etiquette, and secondly because employers like to get the feel of the application in personal terms. A few even submit handwriting for analysis, so this should sharpen up the scribblers and microscopic hieroglyphics writers among us!

- The tone of the letter is properly formal and so the Dear Sir or Dear Madam . . . Yours faithfully salutation and subscription are appropriate.

  While it is not always easy, avoid including too many 'I's in sentence constructions and particularly as the opening words of paragraphs. The British are a funny lot and the ability to blow one's trumpet discreetly is expected in job applications!

- Make sure you convey a sense of being readily available both for interview and to start the job if successful. It does not pay to suggest a starting date betwee[n] the holiday needed after the stress of examinatio[n] and one's customary winter break!

- ALWAYS take photocopies of ALL the docum[ents] despatched in support of a job application. I[f you] are making these thick and fast, you will

JOB SPECIFICATION

Job: Personnel Records Clerk

Duties	Tasks	Knowledge requirements	Skill requirements (ability to:)
(1) Documentation for new employees	(1.1) Sends new employee advice forms to notify Time Officer.	Layout of employee advice forms.	
	(1.2) Makes out rate cards and computer cards.	Layout of computer and rate cards.	Write neatly.
	(1.3) Enters details of new employees in starters book and wage book.	Layout and use of starters book and wage book.	
	(1.4) If employee is disabled enters on registered disabled list.	Method of making entries in disabled list.	
	(1.5) Collects employee's personal documents (i.e. application form, letter of offer, etc) for insertion in personal file.	Documents required. Personal Department filing system.	
	(1.6) Types out absence report form.	Layout and interpretation of forms.	Type accurately complete entries in printed forms.
	(1.7) Sends notification of starter's rate of pay for hourly-paid employees to Head of Department.	Organisation of Departments. Heads of Department. Location of Departments.	
	(1.8) Sends all relevant documents to Wages Department.	Documents required by Wages.	

Extract of a Job Specification reproduced by kind permission of Macdonald & Evans Limited.

otherwise impossible to recall what you wrote – and that is precisely what the interviewers will be scrutinising in front of them when you are being interviewed!

- NEVER send originals of examination certificates etc with job applications. If employers are insistent, say you will bring them with you to any interview. Once lost, some may never be replaced in the same way, and their loss will cause much irritation.

Interviews: general introduction

e interview is used in organisations to meet the needs
ny, quite different, situations. Some interviews
emely formal affairs, where a candidate for a
be examined and evaluated by a board or
rviewers. Others are conducted in a much
atmosphere, in a 'one-to-one' relation-
y, a manager and a subordinate.
it is very difficult to establish where
d the interviewing process begins
working definition of an inter-
es:

two parties meet to
y mutual interroga-

The process is characterised by the posing and answering of questions, or by the giving and receiving of directions, instructions or advice.

In particular, both parties have specific aims to achieve by directing questions and answers to an end known usually to both interviewer and interviewee.

According to the above definition, an interview may, in effect, be taking place far more frequently than we may realise. When, for example, a manager calls a subordinate into his office, invites him to sit down and then says,

'How have things been going, lately, Jim? You've been looking rather unsettled . . .'

a counselling interview is probably about to take place to enable the manager to get to the root of a problem.

So it is that the interview process is employed to obtain information and responses in a wide variety of areas, from sales performance to accounts collection, from disciplinary proceedings to promotion selection, from counselling on personal problems to personnel appointments. The following table indicates some of the principal areas in which the interview is commonly used.

It is therefore important for the members of any organisation to regard the interview not as an intimidating process to be endured, but rather as a tool of communication from the use of which the interviewee

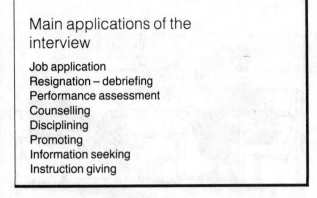

Main applications of the interview

Job application
Resignation – debriefing
Performance assessment
Counselling
Disciplining
Promoting
Information seeking
Instruction giving

has as much to gain as the interviewer. The truth of this observation becomes much more apparent if the interviewee in particular stops to consider that the process *is* two-way.

The following section examines the job application interview process. Careful preparation and probing questions on the part of the interviewee may result in his declining an offered post with a company which is performing poorly and where job prospects exist in theory rather than in practice. It is important, therefore, at the outset to interpret the term, 'interrogation' as 'a two-way channel for finding out'.

The Interview

When interview techniques are being discussed, it is usually the formal interview which is considered. It is important to remember, however, that even in informal interview situations the guide-lines which follow will still hold true in principle, if not in detail.

In any interview, the interviewee will be assessed, either directly or indirectly in these areas:

appearance, deportment, manners, speech, intelligence, judgment, values, commonsense, initiative, resourcefulness, assurance.

Basically, the interviewer will be seeking reassurance or information in line with the questions:

How does the interviewee project himself?

What has he to offer in terms of specialist skills or knowledge?

What has he to offer in terms of personality?

What potential to develop does he display?

Appearance, manners, deportment

As an interviewee, whether making a first job application or an employee, before a promotion panel, your personal appearance matters! Rightly or wrongly other people will make judgments about you, which will be influenced by your appearance. Looking smart and well-groomed is an asset in any situation and is nowhere more important than at an interview.

The way you hold yourself, move and gesture will also affect the way people regard you. In professional and business life attractive people are those who temper assurance with modesty, and who behave calmly, with due consideration for others. On entering the interview room, for example, take care to do so politely but not over-hesitantly, and wait to be proferred a hand to shake or to be invited to take a seat. Once seated, avoid the tendency to slouch or lounge and assume a posture which is comfortable, but alert. Also, it is sensible to hold the hands in the lap, and to return them to this position between any gestures.

It is also important to master any feelings of nervousness. Feeling nervous is natural during an interview and you may be sure that the interviewer is aware of this fact and that he or she will go to some trouble to set you at your ease. Nevertheless, allowing nerves to take over, and displaying signs of tension by hunching into the chair, wringing hands, twisting rings or biting lips not only impairs your performance, but transmits a sense of unease to the interviewer as well. The result may be that you do not do justice to yourself and that you leave doubts about your capacities in the mind of the interviewer.

Listening before speaking

Once the interview is under way, perhaps the best advice is to *listen*! It is all too easy as an interviewee to attend with only half an ear to what is being said or asked. Moreover, you will need to employ all your faculties and to keep extremely alert to ensure that you anticipate, for example, where a sequence of questions is leading you, or to see the probing which may be going on beneath an apparently harmless question!

Listening attentively will also help you to prepare your answer while a question is being framed. It is amazing how fast the brain works in such situations.

Looking at the questioner

Rightly, the ability to 'look someone squarely in the eye' has always been regarded as a sign of honesty and assurance. It helps in any case, during an interview to look at a speaker posing a question since facial expression, gesture or posture often provide valuable insights into what is in an interviewer's mind, and shows that you are paying attention.

Similarly, when providing an answer you should make eye-contact with the questioner, but not to the extent of boring into them with a transfixing stare!

Think before you speak!

This well-worn truism is still excellent advice to the interviewee. Blurting out a nonsense or 'gabbling' on because of nerves are traps into which the unwary often fall. Moreover, it is not possible in an interview to escape from being assessed and both the words you utter and the way in which you express yourself will reveal much about your intelligence, judgment, commonsense and *nous*.

In order to answer questions successfully and in so doing to create a favourable impression, you should ask yourself these questions both before and during your answer:

Have I understood the question?
Do I appreciate what it is driving at?
Are there any traps or pitfalls present in the question?
Can I draw on my own experience to illustrate my answer?
Am I speaking clearly and convincingly?
Have I covered the ground and said enough?

Thinking *while* speaking

Just as the practised reader's eye travels ahead before reading a phrase aloud, so the practised interviewee's mind will be thinking ahead and monitoring what is being said. Additionally, the interviewee's eyes will be looking hard at the interviewer for signs of a favourable response to what is being said.

Sometimes the way in which the spoken word is constructed into phrases or sentences allows for 'rest' or 'pause' expressions to be uttered while the brain composes the next important point:

. . . as a matter of fact I . . .
. . . I accept the truth of that but . . .
. . . although my initial response might be to . . . in this case I would . . .

Also, there are means of delaying arrival at the explicit answer point of a difficult question by means of a sort of delaying tactic:

I suppose it depends to a large degree upon how the term X is interpreted . . .

I don't have an easy or quick answer to that question, but on reflection I . . .

It should be noted that interviewers are only too aware of how much easier it is to pose questions than to answer them, and make natural allowances for initial hesitancy. A word of caution, however: if an interviewee displays a frequent inability to answer questions directly, they are bound to sow in the interviewer's mind seeds of doubt regarding integrity, honesty or, quite simply, lack of knowledge.

Measure what you say

Interviewers are skilled at posing questions which cannot be answered by a simple 'yes' or 'no'. For example, a question would not be phrased:

'Did you enjoy your previous job'

but rather,

'I was rather hoping you would ask me that. Yes . . . and no. I think it really depends on how one views the broader implications. Looking at it objectively, what was the question again? . . .'

'What did you find most satisfying about your previous job?'

In this way the interviewee is invited to expand a reply rather than to offer monosyllabic answers, which inevitably cast doubts upon fluency, knowledge and assurance. It is common, however, for inexperienced interviewees to speak rapidly at great length, as if the assessment were based on words spoken per minute and the range of unrelated topics covered! You must therefore ensure that what you are saying is relevant to the question and forms a summary of the main issues as you see them. It is good practice to pause after having made what you consider an adequate number of points to allow the interviewer either to ask you to continue or to ask another question. Try to strike a happy medium. Saying too little prevents you from demonstrating your knowledge and ability. Saying too much reveals a disorganised and 'butterfly' mind.

Ask *your* questions

Whatever the interviewing situation, the interviewer largely has control of the interview. Nevertheless you should ensure that you make an opportunity to ask the questions *you* have framed. In the context of an application for a job, you wish to establish whether you want the organisation equally as much as it may wish to decide whether it wants you! Such opportunities tend to occur at the end of the interview but clarifying questions may be put throughout.

Useful information for the interviewee

The NIP Seven Point Plan

The following headings summarise an assessment system used in selection processes by interviewers and as a basis for personnel specifications:

Physical make-up
Attainments
General intelligence
Special aptitudes
Interests
Disposition
Circumstances

The application form

The following information is generally required on an application form for a job:

Name
Address
Telephone no.
Age: date of birth
Status: married, single
Maiden name if married woman
Education
Qualifications
Current, previous experience
Present designation or title
Name and address of employers
Details, with dates, of employment since leaving full-time education
Details of salaries in each appointment
Outline of hobbies, interests
Names, addresses and occupations of referees
Date of availability
Signature and achnowledgement of accuracy of data provided

The curriculum vitae

A *curriculum vitae* may be composed by using the following framework:

Personal details
Full name and current address
Telephone number
Age, status – married, single
Nationality
Dependents – wife, husband, children
Education
Secondary school(s)
College(s)⎱ with
University⎰ dates
Post-graduate institution
Main subjects taken
Activities, interests
Post(s) of responsibility
Qualifications
Examination passes indicating grades, dates and examining boards.
Work experience
Usually expressed by starting from immediate past and working backwards.
   Name of organisation, location, job designation, range of duties, extent of responsibilities, reasons for leaving.
Interests
Leisure activities, hobbies, indicating posts of responsibility – e.g. Honorary Secretary of Drama Club – where appropriate.
Circumstances
Period of notice required to be given.
   Mobility – car-ownership, any limiting commitments.

A *curriculum vitae* is usually set out schematically, with appropriate dates and chronological structures.

A golden rule for interviewees

Be yourself!

Pretence or affectation may land you in a job, or with responsibilities which may hang, like the proverbial albatross, around your neck! Hold to what you believe in – it will almost certainly give you a happier and more fulfilled working life.

Assessment questions

1　List with brief notes the major sources of published job applications: (*a*) nationally (*b*) in your locality.
2　What are the principal differences between the services provided by a careers office and a job centre?
3　What do the initials MSC stand for? Outline the range of services which this organisation provides.
4　What is 'an unsolicited letter of application'? What special contribution does it make to the job finding process?
5　What information would you expect to find in:

Who Owns Whom　Who's Who　Kompass　?

6　Make two checklists of the main stages in the job application process from:
　　(*a*)　the applicant's viewpoint
　　(*b*)　the recruiting employer's viewpoint
Include the nature of any documents involved in a particular stage.
7　Explain briefly the function of:
　　(*a*)　a job specification
　　(*b*)　a job description
8　What do you see as the major features a good display job advertisement should embody?
9　In your opinion, what are the principal points a letter of application accompanying a CV and application form should seek to convey?
10　What are the major components of job description?
11　Make a list of the actions you would take to prepare for a job interview once you knew you had been shortlisted.
12　What are the major sections of the NIP Seven Point Plan selection assessment process?
13　If you were an employer, what would be the ten main features you would look for in, say, a college-leaver applying for a trainee manager's job?
14　Outline briefly what a curriculum vitae aims to convey and the main sections a CV typically covers.

Build-up tasks

1　Find out what services are available in your locality either free or in the private sector to provide career counselling and aptitude testing. Report back to your group on what you discover.
2　In small syndicate groups, undertake a survey of the newspapers, magazines and other likely sources which publish both nationally and locally the sort of job opportunities which would be of general interest to your group. When you have carried out your research, write a guide in about 750 words which will provide your group with a source of relevant and practical information.
3　Design and produce for actual use your own curriculum vitae. If you are prepared to share its information, ask your teacher to vet it for you in draft form and then produce it in readiness for your job application programme.
4　Do the same for an unsolicited letter of application which you could send with your CV to appropriate potential employers you have identified.
　　If you prefer, you may produce a simulated CV and letter as a basis for your own real ones to be produced at a later stage.

5　Write a letter to invite a local personnel manager to come and talk to your group on how to succeed as a job interviewee.
6　Make a series of CCTV interview simulations so that each member of your group has a chance to practise being interviewed (and acting as an interviewer). In a subsequent 'wash-up' session, see what constructive suggestions can be made in the light of individual performances. But remember: this assignment is intended to build up confidence and correct unconscious errors, not to cast out motes from the eyes of other group members while ignoring the beams in your own!
7　First conduct your research, then write an article intended for your school/college magazine entitled:

The Do's And Don'ts Of Being Interviewed For Your First Job

8　Assume that you work as the secretary of the board of trustees which is responsible for a series of sheltered home complexes. These homes are sold to retired people and are built in a kind of courtyard and comprise relatively small flats in a three storey building. Part of the attraction of such sheltered homes is that there is a qualified nurse/warden on duty (shift work is involved) who is on hand in case of need or emergency. Residents can call up the warden by pressing a button – one is located in each room of each flat.
　　First research this kind of provision in your locality to find out about conditions of service and the scope of a typical warden's job. Then use this information with that outlined above to:
　　(*a*)　Devise a suitable job specification for a warden to run a new sheltered home complex about to open in your locality.
　　(Note: three wardens will be appointed to work a 24 hour shift system).
　　(*b*)　Design a suitable job description for the post of the senior warden, who will report to the Board of Trustees.
　　(*c*)　Design a display job advertisement for your local weekly newspaper advertising the posts of the three wardens to work in a new sheltered home complex about to open.

Case study

Wanted! Trainee Manager for EXCEL COMPUTERS LTD

The company

Excel Computers Limited manufactures, markets and retails an extensive range of computers and ancillary equipment, selling to both public and private industry.
　　Among its other duties, Excel's Sales Department provides an administrative and information service to its 75 sales representatives. The service helps them to perform effectively in what is a highly sophisticated market – both in terms of advanced product technology and the presentation of technical information.
　　Excel has established a policy of appointing each year, as trainee managers, a number of school and college leavers. They are provided with excellent in-service

training opportunities, including day-release to higher education courses. In addition, their training programmes include experience periods in all departments before taking on specific departmental responsibilities.

The vacancy

Personnel Manager: 'I see young Sara Maxwell has just got the job she's been hoping for in Marketing. I suppose you'll be asking me to find her replacement!'

Sales Manager: 'You're absolutely right! I'll miss Sara, of course, but I suppose Sales' loss is Marketing's gain! Anyway, we ought to get a good response to any advertisement, as it's already August. The school and college leavers should soon have their results. And we don't usually have any trouble in finding the right sort of person. I suppose we ought to check the job description Sara had, and see if the personnel specification needs revising.'

The following was Sara's job description:

```
                    JOB DESCRIPTION

TITLE:          TRAINEE SALES ADMINISTRATION MANAGER

DEPARTMENT:     SALES DEPARTMENT

HOURS OF WORK:  37½ hour week.  Flexible Working Hours:
                Monday – Friday Core Time: 1000 – 1600

RESPONSIBLE TO:  The Assistant Sales Manager

RESPONSIBLE FOR:  Designated junior clerical and secretarial staff.

AUTHORITY OVER:  Designated junior clerical and secretarial staff.

GENERAL DESCRIPTION

To become proficient in performing duties related to sales administration, with particular
regard to providing a supportive service to company sales representatives. To undertake
work delegated by senior Sales Department personnel. To attend in-service training courses
as required. To direct the work of assigned junior clerical and secretarial staff as
requested.

DUTIES AND RESPONSIBILITIES

1  To work within established company regulations and to support determined company
   policies.

2  To develop sales managerial skills, with particular reference to: sales administration
   procedures, product knowledge, marketing activities and sales information systems.

3  To assist in the provision of administration and information services provided to the
   company's sales representative force.

4  To liaise with Marketing Department in communicating sales promotion and advertising
   programmes to company sales representatives.

5  To deal with arising correspondence, memoranda, reports, meetings, documentation etc.

6  To assist the Assistant Sales Manager generally, or any other senior Sales Department
   staff as directed by the Assistant Sales Manager.

7  To assist as required with the processing of sales documentation and sales statistics.

8  To supervise the work of junior staff members as required.

9  To attend courses of training as required.
```

EXCEL COMPUTERS LIMITED

ORGANISATIONAL INFORMATION

HEAD OFFICE: Excel House, Guildford Road, Kingston-upon-Thames,
                 Surrey KT12 6GR
                 Telegrams: Excel, Kingston-upon-Thames
                 Telephone: Kingston 88000
                 Telex: 159621

FACTORIES: Bristol, Liverpool, Leicester

RESEARCH AND
DEVELOPMENT: Excel Laboratories, Harlow New Town

TRAINING
HEADQUARTERS: Moorbridge Manor, Dorchester, Dorset

PERSONNEL: 16 479 Head Office: 643

DEPARTMENTS: Research and Developments, Production, Marketing, Sales, Accounts, Office
                 Administration, Personnel, Distribution and Transport, Training,
                 Communication Services

CONDITIONS OF SERVICE (Head Office Staff)

The company's head office operates a flexible working hours system; staff work in
accordance with a job appraisal scheme — all jobs are graded and promotion/remuneration is
based upon performance assessed at regular intervals.
Company subsidised meals are available in the staff restaurant. Sports and social club
facilities are well catered for in the company's leisure complex adjoining head office
premises.
Paid Leave: junior — training management grades: 3 weeks per annum plus usual bank
holidays.
Company house mortgage loans available at preferential terms.

CAREER OPPORTUNITIES:

The company's employees are encouraged to develop a knowledge of company activities as a
whole and opportunities exist for careers to progress via a number of departments. The
company promotes from within whenever possible.

TRAINING:

Excel Computers Limited maintains an ideally situated Training Centre at Moorbridge Manor,
Dorchester. Residential courses form a central part of management development.
Applications to attend day-release higher education courses are reviewed by a standing
review committee.

SALARIES:

Management salaries are reviewed annually and paid monthly in arrears. Each management
post follows an incremental scale, and annual increases are zoned within defined upper and
lower limits according to performance.
Example: Trainee Manager Grade 6
          Entering salary: £7500 p.a.
          First Increment: £750—1500 p.a.
          Second Increment: £900—1700 p.a.
All incremental scales are reviewed annually.

SALES INFORMATION:

Total sales turnover last year exceeded £420 million. A new MSDOS microcomputer, 'all-
purpose' terminal was introduced recently, together with a portable low-cost personal
computer. Business Computer Systems sales rose by 19% last year. Major customers included
the Bestbuy Supermarkets chain, Sentinel Insurance Limited, Vesco Automotive Products
Limited and Harridges Stores.

FUTURE DEVELOPMENTS:

In March of this year, Sir Peter Henryson, Chairman, announced the Excel was about to enter
overseas markets: 'The time has come for Excel, secure in its very firm UK market, to go on
to the export offensive. We have the people, the products, the marketing and the sales
expertise. We intend to ''excel'' in a number of European and transatlantic markets. Our
plans are well advanced. You are all familiar with the advertisements placed in the
national press reporting the recent Annual General Meeting. Well, I strongly recommend you
to ''Watch This Space!'''

Preliminary assignments

1 Find out about Job Analysis. Check the purpose and structure of job/personnel specifications and job descriptions.

2 Try to obtain a selection of private and public sector job application forms. Compare the types of information they request. What similarities are apparent?

3 Research one of the major computer manufacturers in the UK. Assess its product range and methods of marketing and selling.

Main assignments

1 Compose a personnel specification for the Excel Trainee Sales Administration Manager post, shortly to be advertised.

2 Devise an application form suitable for use in Excel's appointment of the Trainee Sales Administration Manager.

3 Draft an information sheet suitable for sending to candidates who have applied for the Trainee Sales Administration Manager post, outlining the scope of the job and the main features of Excel's business and organisation.

4 Design a display advertisement for the Trainee Manager post and devise an advertising strategy based on your own locality, identifying which newspapers and other media you would use to advertise the post.

5 Make a checklist of questions as follows:

(*a*) questions which Excel interviewers would wish to ask applicants for the Trainee Manager post

(*b*) questions which applicants would wish to ask Excel interviewers

6 Complete the application form devised in 2 above as an applicant for the post. Compose an appropriate *curriculum vitae*. Write a suitable letter of application to:

The Personnel Manager,
Excel Computers Limited,
Excel House,
Guildford Road,
KINGSTON-UPON-THAMES
Surrey
KT12 6GR

7 Set up Excel interviewing panels to evaluate applications received from members of the group. Discuss constructively the strengths and weaknesses of applications.

8 Simulate the interviews for the post of Trainee Sales Administration Manager. Group members should role-play the Excel panel, comprising: the Personnel Manager, the Sales Manager and the Assistant Sales Manager. Other members of the group should role-play successive applicants. Panel interviewers should have time to study applicants' letters and forms. Applicants should also digest the information in the information sheet devised in 3. Observer-role group members should assess the performances of interviewers and interviewees. Simulations may be tape-recorded for subsequent evaluation.

Follow-up assignments

1 Compose an article of between 600 and 800 words, intended for Excel's house magazine, *Input*, entitled:

'Has paper a future in the office?'

Your article should seek to show how the revolution in electronic office equipment is affecting the traditional uses of paper in offices.

2 Write an article of about 700 words for a school and college leavers' careers magazine called *18+* entitled:

'Applying Successfully For Your First Job'.

You should use information acquired while working through the Excel Computer assignments, but should also carry out any additional research you think necessary. In addition, you should keep in mind the age, background and experience of your readership.

3 Discuss the following topic in a general group session:

The job application interview is, at best, a hit and miss affair.

Interview simulation

Assistant required for office administration manager ...

The simulation is designed to involve the whole group. The interviewing panel may comprise up to three members. Authentic roles would be: managing director, personnel manager, office administration manager. Three candidate profiles are outlined below, but more candidate roles may be devised to provide a larger short-list if required. Other members of the group should be divided into two sections – observers of the interviewers and observers of the interviewees. They should meet to decide upon what they will assess and design a check-list to note performances. Each group of observers should report its assessments after the interview simulations have taken place. Interviewers and interviewees should then be asked for their reactions and impressions.

The situation

A post has recently been advertised for an assistant to the Office Administration Manager of Reliant Employment Bureau Ltd. The company has 30 branches throughout the country placing secretarial, clerical and junior management personnel both in full-time and temporary positions.

The job

The duties of the assistant will mainly involve relieving the Office Administration Manager of some of his work-load. Specifically the post will include:

responsibility for the company's stationery supplies, maintenance of existing administration systems, records, filing etc. drafting of correspondence, memoranda, reports, composing advertisements, taking part in meetings, telephone reception. Commercial experience is not essential as training will be given. Shorthand and typewriting skills would be advantageous.

	Candidate A	Candidate B	Candidate C
Age:	18	27	38
Status:	Single	Married (no children)	Divorced (boy 15, girl 10)
Education:	Park View Comprehensive and West Park College of Further Education	Westerham Grammar School	Hightown College and Cumbria University (left after one year to get married)
Qualifications:	4 'O'-levels BTEC National Award in Business and Finance Studies; including Secretarial Studies option	6 'O'-levels 2 'A'-levels Shorthand/Typewriting speeds: 90/40	5 'O'-levels 3 'A'-levels Read English at University
Commercial:	Part-time Holiday Jobs One job as 'Temp' in busy office	4 years in local tax office 2 years as cabin crew member in airline: grounded with blood-pressure: later joined engineering company – made redundant	Housewife until 25 divorced at 30 succession of part-time jobs; refresher shorthand/ typewriting course at local College just completed

Physical Appearance   ⎱ Candidates should decide upon these factors and play a role. For example,
Interests, Circumstances: ⎰ hesitant or assured, social or solitary, flat renter or mortgagee etc.

Note for candidates

Use the above information to provide the basic framework for your 'personality', background and career. Ensure that you have prepared your ground sufficiently.

Note for observers

Every observer should have a full brief of each candidate's background, including any 'skeletons in cupboards' deliberately 'planted' by candidates for interviewers to discover!

13 Meetings

Introduction

The term, 'meeting' is used so widely nowadays, and given so many different interpretations that it has come to mean almost all things to all people. At one end of the meetings' spectrum are those which are formally conducted and governed by rules of procedure as laid down by a company's Memorandum and Articles of Association or the Standing Orders of a county council. At the other end are the easy, informal types of meetings such as the managerial brain-storming meeting at which executives keep making suggestions about, say, product development, in the hope of crystallising a totally new idea or approach.

Some types of limited company and various local government councils are required to hold certain meetings by statute, as a result of government legislation. A company's Articles or a council's Standing Orders will prescribe rules about giving adequate notice of a meeting, what constitutes a quorum (the minimum number of members needed to be present for a meeting to be held), what sort of business a meeting should conduct, and when and where certain types of meeting, such as board meetings or Annual Meetings of a council, should be held. In addition, such rules will indicate what rights the shareholder or member of the public possesses in areas such as voting or admission.

Meetings are held by people from all walks of life and in countless company, public service or sports and leisure contexts. At the top of an organisational pyra-

mid company directors may meet to evolve company policy and decide future strategies. Members of trade unions may meet to hammer out an approach to imminent pay negotiations. Alternatively, members of an angling club committee may meet to discuss the dates and locations of the following season's fishing matches.

Indeed, whether as a tool of management, instruction of local or central government, or forum of the voluntary club, the meeting has, for many years, been employed as a means of making decisions – usually binding, upon those participating in the meeting, of spreading information or a means of resolving a particular problem. Through the medium of the meeting, people are able to make suggestions, voice criticisms and express opinions. Moreover, the physical proximity of people seated round a table to 'thrash things out,' creates a special type of relationship among those present which no form of written exchange or electronic substitutes is able to produce.

Like most communications channels, however, the meeting is also a potential source of communication failure or break-down. It may become sterile and unproductive, costly to call and a source of time-wasting. Much depends upon the qualities of the members attending and their respective skills in communicating effectively through the constraints imposed by rules, procedures or conventions. Certainly all types of meetings share certain common factors which serve to unite those attending and to direct their thoughts and actions.

Common factors of meetings

Goals:	Goals or aims have been identified which the meeting elects to achieve
Outcome:	The members of the meeting have an interest in the outcome of its business
Interests:	Participants represent sectional or official points of view
Action or information:	A problem, situation, plans or attitudes need to be resolved or crystallised; information needs to be imparted and disseminated
Deadlines:	The business of the meeting takes place within a limited time-scale which affects the potential effectiveness of decisions or the relevance of information
Leadership:	Someone has assumed or been assigned the leadership of the meeting

Different types of meeting

Since meetings take place within such a diversity of organisations and are used for so many different purposes, to arrive at a definition true for all types of meeting is virtually impossible, save in the broadest of terms.

Yet, the hostility which the calling of some meetings produces in those required or invited to attend often derives from an inadequate understanding of basics. If the meetings are poorly organised they quickly become 'a waste of time'; if they fail to result in action they are deemed 'pointless'; if the participants bring with them misconceptions about the 'terms of reference' which limit the powers of those attending a meeting, they are likely to become disappointed or embittered about the value or effectiveness of meetings.

It is therefore important to define the nature of certain types of meeting, to appreciate the procedures and conventions which govern their conduct and then to evaluate their effectiveness in contributing to sound decision-making and good administration.

Definitions of meetings

Statutory

A legal definition of a meeting based on case law precedent is:

'the coming together of at least two persons for any lawful purpose'.

To embrace statutory meetings of companies and public institutions, this definition may be enlarged:

an assembly of persons meeting in accordance with legally defined rules and procedures to discharge business as required by law.

Executive

In the on-going administration of companies or local and central government many meetings take place which are participative – all present share in the making of decisions which leads to action being taken:

an assembly of people with common interests arriving at decisions and instituting actions through the process of an exchange of relevant views and information which leads to an agreement favoured by the majority of those present and subsequently supported by all.

Briefing

Some meetings are called, however, within organisations to relay decisions or information from a more senior level:

an assembly of people in a 'reporting to' position within an organisational hierarchy who are summoned to receive, accept and comply with the requirements of formulated decisions or to retain information for use relayed to them by a person in authority over them.

Advisory

In some organisations people meet to generate advice or to make suggestions for submission to a higher authority:

an assembly of people meeting to formulate advice, suggestions or proposals for submission to a higher executive body for ratification.

Managerial

Many informal meetings occur (some arising spontaneously) between a manager and his subordinates or counterparts to exchange opinions, give advice or supply information as part of the managerial decision-making process:

a gathering of people within an organisation (but not necessarily restricted to the organisation) with clearly defined inter-personal relationships, meeting to exchange views, attitudes, or information with a view to making decisions and instituting actions.

Task force, working-party

A modern approach to solving an organisation's problems has been to bring together a group of people with varying responsibilities and from different departments to pursue a particular task or to resolve a specific problem:

an assembly of people drawn from various levels and sectors of an organisation, embodying different specialisms, brought together to find the solution to a problem by working outside the normal administrative structure.

Brain-storming, buzz-groups   Some informal meetings are called with the aim of generating a fresh approach or new ideas relating to organisational activities:

an informal assembly of people who aim to generate ideas, suggestions or approaches to organisational activities from an unrestricted interchange of views, opinions and attitudes.

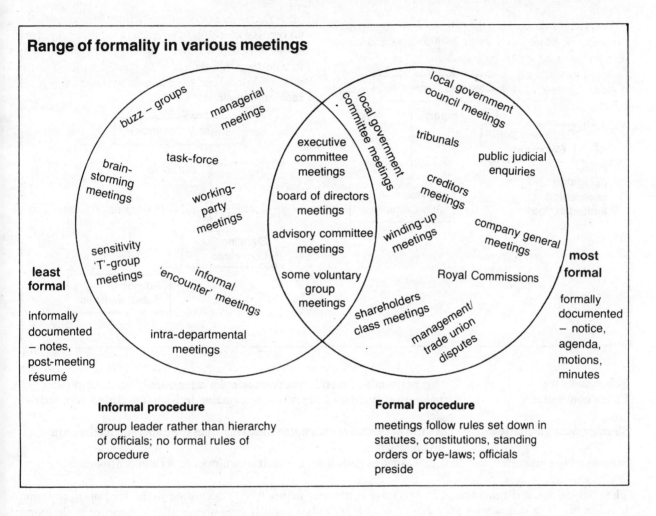

Range of formality in various meetings

buzz – groups

managerial meetings

brain-storming meetings

task-force

working-party meetings

sensitivity 'T'-group meetings

informal 'encounter' meetings

intra-departmental meetings

executive committee meetings

board of directors meetings

advisory committee meetings

some voluntary group meetings

local government committee meetings

local government council meetings

tribunals

public judicial enquiries

creditors meetings

winding-up meetings

company general meetings

Royal Commissions

shareholders class meetings

management/ trade union disputes

least formal

informally documented – notes, post-meeting résumé

most formal

formally documented – notice, agenda, motions, minutes

Informal procedure

group leader rather than hierarchy of officials; no formal rules of procedure

Formal procedure

meetings follow rules set down in statutes, constitutions, standing orders or bye-laws; officials preside

Formal structures and procedures

The preceding definitions and 'range of formality' diagram should be taken as guide-lines since the degree of formality with which a meeting is conducted depends not only upon the existence of a constitution, standing orders or rules, but also upon the climate or atmosphere generated within any organisation.

However, many formal meetings, especially those run by committees, follow broadly similar lines and share equivalent structures and procedures. Generally speaking there is a correlation between the degree of formality of a meeting and the importance of its decisions:

Policy-making
Executive   } affects entire organisation, usually made by a meeting of the board of directors or made by senior or middle management probably affecting departments or divisions

Implementive
Routine   } day-to-day decisions made within departments
Administrative

Executive committee   One which has the power to act upon decisions

Advisory committee
Consultative committee   } One which refers advice to a main, executive committee

Standing committee   One which meets during an indefinite period

Ad hoc committee   A committee constituted to carry out a particular task (from the Latin *ad hoc*: 'for this purpose')

Structure of committee hierarchy

In complex organisations the structures of various committees are fixed in a hierarchy, and their ability to generate action is channelled and controlled:

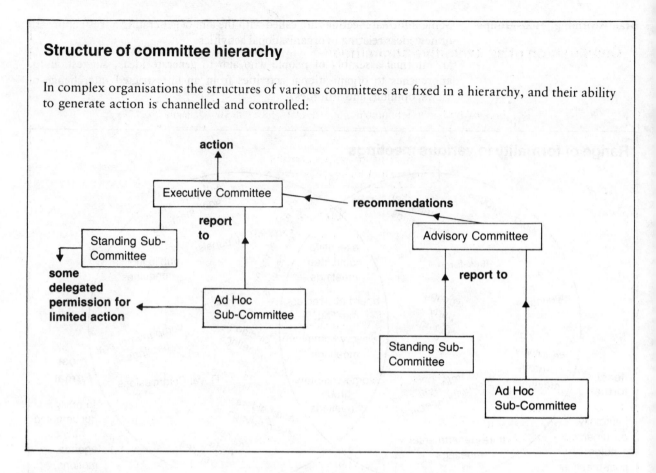

Sub-committee	One performing for and reporting to a main committee
Policy committee	In large organisations, one which takes major decisions affecting future activities
Management committee	A form of executive committee which manages the important affairs of an organisation
Membership committee	Clubs, such as golf clubs, use such committees to vet and control membership

The composition and functions of an executive committee naturally vary according to the type of organisation it is serving. The diagram on page 229 broadly represents a popular type of executive committee to be found in commerce, the public service or voluntary clubs. In large organisations the financial function may be integrated into an accounting department; the committee may be responsible through a board of directors to shareholders, or through a local government council to rate-payers.

Presiding member	In voluntary clubs particularly, a president or captain or captain may act as a figure-head positioned between the executive committee and the club
Chairman	members, although the chairman of the executive committee is responsible for directing its activities and for presiding at its meetings. Some executive
Vice-chairman	committees include a vice-chairman, usually a senior, experienced member, able to stand in for the chairman if need be. The secretary has a close relation-
Secretary	ship with the chairman in planning the business of meetings and generally administering the committee's work, while the treasurer keeps a watching
Treasurer	brief and record of the committee's finances for an annual audit. The members of the committee may be elected or appointed by the general membership,
Committee members	serving for a pre-established term of office. Sometimes committees ask an expert or specialist to join them as a 'coopted member'; he or she may, or
Coopted members	may not, be given the right to vote at committee meetings.
	In the case of voluntary clubs and associations, the annual financial records, expressed by the treasurer in balance sheet form, are checked against receipts by an independently appointed auditor. In this way the general membership
(Auditor)	is reassured of the integrity of its committee.

Composition of an executive committee

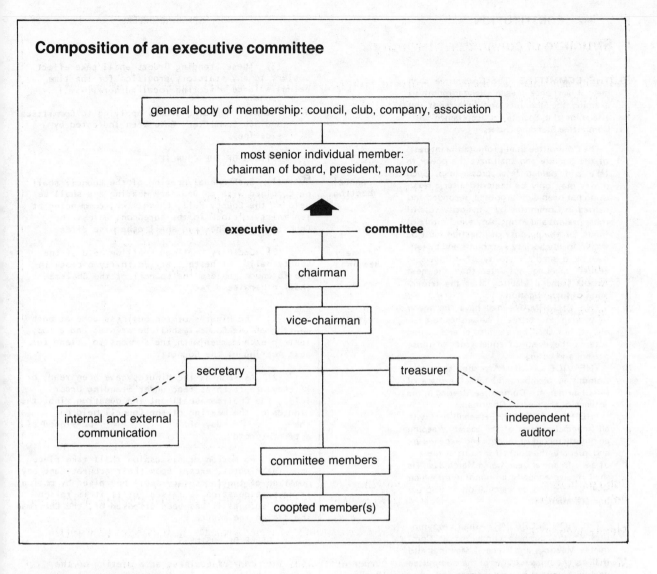

| general body of membership: council, club, company, association |

| most senior individual member: chairman of board, president, mayor |

executive ———— committee

chairman

vice-chairman

secretary — treasurer

internal and external communication

independent auditor

committee members

coopted member(s)

The rules of the game

All meetings, whether statutorily called, run by company departments, or organised by local voluntary clubs, are governed by rules. Sometimes the rules take the form of laws decreed by Act of Parliament, sometimes the form of company regulations lodged with the Registrar of Companies, and sometimes, in the case of a voluntary society, the form of a constitution. Even when no written rules exist – as may be the case in, for example, inter-departmental company meetings – there nevertheless exists a set of 'unspoken rules or conventions' which participants will have learned and which are just as effective in regulating activities.

The best piece of advice for those whose work or whose leisure interests involve them in taking part in meetings, therefore, is:

It pays to know the rules of the game!

An inexperienced company director or county councillor may find him or herself outmanoeuvred or reduced to helpless silence by someone better versed in procedural technicalities – points of order or information – sometimes introduced to win a point or demolish opposition! Even in leisure or voluntary association committee meetings passions have been known to run high over the venue of the annual outing, and even here, it pays to know exactly what the club's constitution has to say on any particular point or procedure.

In the case of those meetings called within the confines of an organisation – a company or local government department – there may be no specific rules to guide procedure at a meeting, although it is held beneath the 'general umbrella' of local government or company law. Here it is much more difficult to grasp the rules of the game, since they are sometimes obscure and capable of change. Such meetings are largely controlled by those members possessing either status or assertive personalities.

In this type of meeting much will depend upon the quality of the chairman, who will need to be a leader, persuader, diplomat, tactician and healer rolled into one!

The inexperienced participator in meetings should, then, take the trouble to learn the rules, written or unspoken, and should 'play himself in' by listening to and observing his fellow-participants in action. Gradually he will perceive the responses and attitudes which motivate his peers, may discern where he will gain a sympathetic ear, and where a rebuff. He should

CONSTITUTION

9. **THE COMMITTEE** The Committee shall meet at least once in each calendar month to examine the accounts and to arrange the affairs of the Society in accordance with Committee Standing Orders.

The Committee shall promote the interests of the Society and shall have the power to take and defend legal proceedings. Such power may only be exercised after a resolution has been duly proposed, seconded and carried in Committee by a majority vote of those present and voting. Any expenditure of funds for the purpose of litigation must be shown in the Society's accounts and be ratified by a simple majority of members in general meeting not later than the next Annual General Meeting after the termination of such litigation.

THE CHAIRMAN—shall have the power of vote in committee if he wishes to exercise it, but shall have a further and casting vote in the event of equal votes of those present and voting.

THE VICE CHAIRMAN—shall serve as a Committee Member and take the place of the Chairman at a Committee Meeting in the absence of the elected Chairman.

THE HON TREASURER—shall deal with all financial matters of the Society, keeping an orderly record of income and expenditure and prepare the books for audit at the end of each financial year, being March 31st. He shall receive annually an honorarium which shall be decided by calculation at 6½p per Society member.

THE HON SECRETARY—shall keep minutes of the business conducted at Committee Meetings and General Meetings and shall carry out instructions of the Committee, deal with general correspondence and other duties which from time to time shall be determined. He shall receive annually an honorarium which amount shall be decided by calculation at 6½p per Society member.

THE HON COMPETITION SECRETARY shall arrange and organise Society and inter-club competitions and visits to other clubs' waters. He shall receive annually an honorarium which amount shall be decided by calculation at 3p per Society member.

APPENDIX
BYE-LAWS

(1) **SUSSEX RIVER AUTHORITY** Each member of the Society shall make himself familiar with the Byelaws of the Sussex River Authority and regard them as additional to the Society's Byelaws.

(2) **BAILIFFS** The Committee shall be empowered to appoint Honorary Bailiffs as is deemed expedient, but members when elected shall undertake the voluntary role of Water Bailiff and will at all times endeavour to prevent poaching and unauthorised fishing on the Society's waters.

(3) **MEMBERS** Members shall at all times behave in an orderly manner or they will become liable for expulsion under the Society's Rule 8. All members are expected, where

STANDING ORDERS

(3) These Standing Orders shall take effect subject to any statutory provision for the time being in force affecting local authorities.

N.B. The main Standing Orders applying to Committees and Sub-Committees have been indicated by sidelines.

MEETINGS OF THE COUNCIL

Annual Meeting
2. (1) Each Annual Meeting of the Council shall be combined with an Ordinary Meeting and shall be held at the County Hall, Chichester, commencing at ten thirty o'clock in the forenoon, unless the Council or the Chairman shall otherwise direct.

Ordinary Meetings
(2) Ordinary Meetings shall be held at the County Hall, Chichester, at ten thirty o'clock in the forenoon, unless the Council or the Chairman shall otherwise direct.

Minutes
9. (1) The Minutes of the business done at each meeting of the Council shall be printed and a copy sent to each member with the summons to attend the next meeting of the Council.

(2) As soon as the Minutes have been read, or if they are taken as read under Standing Order 10(3), the Chairman shall put the question "That the minutes of the meeting of the Council held on the   day of   be signed as a true record".

(3) No motion or discussion shall take place upon the Minutes, except upon their accuracy and any question of their accuracy shall be raised by motion. If no such question is raised, or if it is raised then as soon as it has been disposed of, the Chairman shall sign the minutes.

ORDER OF BUSINESS

Order of Business
10. The order of business at a meeting of the Council shall be:-

(1) To choose a person to preside if the Chairman and Vice-Chairman of the Council be absent;

(2) When required by Statute, to elect a Chairman;

(3) To read the minutes of the last meeting of the Council with a view to their confirmation as a correct record provided that, if so directed by the Council, the whole or any part thereof shall be taken as read;

(4) When necessary, to appoint a member of the Council to be Vice-Chairman;

(5) To deal with business expressly required by Statute to be done at the meeting;

(6) To deal with business specially brought forward by the Chairman;

NOTICES OF MOTION

Procedure
13. (1) Except as provided by Standing Order 15, every notice of motion shall be in writing, signed by the member giving the notice, and shall be delivered at the office of the County Secretary, not less than nine clear days before the next meeting of the Council.

also ensure that he has 'done his homework' before speaking, since if he is to sway his audience, he must first gain their respect. He should also bear in mind that *he* has to become acceptable to his peers before his ideas or suggestions are accepted.

Written rules affecting meetings

Companies   Memorandum and Articles of Association:

Required by Company Law, the Memorandum and Articles define aims, activities and procedure of a company and are lodged with a Registrar of Companies.

Councils   Acts of Parliament and Standing Orders: Much council procedure is governed either by Act of Parliament – Local Government Act 1972, Public Bodies (Admission to Meetings) Act 1960 and approved rules in Standing Orders.

Voluntary bodies   Written constitutions: Voluntary clubs, associations and societies adhere to rules and bye-laws set down in a 'constitution', usually drawn up by founder-members: its rules also govern the composition of committees and meetings procedures.

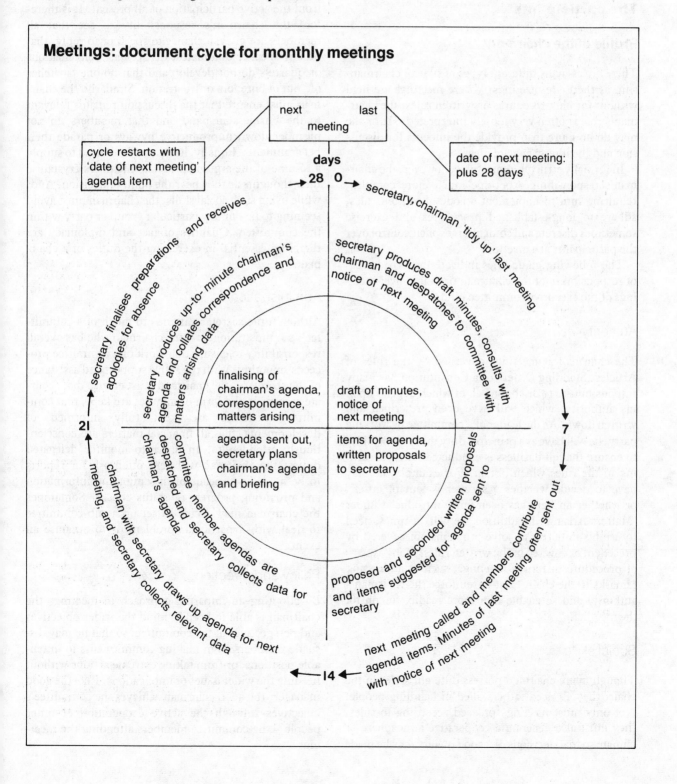

Meetings: document cycle for monthly meetings

next   last
meeting

days

cycle restarts with 'date of next meeting' agenda item

date of next meeting: plus 28 days

28 0

secretary, chairman 'tidy up' last meeting

secretary finalises preparations and receives apologies for absence

secretary produces up-to-minute chairman's agenda and collates correspondence and matters arising data

secretary produces draft minutes, consults with chairman and despatches to committee with notice of next meeting

finalising of chairman's agenda, correspondence, matters arising

draft of minutes, notice of next meeting

21

7

agendas sent out, secretary plans chairman's agenda and briefing

items for agenda, written proposals to secretary

committee member agendas are despatched and secretary collects data for chairman's agenda

chairman with secretary draws up agenda for next meeting, and secretary collects relevant data

proposed and seconded written proposals and items suggested for agenda sent to secretary

next meeting called and members contribute agenda items. Minutes of last meeting often sent out with notice of next meeting

14

Document sequence

1 **Minutes** agreed written record of business of a meeting
2 **Notice** written 'invitation' to meeting's participants
3 **Proposals, agenda items** business proposed for debate at meeting
4 **Committee agenda** list of items of business for discussion
5 **Chairman's agenda** similar to committee agenda, but includes helpful background or briefing notes prepared by Secretary.

Note: Advance notice Some organisations require notices, proposals and agendas to be sent out and received by a fixed number of days in advance of the meeting to which they refer.

The participants

Profile of the chairman

There are as many different types of style of chairmanship as there are meetings. Where meetings are held without formal procedures or written rules, the chairman's role is often very loosely interpreted. He or she may do no more than provide the impetus for discussion and the interchange of ideas.

In formally structured meetings, however, the chairman's responsibilities become much more complex, requiring him to implement a code of written rules, adhere to long-established procedures and exercise sometimes discrete and sometimes explicit control over the participants at a meeting.

The following guide-lines indicate the broad areas of responsibility of the chairman presiding over meetings of the executive committee kind.

Authority

The chairman at meetings governed by the rules of Articles, Standing Orders or a Constitution has many responsibilities to discharge, all of which depend upon his authority, which will have been prescribed and written down. As the leader of a committee or working party, he will have as a principal duty the responsibility to ensure that all business is conducted fairly, according to the rules which obtain. For example, he may have to decide whether a speaker is 'out of order', or whether an item has been fairly introduced under 'Matters Arising'. In addition, he will, at times, need to use his initiative to solve problems not covered by precedent or covered in the written rules. Many aspects of procedure in formal meetings, such as addressing remarks to the chair, exist to reinforce the chairman's authority and so enable him more readily to control the meeting.

Social skills

Though many chairmen possess different styles in the chair, they all need to be skilled in handling people. Not only must meetings proceed according to rules, they must also generate a cooperative atmosphere or climate so that decisions of a good quality may be made

from the active participation of all present. It is therefore the chairman's responsibility to see that all members are given a chance to speak or to reply, that no one speaker dominates, that private conversations or quarrels do not develop and that no-one 'switches off' out of boredom or frustration. Similarly, the chairman must ensure that the discussion remains relevant to the business in hand and that members do not meander down unproductive byways or parade their pet arguments. Equally, he may at times need to supply a résumé of the argument to help members crystallise their thoughts as they near the point of decision. And, while using such social skills, the chairman must avoid seeming to favour any particular group or party within the committee. Qualities of tact and diplomacy are therefore essential in exercising the duties of a chairman.

Administration

Although the secretary attends to much of a committee's administration, it is the chairman who has overall responsibility to ensure that work of a committee proceeds smoothly. With the active support and assistance of the secretary, the chairman must ensure that accurate records in the form of minutes are kept, that committee members are kept fully informed of developments, that all financial matters are conscientiously attended to. In order to monitor delegated duties, the chairman will very often ask for reports to be made as a means of disseminating information and providing progress or status checks. Sometimes the chairman may decide to set up a sub-committee to deal with a particular problem or to organise an event.

Policy and direction

By adopting an impartial approach in meetings the chairman is able to keep in mind the wider objectives and perspectives of the committee, so that he may dissuade members from making commitments to untenable positions, or from taking extreme actions without heeding the wider issues or implications. Like the good manager, the good chairman achieves the committee's objectives through the active cooperation of other people – the committee members attending the meetings.

Profile of the secretary

The secretary is, perhaps, best regarded as the hub of the committee around whom its work revolves. The conscientious secretary undertakes much detailed work, frequently behind the scenes, to ensure that lines of communication between committee members and the organisation as a whole are kept open. In addition, the secretary has a duty to perform administrative tasks punctually and efficiently.

The chairman's 'right hand'

In terms of the seating arrangements of many a committee or working party, the secretary is to be found, quite literally, at the right hand of the chairman. Indeed, this physical proximity is symbolic of the full cooperation and rapport which must exist between chairman and secretary if the work of a committee is to be productive.

Very often, the other duties a chairman may undertake, either at work or in his local community, will mean that much of the routine and detailed work of the committee is left to the secretary. Nevertheless the considerate secretary takes pains to ensure that his chairman is kept fully briefed at all times by means of the chairman's agenda, written briefings, or copies of documents and liaison between meetings. The chairman and the secretary will usually consult over the drafting of minutes, the compilation of an agenda and the calling of meetings.

During the meeting itself, the secretary will keep alert to come to the aid of his chairman, if need be with detailed information, a helpful up-dating or confirmation of any late developments. Moreover, he must be careful to see that such supportive action does not detract in any way from the chairman's control or authority in the meeting but is proffered unobtrusively. Thus the relationship of the secretary to the chairman is largely supportive and it is not always easy for the secretary to accept the constraints which his role imposes. However, the good chairman and secretary realise that they are very much a team and the secretary generally derives much personal satisfaction from being at the centre of the committee's activities.

Administration

Though often enjoying much freedom of action, it is important to remember that the secretary's administrative duties are delegated to him and usually set out, for example, in a society's constitution or in the case of a County Secretary, the council's Standing Orders.

In broad terms, the secretary administers the committee's business. The responsibility includes keeping and distributing records of meetings in the form of minutes and keeping the regular cycle of meetings running smoothly. In this context, the secretary is responsible for producing the minutes of the last meeting to despatch to committee members often with notice of the next. In the case of formal meetings the secretary will accept written proposals from members of the committee to incorporate in a committee agenda, which members must also receive in good time before a meeting. The secretary must also compile a chairman's agenda and attend to any correspondence, written reports or briefings which the committee may need to receive. Before a subsequent meeting, the secretary very often needs to follow up any task delegated to him which may be referred to under 'Matters Arising' and will also need to collect any apologies for absence to pass on to the chairman.

In addition, it usually falls to the secretary to ensure that the venue of the meeting has been booked and that the meeting or conference room itself is fully prepared with a suitable seating arrangement, notepaper, and any further requirements or refreshments which may be needed. The thoughtful secretary also brings copies of relevant documents with him in case committee members arrive without them.

A further duty of the secretary is to see that any absent committee member is kept informed of the business of a meeting and that he receives copies of the appropriate minutes and other documents. As well as servicing the committee in this way, the secretary is also responsible for circulating papers or reports upon request to the organisation's membership and for maintaining any noticeboard which may display committee notices.

Lastly, the secretary has a duty to ensure that he supports the chairman in the sometimes demanding task of conducting a meeting's business in such a way that neither rancour, hostility nor boredom interfere with its work, and that attendance at meetings does not fall off as a result of low morale.

Profile of the treasurer

The treasurer has a crucial part to play in the work of any committee responsible for managing an organisation's funds. He not only keeps careful account of all income and expenditure during a financial year, but also acts as 'watch-dog', monitoring the financial implications of projects and activities, so that the enthusiasm of committee members does not outrun the organisation's financial resources.

Financial administration

The treasurer is expected to keep careful records of all financial transactions which a committee may make on behalf of its members, so that at the end of each year he is able to present a treasurer's report and balance sheet at an Annual General Meeting. Such a duty involves the keeping of all receipts, bills, cheque stubs, bank statements and petty cash records so that his accounts may be substantiated.

In time for the Annual General Meeting, the treasurer of a society will pass his accounts and records to an independent auditor who checks and passes them, so that the integrity both of the treasurer and the committee is preserved when the accounts are presented for the scrutiny of the membership. This function is mirrored in company practice in the work of the accounts or financial director and the company's chartered accountants.

Advisory role

In many situations, the decisions of a committee or working party may involve the spending of money. The treasurer is not only responsible for keeping an up-to-date record of the organisation's financial status – often to be found as an item on the committee agenda – but also to advise the committee on the financial aspects of proposed ventures, even though this may mean 'pouring cold water' on someone's cherished scheme! In this way, the treasurer maintains the solvency of the organisation – essential to almost every undertaking.

Talking point: In meetings chairmen and members tend to deserve each other.

Written documentation

If any committee, working party or convened meeting is to function effectively, it will need to pay careful attention to the range of written documentation it produces, whether a letter, report, agenda or minutes. Where meetings are concerned, written communications either prepare members for business, record business transacted or implement business decided upon. Broadly, the range of written documentation through which a committee will transmit much of its activities is:

1 Notice of meeting
2 Minutes of the last meeting
3 Committee members' agenda
4 Chairman's agenda
5 Chairman's additional briefing
6 Formal, written proposals; motions
7 Correspondence
8 Financial reports
9 Written reports

The secretary produces the first five items, and may ensure that members' proposals are framed appropriately. He or she will also attend to any necessary correspondence, while the treasurer is responsible for financial reports and statements, and the chairman of the committee may oversee the production of any committee report.

Note: There is sometimes confusion over the use of the terms Proposal, Motion and Resolution. It is perhaps helpful to regard the written submission of an item for discussion, before a meeting is held, as a 'proposal'. During the meeting, when the item is brought up for discussion, it is generally referred to as a 'motion'. Whether as a proposal or a motion the item will, in formal meetings, need to be sponsored by a proposer and seconder. If the motion is carried it thereafter becomes a 'resolution' which has been passed by a majority of voters.

The notice

Notices of meetings, despatched in advance according to standing regulations, may be written in one of several formats:

1 A form postcard
Such postcards are pre-printed and used to call routine, perhaps monthly, meetings. Spaces are left for the secretary to enter the committee member's name, and the day, date, time and venue of the meeting. Though there is less of a personal touch, they save the secretary valuable time and effort.

2 Centred notification
Some notices are produced on sheets of A5 landscape headed notepaper. The essential information is imparted in a centred paragraph.

3 Letter format
Sometimes formal meetings are called by means of a personally written letter from the secretary to each committee member on the organisation's headed notepaper.

4 Memorandum
In the case of meetings called by a company or public-service department, the format used is frequently the memorandum.

Agendas

As well as providing a kind of 'early warning system' to help meeting participants to prepare themselves for the topics to be covered, the committee members' agenda acts both as a 'running-order' schedule and time-table during a meeting. The adroit chairman will ensure that agendas are not allowed to become too long or ponderous. Similarly, careful thought may also be given to the position of an item of business on an agenda, where either 'the decks may be cleared' of less important items before a thorny problem is tackled, or where an important item of business is dealt with first, while members are fresh. It is in such instances that the acumen and experience of the chairman is invaluable.

The committee members' agenda

As has already been outlined, committee meetings in

'I didn't bother with an agenda this time – you know how awkward they get when they come prepared. . . .'

particular subscribe to certain formalities. Thus the first three items on a routine agenda tend to be set out as follows:

1 Apologies for absence Having declared the meeting open (while the secretary records the time) the chairman will announce the 'apologies', sent in advance to the secretary, of any member unable to attend the meeting.

2 Minutes of the last meeting Here, the chairman will ask members, who generally will have received a copy of the minutes beforehand, whether they represent a true record of the previous meeting which he may sign. Discussion of this item will be limited to the actual wording of the minutes which must be accurate in fact and fair in implication.

3 Matters arising Some chairmen tend to dislike this item on the grounds that it provides an opportunity for controversial topics to be re-opened for discussion. There are numerous instances, however, when a situation may have developed, or where the secretary or a committee member may have pursued a particular item which arose directly from the last meeting and which should be reported.

Additionally, some committee agendas include as a fourth item, 'Correspondence'. Its inclusion as a regular feature of an agenda depends upon the frequency and extent of any exchange of letters between the committee and third parties.

These three (of four) items on the committee members' agenda represent a kind of ritual opening of the meeting, preserving the integrity and continuity of completed and on-going business before the fresh business which the meeting was primarily called to discharge, commences.

The new business is set out as a number of items in the middle of the agenda. At a meeting of a local branch of a professional institute they might appear as follows:

4 Publicity for new season's programme of events

5 Topic and speaker for meeting: 4 March 19—

6 Visit to business systems exhibition, Olympia

7 Proposal to levy an admission charge at meetings: That an admission charge of 50p per head be levied by the Branch to cover the cost of coffee and biscuits and to contribute towards Branch funds.
Proposer: Mr J Pearson
Seconder: Mrs M Jenkins

Having debated and decided upon action for items 4–7 (for an explanation of proposals, motions and resolutions see above), the new business of the meeting will have been virtually concluded and the chairman will have delegated the actions to be implemented to members. There remain two items on the agenda to be dealt with:

8 Any other business

9 Date of next meeting Some chairmen do not like to include item 8, since it allows members to introduce items without prior notice, may test the patience of members at the end of a meeting or may enable pet schemes and hobby-horses to be paraded for the 'umpteenth' time. On the other hand, such an item does allow a member to introduce a topic which he or she may feel has not been given sufficient attention, or which may have been overlooked entirely. If such a topic is sufficiently important, it may well appear as an item on the agenda of the committee's next meeting. The last duty of the chairman is to decide upon a date for the next committee meeting in consultation with the members. Thereafter the meeting is formally closed, and the secretary records the time.

Note: on some agendas 'Any Other Business' appears as the final item. The ordering of agenda items in this respect seems to be a matter of committee preference.

The chairman's agenda

The chairman's agenda is, essentially, an annotated version of the committee member's agenda. Both will carry identical agenda items in the same sequence. The chairman'a agenda, however, will include after each item sufficient space for the secretary to insert background, briefing notes such as updating information, explanations of newly-developed situations, diplomatic reminders of past personality clashes and so on, to help the chairman to conduct the meeting both authoritatively and tactfully.

The chairman's agenda is particularly invaluable for the chairman whose prestige or status lends respect to the position he occupies, but whose other commitments may prevent him from retaining the detailed knowledge which the secretary readily absorbs from dealing with the committee's administration.

landscape

postcard

memorandum

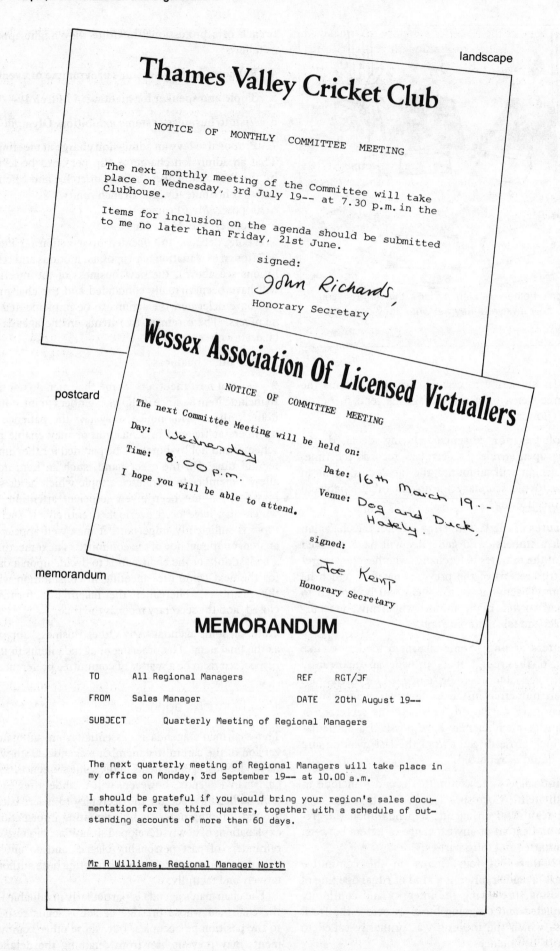

Thames Valley Cricket Club

NOTICE OF MONTHLY COMMITTEE MEETING

The next monthly meeting of the Committee will take
place on Wednesday, 3rd July 19-- at 7.30 p.m. in the
Clubhouse.

Items for inclusion on the agenda should be submitted
to me no later than Friday, 21st June.

signed:

John Richards,
Honorary Secretary

Wessex Association Of Licensed Victuallers

NOTICE OF COMMITTEE MEETING

The next Committee Meeting will be held on:

Day: *Wednesday*

Time: *8.00 p.m.*

Date: *16th March 19.--*

Venue: *Dog and Duck,*
       Hately.

I hope you will be able to attend.

signed:

Joe Kemp
Honorary Secretary

MEMORANDUM

TO	All Regional Managers	REF	RGT/JF
FROM	Sales Manager	DATE	20th August 19--
SUBJECT	Quarterly Meeting of Regional Managers		

The next quarterly meeting of Regional Managers will take place in
my office on Monday, 3rd September 19-- at 10.00 a.m.

I should be grateful if you would bring your region's sales documentation for the third quarter, together with a schedule of outstanding accounts of more than 60 days.

<u>Mr R Williams, Regional Manager North</u>

In this respect the attentive secretary may make an important contribution to the smooth progress of the meeting, although it is only the chairman who will fully appreciate such indispensable 'behind-the-scenes' work.

Special kinds of meetings

In addition to the regular and routine meetings, often held at monthly intervals, through which companies, public service departments and associations carry out their business, circumstances may arise which make it necessary to hold general or 'out-of-the-ordinary', termed 'extraordinary', meetings:

Annual General Meetings

Once a year all the members of an organisation meet to receive activity and financial reports and proposals for future developments and to elect or re-appoint officers.

Extraordinary General Meetings

Sometimes events occur which are sufficiently important and urgent to require the calling of a meeting of all members of an organisation, who may be asked to vote upon a particular matter or to grant special powers to an executive committee or board of directors to enable them to meet a specific contingency.

Creditors' meetings

When companies are unable to continue to trade by reason of insolvency, the official receiver will call a meeting of creditors to appoint a liquidator and arrange for the 'winding-up' of its activities.

Other types of special meeting include Shareholders' Class Meetings, Public Enquiries or occasional *ad hoc* meetings called to conduct business lying outside the normal routines and terms of reference of organisations.

A typical agenda for an Annual General Meeting of a voluntary society

1 Apologies for absence
2 Minutes of the last meeting
3 Matters arising
4 Chairman's report
5 Treasurer's report and presentation of accounts
6 Election of officers
7 (See note below)

Note: There are various ways in which an agenda for an Annual General Meeting may be concluded. For example, item 7 may take the form of, 'Revision of the constitution', or 'Vote of thanks to the president', who may be retiring. In other words, there may be specific business to conduct at any particular Annual General Meeting after more routine matters have been carried.

Some AGM agendas include items such as, 'Any other business' and 'Date of next meeting' to form the conclusion of the meeting. At other Annual General Meetings, however, 'Any other business' may be omitted and discussion and reporting limited to specific items such as those indicated above. Much depends upon the climate, precedents and the composition of constitution in the case of voluntary organisations, or upon the nature of the Articles of Association of a particular company and upon the inclusion, in the notice calling its Annual General Meeting, of additional items of business other than those required by its Articles or by statute.

In the case of Annual General Meetings of the companies governed by the Companies Acts, the usual business conducted includes the receiving of reports upon company progress and performance, the presentation of the company's accounts and dividends (if any are distributed) and the election or appointment of any directors if these are due.

Minutes

Producing the minutes of a meeting is probably the most demanding task assigned to the secretary or his counterpart. In the course of their production, the secretary needs to bear in mind not only that they should be a scrupulous record of the meeting's business, but he should also remember that members will be scrutinising them for any potential slights or reported inaccuracies. In addition, the secretary must appreciate the possible future importance of any set of minutes which may be used as a reference or source of precedent, and also that, while members may exchange mutual insults in the heat of the moment, neither they nor the chairman will thank the secretary for a verbatim report transcribed into reported speech for successive generations of committee members to wonder at!

Why minutes are so important is not difficult to appreciate. They incorporate a number of important functions, essential to the effective working of any meeting or committee. Firstly, the work of a committee or working party is largely evolutionary. Principles are progressively established; rules made and later modified; procedures and attitudes are developed and precedents formed. An ongoing set of minutes, therefore, provides both a source of reference and authority for chairman and members alike. A half-forgotten change made to a constitution which is recorded in the minutes may become crucial at a future date. Without such a source of reference, the work of any committee would be grossly impeded by a return to first principles whenever controversial business arose.

Closely allied to the reference aspect of minutes is their value in other ways as a written record. Human nature being what it is, orally communicated decisions have a way of being 'mis-remembered' when the

The National Institute Of Computer Managers

Newtown Branch

The next Committee Meeting of the Branch will take place on Wednesday 5th June 19-- in the Shelley Room of the White Unicorn Hotel, 7.30 p.m. for 8.00 p.m.

AGENDA

1. Apologies for absence

2. Minutes of the last meeting

3. Matters arising from the minutes

4. Publicity for new season's programme of events

5. Topic and speaker for meeting:
   Wednesday 4th March 19--

6. Visit to business systems

7. Proposal to levy an admission charge at meetings:

   That an admission charge of 50p per head be levied by the Branch as an admission charge to meetings to cover the cost of coffee and biscuits and to contribute towards branch funds

   Proposer: Mr J Pearson
   Seconder: Mrs M Jenkins

8. Any other business

9. Date of next meeting

Chairman: A J Lucas   Vice-Chairman: R T Nicholas

Honorary Secretary: M T Wilkins
Honorary Treasurer: H Jones

Committee Members: E W Booth, F C Carpenter, M Jenkins
Committee Members: G O F Nelson, J Pearson, K D Williams

Honorary Secretary's Address:

'Appletree', Buxton Avenue, Newtown, Surrey, NE12 5AI
Telephone: Business - Newtown 4571   Home - Newtown 46783

THE NATIONAL INSTITUTE OF COMPUTER MANAGERS

Newtown Branch

CHAIRMAN'S AGENDA

For the Branch Committee Meeting of Wednesday
5 June, to be held in the Shelley Room of the
White Unicorn Hotel at 8.00 pm.

CHAIRMAN'S NOTES

1 Apologies For Absence:
   Mr Booth will be visiting his wife in hospital.
   Mr Williams hopes to come but will be late –
   visit to London.

2 Minutes Of The Last Meeting:
   Mr Carpenter has intimated that he was not
   categorically against the change of venue for
   Branch Committee Meetings, and that his remarks
   as they appear in the Minutes of the Last Meeting
   have been misconstrued.

3 Matters Arising:
   Item 6: The manager of the Red Lion has confirmed that the Committee Room of the Blue Boar
   Hotel will be available on the third Wednesday of
   each month from 1 August onwards.

   Excelsior Printing Ltd. have promised the New
   Season's programmes by Friday 26 June at the
   latest.

4 Publicity For New Season's Programme Of Events:
   There does not appear to be any likelihood of the
   Newtown Chronicle repeating last year's price for
   the display advertisement. I spoke to the advertising manager on the 'phone last Thursday.

5 Topic And Speaker For Meeting: Wednesday 4 March 19--
   Lord Grenville has written respectfully to decline
   our invitation to speak. Copy of letter attached.

6 Visit To Business Systems Exhibition, Olympia:
   The Olympia management have confirmed that they
   still have vacancies for parties on Saturday
   25 September. 15% discount on admission
   charges for parties over 25.

7 Proposal To Levy Admission Charge At Meetings:
   As you will recall, John Pearson proposed a
   similar motion at last year's June meeting.
   His motion was defeated last year 6:2

   I understand Harold Jones is concerned about the
   Branch's ability to fund its activities in the
   programme for the New Season

occasion suits. The written record ensures, however, that democratically made decisions cannot be 'overlooked' or unilaterally abrogated by either chairman or caucus. When changes to the rules are sought, the minutes ensure that they are made through established procedures.

The minutes also render each participant at a meeting accountable for his or her utterances. The sure knowledge that an outrageous attitude, surly obstructiveness or domineering interjections are likely to find their way into distributed minutes frequently serves to hold less considerate committee members in check. On the other hand, dissenting members are able to insist on having a particular point minuted either as a source for future reference or to indicate a strong disapproval of a matter at issue.

In some organisations the minutes record only the decision reached, and a veil is drawn over the preceding debate. Such minutes are 'resolution minutes', since a motion which is successfully carried in a meeting is thereafter referred to as a 'Resolution'. Such minutes may be variously expressed:

Resolution minutes:

RESOLVED: That the company's Eastbrook branch be closed with immediate effect.

or,

It was resolved that the company's Eastbrook branch be closed with immediate effect.

Alternatively, the chairman of a committee may prefer to have the interplay of various attitudes leading up to a decision included in the minutes. When the principal viewpoints of members are summarised in this way, the minutes are referred to as 'narrative minutes'.

Narrative minutes:

The chairman invited comment upon the steep decline in the Eastbrook branch's turnover during the past nine months. Mr Weston felt that the branch had always suffered a lack of sufficient advertising support. Mr Hopkins drew attention to the parlous state of the district as a result of urban renewal work.

While generally sympathetic, Mrs Peters alluded to the rapid turnover of staff – six sales assistants in three months. In citing the tendered resignation of the branch manager, Mr Watkins emphasised the gravity of the situation. In summarising, the chairman referred the meeting to company policy, which clearly stated that branch closure was an inevitable consequence of continued trading losses.

By a majority of 7–3, it was decided to close the Eastbrook branch with immediate effect.

The reasons for preferring either resolution or narrative minutes may be briefly summarised as follows:

Resolution minutes

In meetings where it is important for participants to maintain a united front and accept collective responsibility, for example boards of directors or senior officers in public service, then a preference is understandable for a minutes' format which publishes decisions reached, while concealing from junior levels of the organisation strong disagreements or conflicts. In addition, the minutes of formal meetings required by statute may be more appropriately recorded by means of a brief 'resolution statement'. There are also convincing arguments for employing a format which is, above all, succinct and which relates only that information which is neccessary to enable decisions to be implemented.

Narrative minutes

On the other hand, there are many types of meeting for which it would be both more appropriate and, indeed useful, to have a summary of the main points of a discussion which precedes the reaching of a decision. For example, when management decisions are being debated, a managing director may well prefer to have the approaches, attitudes and judgments of his executives recorded in detail, so that individual accountability is recorded for given commitments or objections. In this way, a 'profile' of reliability and soundness of judgment may be identified, even when a single dissenter is in a minority at a meeting but subsequently proved right by a future turn of events. Thus managers, through narrative minutes, are persuaded to make responsible utterances and considered judgments.

Where voluntary bodies are concerned, narrative minutes provide a valuable psychological boost. When committee members give up their spare time to attend meetings, the extent of their motivation and the degree of their commitment may be enhanced by seeing *their* names and synopses of *their* contributions to the work of the club or association and to the decision-making process.

It is much more difficult, of course, for a secretary to write narrative minutes which achieve a successful compromise between terseness and long-windedness, and which report accurately without giving offence or glossing over points of conflict or deep-rooted disagreement.

In some organisations a compromise is achieved between the brevity of resolution minutes and the detail of narrative minutes. Where it is particularly important for executive decisions to be implemented swiftly, and where there is infrequent contact among participants between meetings, then the format sometimes referred to as action minutes may be employed. Here the proceedings are reported briefly and the name of the person delegated to act upon a particular item is entered in a column, usually on the right-hand side of the minutes page, opposite the reference to the item.

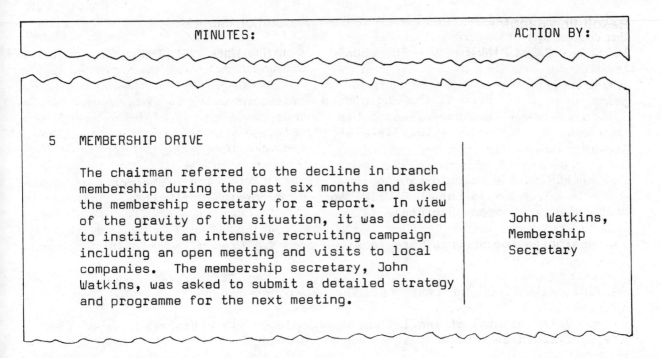

```
MINUTES:                                              ACTION BY:


5    MEMBERSHIP DRIVE

     The chairman referred to the decline in branch
     membership during the past six months and asked
     the membership secretary for a report.  In view
     of the gravity of the situation, it was decided       John Watkins,
     to institute an intensive recruiting campaign         Membership
     including an open meeting and visits to local         Secretary
     companies.  The membership secretary, John
     Watkins, was asked to submit a detailed strategy
     and programme for the next meeting.
```

Action minutes

The advantage of such a format is that it is very clear who has undertaken or been asked to do what. When minutes are circulated, it is immediately clear to a participant whether he has been required to act in any way, or whether he may read and file the minutes on an 'information only' basis. As the minutes format is overtly directional, however, its use is, perhaps, better restricted to those meetings within organisations where there is an obvious 'line authority'. If used in the context of voluntary organisations, there is a possibility of members feeling that they are being coerced and 'driven' rather than wooed and 'led' by the chairman.

Format

There are a number of different ways in which minutes are set out on paper. In some instances, the minutes are numbered and given headings which reproduce exactly the sequence and numbering of the items as they appear on the agenda. In some organisations, however, each minute is numbered consecutively from the very beginning of the first numbered minute of the first meeting onwards. Thus the thirteenth committee meeting may discuss items 261 to 268 on the agenda. In some institutions, particularly in local government, a system is adopted frequently which gives an item on the agenda a number such as, 3.0 or 4.0 or 5.0, followed by its title or heading. Points which are minuted under such headings are then referenced 3.1, 3.2, 3.3 etc.

In the absence of any single, universally adopted format, the following points should be borne in mind:

1 The sequence of items on the agenda should be followed.
2 There should be an intelligent use made of spacing and indentation to help the reader to identify item headings and follow referencing systems.
3 Reported statements should be clearly attributable to identify speakers.
4 Care should be taken to use the correct names of speakers or to identify speakers by their designations – chairman, treasurer, etc.
5 Where names are recorded in lists (for example, of those present) the precedence of officers should be followed by an alphabetical list of members.

Reported speech
The techniques of writing reported speech are examined in detail in the 'Use of English' Topic. It is essential to master these techniques before embarking on the writing of minutes.

Resolution minutes

MINUTES OF THE BOARD OF DIRECTORS MEETING

Held at the Registered Offices of Delta
Business Systems Ltd on Thursday 16th
July 19-- at 10.30 a.m.

PRESENT: R K Baldwin (in the chair); P J Lewis, T A R Sheldon,
J T Talbot, H C Wilkinson, directors; N Cartwright,
Company Secretary

Apologies for absence were received from K T Frewin.

261   MINUTES OF THE LAST MEETING

The minutes of the last meeting, previously circulated, were
taken as read and signed as a true record.

262   MATTERS ARISING

There were no matters arising.

263   COMPANY LOGO, LIVERY AND CORPORATE IDENTITY

It was resolved that the R P Silverton advertising agency be
appointed to develop new company logo and livery designs as
part of the company's policy to revitalise its corporate
identity.

264   INTRODUCTION OF FLEXIBLE WORKING HOURS AT HEAD OFFICE

It was resolved that the system of flexible working hours
agreed be introduced in the company's head office with
effect from 1st September 19--.

265   RELOCATION OF SOUTH WEST REGIONAL OFFICE

It was resolved that the company's South West Regional Office
be relocated at 46-52 Tamar Road, Plymouth, Devon. The office
to be fully operative by 15th August 19--.

266   DATE OF NEXT MEETING

The date of the next meeting of the board of directors was
scheduled for Thursday 13th August 19--.

signed:

R K Baldwin
Managing Director

13th August 19--

Narrative minutes

THE NATIONAL INSTITUTE OF COMPUTER MANAGERS   NEWTOWN BRANCH

MINUTES

Committee Meeting of The National Institute
of Computer Managers, Newtown Branch, held
on Wednesday 5th June 19-- in the Shelley
Room of the White Unicorn Hotel at 8.00p.m.

PRESENT   A.J. Lucas, Chairman; M.T. Wilkins, Hon. Secretary; H. Jones
               Hon. Treasurer; F.C. Carpenter; M. Jenkins; G.O.F. Nelson;
               J. Pearson; K.D. Williams.

1.   APOLOGIES FOR ABSENCE

Apologies for absence were received from R.T. Nicholas, Vice-Chairman, and
E.W. Booth.

2.   MINUTES OF THE LAST MEETING

Mr. Carpenter drew attention to item 6 of the minutes of the last meeting,
Branch Committee Meetings - Change Of Venue. He affirmed that his remarks
had been misinterpreted and that he was not categorically against the
proposed change of venue. By general consent it was agreed to substitute
'had strong reservations about' for 'was categorically against' in Item 6.

3.   MATTERS ARISING

The Secretary reported that in connection with Item 6, the manager of the
Blue Boar was able to offer his hotel's committee room on the third Wednesday of each month from 1st August onwards. The Chairman then requested
the Secretary to confirm acceptance of the offer by letter.

According to the latest information, the Secretary informed the meeting that
Excelsior Printing Ltd. had promised the new season's programmes by Friday
26th June. Mr. Nelson pointed out that it was essential for the programmes
to be available by that date for distribution purposes. The Chairman asked
Mr. Nelson to liaise with the Secretary to ensure that the promised delivery
date was met.

4.   PUBLICITY FOR THE NEW SEASON'S PROGRAMME OF EVENTS

The Chairman, in referring to the branch's advertisements placed with the
Newtown Chronicle, confirmed that the cost of such advertising was certain
to increase. The Treasurer expressed his concern at any prospective increase
in advertising expenditure in view of the agreed increases for speakers'
expenses and mail-shots to members. After a wide-ranging discussion of the
branch's expenditure on publicity, it was decided to place an order for six
advertisements with the Newtown Chronicle instead of the customary seven to
offset the anticipated increase in charges.

5.   TOPIC AND SPEAKER FOR MEETING: WEDNESDAY 4th MARCH 19--

The Chairman asked the Secretary to read to the meeting the letter received from Lord Grenville, who tendered his apologies for having to decline the invitation to speak on 4th March. Suggestions were then requested for possible alternative speakers. Mrs. Jenkins proposed that the Rt. Hon. Charles Hawkins, M.P. for Newtown East be approached, but it was generally agreed that M.P.s were subject to last-minute, unavoidable commitments in Westminster Mr. Williams suggested Mr. John Farnham, Computer Manager for Global Computer an acknowledged expert in developments in computer language. In the absence of any further suggestions, the Chairman requested the Secretary to write to Mr. Farnham inviting him to speak at the 4th March Meeting.

6.   VISIT TO BUSINESS SYSTEMS EXHIBITION, OLYMPIA

The Secretary relayed to the meeting the confirmation from the Olympia management regarding existing vacancies for parties on 25th September 19--. A discount of 15% was offered on admission charges for parties over 25 in number. Strong interest was expressed by all present, and the Chairman asked the Secretary to order 30 tickets at the party rate. Mr. Williams offered to arrange the hiring of a motor-coach and was requested to report progress at the next meeting.

7.   PROPOSAL TO LEVY AN ADMISSION CHARGE AT MEETINGS

The Chairman referred the meeting to Mr. Pearson's proposal on the agenda for the meeting. Before asking Mr. Pearson to speak to his motion, the Chairman reminded the meeting that the subject of admission charges to branch meetings had arisen during the previous season. It was a difficult matter and the financial status of the branch merited that it be re-examined. Mr. Pearson emphasised the rise in the cost of meetings and referred to the minutes of the meeting of Wednesday 17th October 19--, which recorded his prediction that events would prove him right about the need for an admission charge. He was advocating a levy of 50p, which he did not think would prove financially embarrassing to members and would not, in his opinion, result in falling attendances. Opposing the motion, Mr. Nelson felt strongly that members already paid a sufficiently large sum in annual membership fees to the Institute and that branch meetings should be funded from the allocation made to Institute Branches from Computer House. Mrs. Jenkins reminded the meeting that she had opposed the introduction of the charge when it was last debated, but felt that such a levy was the only fair way of keeping the branch solvent during the coming season. The Treasurer echoed Mrs. Jenkins' concern and stated that he was in favour of the motion. In view of the expression of conflicting views, the Chairman asked for a vote on the motion before the meeting. The motion was carried by 5 votes to 3.

8.   ANY OTHER BUSINESS

Mr. Carpenter raised the matter of branch reports submitted to the Institute Journal. He had noted that for the past two quarters, no mention had been made of Newtown branch activities. The Chairman promised to look into the matter and to report back.

Mrs. Jenkins drew the meeting's attention to the new magazine, 'Computer Monthly'. She was personally acquainted with the editor and was able to recommend it to members without reservation.

9.   DATE OF NEXT MEETING

The next Committee Meeting was scheduled for Wednesday 3rd July 19--

Terminology of meetings

The following list includes some of the principal terms used in meetings. This list is by no means exhaustive, however, and you should use it as a basis for your own, more extensive check-list of important technical terms relating to meetings.

Ad hoc from Latin, meaning 'for the purpose of', as for example, when a sub-committee is set up to organise a works outing

Adjourn to hold a meeting over until a later date

Advisory providing advice or suggestion, not taking action

Agenda a schedule of items drawn up for discussion at a meeting

AGM Annual General Meeting; all members are usually eligible to attend

Apologies excuses given in advance for inability to attend a meeting

Articles of Association rules required by Company Law which govern a company's activities

Bye-laws rules regulating an organisation's activities

Chairman leader or person given authority to conduct a meeting

Chairman's Agenda based upon the committee agenda, but containing explanatory notes

Collective responsibility a convention by which all committee members agree to abide by a majority decision

Committee a group of people usually elected or appointed who meet to conduct agreed business and report to a senior body

Consensus agreement by general consent, no formal vote being taken

Constitution set of rules governing activities of voluntary bodies

Convene to call a meeting

Executive having the power to act upon taken decisions

Extraordinary meeting a meeting called for all members to discuss a serious issue affecting all is called an Extraordinary General Meeting; otherwise a non-routine meeting called for a specific purpose

Ex officio given powers or rights by reason of office. For example a trades union convenor may be an ex officio member of a works council

Honorary post a duty performed without payment – Honorary Secretary

Information, point of the drawing of attention in a meeting to a relevant item of fact

Lobbying a practice of seeking members' support before a meeting

Minutes the written record of a meeting; resolution minutes record only decisions reached, while narrative minutes provide a record of the decision-making process

Motion the name given to a 'proposal' when it is being discussed at a meeting

Mover one who speaks on behalf of a motion

Nem. con. from Latin, literally, 'no one speaking against'

Opposer one who speaks against a motion

Order, point of the drawing of attention to a breach of rules or procedures

Other business either items left over from a previous meeting, or items discussed after the main business of a meeting

Proposal the name given to a submitted item for discussion (usually written) before a meeting takes place

Proxy literally, 'on behalf of another person' – 'a proxy vote'

Resolution the name given to a 'motion' which has been passed or carried; used after the decision has been reached

Secretary committee official responsible for the internal and external administration of a committee

Secret ballot a system of voting in secret

Sine die from Latin, literally, 'without a day', that is to say indefinitely, e.g. 'adjourned sine die'

Standing committee a committee which has an indefinite term of office

Seconder one who supports the 'proposer' of a motion or proposal by 'seconding' it

Treasurer committee official responsible for its financial records and transactions

Unanimous all being in favour

Vote, casting when two sides are deadlocked a chairman may record a second or 'casting vote' to ensure a decision is made

Assessment questions

Types of meeting

1 What are the factors common to most meetings which help us to define the purpose of calling a meeting or of holding regular meetings?

2 List as many different types of meeting as you are able to recall.

3   In what circumstances do meetings tend to conduct their business:
(*a*)   with written rules of procedure?
(*b*)   without written rules of procedure?
4   How would you define a formal meeting?
5   What is the point of a 'brain-storming' meeting?
6   Outline as many different reasons as you remember for calling meetings
7   What do you consider to be the advantages and disadvantages of the meeting as a communications medium?

The structure of meetings

8   Illustrate by means of a diagram the relationship between the following: an executive committee; an advisory ad hoc sub-committee; an advisory committee and a standing sub-committee of an executive committee.
9   Explain the meaning of: 'ad hoc'; 'standing'; 'executive'; 'advisory' and 'coopted member'.
10   What are the functions of: a management committee; a policy committee; a membership committee?

The functions of committee officials

11   Explain the principal functions of: a chairman; a secretary; a treasurer.
12   What does an auditor do?
13   Outline the administrative programme followed by a committee secretary between one committee meeting and the next.
14   How would you justify the inclusion of a vice-chairman in a committee?

Rules and regulations

15   Explain the meaning of the following: a statute, a constitution, bye-laws, standing orders, Articles and Memorandum of Association. With what sort of meeting is each associated?
16   What is a quorum?
17   What do you understand by, 'a point of order' and 'a point of information'?
18   At what stages is a formal, written item for discussion at a meeting referred to as a 'proposal', a 'motion' and a 'resolution'?

The written documentation of meetings

19   List the main types of written documentation used in connection with meetings.
20   How does a chairman's agenda differ from a committee member's agenda?
21   List the items which comprise a typical committee member's agenda.
22   Identify the different formats suggested for the notice of a meeting. Suggest a type of meeting appropriate for each different format.
23   List the items of a typical Annual General Meeting agenda of a club or society.
24   What is the difference between resolution and narrative minutes?

25   When would you prefer to use narrative and when resolution minutes format?
26   In what circumstances would you advocate the use of 'action minutes'?
27   Identify three different ways of referencing minutes.
28   What advice would you give to someone about to become a committee secretary?
29   Why do some chairmen dislike 'Matters Arising' and 'Any Other Business'?

Terminology

30   Explain the meaning of: 'collective responsibility'; 'ex officio'; 'honorary'; 'lobbying'; 'nem. con.'; 'sine die'; 'casting vote'; 'extraordinary meeting'.

Build-up tasks and discussion topics

Notice

1   The chairman of the Middletown Traders' Association has recently expressed to you his dissatisfaction with the format of notices sent to committee members to call regular monthly meetings. Several members of the committee have expressed their concern at taking no part in the compilation of committee meeting agendas, despite their attempts to submit agenda items. The chairman has therefore asked you to design a suitable notice format for discussion at the next meeting. The committee has met for some years in the Small Committee Room of the Middletown Town Hall, High Street, Middletown, Midshire MI13 2AC.

Agendas

2   'Ah, Jim, come on in. I've been trying to sort out the items for inclusion in the agenda for the next committee meeting. I saw that written proposal from Jack Burton about changing the date for the Christmas Dance from Saturday 14th December to the 21st. Jack reckons there'll be more of a Christmas spirit nearer the day. You'd better put his proposal into the appropriate format. The seconder is Mrs Bignall. Then there's the complaints about the club-room bar prices. We must deal with that. Oh, and while I remember, I believe you said we've had a number of letters from fixture secretaries asking for dates for next summer's first team cricket fixtures. We ought to settle that one. As you know, I couldn't persuade Ken Palmer not to resign as Hon. Treasurer. You've had four nominations? Yes, well, it's most unfortunate but we can't afford to let the situation drag on. I'll ask Ken meanwhile to act as a caretaker. I think that's about it. Could you draft a committee members' agenda? You'd better give some thought to the running order. I'd help out but I'm late for a section meeting. Thanks a lot!'

As Honorary Secretary of the Lifelong Insurance Co. Ltd Sports & Social Club, Ashburnley Crescent, Richmond, Surrey SU16 4TJ, draft the agenda asked for. The meeting is on Thursday 18 September 19— at 8.00 pm in the Clubhouse Committee Room.

3 The chairman, Mr Peter Turner of the Lifelong Insurance Co. Ltd Sports and Social Club has just telephoned you to say that he won't be able to take the chair at tomorrow's committee meeting. He has asked Mrs Kean, vice-chairman, to take the chair in his absence. As Mrs Kean is not as familiar with the background to the items on the agenda as he is, Mr Turner has asked you to prepare a chairman's agenda for her. The following are the points for her to keep in mind which Mr Turner has suggested:

J Burton proposal – problem of changing band booking – has Gordon Wilson already booked the Post House Hotel ballroom? Jack tends to go on at length when he warms to his theme.

Upset Miss Grainger at the last meeting – her suggestions to form Ladies' Soccer Team.

Bar prices – main source of funds to run club-house – recent poor attendance by members mid-week – charges up by brewery – check Ken Palmer.

Letters from cricket clubs – who is hon. sec. of cricket team? Harry Fielding will know – job needs delegating.

Ken Palmer – resignation – tricky – have been criticisms of Ken's record-keeping – Harry Fielding keen to have office – not nominated – Ken fed up with sniping.

Correspondence

4 At the Lifelong Sports and Social Club committee meeting it was decided not to offer Albion Engineering Sports Club a cricket fixture next summer. After last season's match your clubhouse was left in a damaged state; repairs cost £65.50. Several ladies also complained of the language which was used during the evening at the bar.

As Honorary Secretary, you have been asked to write to the Cricket Club Secretary, declining their offer of a fixture. Coincidentally, Albion Engineering Ltd is a client of Lifelong Insurance!

Report

5 As a development of the Lifelong committee meeting's discussion of the Christmas Dance, it was decided to form an ad hoc sub-committee to arrange it under the chairmanship of Jack Burton. As the sub-committee's secretary, you have been asked to draft a report on the arrangements for submission at the next meeting.

Public address, narrative minutes, meeting simulation

6 As Chairman of the Laystone College Students' Association, you are currently preparing your Chairman's Report for the forthcoming Annual General Meeting. The following are some of the events and topics you have to report upon. You may add others if you wish:

The number of active members has declined during the year – attendance at social events has generally declined.

Criticisms have been levelled at the committee – lack of decent events – programme curtailed – too autocratic.

But – members do not offer help or services – all is left to committee – Social Secretary – organised three discos singlehanded. Three resignations from committee during year – pressure of work – personality clashes.

Liaison with students' associations of neighbouring colleges – three meetings – little progress on joint approach to local accommodation problems – joint social committee formed to plan inter-college social events – starts next session.

Events: Christmas Dance – great success – thanks to Principal and staff for support; Sport – Ladies' Basketball Team won District League – Men came second in Regional Cup – Soccer Team hampered by lack of practice – won 5, lost 6, drew 2; Pram Race – collected £98 for charity – winners – Chris Parker and Susan Curtis; Summer Leavers' Ball – hope as good turnout as for Christmas – tickets still available from Social Secretary.

Financial situation – leave to Treasurer but say balance of £434.28 – thanks to Treasurer and Committee's good management.

Future – emphasise unless better support many facilities and events will die – which now taken for granted – questionnaire being sent out to ask for suggestions for preferred future programme.

Thanks – thank all college staff and committee for help during year – too many to name – wish success to successor.

(*a*) Tape-record or write out in direct speech the chairman's report based on the above topics. Your aims should be to structure the speech logically and to place suitable emphasis on important points.

(*b*) Write out in narrative minutes form the Annual General Meeting's agenda item: Chairman's Report, using the direct speech report in Assignment *a*.

(*c*) Compose a suitable AGM agenda for the meeting of the Laystone College Students' Association and then role-play the meeting. Assume that relations between the committee and the general membership have deteriorated and that some noisy dissatisfaction is voiced from the floor.

(*d*) Write the minutes of your simulated Annual General Meeting in narrative minutes form.

Resolution minutes

7 Write in resolution minutes form minutes appropriate for a board of directors' meeting for the following:

a decision to introduce the post of Communication Co-ordinator into the management structure

the decision to terminate the company's laundering contract with Speedy Cleaning Services Ltd currently due for renewal.

8 Organise a brain-storming meeting aimed at establishing a methodical approach to studying. Produce a study guide for distribution to new students.

Discussion topics

1 'Decisions take too long to reach in committees and when they are arrived at invariably they take the form of harmless compromises.'

2 'Too much store is set by the traditional formal procedures by which some meetings are conducted. All too often they become the means by which the expert "bam-boozles" the layman.'

3 'The most important decisions are usually made before the meeting starts.' Is the practice of lobbying fair? Should it be stopped? Could it be? Does it matter?

4 'If the cost of holding meetings was calculated more frequently, there would soon be fewer of them – and better ones at that!'

5 Of what use is the meeting in all its various forms as a means of democratic decision-making? Where, for example, lies the accountability for decisions made in an organisation by a committee drawn from various departments and levels in the hierarchy? Are effective decisions inevitably 'one man' (or woman) decisions?

Case studies

Mending the cracks in Plastimould

Plastimould Ltd is a company manufacturing a range of household utensils from a chemical base – bowls, buckets, pipes, brushes etc. For the past six weeks it has had a serious industrial dispute on its hands. One of the stages in the production process has been declared 'unsafe' by the unionised factory staff.

This stage concerns the cleaning out of vats which have contained the material for moulding into the various products in the company's range. It is accepted by both management and union representatives that it is possible during the cleaning process for fumes to be generated which are dangerous to the skin and which under no circumstances should be inhaled.

Recently three men have collapsed not long after working on the cleansing of the vats and they are still off work sick. After the third man had fallen ill, the union decided after a full meeting of the factory union membership to ban any of the union's members from working on the vat cleansing process. The effect of this ban was to halt production completely.

The union want an independent enquiry into the dangers and effects to health stemming from the cleansing process. For their part, management have declared that the cleansing process is perfectly safe, provided that the protective clothing and equipment provided is worn and used as specified in company regulations.

The union's position is that the clothing is old-fashioned, having been designed more than ten years previously, and that no-one to their knowledge has carried out any recent tests to confirm the effectiveness of its protection. The men have complained that it is too hot to wear, and that its bulkiness makes it impossible to work in the more inaccessible parts of the vats. The respirators are also, according to the men, inefficient, especially when any physical exertion is required.

Management has pointed out that the protective clothing and equipment conforms to the safety specifications laid down for such work in the relevant section of the industrial safety legislation. The men, says management, have been cutting safety corners to boost bonus earnings by not wearing all the equipment and clothing when there is a clear need to. If there have been instances of men becoming sick, which management will not accept as being a direct consequence of the cleansing process, then it must be the result of contributory negligence.

The union regards this last attitude of management as totally hypocritical. It claims that in the past management has turned 'a blind eye' to total adherence to factory safety regulations. Only now that the company is faced with a law-suit for damages arising from the medical condition of the three workers currently sick in hospital has the accusation of 'contributory negligence' arisen. In any case, the company has failed in its obligation to inform its factory staff adequately of the potential dangers involved in the cleansing process, and now, 'caught red-handed', was trying to prevent an independent enquiry from being set up.

The latest rejoinder from management is that unless a formula can be decided to re-start production with immediate effect, there may well be a possibility that the parent company of Plastimould will divert its production to another factory in another country, thus causing wide-spread redundancy. The union is inclined to see this as bluff, although some members concede that the six-week lay-off must have had crippling effect on the company's financial position.

Assignments

1 Form the management or union team, prepare your case for a 'return-to-work' negotiating meeting and then simulate the meeting. Observers or a team member should take notes and produce narrative minutes.

2 Depending upon the outcome of the meeting draft either a 'joint communiqué' or separate statements for circulation to Plastimould staff.

3 As an individual student write an essay on the problems implicit in the case study and suggest how you think the management and the union would resolve their differences.

Frosty climate at Arctura

Recently, your company, Arctura Refrigeration Ltd has been experiencing a serious problem affecting both its export sales and production departments. The company manufactures a range of refrigerators and freezers, many of which are sold abroad. Of recent months relations have deteriorated between the Export Sales Department and the Production Department. The root of the problem lies in the failure of the company's production department to meet production targets and deadlines for refrigerators and freezers ordered by customers in Middle and Far Eastern markets.

The Export Sales Manager, Mr K D Mears, is receiving letters daily from customers and agents complaining bitterly about broken promises over delivery dates and emphasising the danger of loss of business and the closing of accounts. Until some three months ago, the company's overseas order book had been full, but as a result of the recent poor performance in production, there has been a decline in repeat orders. This situation has been reported by the Export Sales Manager, who drew the Managing Director's attention to the fact that competitors were exploiting the situation to the full.

The Production Manager, Mr J D P Jones, has recently been critical of the poor communications existing between the Export Sales and Production Departments. Orders have been taken, he affirmed, which did not take into account the company's overall production capacity and the production commitment to a more profitable home market. There had also been a spate of late modifications to individual product specifications which had made it impossible to plan an efficient production schedule. Batches of both refrigerators and freezers were being stored because they had not met a modified order requirement.

A further complication lies in the current 'work to rule' being followed by the factory's operatives, members of the Metal Workers' Union, in pursuit of an improved bonus scheme. Talks with the company's management team, headed by the Personnel Manager, Mrs K Wheatley, have broken down over agreement on a revised basic rate of pay and hourly output targets upon which bonus rates are based.

The following are the company's personnel involved principally in the problem:

Mr A Hartley, Managing Director
A N Other, Personal Assistant to the M.D.

Mr K D Mears, Export Sales Manager
Miss A Jameson, Assistant Export Sales Manager
Mrs P Nielson, Export Sales Order Co-ordinator

Mr J D P Jones, Production Manager
Mr R V Kershaw, Assistant Production Manager
Mr N P Oliver, Work Progress Officer

Mrs Wheatley, Personnel Manager
Miss K Bright, Personal Assistant to the Personnel Manager

Mr P R Grimshaw, Works Convener, Metal Workers' Union
Mr J K Briggs, Shop Steward
Mrs R Roberts, Shop Steward

Assignments

1 As Personal Assistant to the Managing Director, you have been asked to draft a memorandum report for Mr Hartley, outlining an approach aimed at solving the problem by 'getting people round a table'. You have been asked to specify the type and number of meetings you would suggest, who should take part and what procedures should be followed in any given meeting.

2 In order to develop this case study further, it is possible to provide additional background and briefing notes for each interested group and then to proceed to a role-playing simulation of one or more meetings. Secretaries may be appointed to *each group* to take minutes of any meeting. Each set of minutes may be produced and circulated to all participants. It may well be instructive to compare the various sets of minutes of the same meeting drawn up by groups with different aims and outlooks. Remember, however, that it is customary to produce only one set of minutes in normal circumstances.

Multi-media assignment

Newbourne Knights – rescued from distress!

Background

The Newbourne Knights is a voluntary charitable society of Newbourne citizens, whose charitable activities are mainly concerned with raising money to provide outings, entertainment and treats for local underprivileged old people and children. Its committee meets monthly in the Committee Room of the Old Town Hall, High Street, Newbourne at 7.30 pm. As a member of the committee, you receive the following telephone call from Mrs Jean Carson, Chairman:

'Sorry to trouble you, but Harold Johnson (Hon. Sec.) has just gone down with 'flu. Do you think you could take over as Acting Honorary Secretary to organise the next committee meeting on the 21st? You'll need to get a notice out as soon as possible – and ask for any agenda items as well, to be sent to you by – well, you fix a deadline.'

A week later, you have a discussion with Jean Carson about the items to be included on the committee agenda. The following points emerge from your conversation:

'It's time we made a date for the annual senior citizens' outing – and I think we'd better set up a sub-committee again to organise it.

'Jack Peters says he'd like to make a Treasurer's Report and also provide a breakdown on the cost of the children's Christmas party – I gather he's a bit fed up because some committee members haven't yet given him their raffle ticket money.

'Mrs Simpson rang to say she's annoyed because her suggestion for holding an Easter Bonnet competition was omitted from Item 6 in last meeting's minutes – Future Programme. Don't forget that we need her support in laying on the refreshments for the Spring Holiday Fete, which we ought to start discussing now.

'Oh, and I mustn't forget to thank Mrs Hargreaves for her recent donation under AOB.

'By the way, here's a letter from the vicar of St Peter's offering his garden for the Spring Bank Holiday Fete again.'

Assume that the committee meeting duly takes place and that its items of business are as indicated on the committee agenda above. Unfortunately, the day before the meeting, Mrs Carson rang you to say she couldn't attend as a relative was seriously ill and she had to visit her. She asked you to prepare a chairman's agenda for Mr John Dickinson, Vice-Chairman, based on the committee agenda, to enable him to chair the meeting.

With Mr Dickinson in the chair, with you as Acting Secretary, and with eight other committee members attending, the meeting proceeds. Amongst other matters agreed, a sub-committee is formed to organise the annual senior citizens' outing.

The selected sub-committee, formed to plan the senior citizens' outing, has been asked to investigate suitable ideas for it, locations, costs, transport, refreshments etc.

Assignments

1   Notice
Draft a suitable notice to call the next committee meeting.

2   Committee agenda
As she was in a hurry to visit the matron of the Newbourne Nursing Home, Mrs Carson has asked you to draw up a committee agenda based on the points raised above, and has asked you to use your discretion in forming a running order of items.

3   Chairman's agenda
Prepare the chairman's agenda requested by Mrs Carson for Mr Dickinson, based on the above committee agenda produced.

4   Meeting simulation
Simulate the committee meeting, having produced and circulated the relevant documents and prepared notes etc.

5   Minutes
Produce narrative minutes of the meeting.

6   Report
Draft a report of the sub-committee's outing plans to submit to the next committee meeting.

14 People, efficiency and effectiveness in organisations

Introduction

The title of this topic may seem a little long-winded, but it has been coined to make an important point. And the point is that being efficient and being effective is not necessarily the same thing. Yet people in organisations must be both if their aims and objectives are to be met. For example, in a sales department there may be a team of sales representatives who are highly efficient in obtaining orders for their company's products. If, however, there is a sloppy back-up of order-processing and despatch administration which fails to keep delivery deadlines or forgets parts of orders, then all the efficient work of the sales representatives will have had little effect, since insufficient goods will have been sold, and customers will go elsewhere.

Similarly, individuals within an office team may be working at their part of the operation in a highly efficient manner, while the overall activity is proving an utter waste of time, as the anecdote on page 252 illustrates.

The role of O and M and work study

Of course, this anecdote is not meant to be taken too literally, but it does highlight the ease with which com-panies or parts of them can slide into inefficient or meaningless routines unless some mechanism exists to ensure that all parts of the organisation are kept under continuous review with a view to maximising:

efficiency and effectiveness

achieved through:

- employing the most economical routines and processes in terms of costs, time and effort or energy
- co-ordinating routines to avoid duplication and overlap
- ensuring that good communication practices avoid breakdowns, ambiguities or exclusions when information is channelled around the organisation
- maximising productivity and minimising waste by scrutinising the ways in which jobs are undertaken and evaluating them to see how they may be done more effectively
- evaluating plant and equipment to ensure that it is being used to its optimum output potential
- appraising the ways in which factories and offices are laid out so that people, machines and materials are harmoniously grouped to minimise delays, bottlenecks or frustrations

Such are the principal considerations of those company

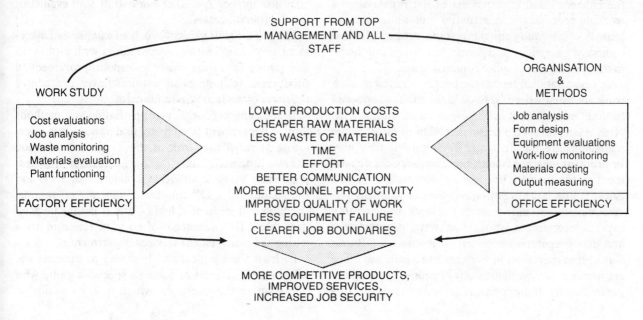

SUPPORT FROM TOP MANAGEMENT AND ALL STAFF

WORK STUDY

ORGANISATION & METHODS

Cost evaluations
Job analysis
Waste monitoring
Materials evaluation
Plant functioning

FACTORY EFFICIENCY

LOWER PRODUCTION COSTS
CHEAPER RAW MATERIALS
LESS WASTE OF MATERIALS
TIME
EFFORT
BETTER COMMUNICATION
MORE PERSONNEL PRODUCTIVITY
IMPROVED QUALITY OF WORK
LESS EQUIPMENT FAILURE
CLEARER JOB BOUNDARIES

Job analysis
Form design
Equipment evaluations
Work-flow monitoring
Materials costing
Output measuring

OFFICE EFFICIENCY

MORE COMPETITIVE PRODUCTS,
IMPROVED SERVICES,
INCREASED JOB SECURITY

Cutting through to the heart of the problem!

There was a large company which had been in the widget manufacturing business for some years. Recently, however, sales had slumped, the percentage of defective widgets being produced had grown alarmingly and overall staff morale had plummeted.

Correspondingly, a team of outside management consultants was called in to go over the company with a fine tooth comb to find out what was going wrong. In part of the team was an Office Administration specialist and his assistant, a kind of apprentice learning the consultancy business.

One day they went into the Widget Evaluation Department, which had a high reputation for efficiency. The young apprentice was deeply impressed. Everywhere she looked she saw smartly dressed personnel beavering away with barely time to acknowledge passing colleagues. In one corner reports were being produced on expensive WP equipment at a high rate of knots, while in another several executives were dictating almost continuously into the latest audio equipment. Further along the office there were the latest filing systems and micro-fiche equipment allied to computers – it was all highly impressive in the eyes of the apprentice consultant. It was obviously impressing her boss, whose eyes roved everywhere, and who asked a series of short but practical questions.

After an hour or two of observation and interview, the consultant specialist said to his assistant:

'Right, I've seen enough. We'll come back tomorrow sharp at nine a.m., and I want you to bring with you two large plastic dustbins and a pair of large shears.'

Mystified, but not daring to question the boss, the apprentice wandered off in search of a hardware shop.

The next morning, just before nine o'clock, master and assistant walked into the Widget Evaluation Department, and to the young lady's horror, the consultant began to sweep whole desk-tops of paperwork and in-trays into the large dustbins. With the shears he cut extension telephone cables and dropped telephones into the bins never minding about terminating peoples' calls in mid sentence! Within minutes the whole department was in uproar and, as the consultant had anticipated, the company's top staff burst into the office, looking either angry, aghast or bewildered.

'What is the meaning of this?' thundered the Managing Director, having got the consultant into the privacy of his own office as quickly as possible.

'Simply,' replied the consultant calmly, 'that in the Widget Evaluation Department you have created an endless loop of activity in which not one sliver of useful information gets out of the office! Those gentlemen over in the far corner, they are all generating audio dictation reports for word processing across the room' he said, referring to the WP staff whose power plugs he had de-activated. 'Which,' he continued dramatically, 'are all filed in those filing cabinets holding the floppy discs at the far end of the office!

'In effect, nothing ever leaves this room – so what's the point? If you had introduced your own Organisation and Methods Unit some while ago, you wouldn't have needed the particular piece of showmanship I indulged in. But I think it did help me to get your undivided attention!'

With that, a duly thoughtful Managing Director and an experienced Management Consultant got down to discussing productively how O&M and Work Study techniques could pull the company round.

or public service personnel whose role is to optimise the efficiency and effectiveness of the organisation's working processes. The activities they undertake are termed 'work study' in the manufacturing side of a company's activities and 'organisation and methods' in the general area of office administration.

In organisational terms, the people engaged in such work are usually deemed to be in the 'staff' as opposed to 'line' management of the organisation and as such often report through a departmental head direct to the managing director. In larger organisations they may be grouped together as a management services department as the diagram on page 253 illustrates. As you can see, in a large organisation, the management services department encompasses the work of accounting experts, economists, systems analysts, programmers and data preparation operatives – in effect a DP unit – as well as specialists in work measurement and office ergonomics (the specialist study of people in a working environment). If the company embodies a manufactur-

ing arm, then the management services department may also include specialist work study staff evaluating production processes.

It is not difficult to justify such an extensive management services operation in companies with multi-million pound turnovers, since a single improvement in production techniques or administrative procedures may save thousands of pounds a day.

In the context of what an organisation and methods unit or department principally undertakes, it is interesting to recall the work of the Topic 'Introduction to Data Processing' since there are a number of correspondences between an O&M evaluation of a job and the creation of a DP routine – both rely on rational thinking and sequential logic – and it is thus no accident that a DP presence is often to be found in firms within the management services department.

Perhaps the simplest and best way to examine the O&M role is in terms of having a specialist group who can examine the questions which follow (or similar

Management services – organisation structure. Work study related to factory-based operations may also be incorporated.

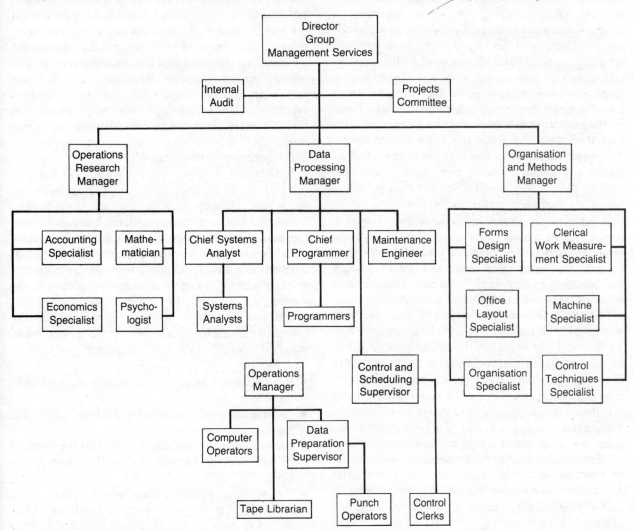

ones) and then proffer answers to them aimed at improving efficiency and effectiveness:

- *Who* actually, precisely and in fine detail is doing what?
- And *what* precisely, actually and in fine detail are they doing?
- *Why* are they doing it? (In what way, following what procedures etc?)
- *When* are they doing it? (At what time intervals, according to what schedules, timetables, cycles of activity?)
- *Where* are they doing it? (Over how many locations, requiring how much movement?)
- *How* are they doing it? (In what sort of work patterns, using what type of equipment, forms, administrative procedures?)
- *To what effect* are they doing it? (Is the operation cost-effective, economical, profitable, achieving quality, worthwhile?)
- *Should it be done at all?* (Who would miss it if it were cut out of company activities?)

The continuous posing of such questions and the attainment of productive answers forms the daily bread-and-butter work of the O&M or Work Study specialist. Historically, the work of staff constantly probing into work routines and practices has not always been managed very well by senior organisational staff. If O&M work is to be truly effective, it has to operate in a climate which is co-operative. If line managers remain suspicious of O&M and factory operatives resentful of enforced work-rates which are imposed rather than negotiated, then the result may be that lip-service is paid to the introduction of revised work routines while, in effect, little changes.

Thus senior management has an obligation to ensure that O&M is not seen as a form of private intelligence to which only the MD is privy and which lies at the root of the imposition of unpopular policies. At the same time, no managing director worth his salt can afford to stand idly by while parts of his or her company lurch cheerfully along, wasting money or failing to make their proper contribution to profits.

Astute senior management has managed to steer a route between these two rock-strewn shores by evolving structures and policies whereby staff at all levels benefit from the introduction of more efficient work practices. For example, part of a departmental manager's salary may be paid on a scale allied to the cost-effectiveness of his department. In production terms this could mean achieving or exceeding production targets or minimising waste and defective products. For the sales manager it may mean achieving his sales target but it might include a reward based on the number of new customers found and the turnover they contribute. For the office administration manager it could mean the running of the administration arm within a total of given expenditure – for payroll, equipment, consumables and repairs, with a bonus relating to any further savings made.

In other words, imaginative management is able to connect all the way down the organisational hierarchy rewards – extra money, holidays, promotion etc – with the achievement of more economic ways of running the business. In this way, the Works Manager may welcome the Work Study Officer with open arms, and not like the way in which the actor John Le Mesurier was received in the Peter Sellers classic comedy 'I'm All Right, Jack!' when as the resident Work Study Officer he was reduced to spying on the factory work force through binoculars at a safe distance! However, it would be oversimplifying the case if the role and functions of trade unions were not to be included in the general mix of O&M and Work Study activities, since the objectives of management and trade union officials may not always entirely coincide. While management may see the introduction of a particular operation as cost-cutting and labour-saving, the trade union involved may regard it as pay-reducing and redundancy-causing.

Thus in many firms the implementation of recommendations made by O&M staff may require an ongoing dialogue and the fostering of good relationships by senior management – as much with their own trade unionist officials/employees as with company staff ignoring the trade union dimension.

Nowhere is this need more apparent than in the manufacturing arms of companies. For very many years, in factories up and down the country, pay has been linked to productivity. The more washers or nuts and bolts an operative could make in an hour, having regard for wastage rates, the more he or she could earn.

As a consequence, factory operatives, charge-hands, foremen, shop-stewards and works managers alike became very much involved in what was termed 'the rate for the job'. In the 1930s and 1940s, the 'labour' side of the manufacturing industry became concerned lest the 'rate for the job' should be 'busted' by operatives demonstrating to work study staff that they could complete a process quicker or turn out products faster. 'Rate-busting' became a dirty word, since it too often came to be accompanied by short-lived increases in bonuses for increased production, while the increased rate soon became the norm.

In the 1950s and 1960s, however, management introduced more sophisticated production incentives which linked quality to output and placed more of the control for performance in the hands of the operatives themselves. A leading car-maker, for instance, introduced a production system in which teams learned to do each others' jobs and between them produced an entire motor-car, and not just a small part of it in endless repetition. Unfortunately, while such production methods were much more job satisfying for individuals, they did not always result in the production of competitively priced motor-cars.

In the office, too, post Second World War management methods became slowly more progressive as employees' job expectations grew and trade unions blossomed in the clerical, secretarial and administrative management sectors. Thus the seemingly endless rows of copy typists which characterised some pre-war large offices gradually became transformed into smaller working units with greater consideration given to their working environment. In 1963 in the UK the Offices, Shops and Railways Act was introduced, which reformed existing legislation about statutory minimum standards for facilities at work, including:

- the minimum floorspace to be allocated to each employee
- the standards to be followed in lighting, ventilating and heating work premises
- the ratio of male and female toilets to the number of staff employed as well as general hygiene provisions
- the inclusion of restrooms in places of work
- regulations to improve working conditions with regard to noise levels, dangerous equipment, first-aid provisions and the like.

In the 1970s, as the cost of office accommodation increased, and as companies wished to become more flexible in their use of floorspace, new approaches to the office as a working environment were introduced. The open-plan office was devised, which functioned without solid partitions, but used plants, filing-cabinets and screens to break down the 'open barn' appearance of large offices. Such developments were followed by what the Germans called 'bürolandschaft' which translates into 'office landscaping' which was achieved through the design of fully integrated office fixtures and fittings, together with acoustic screens which broke down larger spaces into smaller ones without shutting everyone up in self-enclosed rooms. In this system equipment design was also taken into consideration so that tables, desk-tops, power connections and cables were all taken into account and delivered as a co-ordinated package. While such developments were popular both with office architects and employers seeking to contain rental overheads, they did not always meet with the approval of the staff who had to work in them, who sometimes felt they had lost out in the areas of privacy, available floorspace and the loss of confidentiality.

The study of work

Perhaps the greatest single advantage to stem from the industrial disputes about job-rates, manning and output levels in manufacturing industry in the first half of the twentieth century was that it obliged the personnel conducting work study and job analysis surveys to devise some practical means of measuring the processes and practices of production. This work was in a sense begun in the 1920s in the United States by Frederick Taylor, who wrote a treatise on the science of shovelling, after having observed how iron ore was shovelled in the Bethlehem Steel Works. He noticed that experienced shovellers bought in their own shovels made to their preferred dimensions. With superior techniques, they were able to move far more ore or coal than their counterparts with inferior equipment and less technique. With their support, Taylor carried out one of the first scientific and methodical work study analyses, and thereby – almost single-handed – founded the ensuing industrial specialism. Soon after an associate, Frank Gilbreth, conducted a three-year 'time and motion' study into bricklaying. So it was that in the 1920s the foundations of management science were laid. Instead of intuition or 'bully-boy' management practices, a new approach was developed based upon careful and recorded observation, meticulous attention to detail and to the use of statistical and scientific methods to evaluate findings.

No longer was it acceptable to set arbitrary output targets. Instead, existing operations and processes were studied and ways and means identified of streamlining parts of a process or of saving time. Then the new version of the operation would be tested and a new 'rate for the job' set and agreed on both management and labour sides. Of course, human nature is customarily able to set awry even the best of intentions, and cunning and guile were employed on both sides to create a margin of benefit – sometimes the operator was able to convince the work study official that he was working to his upper limit when in reality he wasn't. Thus the rate set for the job had inbuilt into it a margin for extra production which would earn extra bonus!

Nevertheless, a trend was started which enabled both management and staff to improve production and working conditions.

In having to arrive at concrete measurements of work, Work Study and O&M personnel were able to demonstrate to top management:

- the percentage of reduction in costs attained by the introduction of a particular process
- the precise ratio of units produced to defective units scrapped
- the ratio of customer complaints to sales orders processed
- the number of hours of 'downtime' of plant and equipment to hours of continuous use
- the amount of savings made as a proportion of total production costs by switching to an alternative source of raw materials
- the amount of money or man-hours saved by modifying a production or clerical process
- the amount of money saved by introducing a system which requires a lower level of stock holding

and so on.

In this way, the work of Work Study and O&M practitioners became quantifiable and thus straightforward for top management to appreciate – by how much, by how many, by when etc.

The methodology

Much of the work of the management services team is achieved via the successful completion of a project. In 'Organisation and Methods', R. G. Anderson lists the following stages which go to make up an O&M project:

1 Preliminary survey of terms of reference
2 Planning the assignment
3 Collecting the facts
4 Developing the ideas
5 Recording the facts
6 Examining the facts
7 Developing alternative procedures or methods
8 Comparison of costs and benefits of alternative procedures or methods
9 Presenting and selling recommendations (to company personnel)
10 Planning and implementation of recommendations
11 Follow up, updating and review as required

As the checklist illustrates, O&M has everything to do with a factual and rational approach to problem-solving and is very much in tune with the concept of the systems approach to management.

The process of carrying out the O&M project relies on techniques similar to those involved in researching and writing a report, where there is also a fact-finding stage, a stage of collating and synthesising of facts in order of priority and importance, a writing stage and an implementation stage.

O&M and Work Study specialists tend to employ the following techniques of fact-finding:

- observation of staff in action
- observation of plant and equipment in action
- interviews with personnel at all levels
- analysis of operations into each component part or step and timing or measuring its contribution
- checking the flow of work for hold-ups or bottlenecks
- measuring distances walked by staff as part of a work process
- analysing the relationship of the locations of personnel to tools, spares, workbench, equipment, stock etc, and producing work-flow charts for analysis
- comparing the rate of output, cost, reduction in time

ACTIVITY REFERENCE	ACTIVITY	TIME SCHEDULE – NUMBER OF DAYS (5–165)
1	PRELIMINARY SURVEY AND PLANNING THE ASSIGNMENT COLLECT FACTS: (develop ideas for new procedure or method)	
2	Organisation structure	
3	Personnel (staff numbers and job allocations)	
4	Study records and forms	
5	Effectiveness and cost factors	
6	Office layout and work flow	
7	RECORD THE FACTS	
8	VERIFY THE FACTS	
9	EXAMINE THE FACTS	
10	DEVELOP NEW PROCEDURE OR METHODS	
11	DEVELOP ALTERNATIVE PROCEDURES OR METHODS	
12	EVALUATE COSTS AND BENEFITS	
13	SUBMIT PROPOSALS (after writing reports)	
14	ACCEPTANCE OR REJECTION (discussions)	
15	PLAN INSTALLATION	
	INSTALL NEW PROCEDURE OR METHOD:	
16	Prepare new or revised office accommodation	
17	Install new machines and equipment	
18	Prepare new or revised office layout	
19	Trial run	
20	Solve problems	
21	Parallel operation	
	Prove new procedure or method	
	Fully operational (dispense with parallel operation)	
22	FOLLOW-UP	

Assignment bar chart time schedule

or costs etc before and after introducing a modification.

The above illustrations show how a project may be assigned a time schedule and on page 257 how a flow chart works – in this case to record a scrap note procedure. Note here the American Society of Mechanical Engineers (ASME) symbols used in flowcharting to denote an operation, inspection, transport, delay and storage phase. When the many facets of the Work Study and O&M practitioner are seen in the light of the above overview, it is not difficult to understand why the team needs to include:

- a cost accountant familiar with all aspects of production finance
- a statistician and mathematician well versed in analytical and computational techniques
- a group able to devise and implement data processing systems as part of the analytical process
- staff skilled in eliciting information via interviews
- personnel specialising in the operations and technical data of the plant and equipment in use and related to the company's sphere of interest, e.g. printing or injection moulding plant.

If the work of a management services department is seen as a means of transforming loss into profit, waste into finished product and pointless activity into concerted, productive effort, then the entire personnel of any organisation – if they think about it – has good reason to support the O&M and Work Study teams, since they could be the very people who ensure the survival of the works or office complex in the face of stiff competition!

Motivation and job satisfaction

When Henry Ford remarked that his Model T customers could choose 'any colour, so long as it's black', he was certainly being ironic about the limited choice they faced as a result of the new production-line manufacturing methods of the early twentieth century. When Charlie Chaplin became totally taken over by the mesmerising monotony of tightening two nuts with two spanners on a production line in 'Modern Times' so that on leaving work he attacks the twin lines of buttons going down a matronly passer-by's frock, he was definitely making a sardonic criticism of the

FLOW PROCESS CHART-BASIC USE OF SYMBOLS.
SCRAP NOTE PROCEDURE – VALUATION

SCRAP NOTE REFERENCE		DISTANCE-METRES
1 ▷	TO COST OFFICE – RECEIVED FROM FACTORY VIA INSPECTION DEPARTMENT	300
1 □	PLACE IN "IN" TRAY	
1 ○	SORT IN PRODUCT NUMBER SEQUENCE	
2 ○	SORT IN PART NUMBER SEQUENCE BY PRODUCT	6
2 ▷	TO COST RECORDS FILE	
3 ○	SELECT APPROPRIATE COST RECORD SHEET ⎫	
4 ○	RECORD STANDARD COST DATA ⎬ REPEAT FOR EACH SCRAP NOTE	
3 ▷	TO 1ST COMPTOMETER OPERATOR	10
2 □	PLACE IN "IN" TRAY	
5 ○	CALCULATE COST OF SCRAP ⎬ REPEAT FOR EACH SCRAP NOTE	
4 ▷	TO 2ND COMPTOMETER OPERATOR	3
3 □	PLACE IN "IN" TRAY	
1 □	CHECK CALCULATIONS ⎬ REPEAT FOR EACH SCRAP NOTE	
5 ▷	TO COST CLERK	13
4 □	PLACE IN "IN" TRAY	
6 ○	SUMMARISE COST OF SCRAP BY PRODUCT	
7 ○	RECORD COST OF SCRAP ON SCRAP REPORT	
6 ▷	TO FILE	3
▽	FILE SCRAP NOTES	
SUMMARY		
○	OPERATION	7
□	INSPECTION	1
▷	TRANSPORT	6
D	DELAY	4
▽	STORAGE	1
	TOTAL DISTANCE –	METRES 335

in the degree of illumination of the work area and the pattern of the working day. In short, what happened was that productivity increased within the group whether the working conditions were made better or worse. This proved extremely puzzling to the investigators until it was eventually realised that the subject group had been unaccustomed to having any interest taken in them and were unconsciously very supportive of the experiment and as a result determined to make a success of the project no matter what!

This turn of events proved a watershed in management studies of people at work, and in ensuing years a school of human relations management theorists evolved who moved the focus of study of people at work away from scientific recording of data and preoccupation with the economics of work to a deeper interest and concern for the needs of people at work. The Hawthorne Studies revealed that workers could be motivated not out of a sense of coercion and 'stick and carrot' techniques but from a sense of genuine involvement and participation in the work activity allied to being consulted and treated with respect.

Moreover, these studies revealed all sorts of unsuspected – to management anyhow – behavioural patterns within working groups. Unofficial group leaders were identified and unofficial work practices and agreements unearthed to which the workers conformed not because of management's insistence but because of their own codes of practice.

As a result much more attention was paid in the 1940s and 1960s to what motivated workers and how their jobs could be structured so as to provide more satisfaction and hence productivity.

By and large employers in the post-industrial revolution world of industry had considered that the motivator was pay. The more you paid, the harder people worked and the more output rose. Moreover, management cannot be too readily blamed for being naive in this regard, for this is what precisely many industrial operatives have gone on record as confirming with sentiments like:

It's only the thought of the pay that keeps me turning up each day at eight o'clock for an eight hour shift and that keeps me going through the noise and the endless repetition!

Herzberg's Twin Factor Theory: motivators and hygiene factors

Researchers have demonstrated with some effect that whether consciously or unconsciously, workers do have other factors in mind as necessary components of job satisfaction. One American management specialist, Frederick Herzberg, published in the mid 1960s a paper which postulated that there were two sets of factors which related to job satisfaction and the lack of it. They derived from a series of interviews with Pittsburgh engineers and accountants who were requested to identify what it was about their job which

tedious monotony of repetitive production-line manufacturing. Indeed, in a famous survey which later became a part of every management educationalist's repertoire, known as the 'Hawthorne Studies' the case is cited of a series of tests carried out at the Western Electric Company in the 1930s. Here a number of operatives agreed to take part in a set of experiments to see how production might be affected by variations they either found satisfying or, on the contrary, dissatisfying.

Herzberg was able to draw up a table which identified the major 'satisfiers' as:

- achievement in the job
- recognition for doing a good job
- satisfaction deriving from the work itself
- being given responsibility for an area of work
- receiving advancement at work

The factors identified as 'dissatisfiers' were:

- dissatisfaction with company policy and administration
- supervision and technical conditions
- salary rate
- interpersonal relationships with colleagues
- working conditions

Herzberg related the 'satisfiers' with the job the employee does and the 'dissatisfiers' with the environment in which he finds himself. He called the former 'the motivators' and the latter 'the hygiene factors'. His thesis was that the presence of the former would provide a source of motivation, while the presence of positive aspects of the latter – good pay, luxurious office, lovely people to work with – while avoiding active job dissatisfaction would not in themselves motivate and were therefore only 'hygienic' or as we might say today, 'cosmetic', factors. For example, the manager who receives a handsome salary raise may work that much harder for a couple of weeks, but will soon become accustomed to his higher living standard and revert to his former work patterns.

Maslow's Hierarchy of Needs

Another management theorist, A. H. Maslow, evolved a theory on what motivated people based on a hierarchy which started with basic physical needs and which proceeded upwards to what he termed 'self-actualisation' needs:

Maslow's Hierarchy of Needs

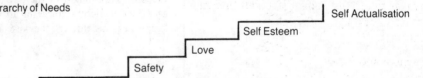

Maslow saw man as 'a perpetually wanting animal'. Thus his needs were inevitably insatiable but were stepped in a series, and for the need next up in the hierarchy to be felt, it was first necessary for the need immediately below (and the others below it) to be satisfied. First an employee requires a meal in his stomach, warm clothes and an absence from sickness. Once these are being met he can consider his position – is he safe or threatened? If so by what? What action can he take to remove the threat? Feeling safe, he will next experience the need to love and be loved. (We might, in the context of work consider whether for 'love' we might substitute 'being liked'.) Perhaps Maslow meant feeling on good terms with those around him. All these needs satisfied, the employee looks for that which will satisfy his self-esteem – perhaps status, a large company car, a bigger office than most! Lastly, all these being satisfied, Maslow says that being fully extended, recognised as one who has achieved – self actualisation – is the supreme need to be met.

What is particularly interesting about Maslow's theory is that if a lower need is threatened, a higher set will be sacrificed to repair the damage to the lower. For example take the need for safety – keeping one's job. A manager rows with his boss over a perceived loss of status or self-esteem, for instance he is instructed to move to a smaller office. They row. The boss says:

'If you don't like it, you can quit!'

The manager by degrees comes round to the view that, actually, it's quite a nice, compact office he is being invited to inhabit!

McGregor's Twin 'X' and 'Y' Theories

Yet another management theorist, Douglas McGregor, published in 1960 a view of human behaviour at work which focused upon two contrasting attitudes of managers towards the staff they managed.

Theory X

Theory X proposed that workers essentially disliked having to work and, given the chance, would avoid it wherever possible.

This being the case, managers were obliged to force employees to do the work required by means of an autocratic approach – threatening, using various levers like promotion or getting a cleaner job to do to get workers to conform to the idea of working according to instructions and not slacking off.

Theory X also propounded the view that generally, employees much preferred a system in which they did as they were told and left decision-making to the managers.

Theory Y

Contrastingly, Theory Y put forward the view that people will bring to work the same interest and energy as they do to their hobbies and interests. Also, that given some form of incentive or reward for good work, the employee will work hard without being under constant, close supervision, and without having the whip constantly cracked at his heels. The employee will flourish under conditions of enlightened management where he or she is given a chance to work on his or her own initiative, to participate in decision-making and to feel a sense of contributing to the overall direction of the undertaking.

Though no entirely conclusive supporting research to support either theory emerged, McGregor did succeed in contributing significantly to the debate in the 1960s on how far management needed to be prescriptive and seen to be firmly in control, and how far authority could be delegated down the chain of command so that management became less obtrusive and shared among more employees. Further, Theory Y gained significant ground in organisations which employ highly qualified people to perform specialist tasks – a trend which IT developments is increasing – since they will not accept highly authoritative management styles.

Since the 1960s, a number of management techniques have been introduced, including management by objectives, which sought to provide staff with clearly defined and attainable objectives to meet, the concept of quality circles which brought together staff from different departments to seek to solve organisational problems and to brainstorm for new ideas. In motivational terms, the idea of the manager providing a 'quid pro quo' or something in return for the subordinate's active cooperation has enjoyed some popularity as a theory of behaviour.

However, today, no particular school of thought holds sway and managers are encouraged to immerse themselves in the wide range of historical and current trends and to bring to bear those management techniques best thought to suit a particular situation.

Job enhancement

In the manufacturing side of industry the problems of repetitiveness in the work routine and the associated boredom it generates, along with poor motivation causing mediocre output, were recognised in the 1960s and efforts were made to increase job satisfaction. In manufacturing industry these centred around:

    job rotation
    job enlargement and
    job enrichment

Job rotation

In this approach, operatives were trained to do several jobs within their competence. For example, the operative might spend one week as a machinist, the next as an overhead crane driver and the third as a packer. The idea was to provide more variety in the work and a change of scenery. A positive spin-off was that companies created much more versatile workforces – sick staff could be replaced quickly and easily. Attitudes changed as staff came to be involved with more of the

total operation and saw more of the problems and difficulties of others.

Unexpectedly, it did not always prove a popular development as some older workers preferred to work day in and day out at the same machine since they could talk to old friends and felt part of a closely-knit team.

Job enlargement and enrichment

Here the idea was to analyse a series of connected jobs to see what skills and activities might be combined so as to create a more demanding and therefore satisfying job. For example, the copy typist might be given some word processing to do and thus extend his or her repertoire and learn fresh skills which counterbalanced longstanding and perhaps stale ones.

The advantages which ensued included not only an increase in job satisfaction, but also the creation of a better qualified workforce.

Thus in general, job rotation, job enlargement and job enrichment were all designed to:

● increase levels of job-satisfaction
● improve employee morale
● develop a more versatile labour force
● improve overall staff competencies

Within some firms, however, such practices were seen as potential job destroyers – it should be borne in mind that the affluent economy of the 1960s had led to overmanning in some organisations and so employees wished to protect their own jobs and were not keen to see other staff acquiring their own skills. Nevertheless, the process did contribute to improving employees' skills and to increasing job satisfaction.

Job enhancement and legislation

Just as managers were devoting more energy to improving their human relations techniques in handling staff, so in post-war Britain was Parliament, through successive governments, reforming and revising company, factory and industrial law to provide better conditions of service. Acts of particular importance were:

Office Shops & Railways Act 1963
Employers' Liability (Compulsory Insurance) Act 1969
Health and Safety at Work Act (HASAW) 1974
Fire Precautions Act 1971
Employment Protection Acts 1975 and (Consolidation) 1978
Data Protection Act 1985

The Health and Safety at Work Act, for example, revised and consolidated previous Factory Acts and laid down essential requirements for both employee and employer in order to secure a safe working environment. For instance, the individual employee was given a responsibility to ensure that he worked safely and with due consideration for the safety of others, and was not able to 'pass the buck' to his employer if an accident arose from his own negligence.

The Employee Protection Acts gave far more job security to employees and established sophisticated mechanisms for grievance and dismissal procedures and recourse to Industrial Tribunals in cases of dispute over dismissal.

The Employers' Liability (Compulsory Insurance Act) 1969, obliged employers to insure all employees against possible injury.

In effect, the legal reforms of the 1960s and 1970s did much to enhance the jobs of employees across the country by giving them more job security, better access to legal redress in cases of dispute and generally improved working conditions.

Job appraisal and job evaluation

Two further aspects of administering people's jobs need to be included in this Topic's survey. They are job appraisal and job evaluation.

Job appraisal

It is one thing to have designed a particular job to a careful specification and to have described its main features. It is quite another to ensure that the job is being steadfastly carried out from one year to another!

If management's interest goes no further than designing the job then there is little or nothing to prevent an employee progressively shedding those bits of his job he does not care for to concentrate upon those he enjoys. And indeed this is what often happens in organisations which fail to monitor their employees' progress and performance. Also, personnel in the private sector in particular tend to be rewarded by promotion or pay rise according to the results they achieve and so it is important to have a system in operation to measure achievement and effectiveness as objectively as possible.

To do this various methods of appraising an employee's performance have been developed. This is generally achieved by the employee and his immediate manager discussing in some detail objectives to be set and met in the coming year. These could include meeting a sales target, completing a project, re-equipping a factory, completing a course of staff development and so on. Additionally, the employee and manager will often discuss the employee's strengths and weaknesses and what actions need to be taken to improve areas of sketchy knowledge or poor communication skills and so on. As a result, a schedule or programme may be drawn up which is agreed to by both parties as a plan of action for the coming year.

At its end, the employee will be invited to an appraisal interview conducted by his immediate superior, but with the boss's own superior in attendance to see fair play and to ensure that neither favouritism nor victimisation arise. The immediate manager will review the year's progress with the employee and either by

means of a form or report will make his appraisal of him or her. A copy of the appraisal will then customarily be given to the employee who will have been invited to signify his acceptance of the appraisal or to add any dissentient views.

This process is referred to as 'open appraisal' since it is achieved with the full knowledge and involvement of the employee. Other appraisal systems may be 'closed' to a greater or smaller degree in that they are produced in whole or part confidentially. Such appraisals may be linked to pay or may be carried out solely as a means of evolving an individual's development programme. Or they may form the basis of a promotion process.

Job evaluation

Here, the range of jobs which span a company's activities are ordered into a kind of league which is then used as a basis for awarding pay and other benefits. Sometimes the ranking order is fairly arbitrary and achieved subjectively – a senior clerk's job is rated lower than a shop foreman's for example.

Alternatively, the precise nature of each job may be measured according to a series of yardsticks universally applied in an effort to be more objective. Such yardstick measurements include:

How many staff and at what levels report to this post?
For how much financial expenditure is the post responsible?
For how much (and costing what) equipment is the post responsible?
For how long last the consequences of the decisions made in this post? How far-reaching is their effect?

and so on. The league of jobs thus ranked and evaluated then provides a basis for ongoing negotiations with trade unions etc on pay and also forms the means of sustaining differentials between jobs in areas like pay and conditions of service.

Design and the office

One of the major factors in creating and maintaining efficiency and effectiveness in office administration lies undoubtedly in the way in which offices are designed and laid out. It may be fairly surmised that Scrooge did not worry himself unduly about Bob Cratchit's working area and we may be quite sure that Scrooge wouldn't have regarded it as worthy of any extended planning or financial investment! Fortunately for today's millions of office workers in the UK, current employers are much more far-sighted than was Ebenezer Scrooge in creating an office environment which would promote productivity and help to minimise staff turnover.

Modern psychological research has demonstrated the effects which colours and textures have on people's moods and attitudes. Red, for example, is seen as a colour tending to agitate and disquiet while green tends to calm and reassure. Strong colours act as a visual distraction while pastel shades are easy to work near.

In equipment terms, the science of ergonomics has resulted in typists' and managers' chairs being better designed for their posture and so as to avoid backache and fatigue. Typewriters, computer keyboards and VDUs incorporate design factors allowing them to be adjusted for different individual use.

British Standards have researched into the lighting needs of office personnel and provided manufacturers with specifications to follow, backed up by legislation.

Government Acts like the HASAW Act have prompted dangerous and untidy trailing cables to be incorporated in walls, floors or furniture by office designers. Further legislation on noise levels has led to the introduction of acoustic covers on noisy printers and acoustic screens around open-plan working areas.

In fact the design and layout of the office has undergone a complete transformation in the past 20 years. Companies have emerged which specialise in office outfitting in a 'turnkey' approach, that is to say they advise on and instal 'the total office', including wiring and telecommunication aspects. The phrase 'systems furniture' has been coined to describe what often looks like the light-coloured Swedish furniture which graces many dining-rooms with its smart and 'up-market' appearance! Indeed, the image which the modern office projects is deemed to be most important both in impressing clients and visitors and in attracting and keeping high-calibre staff.

The components of good office design include:

- satisfying current legislation: toilets, restroom, room-space per employee, adequate heat and light etc
- consideration of personnel work flow associated with moving around the office area so as to avoid congestion and possible accidents
- setting up work groups or teams in clusters; optimising access between staff who work closely
- standardising on equipment to simplify procedures and staff training and to reduce costs
- allowing for privacy and confidentiality – enclosed interview rooms may form part of an open-plan design
- catering for aesthetics by creating pleasing visual and tactile effects with colour, fabrics, surfaces, materials etc
- minimising noise problems with acoustic ceiling-hung baffle panels, acoustic screens and covers
- ensuring that the installation is flexible – panels and screens may be re-sited to provide for a fresh layout in the light of changed needs
- giving employees an opportunity to impose a personal identity on work areas through photographs, brought in flowers, ornaments etc

This checklist – not exhaustive – proves a tall order for employers to satisfy when the constraints are considered:

  Meeting legal requirements
  Minimising costs of floor-space rental, heat, light and rates bills etc
  Affording the 'high-tech' equipment of current electronic office technology
  Coping with the status and hierarchy structures within the company
  Avoiding customers and visitors overhearing either confidential discussions or being embarrassed by heated exchanges among staff

In the context of office design, and the evolution of 'bürolandschaft' and open-plan offices, the needs of the staff and the overall costs of maintaining offices are not easy to reconcile. Indeed, there is nearly always what the Americans call a trade-off to be made. For example, the traditional self-enclosed office box – four walls, a door, and a window looking out over the car-park – minimised the stress of working as part of a group since the occupant could determine whom he saw and who saw him, and could hold confidential discussions without having to use a sotto voce level of conversation. On the other hand, such office boxes did little to promote effective communication face-to-face among personnel, who tended – especially if managers – to become isolated from the daily doings of the work-place, i.e. the general office.

In some open-plan offices, the trade-off is reversed in that while communications and involvement may improve, the qualities of privacy, confidentiality and control of who takes up an individual's time may worsen.

Some 'turnkey' office systems have attempted to resolve this problem by supplying both shoulder-high partitions and plastic corner windows affixed to them as well as more traditional roof-high partitions to form

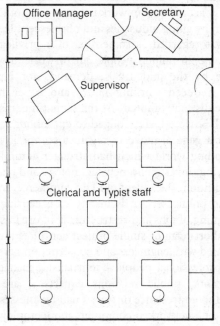

TRADITIONAL OFFICE LAYOUT

LANDSCAPED OFFICE SYSTEMS LAYOUT

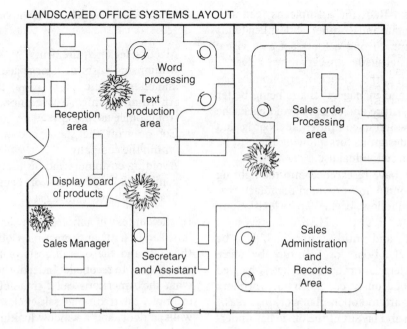

offices for more senior staff, training and conference rooms and so on.

Perhaps the most encouraging trend in the development of modern office layouts is that the lines of demarcation such as seniority and status which separate staff as a whole are becoming much more blurred as both senior and junior staff occupy the same open access areas within a complex, either as offices, restaurants, or social/rest areas.

The impact of change

Industrial relations in the UK in the 1970s and early 1980s changed course perceptibly. The world-wide recession contributed to increasingly high levels of unemployment in the western world, and this factor alone caused widespread changes in management styles and trade union approaches to many aspects of work. The very act of being in work in many areas of Europe, stricken by ailing industries and obsolescent technologies, was regarded as something of a privilege, and with some 20 million people out of work in western Europe by the mid 1980s, demands for increased wages, reduced working hours and other benefits became distinctly muted. At the same time, managers in the UK were being obliged to cut labour forces as part of a general move to regain a competitive edge in a trading world which had stronger commitments to training, investment, new technology and plant.

In addition, the advent of IT in commerce, industry and the public service is in any case causing much redesigning of jobs and restructuring of organisations. More short-term or single project contracts are being negotiated with engineers and construction personnel. More professional people – journalists, management consultants, public relations experts – are being obliged to go freelance or start small businesses. With the aid of a networked computer, more employees are working for longer, if not entirely, from their own homes.

Thus the whole ethos of work is currently undergoing radical change. The possibility that some young people may never work is being looked squarely in the eye. The need for those in work to accept reduced hours and associated lower pay is an option to consider in order to provide more jobs. Traditional jobs and the education and training associated with them are rapidly changing as technology takes away the need for many manually skilled occupations. Without entirely realising the full extent of its global effects and social impact, today's generation of workers is experiencing the turmoil of a second industrial revolution.

In order to come through it securely, directors, managers, supervisors and employees alike will need to co-ordinate their endeavours as never before in the areas of job creation, job design and redesign and staff retraining. Moreover, managers with developed human and industrial relations skills will be needed more than ever to cope successfully with the management of change on a national and international scale.

Assessment questions

1 Explain briefly what is meant in this Topic by the difference between efficiency and effectiveness.
2 What is the principal difference between Work Study and Organisation and Methods?
3 What do you see as the main tasks of an O&M Unit?
4 What main types of post typically form those making up a management services department?
5 Why are Work Study and O&M personnel part of the staff as opposed to the line side of an organisation?
6 What do you understand by the term 'rate-busting'?
7 List the major features of the Office, Shops and Railways Act as outlined in this Topic.
8 What studies did Frederick Taylor undertake in the 1920s which helped to prompt the development of management science?

9 List as many as you can recall of the major phases of an O&M project which R. G. Anderson compiled. Compare your list with his on completion.

10 Through what techniques do Work Study and O&M staff acquire information and data? Make a checklist.

11 For what series of experiments did the Hawthorne Studies become famous? Why?

12 Outline briefly F. Herzberg's theory of what constituted motivating factors at work and what did not, and why not.

13 How does Maslow's Hierarchy of Needs Theory work? Write a short account in your own words.

14 What are 'Theory X' and 'Theory Y'? Who devised this model to explain differing management approaches of how to get people to work?

15 How many Acts of Parliament can you recall enacted since 1960 which improved working conditions?

16 What do HASAW and ASME stand for?

17 Draw up a checklist of factors which should be taken into account in good office design.

18 List four advantages and four disadvantages of the landscape office type of layout.

Discussion topics

1 Is the real reason for the introduction of management services departments into companies the fact that line managers have not been doing their jobs properly?

2 Why are so many developed countries' economies still locked into the production-line means of manufacturing? Surely a better way could have been devised by now!

3 Human relations based management is management gone soft!

4 Given the chance, office workers would rather go back to the old, traditional office layouts. Like the high-rise flats, it's only the people who don't have to live in them or work in them that think they're so wonderful!

5 No matter what the technology or management theory in fashion, employees will always find ways of structuring their jobs the way they want them!

Build-up tasks

1 Invite a local trade unionist active in the industrial sector to give your group a talk about his or her union's perspective of factory jobs and current trends.

2 Make arrangements to interview a local private or public sector management services department manager and find out about his current tasks and preoccupations.

3 First carry out your research and then given an oral presentation supported by audio visual aids on the work of *one* of the following important management theorists:

Frederick Taylor
Henri Fayol
F. Herzberg
A. Maslow
D. McGregor

4 Research one of the following Acts and write a summary of its major features for distribution among your group:

The Health and Safety at Work Act
The Employment Protection Acts
The Offices, Shops and Railways Act

5 Carry out your research, then write an article for your school or college magazine entitled:

'What makes people want to work?'

6 First design an appropriate questionnaire and then do a survey of local people to find out what they find most and least rewarding/satisfying at work. Compare your findings with those of Herzberg's. Your teacher will help you locate them.

7 Arrange to visit a local organisation which has installed an open plan/landscape office layout. Find out how it is generally felt to be working. Write an account of your findings.

8 Do your background work then give your group a 10 minute talk on one of the following:

Has work a future?
How the nature of work will change in the next 20 years
Current approaches to motivation of people at work
How job appraisal works and what it achieves
Changes in work patterns arising from developments in IT

Case study

'What we need is a system!'

Information

Assume that you are the personal assistant of Mr Frank Wainwright, Divisional Sales Manager of Quality Sweets Limited, a manufacturer of sweets and confectioneries. A team of sales representatives promote the product to High Street sweet-shops throughout the country.

Every Monday, Frank Wainwright is obliged to send his weekly sales report to his Regional Manager, summarising the activities of his division's twenty sales representatives, who operate throughout Eastshire, Westshire and Midshire. Each representative makes about 300 calls a month to established and new customers within his district.

One morning you are called into Mr Wainwright's office to be greeted by these words: 'Come in and sit down. Look, there's something that's been getting me down recently and I'd like you to have a go at putting matters right! It concerns my weekly sales report. I'm just about at my wit's end! I don't know how my predecessor managed, but at the moment there's no rhyme or reason in the way the sales reps are writing their weekly reports. What we need is a system – a sort of standardised report form for the whole Division, which would tell me easily and quickly just what I need to know, so that I can collate all 20 reports and write mine for despatch to Regional Office by Monday afternoons. Do you think you could design a working draft that we could try out next month?

'Have a chat with Dick Williams (Divisional Administration Officer). He'll tell you anything you need to know and then see what you can produce. I'd like to be able to look at your draft by next Wednesday. . . .'

Mixed assortment

Your own investigations and conversations with Dick Williams produced the following points:

1   Each sales representative makes an average of some 300 calls each month to established customers and new prospects.

2   There is fierce competition between Quality Sweets and five main competitors.

3   Each sales representative runs a company car. The car is available at week-ends and during evenings for private use. The representatives are required, however, to buy their own petrol for private mileage.

4   The market is frequently dictated by discounted price offers and special offers. It is also subject to swift changes in demand when seasonal novelties and new products are introduced.

5   Sometimes representatives are obliged to stay in hotels or guest-houses overnight.

6   The lines which are most profitable are Devon Cream Toffees, Velveta Boxed Chocolates and a children's favourite, Sunny Snax.

7   Quality Sweets is seeking to expand its business after a very good trading year and also to help guarantee production by increasing orders consistently and smoothly.

8   Representatives take orders from retailers and send them direct to Regional Office for processing. Orders are normally delivered three to four days later from the company's regional warehouse.

9   Quality Sweets sells 36 lines grouped in the following categories:

boiled sweets – 4	chocolates (boxed) – 5
children's sweets – 5	novelties – 4
snack sweets – 3	presentation boxed toffees – 3
wrapped chocolate bars – 3	mixed selections – 5
wrapped chews – 2	seasonal specialities – 2

10   Representatives earn a monthly commission based on the value of orders in excess of pre-determined monthly sales targets.

11   Expenses are paid monthly in arrears from head office after having been authorised at divisional level. Receipts are required.

12   Quality Sweets has a caring attitude towards customer complaints and defective products.

13   Divisional Managers are expected to provide as comprehensive a picture of sales activity within their division as is practicable, so that each Regional Manager is able to establish an up-to-date and informed view of company performance and competitors' activities.

14   Sometimes, Frank Wainwright may not see a sales representative for as long as three weeks. However, he does see them all at least once every month.

Preliminary assignments

1   Collect as many routine report forms as you can. You may expect to find them in areas such as safety inspection, maintenance, work progress, accident reports etc. Compare the ways in which each has been designed. Try to establish what is considered important information in each case.

2   Draw up a checklist of the factors which ought to be taken into account when designing an efficient and easy-to-use report form.

Main assignments

Main Assignments 1 and 2 may be undertaken either by individual students or by groups.

1   Design a weekly report form system which would meet the needs of Mr Wainwright. Bear in mind that your system may need to be easily divided into duplicate sheets for routing to different departments or sections. Consider the use of chemically impregnated paper for providing duplicate copies.

2   Write a commentary to accompany the design of your system of forms, explaining the reasons you have for each entry and the paper dimensions you have chosen.

Follow-up assignments

1   In your general group, discuss the problems encountered by group members in meeting Mr Wainwright's requirements. What aspects need to be borne in mind when seeking to keep sales representatives selling, rather than form-filling? What shortcomings in the design of sales report forms are likely to cause resentment among sales representatives? Is there a danger of trying to obtain too much information as well as too little from such reports?

2   Write an essay entitled:
    The value of the sales report in sales management.

15 Visual and graphical communication

Introduction

The need for the good communicator to have mastered the many applications of visual and graphical communication has increased significantly with the advent of information technology.

For example, in the sales, marketing, production and accounts departments of many firms, extensive use is now made of computer software packages which can display on a VDU screen or in print a wide range of charts, graphs and diagrams to illustrate sales trends, production costs, market shares etc.

In addition, the introduction of the golfball and daisy-wheel into typewriting and word processing made it possible for different varieties of type to be used – often within one paragraph – in order to provide impact or heightened emphasis for a word, phrase or sentence.

There are, therefore, a number of factors for the good communicator to take into account when selecting the best means of imparting information:

1 Should text, numbers or a mixture of both be used?
2 Could varying type styles be used to good effect?
3 In the display of number-based information would a table, bar chart, pie chart or line graph convey the message most effectively?
4 How might colour be introduced?
5 Does the value of the information to be conveyed warrant the time and expense of visual techniques?

There is an old proverb which states: 'a picture is worth ten thousand words'. This is often true of the chart or graph, which in a few moments may convey with much impact what several hundred spoken or written words may fail to impart. It is therefore certainly worthwhile to master the straightforward skills of communicating visually or graphically, especially since almost all office staff today are confronted with such modes of communication daily.

The table

A frequently employed form of visual communication is the table. Simply, the table represents a convenient way of storing and presenting – as well as summarising – number information. Usually, this information is presented in column form with the various number inputs totalled in a variety of meaningful ways. Consider, for example, the following table which has been drawn up to contain a summary of sales for a hardware store over a calendar year, with sales broken down by product:

① Discount Hardware Limited
Sales analysis for year ended 19--

③ Products	② Jan	Feb	Mar	Apr	May	Jun	July	Aug	Sept	Oct	Nov	Dec	④ Sales value in £000
Garden furniture	0.5	0.7	1.2	2.4	3.5	4.6	4.2	2.1	0.6	0.4	0.3	0.1	20.6
Paints	0.8	1.6	2.4	3.5	3.4	2.6	1.7	1.8	1.4	2.1	2.3	0.2	23.8
Tools	0.7	0.5	0.7	0.6	0.5	0.4	0.3	0.3	0.4	0.5	0.7	1.0	6.6
Washing machines	2.0	1.5	2.1	1.7	1.9	2.4	0.8	0.7	0.8	0.6	0.5	0.4	15.4
Refrigerators	2.1	1.4	1.5	1.4	1.8	1.7	1.5	1.7	1.6	1.5	1.4	1.2	18.8
Freezers	1.7	0.6	0.7	0.4	0.4	0.3	0.5	0.9	1.0	0.5	0.6	0.8	8.4
Kitchenware	0.7	0.5	0.3	0.4	0.7	0.5	1.2	0.4	0.5	0.4	0.5	0.8	6.9
Wallpaper	1.1	1.6	1.8	2.2	2.1	1.8	0.6	0.4	0.8	1.2	1.4	0.8	15.8
⑤	9.6	8.4	10.7	12.6	14.3	14.3	10.8	8.3	7.1	7.2	7.7	5.3	116.3 ⑥

The components of the above table may be summarised as follows:

1 A clear title of the function of the table.
2 A scale or interval – here 12 months of the year.
3 A list of items to be compared and totalled.
4 A clear indication of the meaning of the numbers displayed – here they represent pounds sterling in units of a thousand points – £000.
5 The aggregated totals – here shown as monthly totals of all products and annual totals of each
6 product with a final annual total for all sales.

At first glance, the above table appears to be a mass of figures which have little meaning or relationship with one another. A closer examination of the table, however, will reveal much 'concealed' information. For example, can you account for the seasonal fluctuations in the sales of some products? Given equal shares of available floor space, which of the above products would you withdraw in order to introduce a new product? Why? Can you spot any worrying trends in the sale of any of the listed products?

As you have probably concluded by now, tables generally do not display number information with immediate visual impact. The table has to be studied with concentration in order to glean its information. Basically, tables can provide information which states 'more than', 'less than', 'same as' and, after a percentage or fraction calculation, 'by how much'. Tables can also display information in great detail – to four or five decimal points, for instance. Yet they *are* difficult to interpret readily, and lack the visual impact of other forms of visual communication.

The bar chart

A more visually arresting way of conveying visual information is to employ a bar chart. As its name suggests, the bar chart is made up of a series of bars or blocks which represent totals or amounts of items being compared. The bars are read off against a vertical scale in the same way as a column of mercury is read off against the scale of a thermometer.

Below is an example of a bar chart using product sales for August of Discount Hardware Limited:

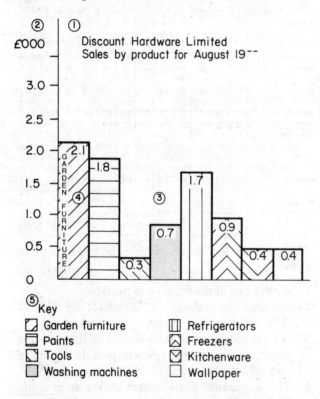

As the bar chart illustrates, comparisons between extremes are much more readily apparent – say garden furniture as opposed to tools. Similarly, the three high selling products 'announce' themselves immediately. Thus the visual impact of the bar chart will rely upon the following factors:

1 A clear, concise title for the chart.
2 A vertical scale showing the unit of measurement (£000s) broken down into a suitable length. Imagine how the bar chart would appear using a scale of £0–£10 000 along 10 centimetres.

3 Bars or blocks of an *equal* lateral dimension. Note, it is not the heights of the bars which is being compared, but their areas. The bars should be distinguished either by colour or contrasting hatching or shading. Also, because of the limitations of the scale used, the total value of each bar is shown within it.
4 On some bar charts, the identity of the bar is given with it – e.g. garden furniture.
5 On other bar charts, the identity of the bars is shown by means of a key.

Bar charts may also be used effectively to show the difference in, say, production of crops 'this year' and 'last year':

Note that some bar charts are drawn in three dimensions to increase their visual impact.

Though bar charts increase the immediacy of visual communication, they are of little visual value when

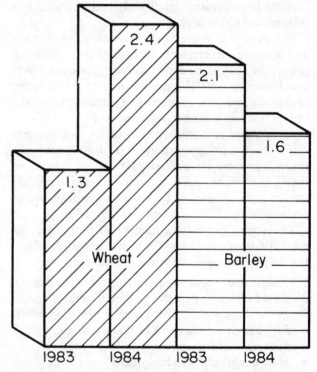

Production of wheat and barley in millions of tonnes

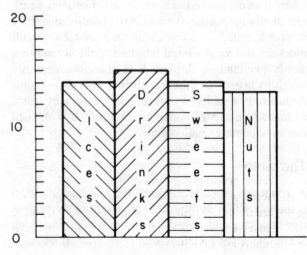

there is almost no difference between the proportions of the items being contrasted.

Can you spot how such a problem could be overcome, still using the bar chart?

Lastly, there are limitations as to the *number* of items which may be effectively compared on a single bar chart which the eye can take in – usually about five to eight bars – provided that they embody sufficient differences in area.

The pie chart

As its name suggests, the pie chart is made up of a circle or 'pie' of information broken into segments of the circle or 'slices' of a pie! Also, the scale in use is circular, representing 360°, rather than linear:

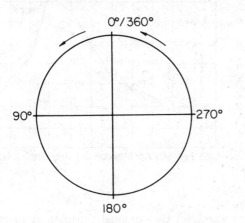

Thus a value of 100 per cent will be equal to 360° on the pie chart.

Four golden rules for devising pie charts

There are four golden rules to remember when the pie chart is considered for illustrating number information visually:

1   The *total value* of the items (100 per cent or 360°) must be known in order to compare items in a pie chart. For example, in comparing the market share of the boot and shoe market controlled by various manufacturers, the total value of *all* boots and shoes sold in the market must be known – and in pie chart terms will equate to the 360° of the circle. This value may be shown in pounds sterling terms or in numbers of pairs of boots and shoes sold. The market share for each manufacturer may then be indicated by a proportional 'slice of the pie'.

2   Each percentage point of the pie chart will be exactly equal to 3.60°. Thus for example 25 per cent will equal 90° (25 × 3.60) or a quarter of the pie.

3   It is very difficult for the human eye to gauge exactly the percentage values of similar-size segments of pie. It is therefore essential that the values of each slice of pie are included clearly in percentage terms, which are themselves given the values of the units in which the pie chart is totalled – here pounds sterling.

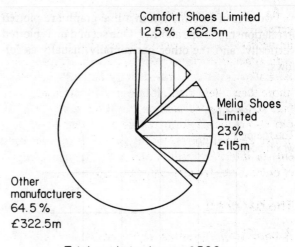

Total market value = £500m

4   Each segment of the pie needs to be identified clearly – ideally in colour, or else in contrasting black/white shadings – and needs to be given clear values, i.e. what the segment represents in percentage and unit values, and what it stands for in the pie chart. As in all charts, clear titles need to be devised and the year, month, quarter, etc when the comparison was made clearly shown.

The following example shows the share of Comfort Shoes Limited's production made up of ladies boots and shoes:

Comfort Shoes Limited
Product share : ladies boots and shoes
Period : 12 months ending December 19--

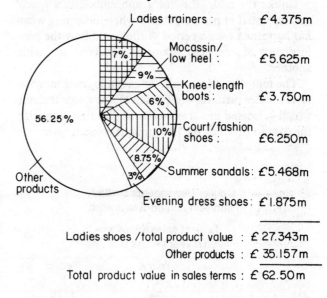

Ladies shoes / total product value : £ 27.343m

Other products : £ 35.157m

Total product value in sales terms : £ 62.50m

The line graph

One of the most frequently employed forms of visual communication used in commerce and the public service is the line graph. It is produced upon a grid of squares of equal size, although this grid is not always shown on the completed graph, though it is certainly needed to plot the positions of points of information which, when connected, go to make up the line or lines of the line graph.

Two sets of information in a line graph are plotted in relationship to one another. One set of data is plotted vertically, and the other horizontally, usually as follows:

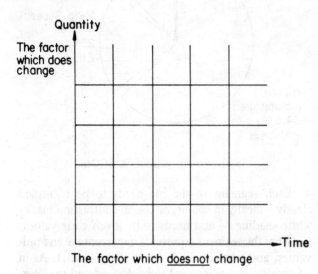

Such line graphs are used in commerce and public administration to display information in a wide variety of activities such as production or output, sales turnover, the incidence of customer complaints, the performance of competing products, the level of absenteeism and so on.

Unlike the table, the line graph embodies a much greater visual impact, especially when indicating what has happened over a period of time, and how the performance of one item compares and contrasts with another.

The following line graph, for example, indicates the level of sales turnover of a branch of a newsagent chain which is located in a seaside resort. But first, consider the data from which the line graph is constructed:

Courier Newsagents Limited
Hamblemouth-on-Sea branch

Table of sales turnover
for years A and B

	Year A £	Year B £
Jan	2080	1770
Feb	1890	2560
Mar	2340	2020
Apr	2860	2760
May	3140	3940
June	4990	3480
July	6630	5760
Aug	7210	5930
Sept	4330	4520
Oct	3150	3870
Nov	1930	2650
Dec	3060	2990

If the table's information is considered, it is by no means immediately apparent what is being conveyed. The human eye simply cannot take in and hold such information while making a comparison of either individual monthly totals or of respective cumulative totals. Similarly, it is not too easy to detect the peaks and troughs of sales performance contained in the tabular information.

In graph form, however, the same information is much more easily read and absorbed by the reader:

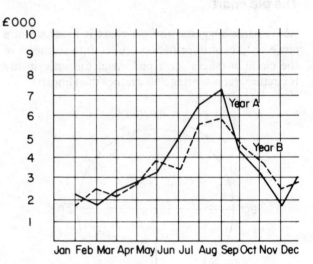

For example, the seasonal fluctuations in sales – doubtless the result of an influx of holiday-makers – becomes instantly apparent, as does the boost in sales due to the Christmas period.

What is *not* so readily apparent in this graph, however, is which year, A or B, was better in total sales terms. Which do *you* think?

In actual fact, the respective turnovers of each 12-month period differ by only £1360, and it is Year A at £43 610 which proved better than Year B at £42 250. Even graphs, therefore, can prove deceptive, and it is necessary almost always to show respective totals:

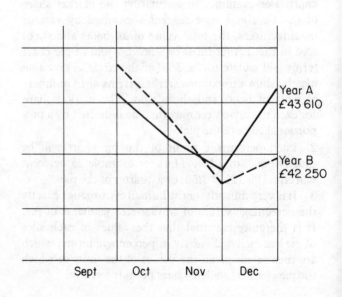

One area – like that of the bar chart – in which graphs have a weakness lies in the size of the vertical scale or axis which it is possible to display. For example, it is not usually possible to provide the fine accuracy of a table when displaying information in graph form – it is not possible for the human eye to detect visually a hundredth or a tenth part of a thousand along a distance, say, of a single centimetre or quarter of an inch. Thus it is often helpful to indicate on a graph the totals represented by each plotted point:

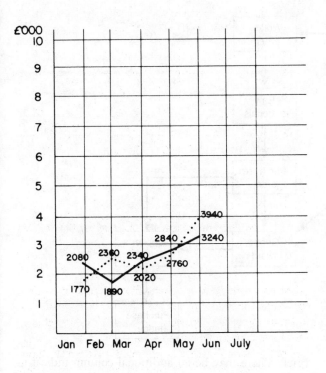

The inclusion of such monthly totals may aid the reader, but they may be intrusive, and obscure the effect of the graph's lines, so it is for the designer of the graph to decide how much detailed information to provide upon it.

A further point to bear in mind when considering the graph as a possible medium for visual communication is that, like the pie chart, it cannot readily or clearly impart too many plotted lines of information:

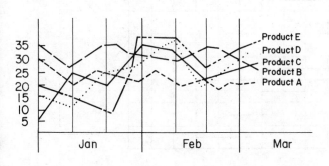

However, one important advantage which the graph *does* possess is its ability to show *trends* clearly. In many graphs, for instance, there may be fluctuations up or down as against one week or month with another, where nevertheless an *overall* trend is clearly discernible as either up or down:

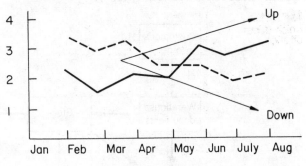

Despite individual peaks and troughs, the above example illustrates the ability of the graph to indicate overall trends or movements which are not at all easily read in a table. Thus, in probability terms, the amounts of July and August of the item shown as a continuous line are likely to occur in the regions of 2–4, whereas those of the broken line are likely to occur in the regions of 0.5 to 2.5 if nothing occurs to change markedly the path of each upward or downward trend. Such a facility in a line graph being plotted in a sales or accounts office may well alert the sales manager or accounts director to, say, a perilous fall in sales at a company branch requiring immediate investigation, or the fact that a company's cash flow is falling to a point where corrective action is needed urgently if events likely to take place in the near future are to be handled correctly and in time! Line graphs, then, are especially helpful in showing up what is likely to happen and thus help forecasts to be made.

'Self programming computers are now just around the corner!

Specimen block diagram in a feasibility report

A specimen block diagram showing the main features of a computerised system for handling customers' orders is shown below. This kind of diagram is frequently included in a feasibility report.

Example of a flow process chart

A procedure analysis chart consists of a list of written descriptions of all the operations in a procedure, with a symbol at the side of each operation indicating its type. The standard BSS work symbols shown on page 271 are used. The descriptions on the chart are very

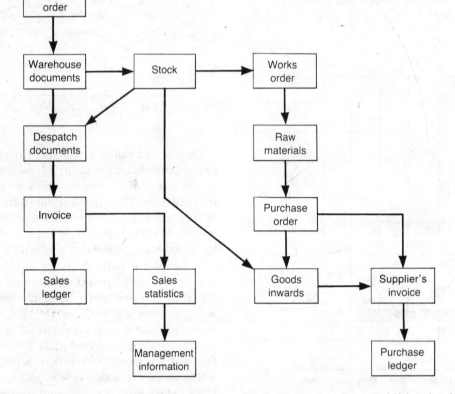

Notice in the above diagram how a visual representation makes each stage of this feasibility study of computerising customers' orders much easier to follow.

Bar chart: time schedule for building

The use of bar charts (see example below) to represent activities which overlap helps to identify potential bottlenecks and to establish priority areas.

brief. There may be an additional column indicating the forms used for each operation.

The purpose of a procedure chart is to aid the study and analysis of the procedure so that the steps involved and their sequence can be seen at a glance. After this comes the difficult task of analysis of faults and making improvements.

	J	F	M	A	M	J	J	A	S	O	N	D
Foundations												
Walls and floors												
Roof												
Electric wiring												
Plumbing												
Gas piping												
Windows and doors												
Glazing												
Plastering												
Decorating, tiling, etc.												

The procedure is analysed in vertical columns for the purpose of diagnosing and assessing faults, In such a chart, the distance travelled by documents and the time taken are recorded by subsequent study.

EXAMPLE OF A FLOW PROCESS CHART

SCRAP NOTE REFERENCE		DISTANCE-METRES
1	TO COST OFFICE – RECEIVED FROM 'FACTORY VIA INSPECTION DEPARTMENT	300
1	PLACE IN "IN" TRAY	
1	SORT IN PRODUCT NUMBER SEQUENCE	
2	SORT IN PART NUMBER SEQUENCE BY PRODUCT	6
2	TO COST RECORDS FILE	
3	SELECT APPROPRIATE COST RECORD SHEET ⎫ REPEAT FOR	
4	RECORD STANDARD COST DATA ⎬ EACH SCRAP NOTE	
3	TO 1ST COMPTOMETER OPERATOR	9
2	PLACE IN "IN" TRAY	
5	CALCULATE COST OF SCRAP ⎬ REPEAT FOR EACH SCRAP NOTE	
4	TO 2ND COMPTOMETER OPERATOR	3
3	PLACE IN "IN" TRAY	
1	CHECK CALCULATIONS ⎬ REPEAT FOR EACH SCRAP NOTE	
5	TO COST CLERK	12
4	PLACE IN "IN" TRAY	
6	SUMMARISE COST OF SCRAP BY PRODUCT	
7	RECORD COST OF SCRAP ON SCRAP REPORT	
6	TO FILE	3
▽	FILE SCRAP NOTES	

SUMMARY		
◯	OPERATION	7
☐	INSPECTION	1
⇨	TRANSPORT	6
D	DELAY	4
▽	STORAGE	1
	TOTAL DISTANCE –	METRES 333

Build-up tasks

1 In small groups, devise a questionnaire (to be completed anonymously) to establish the type of leisure activities which a representative sample of your school's/college's students pursues. You should break down your sample into categories of student – by age, sex, geographical home location etc. When you have obtained the completed questionnaires, set out the information acquired in an appropriate table and provide explanatory notes to detail what you think your data conveys about leisure activities and patterns.

2 Design a series of bar charts which may be constructed from information gained from students in your group on attitudes to national daily newspapers based on the following questions:

(a) Which national newspaper do you prefer to read?
(b) Which national daily newspaper provides:

(i) the best news/information coverage?
(ii) the best sports coverage?
(iii) the best coverage of political affairs?
(iv) the best coverage of women's interest items?

When you have completed your research, write a short article on what you think you have discovered about your group's attitudes to the daily press.

3 For every £100 of expenditure your local district council spends the following on various services:

Council housing	£52.49
Private housing	£8.66
Leisure services	£6.17
Refuse collection	£5.24
Planning	£4.76
Environmental health	£4.54
Financial assistance	£8.32
Other services	£9.82

Devise a pie chart to display this information as clearly as possible.

4 Assume that you work in the training department of International Shipping Limited. As part of a programme to improve the visual communication skills of its supervisors and junior managers, the company is in the process of producing a training manual on 'Effective Visual Communication'. You have been asked to research and to compile a part of the manual which deals with one of the following: (a) the bar chart, (b) the line graph, (c) the pie chart. Devise a suitable structure, content and layout which you think will most readily assist the staff identified to produce and to interpret bar charts, line graphs or pie charts. Compare your effort with those produced by other members of your group and comment upon their likely effectiveness. (*Note:* you may use coloured pens etc if you wish.)

5 You have been called in as business adviser to Mr Jack Green, who owns a large discount electrical goods retail store in the centre of a large conurbation. In the year ended last December, the sales of his principal four products – hi-fi, home computers, televisions and washing machines was as follows:

	Hi-Fi £	Home computers £	Tele-visions £	Washing machines £
Jan	9400	7480	8890	7960
Feb	6750	6760	7760	6740
Mar	7230	5370	7430	6390
Apr	6180	5450	6590	6420
May	5400	6790	4320	5430
June	4950	3860	4160	4330
July	8840	5930	5430	6980
Aug	3790	3220	4380	3140
Sept	5860	4630	4760	4140
Oct	6940	5750	5420	5120
Nov	7880	6890	6130	4980
Dec	10 530	12 430	7130	3760

(a) Construct a line graph illustrating the sales of the above four products for last year.

(b) What does your line graph tell you about the nature of Mr Green's business? Write a brief interpretation to accompany your line graph.

(c) Assuming that each of the four main products enjoys the same profit margin, what advice would you give Mr Green regarding his buying and trading plans for next year? (You should base your advice on the information you have plotted on your line graph.)

(d) What advice could you give Mr Green (based on your graph) about advertising and sales promotion of his four main products for next year?

(e) In view of the nature of the sales of the four main products over the last year, what additional electrical products can you suggest Mr Green should stock to help improve annual sales performance? When would you suggest they be marketed most strongly? Why?

6 What information may be deduced from the graph about the changes in the percentage of employees in various sections of the economy of the United States?

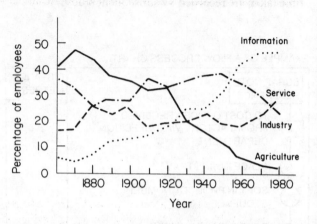

Discussion topics

1 'Numerical and visual communication skills will undoubtedly be needed far more by tomorrow's office worker if he or she is to function effectively!'

2 'Show some people a graph or a chart and they suddenly crumple up!' How might such people best overcome a fear of figures and numbers?

3 How does the use of different sorts of typeface (typography) affect the ways in which a reader reacts to a piece of printed text? Why should this be so? What lessons can the effective communicator learn from this?

4 'For too long English language and number/visual communication subjects have been taught separately. The trends evident in information technology processes and systems emphasise the need to integrate the various strands of communication.'

16 Use of English

Introduction

The ability to use English correctly and effectively is an essential skill which all those working in business or the public service must seek to master.

Many people speak or write English intuitively. They do not realise that often the most effective use of the language is the result of much conscious effort and practice.

Guesses at spellings or 'stabs' at punctuation will not satisfy the conscientious communicator. Neither will rambling sentence-structures nor the inappropriate use of slang find a place in the professional's use of English.

English is the medium through which objectives are achieved, people motivated and productive human relations strengthened. It is therefore essential for the manager, secretary or clerk to appreciate how important it is to speak or write in a way which will achieve positive results.

For example, a business letter may be the only form of contact between a retailing company and a potential customer. The manner in which a friendly and courteous receptionist takes a call may make all the difference to an important buyer. The carefully judged recommendations of a report may have far-reaching consequences. A persuasive sales letter may produce thousands of pounds' worth of orders.

For everyone, then, using English effectively is a vital skill well worth the pains taken to acquire. Like any craft, expertise in English requires a committed apprenticeship. When words are the 'tools of the trade', the good communicator must learn to build structures which are not merely purpose-built but also pleasing and elegant!

Though such skills may take time, patience and effort to secure, the rewards which they bring will be well worth while and last a lifetime.

Grammar

The parts of speech

What is a noun?

Nouns are the naming words in English which act as 'labels' for objects, ideas, people, places, works of art

---

Using English effectively

Syntax and grammar

Understanding the rules which govern the structuring of ideas into accepted sense-groups or patterns of meaning.

Spelling and punctuation

Reproducing words in their accepted form and linking them together clearly and unambiguously.

Vocabulary

Developing a reservoir of general and specialist words and expressions which permit the accurate and effective transmission of the spoken or written word.

Sensitivity and discrimination

Acquiring a feeling for the nuances and shades of meaning which words convey within their contexts.

Style

Appreciating the different effects which various combinations of words, expressions and structures will impart and developing the ability to express ideas in informative, discursive or persuasive ways.

Critical faculties

Being prepared to look critically at what is to be said or written, to measure consciously its likely effect and to modify it where necessary.

Awareness of the recipient

Establishing a rapport with the recipient so that he is receptive to the message.

---

and so on. Nouns which name real, physical things such as 'letter' or 'pen' are called **concrete** nouns. Nouns which express thoughts, ideas and feelings such as 'efficiency' or 'communication' are called **abstract**.

Sometimes nouns are sub-divided into the following categories:

Common: everyday objects or concepts – book, speed, garden

Proper: names for people, places, works of art – John, Pitman 2000, London, the Mona Lisa

(Notice that proper nouns are given capital letters.)

Collective: names for groupings or collections – team, jury, class

What is a pronoun?

Pronouns are also naming or identifying words which can replace nouns. They may refer to people:

I, you, him, her, mine, ours

or to things:

Where is *it*? I don't agree with *that*.

Sometimes they are used in questions:

Who is coming? *What* did you say?

or to complete meanings:

I cut *myself*.

In addition they may be used to introduce further information about a noun:

This is the gentleman *who* earlier wished to see you. The report, *which* concerns office reorganisation, will be ready tomorrow.

What is an article?

Not to be overlooked are the hard-working definite and indefinite articles: *the* job, *a* report, *an* idea.

What is an adjective?

Adjectives are essentially describing words which extend the meaning of nouns or pronouns:

The secretary typed the *important* letter.
A *good* manager looks after *his* staff.
It's only *little* me!

Sometimes adjectives are used to denote possession:

my desk, *their* pay, *your* turn

or to identify a particular object or idea:

this suggestion, *that* idea

or to introduce questions:

What price did you agree?
Which way did he go?

As a general rule, adjectives in English usually come immediately before the noun or pronoun they qualify. But not always:

The office will be *busy* tomorrow.

What is a verb?

Verbs are the words which 'do' – that is, convey actions, identify thought processes or denote states of being:

She *typed* the letter and *posted* it.
He *considered* his next move carefully.
The manager *was* aware of the problem.

Verbs are used in two principal ways:

actively when verbs directly express the actions of the doer:

The manager *dictated* the letter.

or passively when the structure of the sentence is changed to make the doer become the agent by which something is done:

The letter *was dictated* by the manager.

Using verbs passively tends to make the message more impersonal and one trick of its use is that the agent is sometimes omitted:

Your services *are* no longer *required* (by me).

The passive is used in this way as a means of conveying unpopular news, where its communicator pretends not to have been involved.

What is an adverb?

Adverbs are used to extend the meaning of verbs or adjectives:

She can type *quickly*.
He spoke *slowly* and *carefully*.
We need an *extremely* fast photocopier.

Adverbs indicate: How? When? Where? To what extent? How many? etc.

Most adverbs are easily recognised by their -ly endings.

What is a conjunction?

Conjunctions are the linking words which are used to join ideas together:

The report was concise *and* had been clearly constructed. The letter was brief *but* it included the main points.

Some conjunctions – and, but, next, then, yet – are used to link ideas together which could stand independently of one another:

The report was concise. It had been clearly constructed.

Other types of conjunction are used to link together a main and a dependent or subordinate idea:

They decided to repeat the advertisement, *although* the cost had risen sharply.
He decided to answer the letter immediately *because* it was so important.

In order to vary the way in which ideas are presented,

conjunctions introducing dependent ideas sometimes begin sentences:

As you have worked so successfully, I have no hesitation in recommending you for promotion.

Conjunctions frequently used to introduce dependent ideas are:

when, where, why, what, as, since, because, although, though, even though, if, whether, so that, in order that, with the result that, after, unless, as soon as.

Some conjunctions are used as paired sets: either . . . or, neither . . . nor, both . . . and, not only . . . but also.

What is a preposition?

Basically, prepositions are locating words and come immediately in front of nouns or pronouns:

under the blotter, *across* the road, *up* the ladder, *of* him, *to* me, *in* the computer's memory.

Sometimes they are used to form parts of verbs:

to get *down to*, to stand *up to*

What is an interjection?

The interjection is a part of speech which transmits a sense of feeling or emotion: Whew! Ouch! Oh! Ah!

Used most frequently in direct speech, the interjection may express relief:

'Whew! That was close!'

or delight:

'Ah, that's beautiful!'

What is the point?

What, then, are the practical advantages of being able to identify the various parts of speech?

Firstly, with knowledge rather than intuition comes self-confidence in recognising the different components or 'building blocks' of English. Constructions and sense groups appear far less intimidating as the writer begins to feel master of the medium.

In addition, such knowledge has distinct, practical value once the writer has developed the ability to recognise the function of each part of speech. If, for example, he had written or was editing this sentence:

The paint spreads quick and even.

he would recognise that 'quick' and 'even' both modify the verb 'spreads' and so need the -ly ending of an adverb:

The paint spreads quickly and evenly.

Similarly, by knowing that the word 'principle' is *always* used as a noun and 'principal' always as an adjective (save for principals of colleges etc) the two spellings will never be confused.

Syntax

Constructing sentences

Just as there is a practical value in being able to recognise the parts of speech, so it is also important to be able to understand the various ways in which sentences are constructed.

How, for example, does the writer come to recognise that

With reference to your letter of 21st February.

is not a sentence? Intuition may create in him a sense of unease, but there is no substitute for knowing and therefore being able to correct it:

I refer to your letter of 21st February.

What is a sentence?

A useful definition of a sentence is:

A group of words which conveys a complete meaning.

Sentences comprise two basic components:

a subject +	a predicate
Mr Brown	arrived early.
I	am not going.
The last train	has already left.
You	have not signed this letter.

All sentences require a subject – a word which is a noun or a pronoun or a longer group of words which has the force of a noun – and a predicate.

What is a finite verb?

All sentences require a finite verb – a verb which carries out the 'action' of the 'doer' or subject word. Finite verbs need to meet three requirements. They must possess:

A number: singular or plural
A person: first, second or third
A tense: past, present, future or conditional

The verb 'arrived' in the above example is singular, in the third person and in a past tense.

Thus basic sentences need to contain a subject and a finite verb:

He awoke. The visitor left.

When sentences contain a single subject and a single finite verb they are called simple. When more than one subject and finite verb are used in linked sense groups they are called complex.

What is a predicate?

A predicate may include not just a finite verb, but also words which enlarge the verb's meaning:

He awoke *early*.

Useful definitions

A phrase

A phrase is a group of words which are related in sense and are often introduced by a preposition:

at the moment, on his way to the office, in the ledger

or conjunction:

after a busy day's trading, as soon as possible

Phrases do not include finite verbs, but may be introduced by participles:

Turning the corner he saw the factory ahead.

A clause

A clause is a group of words which forms a component of a sentence and possesses both a subject and a finite verb. Clauses are linked in sentences by conjunctions:

He caught the train although *he arrived late at the station.*

A main clause

Main clauses may form complex sentences by being joined together by what are termed coordinating conjunctions:

He stopped and *he called his secretary on the intercom,* then *he resumed drafting the report.*

A dependent clause

Dependent clauses cannot stand alone and are linked by subordinating conjunctions to main clauses in complex sentences:

It is impossible to reach a decision <u>because</u> we lack sufficient information.

As the market is so sluggish, we shall have to reduce our prices, <u>even though</u> it may mean a reduction in our gross profit.

A sentence

A sentence is a group of words which conveys a meaning complete in itself. Every sentence must possess a subject and a finite verb and conventionally they begin with a capital letter and end with a full stop.

(Note that phrases like:

Down in the mouth? You need Fizz, the fun drink!

and,

Rocky and reeling. That was the sad state of Monolithic Enterprises following rumours of a takover bid.

are accepted conventions of advertising and journalism but such techniques are best avoided until the more conventional techniques of sentence-writing have been mastered.)

A simple sentence

A simple sentence is one which contains a single subject and a single finite verb in its predicate.

A complex sentence

A complex sentence is one which comprises two or more clauses which may be main or dependent. It must, however, contain at least one main clause.

Table of verb tenses

Infinitive   to write
Present participle   writing
Past participle   written

Tenses

	Active	Passive
Present	She:	The letter:
simple	writes	is written
continuous	is writing	is being written
Past		
simple	wrote	was written
continuous	was writing	was being written
Perfect		
simple	has written	has been written
continuous	has been writing	
Past perfect		
simple	had written	had been written
continuous	had been writing	
Future		
simple	will write	will be written
continuous	will be writing	
Future perfect		
simple	will have written	will have been written
continuous	will have been writing	
Conditional		
simple	would have written	would have been written
continuous	would have been writing	

or which provide more information about the subject:

The manager felt *irritable*.
Mr Brown is *our chief buyer*.

Some finite verbs need an 'action receiver' or object to complete their meaning:

I have bought *a new typewriter*.

Simple sentences, then, may be constructed as follows:

(*a*) Subject + finite verb
(*b*) Subject + finite verb + enlargers
(*c*) Subject + finite verb + object

What is a subject?

Subjects are the 'doer' words or groups of words which control or govern the actions of finite verbs. They may be common or proper nouns:

The report is on your desk.
Miss Jenkins is in Scotland.

or they may be pronouns:

They thanked him for his help.

In addition they may take the form of a whole phrase:

Complaining about the poor service got him nowhere.

or even a clause:

That you were ignorant of company regulations is no excuse.

(The terms 'phrase' and 'clause' are explained on the previous page.)

In English, subjects normally come immediately before the verbs they govern. Sometimes, however, additional ideas about the subject are inserted between it and its verb:

Miss Johnson, *a most efficient member of staff*, will look after you.
The sales representative, *who was experienced*, soon made the sale.

How are verbs used?

As we have seen, finite verbs in sentences are governed by subjects and need to possess a number, person and tense.

When verbs literally convey ideas of action they are easy to identify:

She *cut* the paper on the guillotine.
Jack *drives* carefully.

Many verbs, however, express abstract ideas:

He *motivates* his staff well.

and some verbs consist of more than one word:

I *shall have left* for Bristol by the time you arrive.

In order to recognise verbs successfully a knowledge of their tenses is necessary, as well as an understanding of their active and passive use.

Active and passive

Verbs which take objects, when used actively, convey the action of the subject or doer on to an action-receiver or object:

Miss Johnson	typed	the report.
subject	finite verb	object

The same idea may, however, be expressed passively, where the object becomes the grammatical subject of the sentence and the active subject becomes an agent in the passive:

The report	was typed	by Miss Johnson.
subject	finite verb	agent

The passive structures of verbs are formed by using the verb 'to be' and, when necessary, the verb 'to have' as well with the past participle of the verb:

is being typed, was typed, has been typed

Verb forms as adjectives and nouns

There are two parts of the verb which are used in sentences, not as verbs, but as nouns or adjectives.

Present participle as an adjective:

The *driving* rain obscured the wind-screen.

Past participle as an adjective:

The *typed* letters are ready to sign.

Present participle form as a noun (gerund):

His *going* surprised us all.

What is an object?

Objects in sentences receive the action of the verb. Certain verbs which need objects to complete their meaning are called transitive. Verbs which are capable of conveying a meaning without the need for an object are called intransitive.

It is sometimes helpful to think of objects as answering the question 'What?':

The manager	arranged	a meeting
subject	finite verb	object

(What did the manager arrange?)

Some objects take the form of word groups:

The personnel manager wrote *a long and difficult letter*.

Objects may sometimes take the form of clauses:

The inspector detected *what appeared to be a flaw in the casing*.

Remember that when transitive verbs are used in the passive, the object of the active voice of the verb becomes the subject:

A long and difficult letter was written by the personnel manager.
What appeared to be a flaw in the casing was detected by the inspector.

As will be seen later, there are a number of uses to which the passive voice of the verb may be put.

Enlarging intransitive verbs

When verbs are used intransitively (when they do not need an object), adverbial words or expressions may be used to extend their meaning:

He awoke *with a start*.
The meeting continued *for quite some time*.

What are complex sentences?

So far we have considered sentences which are called simple – they contain a single subject and predicate. Many sentences are constructed, however, which are composed of two or more clauses with the following relationships:

main clause + main clause
She worked hard on the report
and
she did not finish until 7.30 pm

main clause + dependent clause
He asked her to stay late
because
he needed the report for the next day.

Main and dependent clauses may be combined by using conjunctions in a number of different ways:

Dependent   Although it was not entirely convenient,
Main   she did not mind working late
Dependent   because she realised the importance of completing the report.

Ideas are frequently linked in this way to form complex sentences which provide interest and variety for the reader and which also serve to indicate the relationships between ideas. Remember that dependent clauses cannot stand alone. They need to be accompanied by main clauses. Also, all clauses, whether main or dependent, must possess both a subject and a finite verb.

One of the problems of writing complex sentences is that it is easy to lose control of the meaning by stringing clauses together ungrammatically:

The young typist, who wanted to make a good impression when she arrived for work on her first day, although she was feeling nervous because the surroundings were unfamiliar, despite the friendly greeting she received from the commissionaire when she entered the lofty office block.

Here we wait in vain for the main verb to follow 'the young typist'. It is much better to shorten the structure of the ideas by constructing two sentences:

The young typist wanted to make a good impression when she arrived for work on her first day. She received a friendly greeting from the commissionaire when she entered the lofty office block, but was feeling nervous because the surroundings were unfamiliar.

Practical assignments

Parts of speech

Identify the parts of speech underlined in the following sentences:

1 I asked him to read it.
2 The large envelopes are in the top drawer.
3 The invoices have been checked.
4 He read the report slowly and made his notes methodically.
5 I am pleased to announce that Amalgamated Steel has made extremely good progress during the past year.

6 His instructions were clear.
7 An elderly man carrying a bulky briefcase arrived at reception.
8 Although its price was competitive, the new product sold poorly.
9 Either we increase production or we turn down firm orders.
10 I shall have finished checking the draft by the time you return and then it will be ready for typing.
11 The meeting will require my staying late at the office.
12 'Oh! I never expected such a smart retirement present!'

Syntax

Identify the subject, finite verb, object or adverbial verb enlarger in the following sentences:
1 The last train leaves at ten o'clock.
2 'You have designed a masterpiece!'
3 An increase in output is urgently needed.
4 I followed his instructions precisely.
5 Everyone heard what he said.
6 What he said echoed loudly.
7 The speaker should have arrived last night.
8 The office party has been postponed indefinitely.
9 The performance of the energetic sales force was praised by the managing director.
10 The art of management requires achieving objectives.
11 The word processor saves time.

Clauses and conjunctions

Identify the main and dependent clauses in the following sentences and state which words are the linking conjunctions.
1 If you do not arrive more punctually, I shall be obliged to take further action.
2 Whatever the market research may forecast, the board is determined to go ahead.
3 We shall have to cancel the project as public response has been totally hostile.
4 When he had finished interviewing the last candidate, he reluctantly began to scan his notes because he knew he would not have time tomorrow.
5 As soon as you have time, Mr Jones would like you to see him in his office, which is on the fifth floor.

Sentence structures

What defects in syntax, if any, can you find in the following sentences:
1 Hoping to receive your reply without delay.
2 Unless we hear from you in the meantime.
3 However much we would like to help you.
4 Please let me know as soon as possible.
5 Despite our repeated reminders regarding non-payment of your account, which is long overdue.

6 The prices of our range of kitchen utensils, which, as you know, have not increased, despite the pressure of the increased cost in raw materials.
7 Further to your recent request for samples of our new range of fabrics.
8 Using the microcomputer, the cursor became stuck in the middle of the VDU screen.
9 Having produced a paper print-out, the text was stored in the computer's memory.

Usage: helpful hints

Many writers experience problems with grammar, syntax and usage in the course of composing written documents. Such errors spring from a variety of sources – haste, a failure to read through and check a draft or from simply having missed learning a particular form of accepted usage.

Some of the most frequently encountered problems of usage are as follows:

Agreement

Remember that a plural subject requires a plural verb:

The sales assistant who sold it and the engineer who installed it *are* responsible for the customer's complaint.

Remember also that pronouns should be used consistently and not changed because of an oversight:

I am ~~We are~~ sure you will be pleased with the new model and I look forward to hearing from you.

Incomplete sentences

Incomplete sentences are usually written as a result of haste or a failure to check a draft:

With regard to your recent order for 100 boxes of carbon paper.
Further to your letter of 14 June.

Remember that all sentences require both a subject and a finite verb:

Further to your letter of 14 June, I am pleased to inform you that your order has now been despatched.

Each, everyone, nobody, all

Notice that the following generally take singular verbs:

Each is hand-made.
Everyone is present.
Nobody is willing to stand.

but that 'all' usually takes a plural verb:

All are agreed that the decision should be deferred.

Remember also that collective nouns may, on occasions, take either a singular or a plural verb depending upon the sense – whether the components of the collective noun are seen as a single unified unit or as separate sub-groups:

'*Has* the working party found a solution?'
'No, the working party *are* divided into two distinct camps at present.'

Misrelating the participle and the noun

When beginning sentences with participle constructions care should be taken to ensure that they are not misrelated to the noun immediately following:

Walking along the road, the tile hit him on the head.
Having typed half the letter, the telephone rang insistently.

Clearly, tiles cannot walk and telephones do not type! Such sentences need restructuring to provide the correct subject of 'walking' and 'having typed':

As he was walking down the road, a tile hit him on the head.
Having typed half the letter, the secretary heard the telephone, which rang insistently.

Mixing metaphors

Linking two quite distinct metaphors is often the result of muddled thinking and sometimes produces humorous results:

'You must put your foot down with a firm hand.'
'As long as we all keep our shoulders to the wheel, we'll have a smooth flight.'

Using words wrongly

Some words are frequently used wrongly as a result of confusion over their meaning:

This faint copy is quite ~~unreadable~~ *illegible*!

Placed as he was in a neutral position, he was able to voice an opinion which was quite ~~uninterested~~ *disinterested*.
He was quite ~~effected~~ *affected* receiving so many letters of encouragement.

Who or whom?

Some writers find it difficult in certain sentences to decide whether 'who' or 'whom' is correct: as in

The umbrella belongs to the customer who I served.

A simple rule of thumb will solve this particular problem. In cases of uncertainty, substitute who(m) by either:

he she they = who
or, him her them = whom

in the relevant part of the sentence: I served him. (Clearly it cannot be, 'I served he'.) Thus the correct version in the above sentence is, 'whom'.

Overloading verbs

In some constructions verbs are sometimes overloaded by being required to express two tenses at once:

Property values have and always will rise in an inflationary economy.

Here, the writer has tried to make a false economy by expecting 'rise' to serve not only as a future tense – 'will rise', but as a perfect tense as well – 'have (risen)'. The sentence needs reconstructing:

Property values have always risen and will always rise in an inflationary economy.

Verbs in their noun forms

When verbs are used in their noun forms as gerunds, they are preceded by the possessive form of the personal pronoun used adjectivally:

'I hope you didn't mind ~~me~~ *my* leaving before the end of your talk.'

The absence of Mr Brown will require ~~you~~ *your* taking the chair at the meeting.

Practical assignment

The following sentences contain errors of usage. Rewrite them correctly, changing the sentence-structure as little as possible:

1   So long as you don't object to me going, I would be glad of an opportunity to revisit my home town.
2   Regarding your letter of 21st March 19— concerning the delivery of a defective calculator.
3   As the consignment is already three weeks overdue, I would be grateful if you would ensure prompt delivery.
4   On entering the office late, the busy hubbub stopped and all eyes turned towards her.
5   The secretary who I recently employed is proving most conscientious.
6   Who's coat has been left on the coat-stand?
7   His consistent effort led to him winning the 'Salesman Of The Year' award.
8   Though I have not met the buyer who you refer to, I do know the sales manager.
9   Whatever sales approach one employs, the basic requirement is to get the customer on your side.
10   Every time he opens his mouth, he puts his foot in it!
11   The deeds had laid, undiscovered, for over fifteen years in the trunk.
12   We acknowledge your letter of 28th September and are also in receipt of your order for a Summit adding machine.

Avoiding the cliché

Clichés are expressions which have suffered from over-use. As a consequence they transmit a tired, stale and sometimes irritating meaning:

It has come to my notice
I am writing . . .
with regard to
with reference to
I note that

Most people resort to the cliché occasionally but the effort to express an idea simply and freshly is always well worth while since it helps to maintain the reader's interest.

Punctuation

The system of punctuating written English is perhaps best viewed as a means of ensuring that any message is transmitted both clearly and unambiguously. The system does more than this, however, by providing occasional breathing spaces and by conveying not only what has been written, but, sometimes, the feelings of a writer or speaker.

Basically, there are some eleven major punctuation marks in general use:

.   the full stop
,   the comma
;   the semi-colon
:   the colon
'   the apostrophe
( )   brackets
?   the question mark
!   the exclamation mark
-   the hyphen
–   the dash
" " or ' ' direct speech marks or inverted commas

. The full stop

The full stop has two principal uses. Firstly, it is used to signify the end of a sentence:

He considered his next move carefully. He would call a meeting of his regional managers at the earliest opportunity.

Sometimes a succession of short sentences may be used to obtain a certain effect:

He scanned the memorandum. It told him nothing. He dismissed it entirely.

Although too frequent a use of the above technique may prove irritating, it is generally sound advice to keep sentences short rather than to allow them to ramble. Some researchers have found that constructing sentences with more than 25–30 words leads to comprehension problems on the part of the recipient, particularly if the vocabulary used is multi-syllabic. A useful motto, then, is, 'When in doubt, finish the sentence and start another.'

The other main use of the full stop is to indicate that a word has been abbreviated:

Mr. Rev. Dr. St. i.e. e.g. etc.

It should be borne in mind, however, that some current practices in typing letters embody 'open punctuation' in their format. This format omits full stops (and commas) in those parts of the letter other than its body. Similarly, some abbreviations are currently accepted without full stops, provided that the use is consistent:

OBE Ltd HMS OHMS Mr Mrs

Sometimes abbreviations such as 'a.s.a.p.' are used in messages to indicate 'as soon as possible', but such abbreviations should be avoided in formal documents. Lastly, remember that each sentence begins with a capital letter.

, The comma

The comma is used within sentences to indicate a pause between sense-groups of words:

Reaching the corner he stopped, looked both ways, then crossed.

The comma is also used to separate words (or phrases) put into a list:

The drawer contained paper-clips, rubber-bands, pencils and paper.

Another use of the comma is to show that an enlarging or modifying idea has been inserted between a subject and its verb:

The answer, which had been quite unexpected, took them by surprise.

Note, however, that when such an inserted clause defines a preceding noun, no comma is used:

'The book which you ordered is out of print.'

As a general rule, commas are not needed before conjunctions like 'and', 'or', 'but' or 'then' which link main clauses:

He spoke quietly and they listened intently.
'You must hurry or you will be late.'
The visitor was late but his host displayed no sign of irritation.

Some writers use the comma to separate a dependent clause from a main clause when a sentence is started with the former:

Although he worked at a slow and methodical pace, John could be relied upon to keep going when others wilted.

But this usage is by no means universal:

When he had finished he rang for his secretary.

The use of the comma in such constructions perhaps

coincides with the need for a breathing space in longer sentences.

There are a number of words in frequent use which are employed with one or more commas:

Lastly, the report indicates that . . .
It proved, however, to be of major importance.
Nevertheless, I should be grateful if . . .
The mistake was, moreover, extremely costly.

In direct speech, the comma may be used to indicate an element of hesitancy on the part of the speaker:

'Oh, and another thing, don't forget to ring when you arrive.'

As outlined above, the comma is used to separate lists of words. Sometimes writers employ several adjectives to describe a single noun:

The report was marred by a loose, rambling, disjointed and careless structure.

Heaping such adjectives together may be a deliberate ploy to create a certain effect, but the inclusion of several adjectives before a single noun smacks of 'overkill' rather than good style.

Some writers, though in a minority, insist, and that is not too strong a word, on using the comma, not just when occasion demands, but indiscriminately, with the effect that sentences limp, totter and stumble along, which can be very irritating, and is quite unnecessary!

As the above sentence amply illustrates, the comma should be used sparingly to assist rather than to impede the reader's understanding of what is written.

; The semi-colon

Many writers today tend to shy away from using the semi-colon and it is not used as much as it used to be. It indicates a pause which is longer than the comma but shorter than the full stop. Most frequently it separates main clauses in the following manner:

The sales campaign had been brilliantly conceived; it caught our main competitors completely unprepared.

In such constructions the semi-colon is particularly effective in securing a dramatic pause before the ensuing statement which thus gains in impact. Notice that such a use of the semi-colon requires that the two ideas expressed in the main clauses are closely related and could, if need be, stand as sentences. The semi-colon in the above example could be replaced by 'and' or 'it caught' by 'catching'. The effect, however, would be to lose the emphasis the semi-colon supplies.

: The colon

The colon used to be employed as a stronger stop or break than the semi-colon to separate clauses in a manner similar to that illustrated above. Nowadays it is primarily used to introduce an example or quotation:

I have always found the advice of Polonius in *Hamlet* to be sound: 'Neither a borrower nor a lender be'

or to preface a list. The list may be set out vertically, as in the notice of a bonus award:

The following members of staff won this month's bonus award:
  Mr J Harris
  Mr T Jones . . .

Alternatively, the list may be set out in sentence form:

The exhibition will include: typewriters, word processors, accounting machines, adding machines, audio-dictating equipment and telephone systems.

The inclusion of a dash with the colon :– is now obsolete.

' The apostrophe

The apostrophe has two major uses. The first, used in conjunction with the letter 's', denotes possession:

The secretary's note-book . . . The manager's report

Notice that when the possessor is *singular* – 'of the secretary', 'of the manager', the apostrophe comes *before* the 's' which should be separated from the rest of the word.

To show possession in the plural the apostrophe is positioned immediately *after* the 's' which is added to most nouns to indicate their plural form:

the representatives' calls
the books' prices

Some nouns, however, change in their plural form:

child   children
woman   women

The apostrophe for such nouns is placed immediately after the final 'n' which is followed by an 's':

women's coats
children's shoes

A very useful rule of thumb is: put an apostrophe at the end of the word and add an 's'. If the word already ends in 's' in most cases the second 's' is omitted.

In addition, there are a large number of nouns ending in 'y' which changes to 'ies' in the plural. Such nouns show possession in this way:

ladies' fashions
secretaries' meeting

In cases of uncertainty, a simple test may be applied to a word suspected of needing an apostrophe 's'. Try to substitute 'of the' followed by the word in question in the sentence or phase:

the fashions of the ladies
the meeting of the secretaries
the shoes of the children
the report of the manager

If the wording still makes sense, then the apostrophe is needed!

Remember: that when 'its' means 'of it' the apostrophe is not used.

The other use of the apostrophe is to indicate that a letter (or letters) has been omitted from a word which has been contracted:

do not . . . don't
it's . . . it is
telephone . . . 'phone

Such contractions are very frequently used in spoken English but should not be used in any formal, written documents.

( ) Brackets

Brackets are used to separate what is often a secondary or additional idea from the rest of a sentence:

A shortcut (though this is not recommended for beginners) would be to leave out the second step.

He decided to try (although his chances of succeeding were remote) and entered his name on the list.

Sometimes the brackets enclose a source of reference or information:

The results obtained (Appendix C refers) indicated a distinct preference for the blue colour.

? The question mark

The question mark is placed at the end of the sentences which are structured to form direct questions:

'How many did you sell?'
'When does he leave for London?'

As the above examples illustrate, the stop of the question mark serves to replace any other form of sentence-ending punctuation mark. The following practices should be avoided:

'What did he say?.'
'What did she call you?!'

Sometimes speakers introduce questions known as rhetorical questions into speeches. Such questions are used for effect and do not expect any answer. Nevertheless, they require a question mark:

'An entirely new approach is needed. And who among us would deny that a thorough review is long overdue? Once this need is accepted . . .'

Indirect questions, however, do not require a question mark:

He asked if he might be excused.
She enquired whether the train had left.

! The exclamation mark

Exclamation marks are used to indicate feelings of surprise, astonishment, sarcasm, approval or enthusiasm:

Incredible! No other word would do justice to the performance of the new Magiscribe electronic typewriter.

'Are you going to the meeting?'
. . . 'You can't be serious!'
'So this is the new model. It's beautiful!'

Some writers endeavour to increase the element of surprise or approval by placing several exclamation marks together. Such a practice is an accepted convention in comic books, but has no place in serious writing. Lastly, the exclamation mark suffers from over-use and is best used sparingly.

- The hyphen

The hyphen's function is to link together either words or parts of words. When it is employed to link words together it does so because they have become so closely connected in meaning that they are almost one word:

leap-frog
master-at-arms
turn-table

Some words, however, have been used in conjunction for so long that any hyphen has been dropped: racecourse, turnover, mouthpiece. It is difficult to know for certain when to run words together and when to hyphenate them and in cases of uncertainty the dictionary must be the arbiter.

The other use of the hyphen is to join parts of words together which must each be pronounced separately:

co-edition
co-existence
pre-emptive

Some current writers are tending to drop this use of the hyphen and run words together, but its use is certainly helpful. For example, preeminent is less clear than pre-eminent.

The hyphen is also used in typing and printing to indicate the continuation of a word which starts at the end of one line and finishes on the next.

— The dash

The dash is used in a way similar to that of brackets. It signifies that some utterance or additional statement has been inserted or added:

'I'll come straight to the point – oh, but forgive me, I see your glass is empty.'
The sales of accessories – in fact the entire sales performance – has been extremely satisfying!

' ' Direct speech marks/inverted commas

The use of direct speech marks is restricted to showing exactly which words were spoken by a particular speaker:

'I don't know,' he said, 'but I'll find out.'

When a second speaker is introduced, the spoken words begin a new paragraph. The punctuation of the direct speech is all placed *within* the direct speech marks.

Double or single inverted commas are sometimes used to indicate a quotation or a title:

'Look before you leap' is still good advice.
'Have you read "The Efficient Secretary"?'

Remember

Punctuation is an essential aid to understanding and interpreting the written word correctly. Similarly, the spoken word is conveyed more readily if pauses and intonation are employed to provide oral punctuation.

Practice pieces

1 Set out the following recipient's name and address as it would appear in a business letter employing closed punctuation:

j a crossman esq m sc m b i m sales manager sentinel security ltd 14 kings road maidenhead berks mb142ap

Now set it out according to open punctuation rules.

Punctuate the following:

2 he skimmed rapidly through the article he had found in his morning paper there was nothing on plant bargaining although the articles title had led to suspect there would be

3 choosing his words carefully the chairman of the management committee who was clearly anxious to avert a head on clash expressed his desire for a calm rational and productive discussion

4 the equipment however proved more costly than the production managers estimate

5 however hard it may be keeping the customers good-will is essential in any business

6 the first design which the advertising agency submitted was rejected by the marketing manager

7 if you dont tell him i will avowed john parker the sales manager angrily its ridiculous to set such an impossible target

8 the directors meeting will take place on wednesday 3rd July at 930 am in the boardroom

9 the sales performance for the last quarter has surpassed all expectations turnover has risen by no less than twenty five per cent

10 the following branches exceeded the January sales targets portsmouth aberdeen chester norwich and bath

11 the distribution of the companys branches map page 12 refers now provides a comprehensive nationwide coverage

12 he asked whether he could be heard at the back of the hall

13 i realise your problems and dont forget that i too began as a sales representative and i want to resolve them as quickly as possible

14 is there anyone here at this meeting tonight who seriously believes that such complex problems can be simply solved i very much doubt it

15 Using the closed punctuation system, set out the following typescript section of a business letter in an appropriate format:

your ref fj mg our ref mdf 21st october 19— mrs fiona jackson ba dms personnel manager futura fabrics ltd queens house wellington place london wc2a4tg dear madam personnel management the next decade thank you for your letter of 16th october enquiring about the publication of the above book recently publicised in our autumn catalogue i very much regret that the publication date of gordon richardsons book has been delayed it is however anticipated that it will be available by the end of next january should you experience any difficulty in obtaining a copy from your local bookshop please do not hesitate to contact me in the meantime i enclose a copy of our current personnel management publications catalogue for your consideration please let me know if i may be of any further assistance yours faithfully jean davis mrs assistant sales manager enc

Spelling: some guidelines

The ability to spell correctly is particularly important for the manager or secretary since composing and distributing a wide range of written documents form a central part of their daily work. Moreover, adverse value-judgments are often made about an organisation if documents are received which are marred by spelling errors.

Though the English language is not the easiest to spell, patience, a handy dictionary and the following guide-lines will certainly help in overcoming some of the more common problem areas. It is extremely helpful to keep a record of any irregular spellings or exceptions to spelling rules.

The 100% rules

1 q is always followed by u
2 no English word ends in j
3 no English non-colloquial word ends in v

Plurals

Most English plurals are formed by adding s to the singular:

books   posters   aches

But there are exceptions:

potatoes   brushes   fuzzes

and foreign words with plurals which need to be learnt:

bureaux   stimuli   bases
formulae   stadia   aquaria

(though stadiums is now often seen).

Some words possess irregular plurals:

child/children   ox/oxen   woman/women

Words ending in y in the singular mostly drop the y and add ies in the plural:

secretaries   ladies   hobbies

If the y is preceded by a vowel then the usual s is added.
Note that words ending in: s x z sh ch ss in the singular add es to form the plural:

batches   crosses   mixes

Some words ending in f in the singular discard it for ves in the plural:

scarf scarves   leaf leaves   loaf loaves

Prefixes

An especially helpful rule is that adding a prefix to a word does not alter its basic spelling:

dis/appear   un/necessary   ig/noble
dis/seminate   pro/claim

Note that some prefixes are connected to the base word by a hyphen:

pre-emptive   co-edition

Suffixes

The adverbial -ly ending is added quite straightforwardly to most words:

lively   freely

even those which already end in l:

principally   critically

The -ing ending is also added straight on to the ends of words, except those which end in e, where the e is usually dropped:

moving   scraping   serving

Another very useful guide-line is that when a word ends in a consonant preceded by a vowel, the final consonant is doubled:

fit fitting   tip tipping

This rule is also true of -er, -ed and -est endings:

big bigger   occur occurred   omit omitted

Note that where many verbs end in t, a noun is formed by dropping it for the -sion ending:

convert conversion   divert diversion

The suffix -ness is normally straightforward, but note that when the base word ends in y, it is frequently replaced by an i:

happy happiness   lovely loveliness

Some endings which simply have to be learnt stem from various Latin roots for which the suffixes are:

-able or -ible

commendable   infallible   unavoidable
incomprehensible   divisible

Homophones

The English language abounds with homophones – words which sound the same but which are spelled differently:

air heir   threw through   bite bight   course coarse
what watt

It helps to collect these, to learn their spelling by heart and then to recognise them from the context in which they are used.

Rules of thumb

The soft g sound in a word means that the letter g (or gg) will be followed by: e, i, or y:

impinge   dingy   intelligent

The letter i comes before e, except after c:

conceive   ceiling   deceive

If a word ends in a single l, preceded by a single vowel, then the l will double before any further suffix is added:

typical typically   crystal crystallise
actual actually   unravel unravelled

A word ending in t which has more than one syllable *and* has the accent on the last syllable doubles the t before any further letters are added:

permit permitting

If you are not sure about a word beginning with f or ph, remember that the ph sound stems from Greek, so that it is likely to introduce such word components as:

phil   phono   phen   phal   phos   photo   phys

One further helpful rule of thumb is that a single vowel preceding a double letter consonant is very often short, but when the vowel sound is long, it is very often a single consonant:

fŭnnel fūneral   hămmer lion-tāmer
scrăpping scrāping   fĭlling fīling
spĭnning dīning   ŏtter pōtato

Lastly, in syllables other than the first in a word, the sh sound is most likely to be either: ti, ci, si

spacious notion confusion

Test your spelling power!

The letter total for each word is shown beside it as a number

word		meaning
a....vate	9	make worse exasperate
a....te	7	sportsman
a....alt	7	tar-like material
a....us	9	very wicked/bad
c....ry	8	graveyard
co....on	13	act of looking down on people
d....r	6	one who owes money
d....nt	9	one whom you support
e....ce	10	to bubble
e....nt	9	well-organised
fl....nt	11	luminous
g....e	5	cunning
h....y	9	graded organisation
h....st	8	funny man
in....us	9	very clever/inventive
in....nt	10	payment made in parts
n....l	7	not favouring any side
p....r	9	senior university lecturer
pri....e	9	special given right
p....l	9	in charge of a college
s....e	6	like a sickle
s....tic	9	artificial
t....al	10	like a dictator
w....l	5	spin round very fast
w....e	6	wriggle

Score: 25–20 excellent!
19–15 very good
14–10 encouraging
9–0   stick at it!

existence
foreign
fulfil
gauge
government
grateful
honorary
humorous
illegible
immovable
inconsistent
insistent
intelligible
irresponsible
maintenance
manoeuvre
miscellaneous
mischievous
necessary
negligible
noticeable
occasion
occurred
omission

omitted
parallel
precede
procedure
profess
psychology
receive
recommend
referred
regrettable
resistant
secede
separate
sincerely
skilful
succeed
supersede
technicality
temporary
tragedy
unnecessary
untouchable
woollen
wreath

Assignment

Compose a sentence illustrating the use (or different uses) for each of the words displayed below as pairs.

Once you have used them correctly, you will be well on the way to eliminating fifty troublesome words from the 'problem-pack'!

Check-list of trouble makers

The problem pack

The following words have caused spelling problems for generations of English-writing people. Study them carefully checking especially the parts which have been underlined, since this is where most people go wrong:

accessible	committed
accessory	committee
accommodation	conscious
acquiesce	contemptible
acquire	deceive
address	deferment
aggressive	deferred
analysis	definite
appalling	develop
argument	disappear
beneficial	disseminate
benefited	embarrass
changeable	equipped
chargeable	exaggerate

Double trouble

The following pairs of words are frequently confused. Make sure you know the difference in their meaning and how they are used:

advice	advise
affect	effect
appal	appeal
canvas	canvass
complement	compliment
council	counsel
confidant	confident
continuous	continual
dependant	dependent
decent	descent
draft	draught
faint	feint
forward	foreword
farther	further
licence	license
to lie	to lay
lightening	lightning

lose   loose
passed   past
precede   proceed
principal   principle
practice   practise
stationary   stationery
straight   strait
waver   waiver

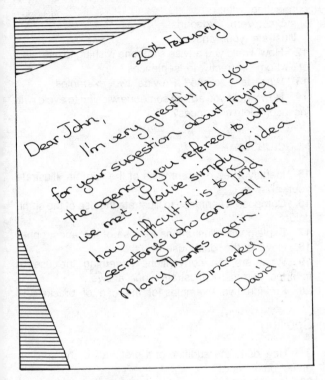

20th February

Dear John,

I'm very greatful to you for your sugestion about trying the agency you refered to when we met. You've simply no idea how difficult it is to find secretaries who can spell !

Many Thanks again.

Sincerely,
David

Reported speech

Reported speech – the system of indirectly conveying what someone has previously said – is frequently used in business and public service organisations.

Many written documents, such as minutes, reports, articles and summaries, report for the benefit of the reader what someone has actually said at an earlier time.

Reported speech is easily recognised by the absence of quotation marks and the introductory 'leaders' such as:

Mr Smith replied that . . .
He said that . . .
She hoped it would not . . .

The system for converting direct speech into reported or indirect speech is generally straightforward, though there are some pitfalls to be avoided.

Person		
	Singular	**Plural**
1st	I	we
2nd	you	you
3rd	he, she	they

Remember that, as a general rule, the first or second persons in direct speech become third persons in reported speech:

'I shall ring you when I reach Bristol.'

He said that he would ring him/her when he reached Bristol.

In addition, it is important to avoid any ambiguities which may result in the change from direct to reported speech:

He thought he ought to resign.

This reported statement could have been as follows in direct speech:

'I think I ought to resign.'
'I think you ought to resign.'
'I think he ought to resign.'

To avoid such ambiguities occurring, it is sometimes necessary to insert a name or an identifying description:

Mr Jones thought Mr Brown ought to resign.
He thought the sales representative ought to resign.
He thought that he, Brown, ought to resign.

Tenses

In reported speech, the tenses of the verbs change as the following table indicates:

Direct speech	Reported speech
I go	He said he . . . went
I am going	he was going
I went	he had gone, he went
I was going	he had been going
I have gone	he had gone
I have been going	he had been going
I had gone	he had gone
I shall go	he would go
I shall be going	he would be going
I shall have gone	he would have gone

Note, however, that sometimes we use the present tense to indicate a customary practice:

'I go to my sports club every Monday.'

He said he was accustomed to going to his sports club every Monday.

The distancing effect

Because the reporting of the direct speech takes place after a lapse of time, some words require to be changed:

'I think this proposal deserves the close attention of everyone here today. I shall be speaking to the staff tomorrow and shall convey to them these suggestions, which have my support.'

He said he thought that proposal deserved the close attention of everyone there that day. He would be speaking to the staff on the following day and would convey to them those suggestions, which had his support.

Note also:

now	becomes	then
yesterday	becomes	the previous day

Using verbs in reported speech

When a lengthy exchange of direct speech is to be converted into reported speech in, say, the minutes of a meeting, it is necessary to avoid the dull repetition of 'he said that' and 'she said that', then 'he said that' . . . More expressive verbs should be used such as: urged that, insisted that, asked whether, to convey the tone of the direct speech.

Assessment questions, discussion topics

Parts of speech

1 Compose a definition for each of the following: noun, pronoun, verb, adverb, adjective, preposition, conjunction, interjection. Give an example of each.
2 Distinguish between a common, proper and collective noun and supply an example of each.

Syntax

3 How would you define the following: a sentence, a subject, a predicate, a finite verb, an object?
   Compose examples of each in suitable sentences and identify them.
4 What is the difference between a transitive and an intransitive verb? Compose two sentences to illustrate your answer.
5 Define: a phrase, a clause.
   Supply an example of each.
6 What is the difference between a simple and a complex sentence? Provide an example of each.
7 What is the difference between a main clause and a dependent clause? Compose a sentence containing one of each.
8 Compose two sentences to show the use of a verb, firstly as an adjective and secondly as a noun (gerund).

9 Explain the difference between a verb used actively and passively and design two sentences to show the use of each.
10 What is the effect of using the passive form of the verb in terms of style?

Usage

11 What do you understand by the term 'agreement' in connection with:
   subject/verb, pronouns
   Illustrate your answer.
12 How would you advise someone wishing to use 'who' or 'whom' correctly in sentences?
13 What is a cliché? Provide two examples.
14 How would you advise someone wishing to avoid writing incomplete sentences?

Punctuation

15 Identify three different uses of the comma. Illustrate your answer.
16 Compose a sentence to illustrate the use of the semicolon.
17 Explain with illustrations the use of the apostrophe.
18 How is the dash used?
19 What are the conventions governing the use of inverted commas? Illustrate your answer.
20 Provide two examples of the use of brackets.

Spelling

21 How does the addition of a prefix affect the spelling of its base word?
22 What happens to a word ending in a consonant and preceded by a single vowel when an -ing, -er, -ed or -est suffix is added to it?
23 What is a homophone? Illustrate your answer.
24 Provide four prefixes beginning with ph.
25 By what alternative letters might the soft g be followed?

Discussion topics

1 Is a knowledge of grammar and syntax of any help to a writer?
2 'You can either spell or you can't!'
3 'It's not what you say, it's the way that you say it!'
4 Provided a message gets across, it matters little how.
5 'I write best when I don't think about it.'

17 Style in English

What is style?

One of the often quoted definitions of style is: 'The best words in the best order'. Style involves the making of a number of deliberate choices:

What sort of words shall I use?
What sentence-structure shall I employ?
What tone shall I adopt?

Style in writing, then, is concerned with the conscious selection of an appropriate vocabulary, the construction of apt sentences and the creation of a fitting tone – the total impact of the message in its context.

Yet style is not an artificial branch of writing skills to be grafted on to a written message. It should be an integral part of the composition of the message and should work towards meeting specific objectives.

The first questions which need, therefore, to be answered are:

In what way should a vocabulary be appropriate?
What constitutes an apt sentence-structure?
What makes a tone fitting?

The end to which style is directed begins and ends with the recipient of the written message. Written communications are composed to satisfy specific aims:

the sender seeks
to inform
to persuade
to motivate
to explain to
to confirm to
to reassure
the recipient of the message

When setting out to compose a written message, it is necessary first to ensure that the essential aims of the message have been identified:

Letter of complaint to complain about a defective purchase and obtain its replacement
Letter of adjustment to redress a customer's complaint and retain his goodwill
Sales letter to persuade a customer to stock a new product

Letter of collection to obtain settlement of an overdue account
Sales memorandum to boost sales representatives' morale after a poor sales performance

If the writer has formulated clear and specific aims to be met by his written message, then he will quickly perceive that the style of, say, a letter of complaint needs to be firm yet not rude, dissatisfied yet not aggressive. Similarly the writer of the letter adjusting the complaint will need to adopt a style which is mollifying and reassuring. The sales letter's author will choose a style which is persuasive and friendly without being unctuous or dishonest, and the sales director's memorandum to his sales force will strive to be positive and encouraging without being complacent or casual. The style, then, of a written message springs directly from its basic aims and is directly concerned with its impact upon the recipient.

In general terms, writers seeking to create a particular style for a given message should ensure that

The message will be clearly understood.
It will be couched in terms which makes its contents acceptable.
The recipient will be motivated to act upon the message or to retain its information.

The recipient

If style of writing is primarily concerned with ensuring that a message is understood, accepted and acted upon by its recipient, then it follows that the writer cannot know too much about the person to whom he is writing!

Of course, circumstances frequently occur when letters, leaflets or articles are written for people whom their authors will never meet and therefore cannot know save in broad, general terms. Nevertheless, very many letters, memoranda, and reports are written by authors who have developed relationships with either clients, customers or colleagues.

It is always helpful, therefore, when choosing an appropriate style for a written message to create as full a profile as possible of the message's intended recipient.

Choosing a style to suit the recipient's profile

Age	People's outlooks and attitudes vary according to their age – a factor to be borne in mind when writing to an older or younger recipient.
Background	People are moulded by their experiences and lifestyles. The metropolitan city-dweller and the rural farmworker inhabit different worlds, as do the small trader and the chairman of the multinational corporation. It is important, therefore, to choose a style and approach in sympathy with the recipient's background.
Education	In our modern, high-technology society there are many different types of education – practical, technical and academic, and not all are linguistic-based. Every effort should therefore be made to express the message in terms which its recipient will understand and readily accept without being either baffled or patronised.
Interests and outlook	It is sometimes helpful to establish a common area of interest with the recipient of the message – not from any sense of seeking to flatter, but rather to establish a rapport. Similarly, knowledge of the recipient's outlook will forestall any tactless observations or remarks.
Specialisms and responsibilities	The nature and extent of the recipient's specialisms and responsibilities also have a bearing on the style with which he is addressed. Doctors, solicitors, surveyors or civil engineers writing to fellow specialists may well employ language which they would understand but which to the layman might appear to be jargon. It is essential, therefore, to use a specialist or general vocabulary with care, so as to avoid obscurity or unnecessary over-simplification.
Relationship of writer and recipient	The style of a communication's message may well be affected by the relationship of writer and recipient. What may be recognised as friendly banter between long-established business associates may be regarded as over-familiarity in another context. In addition, the special relationship, for example, between business and customer may require particular care in establishing an appropriately courteous tone.

Vocabulary

The ability to write effectively – and thus to react and sway the reader – depends to a very large degree upon making sensitive choices from the stock of words or phrases available to create the desired effect.

The English language is particularly rich in synonyms, idiomatic expressions and patterns of syntax (the ways of constructing sentences), so that the writer is supplied with a large number of permutations through which to convey his meaning. The practised writer is able to impart delicate nuances and shades of meaning, to select at will words which will be either sympathetic or cutting, minutely exact or broadly sweeping, aimed at the intellect or appealing to the heart. The writer must, therefore, constantly monitor his choice of vocabulary to ensure that he creates the desired tone and imparts the required meaning. By asking questions like the following at the point of composition, the writer will become much more sensitive to the power of the words he uses, and thus much more effective:

Will the recipient understand this word or phrase?
Is its meaning specific and unambiguous?
Am I seeking chiefly to inform or to persuade?
Does the word or phrase convey overtones or innuen-

does to which the reader may object?
Is the word or phrase tactfully chosen?
Is it the most effective choice or am I being lazy?
Is it sufficiently precise/warm/objective/persuasive/accurate/uplifting etc?

The likely effect of a word or phrase upon the reader will depend upon his ability to comprehend it and upon the associations it has for him. The following table illustrates some of the alternative characteristics which words possess:

Word characteristics

long	short
polysyllabic	monosyllabic
abstract	concrete
objective	subjective
denotative	connotative
informative	persuasive
rational	emotive
old-established	new
formal	familiar, colloquial
indigenous	foreign
Old English roots	Latin/Greek roots
technical	general
abstruse	direct

The appropriate selection of a word or phrase depends very much upon the context of the message and the response sought from the reader:

Document	Context	Tone	Vocabulary bias
report	sales analysis	neutral	objective, informative
unsolicited sales letter	advertising	inducing to buy	subjective, persuasive, emotive
article	publicising company expansion	friendly	direct, persuasive, colloquial

Certain combinations reflected in a word – long, polysyllabic, abstract, Latin-rooted – may make strenuous comprehension demands upon the reader, while other combinations – short, monosyllabic, concrete, Old English-rooted – may be much easier to understand. Moreover, this latter combination may also subject the reader to emotional overtones of meaning stemming from the deep associations which the words possess:

residence/house
domicile/home
capitulate/give in
conflagration/fire
extinguish/put out

'He seems to have found a whole new purpose in life.'

Vocabulary style check

length · syllable count · simple–abstruse · emotive–persuasive · objective–informative · specialist–general · formal–colloquial

Using the Word Characteristics chart as a guide, analyse the following groups of words:

Advertising	Management	Reporting	Selling	Industrial
new	job-appraisal	investigate	discount	strike
wonder	motivate	interpret	special offer	slump
fantastic	enrichment	infer	de luxe	dole
big value	objectives	qualify	sample	lock-out
better	morale	indicate	extras	inflation
magic	aptitude	sample	desirable	bosses
love	target	questionnaire	exclusive	confetti money
warm	deadline	research	family-size	negotiate
cool	efficient	cross-section	fully-guaranteed	unofficial
fresh	effectiveness	value-judgment	personalised	go-slow
sunshine	job-satisfaction	recommendation	custom-built	productivity
tingling	delegate	evaluate	hand-made	piece-work
enjoyment	authorise	analysis	quality	picket
join	accountability	comparatively	performance	provocation
together	enthuse	predominantly	export model	labour
even whiter	analyse	logical	bargain	staff

Study the following extracts and comment upon the vocabulary and its intended effect upon the reader:

Sales report

... The effect of the new bonus incentive scheme has been to increase December sales of products generating optimum gross profit by 17% compared with November. ... The response of sales representatives to the Head Office directive requiring a reduction in days of credit has exceeded expectations. The target of 28 days has been attained. The regional mean average now stands at 26 days ...

Unsolicited sales letter advertising perfume

... The magic of Michèle, an exquisite new perfume from France, has been especially created for women like you. Michèle is the fragrance of a misty morning, the mystery of warm, scented nights. The magic of Michèle tells him you care, when words would break the spell!

Article in a house journal describing a factory construction programme

What is five foot two high, has big, staring eyes and a gaping mouth?

Yours truly! Well, that's how I must have looked when they said, 'Get down to Welborough New Town and find out what the place is like where they're building our brand new factory.'

What is six feet tall and bounces and whistles?

Yes, you've guessed it! Me again, when I'd looked round Welborough. What a place! It's clean, bright as a new pin and already a thriving centre of commerce and culture. ...

Sentence structure

The ability to transmit a written message effectively to its reader depends not only upon choosing the right words, but also upon constructing suitable sentences.

As a general rule, the shorter the sentence and the fewer the number of syllables per word, the easier it will be to understand. Indeed, some researchers consider that sentences of more than twenty-five words begin to pose comprehension problems for their readers. Much depends, however, upon the clarity and control of the sentence structure.

Composing sentences effectively in continuous prose also relies very much upon using structures which are varied and upon creating a sense of balance within each sentence's design. For example, a succession of very short, simple sentences quickly becomes boring and makes their writer seem immature:

Thank you for your letter of 3rd July 19--. You enquire in it about the cost of Ariel car radios.

There are two models. One is the Ariel Tourist. The other is the Ariel Europa. The Tourist costs £39.00. The Europa costs £64.00. It has the added feature of pre-selected station tuning buttons. The radios are guaranteed for twelve months. The prices include postage and packing costs.

I enclose a catalogue featuring both models. I look forward to hearing from you.

The above example is made up of twelve sentences, the average length of which is about seven words. The reason for its seeming immaturity stems from the shortness of the sentences and the simplicity of much of

---

Sentence structure style check
length · simple—complex · clause order · variety · balance · linking words

the vocabulary. Together they demand a reading age of between nine and eleven.

Consider the same message with a more complex sentence structure:

Thank you for your letter of 3rd July 19–– enquiring about the cost of Ariel car radios.

I recommend both the Ariel Tourist, which costs £39.00, and the Europa, which has the added feature of pre-selected station tuning buttons, and costs £64.00. Both radios are guaranteed for 12 months and prices include postage and packing costs.

I enclose a catalogue featuring both models and look forward to hearing from you.

The effect of this restructuring is to make the message more interesting and acceptable to the reader. The letter's message is more fluent and the balance of each sentence has improved. Part of the reason for its improved readability is that the reading age has become much more adult.

There are, of course, dangers in allowing sentence structures to run out of control:

As the above facts indicate, the effectiveness of the proposed advertising campaign would depend not only upon the timing of the national press advertisements, where co-ordination would be essential, but also upon the extent of the budget which would be allocated to the commissioning of a series of linked television commercials, both of which would be aimed at securing the interest of the teen-age market as well as the young married couples in their twenties who also share similar tastes in clothing.

The above example is a single sentence of some 82 words! Such a sentence length places undue demands upon the reader in remembering the sense of all its component phrases and clauses. Thus, as another general rule, the longer the sentence, and the more numerous the dependent clauses, the more difficult will it be to understand – especially if there are many long words.

When constructing sentences within paragraphs or a piece of continuous prose, the writer must also aim to create variety and balance in the structure of his sentences. In addition, care must be taken to ensure that the ideas in any passage flow smoothly and easily, so that sentences are linked and the thread of argument remains intact.

As the car radios example illustrates, ideas soon become plodding and boring if expressed in a series of short, simple sentences comprising single main clauses. Many writers therefore try to link two or more ideas in sentences by constructing sentences as follows:

main clause + dependent clause

dependent clause + main clause + dependent clause

Delivery has regrettably been delayed because spare parts are in short supply.
After the automatic key has been depressed, the copier
will continue to print copies until the pre-set number has been reached.

Notice that when the dependent clause precedes the main clause, the effect is to emphasise the main clause and especially those words which end the sentence:

Whatever the outcome may be, the board has decided to go ahead with the project.
As your sales record has been outstanding this year, I am pleased to award you a bonus of £500.
Although sales fell last month, total sales to date are 20% up on last year.

One way, therefore, of achieving variety in sentence-structure is to alternate the positioning of clauses in sentences which follow each other.

Whatever the outcome may be, the board has decided to go ahead with the project. Moreover, it wishes to place on record that it has complete trust in the Marketing Department.
Though its development will not be easy, the board is confident that the new product will prove a success.

Notice also in the above example the emphasis placed upon 'prove a success' as the last words in a finishing main clause.

Another means of creating interesting complex sentences is to insert a dependent clause between a subject and its verb:

The merchandiser, which is supplied free of charge, stands approximately two metres high.

If, however, a main clause is followed by one or more dependent phrases or clauses, the effect is for the impact of the sentence to tend to tail off:

The sales target of £250 000 has been reached, although competition was fierce from companies which traditionally trade in our markets.

A sense of anticipation and suspense is created when the order of the clauses in the above example is reversed.

Balance in sentence structure may be achieved in a number of ways and constructions like the following are often helpful:

not only ... but also, both ... and, either ... or, although ... nevertheless

The colours not only remain fast in the wash, but are also resistant to fading in bright light.

Either we reduce our prices across our whole product range, or we run the risk of becoming uncompetitive.

Our designers have improved both the accuracy and the elegance of our new Chronos wrist watch.

Alternatively, the semi-colon may be used as a pivot upon which to balance a sentence:

The Faragucchi Bullet has been built to last; it has a rust-resistant sub-frame and is meticulously undersealed.

Tone

The creation of an appropriate tone in a piece of writing is largely cumulative – it is the total effect of the message upon the reader and stems not only from what is transmitted but also from how the message is expressed.

Tone is created by the interaction of a number of factors:

Tone check-list

The context of the message

Choice of vocabulary, terminology

Sentence-structure, syntax, rhythms

Bias of the language: emotive, informative, persuasive, neutral, objective etc.

Relationship of writer and reader: rapport or hostility etc.

The recipient of a message identifies its tone by the way he reacts to it. It is either warm and friendly or cool and distant, formal or informal, terse or reassuring, pompous or modest, rude or courteous. The efficient writer is constantly monitoring the tone of his writing to ensure that he does not inadvertently fail to meet the aim of his message by offending the reader or by evoking a negative response as a result of couching his message in an inappropriate tone.

Consider the following letter of adjustment to a customer who has experienced problems in operating a new cassette-recorder:

Dear Sir,

The problem of operating our Akustik cassette-recorder, of which you complain in your letter of 13th July 19––, is simply remedied.

It is merely a matter of depressing the 'Play' and 'Record' buttons simultaneously. Page 2 of the Operating Manual explains the procedure quite straightforwardly.

I trust you will experience no further difficulties.

Yours faithfully,

The writer of the above letter adopts a pompous and condescending tone towards a customer who has experienced difficulty in carrying out what may be a simple operating procedure. As a consequence of the tone of the explanation, the customer is made to feel totally incompetent and the writer's brusque manner does nothing to cement customer relations. How much better would the adjustment letter have been if the writer had created a more helpful and courteous tone:

Dear Mr Gray,

I was sorry to read in your letter of 13 July 19–– of the trouble you are experiencing in operating the Akustik cassette-recorder.

Operating an unfamiliar piece of equipment does, I know, sometimes cause initial difficulties. In order to record on the Akustik, it is necessary to depress both the 'Play' and the 'Record' buttons at the same time. You will be able to check that you are recording successfully by noting the movement on the sound level meter's needle. The photographs on page 2 of the Operating Manual are helpful here.

I hope this explanation will enable you to gain much pleasure from your new Akustik. Please let me know if I may be of any further help.

Yours sincerely,

Very often, the choice of an appropriate tone for a particular document springs naturally from its intended use. We expect, for example, that a report will be factual and objective and that the creation of a suitable tone will make use of impersonal and passive verb constructions:

It was evident that . . .
The interviews revealed that . . .
The branch manager, Mr Wilkins, was asked for his views on the reasons for the recent increase in staff turnover . . .
If the problem is to be resolved, the following action needs to be taken: . . .

We also expect a press-release to be broadly factual, although it seeks to present, say, an insurance company in a good light:

. . . The Castle Insurance Company will be moving into the new Castlemount office block during the week-end of 24th–25th March, to ensure a minimum of inconvenience to its customers.

Relays of volunteer staff will be transferring the company's computerised records to their new home in the Computer Centre housed in the basement of the twenty-one storey building. The Castlemount offices are protected by one of the latest thermostatically controlled and smoke-sensitive fire alarm systems . . .

Equally, we expect personal letters from colleagues to be expressed in an appropriately direct and sincere tone:

I was very sorry to learn of your intention to resign. Though I shall miss your help and advice very much, I realise that you are now anxious to take on a post of more responsibility. I sincerely regret that, at this time, I am unable to offer you an appointment which would enable the company to keep your valued services. . . .

Whatever the situation, most recipients of written documents are quick to perceive when a tone is glib, insincere, dishonest or hypocritical:

I was indeed sorry to hear of your intention to resign. The company is particularly fortunate that John Parker is more than ready to take over your department in your stead.

I wish you well in your future post and hope it affords you the satisfaction you have been unable to find here at Marshalls.

If we accept that producing written documents is expensive, time-consuming and essential – both in terms of achieving organisational objectives and fostering human relations – then the creation of a suitable tone in whatever we write is of paramount importance!

Paragraph structures

One further aspect of style concerns the structuring of ideas not only within sentences, but also within paragraphs. Just as the creation of variety is important in sentence structure, so it is in paragraph design. The following diagram illustrates the various effects of structuring paragraphs with the 'key' or 'topic' sentence occurring either at the opening, in the middle or at the close of the paragraph. Each adjacent graph indicates the likely effect of the reader's interest in each case.

The reader's interest tends to be at its height where the paragraph's most important 'key' sentence makes its impact. Thus opening paragraphs in a passage often start with an arresting key sentence to secure the reader's attention and finishing paragraphs often keep the reader in suspense until a concluding key sentence point is made. Varying paragraph structures helps to create emphasis and to keep the reader's interest alive.

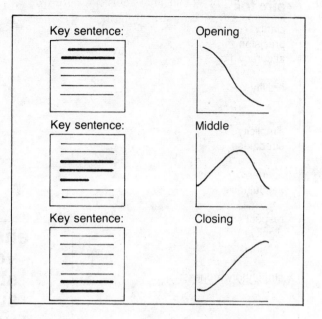

Style checks

aim for		avoid
clarity		irrelevance
precision		vagueness
accuracy		ambiguity
brevity		longwindedness
		rambling
simplicity		obscurity
directness		complexity
courtesy		rudeness
helpfulness		sarcasm
respect		pomposity
dignity		condescension
	ensure	
	your	
straightforwardness	**style**	jargon
	suits	officialese
	your	
	aims	
freshness		clichés
caring		stock responses
appropriate		over-formality
tone		over-familiarity
appropriate		inappropriate
language		colloquialisms
		slang
honesty		hypocrisy
integrity		insincerity
lead to		**lead to**
understanding		irritation
acceptance		rejection
action		delay

Keep a constant style check on:

vocabulary	is it	obscure? over-simple? accurate? lazy? too abstract? too colloquial? too formal? jargon? precise?
expression	is it	straightforward? pompous? full of clichés? simple? abstruse? stale? ambiguous? clear? fresh?
sentence-structure	is it	too long? rambling? too short? easy to follow? too complex? direct? out of control?
tone	is it	creating the desired effect? warm? aloof? friendly? cold? rude? aggressive? courteous? insincere? honest? not firm enough? hypocritical? over-familiar? too formal?

Your style should reinforce the aims of your message!

Extracts for analysis

What criticisms can you make of the style, tone and use of language in the following extracts? Either discuss or write an account of your findings. Rewrite each extract in what you consider a more appropriate style.

I have to inform you that your enquiry will be dealt with in due course.

I must apologise for the delay in your receiving your vehicle after service.

As you will readily appreciate, motor-vehicle wheels need to be balanced dynamically as well as statically to avoid the transmission of vibration through the steering linkage.

Moreover, the diagnosis of mis-alignment in the nearside front wheel revealed that feathering and premature wear had been caused to the tyre, which as you realise, being asymmetrical in tread design is incompatible with tyres of another make.

I trust this explanation will satisfactorily account for the delay.

The reason I am writing to you on a plain piece of notepaper is because of the incompetence of your firm in supplying my order for company stationery, which you may just recall you received last December.

'Mr Johnson said to tell you we seem to have dropped a bit of a clanger over the grinding machine. The drive belt's come adrift and we're up the creek for a spare. He says we're due for a drop next Monday and he'll give you a tinkle, OK?'

It has come to my attention that departmental staff are in breach of their conditions of service as a result of unpunctuality.

Unless a substantial improvement is discerned in the immediate future, disciplinary measures will be taken.

'Thank you for your enquiry, but my company only deals in genuine antiques.'

Our current inability to meet the requirements of your recently remitted order is occasioned by an unanticipated shortage of the spare parts specified.

Due to circumstances beyond our control, there has been a temporary delay in effecting repairs to your lawn-mower, which we hope to rectify as soon as the situation eases.

Assuring you of our best attention at all times.

Further to your memorandum of 14 June 19––.

Of course, in normal circumstances my department would be only too pleased to be of assistance with the provision of advertising material for your display on 21st August.

Regretfully, however, only reference copies of such material are kept centrally. You may care to try Sales.

Do let me know if I may be of any assistance in any other sphere.

RECOMMENDATIONS

Any future improvement in company turnover is entirely dependent upon either lowering or
raising the price or the quality
of our current product range.

If the latter option is adopted,
the prospect of increased competition or a reduction in gross
profits must be faced.

In such a clear-cut situation,
the action needed to resolve
the problem is self-explanatory.

Much as I sympathise with your predicament, I do feel that I am not in a position to grant you further leave of absence to nurse your sick parent. I am sure you will see the difficult position in which I feel myself to be placed in that I do not consider myself to be entirely unfeeling in such matters, having experienced a similar situation myself. Perhaps if you call in to see me a solution will readily suggest itself, which will prove acceptable to you yourself.

18 Integrated Assignments

Case study
The Midstead Chronicle

Gartholme – Sir Christopher condemns the 'cosy conservationists'

The controversial industrial development project centred at Gartholme Meadows on the western approaches to Midstead last night had a noisy public airing.

As this newspaper last week predicted, the Town Hall was packed to capacity for a public meeting chaired by Lord Forderdale. Over 450 local residents arrived anxious to listen to both sides of the argument over the proposed building of an industrial estate on Gartholme Meadows.

Ardent conservationists have been locked in combat with local businessmen during the past three months. The nub of the controversy – which has divided local families – centres upon the proposed demolition of Garth Cottage, which dates back to the 17th century, and the adjacent blacksmith's forge, last used in 1948.

Hard-hitting speech

Development plans also include the construction of a bypass running south and west of Midstead, passing through Denholme Park, a favourite Sunday strolling spot for local residents. Denholme Park was formerly the home of the dukes of Midshire.

One of last night's principal speakers was Sir Christopher Crawshaw, local businessman and chairman of the Gartholme Development Consortium. He concluded a hard-hitting and controversial speech with these words:

'And so, ladies and gentlemen, I would put the following alternatives to you. The conservationists may win. A single period cottage may remain as a silent reminder of the blinkered forces of reaction and stagnation. The six hundred unemployed people in this town may feel reassured, as they continue to search for non-existent jobs, that the honeysuckle still entwines Garth Cottage, and that the disused blacksmith's forge remains preserved for a car-owning pos-

terity. It may be that the backward-looking forces of the cosy conservationists may triumph.'

Employment for all

'Alternatively, the proposed industrial estate at Gartholme Meadows may receive planning permission, in which case, Midstead will once again enjoy full employment and the exciting prospect of affluence and expansion. The proposed tannery alone will employ at least fifty people. Moreover, the access route to the Estate, running off the bypass in Denholme Park will relieve congestion around the Market Cross in the town centre. The entire construction of this much-needed bypass will only affect a very few old, decaying properties. The industrial estate and bypass will supply a very much needed 'shot in the arm' for Midstead, which every sensible resident will agree is at present suffering from a severe shortage of jobs and a hardening of its road arteries!

Noisy heckling

'What Midstead needs, then, is not some form of "mothballing" to preserve a few unremarkable examples of an indifferent architectural heritage, but the provision of industrial and communication amenities which will give local working people and their children the means of securing a happy and prosperous future!'

Sir Christopher's speech was punctuated with noisy heckling and has certainly added more fuel to the fire of controversy raging over Gartholme Meadows. Next week's council elections will give Midstead voters a chance to have *their* say and to tell the Town Hall in no uncertain terms what *they* want!

Preliminary assignments

1 Find out how public meetings are called and held in your town. Report your findings orally to your group.

2 Find out how your local council elections are held and how issues of local importance are aired in the run-up. Deliver your findings in an oral briefing to your group.

Main assignments

1 In groups, study the extract of Sir Christopher's speech and discuss its potential effectiveness upon the Midstead audience. Your examination of the extract should pay particular attention to:

(a) appeals to the audience's emotions
(b) tricks of public address rhetoric
(c) examples of 'loaded' vocabulary
(d) the overall tone of the speech.

Discuss your findings in a general group session.

2 Draft the opposing main speech given by Miss Penelope Carstairs, President of the Midstead Conservation Society after Sir Christopher had spoken.

Simulate the Midstead Public Meeting, starting at the stage where Sir Christopher has spoken, and Miss Carstairs delivers her opposing speech. Group students should prepare questions to ask 'from the floor' to a panel comprising: Lord Forderdale (chairman), Sir Christopher Crawshaw, Miss Penelope Carstairs and Mr F Shaw, District Surveyor.

3 Successive students should record a version of Miss Carstairs' speech either on video or audio-tape for the general group to assess in the context of influencing the Midstead audience.

4 Either as a supporter of Sir Christopher or Miss Carstairs, write a letter to: The Editor, *The Midstead Chronicle*, 6 St Peter's Road, Midstead, Midshire MS14 3PR. Your letter should aim to reinforce the developers' or conservationists' viewpoint and you should bear in mind that, if printed, your letter will appear in the edition of the newspaper which is sold on the day before the local elections.

5 As a retired householder living in one of the 'old, decaying properties' referred to by Sir Christopher, write a letter to *The Midstead Chronicle* expressing *your* views on the proposed development scheme.

6 As Mr Fred Parker, independent candidate in the forthcoming council elections, write a letter to *The Midstead Chronicle* outlining your own position on the Gartholme Meadows project.

7 Form groups, each one representing the committee of the Midstead Conservation Society. In an effort to influence matters in the run-up to the local council elections, you have decided to produce a leaflet for distribution to all local residents, putting the conservationist viewpoint as forcefully as possible. Design a suitable leaflet and then compare it with those produced by other groups in a general group session.

8 Assume that the local council election has been held and that councillors sympathetic to the development of Gartholme Meadows have won the day. As editor of *The Midstead Chronicle*, draft an editorial commenting on the effect of the elections upon the development plans. Research editorials in your own local weekly papers before attempting this assignment. Compare the use of language of your editorial with that of other versions in your group.

Follow-up assignments

1 Discuss the following topic in a general group session:
One of the benefits of our local government democracy is the freedom given to local interest and pressure groups to put forward their opinions in the forum of local debate.

2 Write an essay entitled:
How can local media resources help to publicise the views of public pressure groups? How may they be used to best effect?

What advertising does

A great deal has been written about advertising. Some has been informative, some constructively critical and some destructively ill-informed. This booklet is a simple introduction to some of the things advertising can and cannot do.

What advertising does is not a new title in the series of IPA publications. Some 50 000 copies of the first and second editions have been distributed since it was originally published in 1959.

It has been used by students as an introduction to the subject, by advertisers to explain the value of advertising to their employees, and by advertising agencies to give basic information to new recruits.

This new edition takes into account a number of changes in the advertising industry which have developed in recent years, and adds a reading list for those who wish to find out more.

The function of advertising

Advertisements are a form of communication. The country's largest advertiser is the Government. It advertises to tell people of their right to a rent rebate, to encourage investment in National Savings or Premium Bonds, to persuade drivers to wear seat belts and householders to save fuel, and for many other reasons. Employees advertise to recruit staff. Charities advertise to attract donations. Pressure groups and political parties advertise for support. Individuals advertise to sell a second-hand car.

Although advertisements like these are in the majority, what most people understand by advertising is manufacturers talking to their customers. The primary purpose of this kind of advertising is to sell goods or services at a profit to the company manufacturing or providing them.

As far as the public is concerned, advertisements offer a wide variety of suggestions to people with money to spend so that they can choose for themselves the benefits or pleasures they wish to get with their money.

There are, of course, wider ramifications to the complex business of advertising. It is used to keep established brands fresh in their customers' minds, and to introduce them to new customers. It informs appropriate sections of the public of new products or services and of improvements to existing ones, stimulating innovation and product development. It helps to maintain confidence in companies which is vital to attracting both new custom and new investment.

The list could be considerably extended, but this booklet will concentrate on one basic job of advertising: to sell things profitably for the advertiser.

The economic force of advertising

The production index of a nation is one common standard by which to evaluate the strength of the economy, both against past achievements and the performance of other countries.

Goods are not produced to increase production figures and to fill warehouses. They are produced to be bought, used and enjoyed and – in the final analysis – to be sold. So if the selling effort of a nation does not match its production achievement, the latter will inevitably suffer.

Advertising is the mass method of selling. It is a vital bulwark of the country's selling performance. It provides a growth factor, therefore, that is indispensable to the stability and expansion of the economy, at home and abroad.

The country's future depends on the success of our export trade. Exports are not just bought: they must be sold. The advertising talents, skills, judgement and experience gained in selling to domestic markets are increasingly devoted to expanding overseas sales.

Advertising helps to provide jobs, too. By stimulating demand (thereby increasing production) employment is stabilised. Increased sales mean more jobs.

What is good advertising?

Good advertising presents the most persuasive possible selling message to the right target group for the product or service at the lowest possible media cost.

This rather formal definition needs analysis.

'*Persuasive selling message*'. Advertisements should aim to promise the people to whom they are addressed a genuinely desirable and believable benefit which is genuinely delivered by the product or service.

This benefit should be presented in a way that compels the attention of the target audience and carries conviction.

Both the benefit and the way it is presented should be consistent with the long-term 'brand-image' or personality which enhances both the product or service itself and the company providing it.

'*The right target group*'. Marketing identifies the sections of the consumer universe which are most likely to be customers for the advertised brand: the target group. In the case of a washing powder, this could include most households in the country. In the case of executive helicopters, the number would be very small.

Very few advertisements are directed to the population as a whole. The content of each one and the medium in which it appears direct it to one particular and appropriate target group.

'*At the lowest possible media cost*'. Expenditure on advertising must contribute to the advertiser's profits. When new products are being introduced, the initial advertising is part of the total expenditure the company must make. As quickly as possible it has to earn a return on that initial investment, and contribute to the company's financial stability.

Therefore the size of the advertising appropriation is very carefully related to the market potential and the particular marketing objectives to be achieved.

How that money is allocated between the choices of media available depends on a number of factors: how best to reach the target group, the creative requirements for effective presentation of the selling message, the frequency of impact needed, and so on.

What advertising can't do

A great deal of nonsense is talked and written about advertising. At one extreme, some say that advertising is a complete waste; at the other, that advertising possesses mystic powers which hoodwink the public into doing anything. (Not infrequently, these contradictory points of view are expressed by the same people, and not always at different times.)

Perhaps some of this criticism can be countered by stating categorically three things which advertising cannot do.

1 Advertising cannot get repeat business for a product or service which does not represent real value to the consumer. The greater the amount of advertising put behind poor value items, the larger the financial loss to the advertiser. The consumer decides.

2 Advertising, on its own, cannot always make instant sales. It takes time to build a business and a reputation. So it is important for advertising to be continuous.

3 Advertising cannot sell things which are not available in the kinds of shops or outlets where consumers normally expect to find them. Only in rare cases could advertising succeed in encouraging a housewife to search for a particular product and accept no substitute.

What advertising can do

There are a number of things that advertising can achieve, and very effectively.

Advertising develops a direct bond between producer and customer. In many cases this franchise is more valuable to a company than its physical installations. If machinery is damaged, it can be repaired or replaced. If the public reputation of a company is destroyed or allowed to lapse, the business may never recover.

Advertising is, in a very direct way, a form of guarantee that the product or service it promotes will deliver value to its users and maintain its standards. No rational businessman invests money in advertising unless he is convinced that what he offers his customers is of sufficient worth to command a continuing market. Should he discover this is not the case, he ceases to advertise and the product is withdrawn.

Advertising ensures that people are aware that they have a choice: a real choice to select what they want in a wide range of purchases, and to reject those which are inappropriate to their lives. Individuals are very different. A product which is eminently satisfactory to one housewife may not be given houseroom by another.

In a free society, both must be given the opportunity to suit their own preferences, exercise their own judgements and cast their own votes for the brand by buying or refusing to buy. Encouraging such choices develops consumer discrimination.

Advertising is an essential part of competition, and competition is essential to choice. Every day, advertising demonstrates that it can sell an enormous range of products and services to millions of people, to the benefit of the countless businesses that use it. This advertising stimulates increased production (and therefore employment), and the economies of scale which help to stabilise prices and encourage wide distribution. It also encourages manufacturers to compete through product improvement and innovation, offering better products at better value.

Advertising not only increases sales for individual companies, but also expands total markets. Convenience foods, freezers, hi-fi equipment and holidays abroad are examples of products and services that have ceased to be for a favoured few and have become widely available and widely used.

Advertising maintains the independence of the press and broadcasting media. Income from advertisements keeps media independent of government influence, and makes a wide and varied choice available to the public at lower cost. Without this advertisement income, the reader would pay a great deal more for a smaller, less colourful publication and commercial television and radio would disappear altogether.

Advertising's role in the marketing complex

So far, advertising has been discussed as if it somehow functions independently, divorced from the total marketing effort of business. In fact it is an integral part, and cannot operate in isolation.

Advertising is only one aspect of the marketing complex. Its effectiveness depends not only on the persuasiveness of its message, the accuracy of its direction to the target group and the economy of its media choice. It also depends on product and market research, production, sales and distribution, financial control and all the other ingredients of the total marketing operation.

Within this complex, the contribution of advertising experts may range over many areas; but their most significant contribution is their insistence on the overriding importance of the consumer to the success of the enterprise. Differences of opinion between a company's marketing, production, sales and financial executives are productive and healthy. Each has special interests and special knowledge. So has the advertising specialist: the awareness of what the consumer wants and the need to strike a balance between how the manufacturer can best meet those wants, and what the consumer can afford to pay.

The cost of advertising

Advertising costs money, as does capital, manpower, raw materials, packaging, transport and all the other essential parts of the total manufacturing and marketing process. The funds apportioned to advertising are concerned with creating and maintaining markets for the goods produced.

Without advertising as a method of achieving volume sales comparatively quickly, the very expensive business of launching new products or services would be greatly limited and those which saw the light of day would be very expensive. It is only when sales have reached certain levels that large-scale production, packaging and distribution are economic propositions. When this happens, prices tend to come down, or quality or quantity is improved, or all these combine, to the benefit of the consumer.

Truth in advertising

There are a number of laws and statutory instruments which control the content of advertisements. Far more important to all those working in advertising – whether for advertisers, agencies or media – are the stringent requirements of the self-regulatory controls embodied in the British Code of Advertising Practice.

The Code has two functions. For those in advertising, it lays down criteria for professional conduct and the maintenance of high standards. For the general public, it defines the self-imposed limitations to which those using or working in advertising must conform.

The Code complements the law. It is more easily adaptable to changing social and economic conditions and can act faster to stamp out any dubious practices. It can also control areas which defy legal definition: questions of taste and decency, for example.

When breaches of the Code occur, advertisers are quick to amend or withdraw the advertisements concerned. Should they not, media agree not to sell them advertising space or airtime, and they would risk unwelcome publicity by the Advertising Standards Authority which publishes regular reports of its investigations.

In the case of television commercials, every film must be approved for transmission before it can be screened, to ensure that it complies with the Independent Broadcasting Authority's Code.

In practice, it is clearly in the interests of advertisers

and their agencies to ensure that potential customers are neither misled nor disappointed by a discrepancy between an advertisement's promise and the product's performance.

What advertising can achieve

Advertising is a dynamic factor in the domestic economy and it is vital to exports.

Like all activities which take place very publicly, advertising is often criticised – and sometimes justly. There is 'good' and 'bad' advertising. As any other powerful tool, it attracts a minority who misuse it. Today there is an increasingly vigilant body determined to stamp out such abuses.

There may be waste as well as productivity. Advertisements may irritate as well as persuade. Their desire to capture the attention may seem too aggressive on occasions.

Nevertheless, for the vast majority of manufacturers, it is advertising that sells their goods and services on a large enough scale for them to make the most of the economies of large scale production and distribution, and to share those economies with their customers. It is advertising that keeps their workforce busy and steadily employed, that allows them to recover their investment in expensive plant and machinery and to earn a reasonable return on their business capital. And it is advertising that ensures consumers have a choice, spending their own money in their own way, and getting value for it.

Assignments

Preliminary assignments

1   Find out what the British Code of Advertising Practice covers and give a talk to your group on its effect upon advertisers.

2   Find out:

(a) How much money was spent in the UK on advertising last year?

(b) What is the current cost of a 30 second TV advertising spot at peak viewing time?

(c) Which advertising medium was most popular with advertisers last year?

(d) What do the initials IBA stand for? What is the role of this organisation?

(e) What is the main function of the I.S.B.A.?

Main assignments

1   You work as assistant to Jack Jervis, Advertising Manager of Glowbright Products Limited, which manufactures a range of household cleaners and polishes. Jack is due to meet Glowbright's Board of Directors next week to seek a larger investment of company cash in advertising – an investment which Jack considers essential if the company is to survive increasing competition. Until some nine months ago, Glowbright

enjoyed a steady if undramatic increase in sales and profits. It has become clear over past months, however, that competing firms are ousting Glowbright products from retailers' shelves and customers' minds. The Glowbright Board are inclined to think that what is needed is higher quality in the products. Jack firmly believes the products to be every bit as good as the competition's, but that they are not being sufficiently exposed to the public.

Jack has fetched from his office shelf an article entitled 'What Advertising Does', produced by the Institute of Practitioners in Advertising.

He has asked you to make careful notes of the points which you think tend to show the value of advertising to a manufacturer. He then wants you to draft a memorandum of about 300 words to the Board of Directors, based on your notes, summarising the main advantages to manufacturers of advertising products adequately. The memorandum is to be sent out in Jack Jervis's name.

2   Jack has also asked you to produce for him a schematically laid out set of points on the same subject, which you consider important, and which he could use when making his presentation to the Board next week.

3   You were pleased to be handed the article, since you have been pondering on how to give a ten minute talk in a fortnight's time to the local consumers' association entitled, 'The Benefits of Advertising to the Consumer'. Your talk is to preface a Question and Answer Forum, when a panel of three speakers answers questions from the floor about advertising.

Using material you think helpful from the article together with any additional information you are able to find, draft your notes for the ten minute talk. Various versions of the talk may be tape-recorded for general group evaluation.

4   Simulate the consumers' association meeting. Three group members should assume the panel roles, and a fourth role of chairman. What type of person might be chosen to sit on such a panel? The simulation may commence with the ten minute speech or at a stage when questions are answered from the floor. Such questions should be prepared in advance by members of the group. Panellists should have time to prepare a case for or against the place of advertising in consumer markets.

The following questions and responses should help to get the Forum going!

(a) 'In my opinion, advertising persuades people to buy things they don't want, with money they haven't got, to fill a need they didn't know they had – until the advertisers got at them!'

(b) 'If advertising is such a good thing, why is it that most advertisements contain so little "hard" information about prices, specifications and so on?'

(c) 'In my view advertisements treat us all like little kids! Don't the advertisers realise we've minds of our own? It's maddening, the way some of them talk down to people!'

(d) 'Regardless of what their shortcomings might be, if advertisements were suddenly banned, prices would rocket and the essential competitiveness from which consumers benefit would disappear.'

(e) 'It's their language which bothers me. Everything is "new" or "super" or "extra white" or "fabulous" – and what about the way advertisers spell? Take words like "pinta", "eezee", "to-nite", "kreemy" and so on. No wonder our children find spelling so difficult!'

Follow-up assignments

1 Assume that you work for the Public Relations Department of the National Association of Retail Customers (NARC). Write an article of about 800 words which presents an alternative point of view to that expressed in the above article. Yours is intended for publication in the next edition of *Retail Review* and you have been asked to write on the subject:

Is the retail customer getting what he wants from advertising?

2 Hold a general group discussion on one or more of the following topics:

(*a*) If advertising were banned, would the wheels of industry grind to a halt?

(*b*) If good products are supposed to sell themselves, why are advertising agencies so keen to persuade manufacturers that their services are indispensable?

(*c*) The creation of new markets and products, aided by advertising, is essential to maintaining employment and achieving growth in today's economy.

Case study

The Harris Case

On Tuesday 1st February 19—, Jack Harris, a machine operator at Advance Engineering Company Limited, was summarily dismissed....

'D' Machines – Extract of company regulations

Extract from the Company Regulations of Advance Engineering Company Limited:

'Try not to worry ...'

An extract from a conversation which took place in the surgery of Jack Harris's family doctor on Wednesday 19th January 19—:

Doctor Grant:
'Well, Mr Harris, I think I'd better put you on a course of anti-depressants. I don't think you need to stay at home – especially while your wife is in hospital – but you must take things steadily. The pills I am prescribing will help you to do just that. And don't worry about Mrs Harris – she's going to be all right....'

Jack Harris:
'Thank you, Doctor, I'm very grateful. It's been a worrying time ever since the wife was taken ill. Still, they told me this morning she could be out of the intensive care unit in a few days' time, if all goes well....'

'Give us a break!'

An extract from a conversation between Alec Baker, Supervisor, and Jack Harris in the works staff restroom, Tuesday 1st February 19— at 15.35 hours:

Alec Baker:
'Right, Harris, you've had it this time! This time I'm going to have to report you to Mr Watkins! You'd better put that fag out and come with me to his office – straightaway!'

Jack Harris:
'Aw, give us a break, Mr Baker, I've only just.... You see, I've had a lot.... Well, I've not been....'

Alec Baker:
'Save it for Mr Watkins! Come on. It's not as if you haven't been warned about leaving a 'D' classified machine unattended. The line was clearly working when I spotted you missing! Total disregard for your workmates – that's what beats me!'

```
VI   SAFETY PROCEDURES

...3  Operation of Classified Machinery

     Certain production processes (specified below) are effected by machines having a 'D'
     (Danger) classification. Under no circumstances may such machines be left unattended
     by operatives while assembly-line work is in progress.

     (a)  Relief Summoning Procedures

          Operatives working 'D' classified machines are required to summon a relief
          operator before leaving the machine for any reason while work is in progress.

     (b)  Summary Dismissal

          In view of the danger to personnel working in the vicinity of 'D' classified
          machines, operatives who leave them negligently unattended render themselves
          liable to summary dismissal.

                                                    Revised:  1st January 19—
```

Summary dismissal

Mr Watkins' reaction on hearing of the incident from Alec Baker in the Works Manager's Office. Tuesday 1st February 19— at 1555 hours:

'Found smoking you say. In the restroom. Well, it all seems pretty clear-cut to me! Left his 'D' machine unattended and the line in progress when you spotted his absence. You'd think they'd have more sense! Especially after my recent reminder. You'd better wheel him in, Mr Baker!...'

The EWA steps in

Extract of a conversation between Jack Harris and Vic Cooper, Convenor of the Engineering Workers' Association at Advance Engineering, Tuesday 1st February 19— at 1635 hours:

Jack Harris:
'He never gave me a chance, Vic, nor did Watkins! I dunno, I just came over sort of shaky. There was a stoppage further up the line, so I thought I'd just have a quick sit-down in the restroom. I never meant to be away more than a minute or two...'

'D' Machines – Notice to all works personnel

Notice to all Advance Engineering Works Personnel posted on general works noticeboard 24th January 0900 hours (see below).

Vic Cooper:
'Absent only a minute or two you say. Line stopped – again! Didn't you tell 'em you weren't feeling well? Anyway, anyone can see you're not right – not by a long chalk. Didn't give you a chance? Jack, you should have spoken up! Well, I think it's a clear case of victimisation! You'd best go home now. Charlie'll go with you. But don't you worry, you'll keep your job – or my name's not Vic Cooper! Now, I've got some telephoning to do to District Office!...'

'... on the grounds of unfair dismissal ...'

Conversation between John Watkins, Works Manager, and Dennis Brooke, Managing Director of Advance Engineering in his office, Friday 4th February 19— at 1015 hours:

John Watkins:
'Bad business. Not made any easier by Peter Taylor's absence (Advance's Personnel Manager, absent since Christmas because of illness). We could have done with his expertise. Of course, we had to take a firm line. If company regulations are seen to be openly flouted.... Open and shut case I'd say.'

Dennis Brooke:
'I'm not so sure. I know things have been too lax in the Works, but by all accounts, Jack Harris was regarded as being conscientious. I hope we haven't acted hastily over this.... I've a letter here from the EWA informing me of their intention to advise Mr Harris to take his case to the Industrial Tribunal and to claim unfair dismissal.

```
                        MEMORANDUM


To:    ALL WORKS PERSONNEL            Ref:   JK/RG HSAW 24

From:  WORKS MANAGER'S OFFICE         Date:  24 January 19—


                OPERATION OF 'D' CLASSIFIED
                         MACHINES

All Works Personnel are reminded of Section VI, Para 3, Sub-sections (a) and (b) of the
revised Company Regulations issued earlier this month.

Recently, instances have occurred when 'D' classified machines have been left unattended.
Such acts of negligence on the part of machine operative staff could well lead to serious
injury or even fatality.

All works personnel are therefore reminded that failure to comply with the above
regulations will render them liable to summary dismissal.


                                        JK Watkins

                                   J. K. Watkins
                                   Works Manager
```

According to them, Harris was unwell at the time of the incident. Your "open and shut case" had better be as good as you think it is!'

Prior to the Industrial Tribunal's hearing, the EWA secured a written statement from Jack Harris's doctor, to the effect that Jack had been prescribed medication to alleviate anxiety caused by his wife's ill-health.

Assignments

Preliminary assignments

1   Research the following Acts of Parliament from the point of view of dismissal:

- (a) Trade Union and Labour Relations Act 1974
- (b) Employment Protection Acts 1975 and 1978
- (c) Health and Safety at Work Act 1974, Sections 7 and 8.

2   Find out about current practices regarding industrial grievance and dismissal procedures. Give an oral report of your findings to the group.

3   Find out about the role of a works committee in a large, manufacturing company.

4   Find out how an Industrial Tribunal works, and how cases of unfair dismissal are heard and adjudicated.

5   By arrangement, visit a factory in your locality to see production processes in action. Talk to the management and works staff about potential dangers and the measures taken to prevent accidents.

Either: Write a report on your findings
Or: Give an oral account of your visit to your group.

Main assignments

1   In groups, study, from both the management and trade union point of view, the background and events leading to Jack Harris's summary dismissal. Consider, also, the dismissal from Jack Harris's personal point of view. Make notes of your conclusions for a general group discussion.

2   Form groups to represent:

- (a) the management of Advance Engineering
- (b) the District Officers and Advance shop stewards of the EWA.

Assuming that Jack Harris's case is shortly to be heard by an Industrial Tribunal, prepare either the management or the trade union case to put to the hearing. Base your case on the information given and on any additional relevant information you research.

3   Simulate the Industrial Tribunal hearing. Students should prepare to role-play the various participants. Note that the tribunal panel comprises three members and that its chairman will be qualified in law. Organisations or individuals appearing may be legally represented and advised by appropriate associations. Participants in the simulation should include:

- (a) the Industrial Tribunal Panel
- (b) representatives for Advance Engineering
- (c) representatives for the Engineering Workers' Association
- (d) Jack Harris
- (e) witnesses.

Other students should assume observer roles to evaluate the effectiveness of presentation of cases and judgments by the participants. The simulation should subsequently be evaluated by the general group, when observers should present their opinions.

4   Assume that you are chairman of the Industrial Tribunal. 'Write a summary of your Tribunal's findings and its judgment. Base your summary upon the evidence given in the simulation role-play in 3.

5   Design a poster for display in a factory working area emphasising the need for safety consciousness and the possible consequences of carelessness.

6   Study carefully the wording of the notice to all works personnel written by John Watkins and consider any shortcomings it might embody. Re-write the notice in a style you think would be more effective in the situation.

7   Role-play the interview between Jack Harris and the District Officer of the EWA prior to the tribunal hearing.

8   Role-play the interview between Alec Baker and John Watkins before Jack Harris is brought in.

9   Write Alec Baker's report, which John Watkins has requested, of the incident involving Jack Harris.

Follow-up assignments

1   Write an essay entitled:

Current dismissal procedures and their implications for industrial managers and trade unionists.

2   Discuss the following topics in a general group session:

- (a) What are the likely effects of poor communication on the shop floor.
- (b) Could 'The Harris Case' have been avoided? If so, how?
- (c) Assuming that the Industrial Tribunal recommended Jack Harris's reinstatement, what problems might ensue?

4   Write an article for the Engineering Workers' Association journal entitled:

'Unfair Dismissal – How to Prepare for an Industrial Tribunal Hearing'

5   Write an article for the Society of Works Managers' quarterly journal entitled:

'Grounds for Summary Dismissal'

Case study

Flair Heating (Nottingham) Limited

The success of Flair Heating (Nottingham) Limited really stemmed from a decision to diversify the range of its products. The company had for many years concentrated on manufacturing industrial gas-burning heating appliances used in factories, armed forces workshops with hangars and various construction sites. The advent of North Sea gas had been accompanied by an increase in demand for gas-burning appliances both in the home and in the growing leisure industry of camping and caravanning. Consequently, Flair Heating set out to design and manufacture a range of gas-fires, heaters, lamps and other gas-burning appliances to meet this demand – a demand which had benefited both the employees and shareholders of Flair Heating alike.

Recently, Flair Heating, upon the advice of the Financial Director, introduced Value Added into its accounting procedures. One of the newer accounting concepts, Value Added indicates how the difference between sales and *direct costs* (other than wages) is shared out among the various interested parties, as the following table shows:

Flair Heating (Nottingham) Limited
Statement of value added

	This Year £ million	Last Year £ million
Sales	877	700
less cost of materials and services	417	300
Value Added	460	400
Disbursed as follows:		
To employees	358	312
To Government (taxation)	32	30
To providers of loans	12	10
To shareholders	18	15
And retained in the business:		
As depreciation/ replacements	20	18
As reserves	20	15
	460	400

Abridged Profit and Loss Account for this year and last year

	This Year £ million	Last Year £ million
Turnover	877	700
Surplus from trading	82	70
Interest paid	12	10
Profit before tax	70	60
Taxation	32	30
Profit after tax – attributable to shareholders	38	30
Dividends paid or recommended		
Preference	1	1
Ordinary – interim paid (3.122p)	6	5
proposed final (5.8923p)	11	9
Transfer to reserve	20	15
Capital employed financed by:	£ million	£ million
Shareholders' funds	330	270
Debentures	110	90
	440	360

How the £460 million value added was allocated this year:

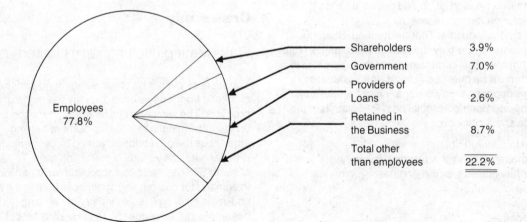

Employees	77.8%
Shareholders	3.9%
Government	7.0%
Providers of Loans	2.6%
Retained in the Business	8.7%
Total other than employees	22.2%

Flair Heating (Nottingham) Limited: the annual general meeting

At this year's Annual General Meeting, Captain Richard Kirkwright, Flair's newly appointed Chairman, made reference, not only to the large increase in turnover and the increased number of peronnel employed, coupled with improved investment, but also to the increase in profit before tax of 16.7% and the substantial payments made in dividends and wages.

As he sat down, he privately congratulated himself on having delivered a particularly fine speech. He was consequently somewhat taken aback when addressed by a shareholder from the back of the hall:

'Mr Chairman, in spite of your glowing report of the past year's activities, would you mind explaining to me why the profitability of the company has fallen? According to my calculations, based on the Published Profit and Loss Account sent to me before this meeting, the company's profitability seems to have fallen by almost one per cent!'

During the commotion which followed the delivery of this 'bombshell', Dr Grimshaw, Flair Heating's Finance Director, managed to pass a note to the Chairman (to save his embarrassment) which contained several important facts.

Summoning the meeting to order, Captain Kirkwright rose, composed himself, and delivered the new facts to the complete satisfaction of all present.

After the annual general meeting

After the AGM a top management meeting was called at Flair's Head Office to investigate the causes of the fall in profitability. Although Dr Grimshaw's accounting information was correct, the Board of Directors had indicated that they were not satisfied, especially since the Annual General Meeting had been given some unwelcome publicity in the financial press.

The following points emerged:

1   There had been a rise in absenteeism and a fall in voluntary overtime.
2   The number of industrial accidents, although of a minor nature, had risen from 20 last year to 60 this year and particularly involved the much-used new welding equipment.
3   The Works Manager complained that there had been frequent delays in receiving materials, as well as technical information about newer products.
4   The Cost Control Manager reported that, due to a shortage of staff, Variance Analysis reports* had been subject to considerable delay and the reports which had been completed showed an increasing proportion of Adverse Material variances.

Assignments

Preliminary assignments

1   Find out how companies conduct the business of their Annual General Meetings. Report your findings orally to your group.

(*Note: A Variance Analysis Report indicates the difference between forecast costs and actual costs incurred.)

2   Research the usefulness of employing the Value Added accounting approach. Make notes of your findings to distribute to your group.

Main assignments

1   Flair Heating publishes a monthly house magazine, *Flair-Up* which is given to all company employees throughout the country.

Write a short article for inclusion in next month's issue to explain the usefulness of a Value Added Statement and include a pie-chart to illustrate Flair Heating's figures for last year.

As your article will be read by non-accountants, you should take care to ensure that its language is appropriately clear and simple.
2   Having studied carefully the accounting information reproduced in the case study, draft the note which you think Dr Grimshaw would have passed to Captain Kirkwright.

Compare your draft with those produced by the rest of your group, and discuss what information the note ought to convey.
3   Discuss the items referred to in the Chairman's report and the probable contents of Dr Grimshaw's note. Draft that part of the Chairman's Report which refers to the figures given and include the calculation of relevant ratios, stressing those omitted originally and making comparison with last year's figures.
4   In groups, discuss the possible underlying reasons for deficiencies recorded in the four points which emerged from the top management meeting.

Compare your findings in a general group session.
5   Assume that Flair Heating's Managing Director is anxious to get to the root of the problems which came to light after the AGM and that he has asked you to devise a questionnaire to be completed by departmental managers under the following headings:

   1 Absenteeism   2 Accident rate
     3 Material/information delays
     4 Variance analysis reports

Provide suggested answers to the questionnaires.

6   Draft a questionnaire aimed at obtaining background information relevant to 5 above. It will be sent to Flair Heating's production workers. Bear in mind that their goodwill needs to be retained if your questionnaires are to be completed!
7   Compose a circular letter which will be sent to all production personnel to accompany the questionnaire in 6. Your letter should explain the need for collecting the information and the use to which it will be put.
8   Assume that the Engineering Workers' Association Shop Stewards' Committee has been passed a copy of the questionnaire referred to in 6. The Committee is concerned about the nature and intent of the questions and decides to hold a meeting to discuss the implications for their members.

Using a selected questionnaire, simulate the meeting.
9   Draft minutes of the meeting (see 8 above) to be sent to District Office.

Follow-up assignments

1   Collect a number of company Annual General Reports. (Extracts are frequently published in the national press and your library will be able to help). Analyse the type of information presented and the styles of English employed. Consider the reasons for the conclusions you draw.

2   Discuss the following topics in a general group session:

(a)   What factors are likely to inhibit a free exchange of information between management and workers in a large manufacturing company?

(b)   How important to large organisations are house magazines and journals?

Case study

Intercontel

Containerisation. An ugly word, but a streamlined concept for moving goods quickly and easily around the world's crowded roads and shipping lanes. The idea of transporting goods in sealed containers, from manufacturer to destination has aroused a good deal of controversy, yet the firms constructing the containers have somehow managed to avoid the headlines. Such a firm is Intercontel Containers Limited, based in Northampton. Intercontel's containers are used by all kinds of manufacturers and distributors both in the UK and overseas. Indeed, the initial export of containers had proved so successful for Intercontel, that the Board of Directors was convinced of the advisability of expanding this area of Intercontel's sales.

Recently, for example, Intercontel received a substantial order from a company in Holland for the manufacture and delivery to Rotterdam of 200 of its 'Jumbo' containers. After securing this order, Mr Colin Cantell, Intercontel's chief salesman, visited other European industrial cities and ports and, having made contact with a number of potential customers, foresaw the enormous export potential for Intercontel containers. His subsequent report to the Managing Director, Mr David Taylor, included estimates of demand over the next three years from firms in West Germany, Holland, France, Belgium, Denmark and Spain. The projected estimates were, respectively, for next year: 1000, 300, 600, 400, 200 and 200.

Intercontel's Board soon realised that their manufacturing capacity at Northampton, already working at almost maximum levels of output, would not be able to cope with any significantly increased demand – especially when delivery dates would have to be guaranteed. Moreover, the Board felt that Intercontel would be at a cost disadvantage if containers destined for Europe had to be manufactured at a site, as far inland as Northampton.

Accordingly, a search was started for a suitable site for a new factory from which to mount an export drive into Europe. After careful enquiries, the most appropriate location appeared to be in Valengate, a small seaside town, only ten miles from Newhampton on the south coast, a large industrial town with excellent port facilities and established shipping routes to a number of European ports.

Valengate

Valengate (population 32 000) had been a fashionable resort in Edwardian days, but a lack of investment in hotels and leisure facilities had caused a slow but sure decline in the town's tourist trade. For the past ten years it has increasingly become a favourite place for people to retire to. Valengate has some light industry – boat-building and electronic engineering – but is currently suffering from a high level of unemployment.

Valengate: Distribution of Population

Ages	Number	Percentage Unemployed (16–65)
0–15	3 000	–
16–21	4 000	20
22–45	7 000	15
46–65	8 000	10
over 65	10 000	–

Many young people are currently leaving the district, since there are few job prospects in Valengate. Some school-leavers are pursuing courses at Valengate College of Further Education, which has, among others, a competent Engineering Department, concentrating on marine engineering.

The map (see page 309) illustrates the physical characteristics of Valengate and indicates the two possible sites where Intercontel might be able to construct their new factory.

The sites: Park Rise and Valen Flats

On a fact-finding visit to Valengate, Mr Taylor was briefed on the two sites, Park Rise and Valen Flats by Mr Grimwade, of Grimwade and Shankley, Estate Agents:

'What I have termed "Site 1", the Park Rise site, lies at the, ah, "better" end of Valengate. It's a plot of rising ground, situated between the western end of town and Valen Park – a rather plush development, the sort of place where your senior managers might wish to reside. As a matter of fact, we have some very desirable properties on our books right now... But where was I? Well, land values to the west are rather more expensive, but the site is handy for the inner distribution road, lying between it and the B3534, which runs round Valen Head to Sunnydays Holiday Camp – about the only real tourist attraction left in Valengate of any consequence, I'm sad to say. Then there's the railway line to the north – runs across to Westquay, but it's not much used – probably only a matter of time before some Whitehall bureaucrat gets his axe into it!... Valengate Bus Company provides quite a good service up to Valen Park – shopping and schoolchildren, the usual sort of thing. There's just one, ah, consideration ... the Park Rise site is, what shall I say ... rather prominent, overlooking the town as it does. The Council might think your buildings would be a little "obvious", if you see what I mean. Still, with the job situation being what it is, I don't suppose they'd be too fussy ...

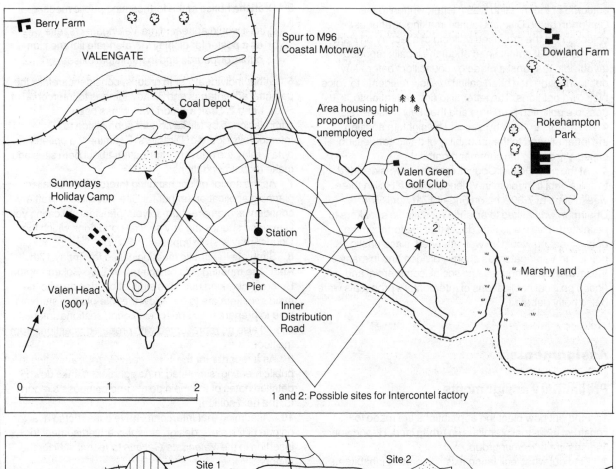

VALENGATE from the sea showing contours

'Now, "Site 2", Valen Flats, lies at the other end of town, or rather somewhat beyond it, just west of the river Valen, and on the other side of the gasworks. The land is flat – lowish really – but I'm reliably informed that there'd be no problems a good construction engineer couldn't sort out. And of course, there's almost twice the acreage. Unlike Site 1, which is privately owned, Site 2 currently belongs to the Council. At one time, when it looked as though Valengate might expand, there were plans to site a new, ah, sewage farm there . . . but that came to nothing. . . . In my estimation, the land might well be obtained at a cheaper price per acre than that of Site 1.

'In the last analysis, it's really up to *you*. Each site has its pros and cons, and you know the needs of your business better than I do, I feel sure. Perhaps the best next step would be to seek outline planning permission in respect of both sites, while you consider each in more detail.'

Mr Taylor thought that Mr Grimshaw's advice seemed sound and instructions were issued by Intercontel for the planning applications to be made.

The sequence of events

1   The notices of application duly appeared in the *Valengate Gazette* and the *Newhampton Times* carried a story at the same time about the interest Intercontel was showing in the area. The report was generally favourable and the venture was seen as a potential injection of new industrial life into Valengate. A further article, based upon an Intercontel press-release, revealed that the factory anticipated employing some 50 skilled and 250 semi-skilled workers (with job-training provided if required). In addition there would be about 20 administrative staff.
2   The majority of the Valengate District Councillors were in favour of Intercontel moving into the area – especially those with wards on the eastern side of Valengate. Some, however, expressed reservations about the siting of the proposed factory.
3   The application notices were read by Major James Hammersley (Ret'd), Chairman of the Valen Park Residents' Association, who snorted his disapproval over breakfast to Mrs Hammersley, and decided to call a meeting of the Residents' Committee without delay. The

outcome of the meeting was a letter, written to the Chairman of the District Council, making strenuous objections to the proposed building of a factory on Park Rise (Site 1). It complained about the locally reported favourable responses made by councillors before any public meeting had been called to allow residents to voice their own opinions. The letter also drew attention to possible pollution problems and the likely noise levels which might continue by day and by night. In addition, the letter alluded to the probability of traffic congestion, especially during the summer months.

4   At the next District Council meeting, it was decided to call a public meeting in Valengate Town Hall in three weeks' time at 7.30 p.m. on Friday 17th April. The Chairman was asked to arrange for suitable speakers to be invited. There was little doubt that the forthcoming public meeting would be well-attended, since public opinion in Valengate was sharply divided and in many of the town's public houses, the social, commercial and (local) political implications of Intercontel's proposals were being hotly debated.

Assignments

Preliminary assignments

1   Find out how planning applications are made to construct industrial premises on urban land. Report your findings orally to your group.

2   Find out what legislation exists to protect inhabitants and surroundings from pollution of the environment. Compose a hand-out of your findings for distribution to your group.

3   Find out what 'action groups' exist in your locality to protect sectional and local interests. Make a checklist of the scope of their activities aimed at influencing public opinion.

Main assignments

1   Design a bar chart to display the information of the Valengate Distribution of Population table. Discuss the advantages and disadvantages of presenting the information either in table or bar chart form and in what circumstances you would opt for the one or the other format.

2   Draft Mr Cantell's report for Mr Taylor. It should be based on the figures given, which project an increase in container exports to the European countries specified of approximately 25% per annum for the next three years. Your report's statistics should be set out in tabular and graph formats.

3   Compose one of the notices publishing the outline planning application for Park Rise (Site 1) or Valen Flats (Site 2). Consult your local weekly paper before attempting this assignment.

4   Compose the letter which was sent by the Valen Park Residents' Association to the Chairman, Mr Richard Jackson, of the Valengate District Council.

5   Draft the notice of the forthcoming public meeting:

   (a) as it would appear in the *Valengate Gazette*
   (b) as a poster for display in Valengate libraries, on public billboards and in municipal offices.

6   Either individually or in groups, consider carefully the potential advantages and disadvantages to Intercontel of Sites 1 and 2. Draft a report (which has been commissioned by Mr Taylor) for submission to Intercontel's Board of Directors. Examine the options in detail, relay the relevant information about both sites and make recommendations.

7   As the senior officer handling Intercontel's detailed planning application (either for Site 1 or Site 2), draft a confidential memorandum to your principal indicating your views and suggesting any special conditions which the Council may wish to impose.

8   Simulate the public meeting called for Friday 17th April. The meeting is to be chaired by Lord Rokehampton. Before embarking upon the simulation, decide who the main speakers are to be. Allow the role-playing students time to prepare their speeches. Local, sectional interests should also be represented with prepared questions from the floor.

9   As a reporter for the *Valengate Gazette* attending the public meeting, simulated in Assignment 8, take down detailed notes of the main points and compose a report for the next edition.

10   Assuming that Intercontel have constructed a factory on one of the sites, design a display advertisement for insertion in the *Valengate Gazette* to recruit staff for the factory.

11   Study carefully the words of Mr Grimwade to Mr Taylor, outlining the nature of both sites. Consider his observations from the point of view of:

   (a) Salesmanship
   (b) Objectivity
   (c) Helpfulness
   (d) Clarity and comprehensiveness

Assume that Grimwade and Shankley have been retained as estate agents for both sites.

Follow-up assignments

1   Write an essay entitled:

   The factors to be considered when planning the construction of a new factory.

2   Discuss the following topics in a general group session:

   (a) What public relations exercises might Intercontel undertake in the Valengate district to help them to succeed in establishing their proposed factory?
   (b) What are the economic advantages to Valengate of Intercontel building a new factory there? Are there any disadvantages?
   (c) What part could the Valengate College of Further Education and the Manpower Services Commission play in the development of Intercontel's operation in Valengate?